JEREMY & DAD

Also by Jerry Scott and Jim Borgman

Zits: Sketchbook 1
Growth Spurt: Zits Sketchbook 2
Don't Roll Your Eyes at Me, Young Man! Zits Sketchbook 3
Are We an "Us"? Zits Sketchbook 4
Zits Unzipped: Zits Sketchbook 5
Busted! Zits Sketchbook 6
Road Trip: Zits Sketchbook 7
Teenage Tales: Zits Sketchbook 8
Thrashed: Zits Sketchbook No. 9
Pimp My Lunch: Zits Sketchbook No. 10
Are We Out of the Driveway Yet? Zits Sketchbook No. 11
Rude, Crude, and Tattooed: Zits Sketchbook No. 12
Jeremy and Mom
Pierced
Lust and Other Uses for Spare Hormones

Treasuries
Humongous Zits
Big Honkin' Zits
Zits: Supersized
Random Zits
Crack of Noon
Alternative Zits
My Bad

Gift Book
A Zits Guide to Living with Your Teenager

JEREMY & DAD

A ZITS® Tribute-ish to Fathers and Sons

by Jerry Scott and Jim Borgman

Andrews McMeel
Publishing, LLC

Kansas City • Sydney • London

Zits® is syndicated internationally by King Features Syndicate, Inc. For information, write King Features Syndicate, Inc., 300 West Fifty-Seventh Street, New York, New York 10019.

Andrews McMeel Publishing, LLC
an Andrews McMeel Universal company
1130 Walnut Street, Kansas City, Missouri 64106

www.andrewsmcmeel.com

11 12 13 14 SDB 10 9 8 7 6 5 4 3 2

ISBN: 978-0-7407-9155-0

Library of Congress Control Number: 2009943085

Zits® may be viewed online at
www.kingfeatures.com.

Special thanks to Nancy Evans for her design and production brilliance on this book.
She joins an army of people who make us look better than we are.

For Pop and Big Jim, from your boys

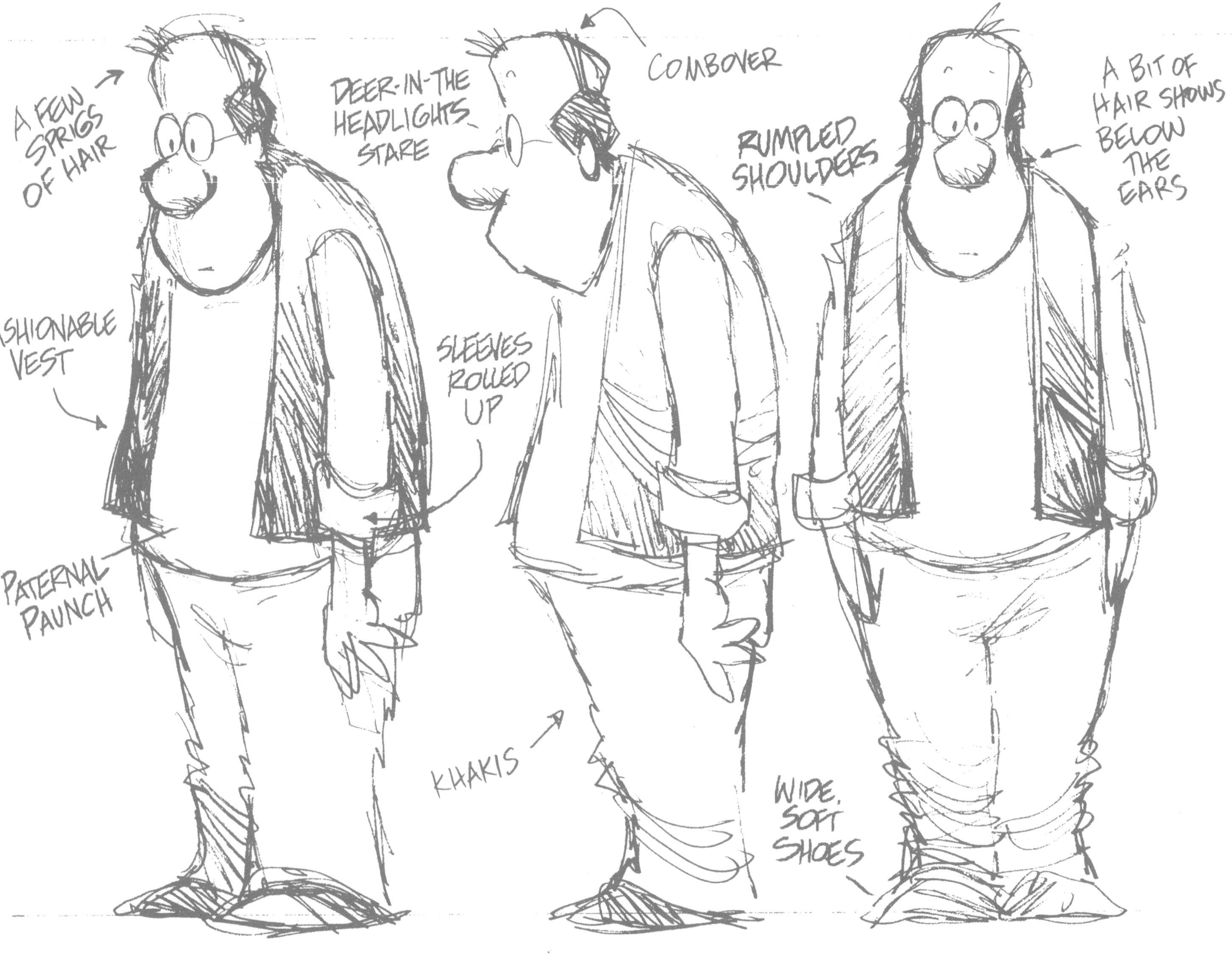

A FEW SPRIGS OF HAIR
DEER-IN-THE HEADLIGHTS STARE
COMBOVER
RUMPLED SHOULDERS
A BIT OF HAIR SHOWS BELOW THE EARS
FASHIONABLE VEST
SLEEVES ROLLED UP
PATERNAL PAUNCH
KHAKIS
WIDE, SOFT SHOES

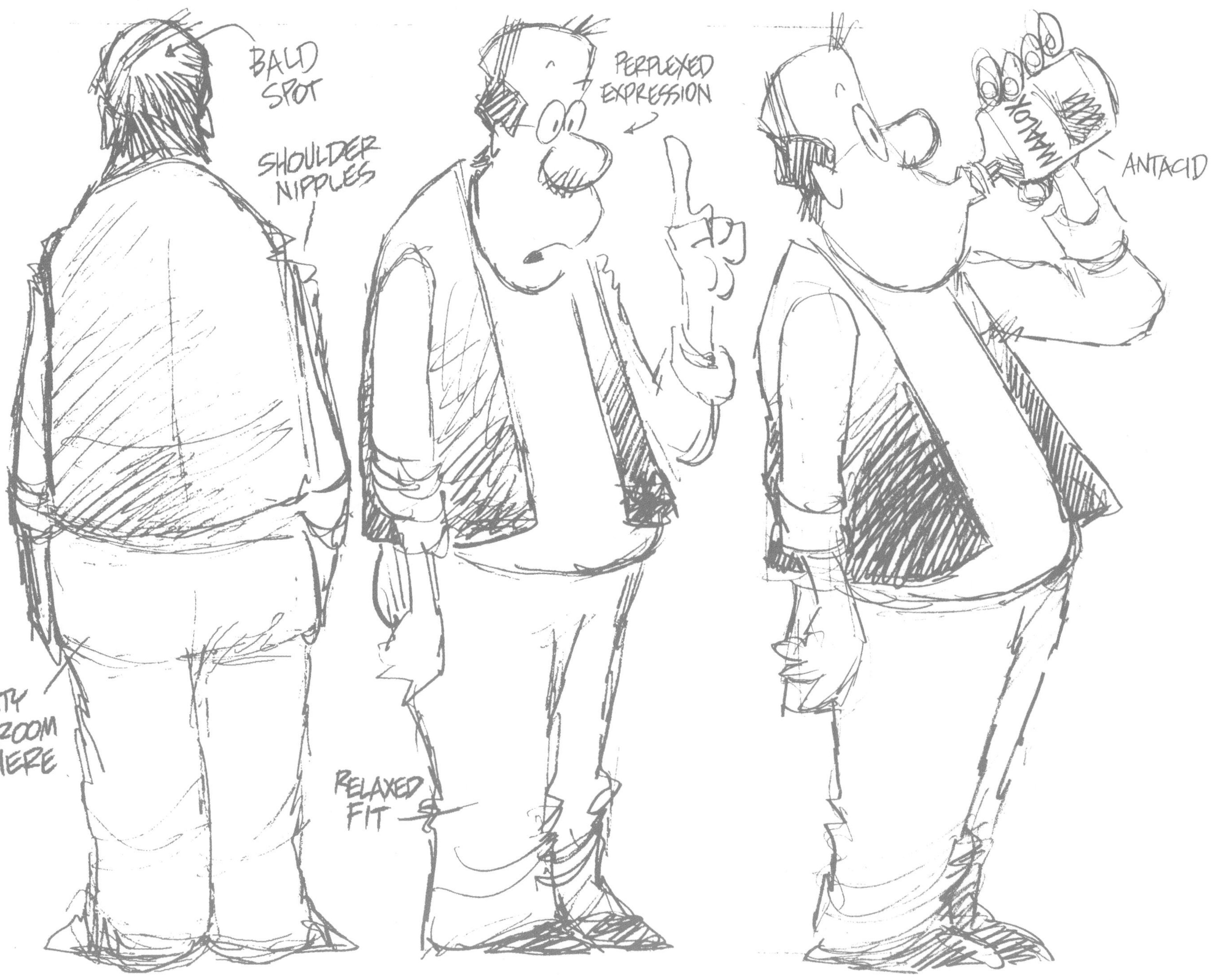
BALD SPOT
PERPLEXED EXPRESSION
SHOULDER NIPPLES
MAALOX
ANTACID
PLENTY OF ROOM IN THERE
RELAXED FIT

Jerry: This is one of the very first strips that helped set the tone for *Zits*. It's been one of our most requested reprints.

WHAT'S UP, SON?
I KEEP GETTING THE SAME ERROR CODE, AND I CAN'T FIGURE OUT WHY.
WELL, I DON'T KNOW TOO MUCH ABOUT THESE THINGS, BUT HAVE YOU CHECKED THE GIGABYTES?

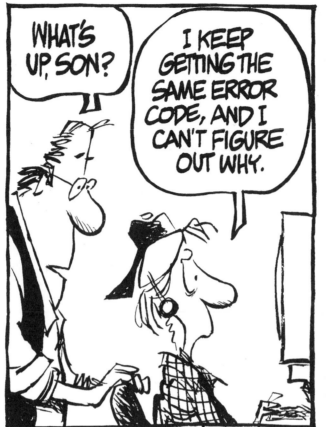

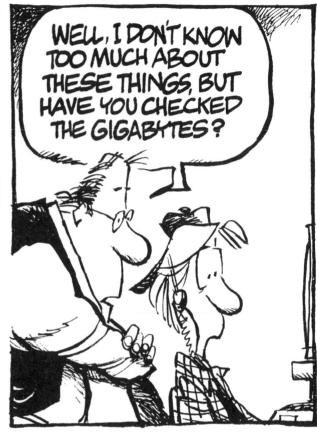

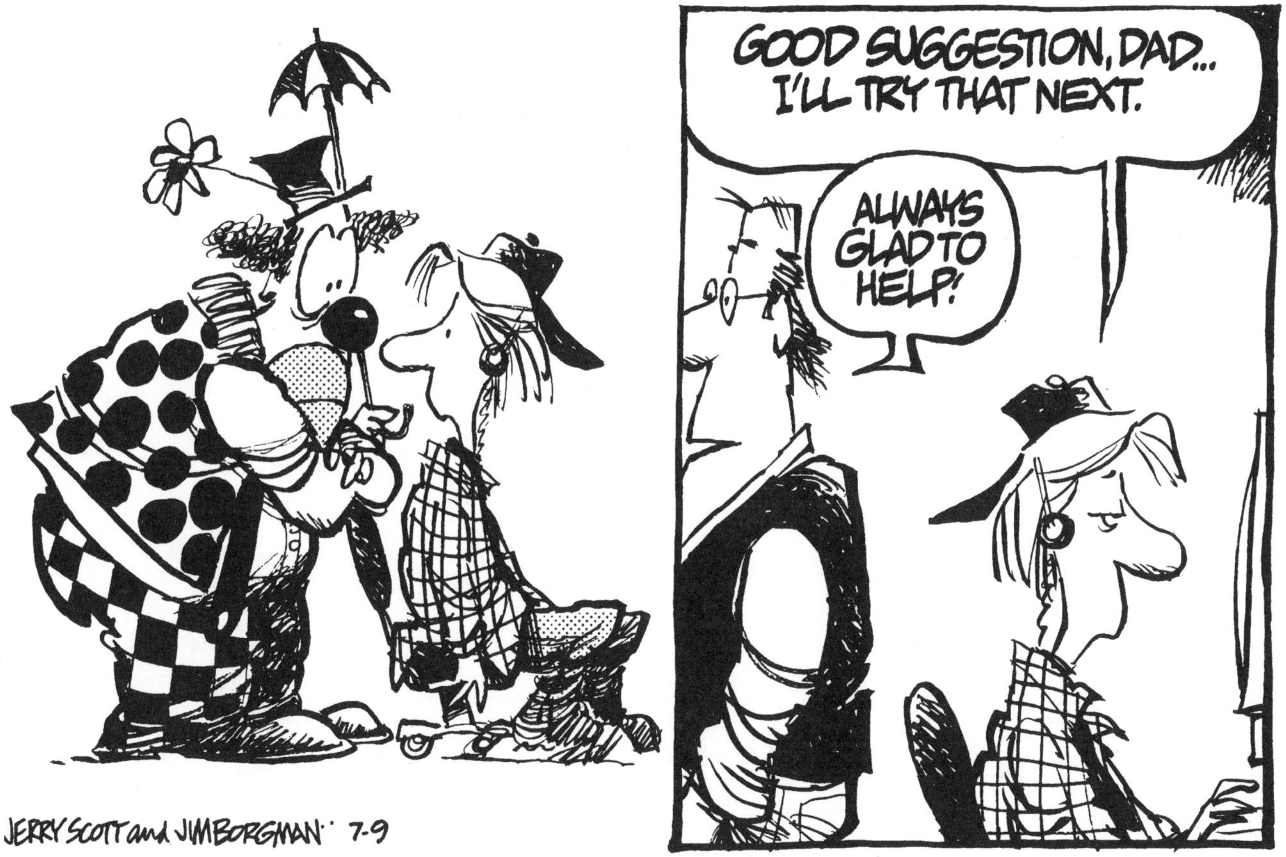
JERRY SCOTT and JIM BORGMAN 7-9
GOOD SUGGESTION, DAD... I'LL TRY THAT NEXT.
ALWAYS GLAD TO HELP!

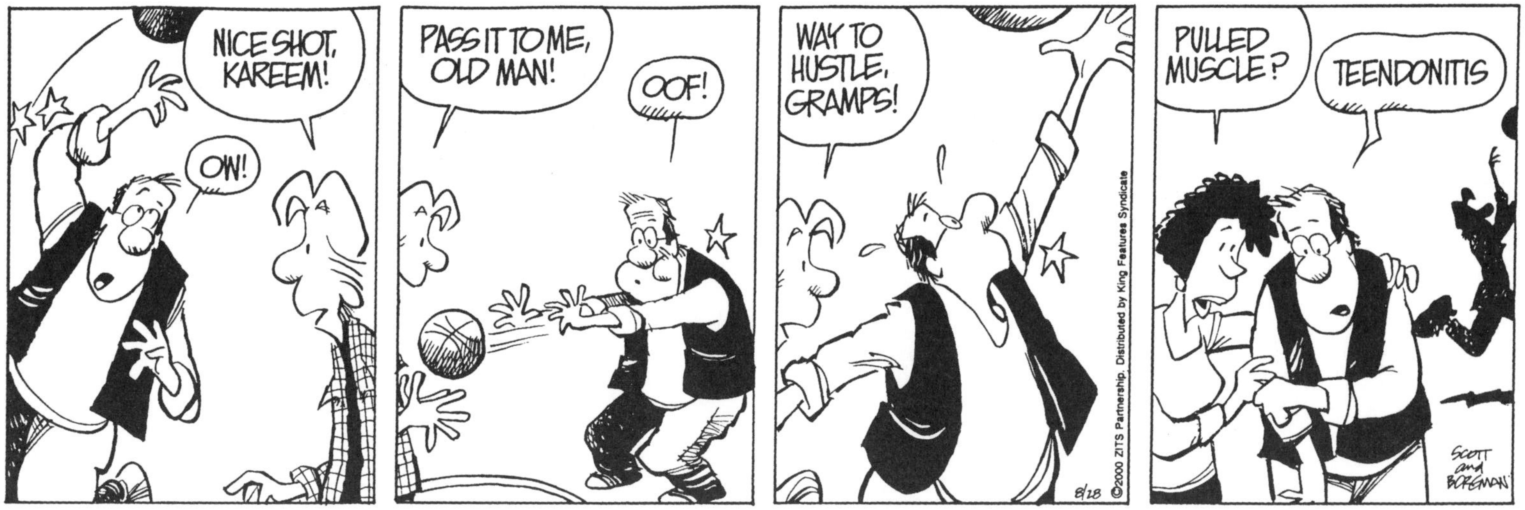
NICE SHOT, KAREEM!
OW!
PASS IT TO ME, OLD MAN!
OOF!
WAY TO HUSTLE, GRAMPS!
!
©2000 ZITS Partnership. Distributed by King Features Syndicate
8/28
PULLED MUSCLE?
TEENDONITIS
SCOTT and BORGMAN

SCOTT AND BORGMAN
©2002 ZITS Partnership. Distributed by King Features Syndicate
JEREMY'S ROOM — KEEP OUT!
3/17
YOU'RE KIDDING! THIS IS HOW THE WORLD LOOKS TO YOU??
WHY? WHAT'S FUNNY?

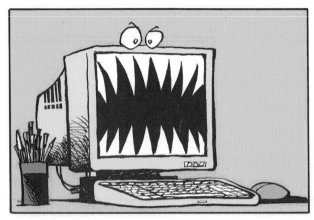

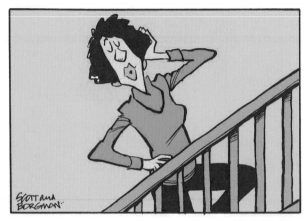

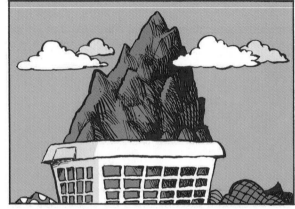

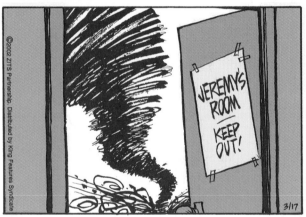

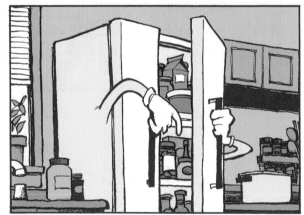

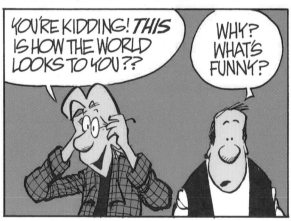

Jim: From the very beginning of *Zits*, we imagined Dad as a technological footdragger. He is also the launderer in the Duncan household. There, straight out of the gate, are two reasons why he is unfathomable to his son.

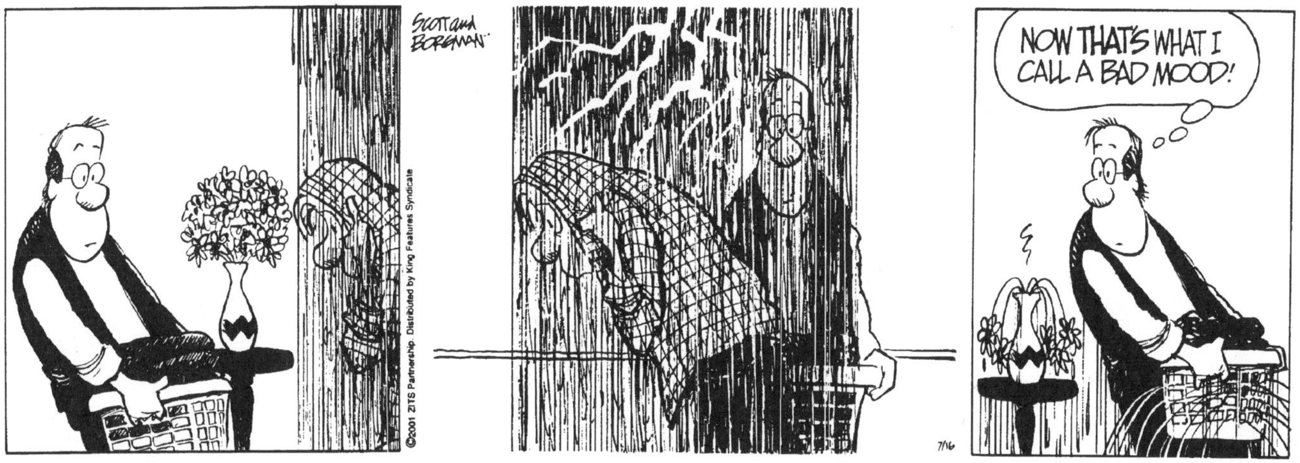
SCOTT and BORGMAN
©2001 ZITS Partnership. Distributed by King Features Syndicate
7/16
NOW THAT'S WHAT I CALL A BAD MOOD!

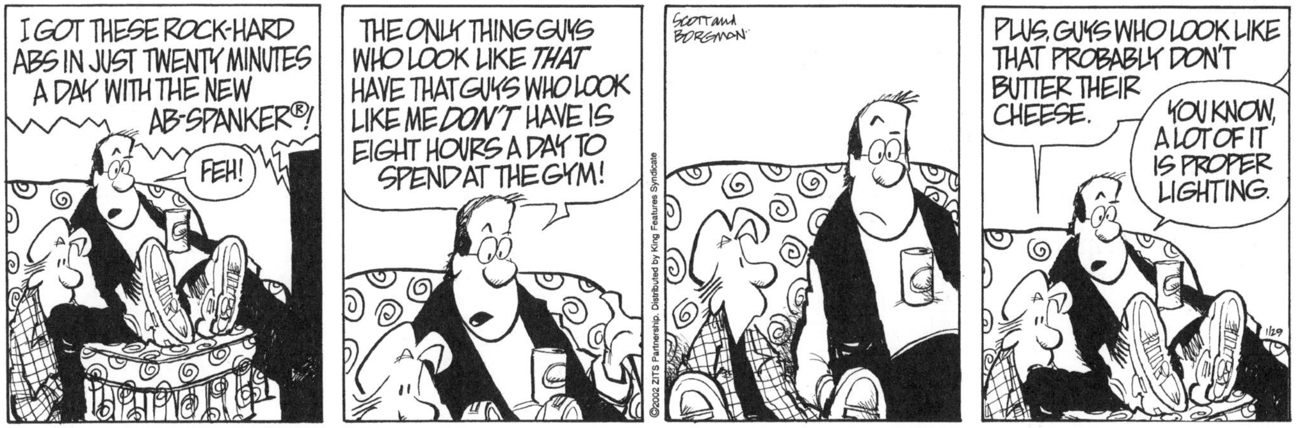
I GOT THESE ROCK-HARD ABS IN JUST TWENTY MINUTES A DAY WITH THE NEW AB-SPANKER®!
FEH!
THE ONLY THING GUYS WHO LOOK LIKE *THAT* HAVE THAT GUYS WHO LOOK LIKE ME *DON'T* HAVE IS EIGHT HOURS A DAY TO SPEND AT THE GYM!
©2002 ZITS Partnership. Distributed by King Features Syndicate
SCOTT and BORGMAN
PLUS, GUYS WHO LOOK LIKE THAT PROBABLY DON'T BUTTER THEIR CHEESE.
YOU KNOW, A LOT OF IT IS PROPER LIGHTING.
1/29

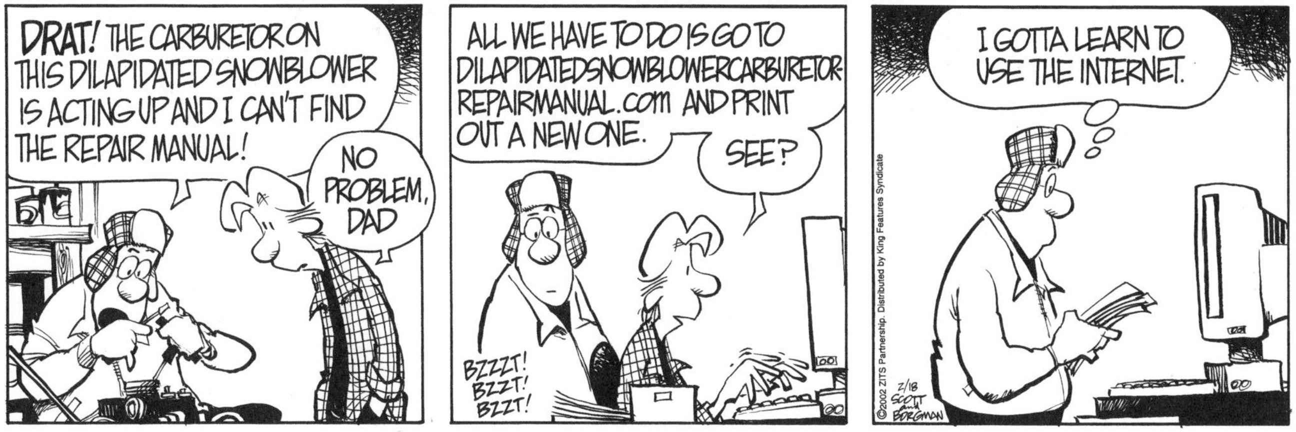
DRAT! THE CARBURETOR ON THIS DILAPIDATED SNOWBLOWER IS ACTING UP AND I CAN'T FIND THE REPAIR MANUAL!
NO PROBLEM, DAD
ALL WE HAVE TO DO IS GO TO DILAPIDATEDSNOWBLOWERCARBURETOR-REPAIRMANUAL.com AND PRINT OUT A NEW ONE.
SEE?
BZZZT! BZZT! BZZT!
©2002 ZITS Partnership. Distributed by King Features Syndicate
2/18
SCOTT and BORGMAN
I GOTTA LEARN TO USE THE INTERNET.

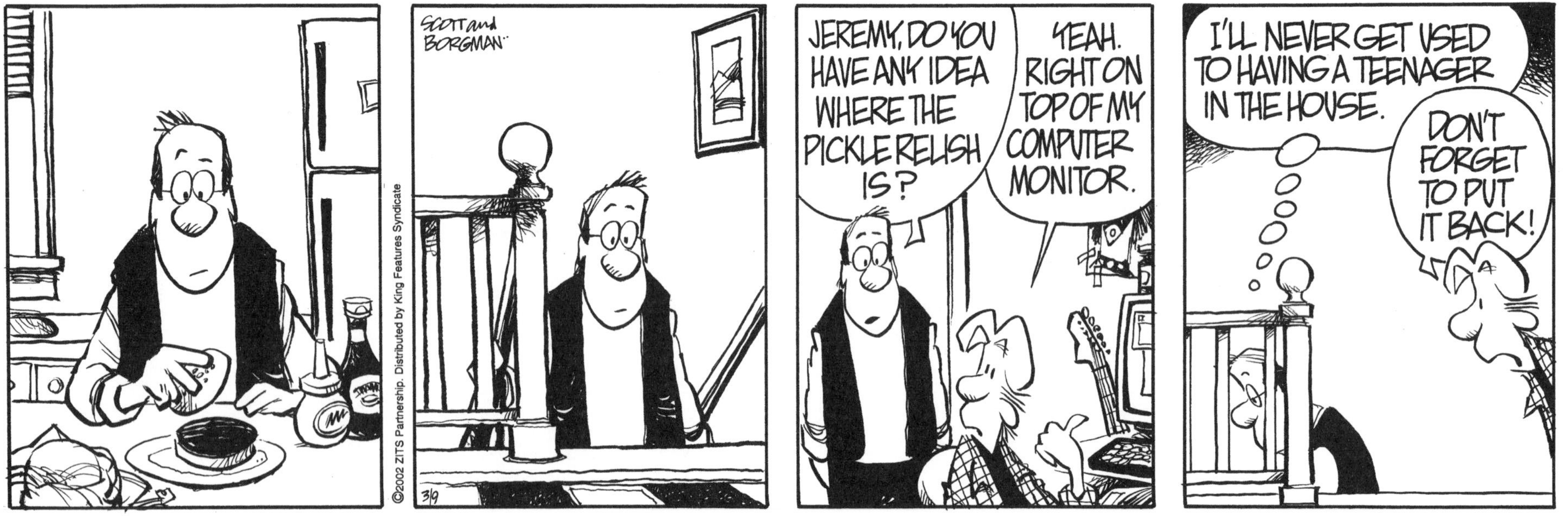
SCOTT and BORGMAN
©2002 ZITS Partnership. Distributed by King Features Syndicate
3/9
JEREMY, DO YOU HAVE ANY IDEA WHERE THE PICKLE RELISH IS?
YEAH. RIGHT ON TOP OF MY COMPUTER MONITOR.
I'LL NEVER GET USED TO HAVING A TEENAGER IN THE HOUSE.
DON'T FORGET TO PUT IT BACK!

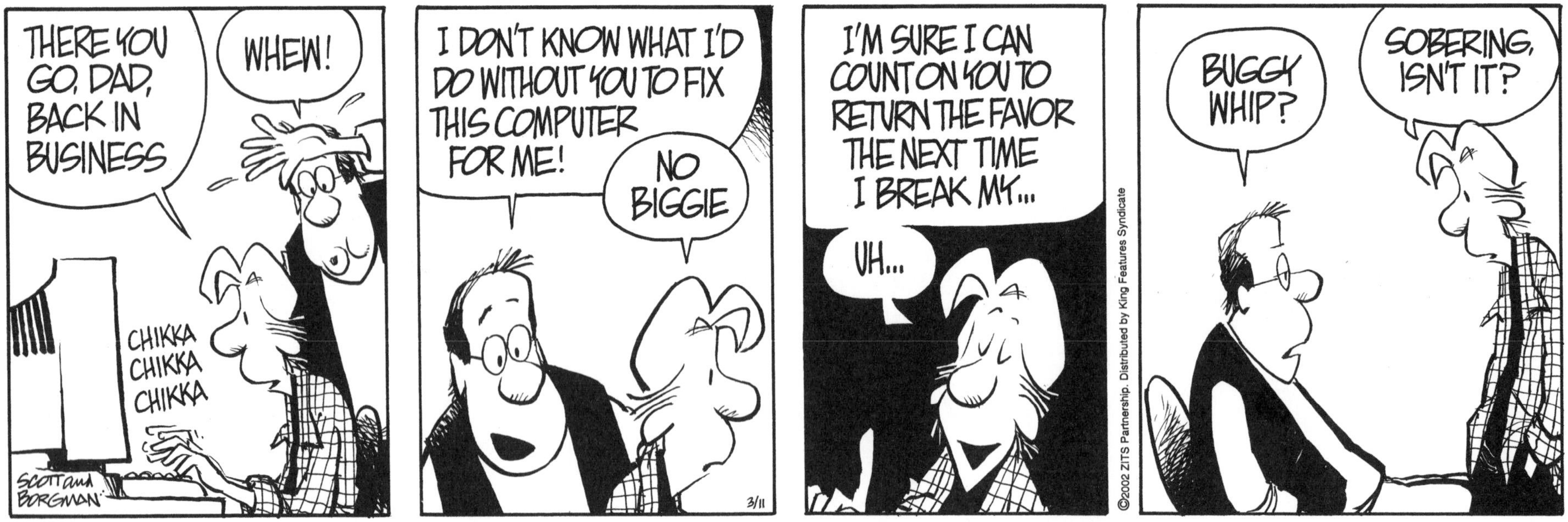
THERE YOU GO, DAD, BACK IN BUSINESS
WHEW!
CHIKKA CHIKKA CHIKKA
SCOTT and BORGMAN
I DON'T KNOW WHAT I'D DO WITHOUT YOU TO FIX THIS COMPUTER FOR ME!
NO BIGGIE
3/11
I'M SURE I CAN COUNT ON YOU TO RETURN THE FAVOR THE NEXT TIME I BREAK MY...
UH...
©2002 ZITS Partnership. Distributed by King Features Syndicate
BUGGY WHIP?
SOBERING, ISN'T IT?

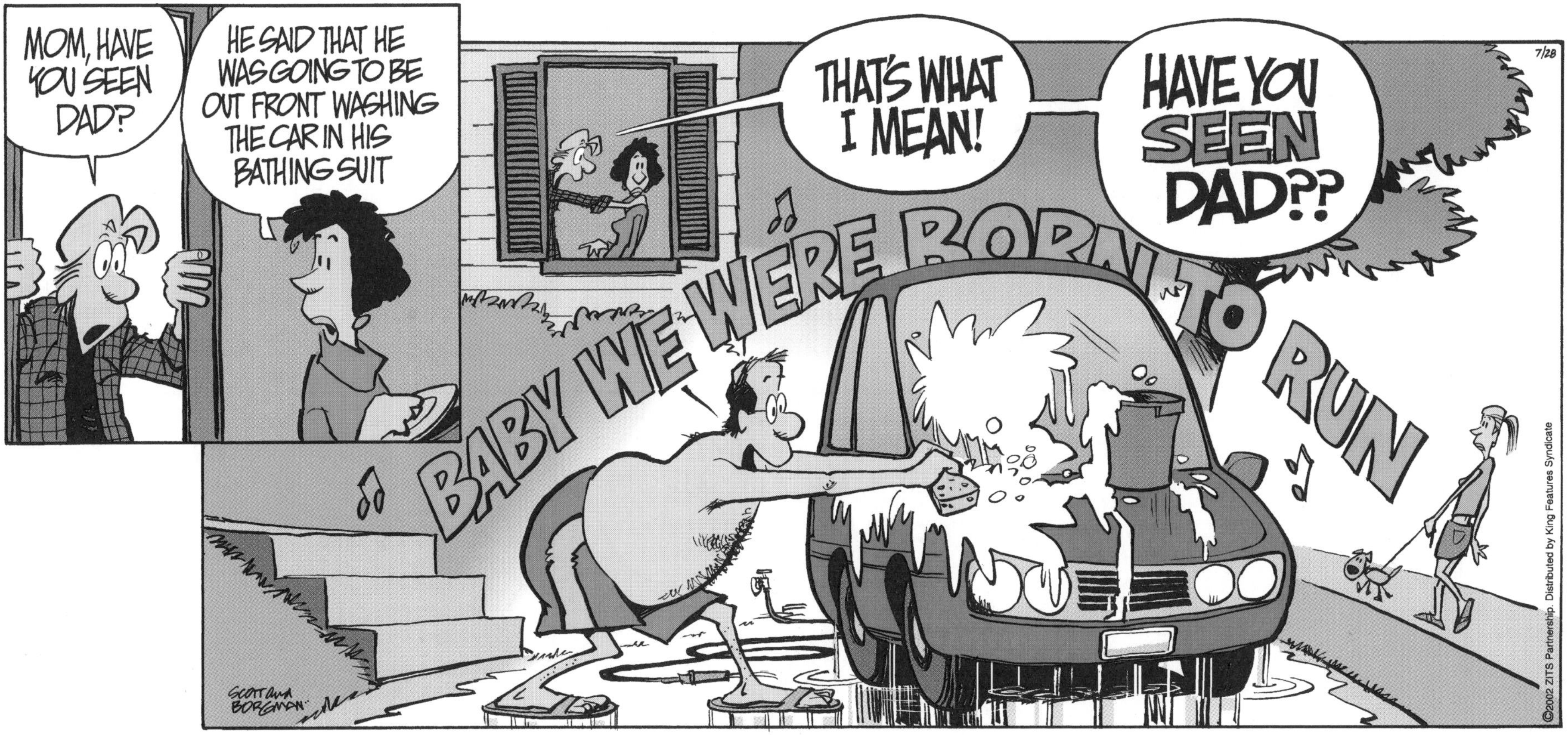
MOM, HAVE YOU SEEN DAD?
HE SAID THAT HE WAS GOING TO BE OUT FRONT WASHING THE CAR IN HIS BATHING SUIT
THAT'S WHAT I MEAN!
HAVE YOU SEEN DAD??
BABY WE WERE BORN TO RUN
7/28
SCOTT AND BORGMAN
©2002 ZITS Partnership. Distributed by King Features Syndicate

Jim: Part of the responsibility of being a dad is to regularly embarrass your kids. And, by the way, any rumors regarding physical resemblances between Walt and myself are highly exaggerated.

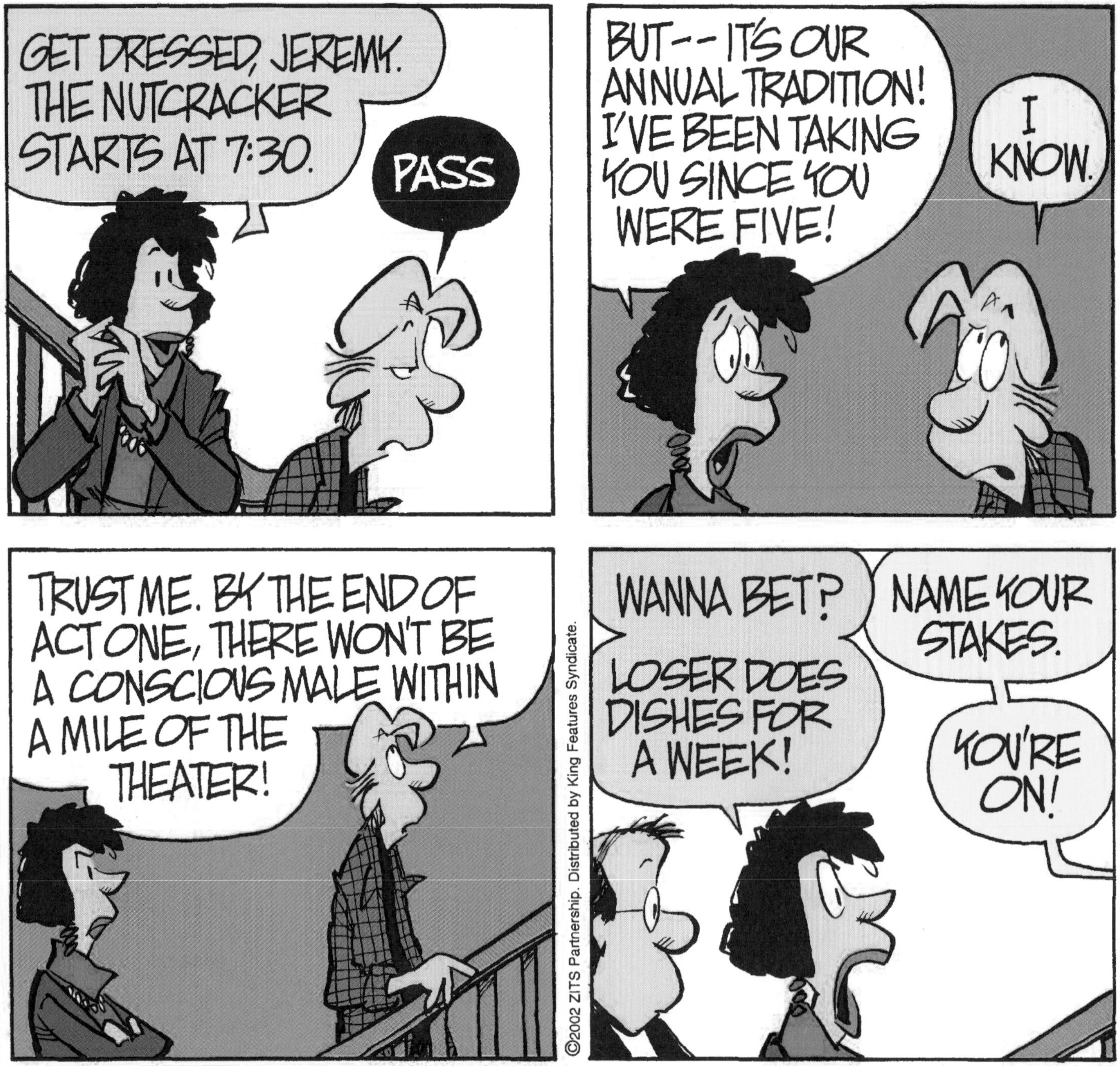
GET DRESSED, JEREMY. THE NUTCRACKER STARTS AT 7:30.
PASS
BUT-- IT'S OUR ANNUAL TRADITION! I'VE BEEN TAKING YOU SINCE YOU WERE FIVE!
I KNOW.
TRUST ME. BY THE END OF ACT ONE, THERE WON'T BE A CONSCIOUS MALE WITHIN A MILE OF THE THEATER!
WANNA BET?
NAME YOUR STAKES.
LOSER DOES DISHES FOR A WEEK!
YOU'RE ON!
©2002 ZITS Partnership. Distributed by King Features Syndicate.

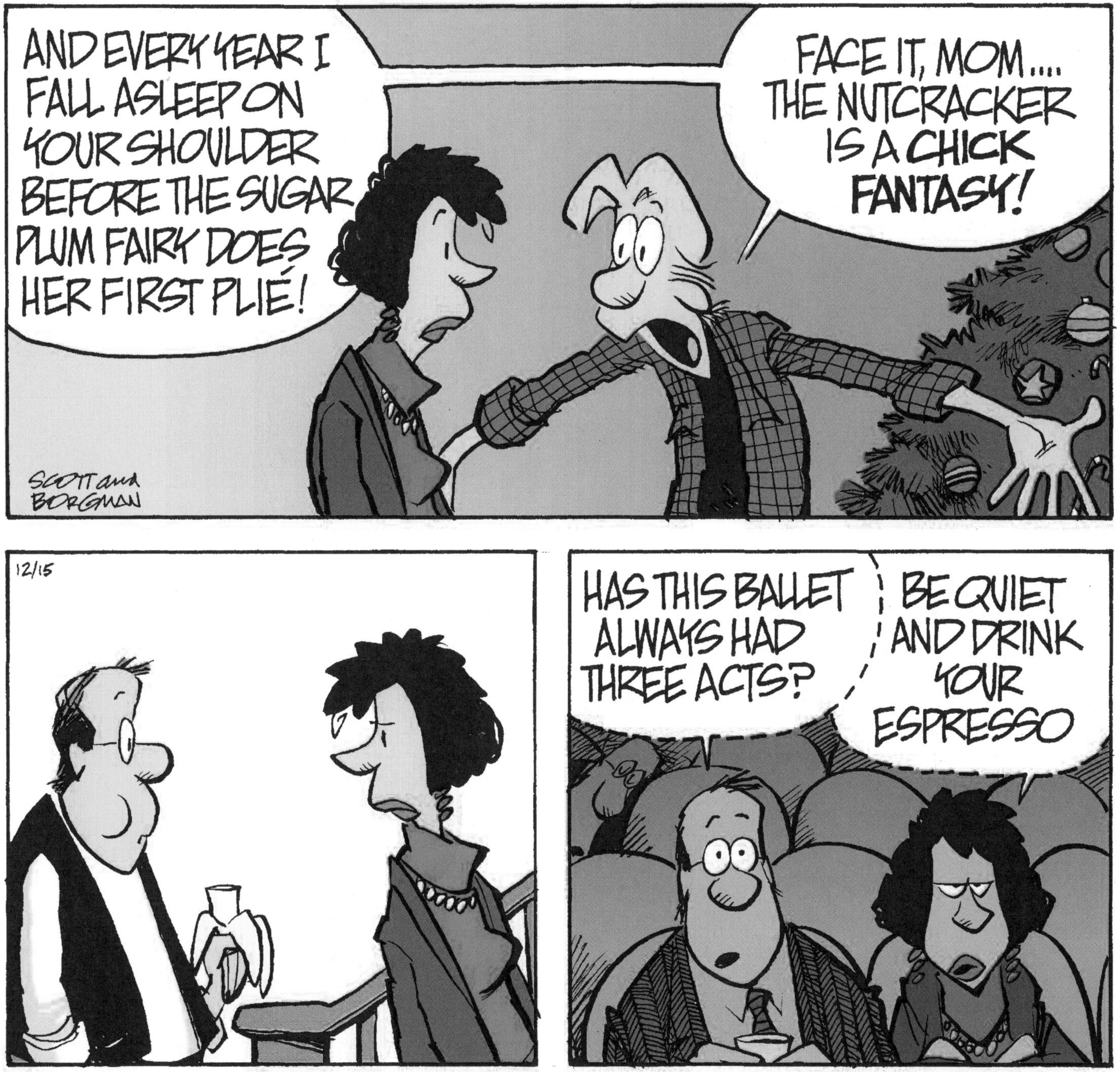
AND EVERY YEAR I FALL ASLEEP ON YOUR SHOULDER BEFORE THE SUGAR PLUM FAIRY DOES HER FIRST PLIÉ!
FACE IT, MOM.... THE NUTCRACKER IS A CHICK FANTASY!
SCOTT and BORGMAN
12/15
HAS THIS BALLET ALWAYS HAD THREE ACTS?
BE QUIET AND DRINK YOUR ESPRESSO

Jerry: Jeremy's look was a little dorkier back when this one was drawn. In current strips, Jeremy's hair is longer, shaggier, and cooler, while Dad's comb-over is less convincing.

STILL NO EXPRESS PACKAGE FOR ME?
NOT TODAY
THAT DOES IT! I'M CALLING THEIR COMPLAINT DEPARTMENT RIGHT N--
BIP BEEP BIP
EXPRESS PACKAGE?
OH, WAIT...
©2002 ZITS Partnership. Distributed by King Features Syndicate
SOME GUY DELIVERED THIS ON TUESDAY AS I WAS ON MY WAY UP TO MY ROOM.
SCOTT and BORGMAN
3/15
OVERNIGHT FROM SEATTLE TO OUR FRONT DOOR, AND THREE DAYS FROM JEREMY'S HANDS TO MINE.
SORRY ABOUT THE PEANUT BUTTER STAINS

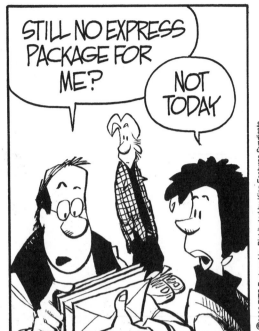

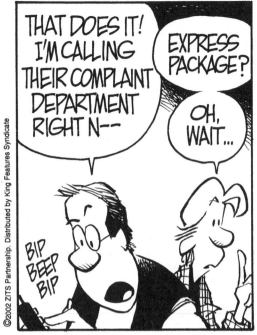

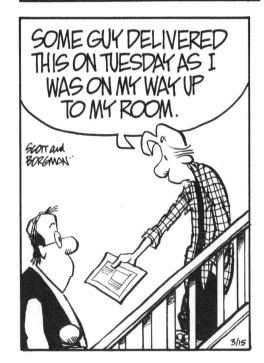

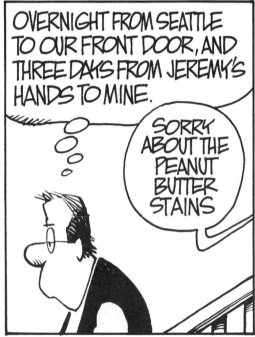

SCOTT and BORGMAN
DING! DONG!
3/22
©2002 ZITS Partnership. Distributed by King Features Syndicate
WHO WAS IT?
NOT THE PIZZA GUY
AND IT'S GOOD TO BE HOME, TOO.

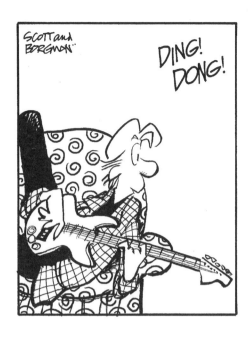

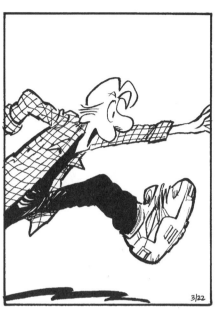

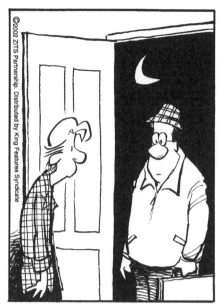

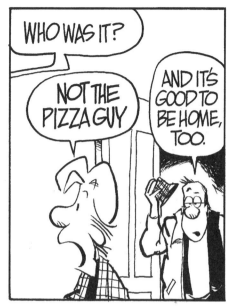

Jim: In drawing Walt, I look for emblems that mark him as a baby boomer with a dated wardrobe—the way all dads look to their teenagers. Does anyone actually still wear plaid hats like this? Come on, let's see those hands.

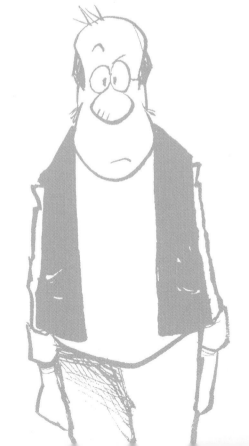

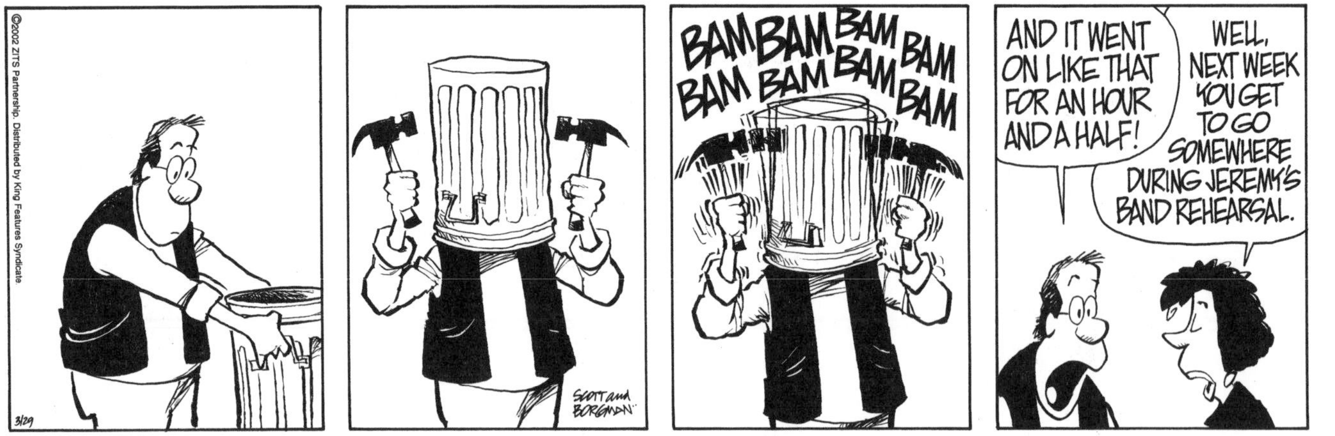
©2002 ZITS Partnership. Distributed by King Features Syndicate
3/29
SCOTT AND BORGMAN
BAM BAM BAM BAM BAM BAM BAM BAM
AND IT WENT ON LIKE THAT FOR AN HOUR AND A HALF!
WELL, NEXT WEEK YOU GET TO GO SOMEWHERE DURING JEREMY'S BAND REHEARSAL.

Jerry: I used to have a riding mower like this and felt pretty good about it until I saw my reflection in a window. It immediately became a Dad thing in the strip.

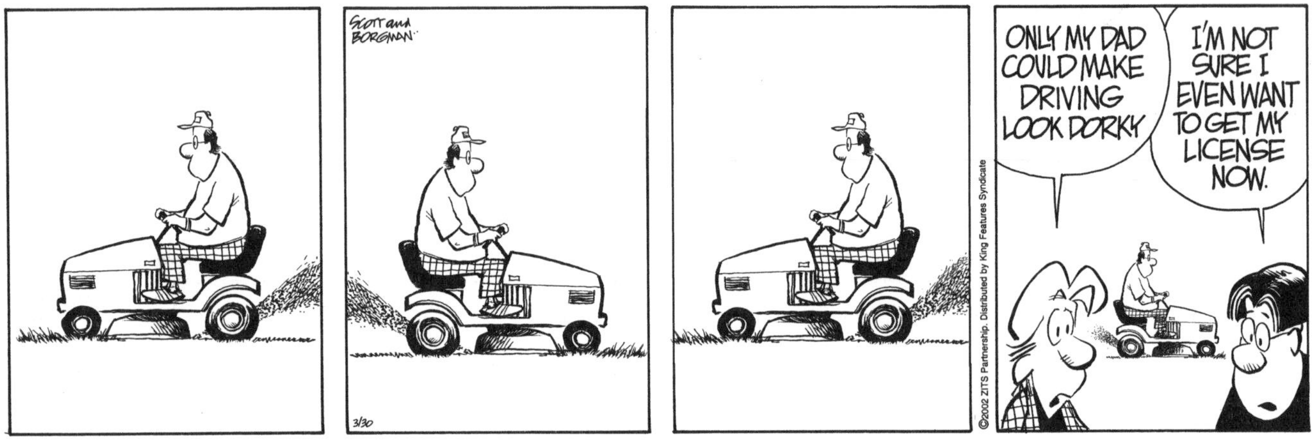
SCOTT AND BORGMAN
3/30
©2002 ZITS Partnership. Distributed by King Features Syndicate
ONLY MY DAD COULD MAKE DRIVING LOOK DORKY
I'M NOT SURE I EVEN WANT TO GET MY LICENSE NOW.

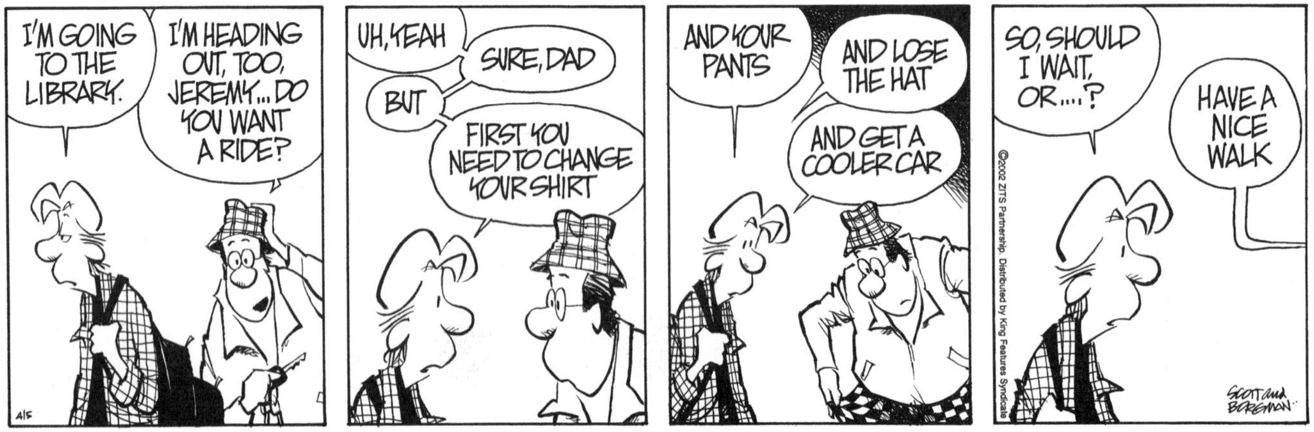
I'M GOING TO THE LIBRARY.
I'M HEADING OUT, TOO, JEREMY... DO YOU WANT A RIDE?
4/5
UH, YEAH
SURE, DAD
BUT
FIRST YOU NEED TO CHANGE YOUR SHIRT
AND YOUR PANTS
AND LOSE THE HAT
AND GET A COOLER CAR
©2002 ZITS Partnership. Distributed by King Features Syndicate
SO, SHOULD I WAIT, OR....?
HAVE A NICE WALK
SCOTT AND BORGMAN

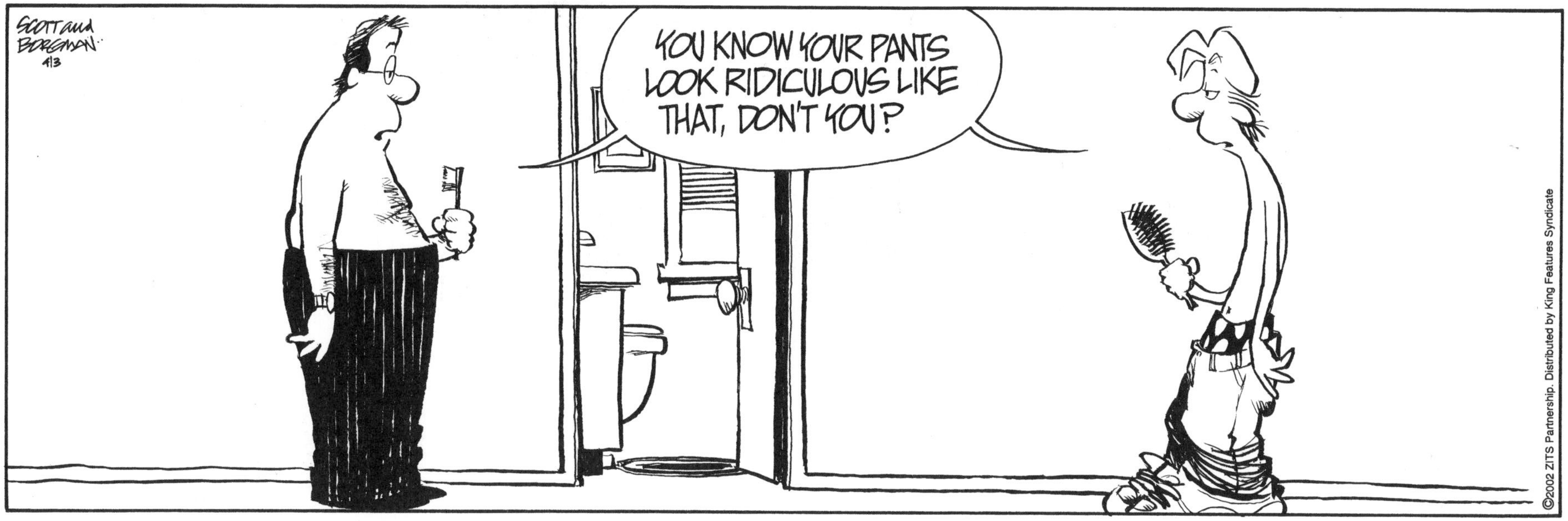
YOU KNOW YOUR PANTS LOOK RIDICULOUS LIKE THAT, DON'T YOU?
©2002 ZITS Partnership. Distributed by King Features Syndicate

Jim: I am never more comfortable drawing *Zits* than when Dad is onstage. He relates to the world through '60s music, loose clothing, and snacks.

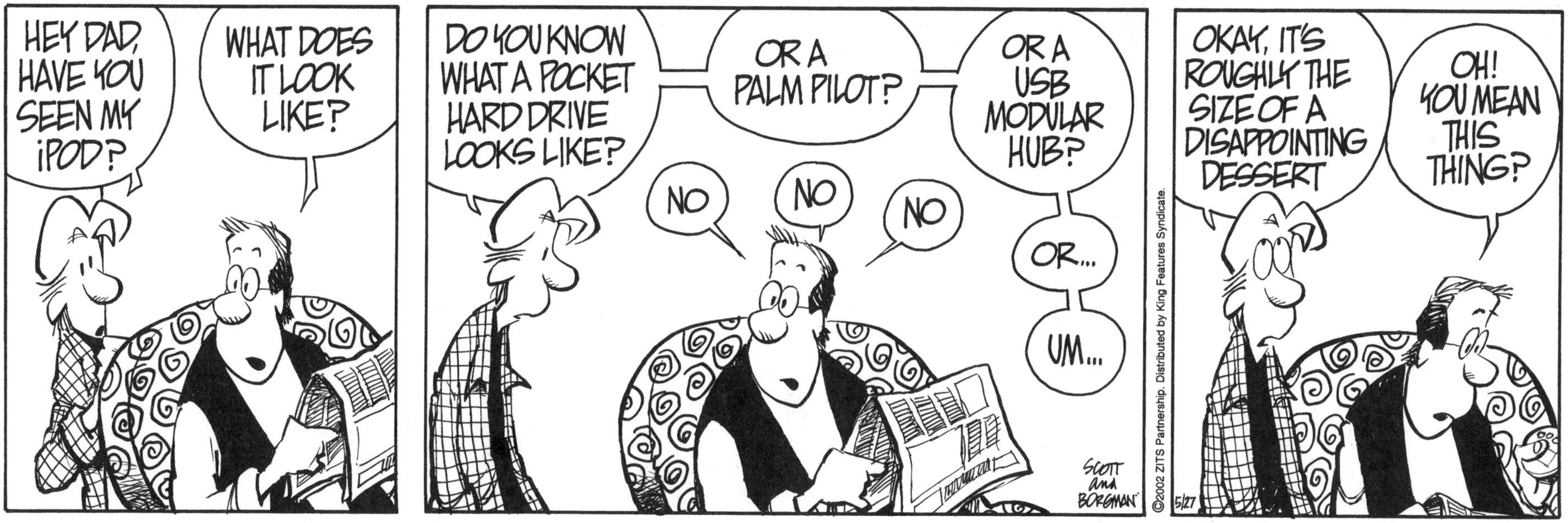
HEY DAD, HAVE YOU SEEN MY iPOD?
WHAT DOES IT LOOK LIKE?
DO YOU KNOW WHAT A POCKET HARD DRIVE LOOKS LIKE?
NO
OR A PALM PILOT?
NO
OR A USB MODULAR HUB?
NO
OR...
UM...
SCOTT and BORGMAN
©2002 ZITS Partnership. Distributed by King Features Syndicate.
OKAY, IT'S ROUGHLY THE SIZE OF A DISAPPOINTING DESSERT
OH! YOU MEAN THIS THING?

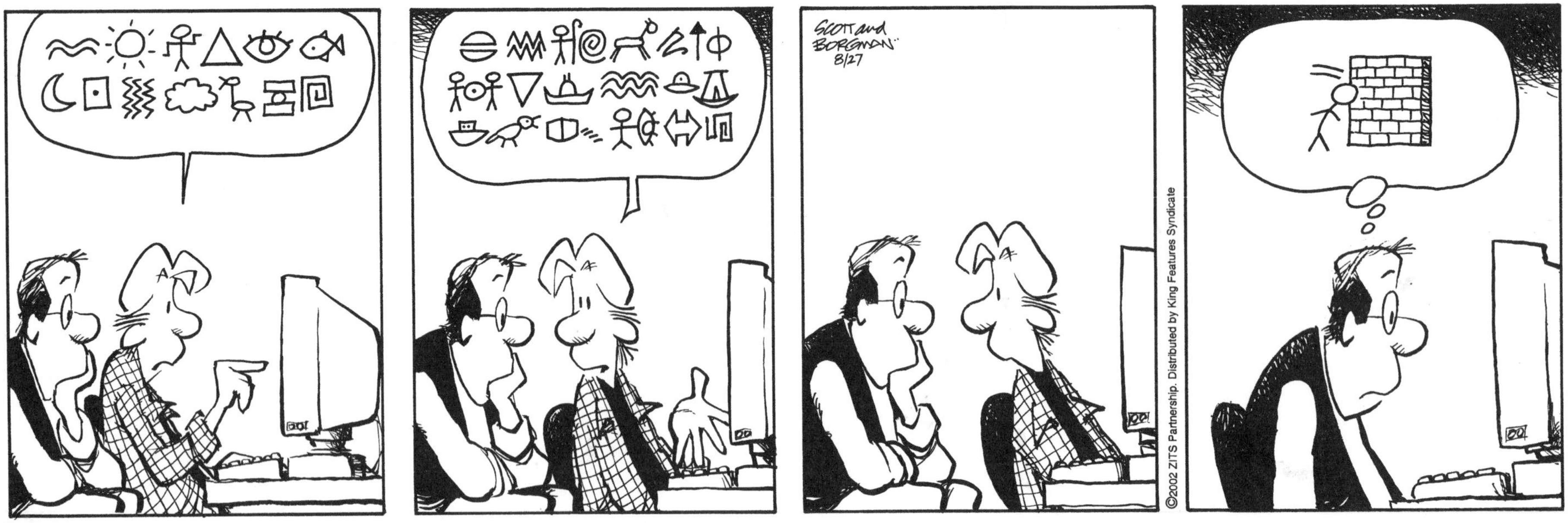
SCOTT and BORGMAN
8/27
©2002 ZITS Partnership. Distributed by King Features Syndicate

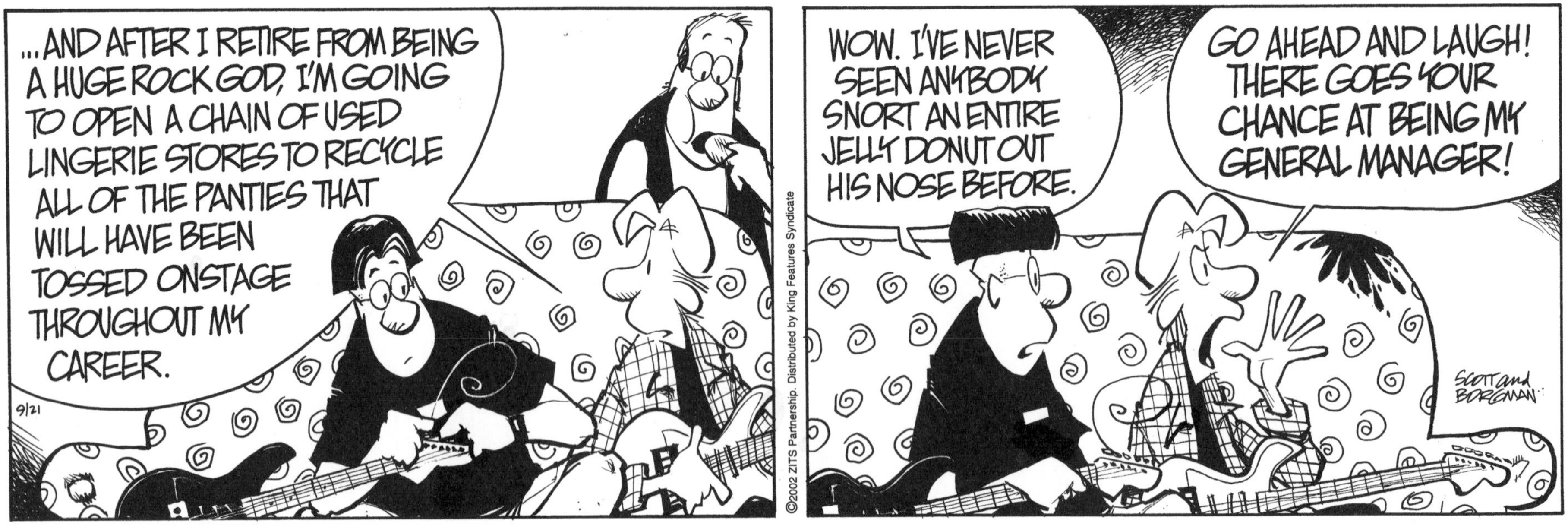
...AND AFTER I RETIRE FROM BEING A HUGE ROCK GOD, I'M GOING TO OPEN A CHAIN OF USED LINGERIE STORES TO RECYCLE ALL OF THE PANTIES THAT WILL HAVE BEEN TOSSED ONSTAGE THROUGHOUT MY CAREER.
9/21
©2002 ZITS Partnership. Distributed by King Features Syndicate
WOW. I'VE NEVER SEEN ANYBODY SNORT AN ENTIRE JELLY DONUT OUT HIS NOSE BEFORE.
GO AHEAD AND LAUGH! THERE GOES YOUR CHANCE AT BEING MY GENERAL MANAGER!
SCOTT and BORGMAN

IT'S 9:30
SHOULDN'T YOU BOYS BE IN BED?
TYPE! TYPE! TYPE! TYPE! TYPE! TYPE! TYPE!
SEND
SCROLL! SCROLL! SCROLL! SCROLL!
SCOTT AND BORGMAN
11/2
BWA-HAHAHAHAHA!
©2003 ZITS Partnership. Distributed by King Features Syndicate.
I THINK I'VE JUST BEEN DIGITALLY DISRESPECTED!
PERSONALLY, I FIND IT LESS ANNOYING THAN THE ANALOG METHOD.

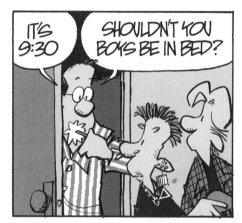

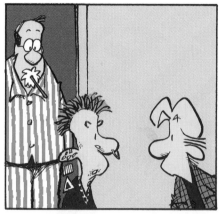

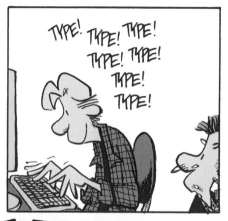

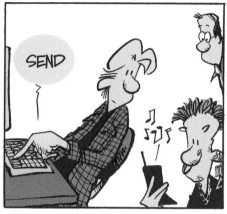

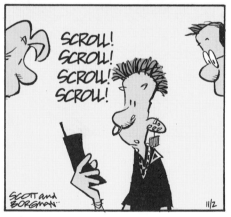

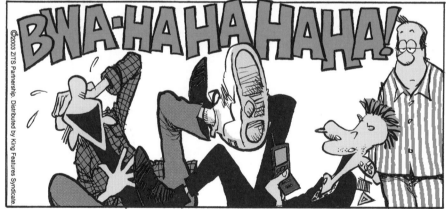

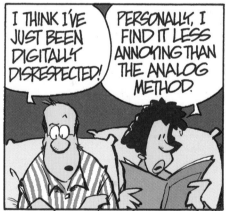

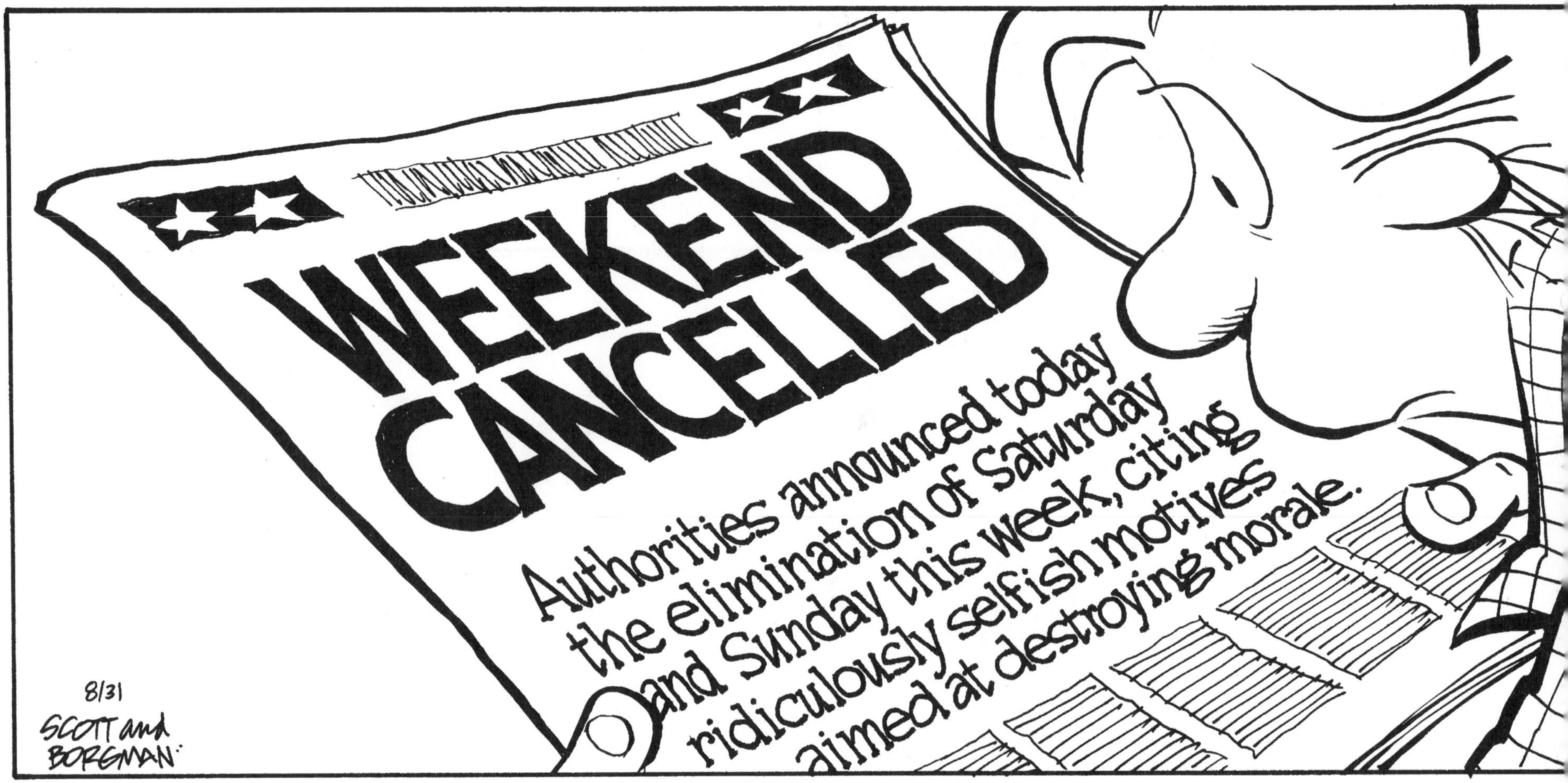
WEEKEND CANCELLED
Authorities announced today the elimination of Saturday and Sunday this week, citing ridiculously selfish motives aimed at destroying morale.
8/31
SCOTT and BORGMAN

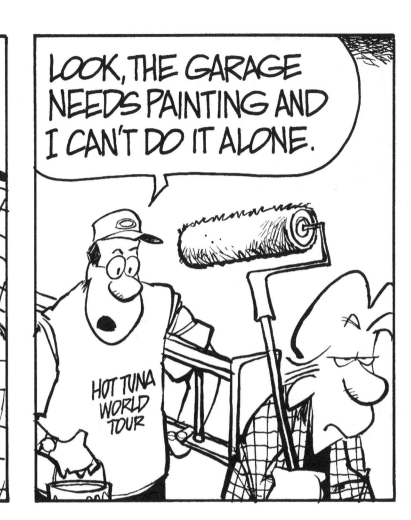

LOOK, THE GARAGE NEEDS PAINTING AND I CAN'T DO IT ALONE.
HOT TUNA WORLD TOUR

Jim: I started putting old '60s band names on Dad's T-shirts to establish him as a baby boomer, but over time it became an exercise in nostalgia for me. Moby Grape, the Electric Prunes, Humble Pie, Strawberry Alarm Clock, and the Moody Blues have all made appearances on his shirts. (In case you were wondering, the Hot Tuna Reunion Tour of 1983 bombed when the band switched its emphasis from country blues to heavy metal.)

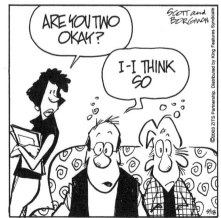

ARE YOU TWO OKAY?
I-I THINK SO
SCOTT and BORGMAN
©2003 ZITS Partnership. Distributed by King Features Syndicate
9/18
JEREMY AND I WERE SITTING HERE TALKING, AND BAM!
IT JUST HAPPENED!
WHAT HAPPENED?
WE AGREED ON SOMETHING
SO...
WOOZY...

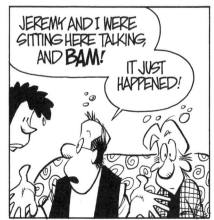

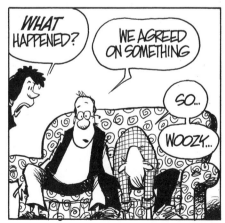

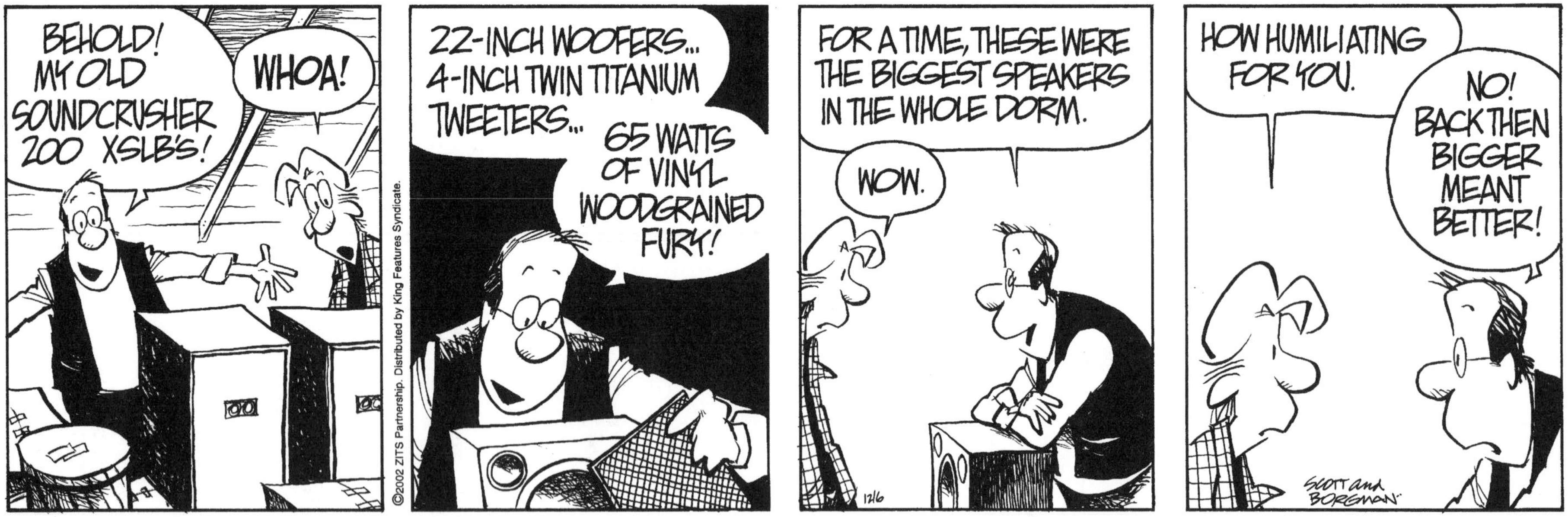
BEHOLD! MY OLD SOUNDCRUSHER 200 XSLB'S!
WHOA!
22-INCH WOOFERS... 4-INCH TWIN TITANIUM TWEETERS...
65 WATTS OF VINYL WOODGRAINED FURY!
FOR A TIME, THESE WERE THE BIGGEST SPEAKERS IN THE WHOLE DORM.
WOW.
HOW HUMILIATING FOR YOU.
NO! BACK THEN BIGGER MEANT BETTER!
©2002 ZITS Partnership. Distributed by King Features Syndicate.
12/6
SCOTT and BORGMAN

Jerry: I think I still have a pair of speakers like this in the attic.

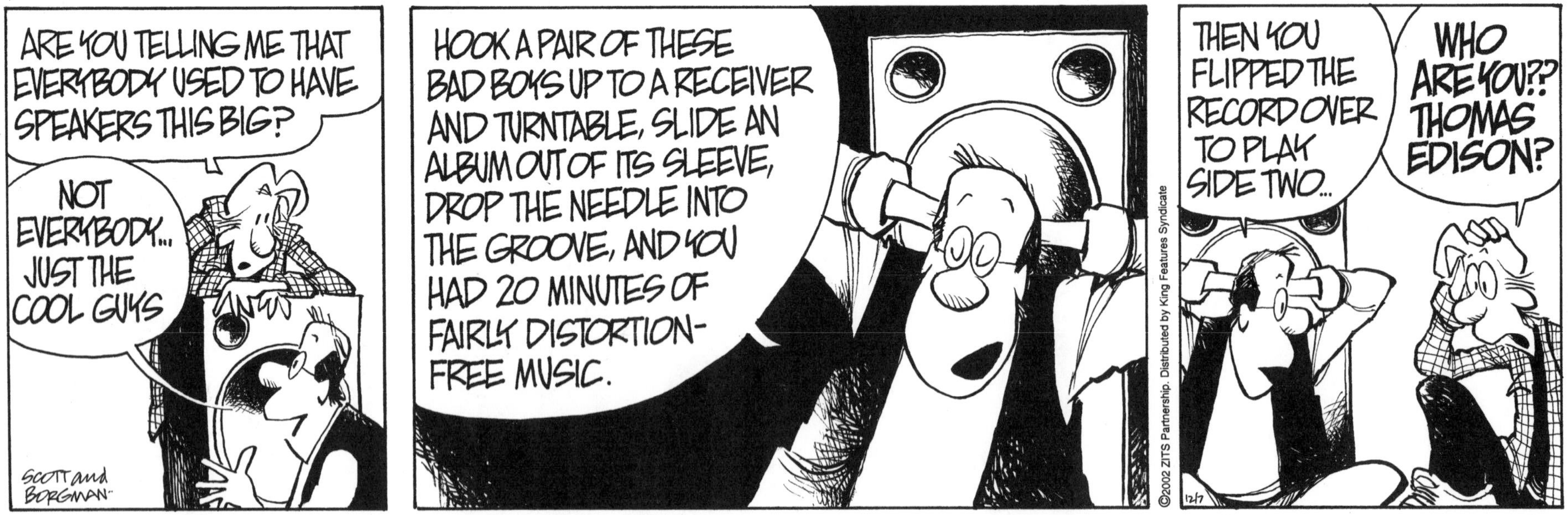
ARE YOU TELLING ME THAT EVERYBODY USED TO HAVE SPEAKERS THIS BIG?
NOT EVERYBODY... JUST THE COOL GUYS
SCOTT and BORGMAN
HOOK A PAIR OF THESE BAD BOYS UP TO A RECEIVER AND TURNTABLE, SLIDE AN ALBUM OUT OF ITS SLEEVE, DROP THE NEEDLE INTO THE GROOVE, AND YOU HAD 20 MINUTES OF FAIRLY DISTORTION-FREE MUSIC.
THEN YOU FLIPPED THE RECORD OVER TO PLAY SIDE TWO...
WHO ARE YOU?? THOMAS EDISON?
©2002 ZITS Partnership. Distributed by King Features Syndicate
12/7

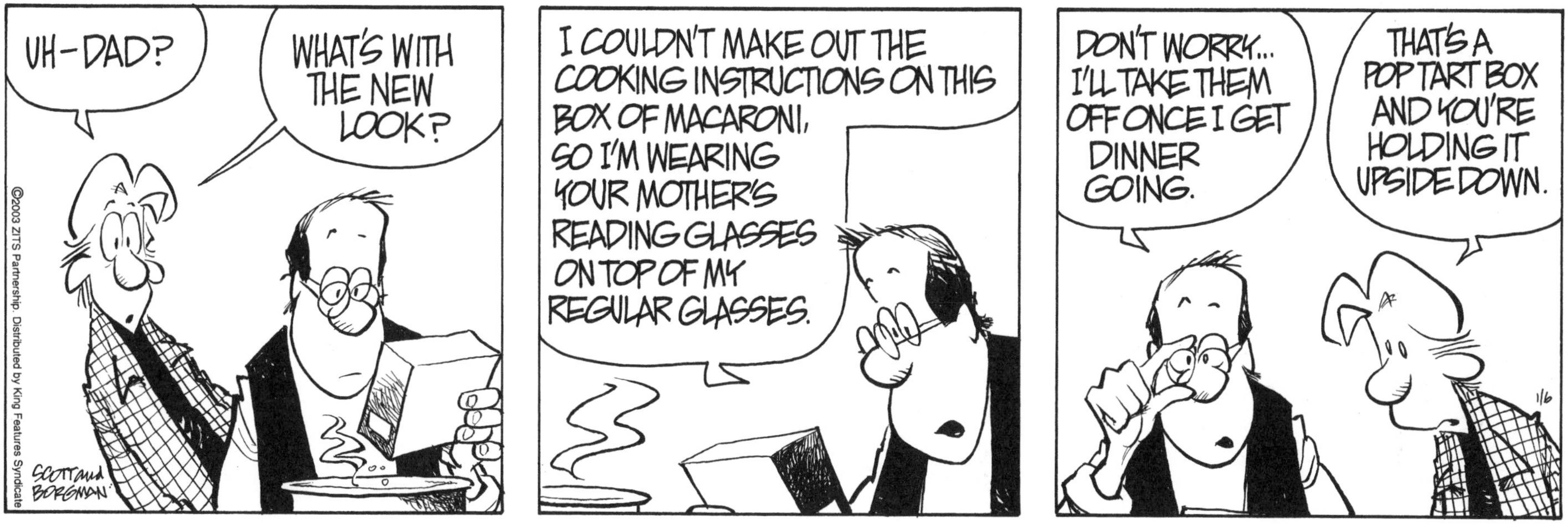
UH-DAD?
WHAT'S WITH THE NEW LOOK?
©2003 ZITS Partnership. Distributed by King Features Syndicate.
SCOTT AND BORGMAN
I COULDN'T MAKE OUT THE COOKING INSTRUCTIONS ON THIS BOX OF MACARONI, SO I'M WEARING YOUR MOTHER'S READING GLASSES ON TOP OF MY REGULAR GLASSES.
DON'T WORRY... I'LL TAKE THEM OFF ONCE I GET DINNER GOING.
THAT'S A POP TART BOX AND YOU'RE HOLDING IT UPSIDE DOWN.
1/6

Jim: What father among us hasn't sported the specs-on-specs look when reading, say, instructions on a Lipitor bottle?

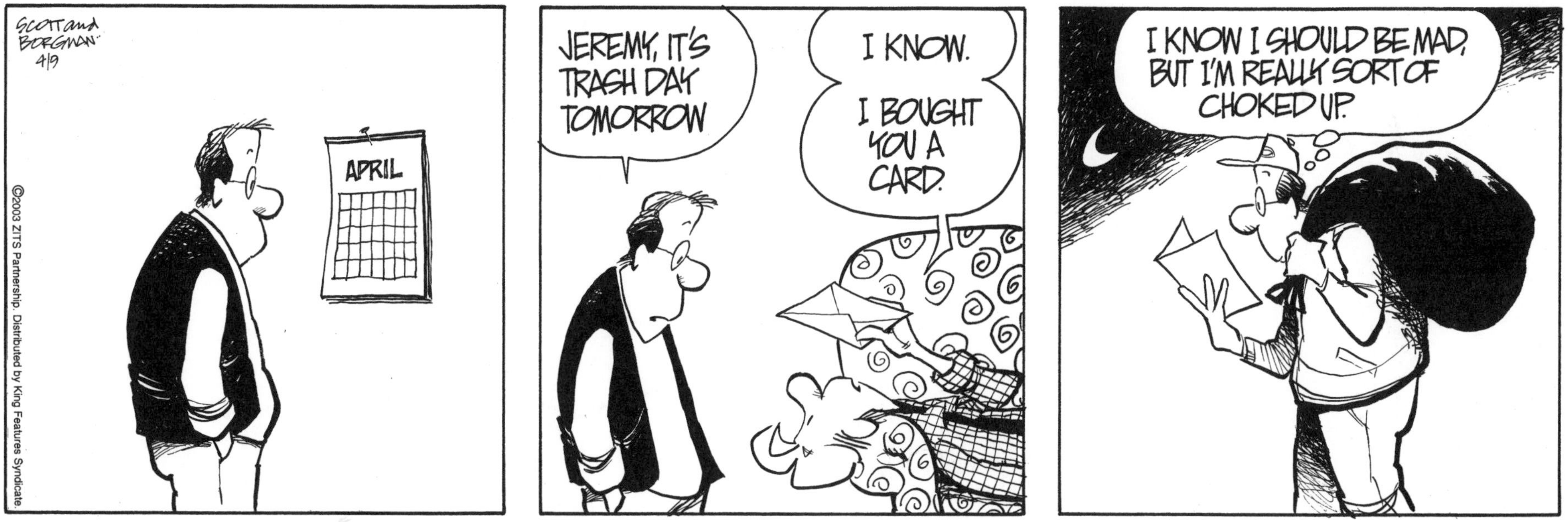
SCOTT AND BORGMAN 4/9
©2003 ZITS Partnership. Distributed by King Features Syndicate.
APRIL
JEREMY, IT'S TRASH DAY TOMORROW
I KNOW.
I BOUGHT YOU A CARD.
I KNOW I SHOULD BE MAD, BUT I'M REALLY SORT OF CHOKED UP.

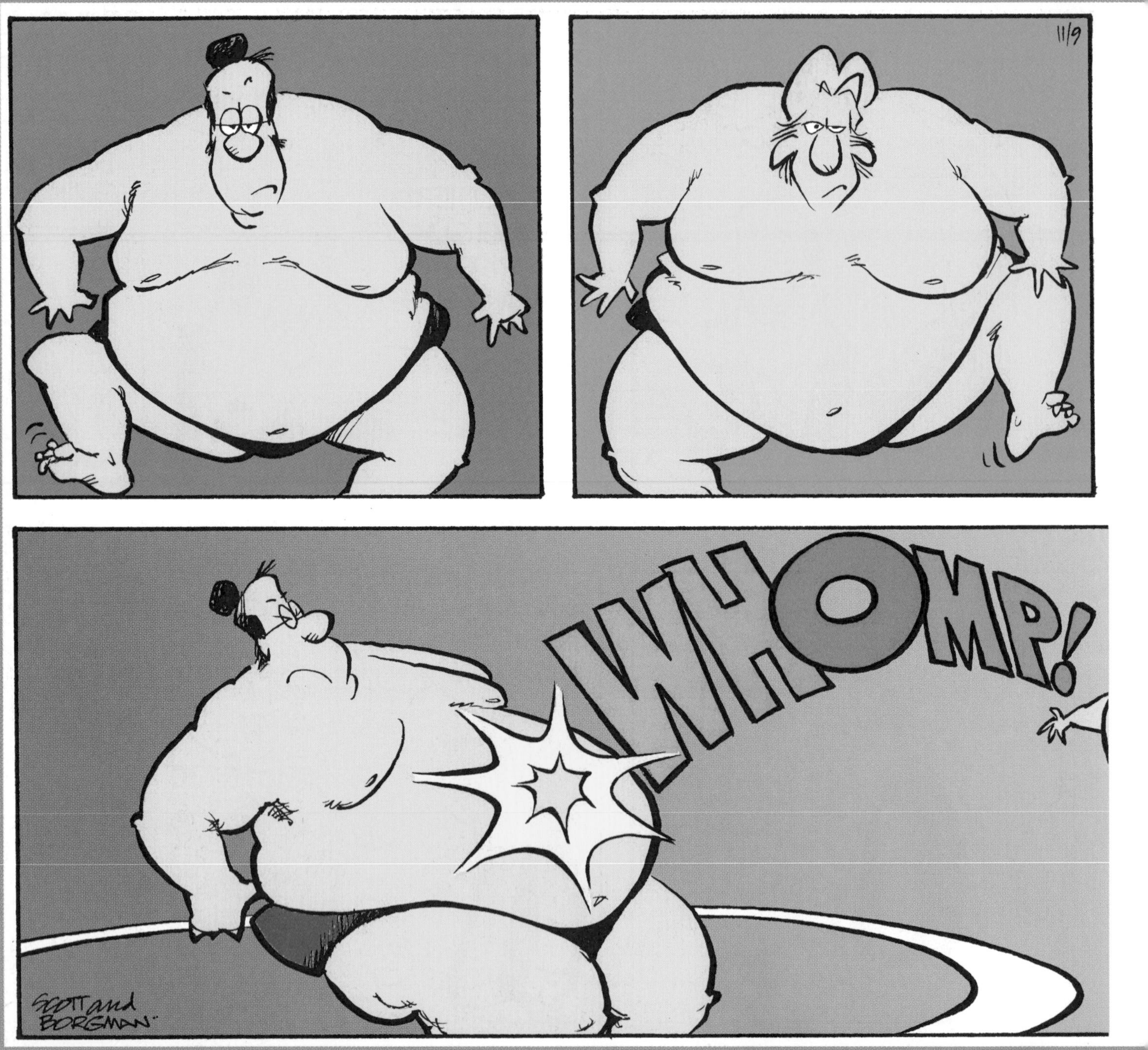
11/9
WHOMP!
SCOTT and BORGMAN

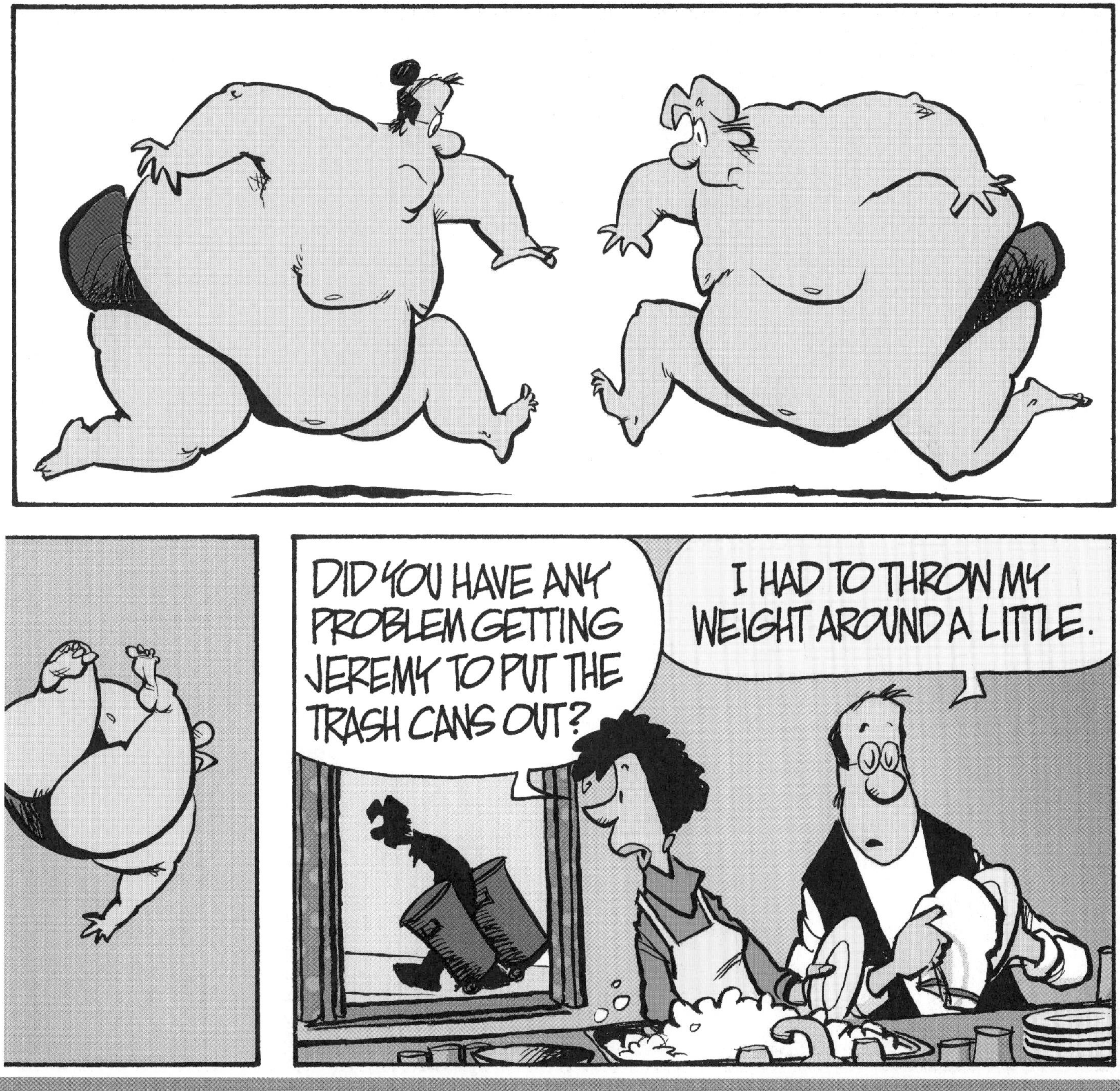
DID YOU HAVE ANY PROBLEM GETTING JEREMY TO PUT THE TRASH CANS OUT?
I HAD TO THROW MY WEIGHT AROUND A LITTLE.

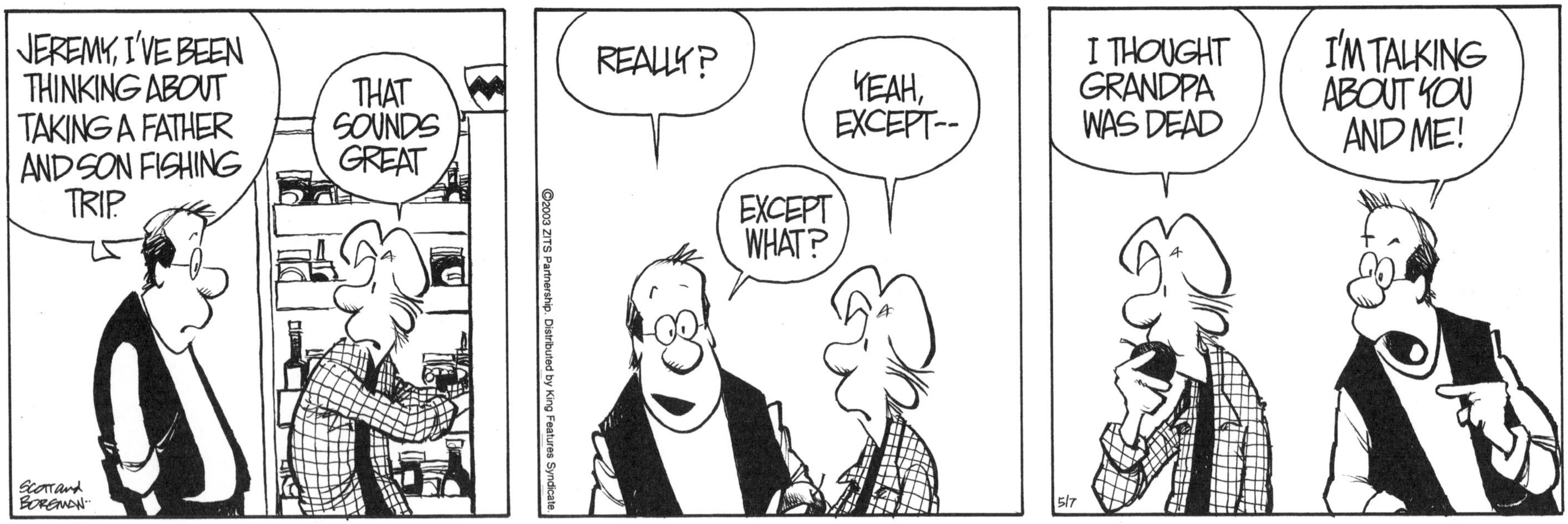
JEREMY, I'VE BEEN THINKING ABOUT TAKING A FATHER AND SON FISHING TRIP.
THAT SOUNDS GREAT
SCOTT and BORGMAN
REALLY?
YEAH, EXCEPT--
EXCEPT WHAT?
©2003 ZITS Partnership. Distributed by King Features Syndicate.
I THOUGHT GRANDPA WAS DEAD
I'M TALKING ABOUT YOU AND ME!
5/7

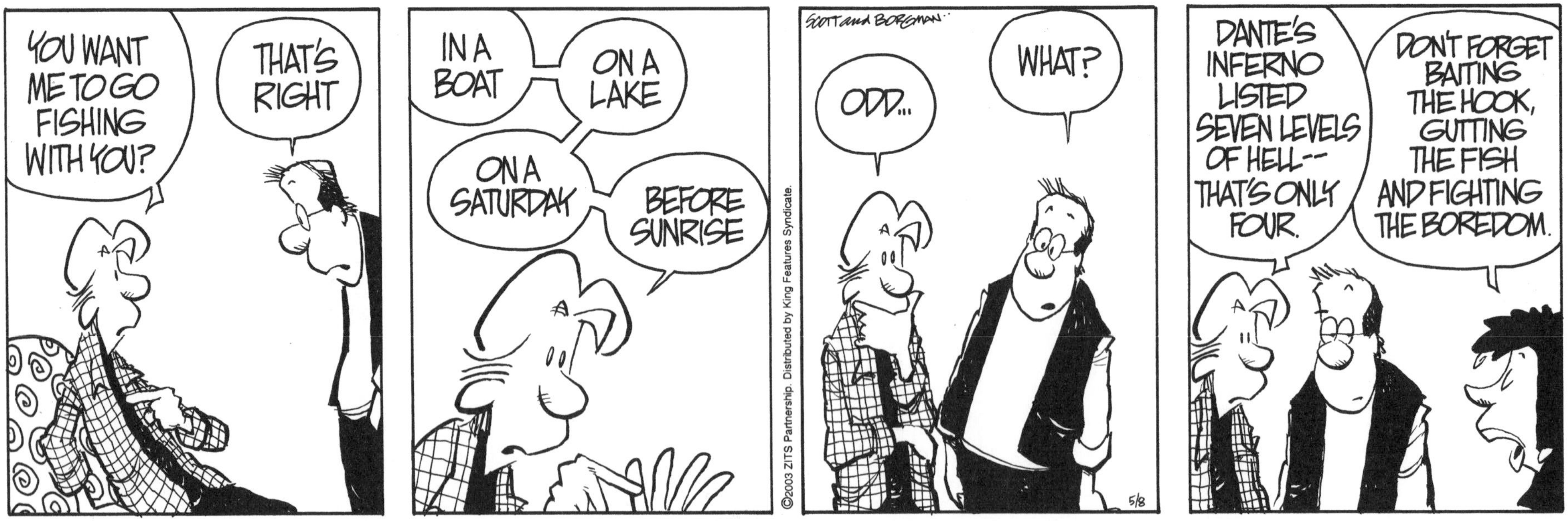
YOU WANT ME TO GO FISHING WITH YOU?
THAT'S RIGHT
IN A BOAT
ON A LAKE
ON A SATURDAY
BEFORE SUNRISE
©2003 ZITS Partnership. Distributed by King Features Syndicate.
SCOTT and BORGMAN
ODD...
WHAT?
5/8
DANTE'S INFERNO LISTED SEVEN LEVELS OF HELL-- THAT'S ONLY FOUR.
DON'T FORGET BAITING THE HOOK, GUTTING THE FISH AND FIGHTING THE BOREDOM.

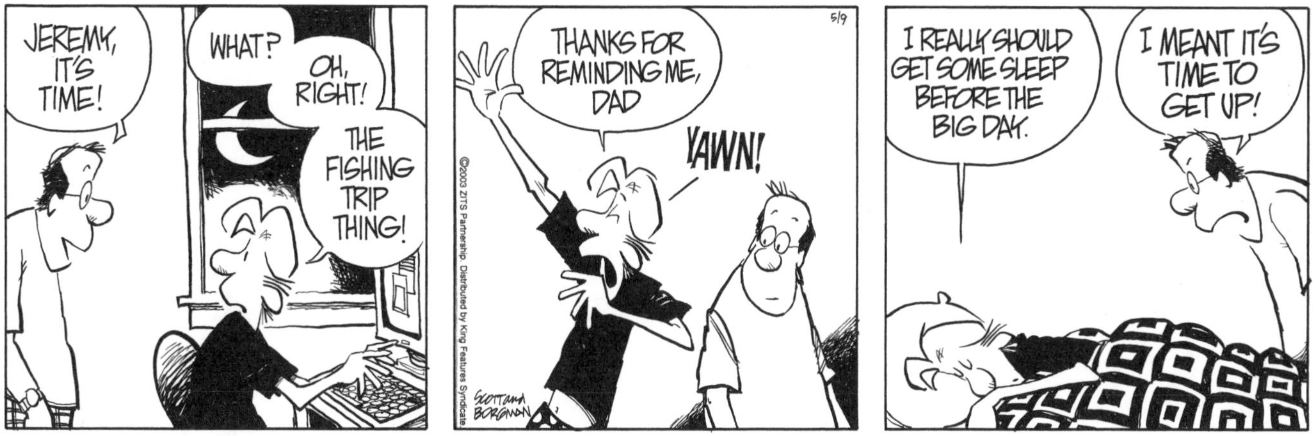
JEREMY, IT'S TIME!
WHAT?
OH, RIGHT!
THE FISHING TRIP THING!
THANKS FOR REMINDING ME, DAD
YAWN!
I REALLY SHOULD GET SOME SLEEP BEFORE THE BIG DAY.
I MEANT IT'S TIME TO GET UP!
SCOTT AND BORGMAN
5/9

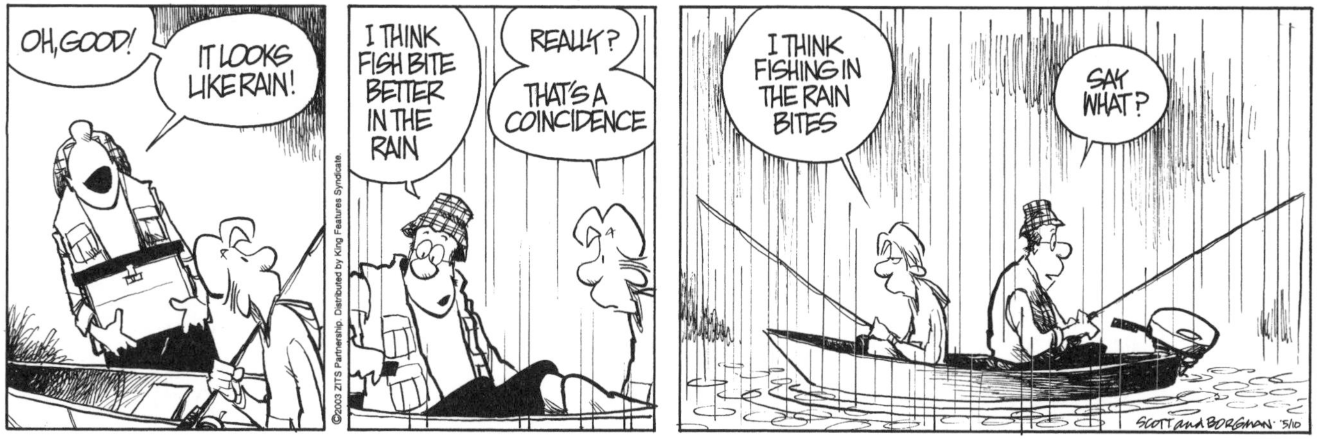
OH, GOOD!
IT LOOKS LIKE RAIN!
I THINK FISH BITE BETTER IN THE RAIN
REALLY?
THAT'S A COINCIDENCE
I THINK FISHING IN THE RAIN BITES
SAY WHAT?
SCOTT AND BORGMAN 5/10

Jerry: This series where Jeremy and Dad have "The Talk" was fun to write. Awkward moments usually equal juicy humor possibilities.

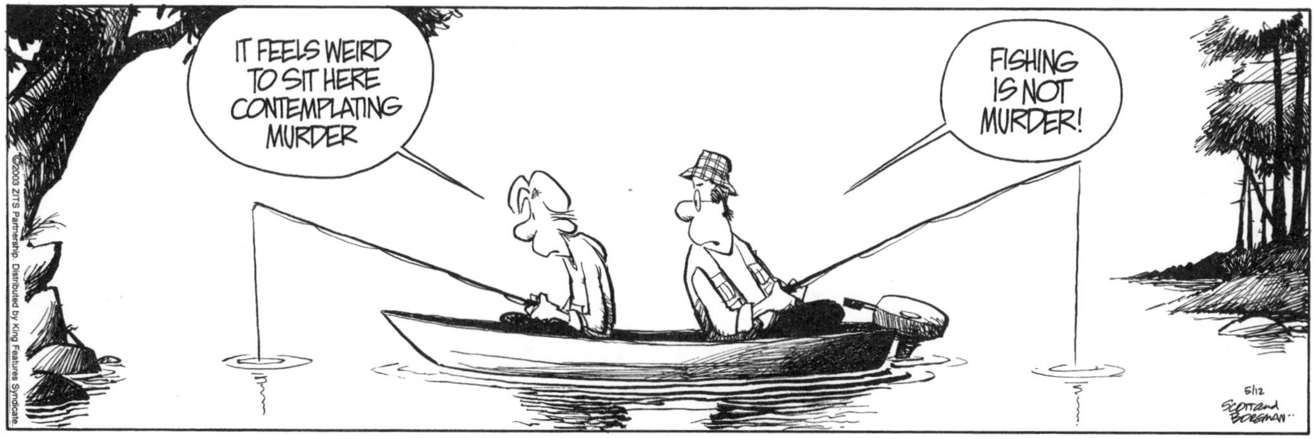
IT FEELS WEIRD TO SIT HERE CONTEMPLATING MURDER
FISHING IS NOT MURDER!
5/12
SCOTT AND BORGMAN

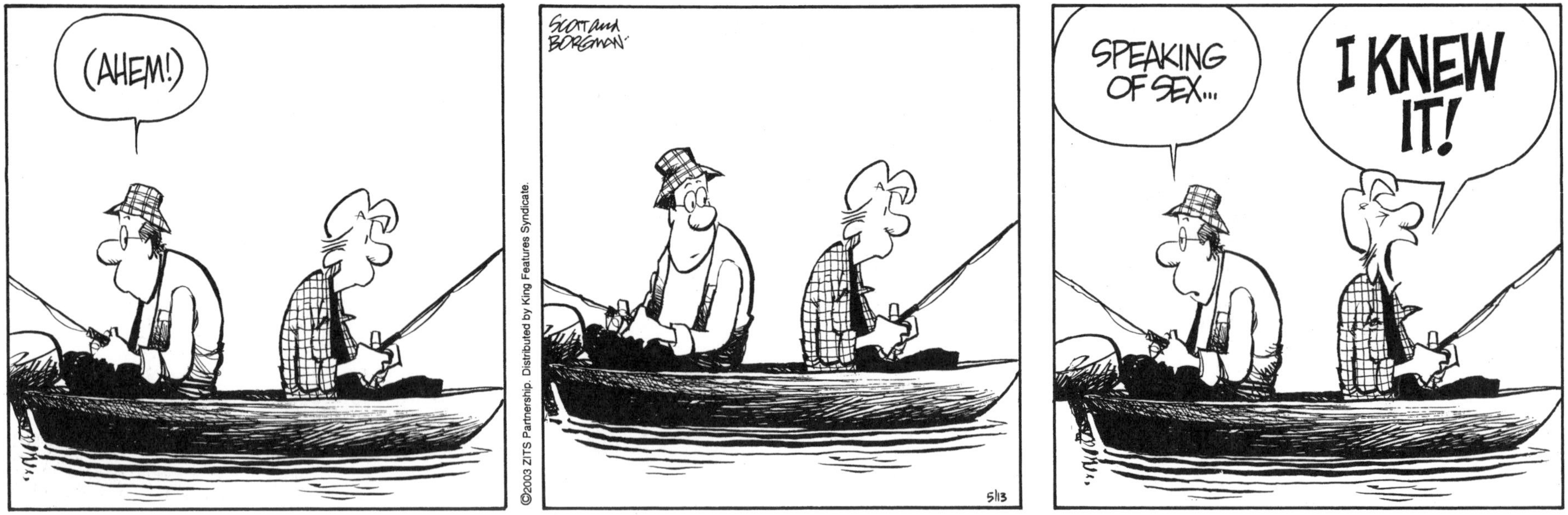
(AHEM!)
SCOTT and BORGMAN
©2003 ZITS Partnership. Distributed by King Features Syndicate.
5/13
SPEAKING OF SEX...
I KNEW IT!

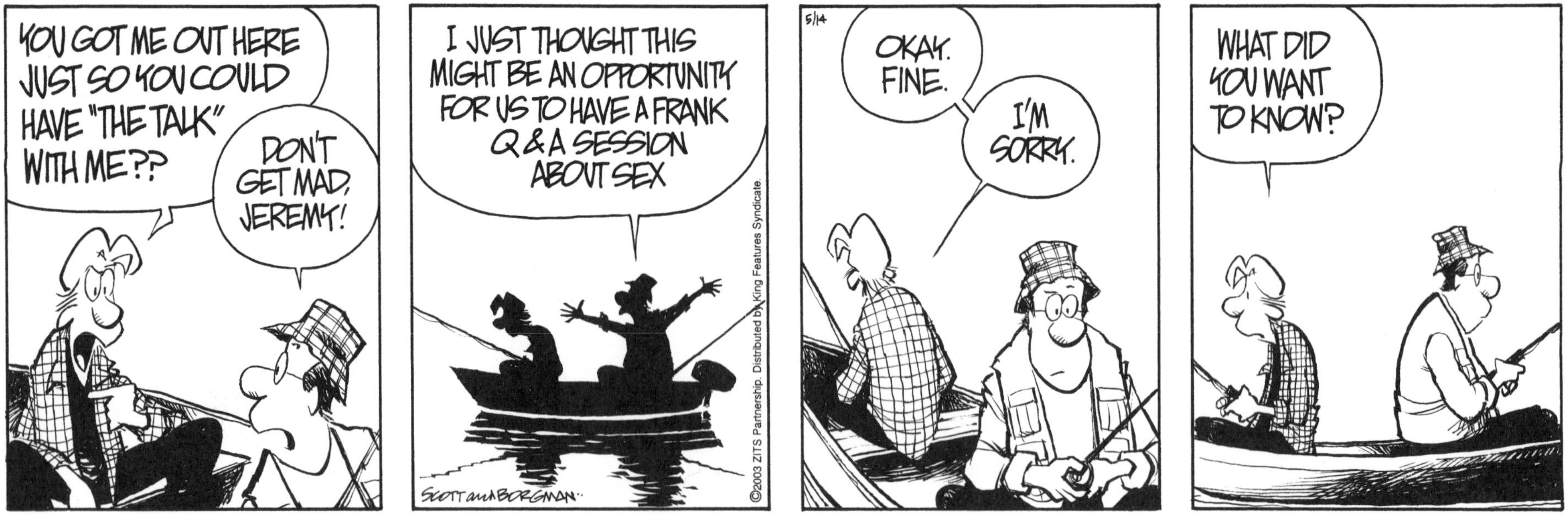
YOU GOT ME OUT HERE JUST SO YOU COULD HAVE "THE TALK" WITH ME??
DON'T GET MAD, JEREMY!
I JUST THOUGHT THIS MIGHT BE AN OPPORTUNITY FOR US TO HAVE A FRANK Q & A SESSION ABOUT SEX
SCOTT and BORGMAN
©2003 ZITS Partnership. Distributed by King Features Syndicate.
5/14
OKAY. FINE.
I'M SORRY.
WHAT DID YOU WANT TO KNOW?

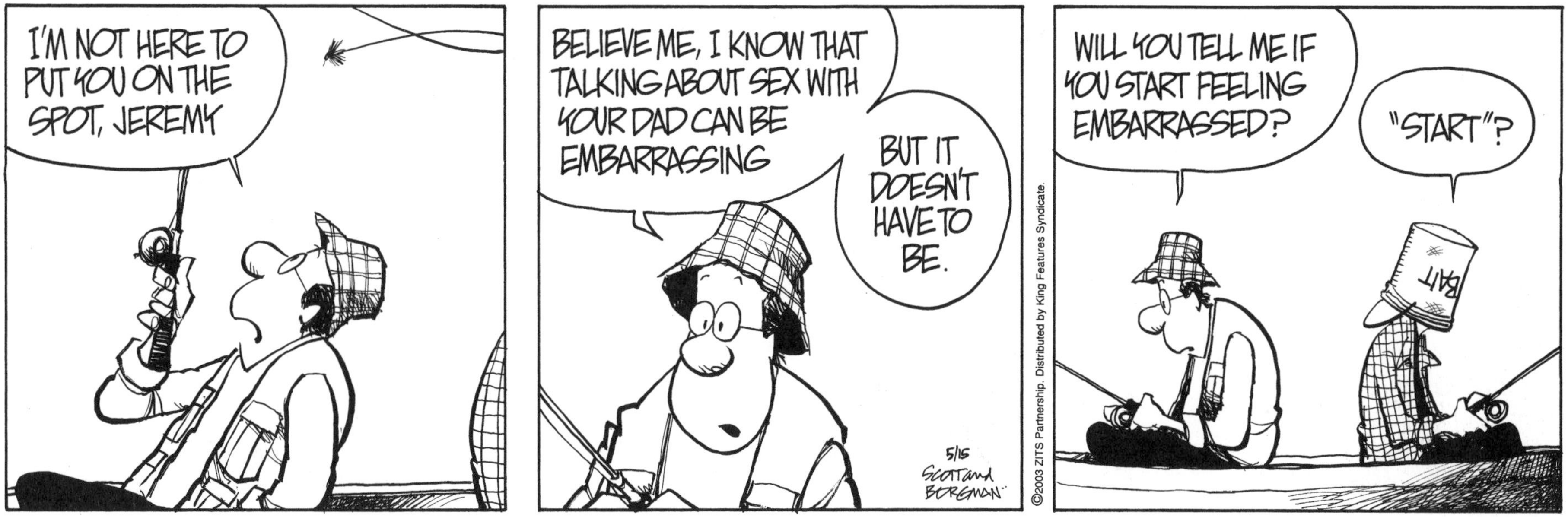
I'M NOT HERE TO PUT YOU ON THE SPOT, JEREMY
BELIEVE ME, I KNOW THAT TALKING ABOUT SEX WITH YOUR DAD CAN BE EMBARRASSING
BUT IT DOESN'T HAVE TO BE.
5/15 SCOTT and BORGMAN
©2003 ZITS Partnership. Distributed by King Features Syndicate.
WILL YOU TELL ME IF YOU START FEELING EMBARRASSED?
"START"?
BAIT

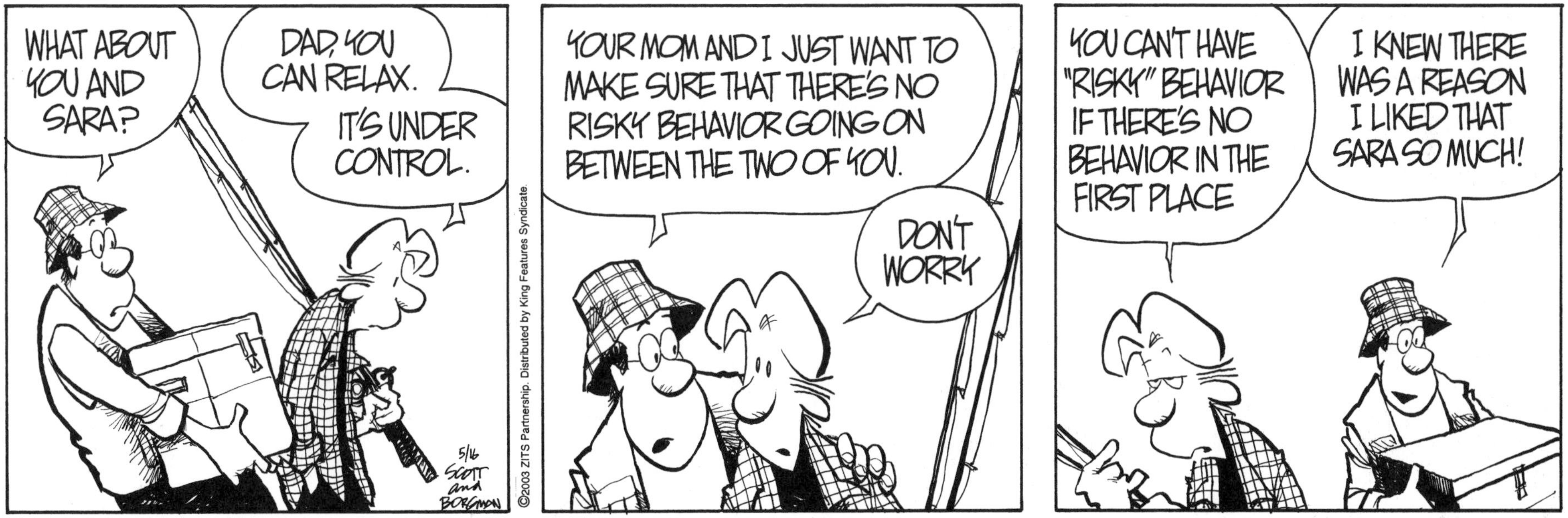
WHAT ABOUT YOU AND SARA?
DAD, YOU CAN RELAX.
IT'S UNDER CONTROL.
5/16 SCOTT and BORGMAN
©2003 ZITS Partnership. Distributed by King Features Syndicate.
YOUR MOM AND I JUST WANT TO MAKE SURE THAT THERE'S NO RISKY BEHAVIOR GOING ON BETWEEN THE TWO OF YOU.
DON'T WORRY
YOU CAN'T HAVE "RISKY" BEHAVIOR IF THERE'S NO BEHAVIOR IN THE FIRST PLACE
I KNEW THERE WAS A REASON I LIKED THAT SARA SO MUCH!

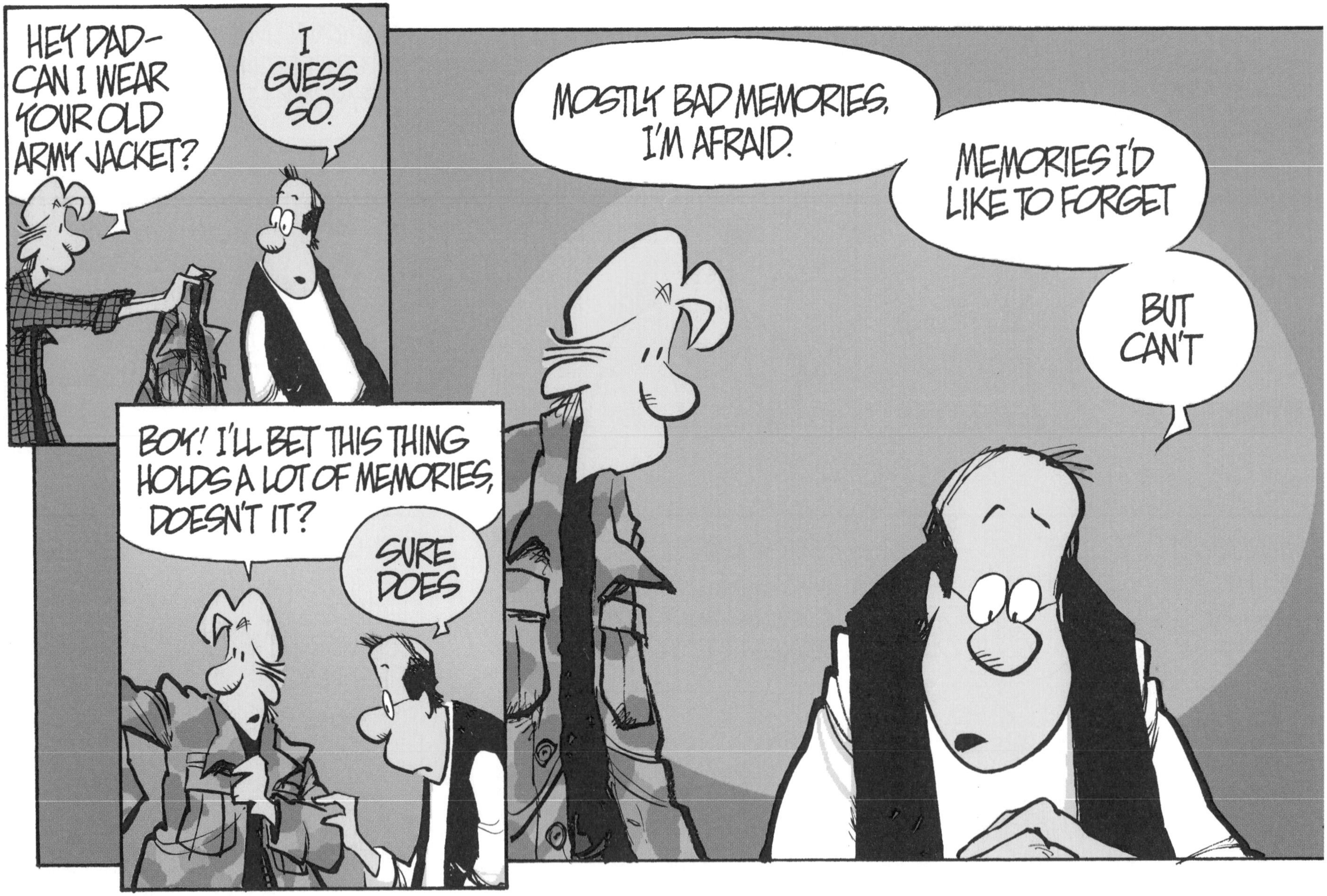
HEY DAD- CAN I WEAR YOUR OLD ARMY JACKET?
I GUESS SO.
BOY! I'LL BET THIS THING HOLDS A LOT OF MEMORIES, DOESN'T IT?
SURE DOES
MOSTLY BAD MEMORIES, I'M AFRAID.
MEMORIES I'D LIKE TO FORGET
BUT CAN'T

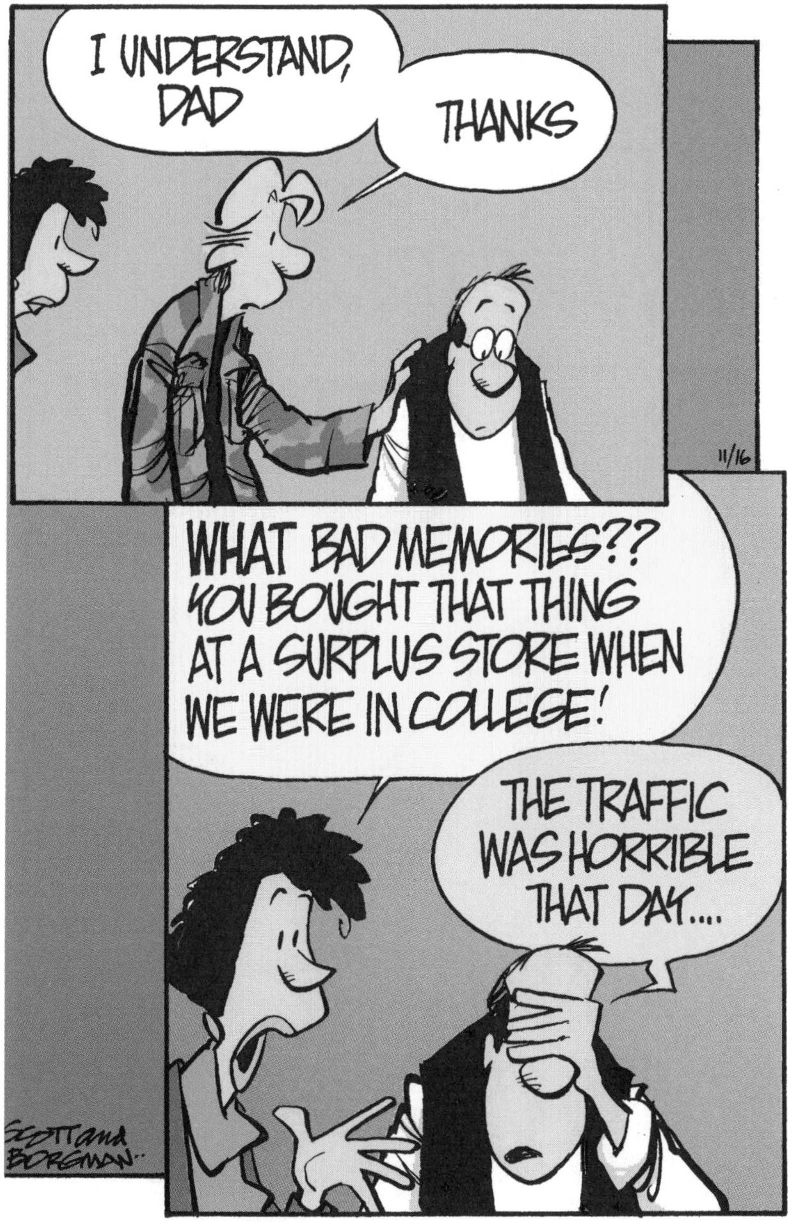
I UNDERSTAND, DAD
THANKS
11/16
WHAT BAD MEMORIES?? YOU BOUGHT THAT THING AT A SURPLUS STORE WHEN WE WERE IN COLLEGE!
THE TRAFFIC WAS HORRIBLE THAT DAY....
SCOTT and BORGMAN

Jim: While I work hard to dress the teenagers in *Zits* in plausibly current fashions, I just clothe Dad from my own closet. I retired my vest in the '80s but Dad's still seems comfortable.

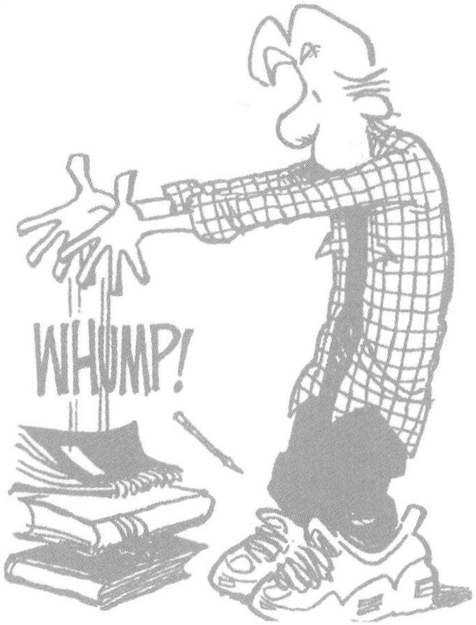
WHUMP!

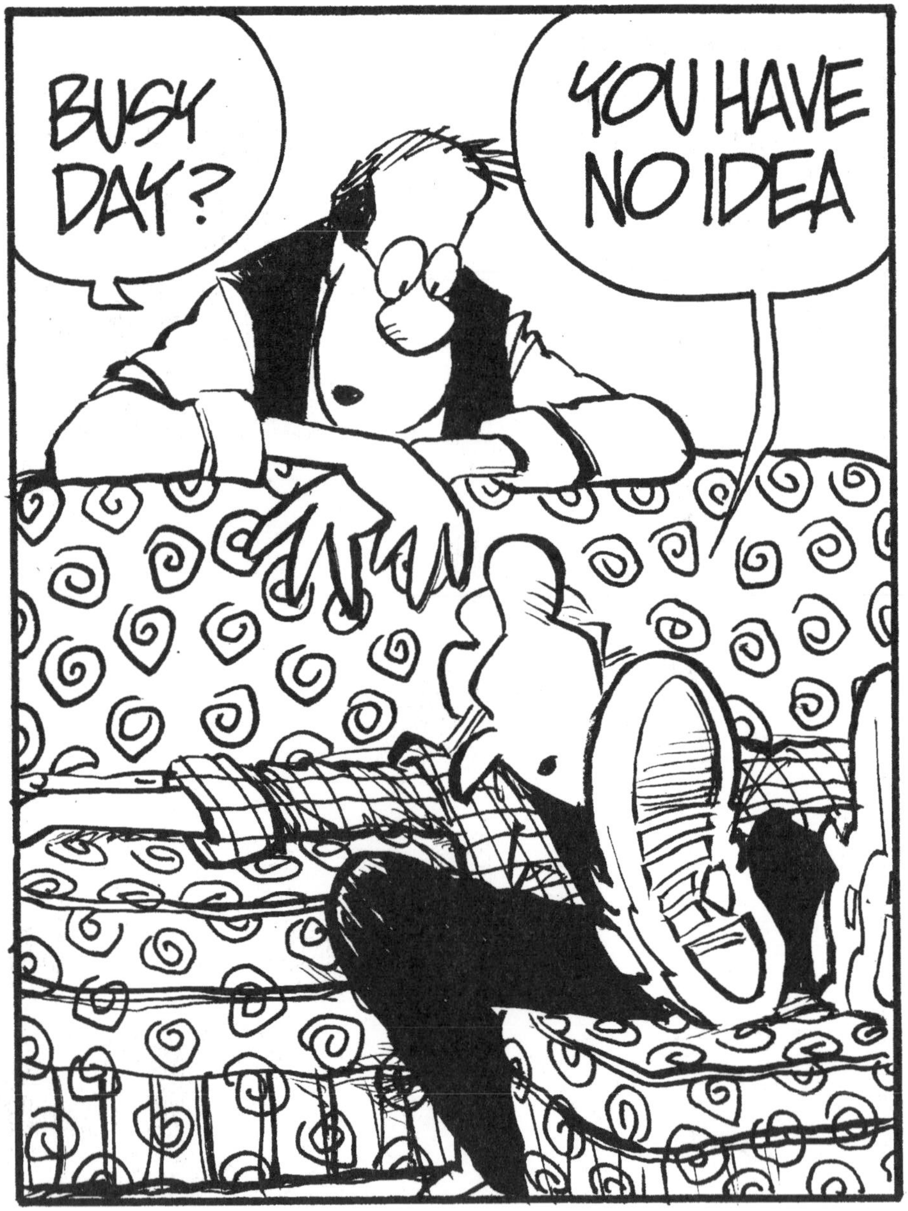
BUSY DAY?
YOU HAVE NO IDEA
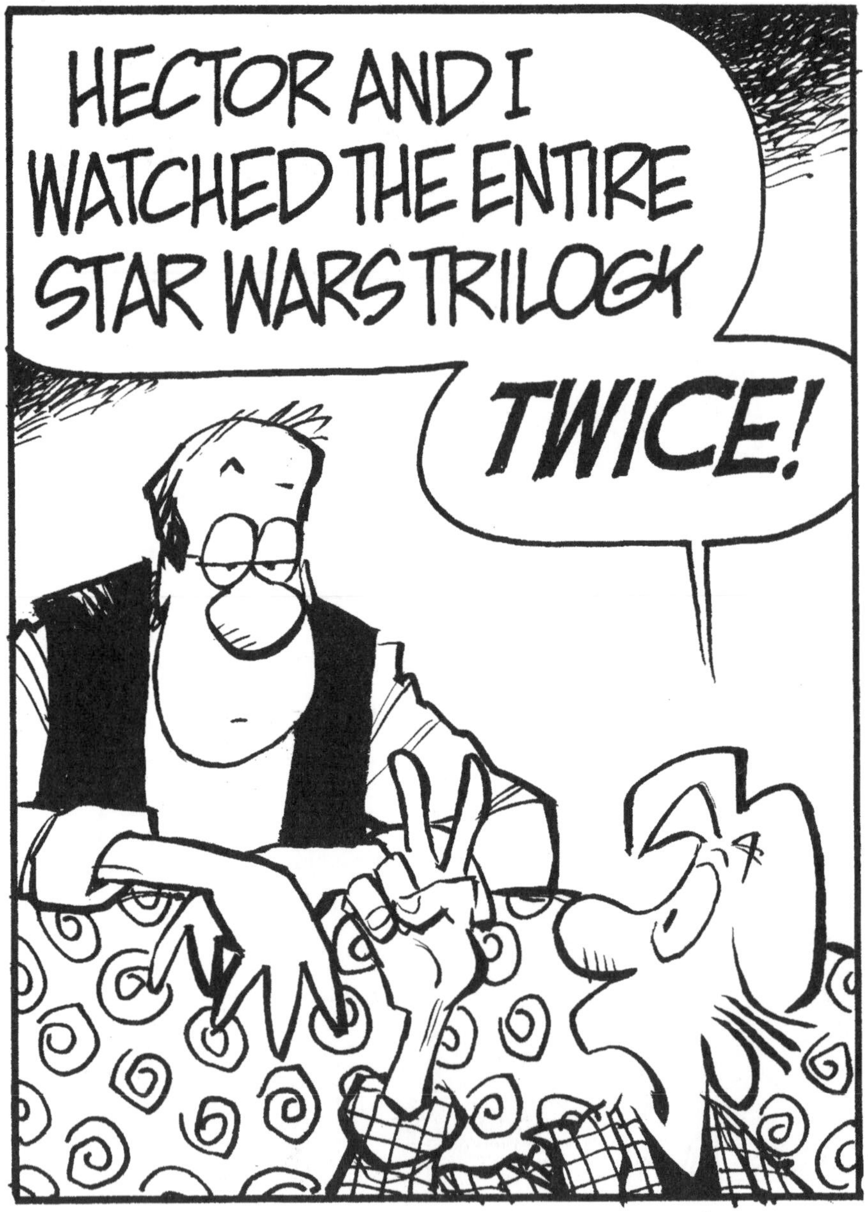
HECTOR AND I WATCHED THE ENTIRE STAR WARS TRILOGY
TWICE!

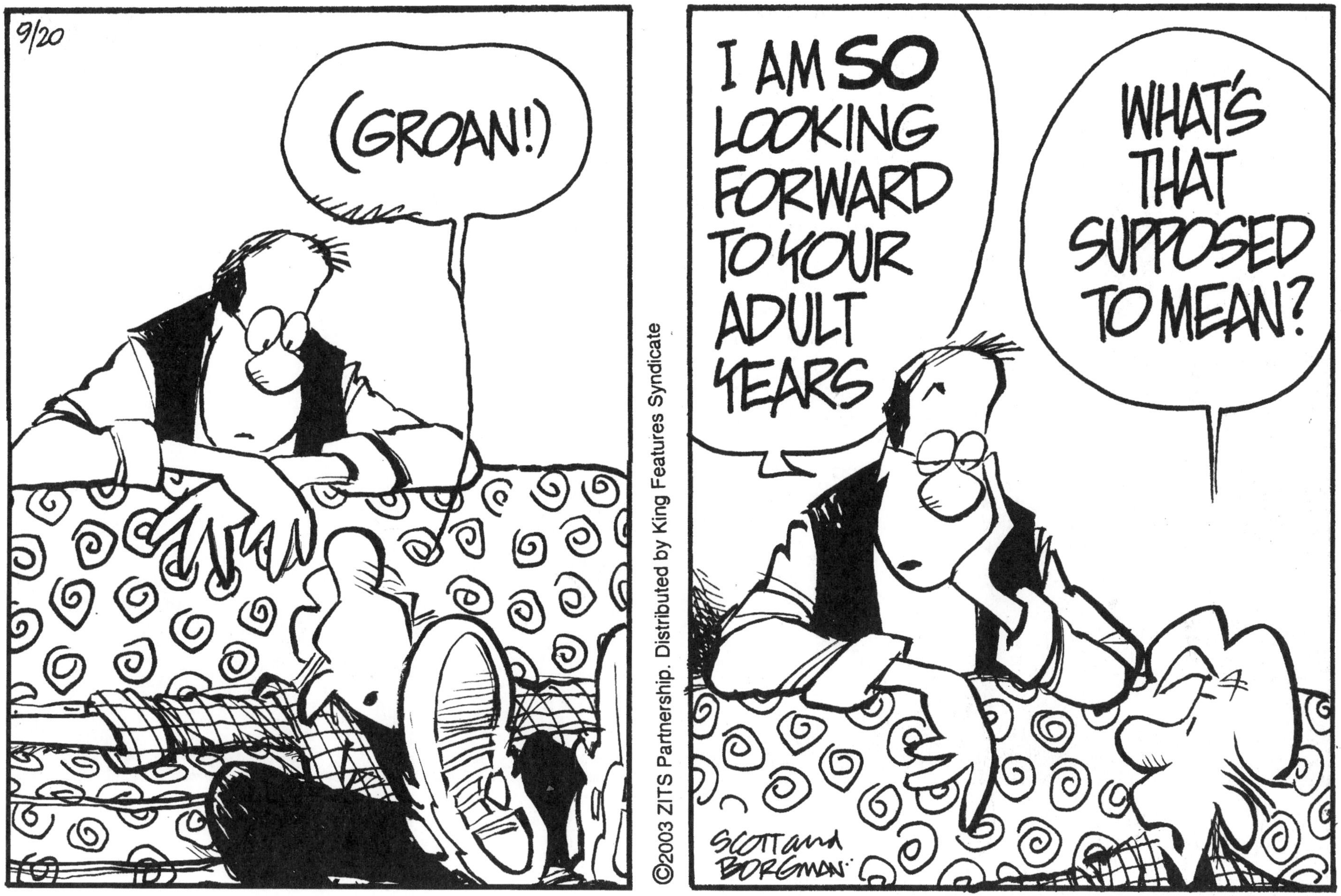
9/20
(GROAN!)
©2003 ZITS Partnership. Distributed by King Features Syndicate
I AM SO LOOKING FORWARD TO YOUR ADULT YEARS
WHAT'S THAT SUPPOSED TO MEAN?
SCOTT and BORGMAN

Jerry: Comic strips should be fun to look at. One of my favorite things about the strip is how Jeremy can strike poses usually associated only with contortionists and boneless chickens.

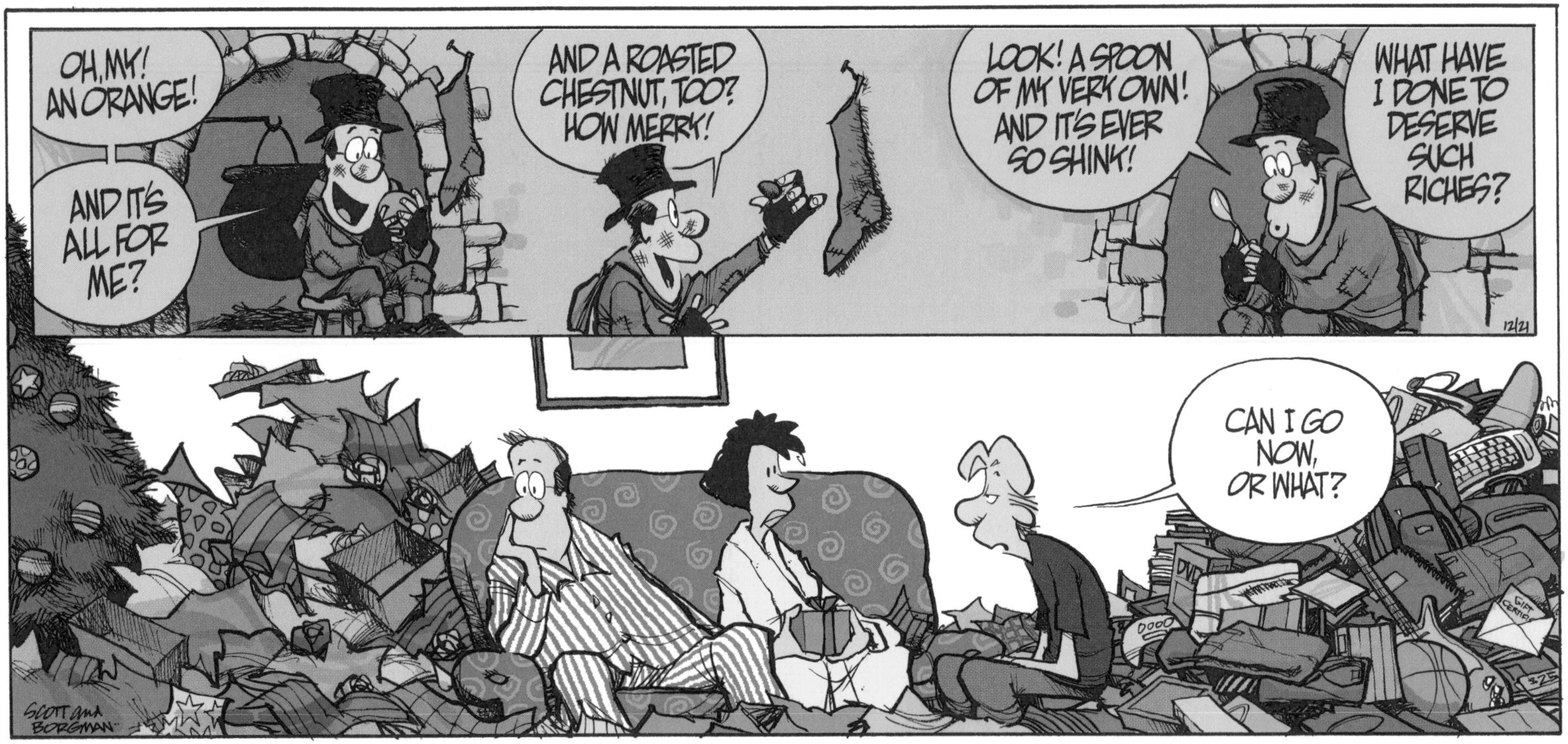
OH, MY! AN ORANGE!
AND IT'S ALL FOR ME?
AND A ROASTED CHESTNUT, TOO? HOW MERRY!
LOOK! A SPOON OF MY VERY OWN! AND IT'S EVER SO SHINY!
WHAT HAVE I DONE TO DESERVE SUCH RICHES?
12/21
CAN I GO NOW, OR WHAT?
SCOTT AND BORGMAN

Jim: My daughter is mentally assembling a volume she calls *Dad's Big Book of Pathetic Childhood Stories* based on my tales of woe and deprivation. Even so, I'm not sure we're doing our kids any favors burying them in material riches.

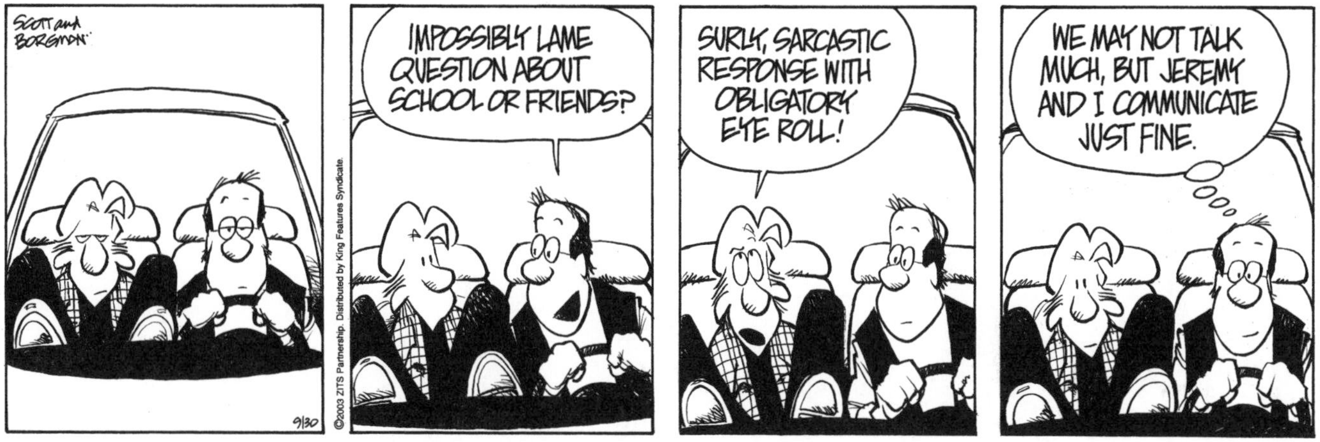
SCOTT and BORGMAN
9/30
©2003 ZITS Partnership. Distributed by King Features Syndicate.
IMPOSSIBLY LAME QUESTION ABOUT SCHOOL OR FRIENDS?
SURLY, SARCASTIC RESPONSE WITH OBLIGATORY EYE ROLL!
WE MAY NOT TALK MUCH, BUT JEREMY AND I COMMUNICATE JUST FINE.

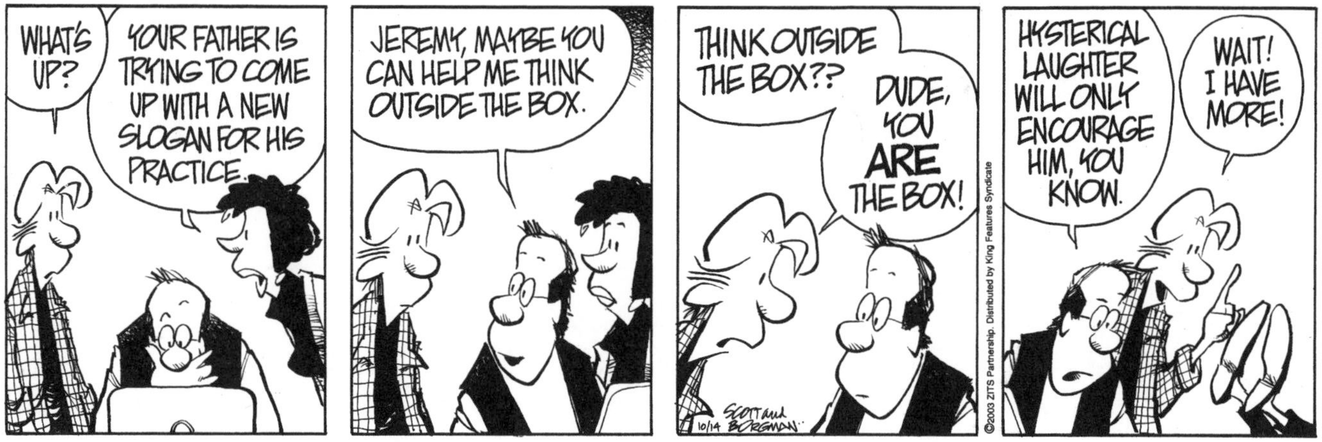
WHAT'S UP?
YOUR FATHER IS TRYING TO COME UP WITH A NEW SLOGAN FOR HIS PRACTICE.
JEREMY, MAYBE YOU CAN HELP ME THINK OUTSIDE THE BOX.
THINK OUTSIDE THE BOX??
DUDE, YOU **ARE** THE BOX!
SCOTT and BORGMAN
10/14
©2003 ZITS Partnership. Distributed by King Features Syndicate
HYSTERICAL LAUGHTER WILL ONLY ENCOURAGE HIM, YOU KNOW.
WAIT! I HAVE MORE!

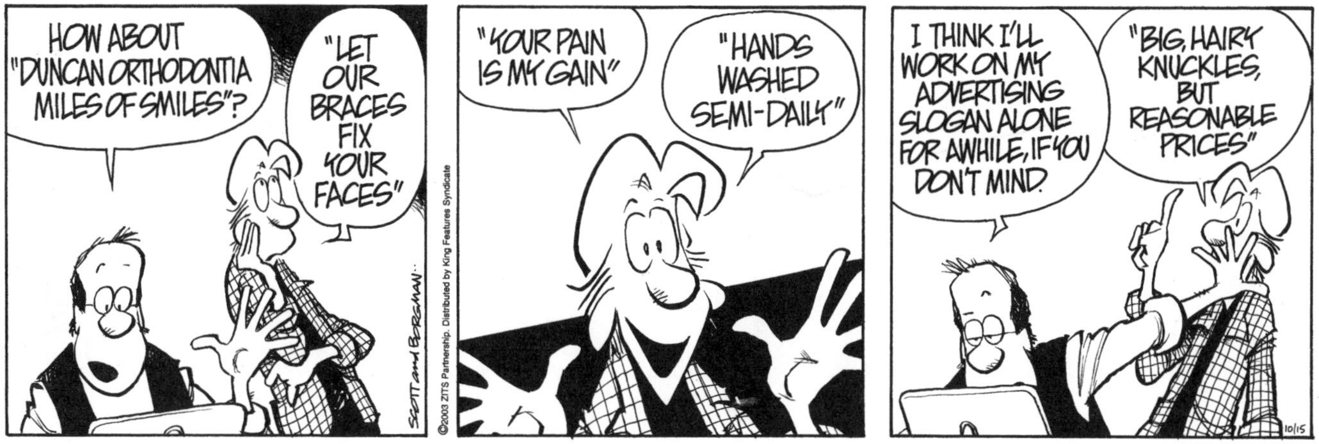
HOW ABOUT "DUNCAN ORTHODONTIA MILES OF SMILES"?
"LET OUR BRACES FIX YOUR FACES"
SCOTT and BORGMAN
©2003 ZITS Partnership. Distributed by King Features Syndicate
"YOUR PAIN IS MY GAIN"
"HANDS WASHED SEMI-DAILY"
I THINK I'LL WORK ON MY ADVERTISING SLOGAN ALONE FOR AWHILE, IF YOU DON'T MIND.
"BIG, HAIRY KNUCKLES, BUT REASONABLE PRICES"
10/15

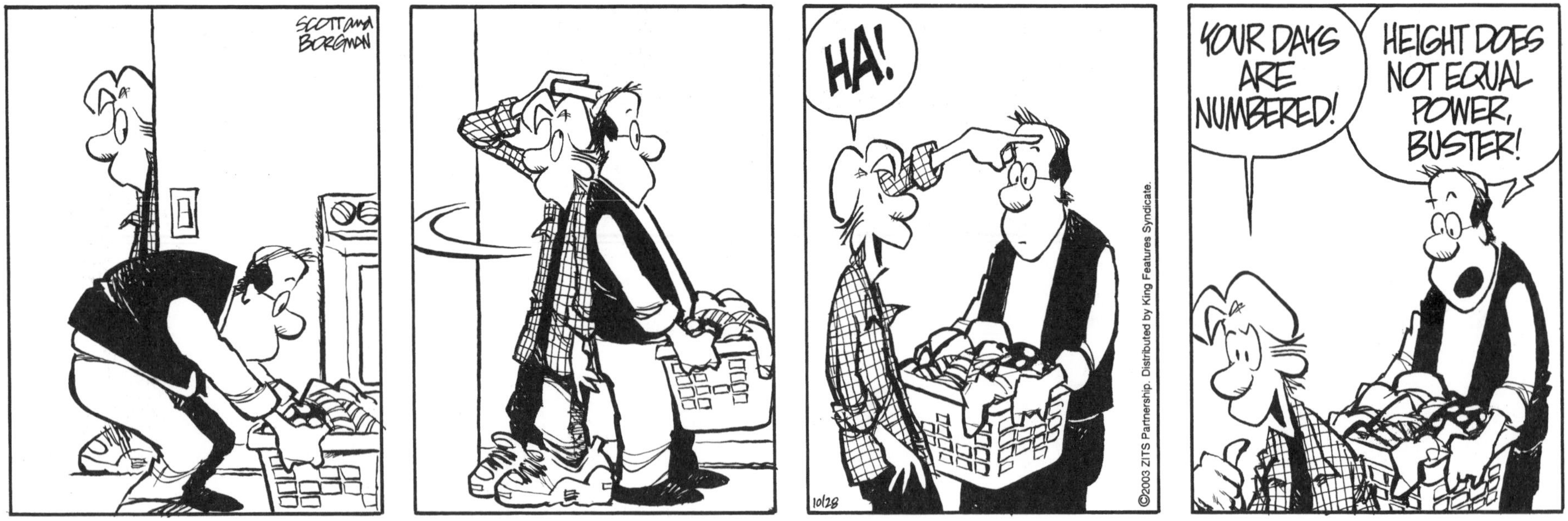
SCOTT and BORGMAN
HA!
10/28
©2003 ZITS Partnership. Distributed by King Features Syndicate.
YOUR DAYS ARE NUMBERED!
HEIGHT DOES NOT EQUAL POWER, BUSTER!

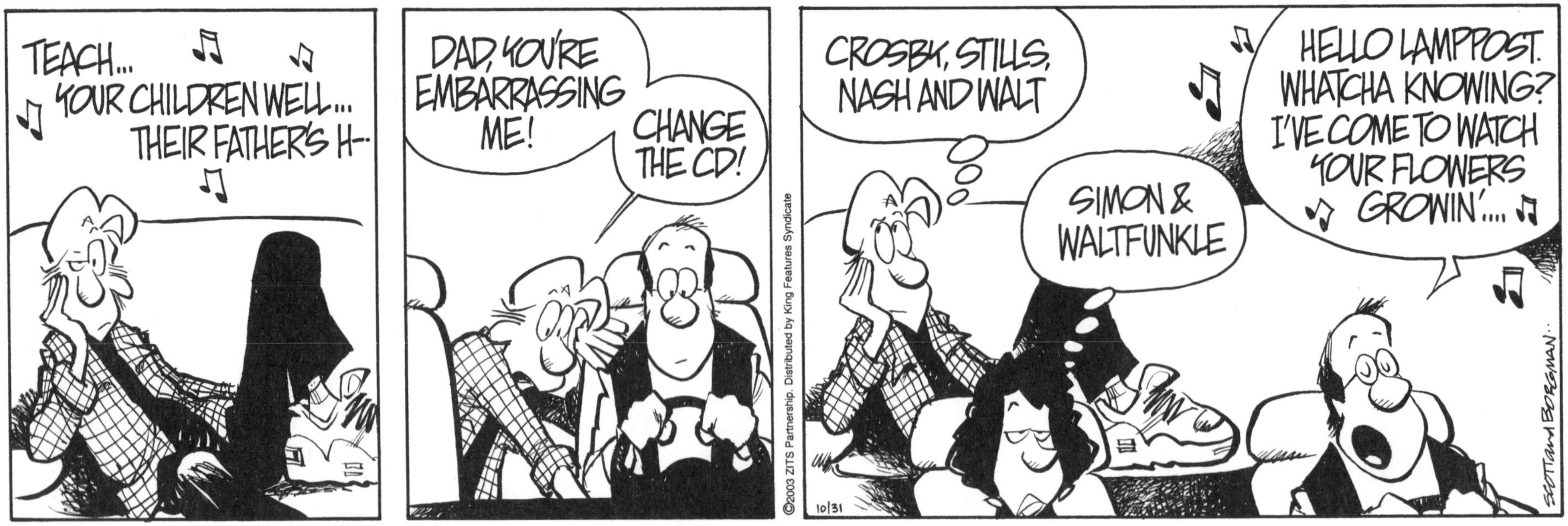
TEACH... YOUR CHILDREN WELL... THEIR FATHER'S H--
DAD, YOU'RE EMBARRASSING ME!
CHANGE THE CD!
©2003 ZITS Partnership. Distributed by King Features Syndicate
10/31
CROSBY, STILLS, NASH AND WALT
SIMON & WALTFUNKLE
HELLO LAMPPOST. WHATCHA KNOWING? I'VE COME TO WATCH YOUR FLOWERS GROWIN'....
SCOTT and BORGMAN

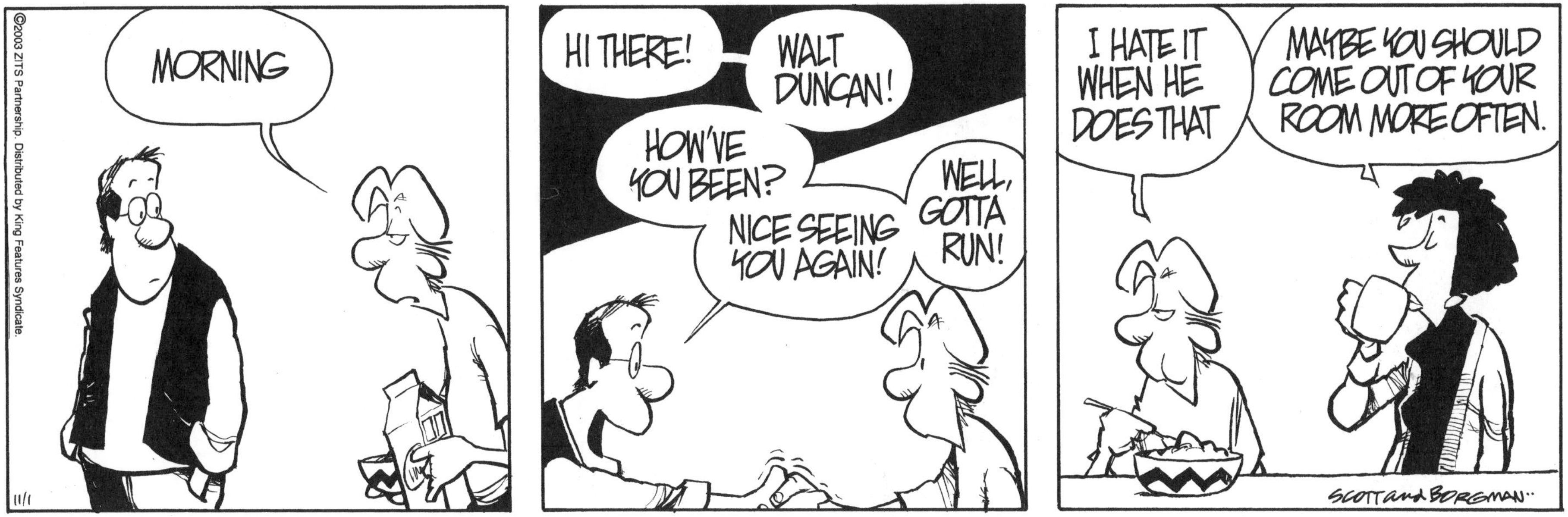
©2003 ZITS Partnership. Distributed by King Features Syndicate.
MORNING
11/1
HI THERE!
WALT DUNCAN!
HOW'VE YOU BEEN?
NICE SEEING YOU AGAIN!
WELL, GOTTA RUN!
I HATE IT WHEN HE DOES THAT
MAYBE YOU SHOULD COME OUT OF YOUR ROOM MORE OFTEN.
SCOTT and BORGMAN

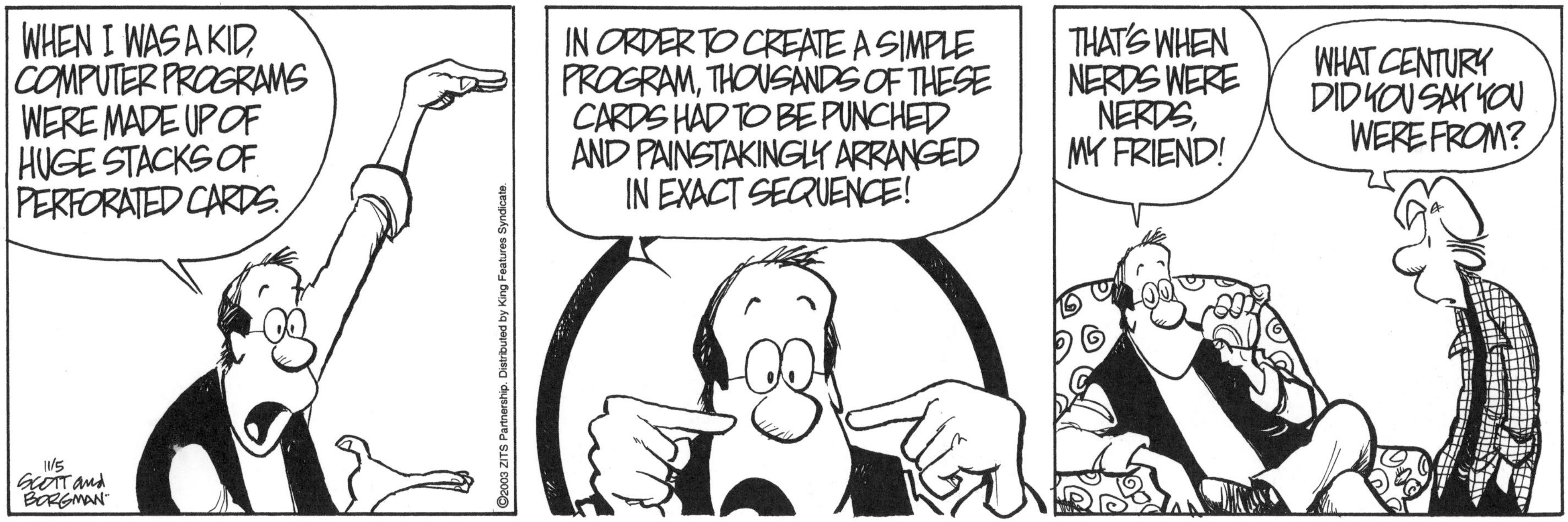
WHEN I WAS A KID, COMPUTER PROGRAMS WERE MADE UP OF HUGE STACKS OF PERFORATED CARDS.
11/5
SCOTT and BORGMAN
©2003 ZITS Partnership. Distributed by King Features Syndicate.
IN ORDER TO CREATE A SIMPLE PROGRAM, THOUSANDS OF THESE CARDS HAD TO BE PUNCHED AND PAINSTAKINGLY ARRANGED IN EXACT SEQUENCE!
THAT'S WHEN NERDS WERE NERDS, MY FRIEND!
WHAT CENTURY DID YOU SAY YOU WERE FROM?

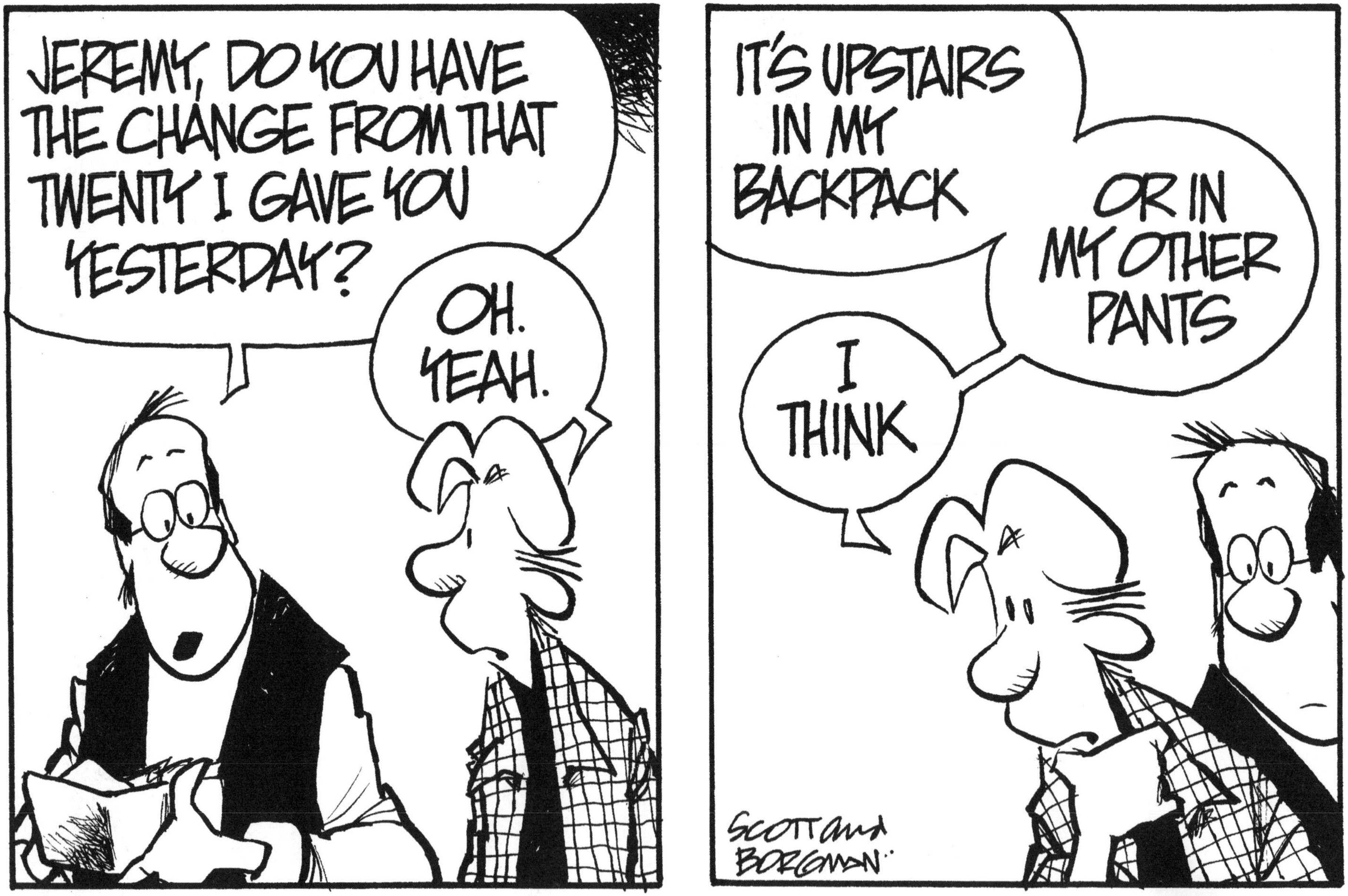
JEREMY, DO YOU HAVE THE CHANGE FROM THAT TWENTY I GAVE YOU YESTERDAY?
OH. YEAH.
IT'S UPSTAIRS IN MY BACKPACK
OR IN MY OTHER PANTS
I THINK
SCOTT and BORGMAN

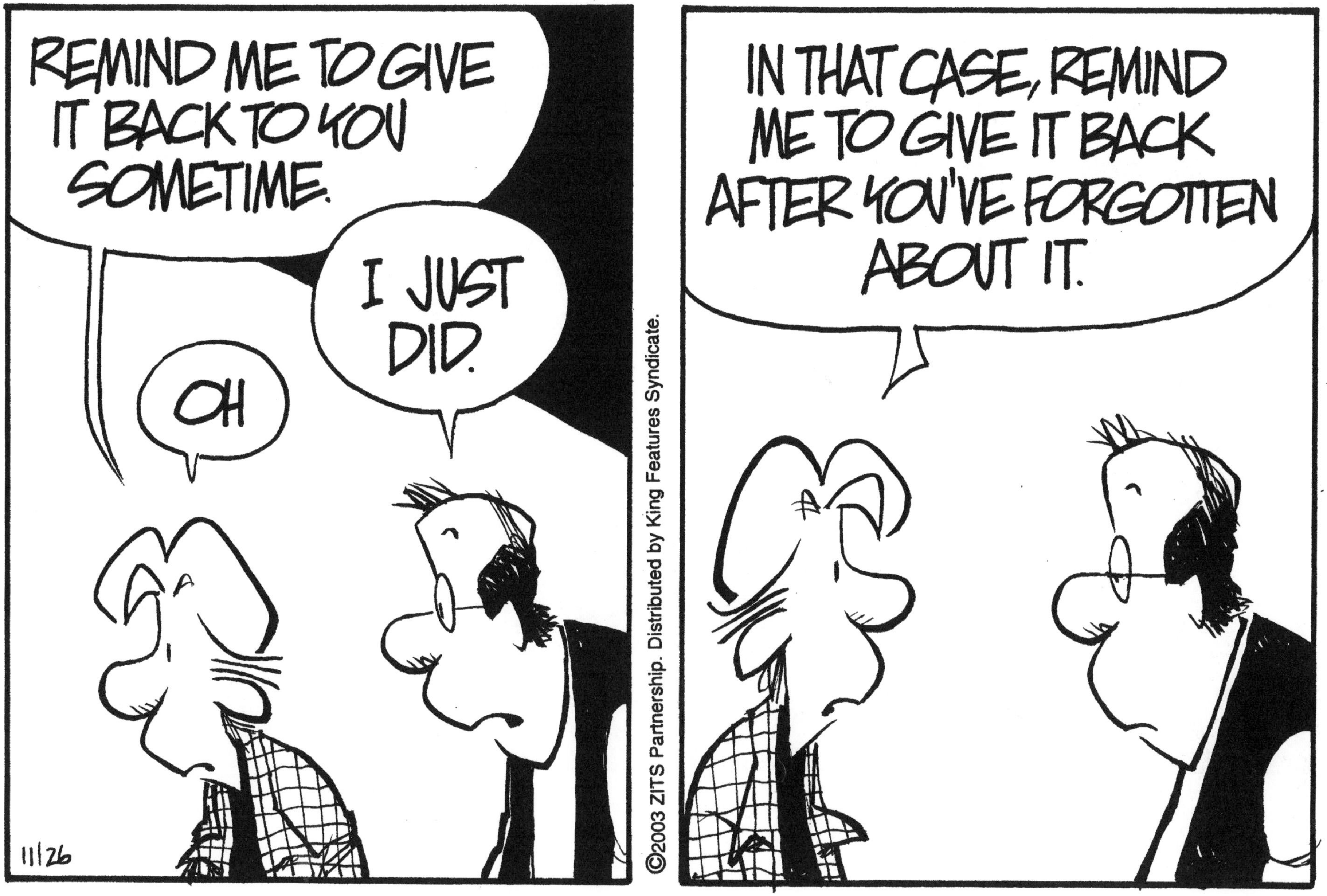
REMIND ME TO GIVE IT BACK TO YOU SOMETIME.
OH
I JUST DID.
11/26
IN THAT CASE, REMIND ME TO GIVE IT BACK AFTER YOU'VE FORGOTTEN ABOUT IT.

Jerry: I'm sure my daughter has doubled her allowance over the years by "forgetting" to give me my change. Heck, she's probably started a hedge fund by now.

OKAY, LET'S REVIEW.
WITH YOUR RIGHT BLINKER ON, TURN THE STEERING WHEEL ONE TURN TO THE RIGHT.
BACK UP SLOWLY, THEN STOP WHEN YOU CAN SEE THE REAR BUMPER OF THE CAR BESIDE YOU. THEN---
DAD!
I KNOW HOW TO PARALLEL PARK, OKAY??
I JUST NEED TO PRACTICE.
FROM NOW ON, PRACTICE IN YOUR MOTHER'S CAR.
SCOTT AND BORGMAN 3/21
©2004 ZITS Partnership. Distributed by King Features Syndicate.

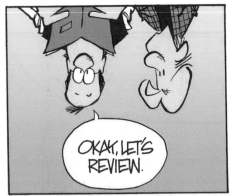

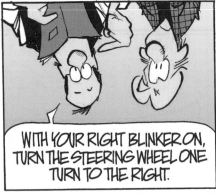

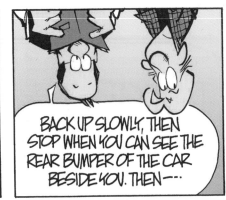

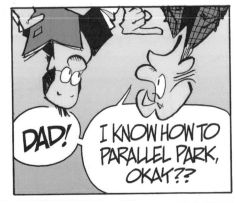

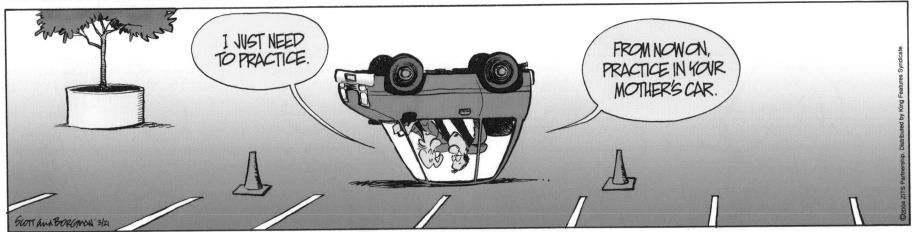

Jerry: I still get dizzy when I look at this strip.

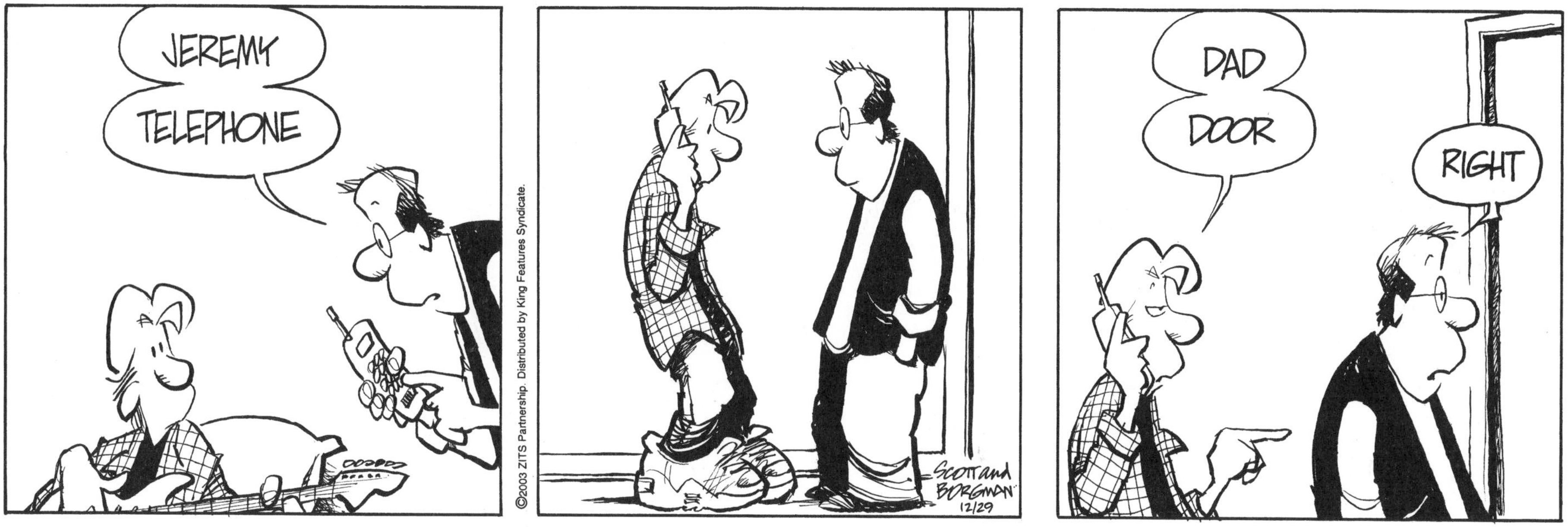
JEREMY
TELEPHONE
DAD
DOOR
RIGHT
SCOTT and BORGMAN 12/29

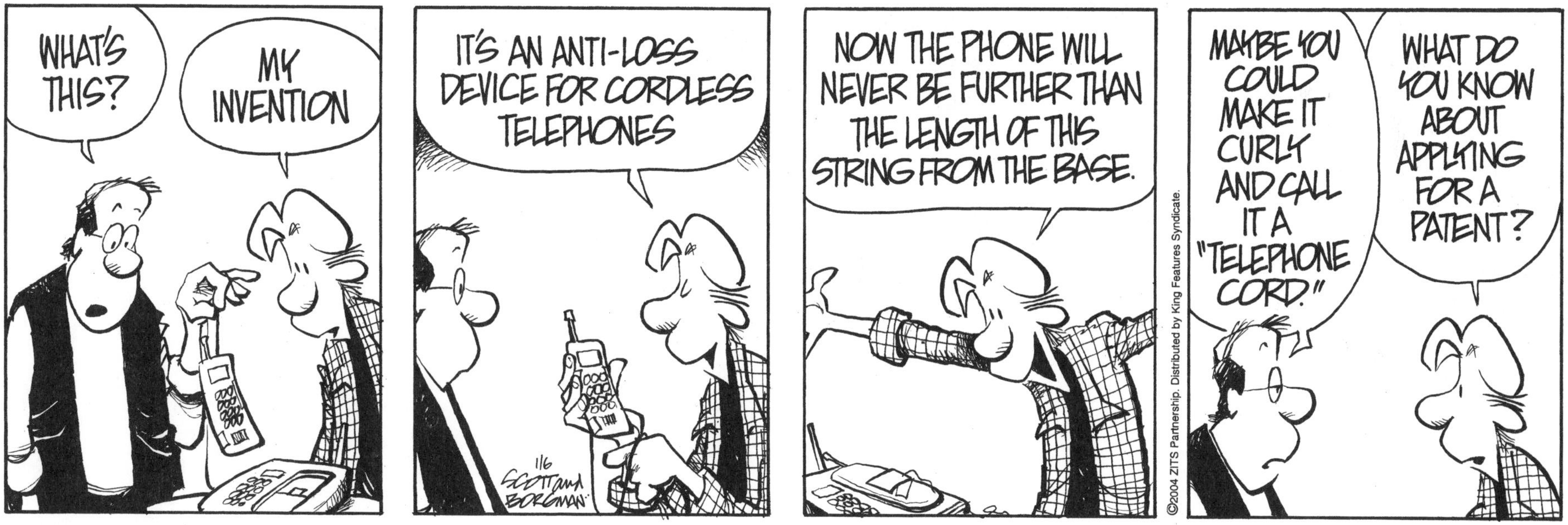
WHAT'S THIS?
MY INVENTION
IT'S AN ANTI-LOSS DEVICE FOR CORDLESS TELEPHONES
1/6 SCOTT and BORGMAN
NOW THE PHONE WILL NEVER BE FURTHER THAN THE LENGTH OF THIS STRING FROM THE BASE.
MAYBE YOU COULD MAKE IT CURLY AND CALL IT A "TELEPHONE CORD."
WHAT DO YOU KNOW ABOUT APPLYING FOR A PATENT?

Jim: If you feel your life is going too smoothly, teach your teenager to drive a standard transmission.

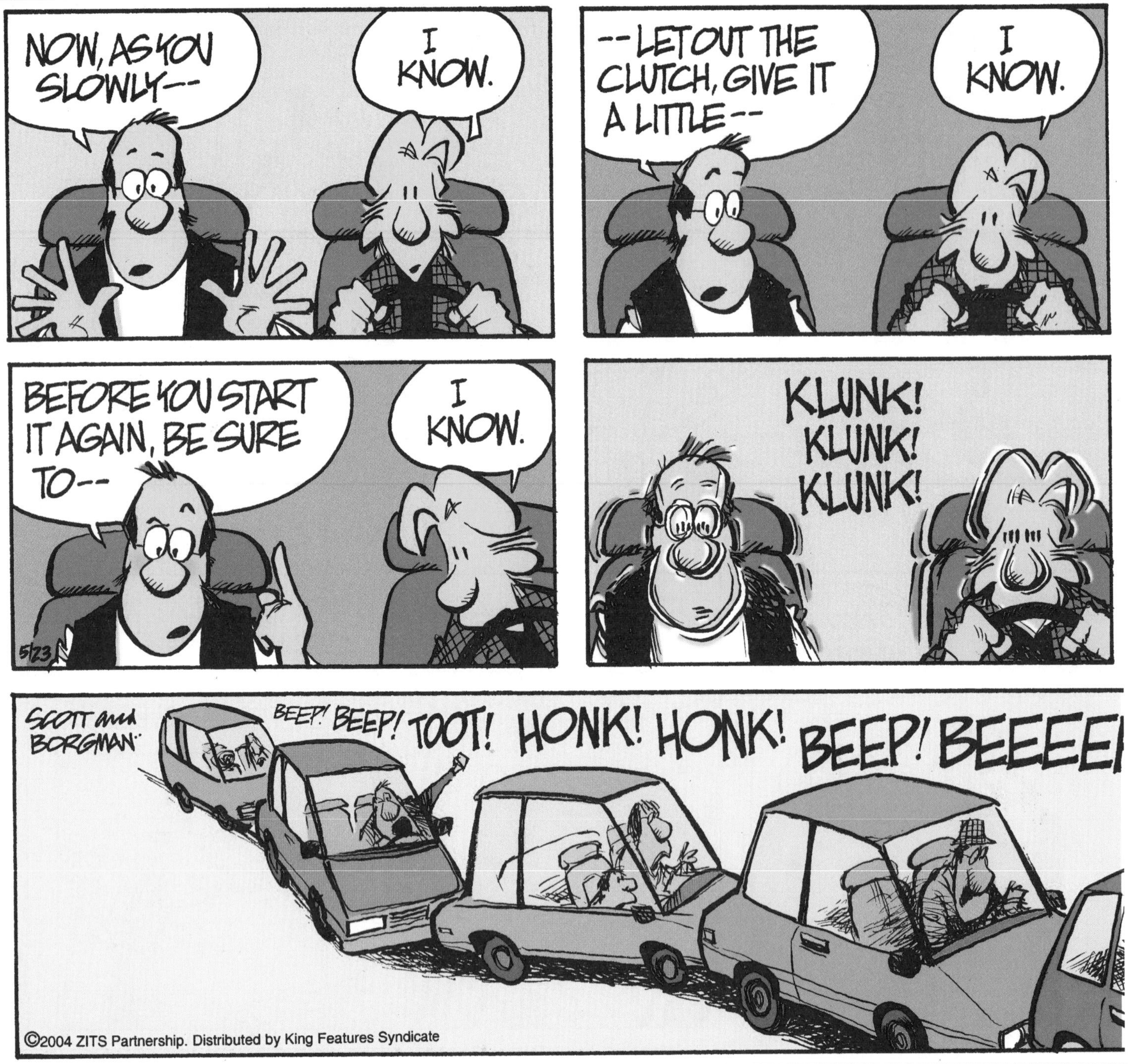
NOW, AS YOU SLOWLY--
I KNOW.
--LET OUT THE CLUTCH, GIVE IT A LITTLE--
I KNOW.
BEFORE YOU START IT AGAIN, BE SURE TO--
I KNOW.
5/23
KLUNK! KLUNK! KLUNK!
SCOTT and BORGMAN
BEEP! BEEP! TOOT! HONK! HONK! BEEP! BEEEEE
©2004 ZITS Partnership. Distributed by King Features Syndicate

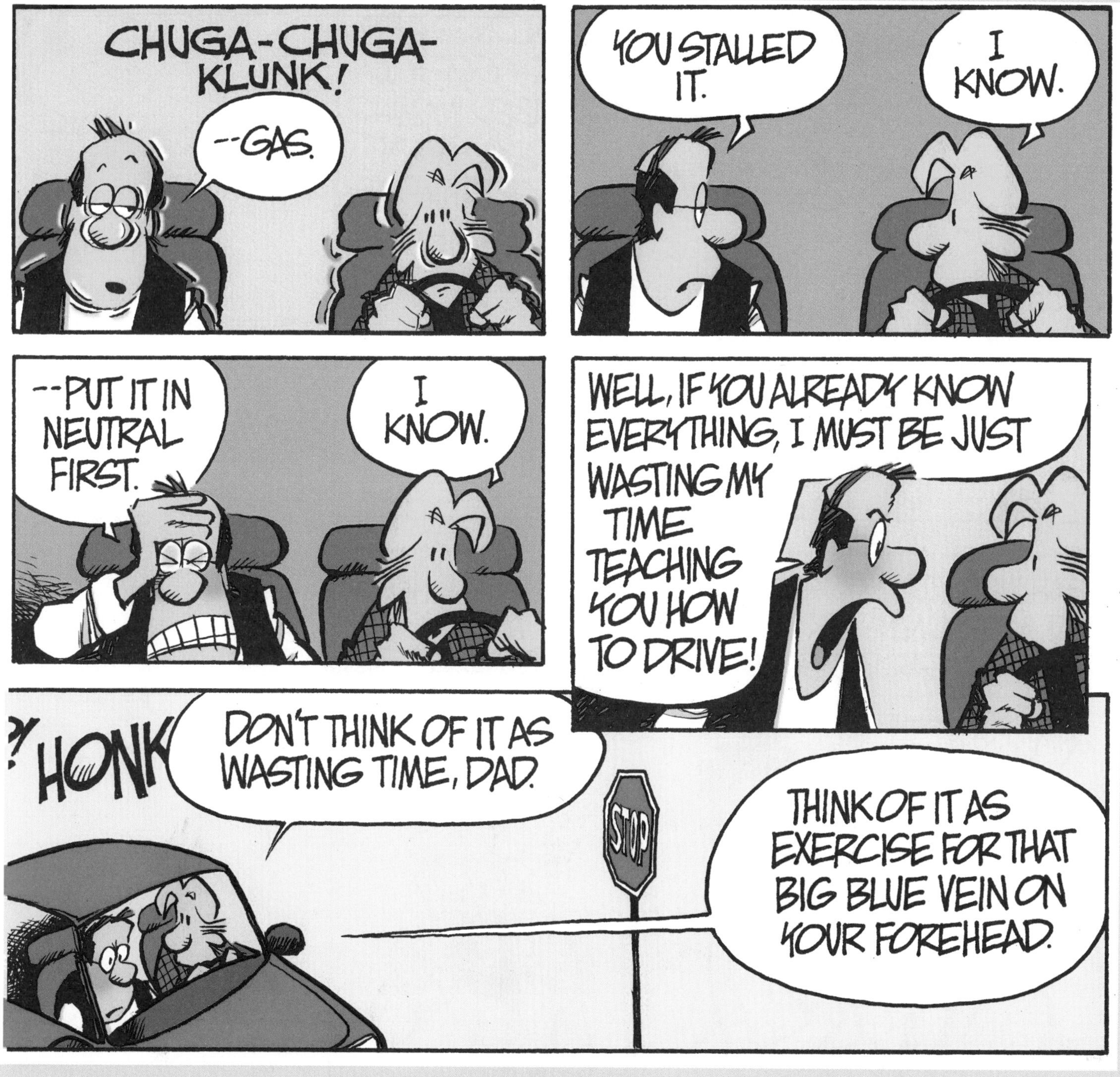
CHUGA-CHUGA-KLUNK!
--GAS.
YOU STALLED IT.
I KNOW.
--PUT IT IN NEUTRAL FIRST.
I KNOW.
WELL, IF YOU ALREADY KNOW EVERYTHING, I MUST BE JUST WASTING MY TIME TEACHING YOU HOW TO DRIVE!
HONK
DON'T THINK OF IT AS WASTING TIME, DAD.
STOP
THINK OF IT AS EXERCISE FOR THAT BIG BLUE VEIN ON YOUR FOREHEAD.

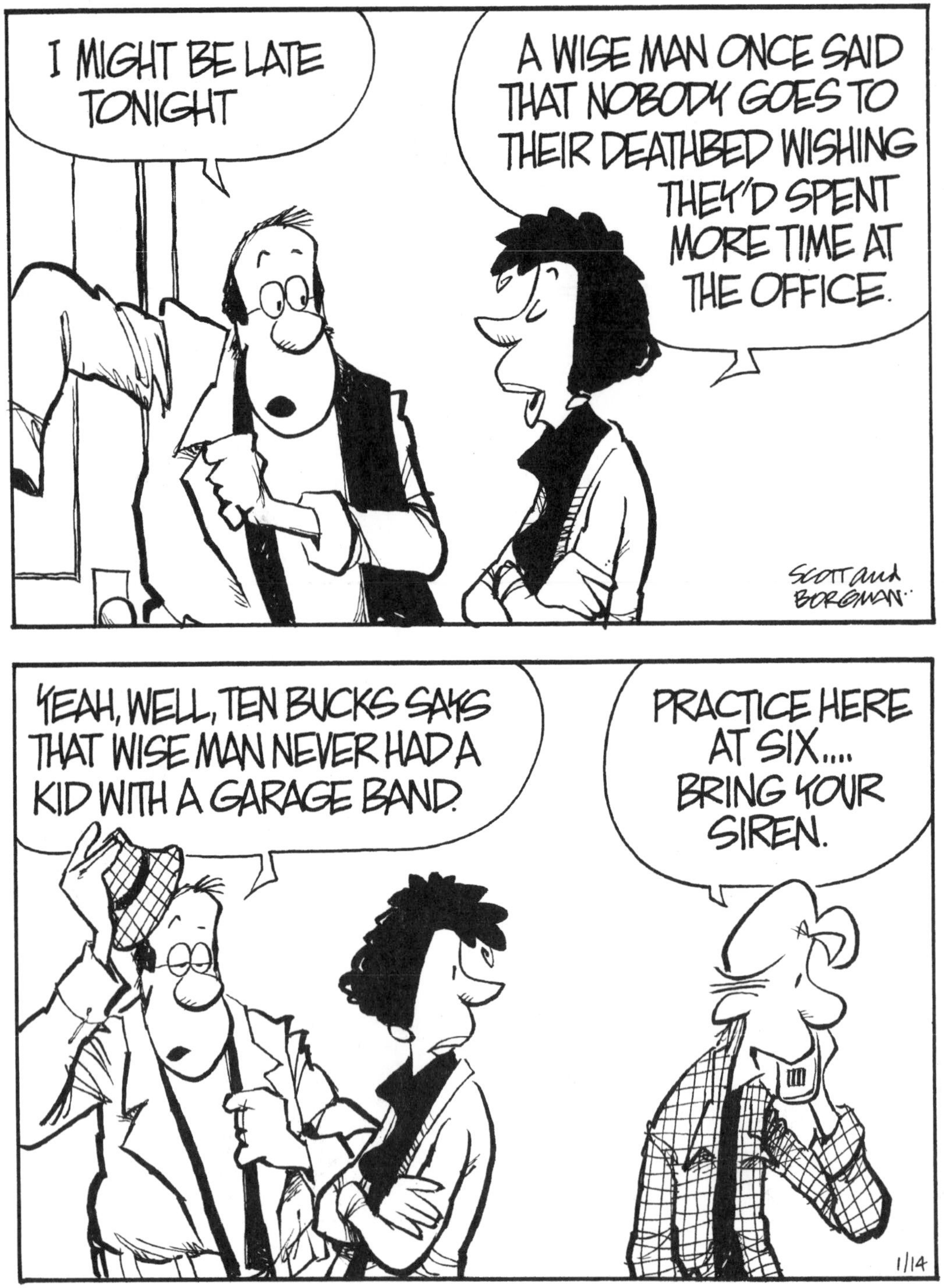
I MIGHT BE LATE TONIGHT
A WISE MAN ONCE SAID THAT NOBODY GOES TO THEIR DEATHBED WISHING THEY'D SPENT MORE TIME AT THE OFFICE.
SCOTT AND BORGMAN
YEAH, WELL, TEN BUCKS SAYS THAT WISE MAN NEVER HAD A KID WITH A GARAGE BAND.
PRACTICE HERE AT SIX.... BRING YOUR SIREN.
1/14

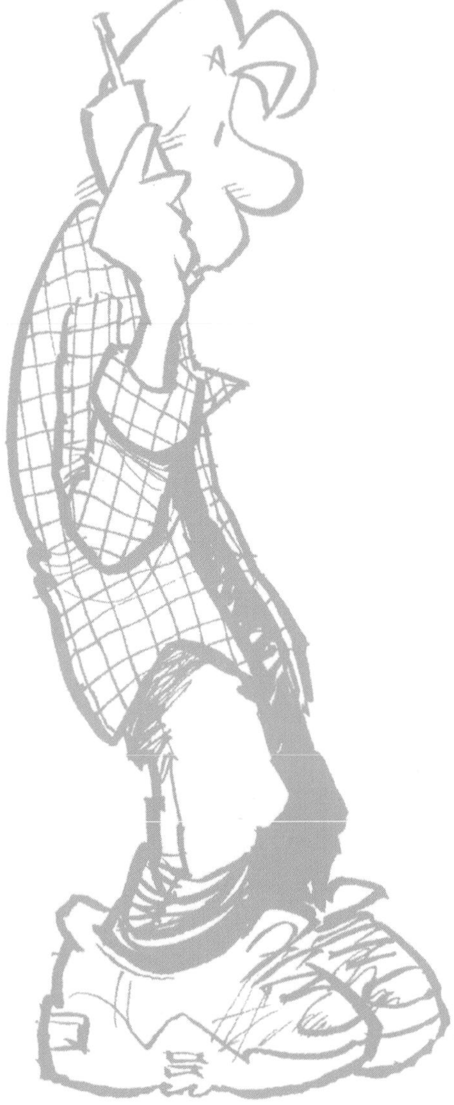

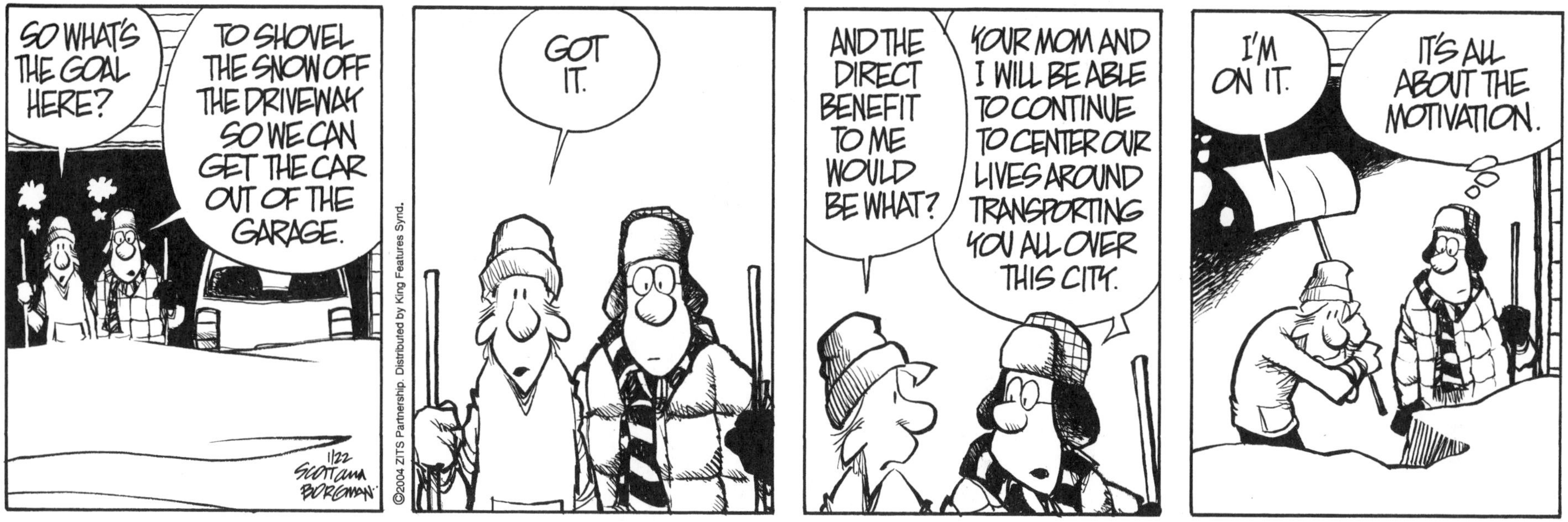
SO WHAT'S THE GOAL HERE?
TO SHOVEL THE SNOW OFF THE DRIVEWAY SO WE CAN GET THE CAR OUT OF THE GARAGE.
GOT IT.
AND THE DIRECT BENEFIT TO ME WOULD BE WHAT?
YOUR MOM AND I WILL BE ABLE TO CONTINUE TO CENTER OUR LIVES AROUND TRANSPORTING YOU ALL OVER THIS CITY.
I'M ON IT.
IT'S ALL ABOUT THE MOTIVATION.
©2004 ZITS Partnership. Distributed by King Features Synd.

Jerry: There's that hat thing again with Dad. Dude, buy a mirror!

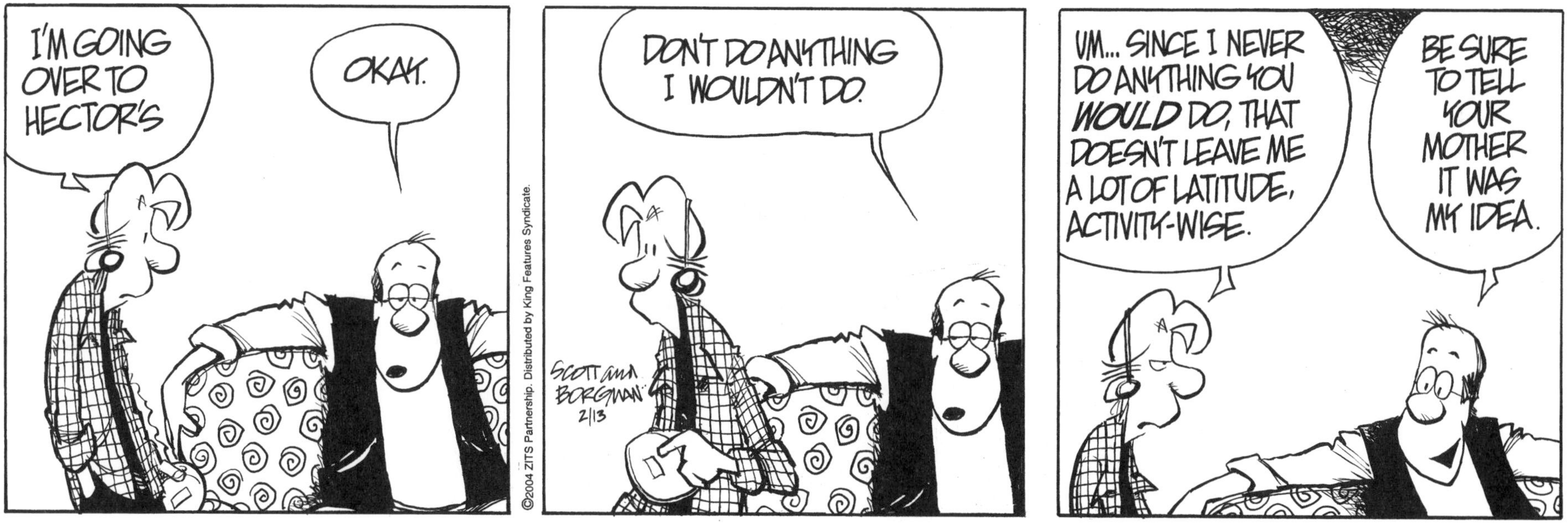
I'M GOING OVER TO HECTOR'S
OKAY.
DON'T DO ANYTHING I WOULDN'T DO.
UM... SINCE I NEVER DO ANYTHING YOU *WOULD* DO, THAT DOESN'T LEAVE ME A LOT OF LATITUDE, ACTIVITY-WISE.
BE SURE TO TELL YOUR MOTHER IT WAS MY IDEA.
©2004 ZITS Partnership. Distributed by King Features Syndicate.

SO WHAT DO YOU WANT FOR FATHER'S DAY, DAD?

WELL, I'VE SORT OF HAD MY EYE ON THE SPINNING REEL IN THIS MAGAZINE.

THREE HUNDRED BUCKS!?!?

ANYTHING ELSE?

YEAH. I'D LIKE TO BE RIGHT ABOUT SOMETHING.

IT DOESN'T MATTER WHAT IT IS.

I JUST WANT TO MAKE ONE DECISION OR ONE STATEMENT WITHOUT BEING CRITICIZED, CORRECTED OR RIDICULED.

SCOTT and BORGMAN

6/20

LET ME HAVE ANOTHER LOOK AT THAT MAGAZINE.

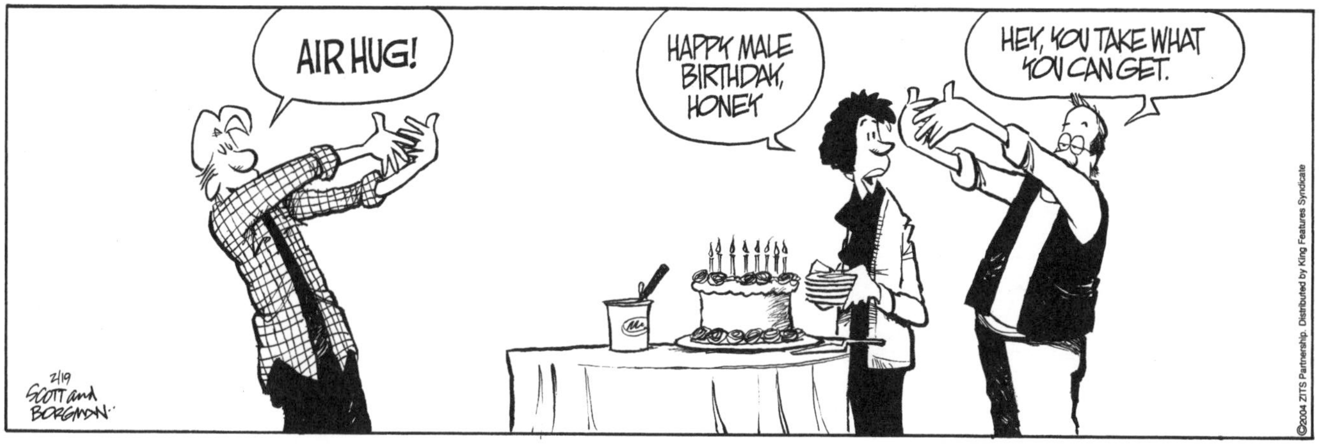
AIR HUG!
HAPPY MALE BIRTHDAY, HONEY
HEY, YOU TAKE WHAT YOU CAN GET.
2/19 SCOTT and BORGMAN
©2004 ZITS Partnership. Distributed by King Features Syndicate

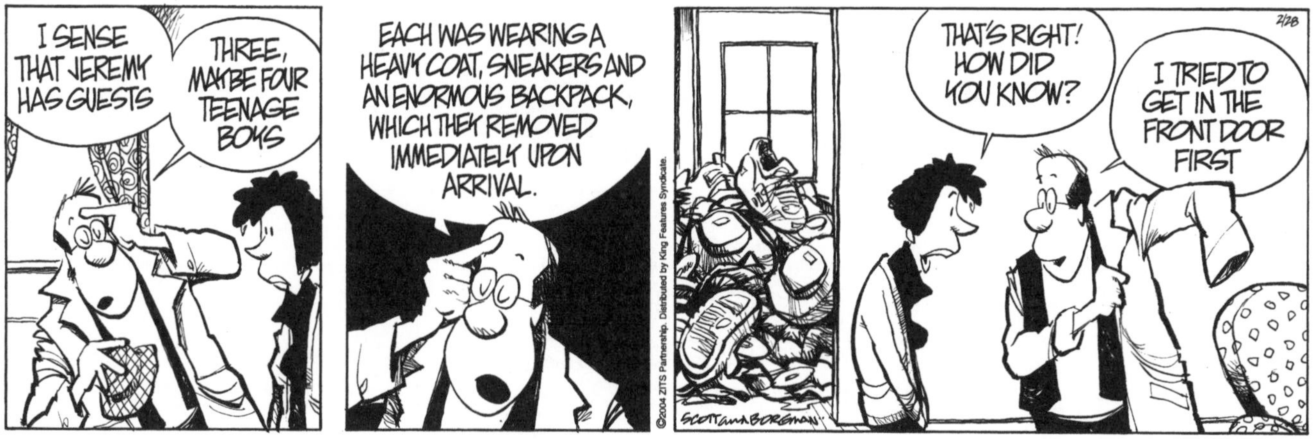
I SENSE THAT JEREMY HAS GUESTS
THREE, MAYBE FOUR TEENAGE BOYS
EACH WAS WEARING A HEAVY COAT, SNEAKERS AND AN ENORMOUS BACKPACK, WHICH THEY REMOVED IMMEDIATELY UPON ARRIVAL.
©2004 ZITS Partnership. Distributed by King Features Syndicate.
2/28
THAT'S RIGHT! HOW DID YOU KNOW?
I TRIED TO GET IN THE FRONT DOOR FIRST
SCOTT and BORGMAN

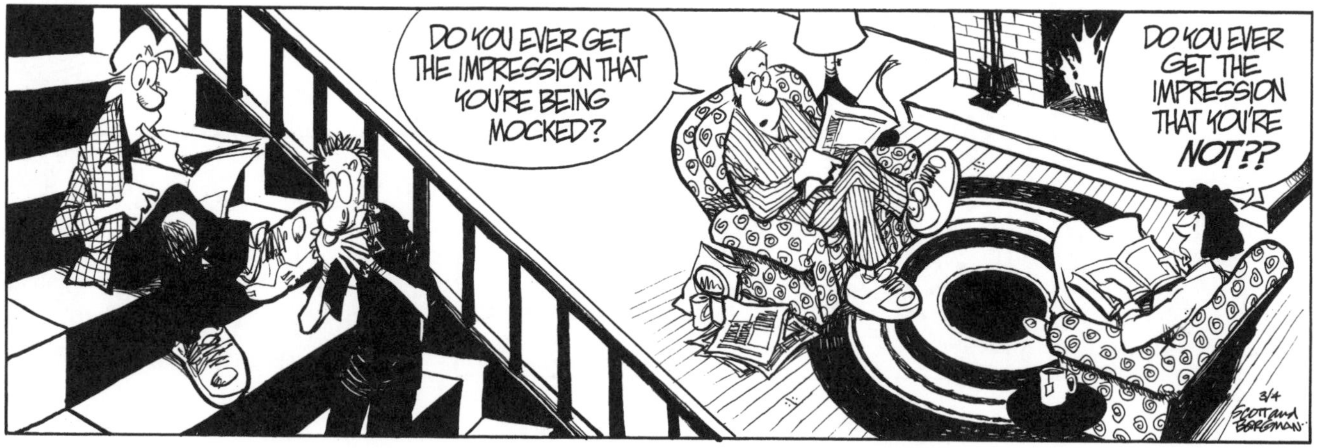
DO YOU EVER GET THE IMPRESSION THAT YOU'RE BEING MOCKED?
DO YOU EVER GET THE IMPRESSION THAT YOU'RE ***NOT??***
3/4 SCOTT and BORGMAN

Jerry: Dad-mocking isn't a choice for teenagers, it's an obligation.

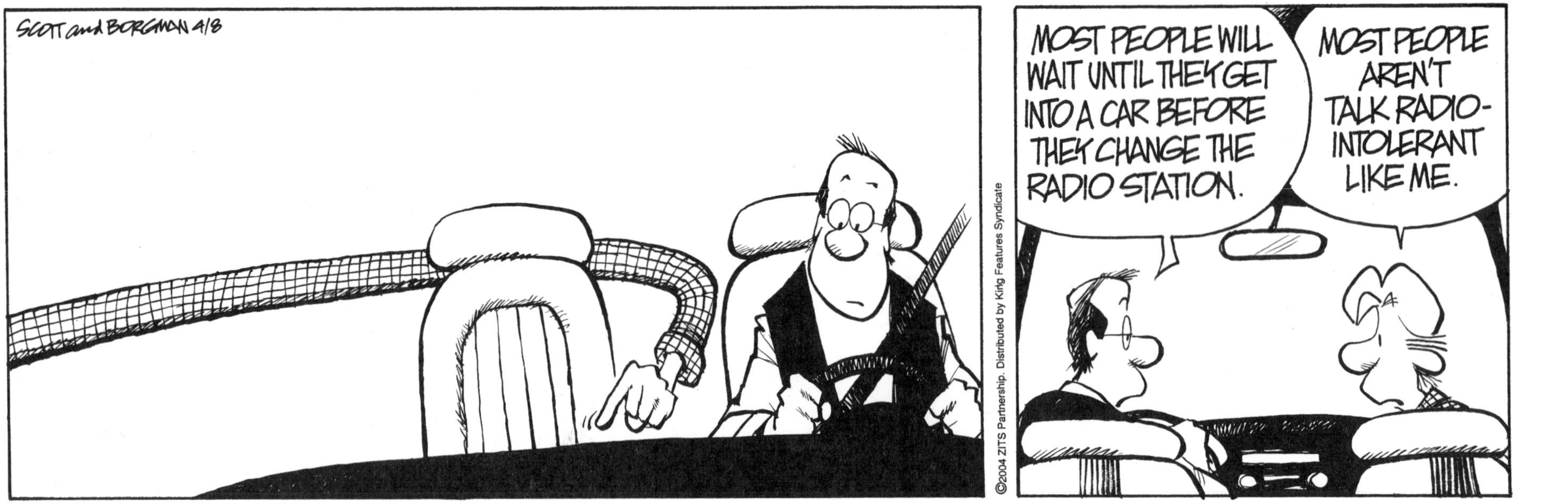
SCOTT and BORGMAN 4/8
MOST PEOPLE WILL WAIT UNTIL THEY GET INTO A CAR BEFORE THEY CHANGE THE RADIO STATION.
MOST PEOPLE AREN'T TALK RADIO-INTOLERANT LIKE ME.
©2004 ZITS Partnership. Distributed by King Features Syndicate

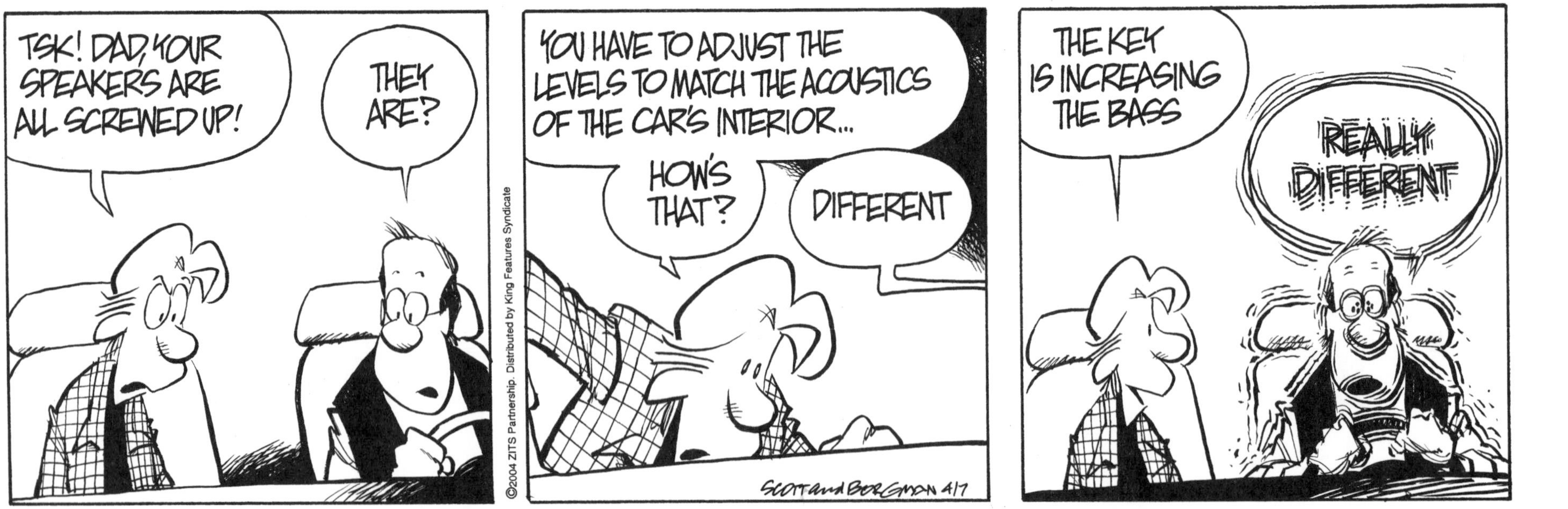
TSK! DAD, YOUR SPEAKERS ARE ALL SCREWED UP!
THEY ARE?
©2004 ZITS Partnership. Distributed by King Features Syndicate
YOU HAVE TO ADJUST THE LEVELS TO MATCH THE ACOUSTICS OF THE CAR'S INTERIOR...
HOW'S THAT?
DIFFERENT
SCOTT and BORGMAN 4/7
THE KEY IS INCREASING THE BASS
REALLY DIFFERENT

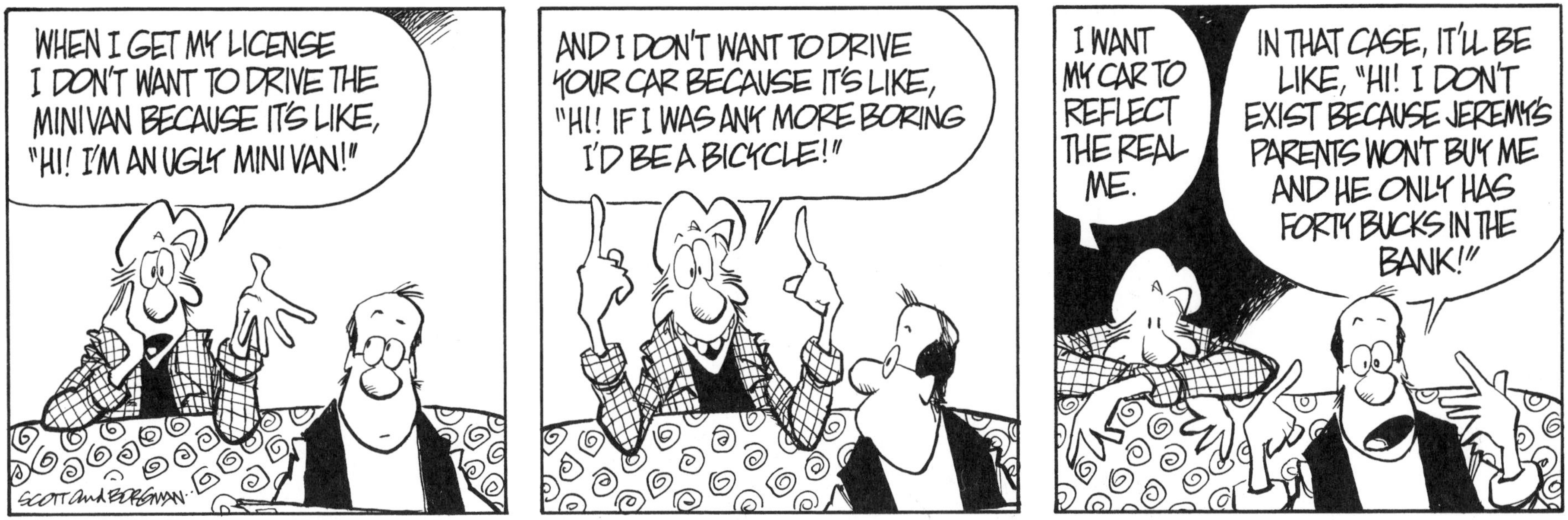
WHEN I GET MY LICENSE I DON'T WANT TO DRIVE THE MINIVAN BECAUSE IT'S LIKE, "HI! I'M AN UGLY MINI VAN!"
SCOTT and BORGMAN
AND I DON'T WANT TO DRIVE YOUR CAR BECAUSE IT'S LIKE, "HI! IF I WAS ANY MORE BORING I'D BE A BICYCLE!"
I WANT MY CAR TO REFLECT THE REAL ME.
IN THAT CASE, IT'LL BE LIKE, "HI! I DON'T EXIST BECAUSE JEREMY'S PARENTS WON'T BUY ME AND HE ONLY HAS FORTY BUCKS IN THE BANK!"

Jim: Oops. The mocking gene must be inherited.

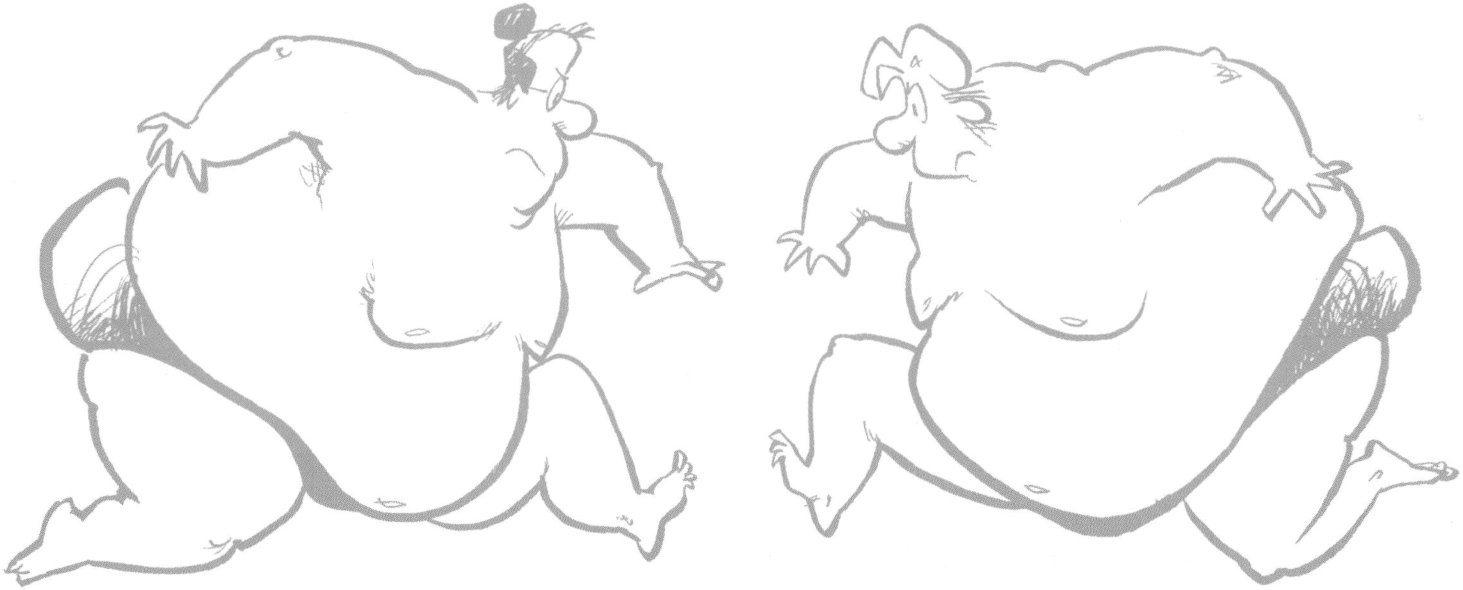

DAD!
DAD!
DAD? YOU'RE OKAY??
I'M FINE. WHY WOULDN'T I BE?
I SENT YOU A MESSAGE, AND WHEN I DIDN'T HEAR BACK FROM YOU, WELL, NATURALLY I ASSUMED THE WORST!
I'M SO RELIEVED TO SEE THAT YOU'RE NOT DEAD OR LYING AT THE BOTTOM OF AN ABANDONED MINE-SHAFT SOMEWHERE!
WHICH IS THE ONLY LOGICAL REASON IT WOULD TAKE SOMEBODY SO LONG TO HIT "REPLY"!
NOT EVERYBODY CHECKS THEIR E-MAIL EVERY 15 SECONDS LIKE YOU DO, JEREMY.
10/10
SCOTT AND BORGMAN

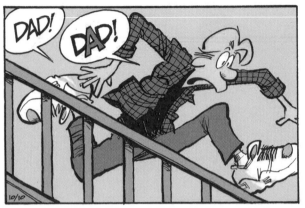

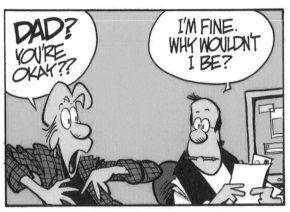

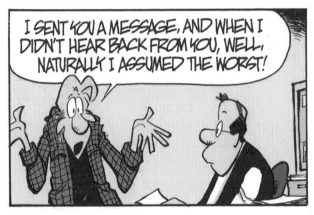

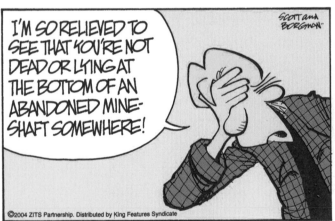

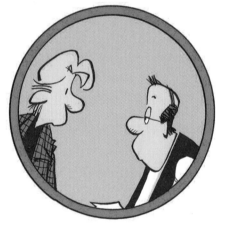

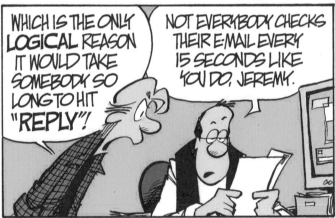

Jerry: From the days when e-mail was cool.

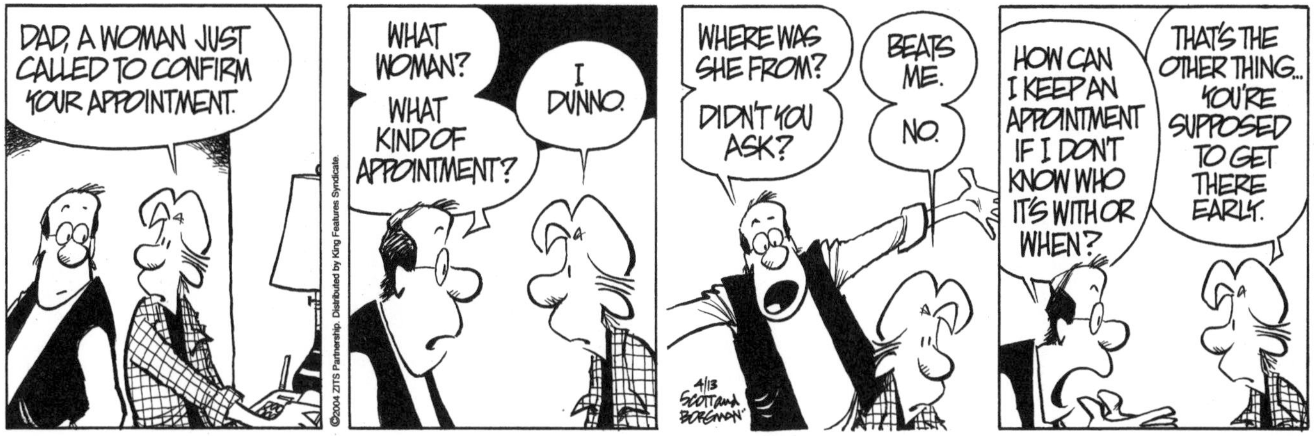
DAD, A WOMAN JUST CALLED TO CONFIRM YOUR APPOINTMENT.
WHAT WOMAN?
WHAT KIND OF APPOINTMENT?
I DUNNO.
WHERE WAS SHE FROM?
BEATS ME.
DIDN'T YOU ASK?
NO.
HOW CAN I KEEP AN APPOINTMENT IF I DON'T KNOW WHO IT'S WITH OR WHEN?
THAT'S THE OTHER THING... YOU'RE SUPPOSED TO GET THERE EARLY.
©2004 ZITS Partnership. Distributed by King Features Syndicate.
4/13 SCOTT AND BORGMAN

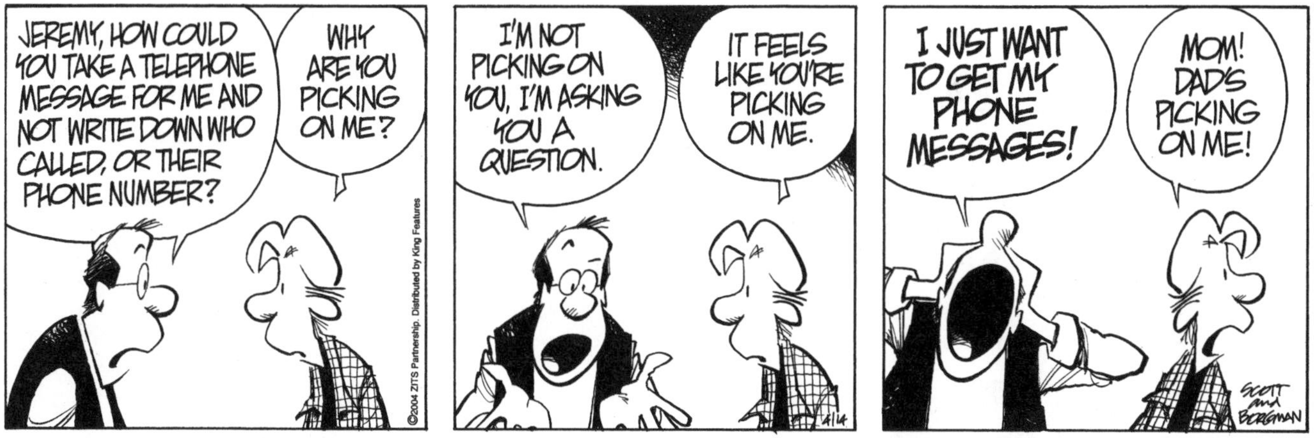
JEREMY, HOW COULD YOU TAKE A TELEPHONE MESSAGE FOR ME AND NOT WRITE DOWN WHO CALLED, OR THEIR PHONE NUMBER?
WHY ARE YOU PICKING ON ME?
I'M NOT PICKING ON YOU, I'M ASKING YOU A QUESTION.
IT FEELS LIKE YOU'RE PICKING ON ME.
I JUST WANT TO GET MY PHONE MESSAGES!
MOM! DAD'S PICKING ON ME!
©2004 ZITS Partnership. Distributed by King Features
4/14
SCOTT and BORGMAN

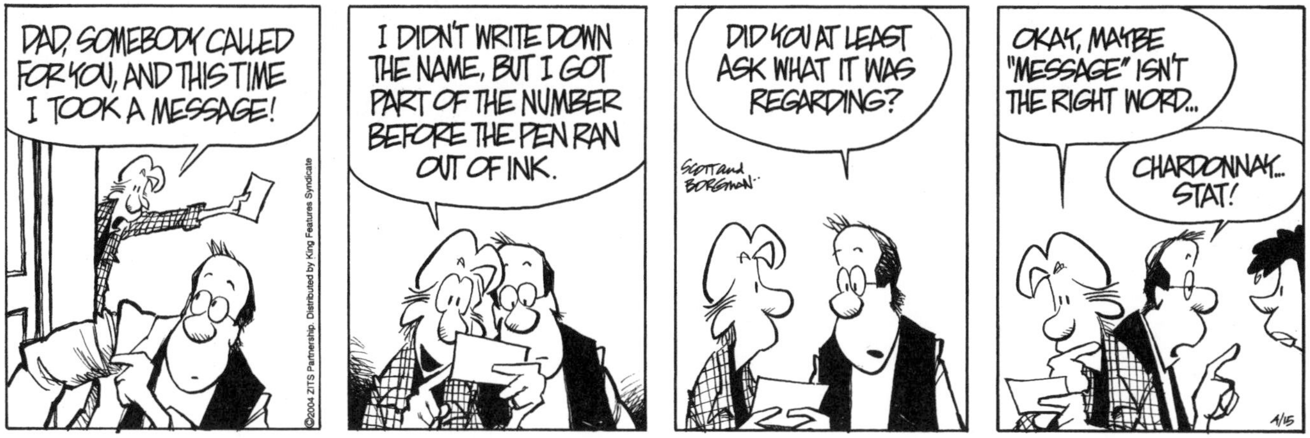
DAD, SOMEBODY CALLED FOR YOU, AND THIS TIME I TOOK A MESSAGE!
I DIDN'T WRITE DOWN THE NAME, BUT I GOT PART OF THE NUMBER BEFORE THE PEN RAN OUT OF INK.
DID YOU AT LEAST ASK WHAT IT WAS REGARDING?
OKAY, MAYBE "MESSAGE" ISN'T THE RIGHT WORD...
CHARDONNAY... STAT!
©2004 ZITS Partnership. Distributed by King Features Syndicate
SCOTT and BORGMAN
4/15

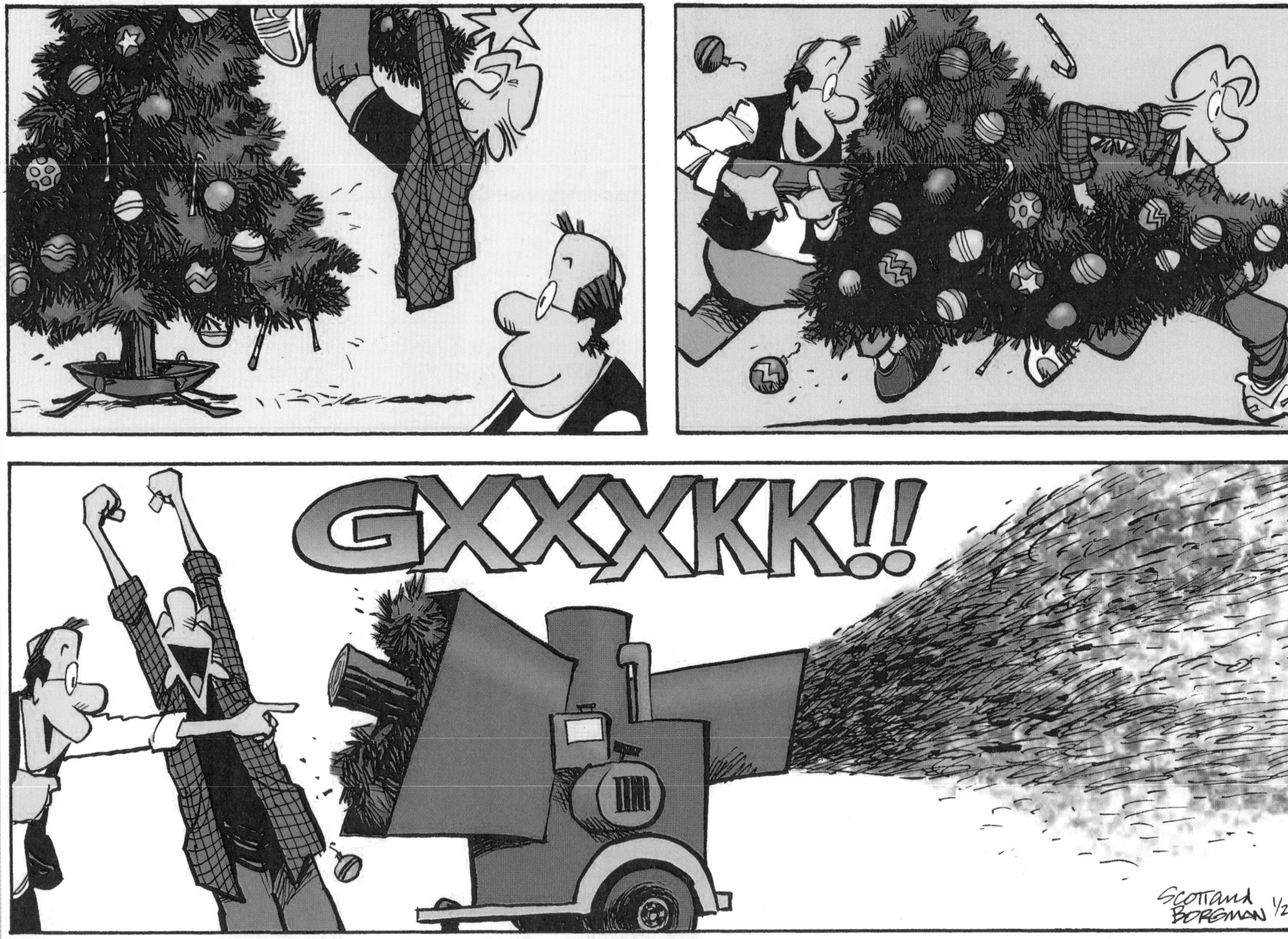
GXXXKK!!
SCOTT and BORGMAN 1/2

Jim: I'm fond of these strips where Jeremy and Dad are on the same side of an issue.

WHAT COULD BE MORE SATISFYING THAN GETTING ALL OF THE CHRISTMAS DECORATIONS PUT SAFELY BACK IN THEIR ORIGINAL BOXES?

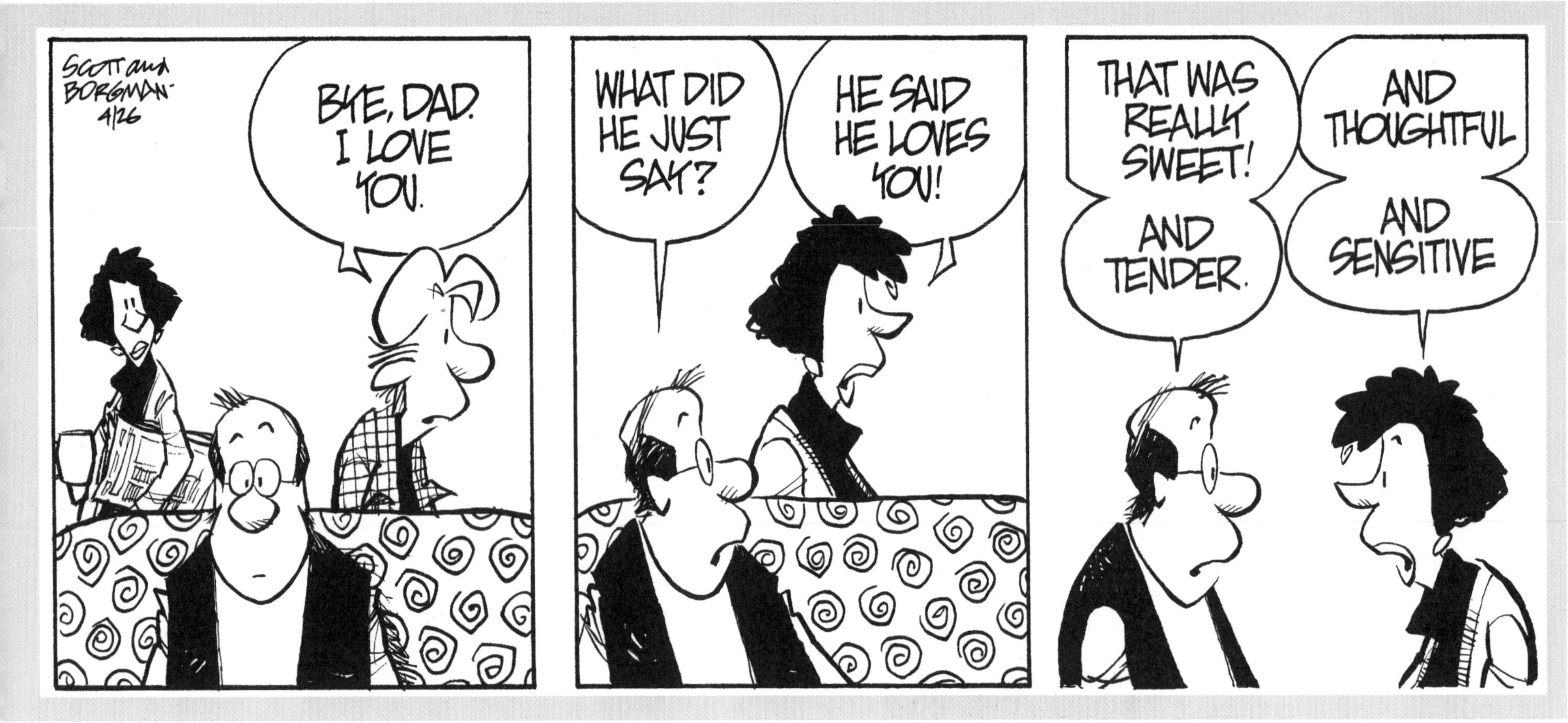
SCOTT and BORGMAN 4/26
BYE, DAD. I LOVE YOU.
WHAT DID HE JUST SAY?
HE SAID HE LOVES YOU!
THAT WAS REALLY SWEET!
AND TENDER.
AND THOUGHTFUL
AND SENSITIVE

Jerry: Sudden sweetness should always be accepted graciously with suspicion and caution.

NO GOOD CAN COME FROM THIS.
WE'VE GOT OUR EYE ON YOU, MISTER!

DAD! QUICK! SIGN MY TEST PAPER!
WHAT? WHY?
HURRY! THE PEOPLE BEHIND YOU ARE HONKING!
I DON'T EVEN KNOW WHAT I'M SIGNING!
IT'S JUST TO PROVE THAT I SHOWED IT TO YOU AND THAT YOU'RE SATISFIED WITH MY KNOWLEDGE OF THE SUBJECT.
BUT YOU--
GOTTA GO!
WALT DUNCAN...
CARPOOL AND PERJURY, AT YOUR SERVICE.
©2004 ZITS Partnership. Distributed by King Features Syndicate.

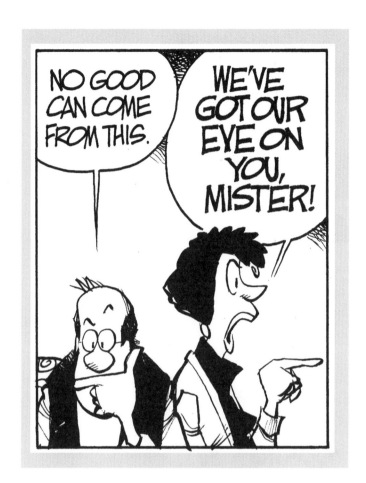

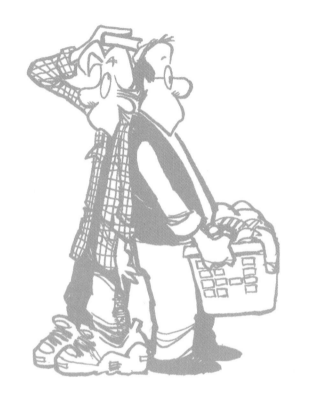

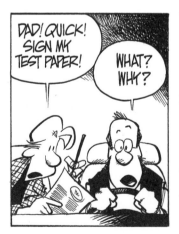

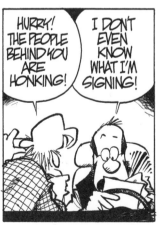

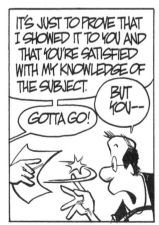

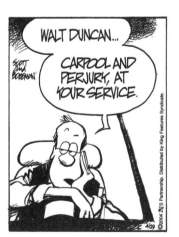

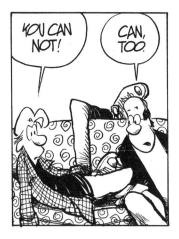

YOU CAN NOT!
CAN, TOO.
YOU'RE SAYING THAT YOU CAN LEVITATE A HUMAN BEING WITHOUT TOUCHING THEM.
PROVE IT.
RIGHT.
SCOTT and BORGMAN 4/30
BEEP BIP BEEP BOOP BIP BIP BIP
RI-I-I-I-I-ING!
I'LL GET IT!

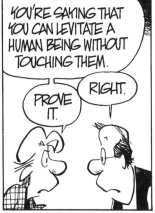

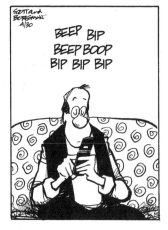

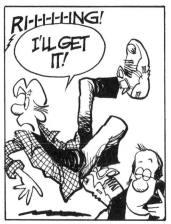

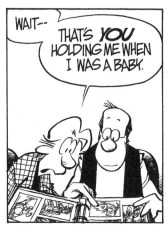

WAIT--
THAT'S YOU HOLDING ME WHEN I WAS A BABY.
THIS PICTURE WAS TAKEN FIFTEEN YEARS AGO, BUT YOU LOOK, LIKE SIXTY YEARS YOUNGER!
THAT SETTLES IT... I AM NEVER HAVING KIDS!
SCOTT and BORGMAN 5/25
©2004 ZITS Partnership. Distributed by King Features Syndicate.
BIRTH CONTROL BY PHOTO ALBUM?
WHATEVER WORKS

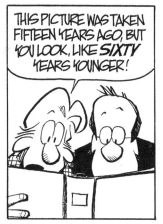

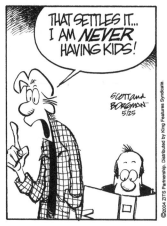

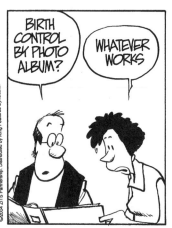

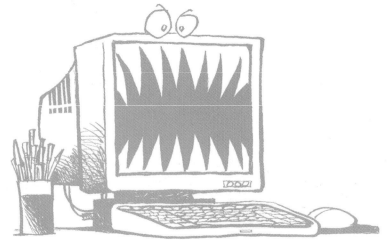

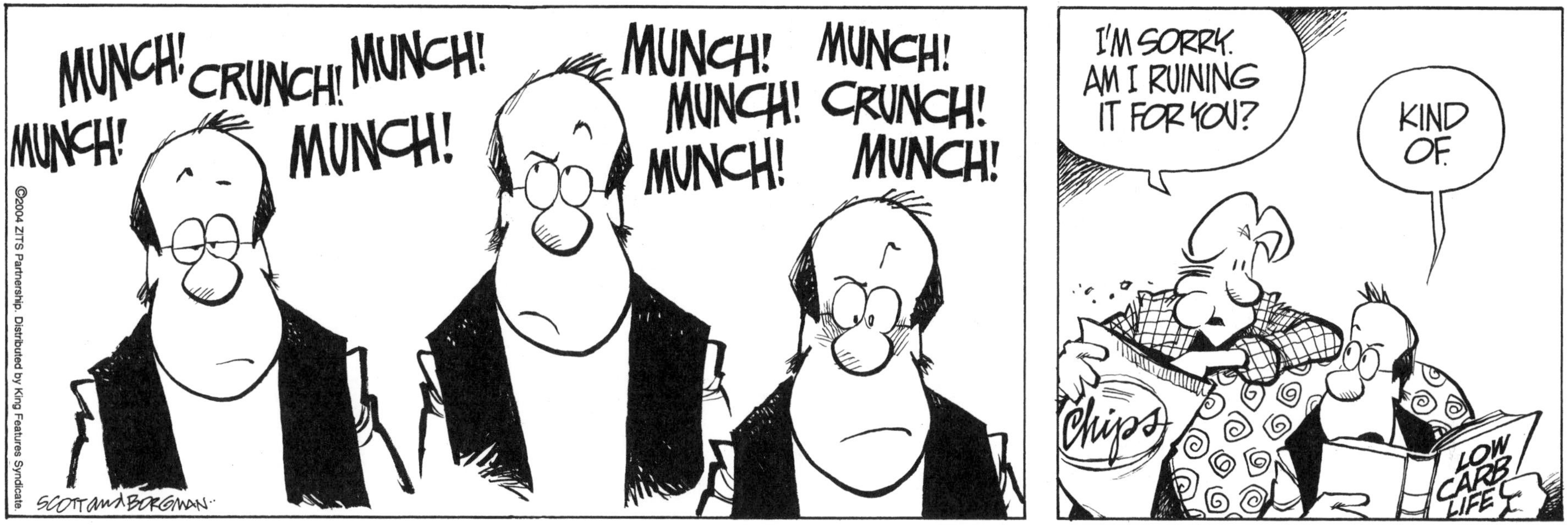
MUNCH!
MUNCH! CRUNCH! MUNCH!
MUNCH!
MUNCH!
MUNCH!
MUNCH!
MUNCH!
CRUNCH!
MUNCH!
©2004 ZITS Partnership. Distributed by King Features Syndicate.
SCOTT and BORGMAN
I'M SORRY. AM I RUINING IT FOR YOU?
KIND OF.
Chips
LOW CARB LIFE

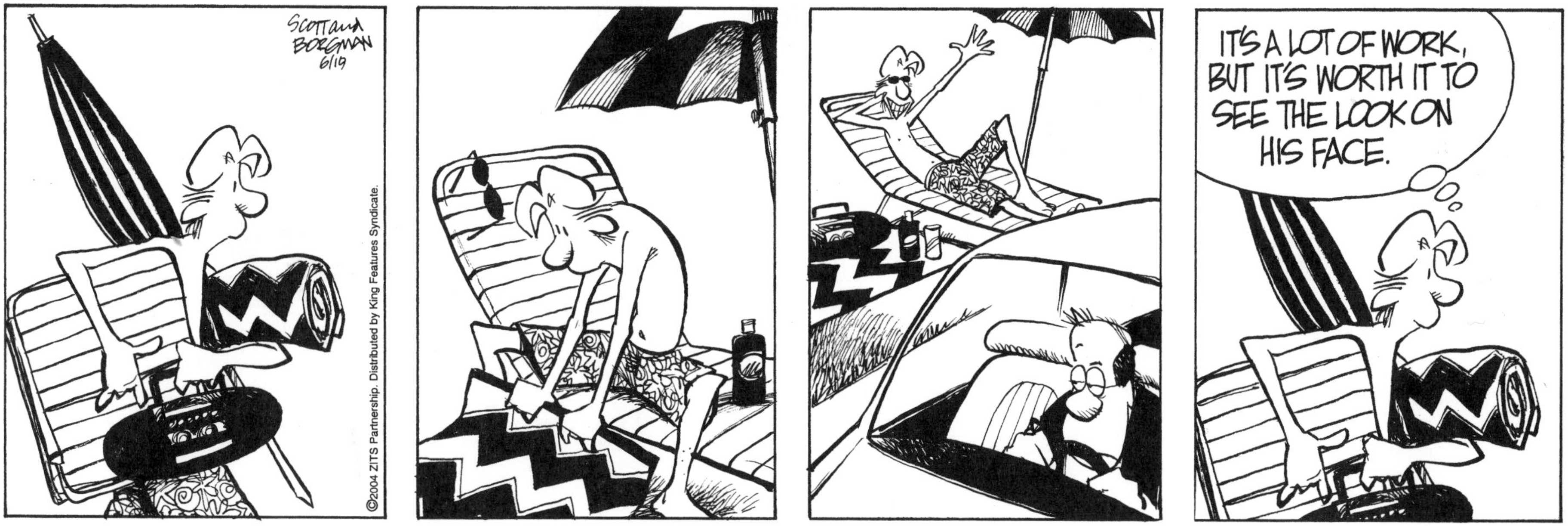
SCOTT and BORGMAN 6/19
©2004 ZITS Partnership. Distributed by King Features Syndicate.
IT'S A LOT OF WORK, BUT IT'S WORTH IT TO SEE THE LOOK ON HIS FACE.

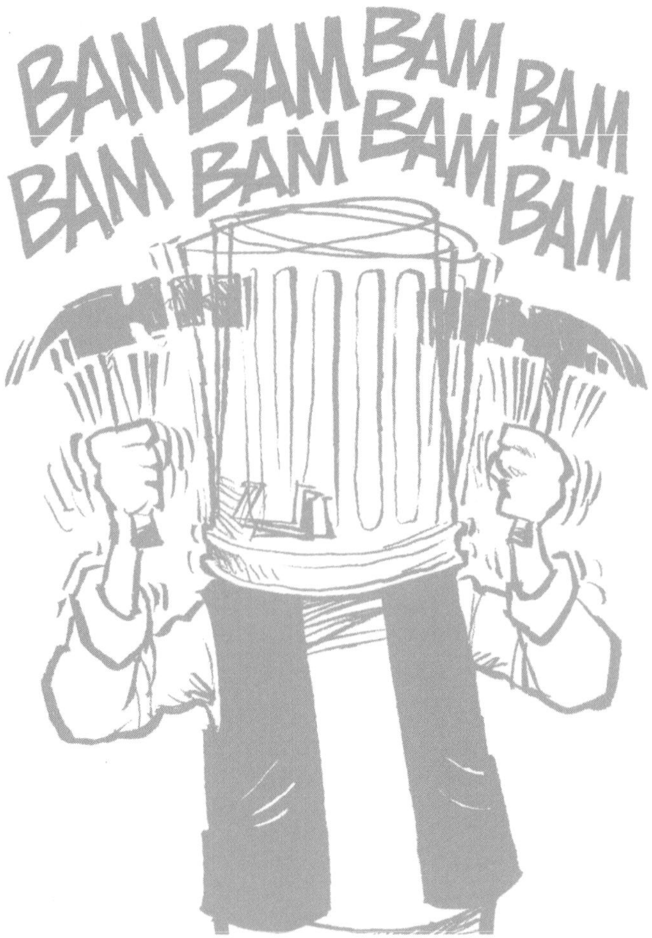
BAM BAM BAM BAM
BAM BAM BAM BAM

Jim: I wore a very comfortable T-shirt to bed for years that my kids later told me they hoped never to touch.

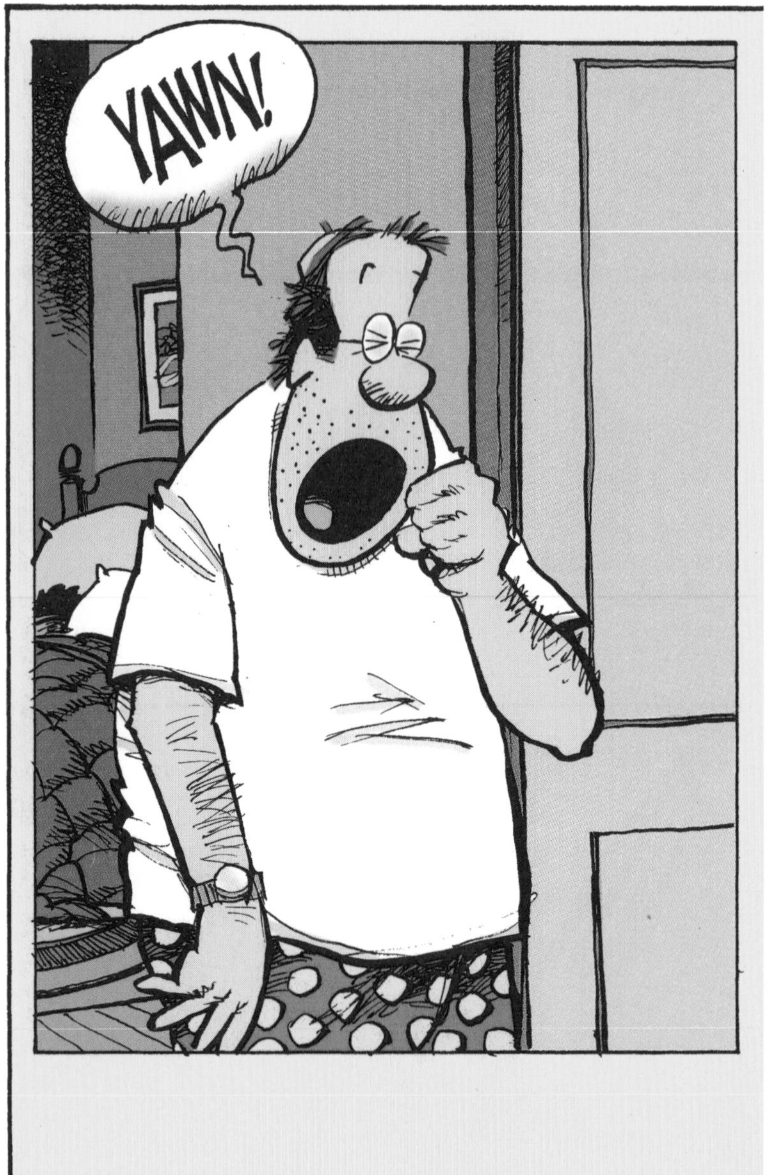
YAWN!

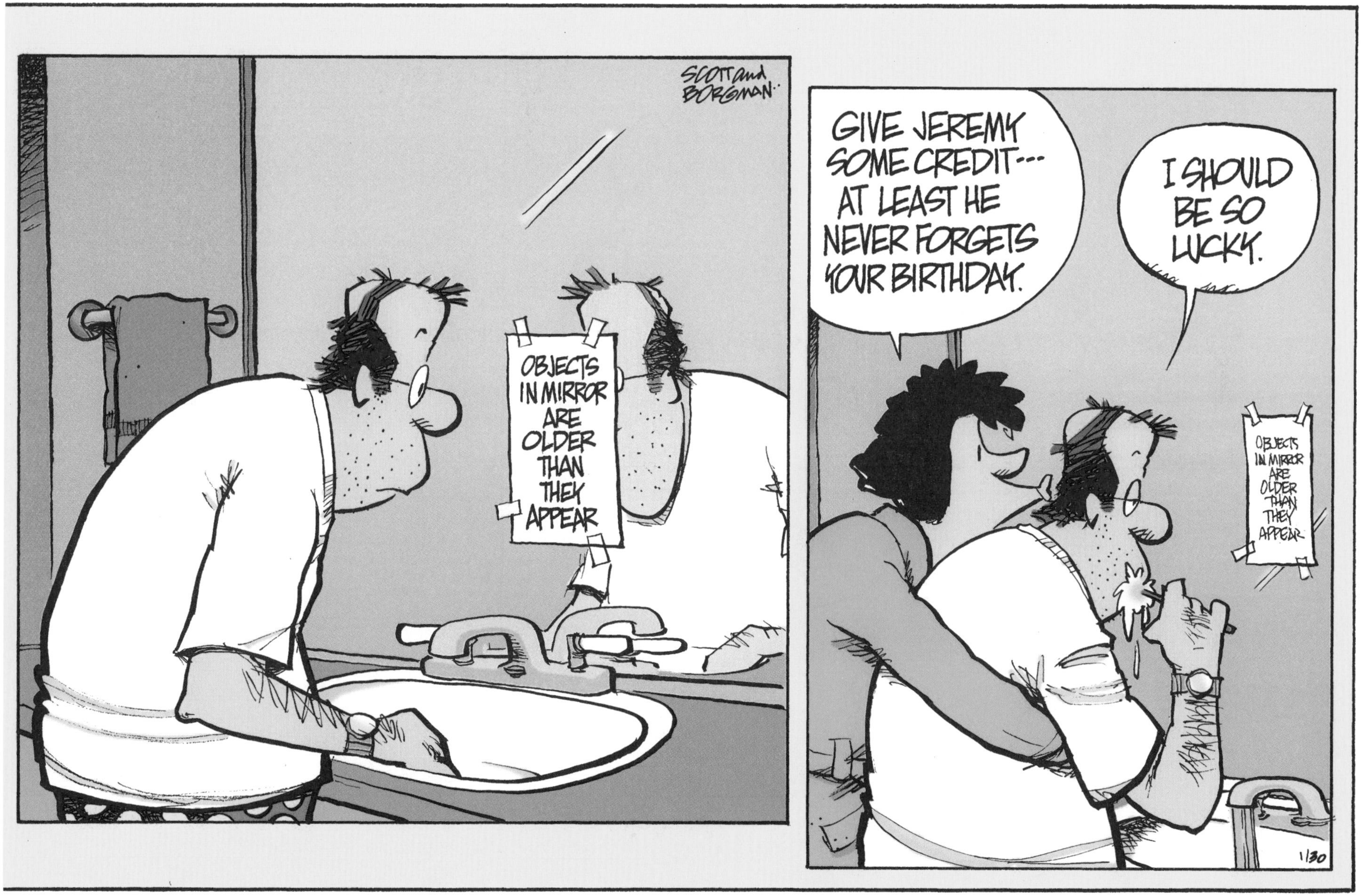
SCOTT and BORGMAN
OBJECTS IN MIRROR ARE OLDER THAN THEY APPEAR
GIVE JEREMY SOME CREDIT--- AT LEAST HE NEVER FORGETS YOUR BIRTHDAY.
I SHOULD BE SO LUCKY.
OBJECTS IN MIRROR ARE OLDER THAN THEY APPEAR
1/30

SCOTT AND BORGMAN
DAD, CAN YOU SHOW ME HOW TO PUT THIS TOGETHER?
WELL, FIRST YOU--
THAT'S NOT RIGHT.
7/1
©2004 ZITS Partnership. Distributed by King Features Syndicate.

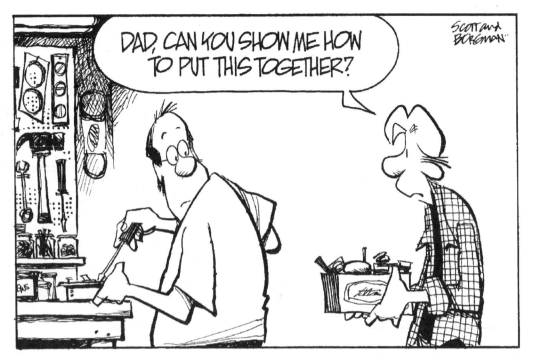

Jim: I didn't inherit my dad's handyman gene, and I fear our kids may be even worse. My dad always seemed to be puttering at his workbench; he could fix anything in our house. He and his buddies built a garage in our backyard when I was ten. I've become That Guy who pays someone else to change my oil.

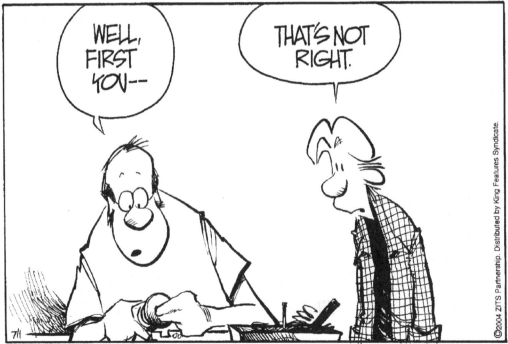

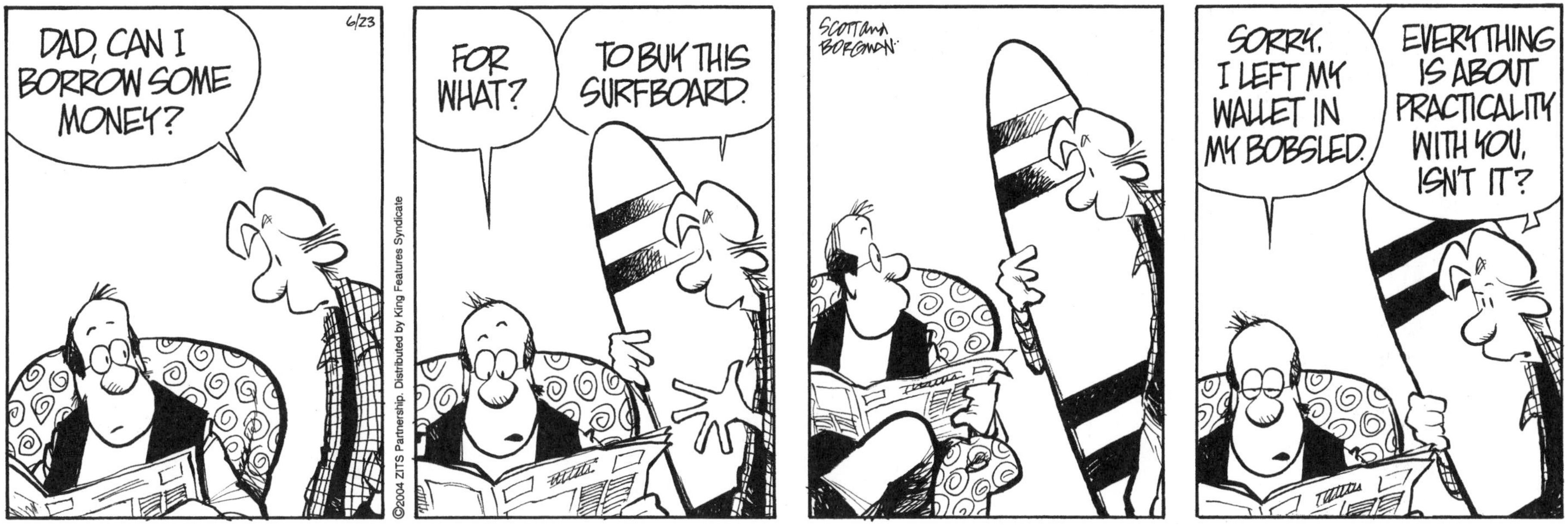
6/23
DAD, CAN I BORROW SOME MONEY?
FOR WHAT?
TO BUY THIS SURFBOARD.
SCOTT and BORGMAN
SORRY. I LEFT MY WALLET IN MY BOBSLED.
EVERYTHING IS ABOUT PRACTICALITY WITH YOU, ISN'T IT?
©2004 ZITS Partnership. Distributed by King Features Syndicate

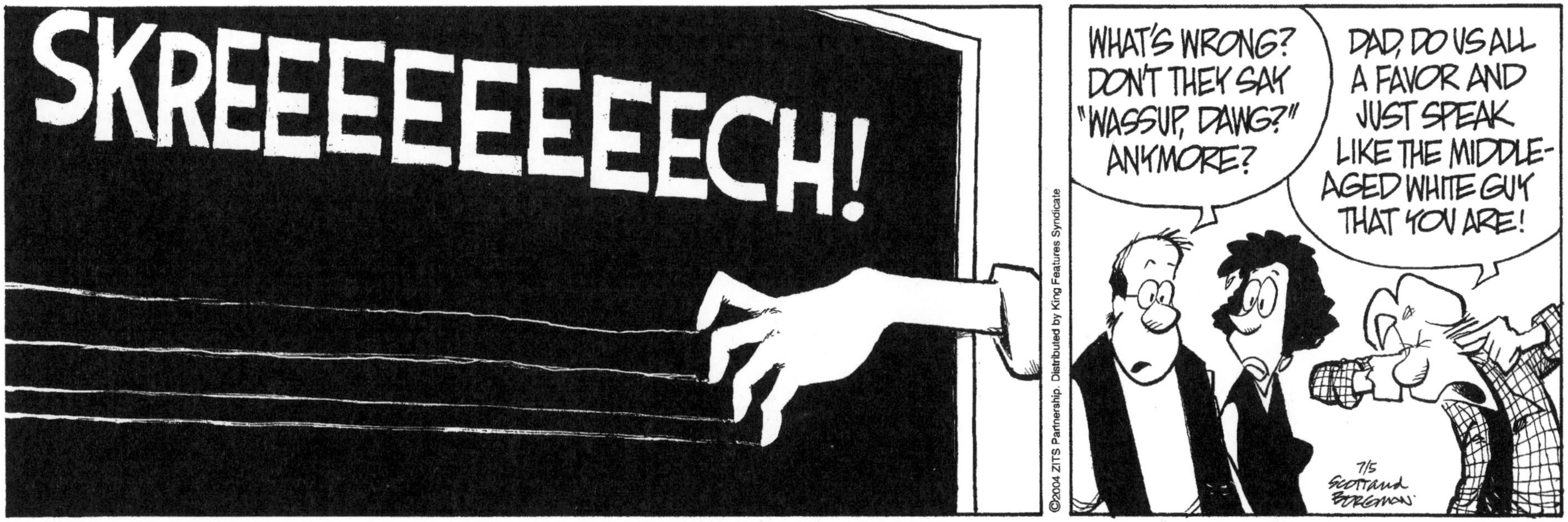
SKREEEEEEEEECH!
©2004 ZITS Partnership. Distributed by King Features Syndicate
WHAT'S WRONG? DON'T THEY SAY "WASSUP, DAWG?" ANYMORE?
DAD, DO US ALL A FAVOR AND JUST SPEAK LIKE THE MIDDLE-AGED WHITE GUY THAT YOU ARE!
7/5
SCOTT and BORGMAN

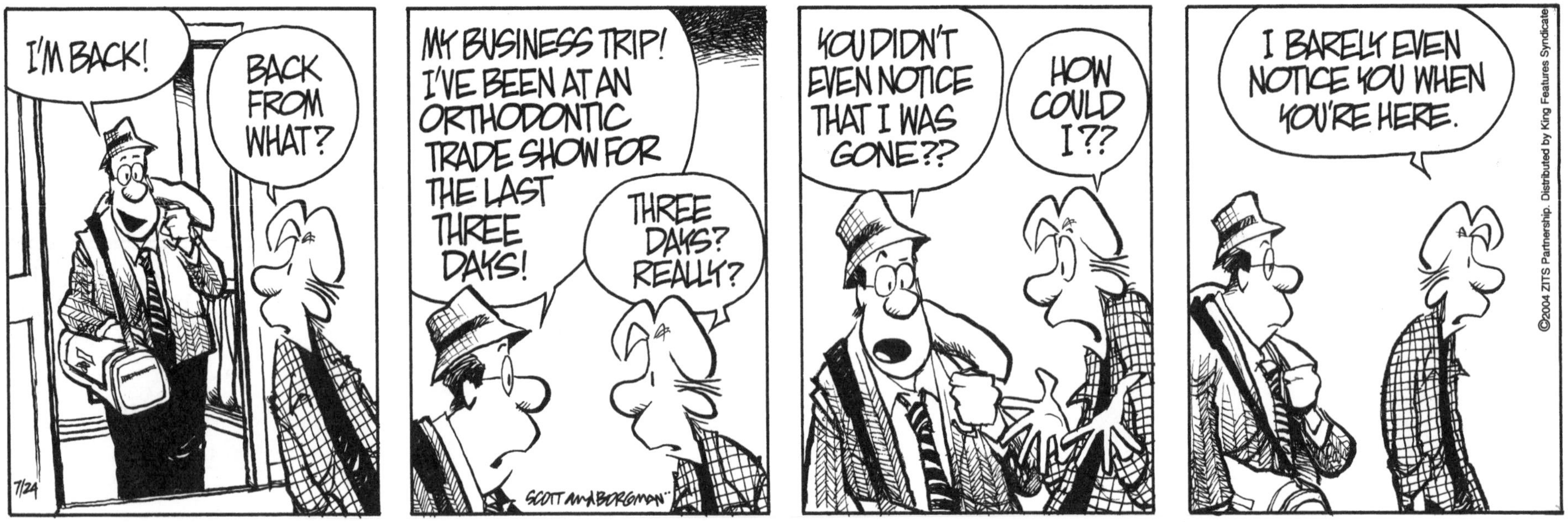
I'M BACK!
BACK FROM WHAT?
MY BUSINESS TRIP! I'VE BEEN AT AN ORTHODONTIC TRADE SHOW FOR THE LAST THREE DAYS!
THREE DAYS? REALLY?
YOU DIDN'T EVEN NOTICE THAT I WAS GONE??
HOW COULD I??
I BARELY EVEN NOTICE YOU WHEN YOU'RE HERE.
7/24
SCOTT and BORGMAN
©2004 ZITS Partnership. Distributed by King Features Syndicate

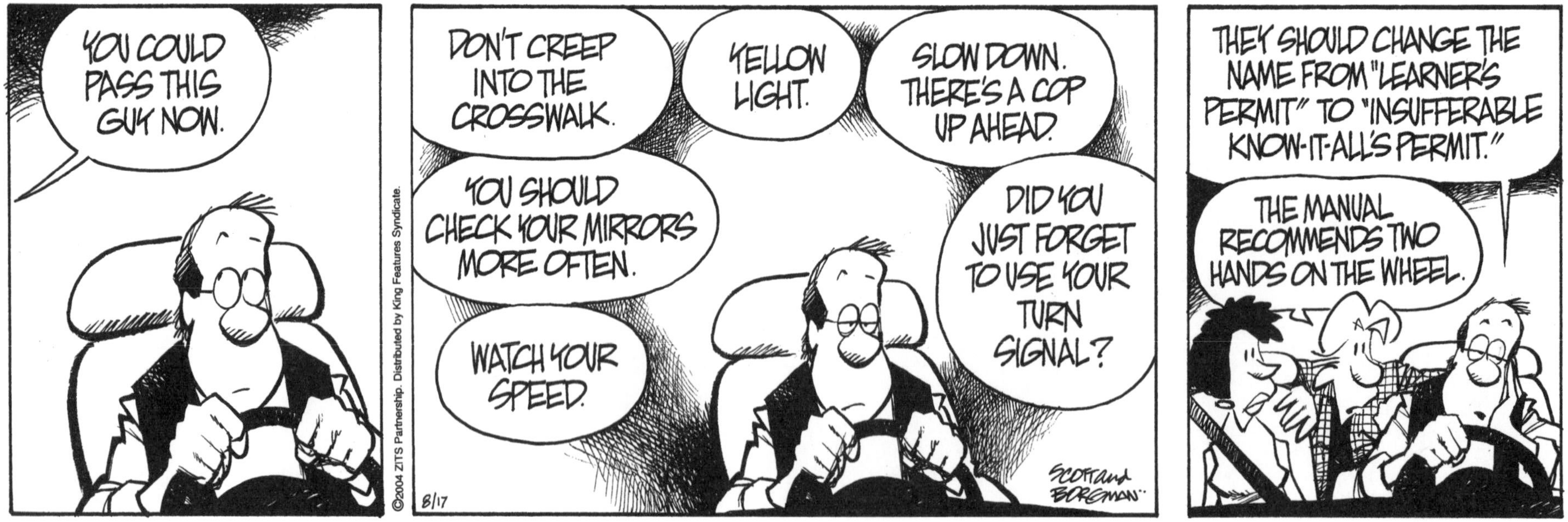
YOU COULD PASS THIS GUY NOW.
©2004 ZITS Partnership. Distributed by King Features Syndicate.
DON'T CREEP INTO THE CROSSWALK.
YELLOW LIGHT.
SLOW DOWN. THERE'S A COP UP AHEAD.
YOU SHOULD CHECK YOUR MIRRORS MORE OFTEN.
DID YOU JUST FORGET TO USE YOUR TURN SIGNAL?
WATCH YOUR SPEED.
8/17
SCOTT and BORGMAN
THEY SHOULD CHANGE THE NAME FROM "LEARNER'S PERMIT" TO "INSUFFERABLE KNOW-IT-ALL'S PERMIT."
THE MANUAL RECOMMENDS TWO HANDS ON THE WHEEL.

JEREMY KNOWS SO MUCH ABOUT TECHNOLOGY THAT IT'S ALMOST SCARY.
YUP.
AND HIS GRADES ARE AMAZING, TOO.
HE'S HOLDING A 4.0 GPA WITH THREE A.P. CLASSES.
I'VE NOTICED THAT HE'S GETTING PRETTY TALL, TOO.
PLUS, HE HAS GREAT HAIR, A HANDSOME FACE, AND MUSICAL TALENT COMING OUT OF HIS EARS!
MAKES YOU PROUD, DOESN'T HE?
YOU BET.
AND IF HE WASN'T MY SON, I'D HATE HIS GUTS.
NOW, NOW... THAT'S JUST THE CHOLESTEROL TALKING.
©2005 ZITS Partnership. Distributed by King Features Syndicate.
SCOTT AND BORGMAN

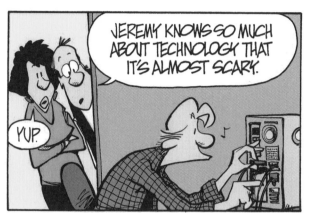

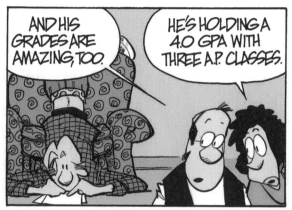

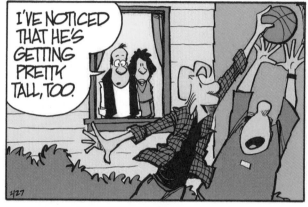

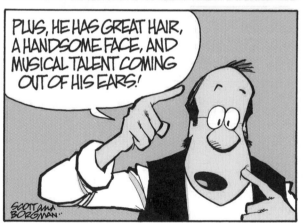

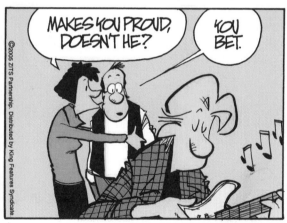

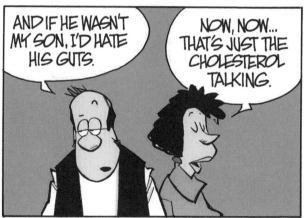

Jim: It's a powerful and mixed feeling when you see your teenager begin to eclipse you.

DEEDLE! DEEDLE! DEEDLE!
DEEDLE! DEEDLE! DEEDLE!
OW!
DEEDLE! DEEDLE! DEEDLE!
BAM!
DEEDLE! DEEDLE! DEEDLE!
WHUMP!
3/13
DEEDLE! DEEDLE! DEEDLE!
HELLO? HELLO?
JEREMY, DID YOU CALL YOUR FATHER FOR DINNER LIKE I ASKED YOU TO?
YEAH. BUT FOR SOME REASON HE HUNG UP ON ME.
SCOTT AND BORGMAN
©2005 ZITS Partnership. Distributed by King Featu

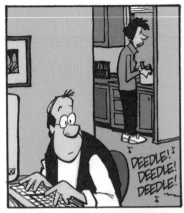

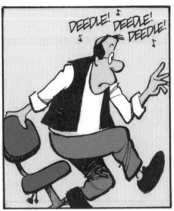

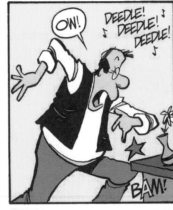

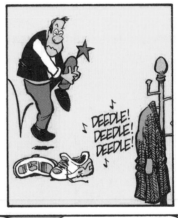

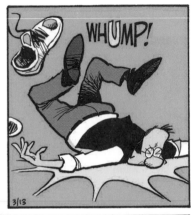

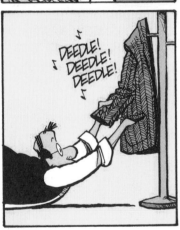

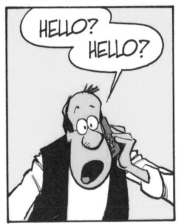

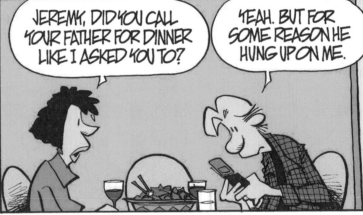

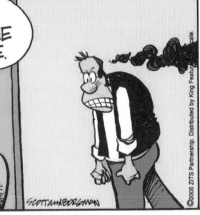

I get your comic strip in the London Free Press. I would just like to say that this is by far the best strip I have ever read. I first started reading comics every day when high school started for me (six years ago), and when Zits showed up in my paper four years ago, the cartoon section became a lot funnier.

Your cartoon also helps out with my family life, because every once in a while I have proof that I'm not the only kid on this planet who acts like me.

Anyway, keep up the good work.

Your Fan,

M.W.

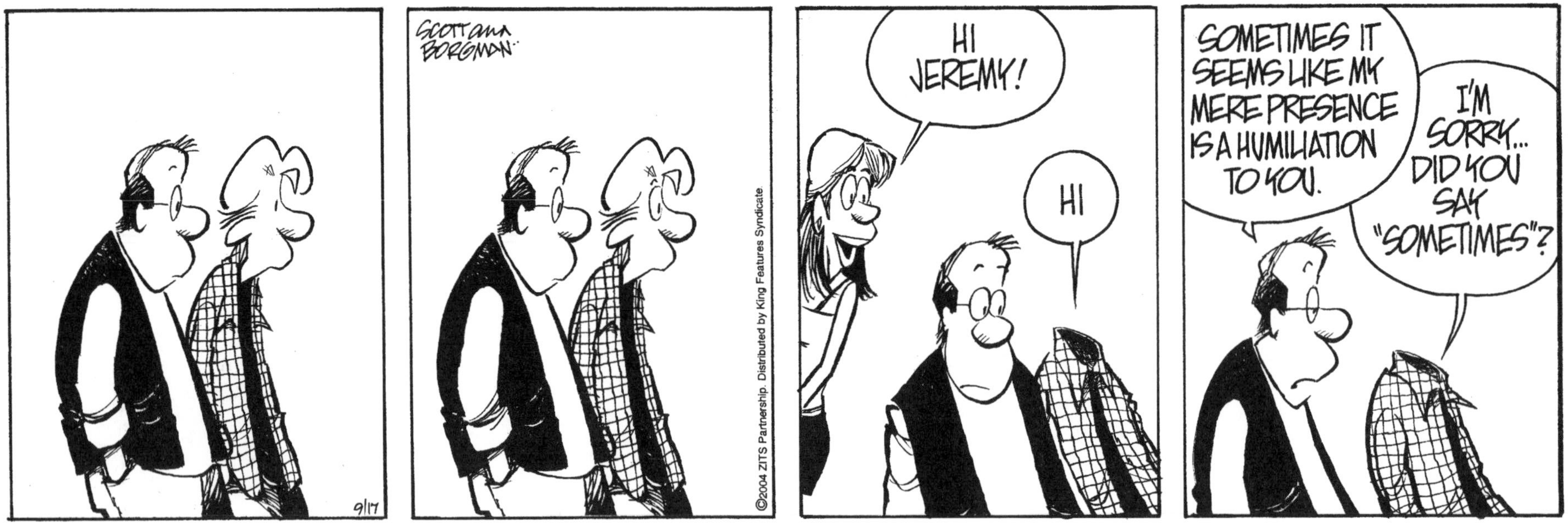
9/17
SCOTT and BORGMAN
©2004 ZITS Partnership. Distributed by King Features Syndicate
HI JEREMY!
HI
SOMETIMES IT SEEMS LIKE MY MERE PRESENCE IS A HUMILIATION TO YOU.
I'M SORRY... DID YOU SAY "SOMETIMES"?

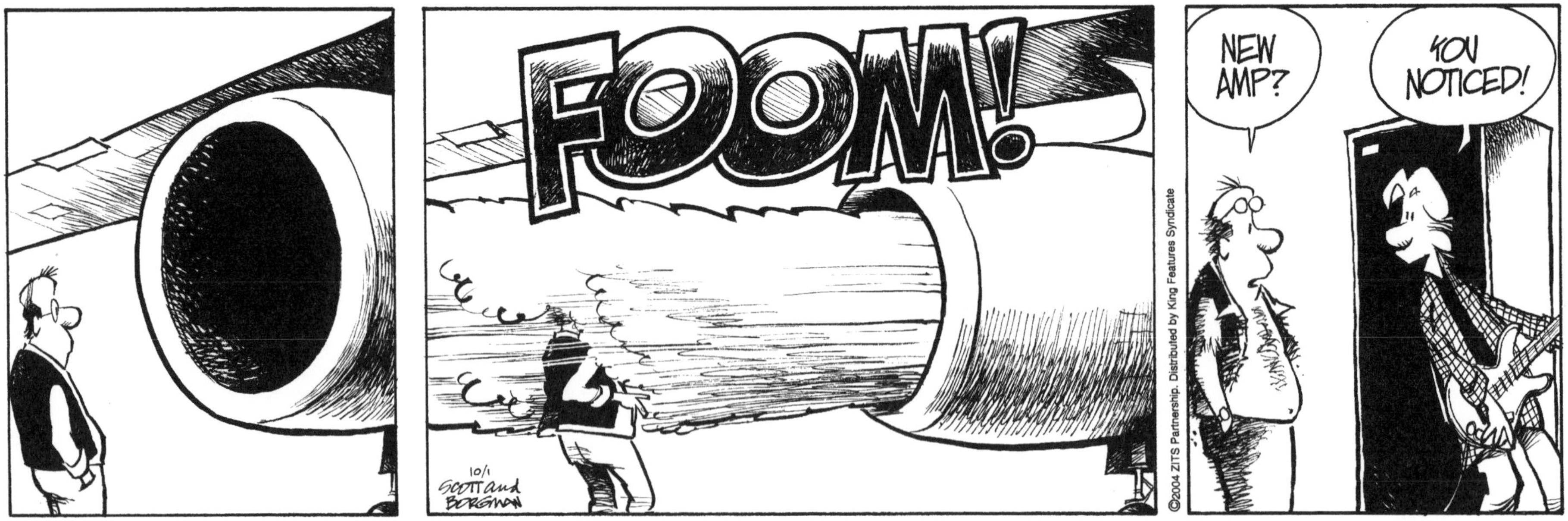
FOOM!
10/1
SCOTT and BORGMAN
©2004 ZITS Partnership. Distributed by King Features Syndicate
NEW AMP?
YOU NOTICED!

HEY DAD-
WHAT'S YOUR ALL-TIME FAVORITE TV SHOW?
M*A*S*H
M*A*S*H?
M*A*S*H.
OOOOOOOHH!
YOU WERE ALIVE WHEN M*A*S*H WAS ON?
THAT'S NOTHING! MY GRANDPA REMEMBERS LAUGH-IN!
10/12
SCOTT and BORGMAN
©2004 ZITS Partnership. Distributed by King Features Syndicate

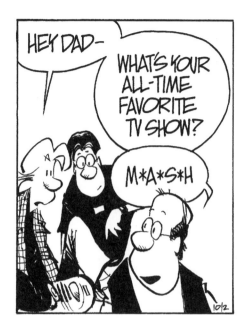

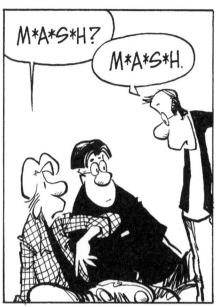

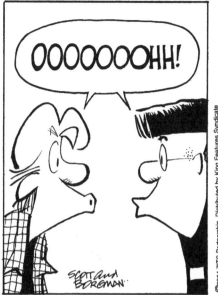

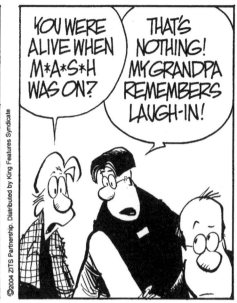

Jim: We've sometimes heard the complaint that Walt is yet another bumbler in a culture that disrespects dads. We've never seen him that way. Sure, Walt's frame of reference is hopelessly stuck in the past when it comes to TV, technology, and jargon. But he's an involved dad who spends time with his son, and we like to think he provides ballast for the Duncan family.

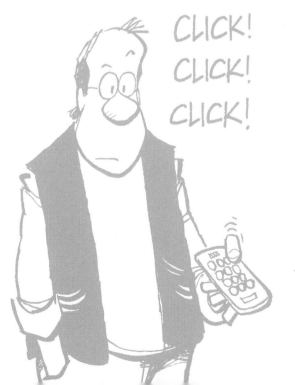

CLICK!
CLICK!
CLICK!

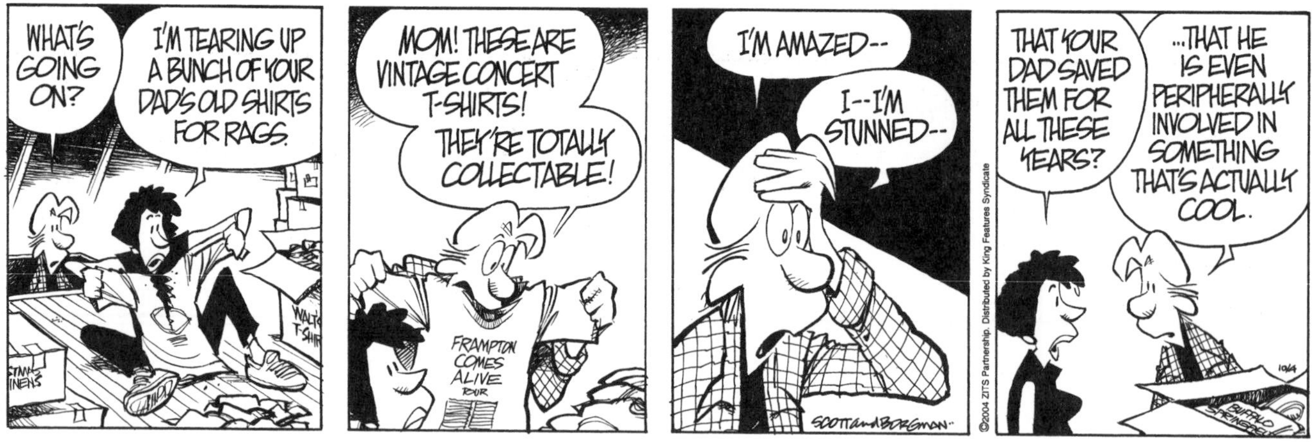
WHAT'S GOING ON?
I'M TEARING UP A BUNCH OF YOUR DAD'S OLD SHIRTS FOR RAGS.
MOM! THESE ARE VINTAGE CONCERT T-SHIRTS!
THEY'RE TOTALLY COLLECTABLE!
FRAMPTON COMES ALIVE TOUR
I'M AMAZED--
I--I'M STUNNED--
SCOTT and BORGMAN
THAT YOUR DAD SAVED THEM FOR ALL THESE YEARS?
...THAT HE IS EVEN PERIPHERALLY INVOLVED IN SOMETHING THAT'S ACTUALLY COOL.
©2004 ZITS Partnership. Distributed by King Features Syndicate
10/4

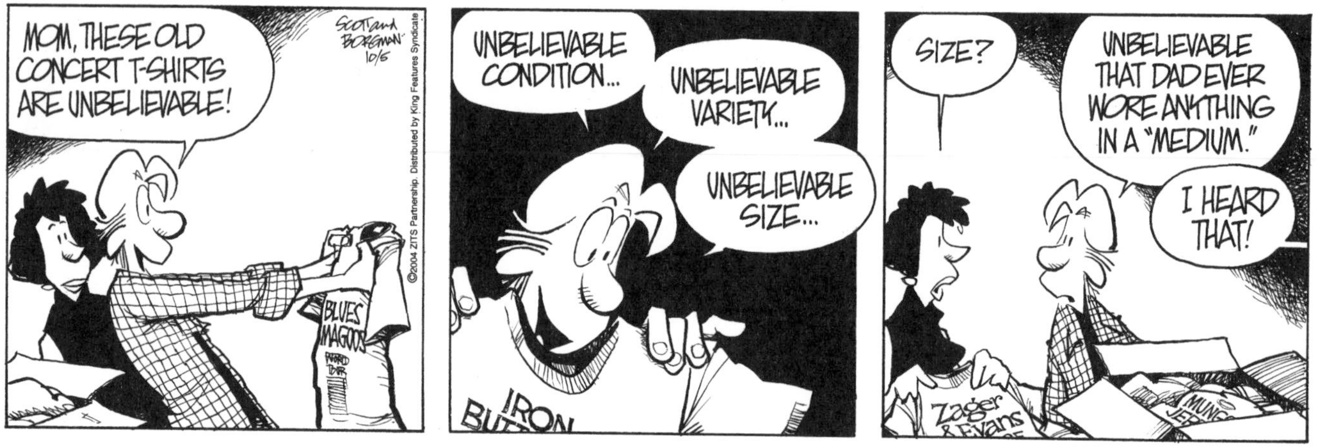
MOM, THESE OLD CONCERT T-SHIRTS ARE UNBELIEVABLE!
SCOTT and BORGMAN 10/5
©2004 ZITS Partnership. Distributed by King Features Syndicate
BLUES MAGOOS
UNBELIEVABLE CONDITION...
UNBELIEVABLE VARIETY...
UNBELIEVABLE SIZE...
SIZE?
UNBELIEVABLE THAT DAD EVER WORE ANYTHING IN A "MEDIUM."
I HEARD THAT!
Zager & Evans

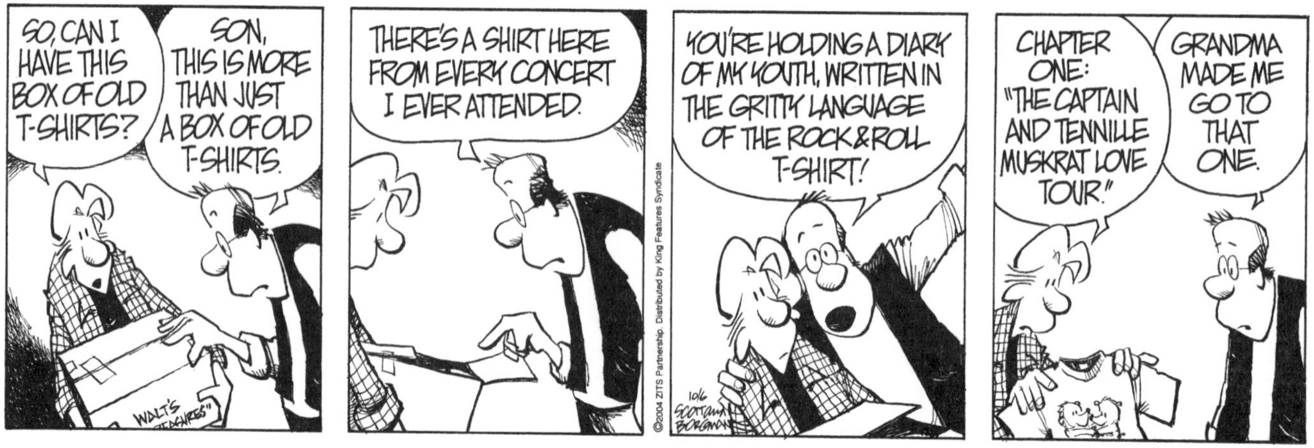
SO, CAN I HAVE THIS BOX OF OLD T-SHIRTS?
SON, THIS IS MORE THAN JUST A BOX OF OLD T-SHIRTS.
THERE'S A SHIRT HERE FROM EVERY CONCERT I EVER ATTENDED.
©2004 ZITS Partnership. Distributed by King Features Syndicate
YOU'RE HOLDING A DIARY OF MY YOUTH, WRITTEN IN THE GRITTY LANGUAGE OF THE ROCK & ROLL T-SHIRT!
10/6 SCOTT and BORGMAN
CHAPTER ONE: "THE CAPTAIN AND TENNILLE MUSKRAT LOVE TOUR."
GRANDMA MADE ME GO TO THAT ONE.

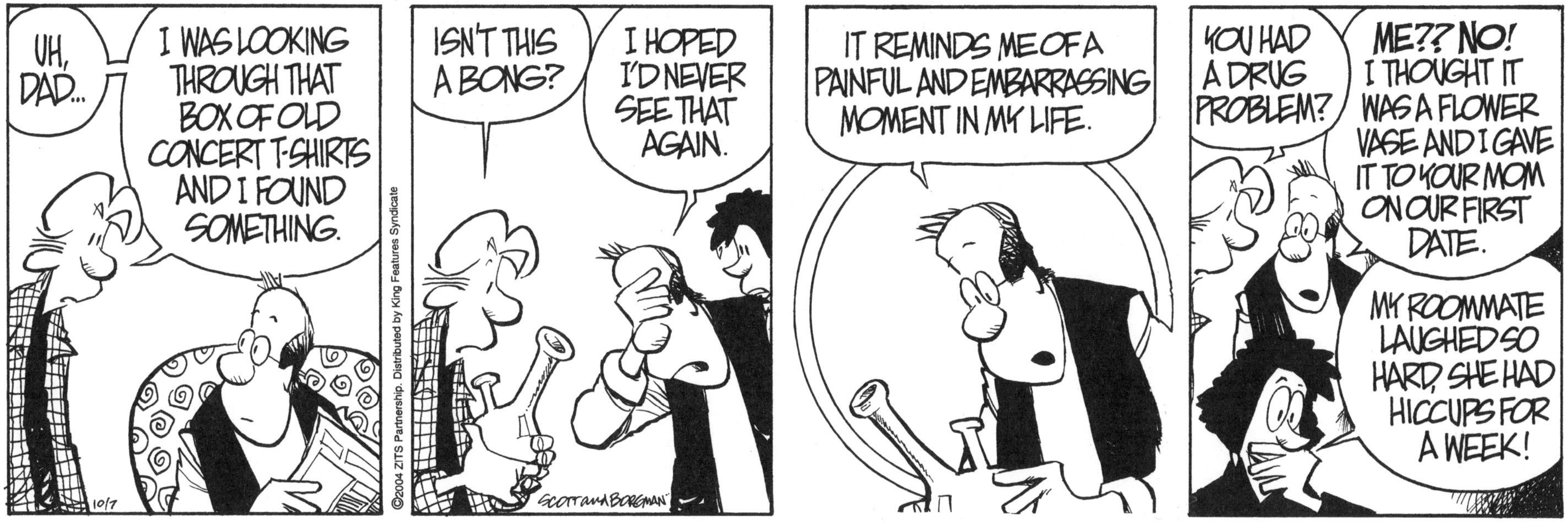
UH, DAD...
I WAS LOOKING THROUGH THAT BOX OF OLD CONCERT T-SHIRTS AND I FOUND SOMETHING.
10/7
©2004 ZITS Partnership. Distributed by King Features Syndicate
ISN'T THIS A BONG?
I HOPED I'D NEVER SEE THAT AGAIN.
SCOTT and BORGMAN
IT REMINDS ME OF A PAINFUL AND EMBARRASSING MOMENT IN MY LIFE.
YOU HAD A DRUG PROBLEM?
ME?? NO! I THOUGHT IT WAS A FLOWER VASE AND I GAVE IT TO YOUR MOM ON OUR FIRST DATE.
MY ROOMMATE LAUGHED SO HARD, SHE HAD HICCUPS FOR A WEEK!

Jerry: Members of the Blues Magoos contacted us after seeing their name in the strip on the opposite page. We've also heard from Moby Grape. No word yet from the Electric Prunes.

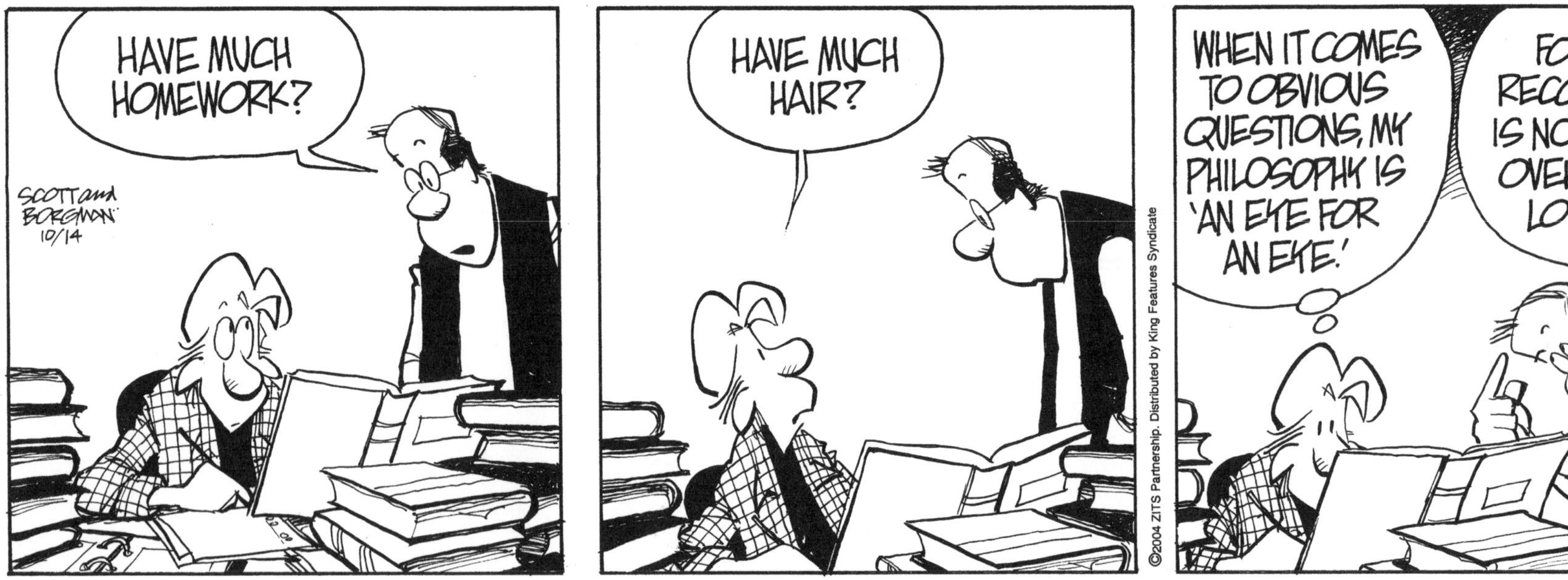
HAVE MUCH HOMEWORK?
SCOTT and BORGMAN 10/14
HAVE MUCH HAIR?
©2004 ZITS Partnership. Distributed by King Features Syndicate
WHEN IT COMES TO OBVIOUS QUESTIONS, MY PHILOSOPHY IS 'AN EYE FOR AN EYE.'
FOR THE RECORD, THIS IS NOT A COMB-OVER, IT'S A LOW PART!

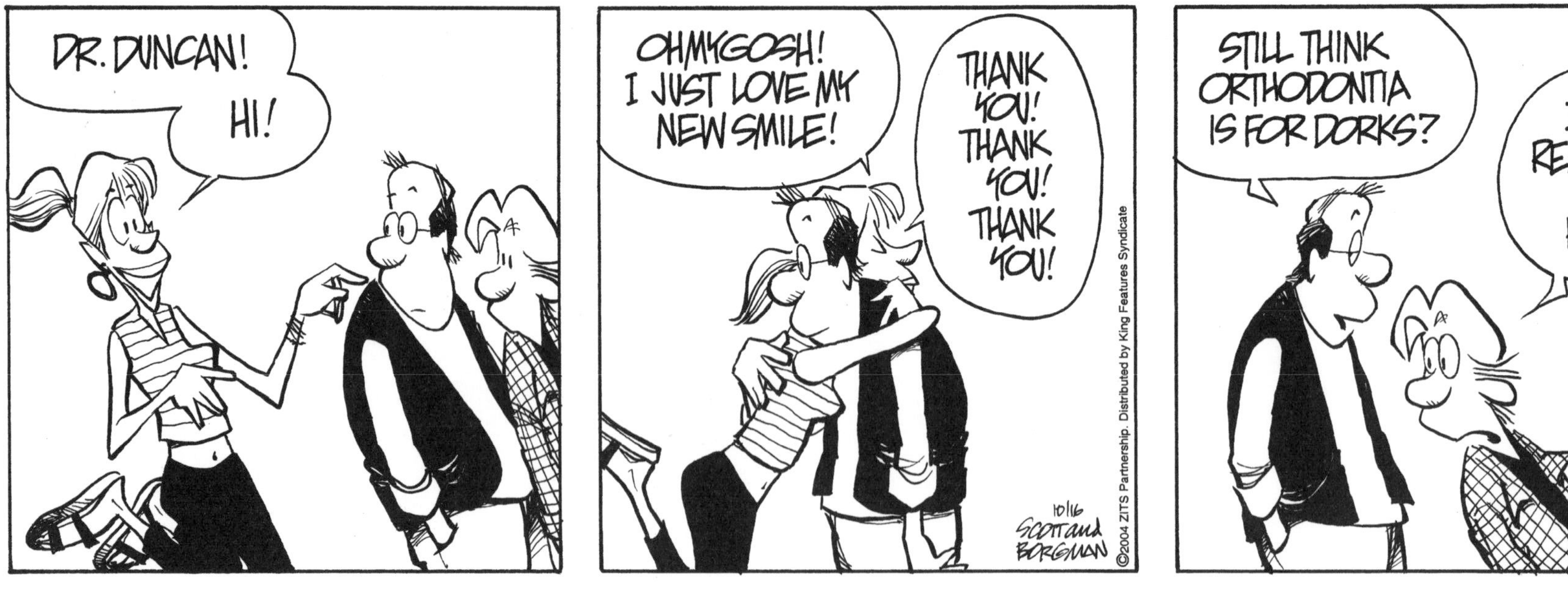
DR. DUNCAN!
HI!
OHMYGOSH! I JUST LOVE MY NEW SMILE!
THANK YOU! THANK YOU! THANK YOU!
10/16 SCOTT and BORGMAN
©2004 ZITS Partnership. Distributed by King Features Syndicate
STILL THINK ORTHODONTIA IS FOR DORKS?
I MAY BE REASSESSING MY POSITION.

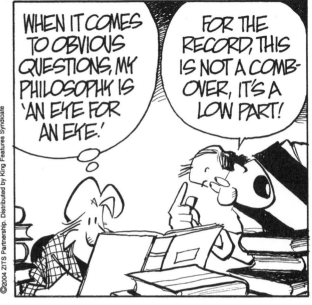

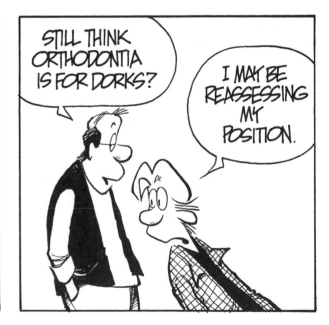

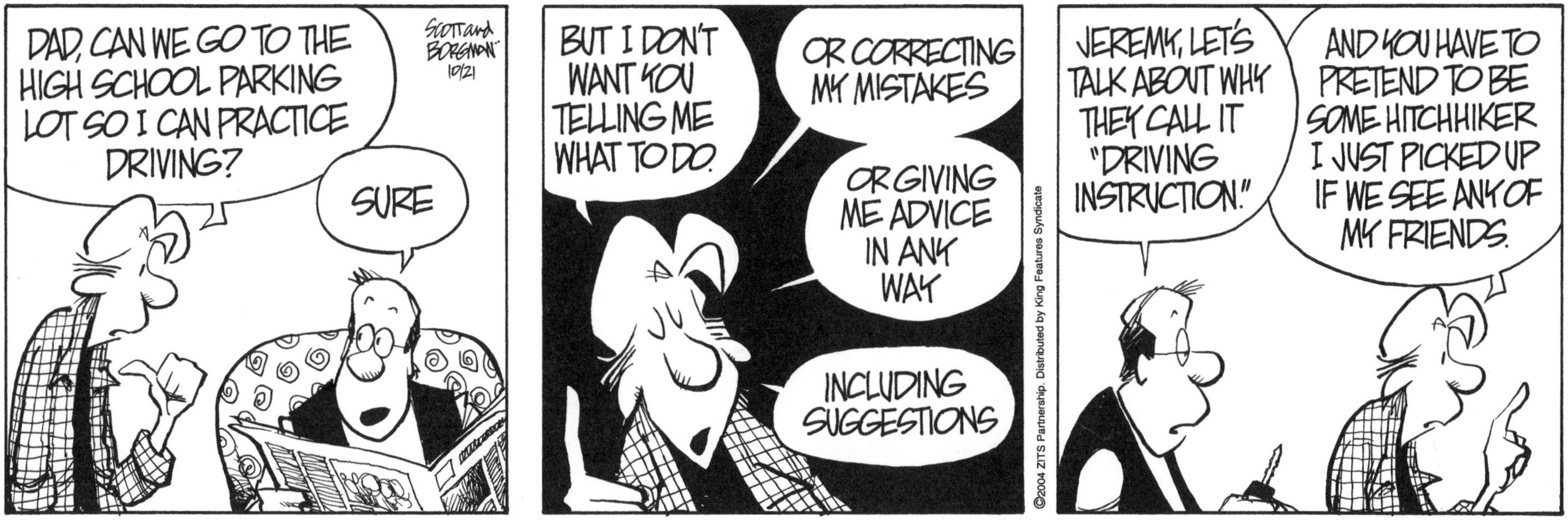
DAD, CAN WE GO TO THE HIGH SCHOOL PARKING LOT SO I CAN PRACTICE DRIVING?
SCOTT and BORGMAN 10/21
SURE
BUT I DON'T WANT YOU TELLING ME WHAT TO DO.
OR CORRECTING MY MISTAKES
OR GIVING ME ADVICE IN ANY WAY
INCLUDING SUGGESTIONS
©2004 ZITS Partnership. Distributed by King Features Syndicate
JEREMY, LET'S TALK ABOUT WHY THEY CALL IT "DRIVING INSTRUCTION."
AND YOU HAVE TO PRETEND TO BE SOME HITCHHIKER I JUST PICKED UP IF WE SEE ANY OF MY FRIENDS.

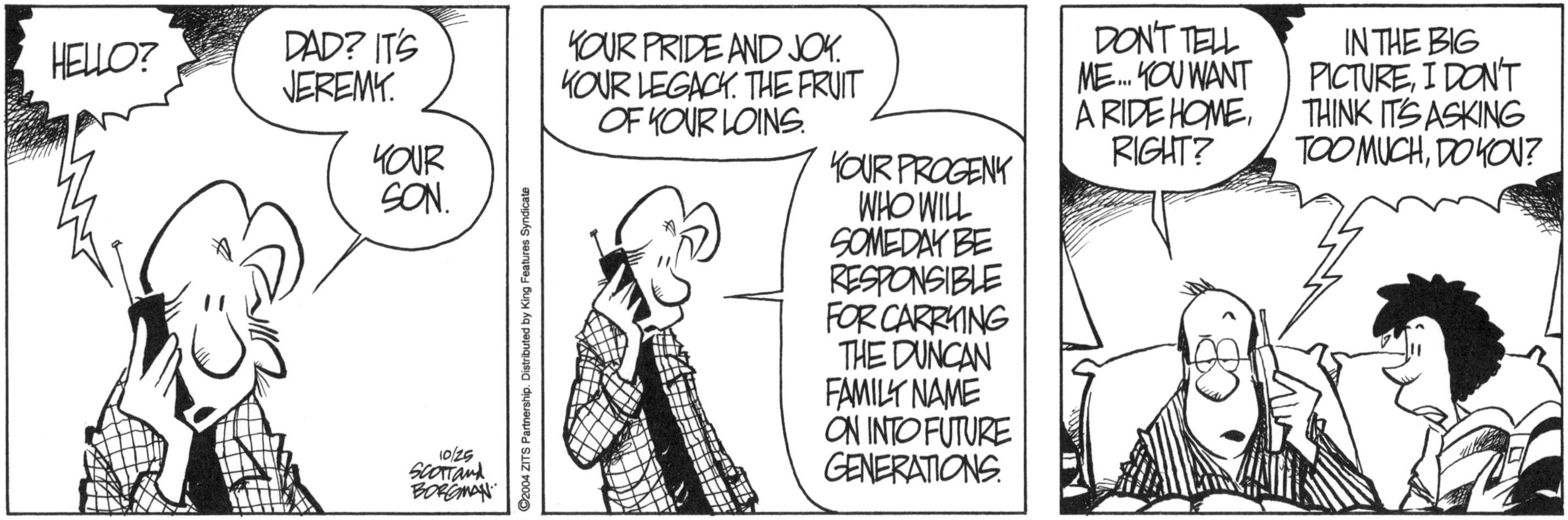
HELLO?
DAD? IT'S JEREMY.
YOUR SON.
10/25 SCOTT and BORGMAN
©2004 ZITS Partnership. Distributed by King Features Syndicate
YOUR PRIDE AND JOY. YOUR LEGACY. THE FRUIT OF YOUR LOINS.
YOUR PROGENY WHO WILL SOMEDAY BE RESPONSIBLE FOR CARRYING THE DUNCAN FAMILY NAME ON INTO FUTURE GENERATIONS.
DON'T TELL ME... YOU WANT A RIDE HOME, RIGHT?
IN THE BIG PICTURE, I DON'T THINK IT'S ASKING TOO MUCH, DO YOU?

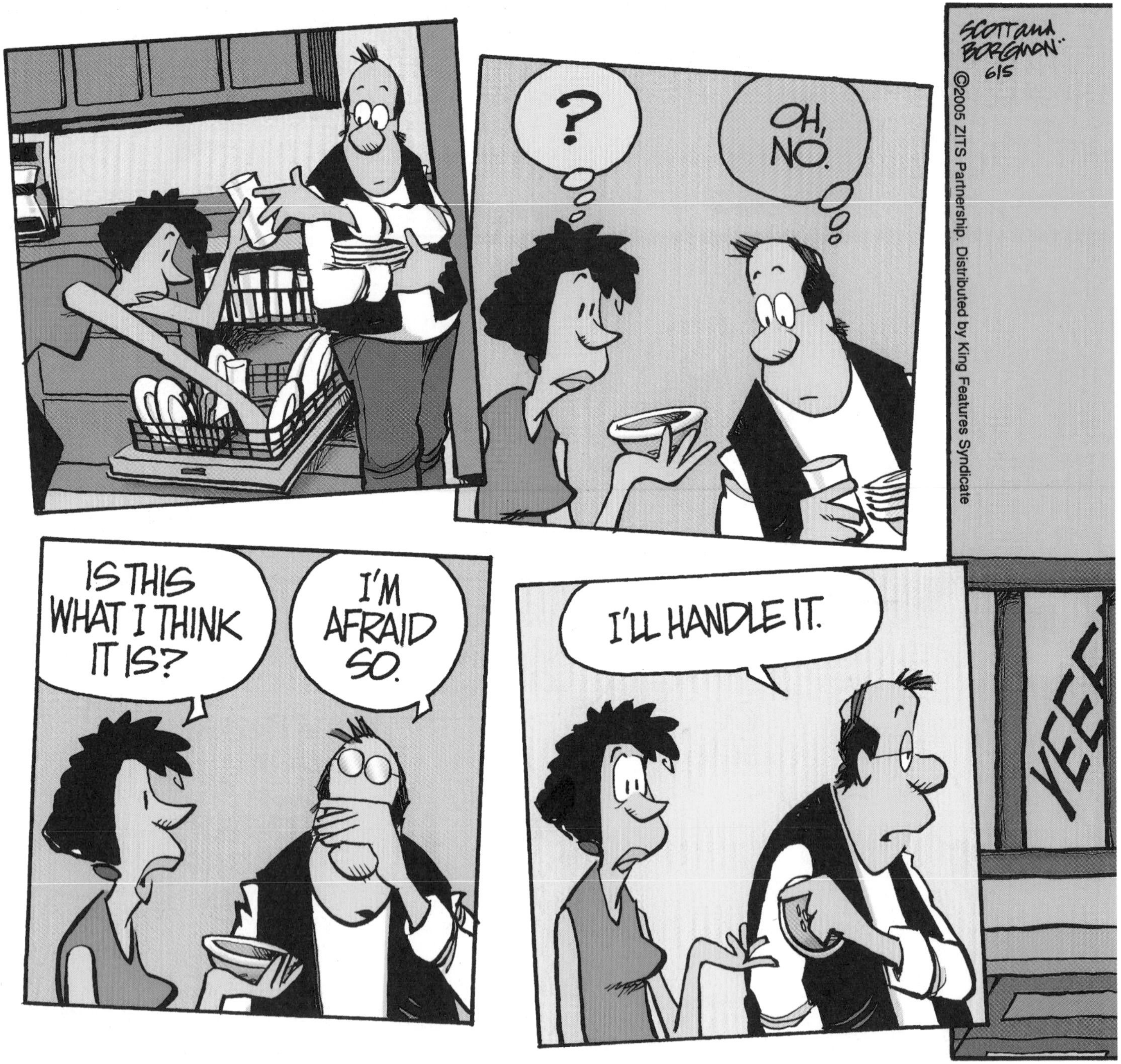
?
OH, NO.
IS THIS WHAT I THINK IT IS?
I'M AFRAID SO.
I'LL HANDLE IT.
©2005 ZITS Partnership. Distributed by King Features Syndicate
YEEE

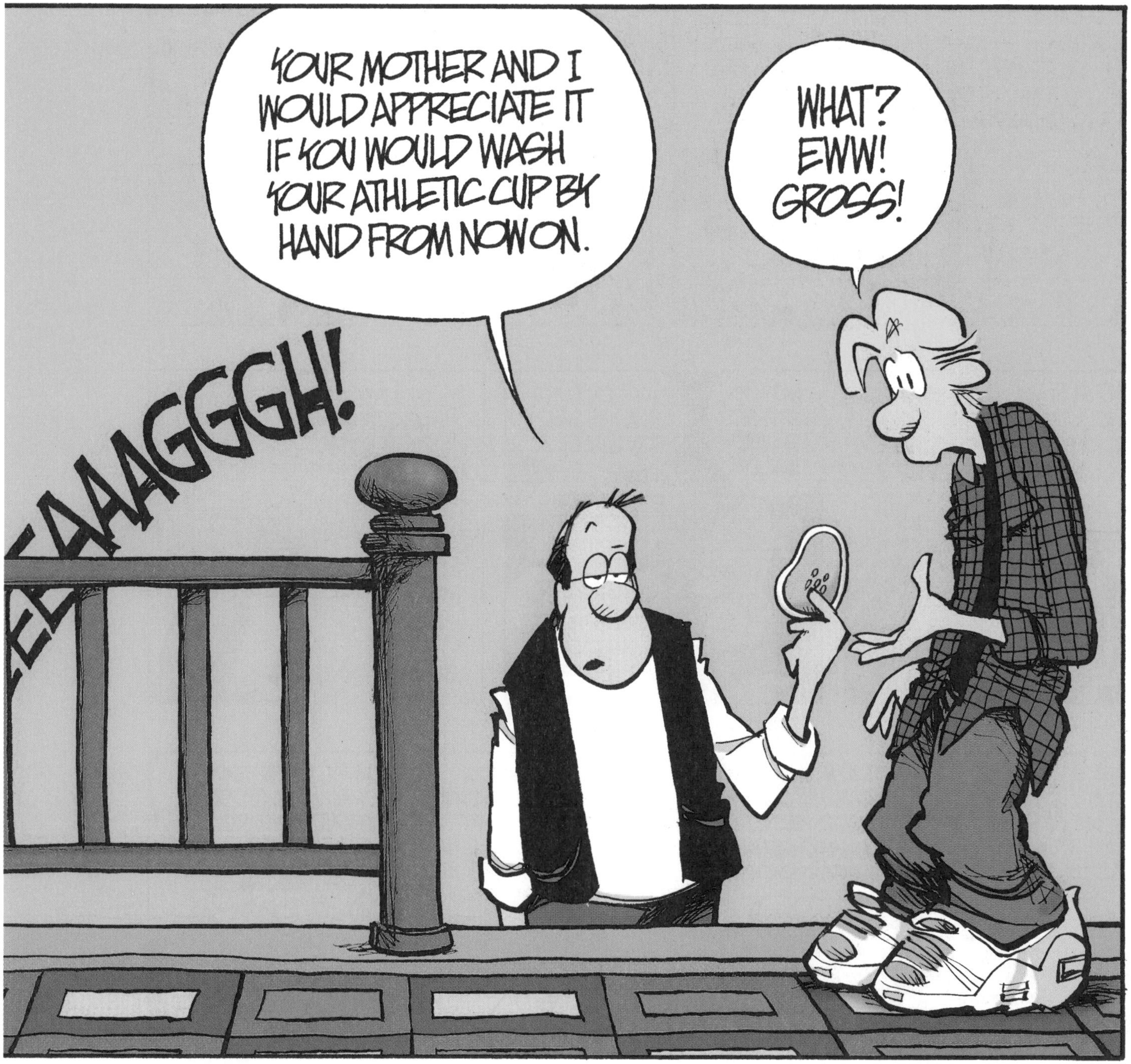
YOUR MOTHER AND I WOULD APPRECIATE IT IF YOU WOULD WASH YOUR ATHLETIC CUP BY HAND FROM NOW ON.
WHAT? EWW! GROSS!
EEAAAGGGH!

Jim: We're sometimes asked if the ideas in *Zits* strips come from life in our homes. This one, alas, is direct from my kitchen almost word for word. No one drank from our glasses for a month following that incident.

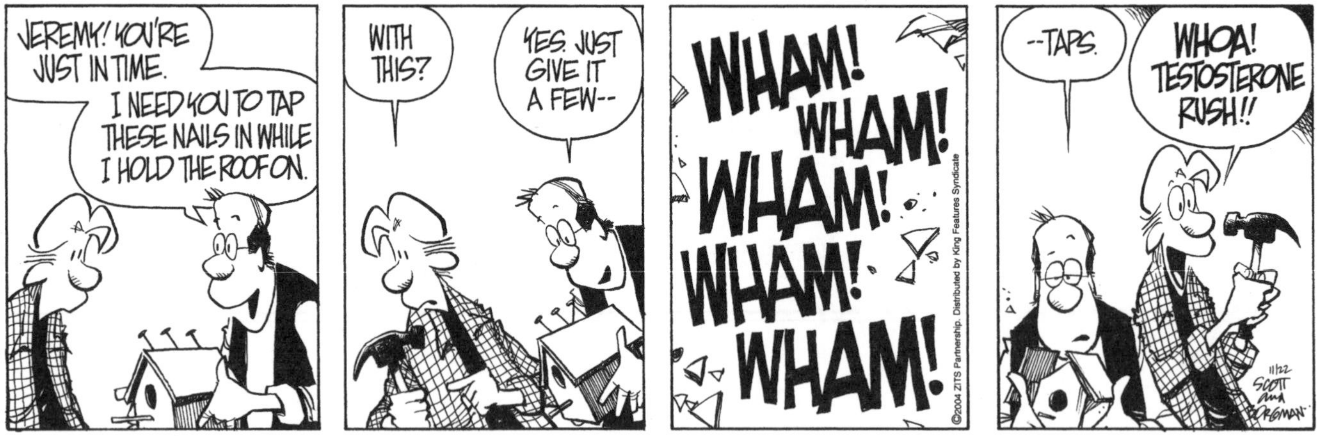
JEREMY! YOU'RE JUST IN TIME.
I NEED YOU TO TAP THESE NAILS IN WHILE I HOLD THE ROOF ON.
WITH THIS?
YES. JUST GIVE IT A FEW--
WHAM! WHAM! WHAM! WHAM! WHAM!
--TAPS.
WHOA! TESTOSTERONE RUSH!!
©2004 ZITS Partnership. Distributed by King Features Syndicate
11/22 SCOTT AND BORGMAN

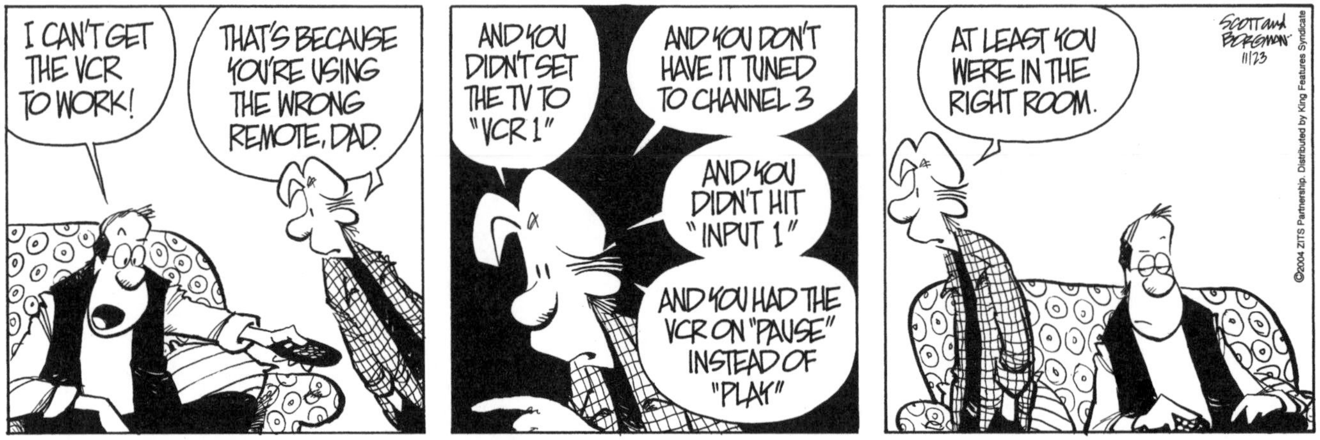
I CAN'T GET THE VCR TO WORK!
THAT'S BECAUSE YOU'RE USING THE WRONG REMOTE, DAD.
AND YOU DIDN'T SET THE TV TO "VCR 1"
AND YOU DON'T HAVE IT TUNED TO CHANNEL 3
AND YOU DIDN'T HIT "INPUT 1"
AND YOU HAD THE VCR ON "PAUSE" INSTEAD OF "PLAY"
AT LEAST YOU WERE IN THE RIGHT ROOM.
SCOTT AND BORGMAN 11/23
©2004 ZITS Partnership. Distributed by King Features Syndicate

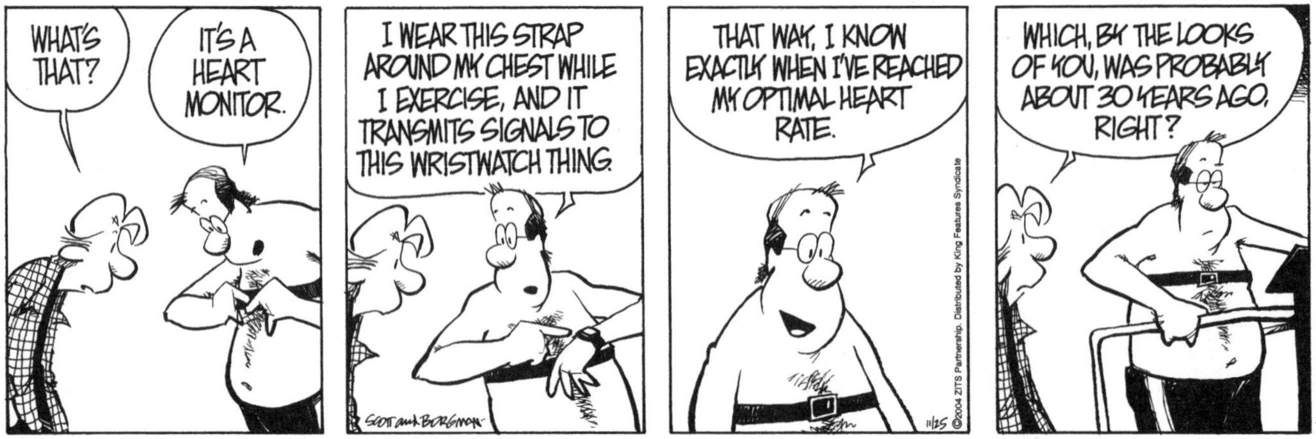
WHAT'S THAT?
IT'S A HEART MONITOR.
I WEAR THIS STRAP AROUND MY CHEST WHILE I EXERCISE, AND IT TRANSMITS SIGNALS TO THIS WRISTWATCH THING.
SCOTT AND BORGMAN
THAT WAY, I KNOW EXACTLY WHEN I'VE REACHED MY OPTIMAL HEART RATE.
©2004 ZITS Partnership. Distributed by King Features Syndicate
11/25
WHICH, BY THE LOOKS OF YOU, WAS PROBABLY ABOUT 30 YEARS AGO, RIGHT?

Jim: So many remotes, so little time. Dad the Technoklutz never seems to get old for readers, as long as we all continue to bumble toward the future with him.

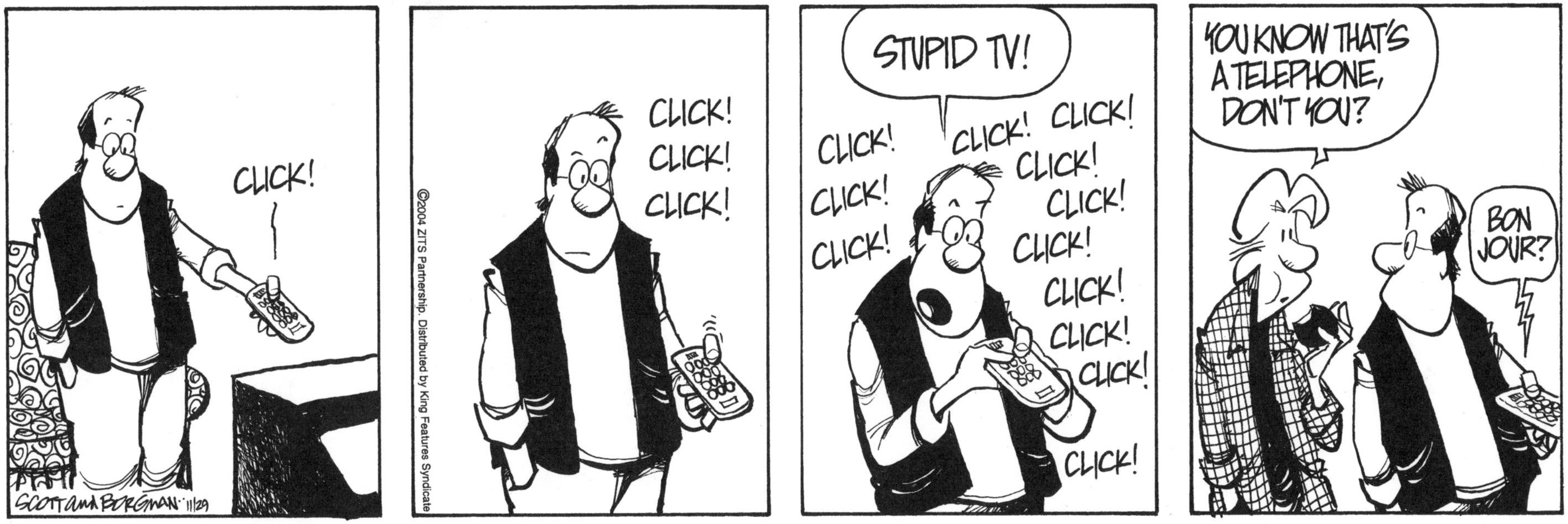
CLICK!
SCOTT and BORGMAN 11/29
CLICK! CLICK! CLICK!
©2004 ZITS Partnership. Distributed by King Features Syndicate
STUPID TV!
CLICK! CLICK! CLICK! CLICK! CLICK! CLICK! CLICK! CLICK! CLICK! CLICK! CLICK! CLICK! CLICK!
YOU KNOW THAT'S A TELEPHONE, DON'T YOU?
BON JOUR?

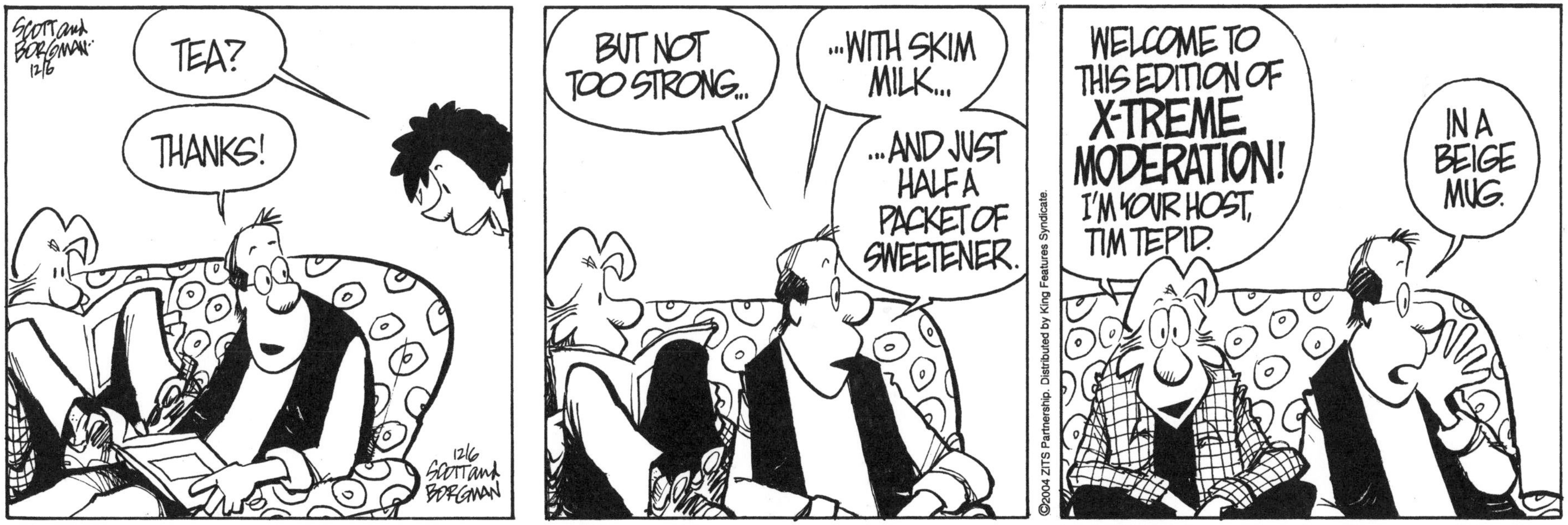
SCOTT and BORGMAN 12/6
TEA?
THANKS!
12/6 SCOTT and BORGMAN
BUT NOT TOO STRONG...
...WITH SKIM MILK...
...AND JUST HALF A PACKET OF SWEETENER.
©2004 ZITS Partnership. Distributed by King Features Syndicate.
WELCOME TO THIS EDITION OF X-TREME MODERATION! I'M YOUR HOST, TIM TEPID.
IN A BEIGE MUG.

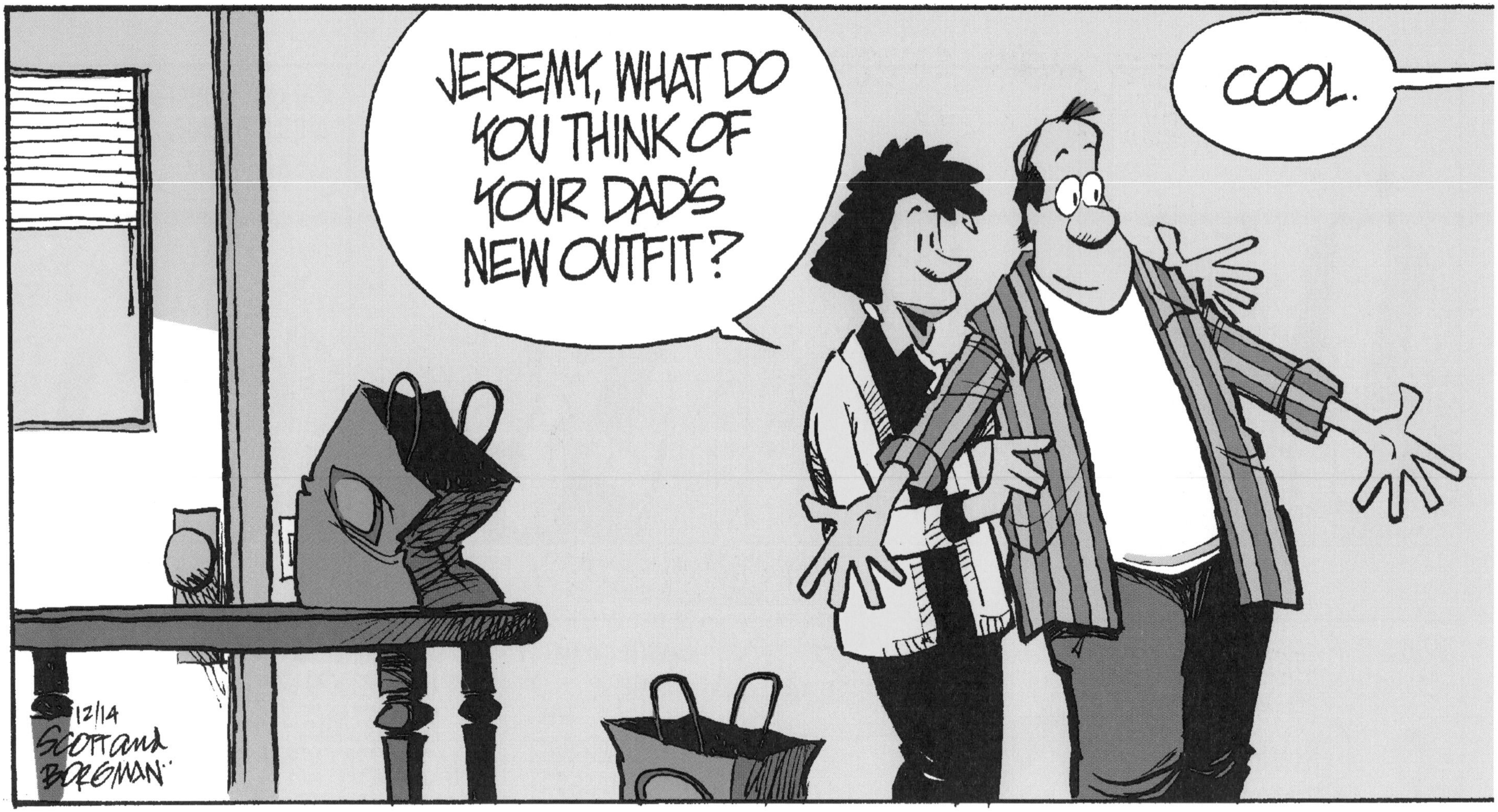
JEREMY, WHAT DO YOU THINK OF YOUR DAD'S NEW OUTFIT?
COOL.
12/14
SCOTT and BORGMAN

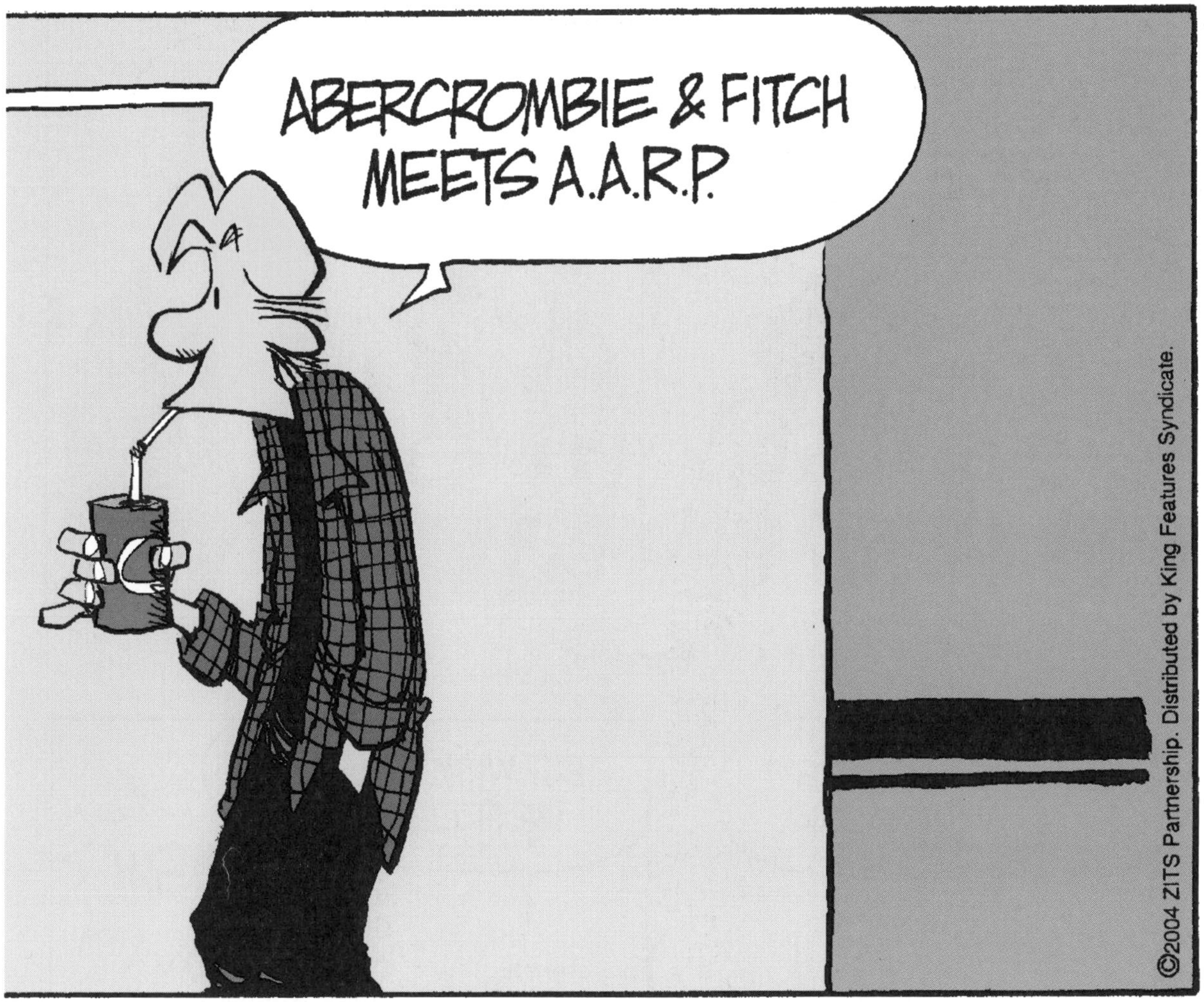
ABERCROMBIE & FITCH MEETS A.A.R.P.
©2004 ZITS Partnership. Distributed by King Features Syndicate.

Jim: Forget it. No one over twenty-one looks cool in A&F, and the sooner you learn that, the happier everyone will be.

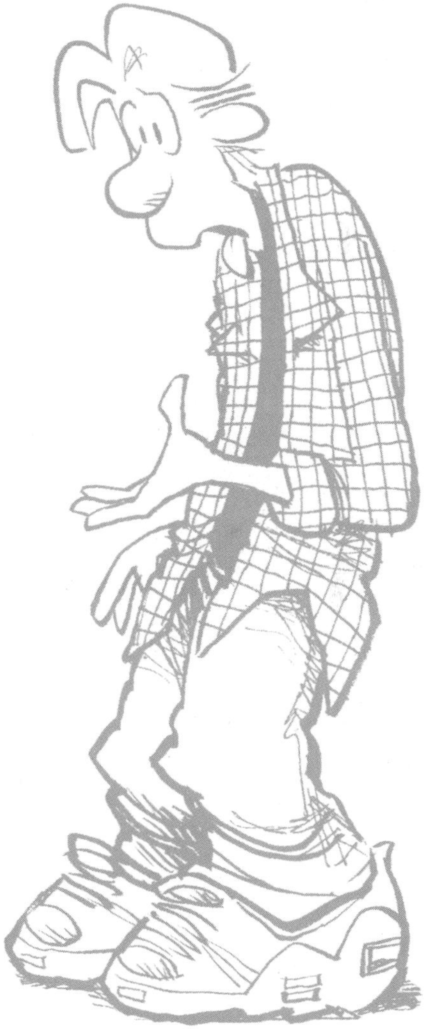

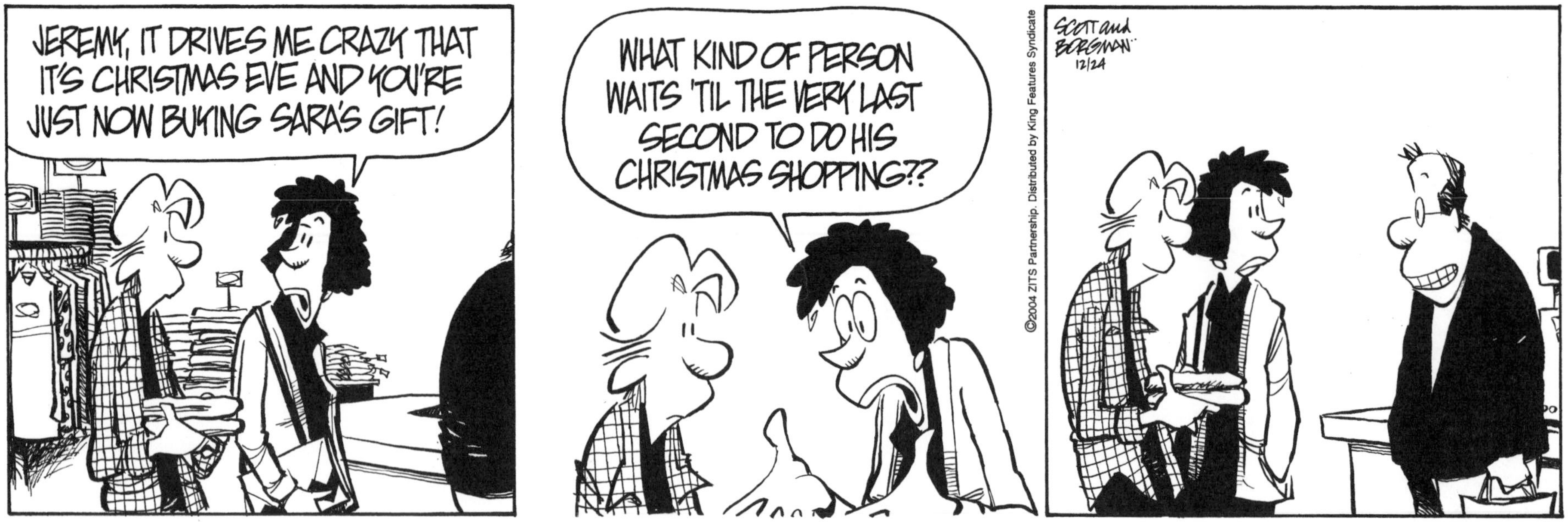
JEREMY, IT DRIVES ME CRAZY THAT IT'S CHRISTMAS EVE AND YOU'RE JUST NOW BUYING SARA'S GIFT!
WHAT KIND OF PERSON WAITS 'TIL THE VERY LAST SECOND TO DO HIS CHRISTMAS SHOPPING??
©2004 ZITS Partnership. Distributed by King Features Syndicate
SCOTT and BORGMAN 12/24

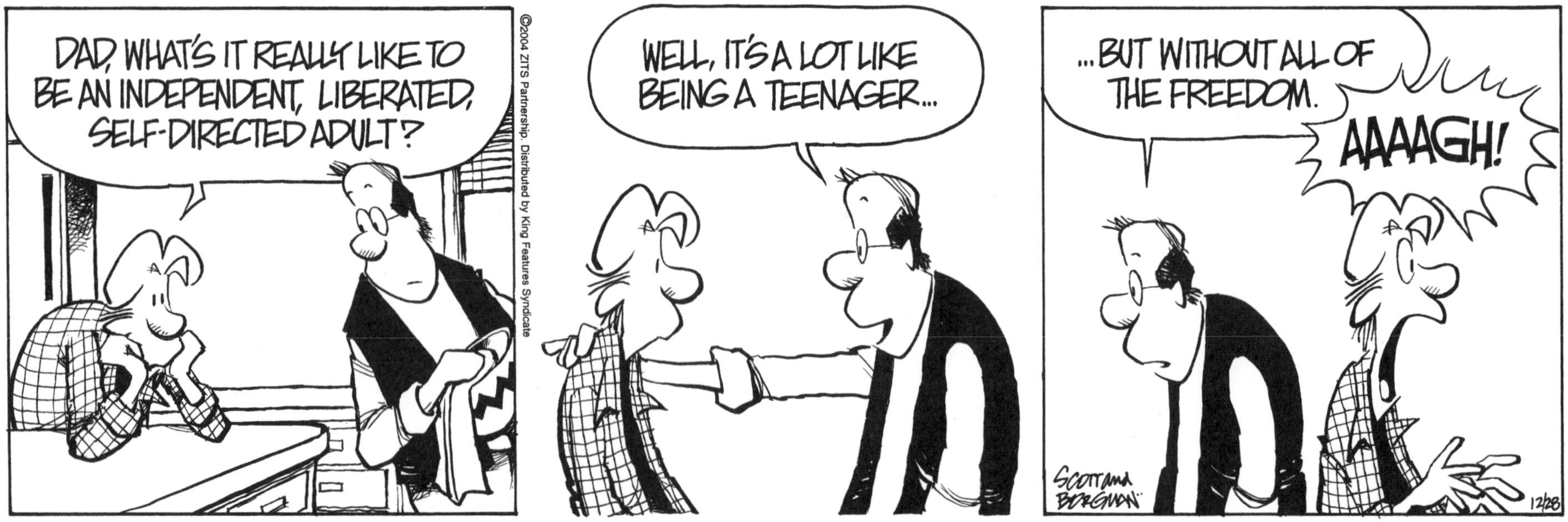
DAD, WHAT'S IT REALLY LIKE TO BE AN INDEPENDENT, LIBERATED, SELF-DIRECTED ADULT?
©2004 ZITS Partnership. Distributed by King Features Syndicate
WELL, IT'S A LOT LIKE BEING A TEENAGER...
...BUT WITHOUT ALL OF THE FREEDOM.
AAAAGH!
SCOTT and BORGMAN 12/28

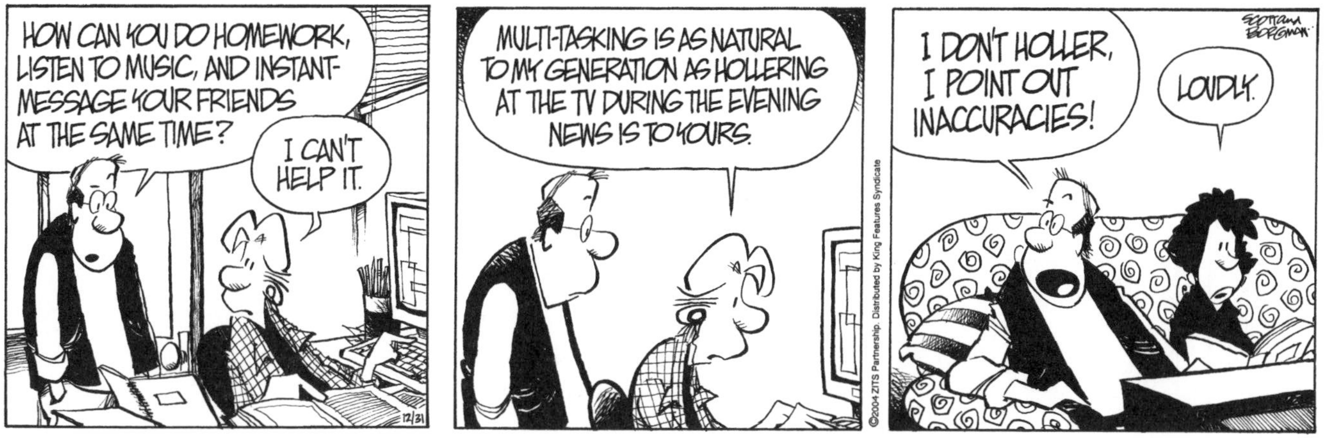
HOW CAN YOU DO HOMEWORK, LISTEN TO MUSIC, AND INSTANT-MESSAGE YOUR FRIENDS AT THE SAME TIME?
I CAN'T HELP IT.
12/31
MULTI-TASKING IS AS NATURAL TO MY GENERATION AS HOLLERING AT THE TV DURING THE EVENING NEWS IS TO YOURS.
©2004 ZITS Partnership. Distributed by King Features Syndicate
SCOTT and BORGMAN
I DON'T HOLLER, I POINT OUT INACCURACIES!
LOUDLY.

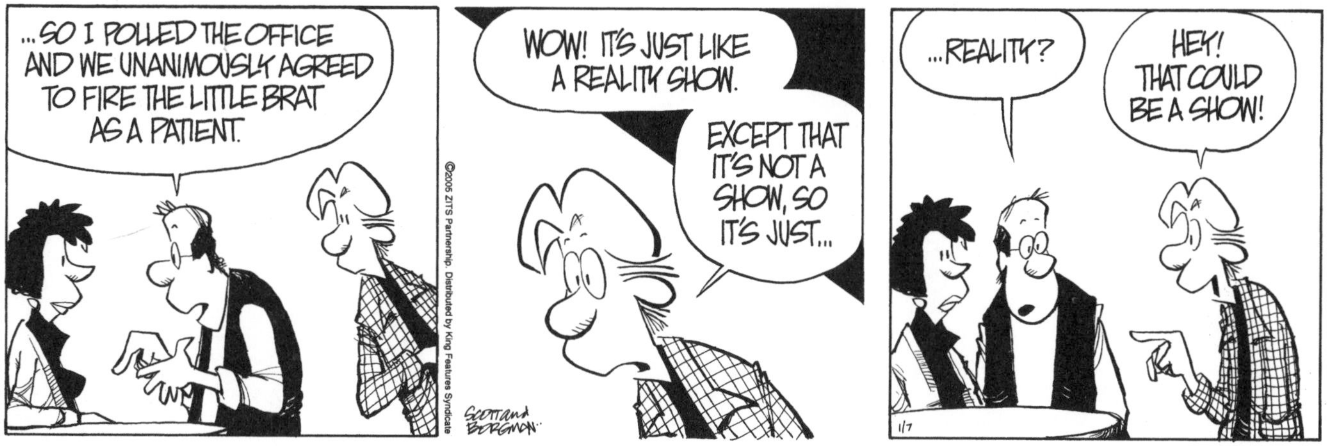
...SO I POLLED THE OFFICE AND WE UNANIMOUSLY AGREED TO FIRE THE LITTLE BRAT AS A PATIENT.
©2006 ZITS Partnership. Distributed by King Features Syndicate
SCOTT and BORGMAN
WOW! IT'S JUST LIKE A REALITY SHOW.
EXCEPT THAT IT'S NOT A SHOW, SO IT'S JUST...
...REALITY?
HEY! THAT COULD BE A SHOW!
1/7

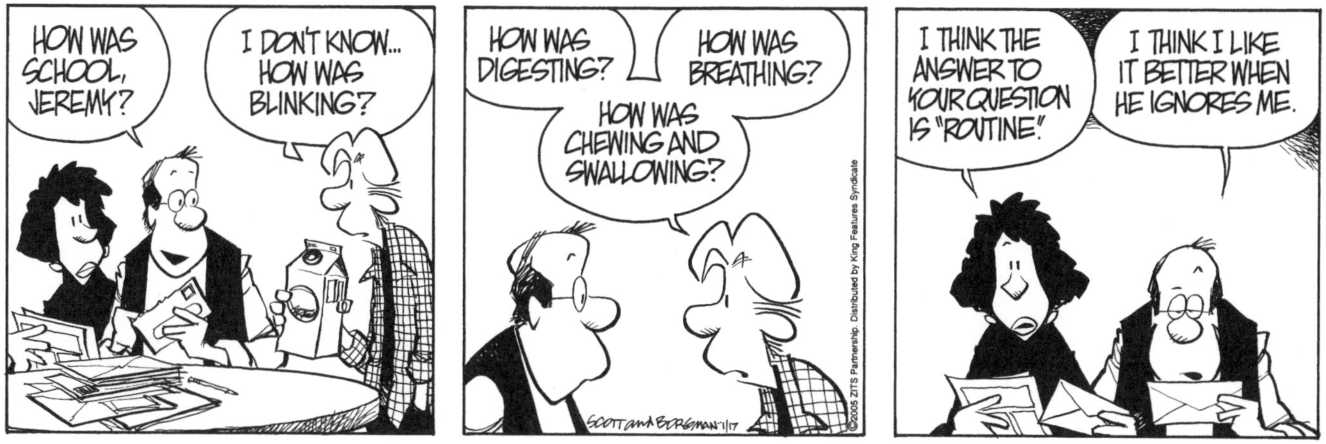
HOW WAS SCHOOL, JEREMY?
I DON'T KNOW... HOW WAS BLINKING?
HOW WAS DIGESTING?
HOW WAS BREATHING?
HOW WAS CHEWING AND SWALLOWING?
SCOTT and BORGMAN 1/17
©2005 ZITS Partnership. Distributed by King Features Syndicate
I THINK THE ANSWER TO YOUR QUESTION IS "ROUTINE."
I THINK I LIKE IT BETTER WHEN HE IGNORES ME.

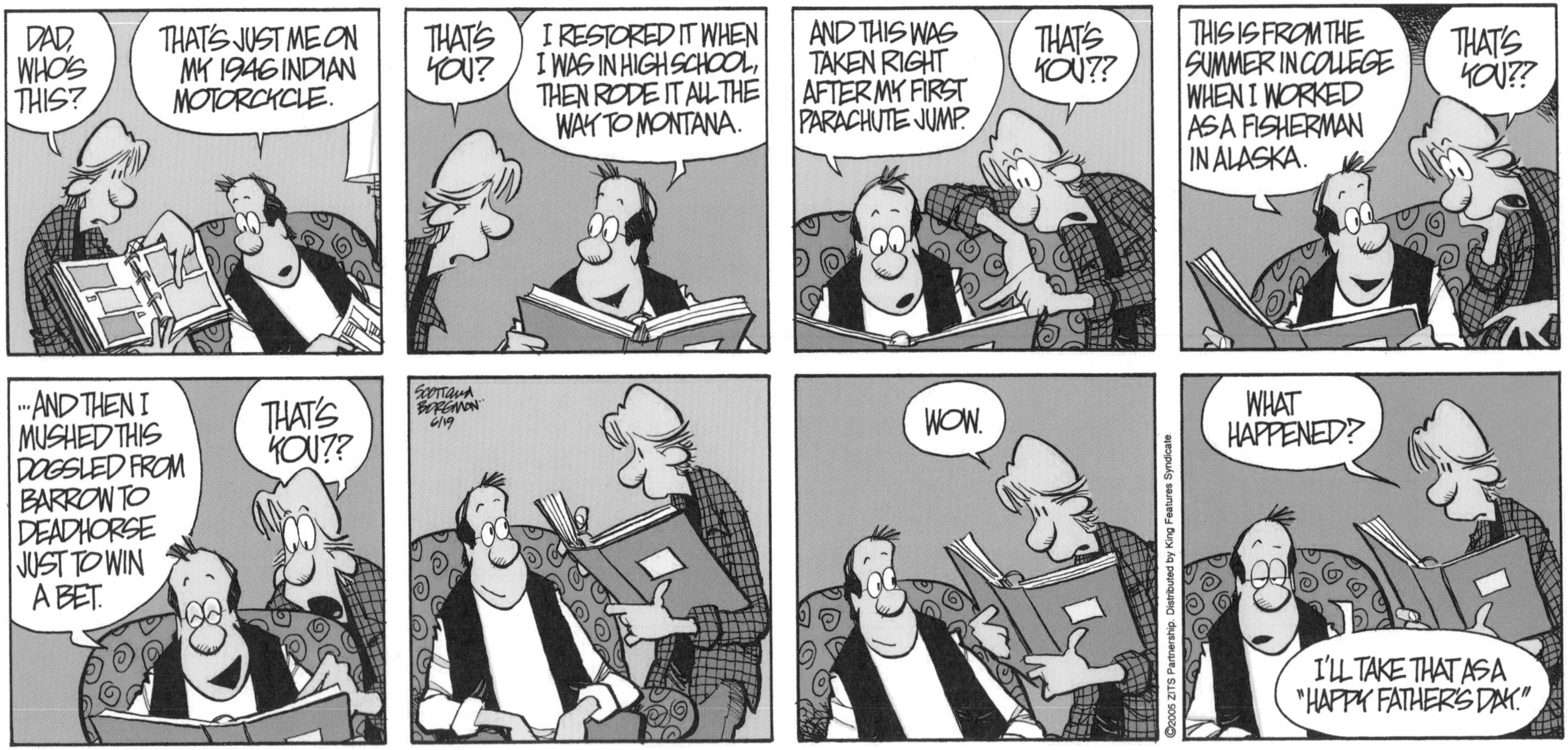
DAD, WHO'S THIS?
THAT'S JUST ME ON MY 1946 INDIAN MOTORCYCLE.
THAT'S YOU?
I RESTORED IT WHEN I WAS IN HIGH SCHOOL, THEN RODE IT ALL THE WAY TO MONTANA.
AND THIS WAS TAKEN RIGHT AFTER MY FIRST PARACHUTE JUMP.
THAT'S YOU??
THIS IS FROM THE SUMMER IN COLLEGE WHEN I WORKED AS A FISHERMAN IN ALASKA.
THAT'S YOU??
...AND THEN I MUSHED THIS DOGSLED FROM BARROW TO DEADHORSE JUST TO WIN A BET.
THAT'S YOU??
WOW.
©2005 ZITS Partnership. Distributed by King Features Syndicate.
WHAT HAPPENED?
I'LL TAKE THAT AS A "HAPPY FATHER'S DAY."

Jerry: Another strip torn directly from the pages of our lives. All true . . . except that my bike was a 1968 250cc Yamaha. And neither of us has ever parachuted. Or fished in Alaska. Shoot . . . maybe we saw the whole thing on TV.

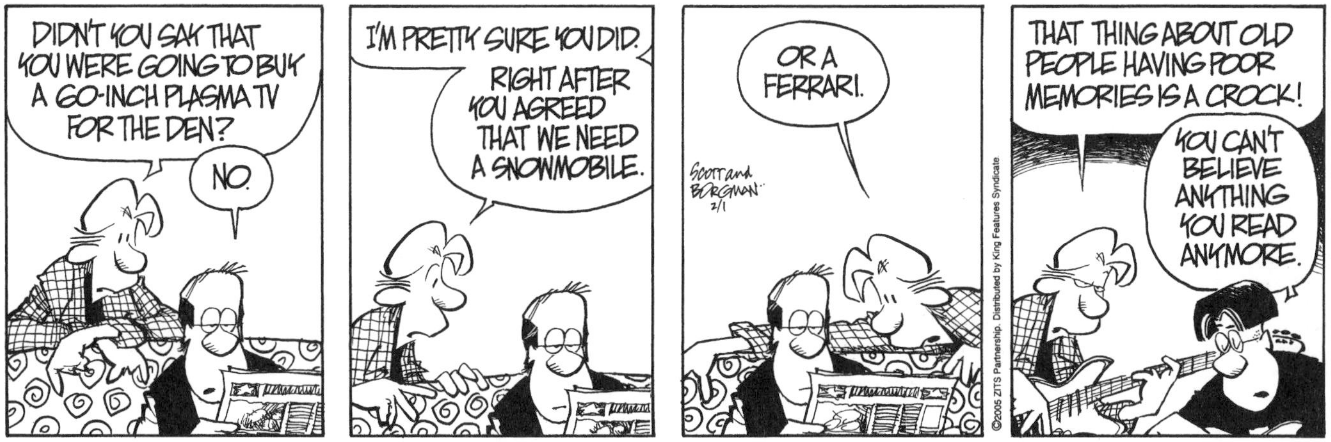
DIDN'T YOU SAY THAT YOU WERE GOING TO BUY A 60-INCH PLASMA TV FOR THE DEN?
NO.
I'M PRETTY SURE YOU DID.
RIGHT AFTER YOU AGREED THAT WE NEED A SNOWMOBILE.
SCOTT and BORGMAN 2/1
OR A FERRARI.
THAT THING ABOUT OLD PEOPLE HAVING POOR MEMORIES IS A CROCK!
YOU CAN'T BELIEVE ANYTHING YOU READ ANYMORE.
©2005 ZITS Partnership. Distributed by King Features Syndicate

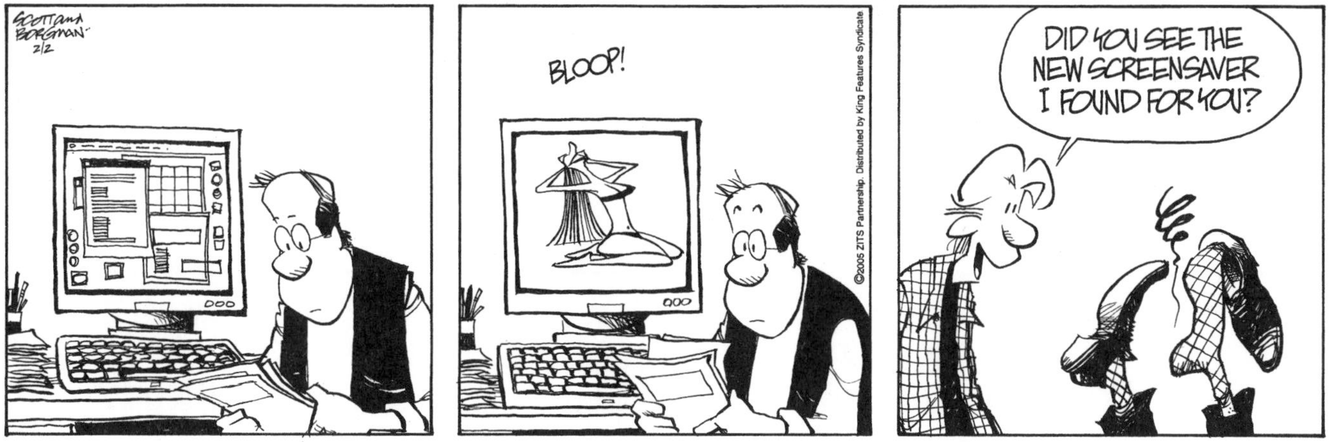
SCOTT and BORGMAN 2/2
BLOOP!
©2005 ZITS Partnership. Distributed by King Features Syndicate
DID YOU SEE THE NEW SCREENSAVER I FOUND FOR YOU?

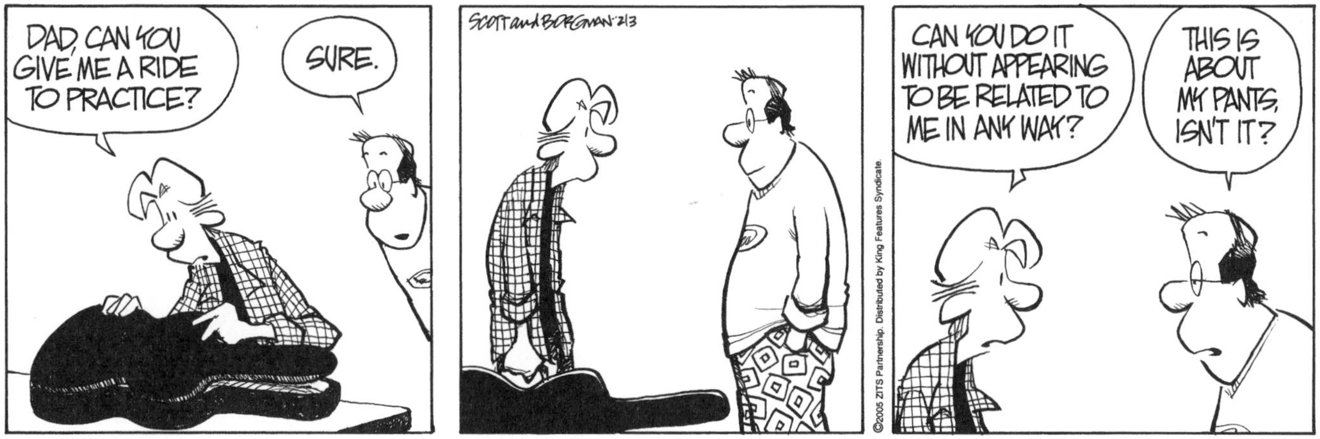
DAD, CAN YOU GIVE ME A RIDE TO PRACTICE?
SURE.
SCOTT and BORGMAN 2/3
©2005 ZITS Partnership. Distributed by King Features Syndicate.
CAN YOU DO IT WITHOUT APPEARING TO BE RELATED TO ME IN ANY WAY?
THIS IS ABOUT MY PANTS, ISN'T IT?

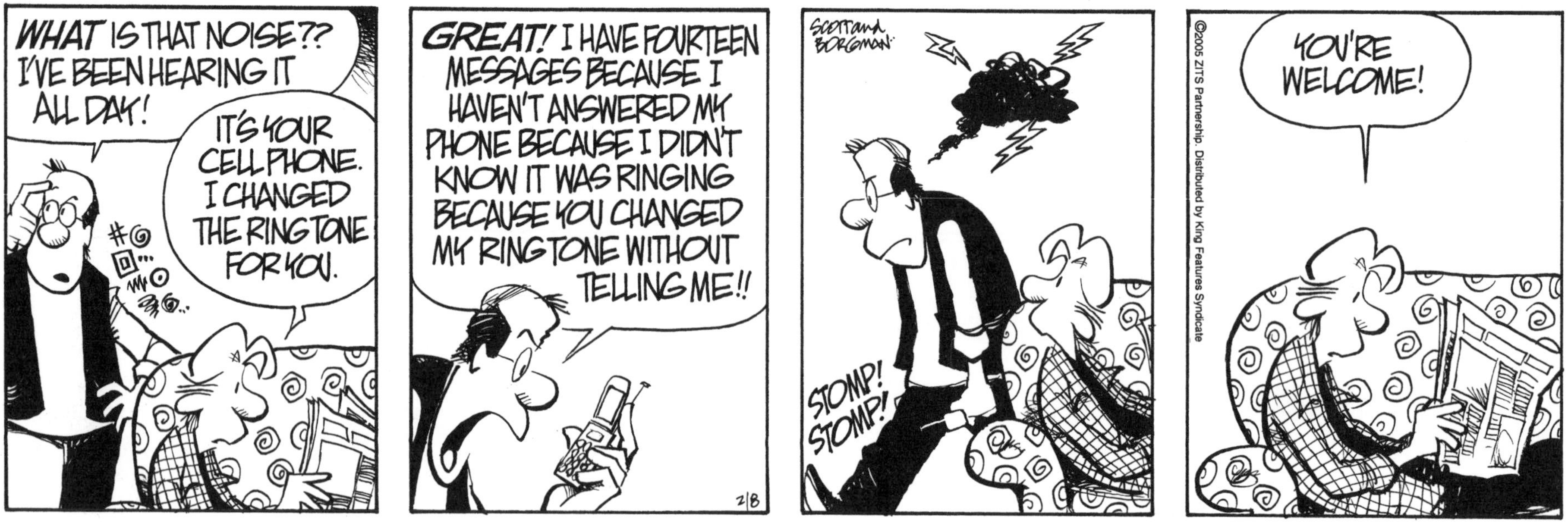
WHAT IS THAT NOISE?? I'VE BEEN HEARING IT ALL DAY!
IT'S YOUR CELL PHONE. I CHANGED THE RINGTONE FOR YOU.
GREAT! I HAVE FOURTEEN MESSAGES BECAUSE I HAVEN'T ANSWERED MY PHONE BECAUSE I DIDN'T KNOW IT WAS RINGING BECAUSE YOU CHANGED MY RINGTONE WITHOUT TELLING ME!!
2/8
SCOTT and BORGMAN
STOMP! STOMP!
©2005 ZITS Partnership. Distributed by King Features Syndicate
YOU'RE WELCOME!

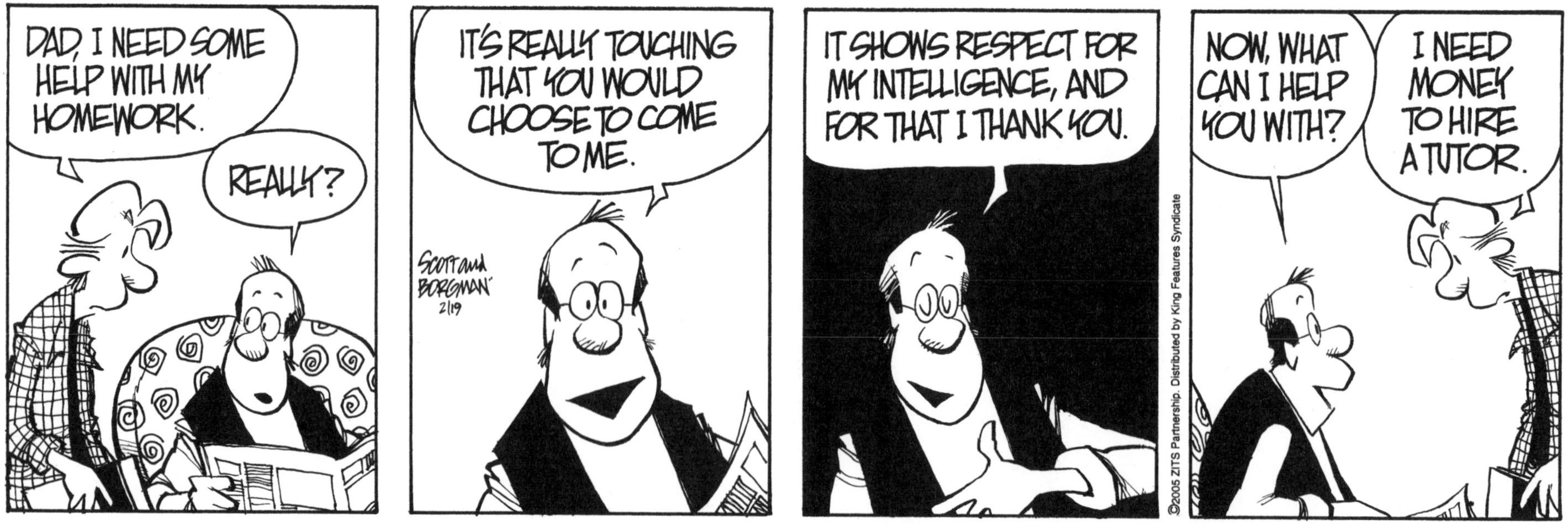
DAD, I NEED SOME HELP WITH MY HOMEWORK.
REALLY?
IT'S REALLY TOUCHING THAT YOU WOULD CHOOSE TO COME TO ME.
SCOTT and BORGMAN
2/19
IT SHOWS RESPECT FOR MY INTELLIGENCE, AND FOR THAT I THANK YOU.
©2005 ZITS Partnership. Distributed by King Features Syndicate
NOW, WHAT CAN I HELP YOU WITH?
I NEED MONEY TO HIRE A TUTOR.

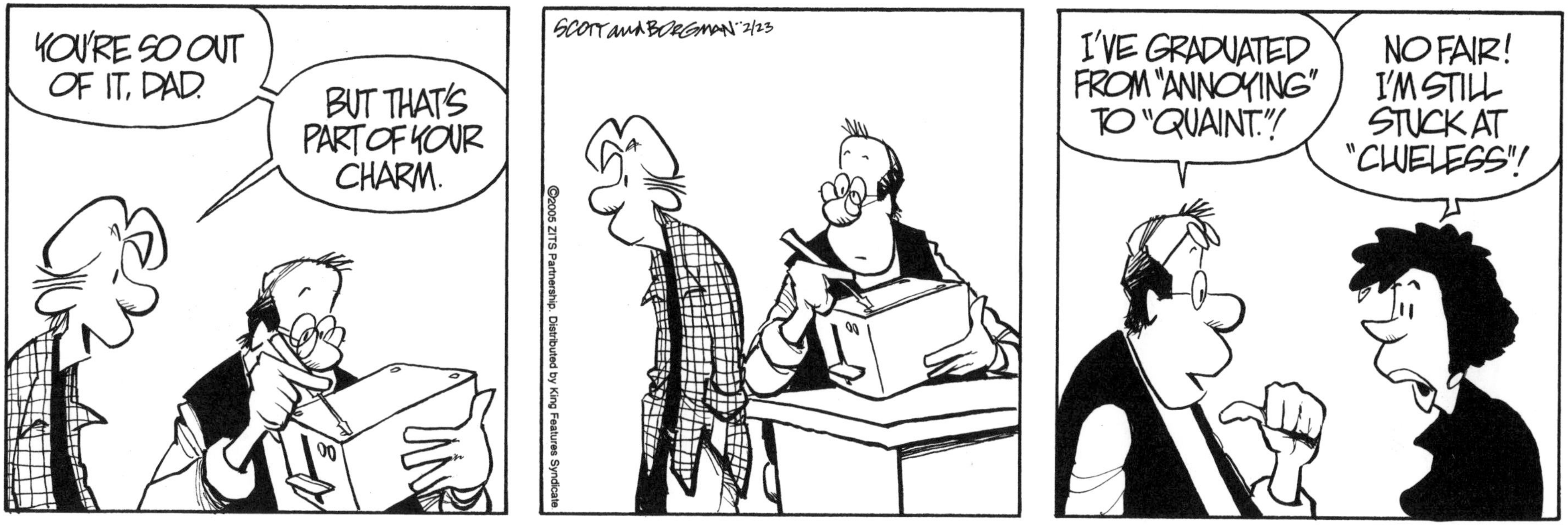
YOU'RE SO OUT OF IT, DAD.
BUT THAT'S PART OF YOUR CHARM.
SCOTT and BORGMAN 2/23
©2005 ZITS Partnership. Distributed by King Features Syndicate
I'VE GRADUATED FROM "ANNOYING" TO "QUAINT."!
NO FAIR! I'M STILL STUCK AT "CLUELESS"!

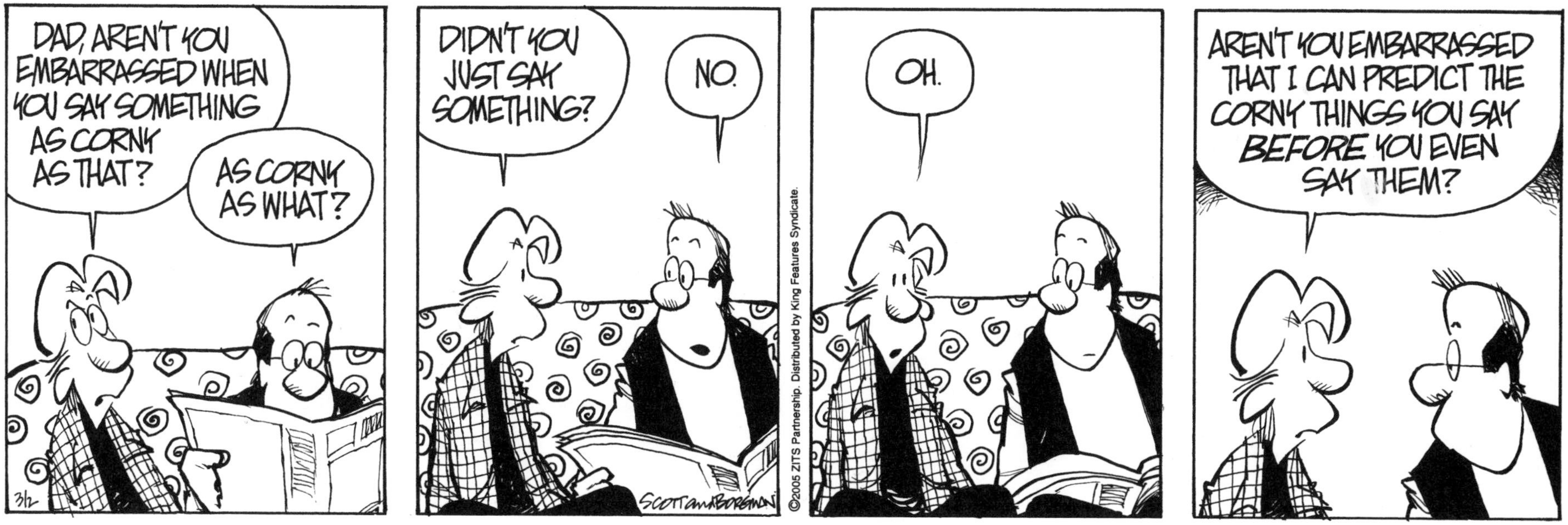
DAD, AREN'T YOU EMBARRASSED WHEN YOU SAY SOMETHING AS CORNY AS THAT?
AS CORNY AS WHAT?
3/2
DIDN'T YOU JUST SAY SOMETHING?
NO.
SCOTT and BORGMAN
©2005 ZITS Partnership. Distributed by King Features Syndicate.
OH.
AREN'T YOU EMBARRASSED THAT I CAN PREDICT THE CORNY THINGS YOU SAY *BEFORE* YOU EVEN SAY THEM?

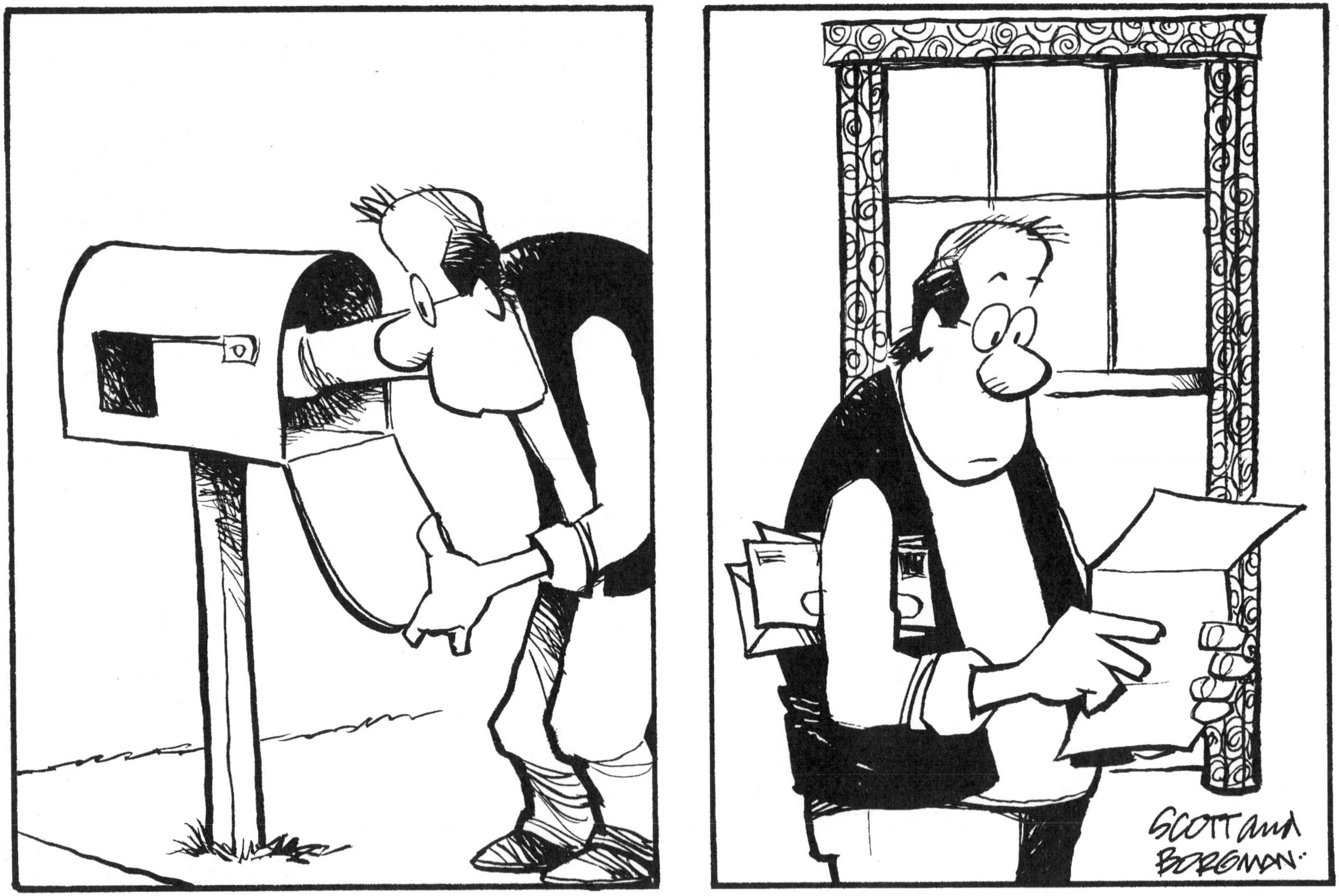
SCOTT and BORGMAN

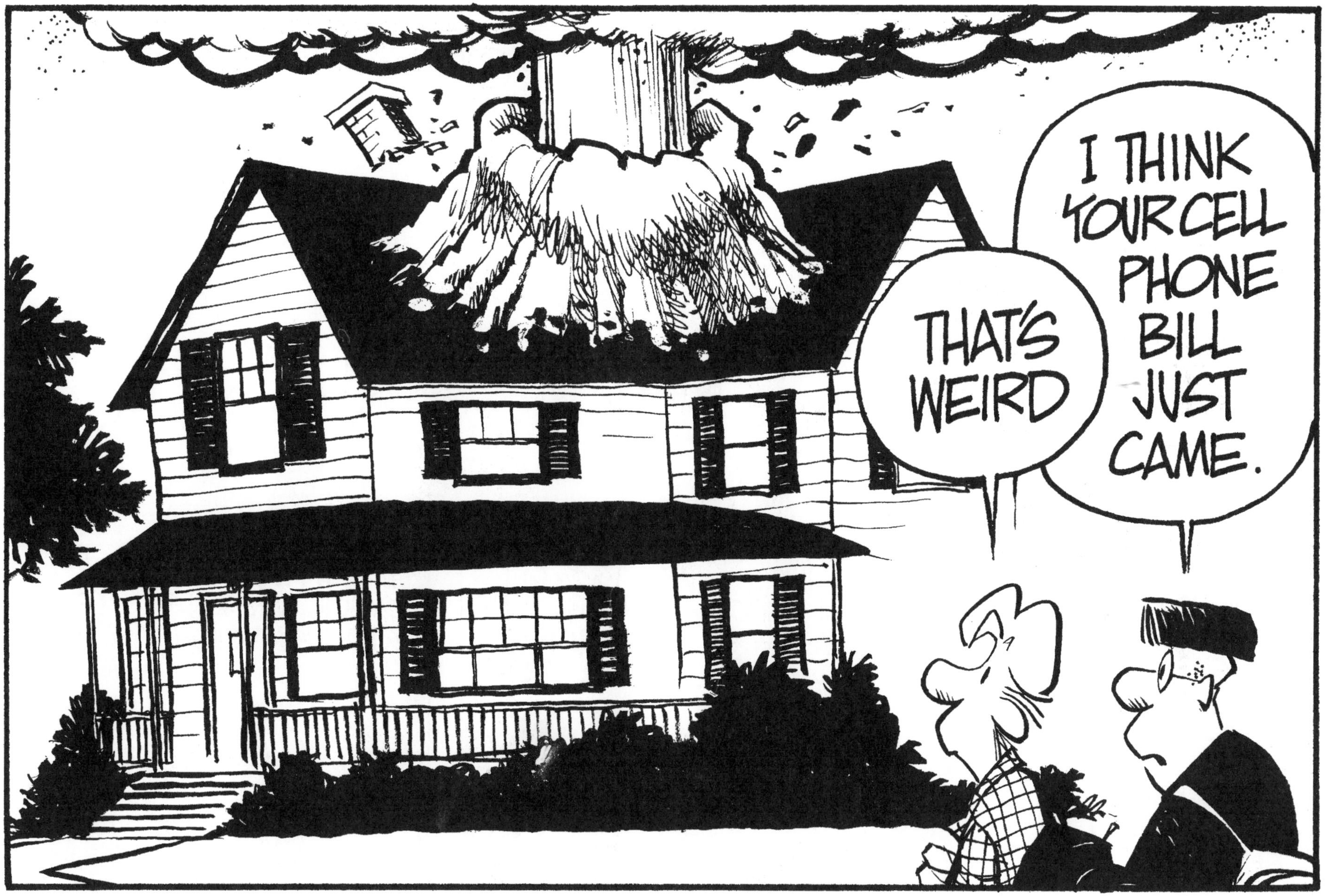
THAT'S WEIRD
I THINK YOUR CELL PHONE BILL JUST CAME.

Jerry: Before cell packages grew up, every family had a horror story to tell about enormous surprise bills for thousands of texts run up by crazed teens. The phone companies made texting free when everyone converted to Facebook.

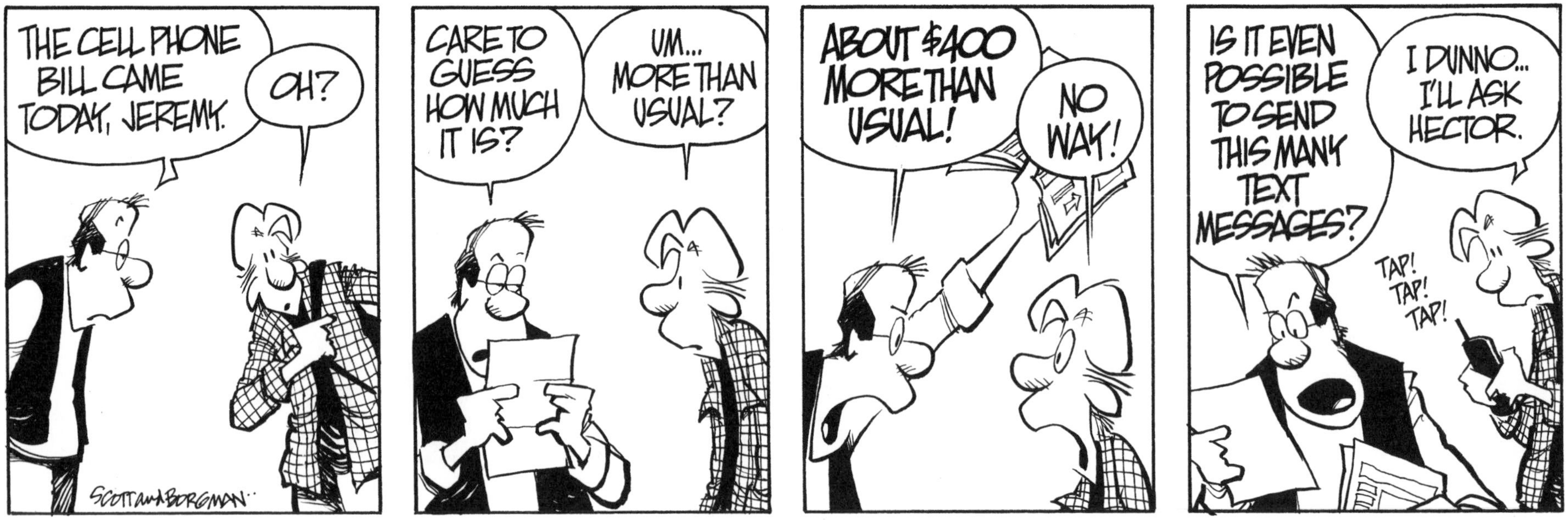
THE CELL PHONE BILL CAME TODAY, JEREMY.
OH?
CARE TO GUESS HOW MUCH IT IS?
UM... MORE THAN USUAL?
ABOUT $400 MORE THAN USUAL!
NO WAY!
IS IT EVEN POSSIBLE TO SEND THIS MANY TEXT MESSAGES?
I DUNNO... I'LL ASK HECTOR.
TAP! TAP! TAP!
SCOTT and BORGMAN

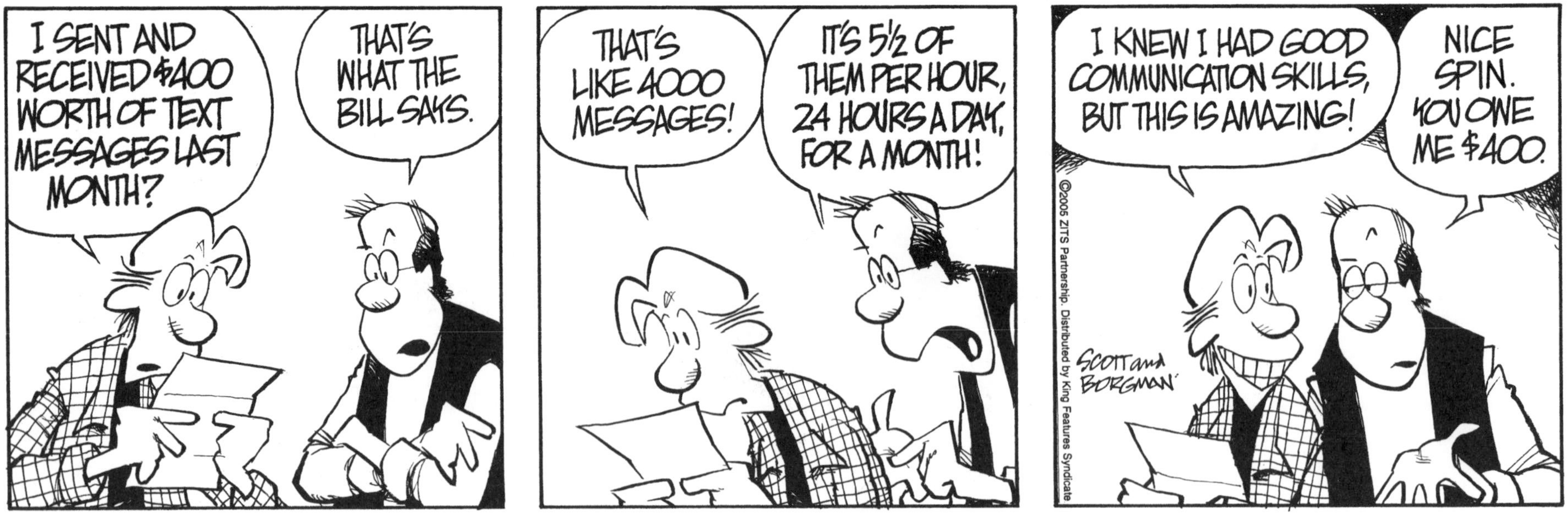
I SENT AND RECEIVED $400 WORTH OF TEXT MESSAGES LAST MONTH?
THAT'S WHAT THE BILL SAYS.
THAT'S LIKE 4000 MESSAGES!
IT'S 5½ OF THEM PER HOUR, 24 HOURS A DAY, FOR A MONTH!
I KNEW I HAD GOOD COMMUNICATION SKILLS, BUT THIS IS AMAZING!
NICE SPIN. YOU OWE ME $400.
SCOTT and BORGMAN
©2005 ZITS Partnership. Distributed by King Features Syndicate

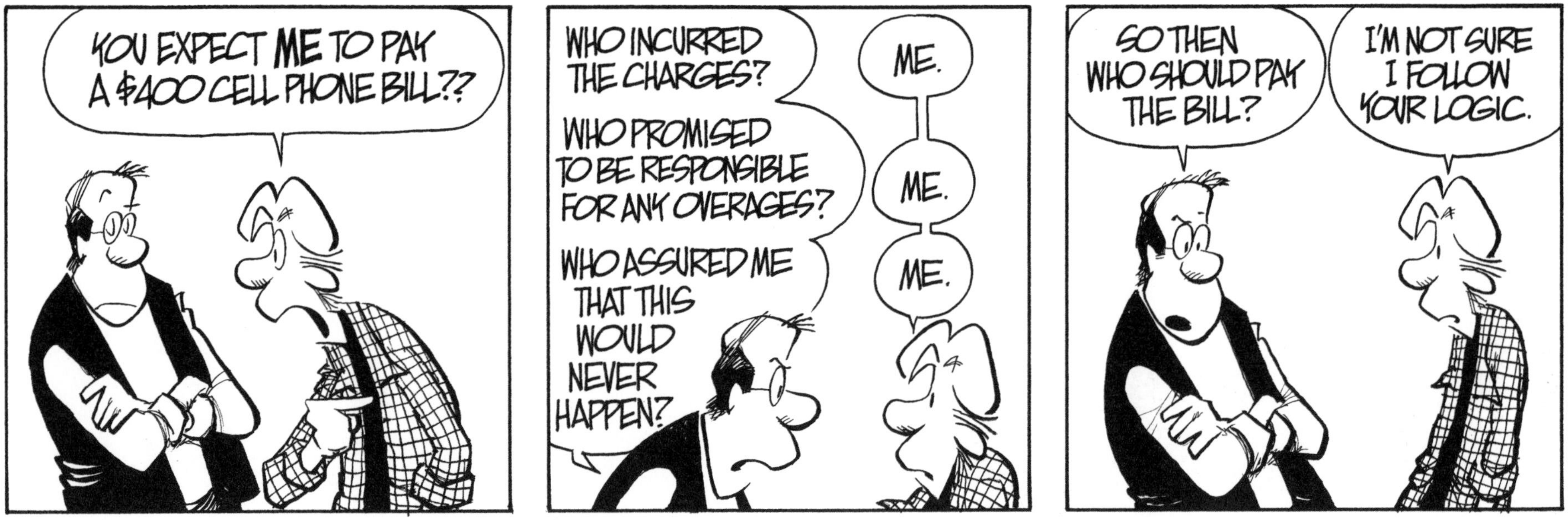
YOU EXPECT ME TO PAY A $400 CELL PHONE BILL??
WHO INCURRED THE CHARGES?
ME.
WHO PROMISED TO BE RESPONSIBLE FOR ANY OVERAGES?
ME.
WHO ASSURED ME THAT THIS WOULD NEVER HAPPEN?
ME.
SO THEN WHO SHOULD PAY THE BILL?
I'M NOT SURE I FOLLOW YOUR LOGIC.

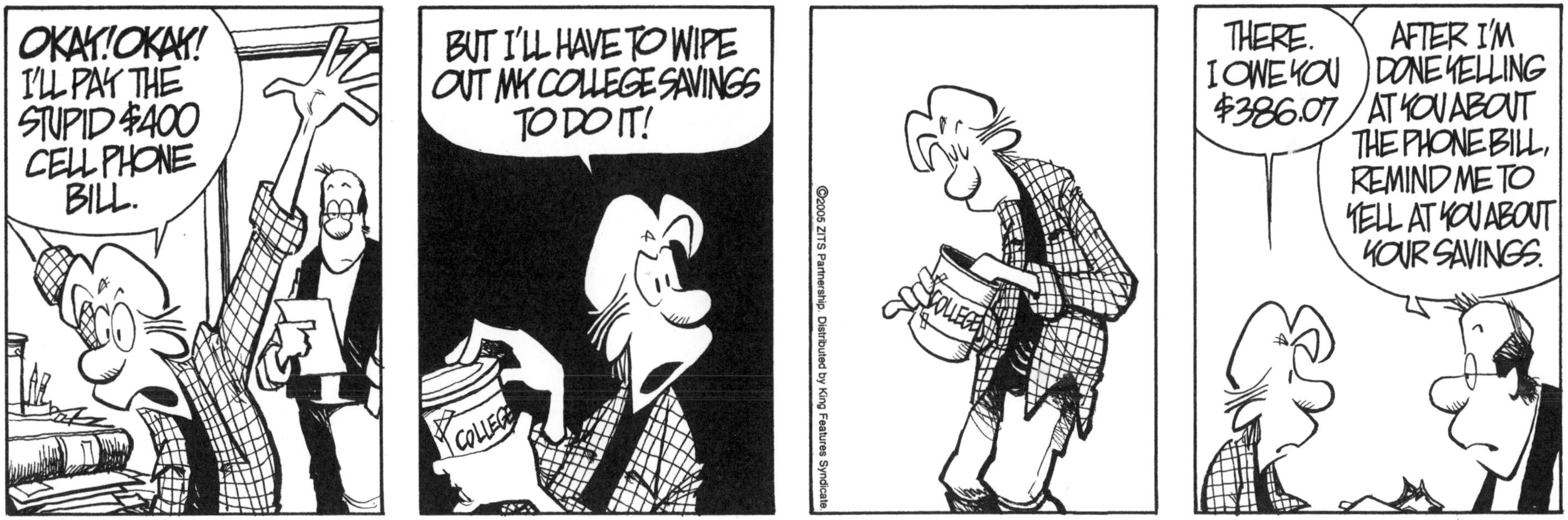
OKAY! OKAY! I'LL PAY THE STUPID $400 CELL PHONE BILL.
BUT I'LL HAVE TO WIPE OUT MY COLLEGE SAVINGS TO DO IT!
COLLEGE
©2005 ZITS Partnership. Distributed by King Features Syndicate
COLLEGE
THERE. I OWE YOU $386.07
AFTER I'M DONE YELLING AT YOU ABOUT THE PHONE BILL, REMIND ME TO YELL AT YOU ABOUT YOUR SAVINGS.

JEREMY? ARE YOU OKAY?
I'M FINE. JUST WARMING UP.
WARMING UP FOR WHAT?
I'M HOME!
HEY DOOD! WHAT UP?
OH.
9/25
SCOTT and BORGMAN
©2005 ZITS Partnership. Distributed by King Features Syndicate

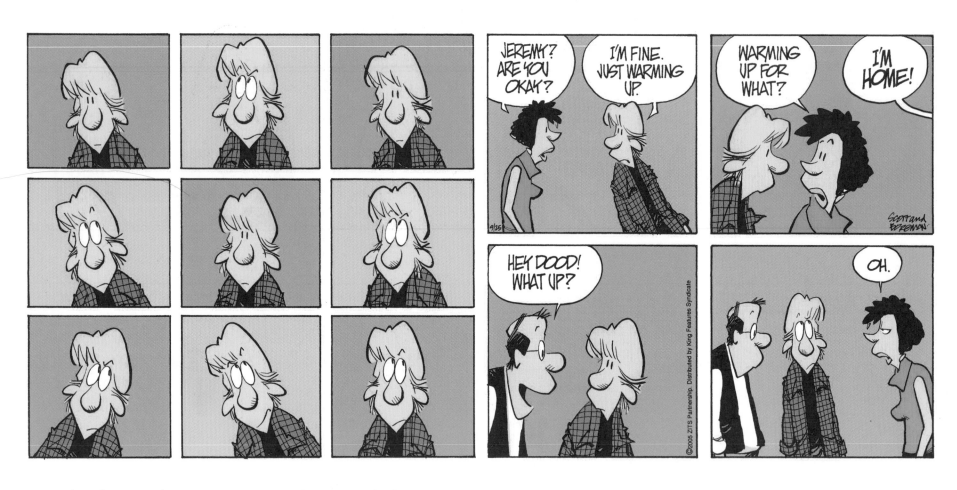

Jim: Abandon any dream you ever secretly nurtured of being the Cool Dad. Not gonna happen.

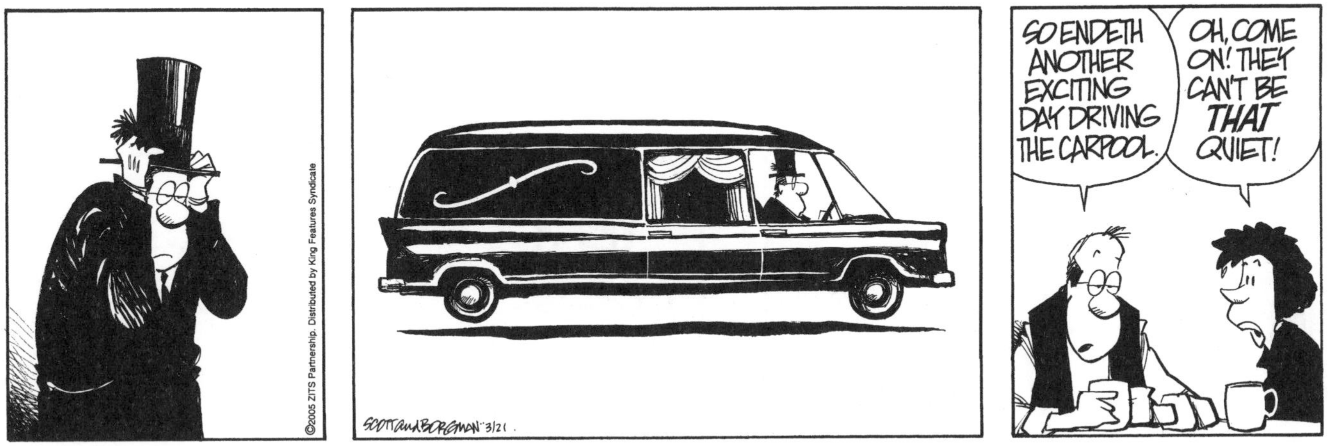
©2005 ZITS Partnership. Distributed by King Features Syndicate
SO ENDETH ANOTHER EXCITING DAY DRIVING THE CARPOOL.
OH, COME ON! THEY CAN'T BE *THAT* QUIET!

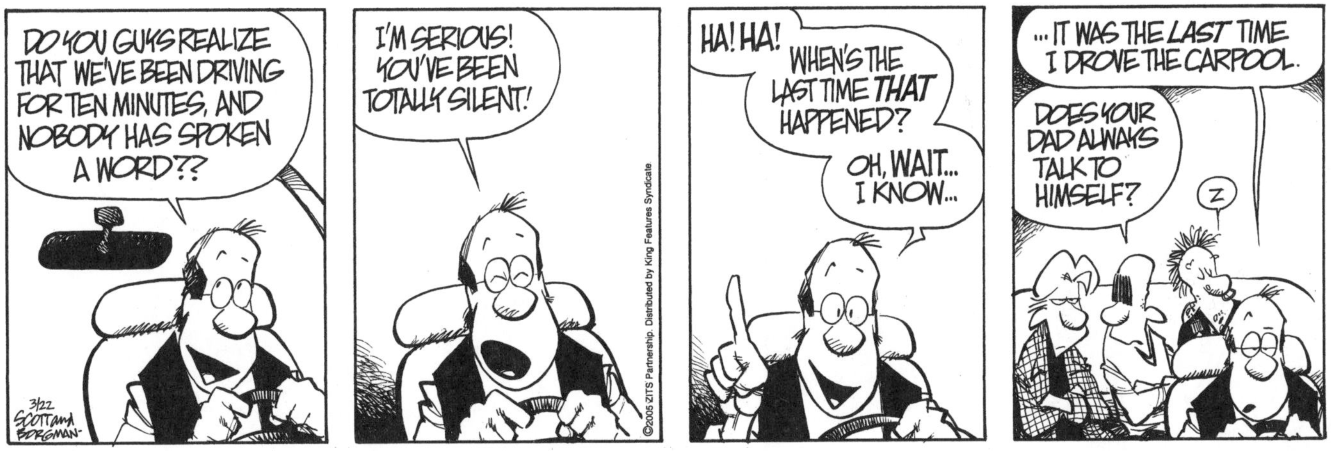
DO YOU GUYS REALIZE THAT WE'VE BEEN DRIVING FOR TEN MINUTES, AND NOBODY HAS SPOKEN A WORD??
I'M SERIOUS! YOU'VE BEEN TOTALLY SILENT!
©2005 ZITS Partnership. Distributed by King Features Syndicate
HA! HA!
WHEN'S THE LAST TIME *THAT* HAPPENED?
OH, WAIT... I KNOW...
...IT WAS THE *LAST* TIME I DROVE THE CARPOOL.
DOES YOUR DAD ALWAYS TALK TO HIMSELF?
Z

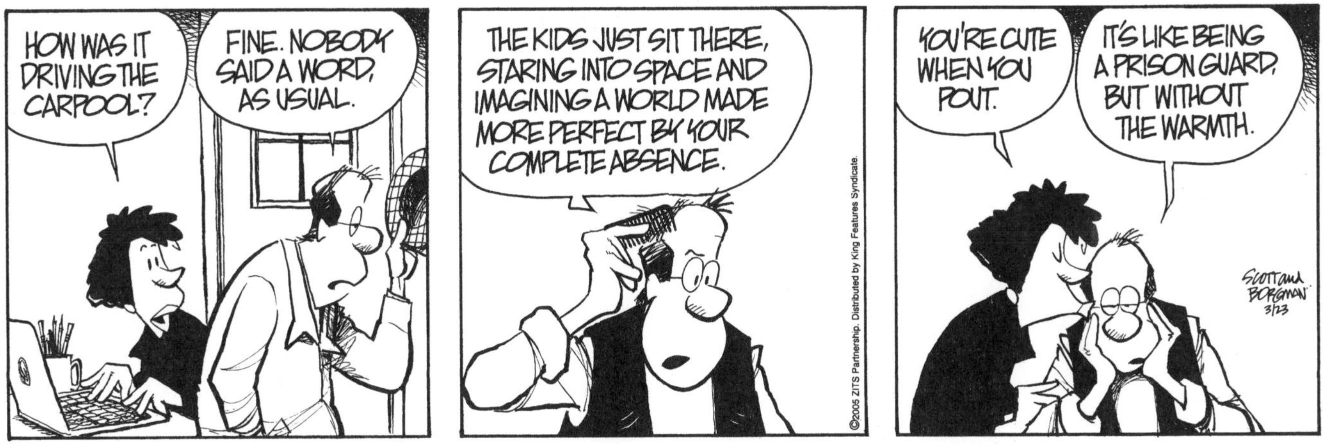
HOW WAS IT DRIVING THE CARPOOL?
FINE. NOBODY SAID A WORD, AS USUAL.
THE KIDS JUST SIT THERE, STARING INTO SPACE AND IMAGINING A WORLD MADE MORE PERFECT BY YOUR COMPLETE ABSENCE.
©2005 ZITS Partnership. Distributed by King Features Syndicate
YOU'RE CUTE WHEN YOU POUT.
IT'S LIKE BEING A PRISON GUARD, BUT WITHOUT THE WARMTH.

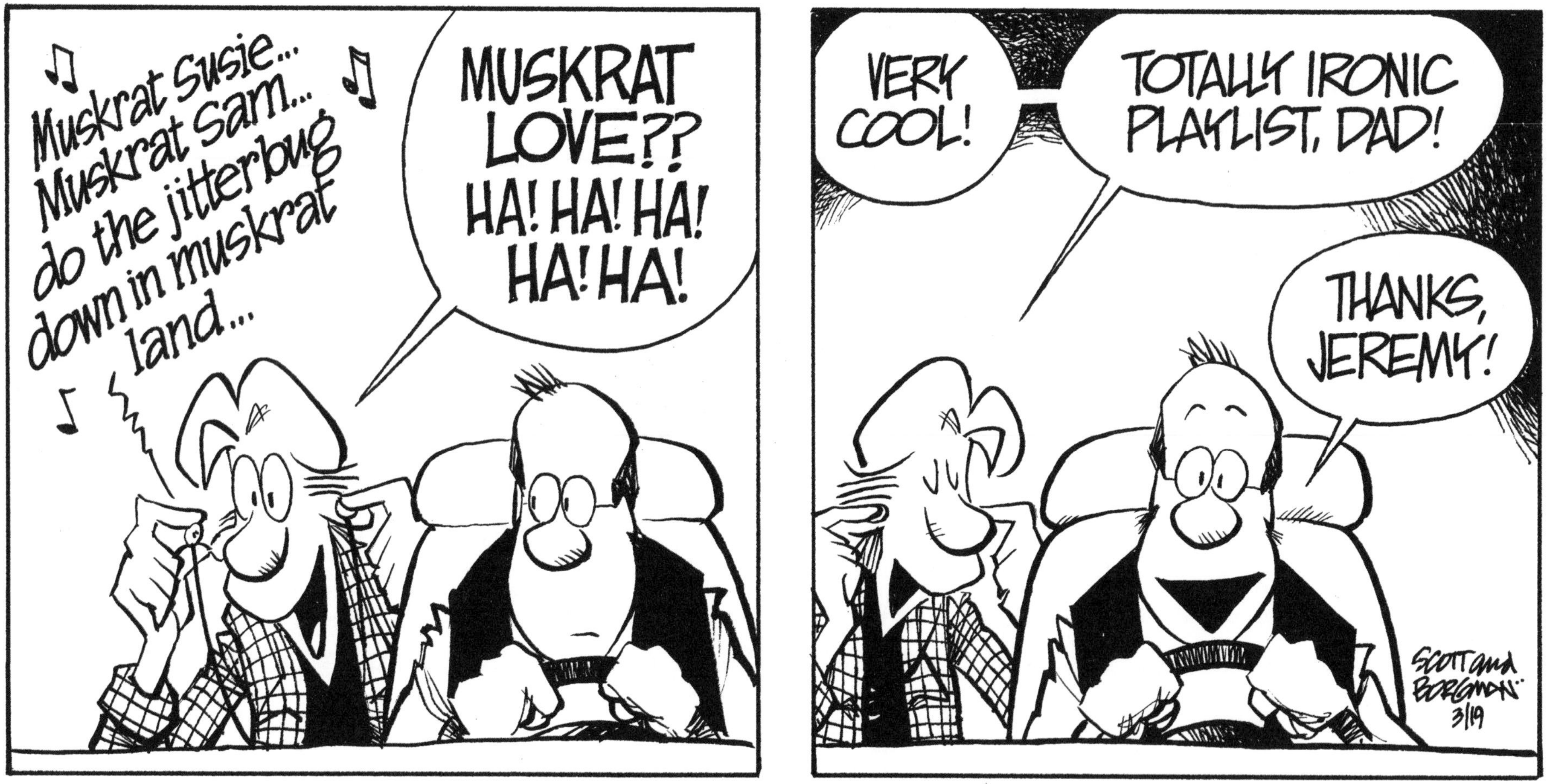
Muskrat Susie... Muskrat Sam... do the jitterbug down in muskrat land...
MUSKRAT LOVE?? HA! HA! HA! HA! HA!
VERY COOL!
TOTALLY IRONIC PLAYLIST, DAD!
THANKS, JEREMY!
SCOTT and BORGMAN 3/19

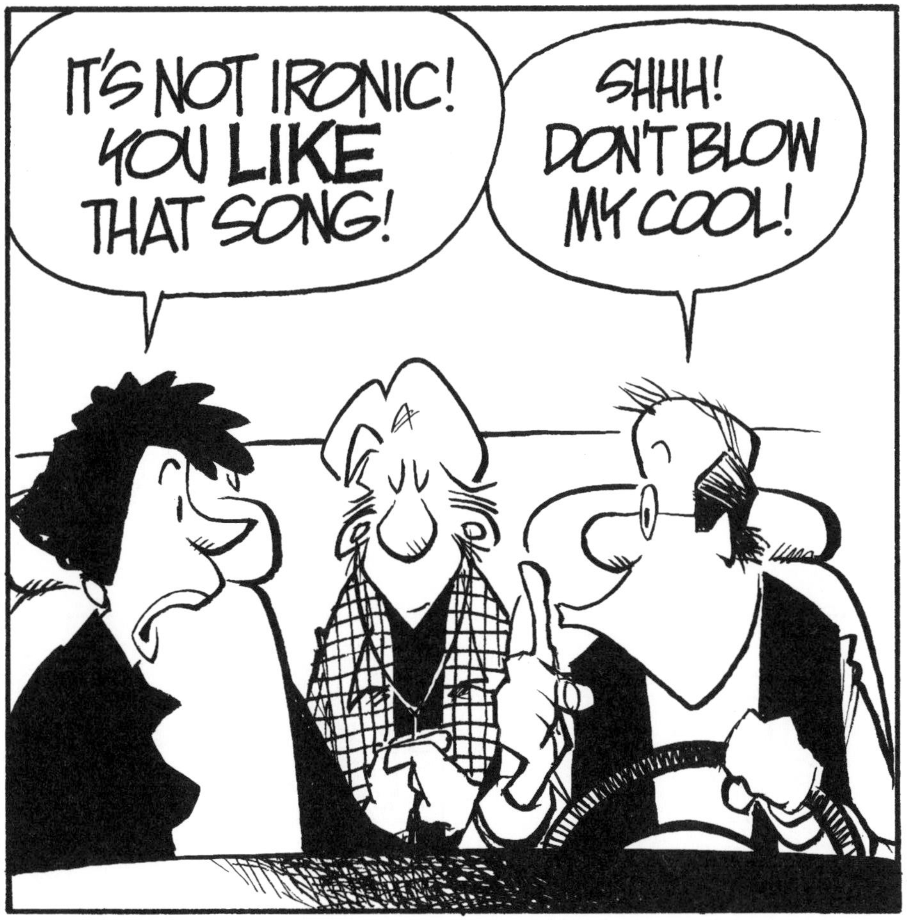
IT'S NOT IRONIC! YOU LIKE THAT SONG!
SHHH! DON'T BLOW MY COOL!

Jim: Payback is slow, but rest assured that someday your son's kids will mock him for knowing the words to Rob Zombie songs.

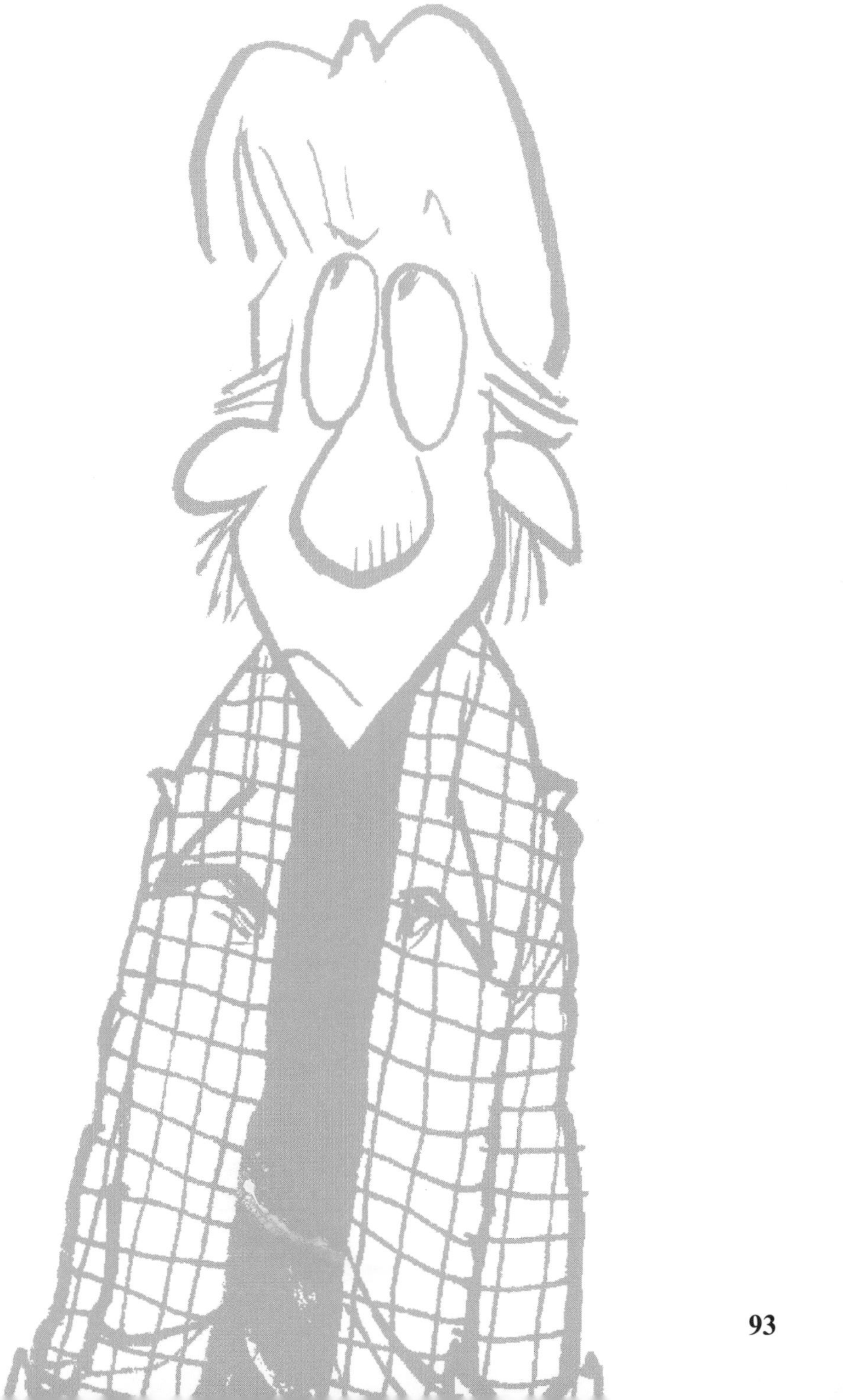

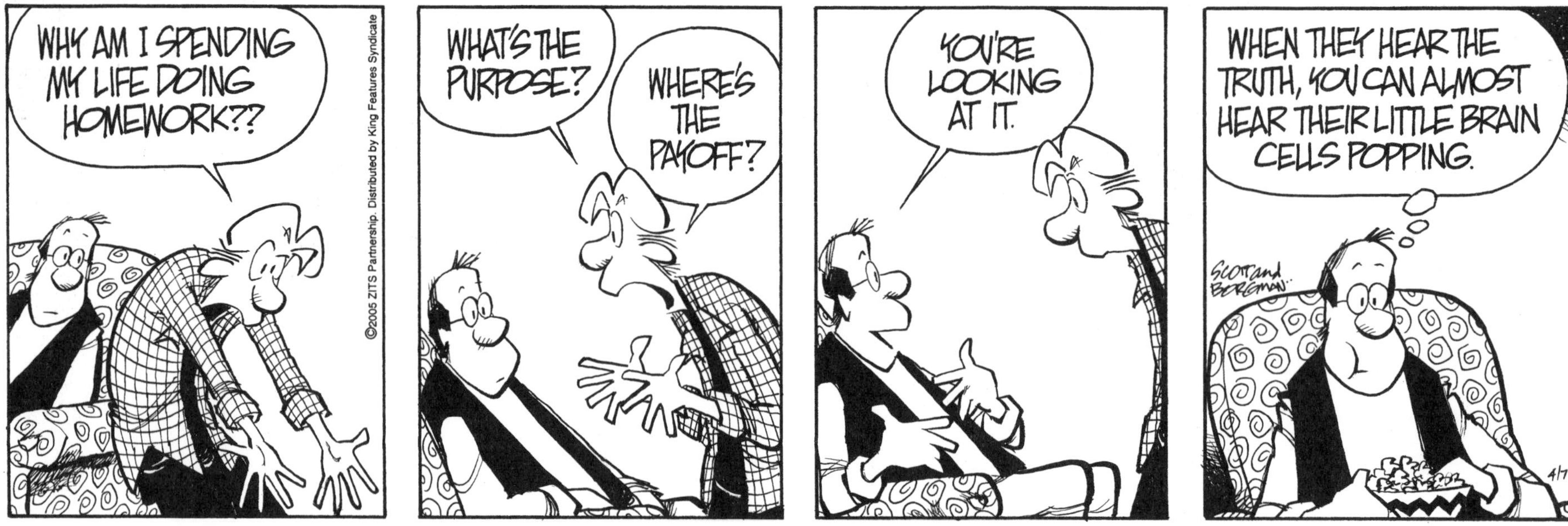
WHY AM I SPENDING MY LIFE DOING HOMEWORK??
WHAT'S THE PURPOSE?
WHERE'S THE PAYOFF?
YOU'RE LOOKING AT IT.
WHEN THEY HEAR THE TRUTH, YOU CAN ALMOST HEAR THEIR LITTLE BRAIN CELLS POPPING.
©2005 ZITS Partnership. Distributed by King Features Syndicate
SCOTT and BORGMAN
4/7

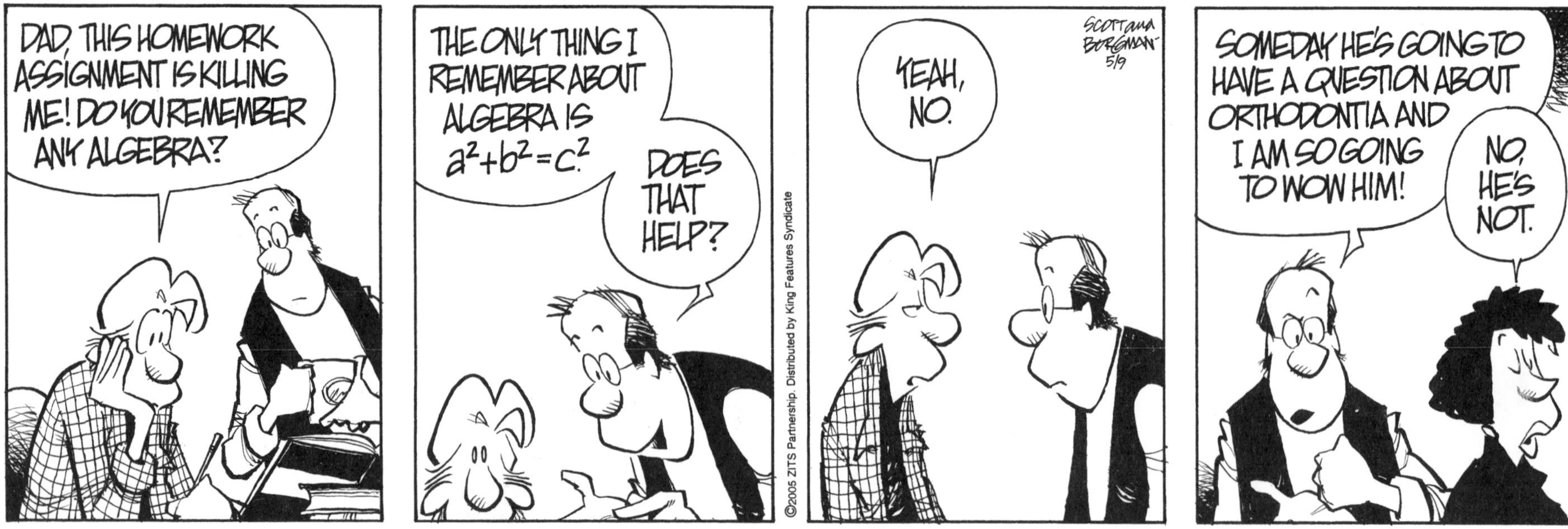
DAD, THIS HOMEWORK ASSIGNMENT IS KILLING ME! DO YOU REMEMBER ANY ALGEBRA?
THE ONLY THING I REMEMBER ABOUT ALGEBRA IS a²+b²=c².
DOES THAT HELP?
YEAH, NO.
SOMEDAY HE'S GOING TO HAVE A QUESTION ABOUT ORTHODONTIA AND I AM SO GOING TO WOW HIM!
NO, HE'S NOT.
©2005 ZITS Partnership. Distributed by King Features Syndicate
SCOTT and BORGMAN
5/9

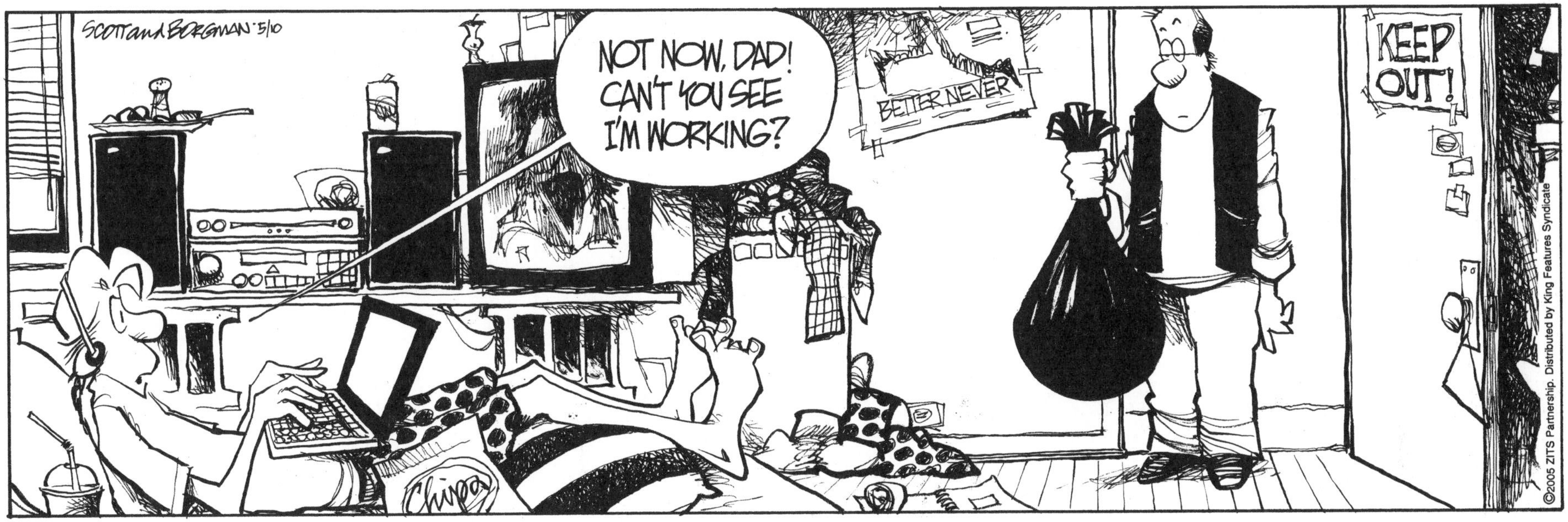
SCOTT and BORGMAN 5/10
NOT NOW, DAD! CAN'T YOU SEE I'M WORKING?
BETTER NEVER
KEEP OUT!
Chips
©2005 ZITS Partnership. Distributed by King Features Syndicate

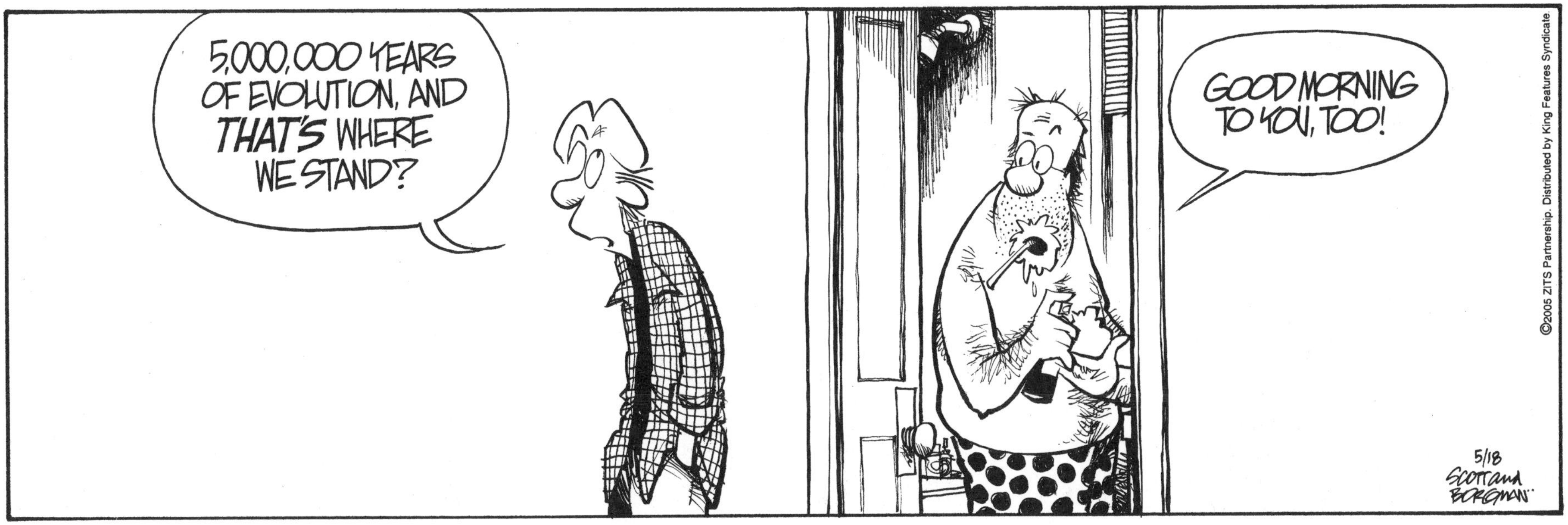
5,000,000 YEARS OF EVOLUTION, AND *THAT'S* WHERE WE STAND?
GOOD MORNING TO YOU, TOO!
©2005 ZITS Partnership. Distributed by King Features Syndicate
5/18 SCOTT and BORGMAN

Jim: In rare moments, Walt flashes his Homer side. Usually he's a tad less oafish and tends more to Toasted Head than Duff's, but the parallel has not entirely escaped us.

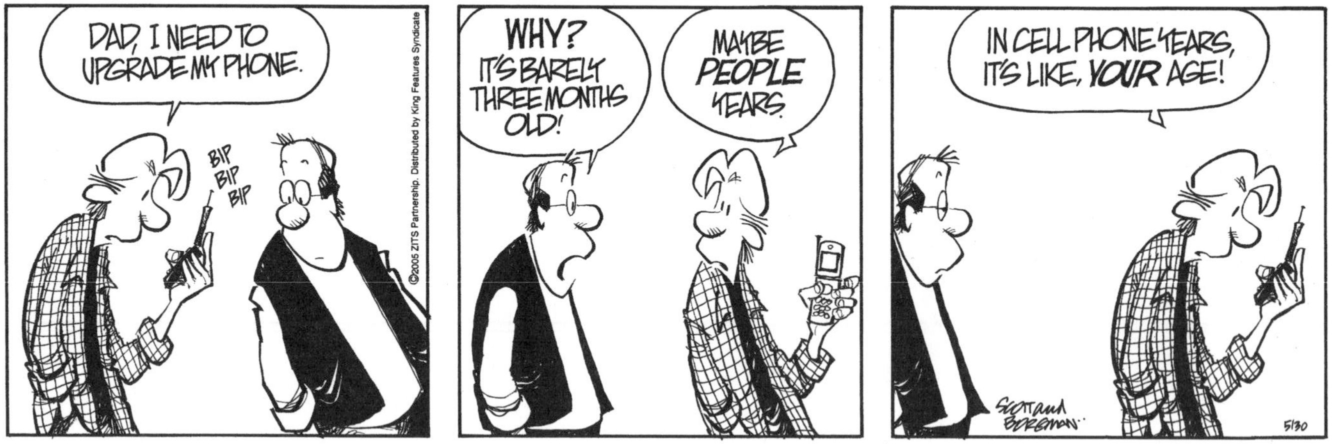
DAD, I NEED TO UPGRADE MY PHONE.
BIP BIP BIP
©2005 ZITS Partnership. Distributed by King Features Syndicate
WHY? IT'S BARELY THREE MONTHS OLD!
MAYBE PEOPLE YEARS.
IN CELL PHONE YEARS, IT'S LIKE, YOUR AGE!
SCOTT and BORGMAN
5/30

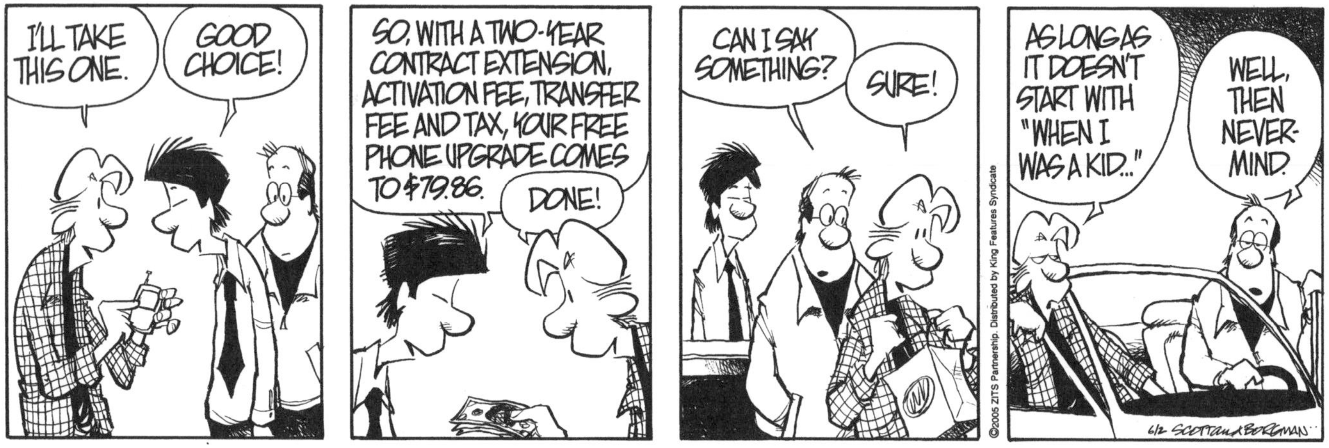
I'LL TAKE THIS ONE.
GOOD CHOICE!
SO, WITH A TWO-YEAR CONTRACT EXTENSION, ACTIVATION FEE, TRANSFER FEE AND TAX, YOUR FREE PHONE UPGRADE COMES TO $79.86.
DONE!
CAN I SAY SOMETHING?
SURE!
©2005 ZITS Partnership. Distributed by King Features Syndicate
AS LONG AS IT DOESN'T START WITH "WHEN I WAS A KID..."
WELL, THEN NEVER-MIND.
6/2 SCOTT and BORGMAN

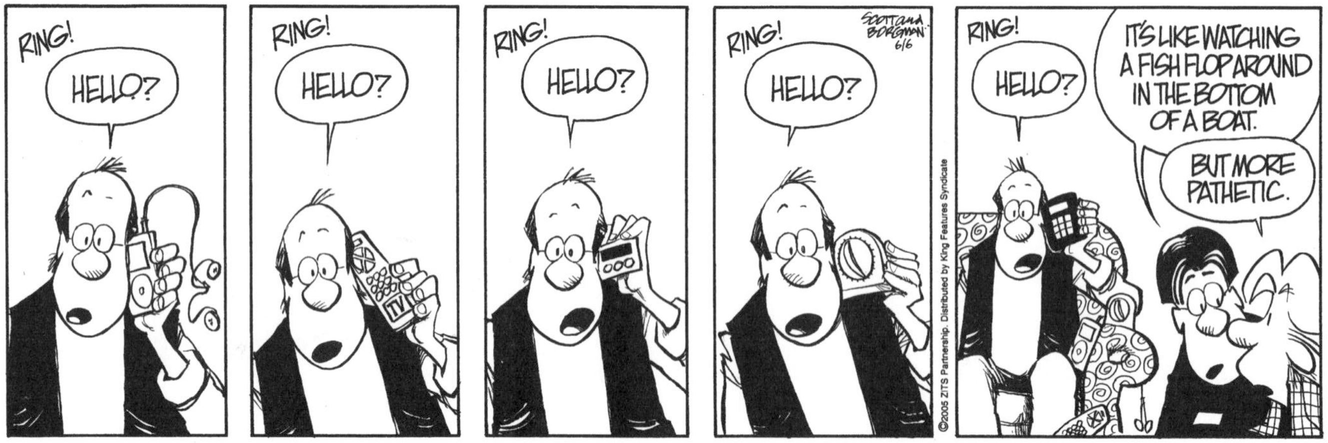
RING!
HELLO?
RING!
HELLO?
TV
RING!
HELLO?
SCOTT and BORGMAN 6/6
RING!
HELLO?
©2005 ZITS Partnership. Distributed by King Features Syndicate
RING!
HELLO?
IT'S LIKE WATCHING A FISH FLOP AROUND IN THE BOTTOM OF A BOAT.
BUT MORE PATHETIC.

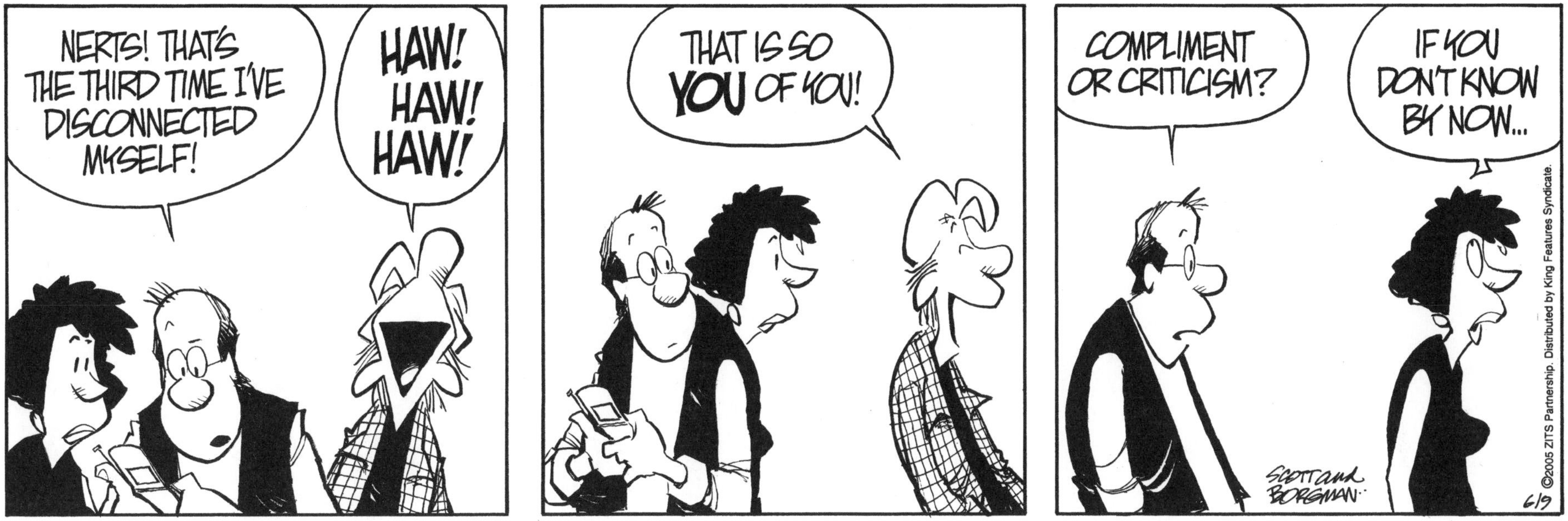
NERTS! THAT'S THE THIRD TIME I'VE DISCONNECTED MYSELF!
HAW! HAW! HAW!
THAT IS SO YOU OF YOU!
COMPLIMENT OR CRITICISM?
IF YOU DON'T KNOW BY NOW...
SCOTT and BORGMAN
6/9
©2005 ZITS Partnership. Distributed by King Features Syndicate.

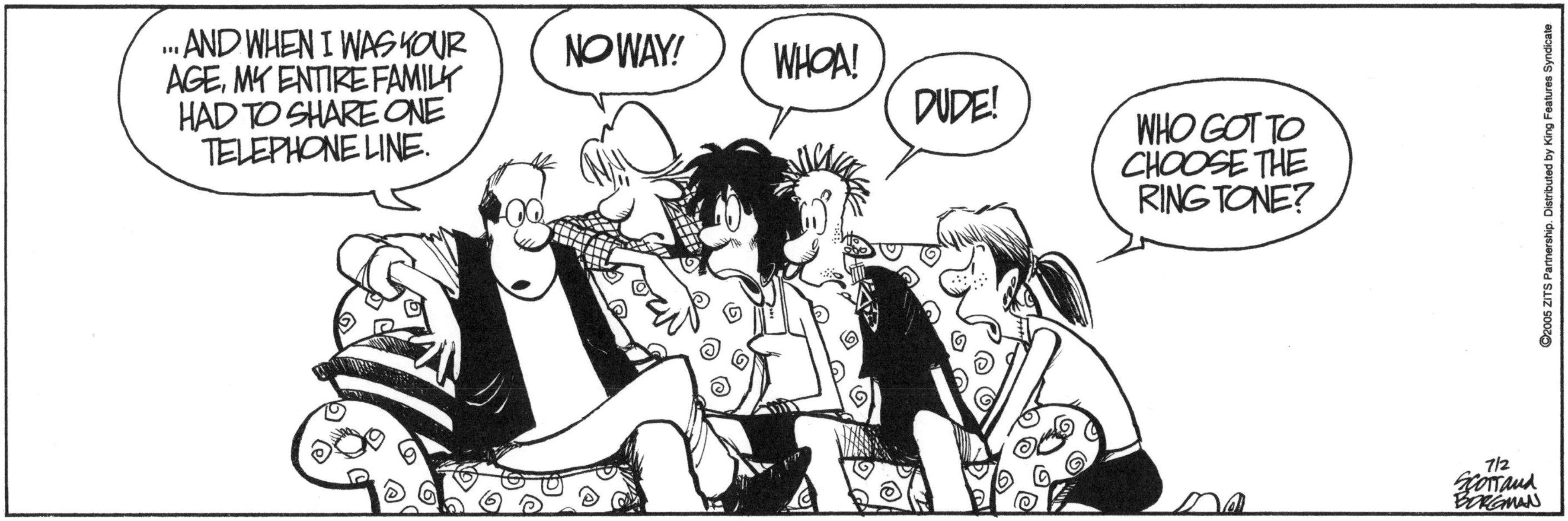
...AND WHEN I WAS YOUR AGE, MY ENTIRE FAMILY HAD TO SHARE ONE TELEPHONE LINE.
NO WAY!
WHOA!
DUDE!
WHO GOT TO CHOOSE THE RING TONE?
7/2
SCOTT and BORGMAN
©2005 ZITS Partnership. Distributed by King Features Syndicate

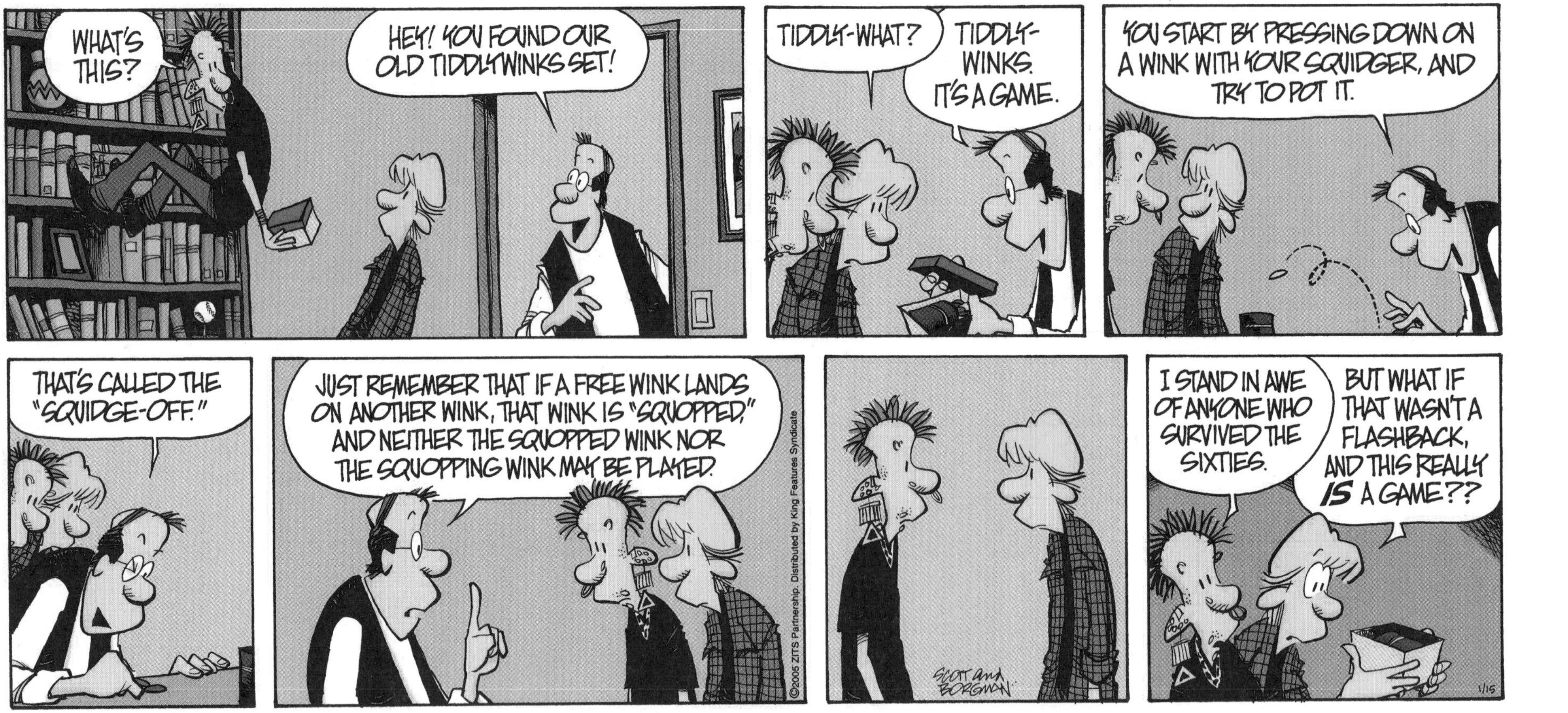
WHAT'S THIS?
HEY! YOU FOUND OUR OLD TIDDLYWINKS SET!
TIDDLY-WHAT?
TIDDLY-WINKS. IT'S A GAME.
YOU START BY PRESSING DOWN ON A WINK WITH YOUR SQUIDGER, AND TRY TO POT IT.
THAT'S CALLED THE "SQUIDGE-OFF."
JUST REMEMBER THAT IF A FREE WINK LANDS ON ANOTHER WINK, THAT WINK IS "SQUOPPED," AND NEITHER THE SQUOPPED WINK NOR THE SQUOPPING WINK MAY BE PLAYED.
©2005 ZITS Partnership. Distributed by King Features Syndicate
SCOTT AND BORGMAN
I STAND IN AWE OF ANYONE WHO SURVIVED THE SIXTIES.
BUT WHAT IF THAT WASN'T A FLASHBACK, AND THIS REALLY ***IS*** A GAME??
1/15

Jerry: I was thinking about tiddlywinks one morning, Googled it, and came up with this strip (do I have a great job, or what?). I can't picture anyone but Dad saying "squidge-off."

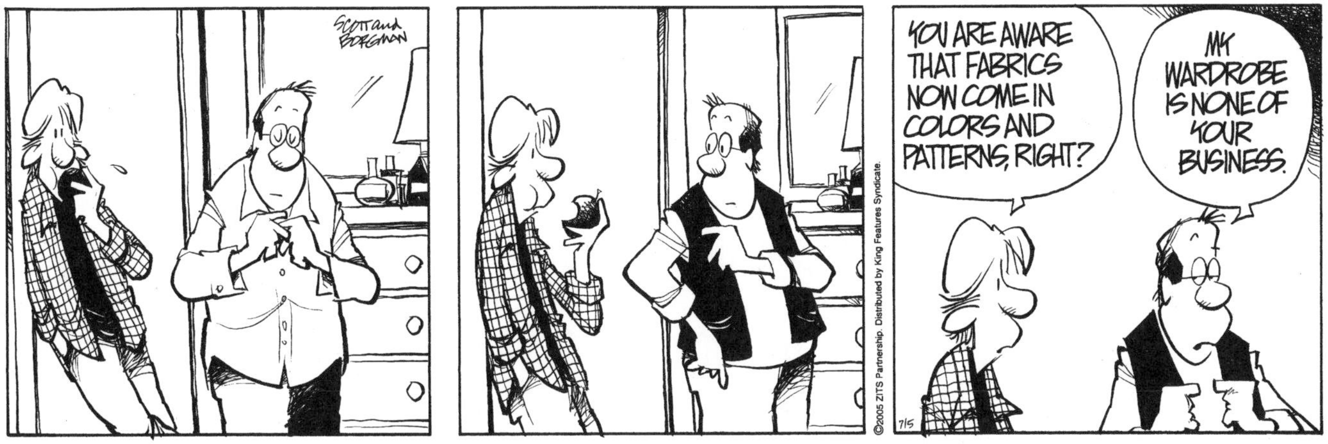
SCOTT AND BORGMAN
©2005 ZITS Partnership. Distributed by King Features Syndicate.
7/5
YOU ARE AWARE THAT FABRICS NOW COME IN COLORS AND PATTERNS, RIGHT?
MY WARDROBE IS NONE OF YOUR BUSINESS.

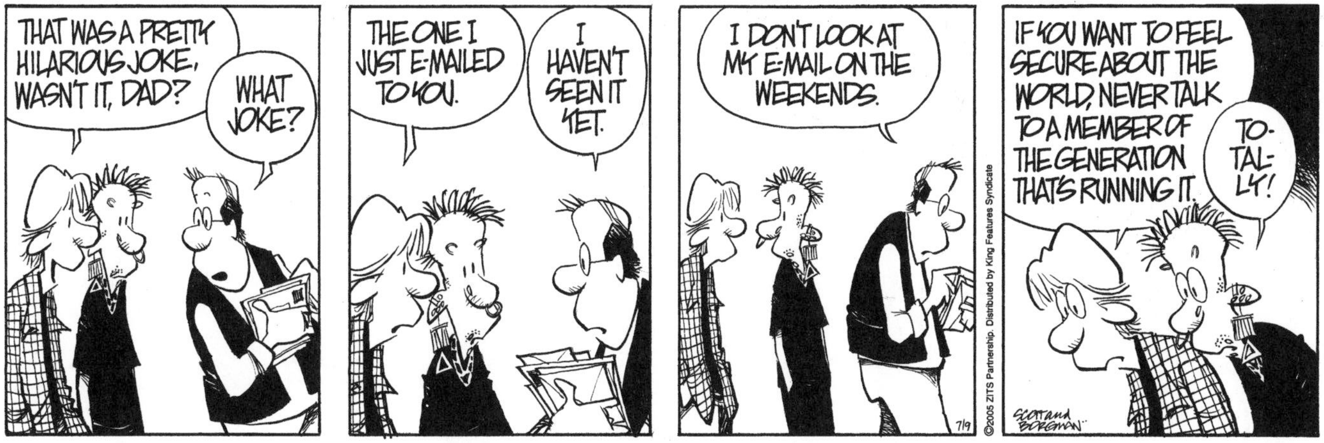
THAT WAS A PRETTY HILARIOUS JOKE, WASN'T IT, DAD?
WHAT JOKE?
THE ONE I JUST E-MAILED TO YOU.
I HAVEN'T SEEN IT YET.
I DON'T LOOK AT MY E-MAIL ON THE WEEKENDS.
7/9
©2005 ZITS Partnership. Distributed by King Features Syndicate
IF YOU WANT TO FEEL SECURE ABOUT THE WORLD, NEVER TALK TO A MEMBER OF THE GENERATION THAT'S RUNNING IT.
TO-TAL-LY!
SCOTT AND BORGMAN

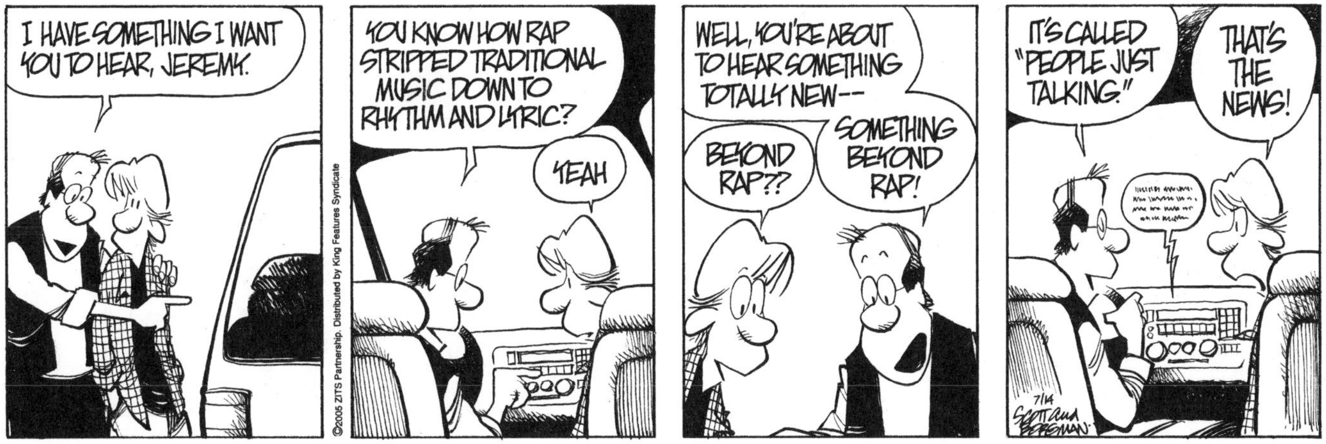
I HAVE SOMETHING I WANT YOU TO HEAR, JEREMY.
©2005 ZITS Partnership. Distributed by King Features Syndicate
YOU KNOW HOW RAP STRIPPED TRADITIONAL MUSIC DOWN TO RHYTHM AND LYRIC?
YEAH
WELL, YOU'RE ABOUT TO HEAR SOMETHING TOTALLY NEW--
SOMETHING BEYOND RAP!
BEYOND RAP??
IT'S CALLED "PEOPLE JUST TALKING."
THAT'S THE NEWS!
7/14
SCOTT AND BORGMAN

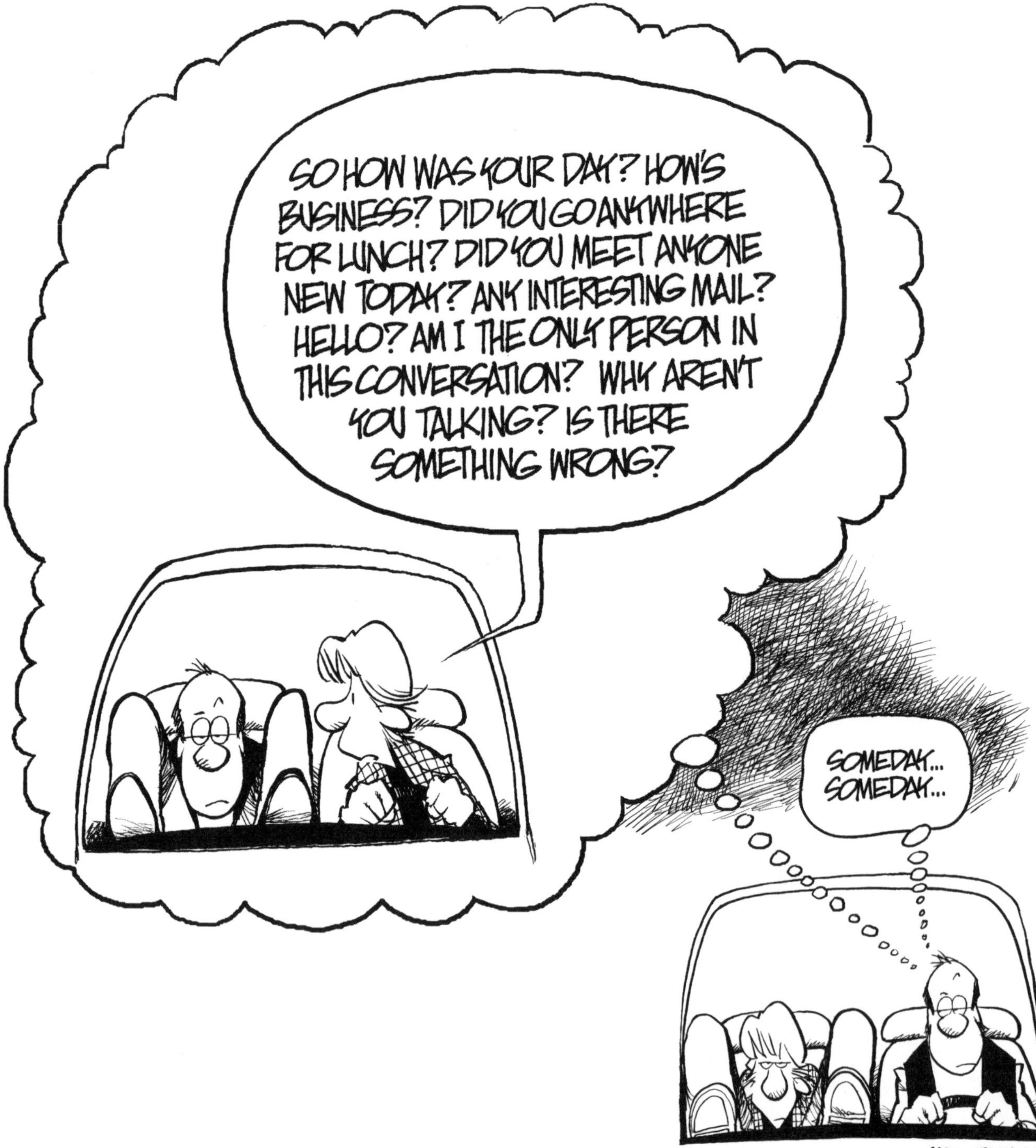
SO HOW WAS YOUR DAY? HOW'S BUSINESS? DID YOU GO ANYWHERE FOR LUNCH? DID YOU MEET ANYONE NEW TODAY? ANY INTERESTING MAIL? HELLO? AM I THE ONLY PERSON IN THIS CONVERSATION? WHY AREN'T YOU TALKING? IS THERE SOMETHING WRONG?
SOMEDAY... SOMEDAY...

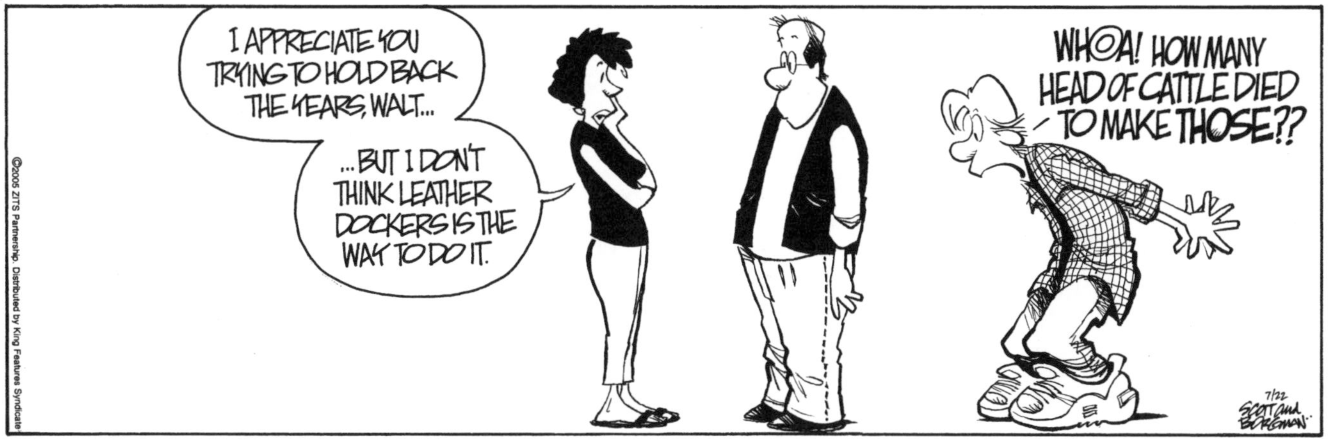
I APPRECIATE YOU TRYING TO HOLD BACK THE YEARS, WALT...
...BUT I DON'T THINK LEATHER DOCKERS IS THE WAY TO DO IT.
WHOA! HOW MANY HEAD OF CATTLE DIED TO MAKE THOSE??
©2005 ZITS Partnership. Distributed by King Features Syndicate
7/22 SCOTT AND BORGMAN

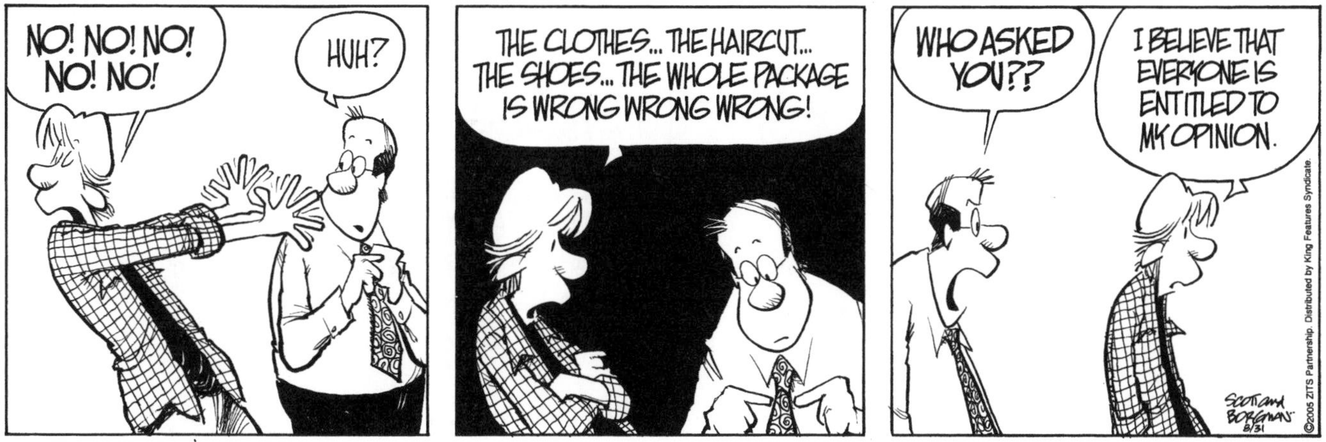
NO! NO! NO! NO! NO!
HUH?
THE CLOTHES... THE HAIRCUT... THE SHOES... THE WHOLE PACKAGE IS WRONG WRONG WRONG!
WHO ASKED YOU??
I BELIEVE THAT EVERYONE IS ENTITLED TO MY OPINION.
SCOTT AND BORGMAN 8/31
©2005 ZITS Partnership. Distributed by King Features Syndicate.

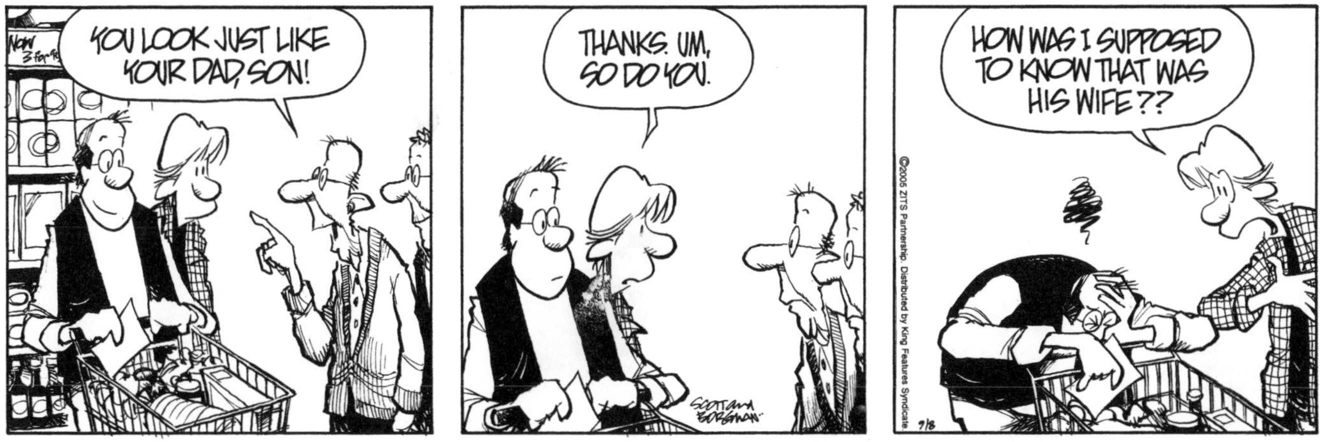
YOU LOOK JUST LIKE YOUR DAD, SON!
THANKS. UM, SO DO YOU.
SCOTT AND BORGMAN
HOW WAS I SUPPOSED TO KNOW THAT WAS HIS WIFE??
©2005 ZITS Partnership. Distributed by King Features Syndicate
9/8

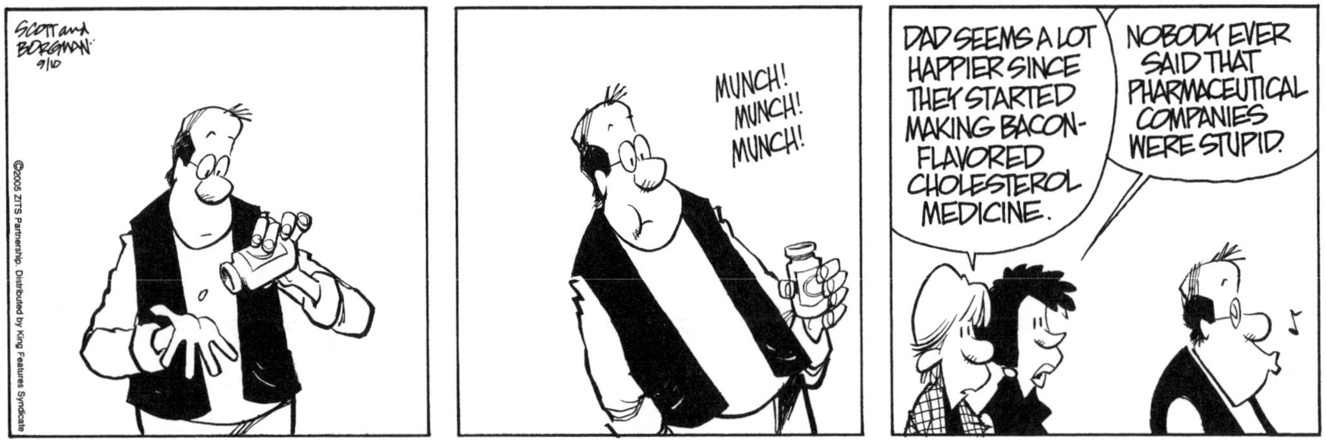
SCOTT and BORGMAN 9/10
©2005 ZITS Partnership. Distributed by King Features Syndicate
MUNCH! MUNCH! MUNCH!
DAD SEEMS A LOT HAPPIER SINCE THEY STARTED MAKING BACON-FLAVORED CHOLESTEROL MEDICINE.
NOBODY EVER SAID THAT PHARMACEUTICAL COMPANIES WERE STUPID.

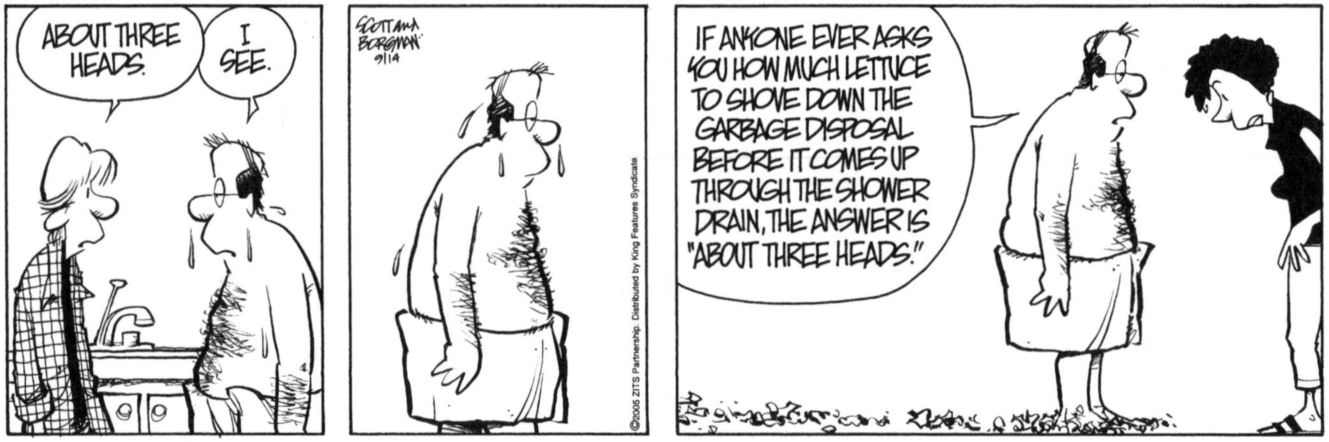
SCOTT and BORGMAN 9/14
©2005 ZITS Partnership. Distributed by King Features Syndicate
IF ANYONE EVER ASKS YOU HOW MUCH LETTUCE TO SHOVE DOWN THE GARBAGE DISPOSAL BEFORE IT COMES UP THROUGH THE SHOWER DRAIN, THE ANSWER IS "ABOUT THREE HEADS."
ABOUT THREE HEADS.
I SEE.

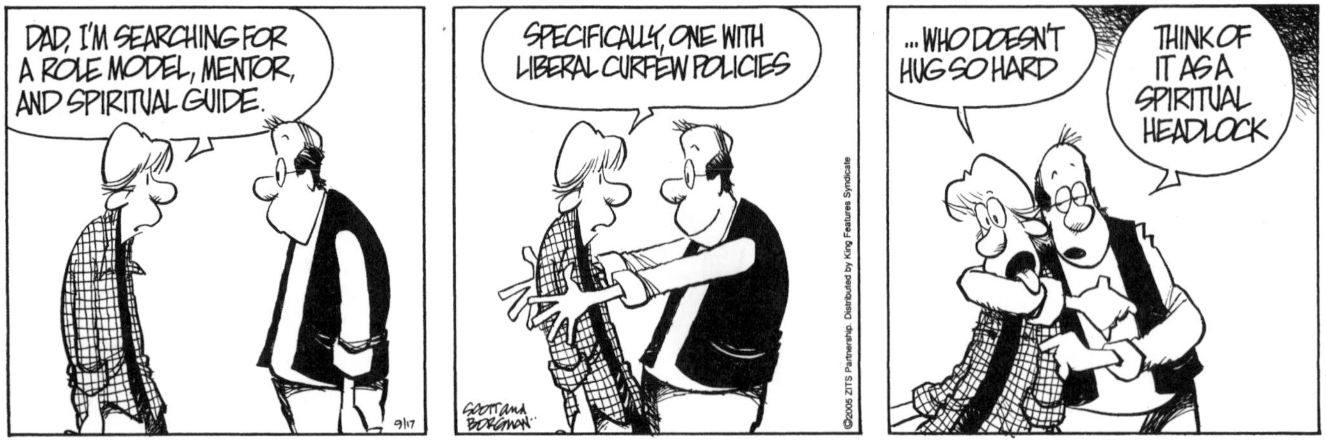
DAD, I'M SEARCHING FOR A ROLE MODEL, MENTOR, AND SPIRITUAL GUIDE.
SPECIFICALLY, ONE WITH LIBERAL CURFEW POLICIES
SCOTT and BORGMAN 9/17
©2005 ZITS Partnership. Distributed by King Features Syndicate
...WHO DOESN'T HUG SO HARD
THINK OF IT AS A SPIRITUAL HEADLOCK

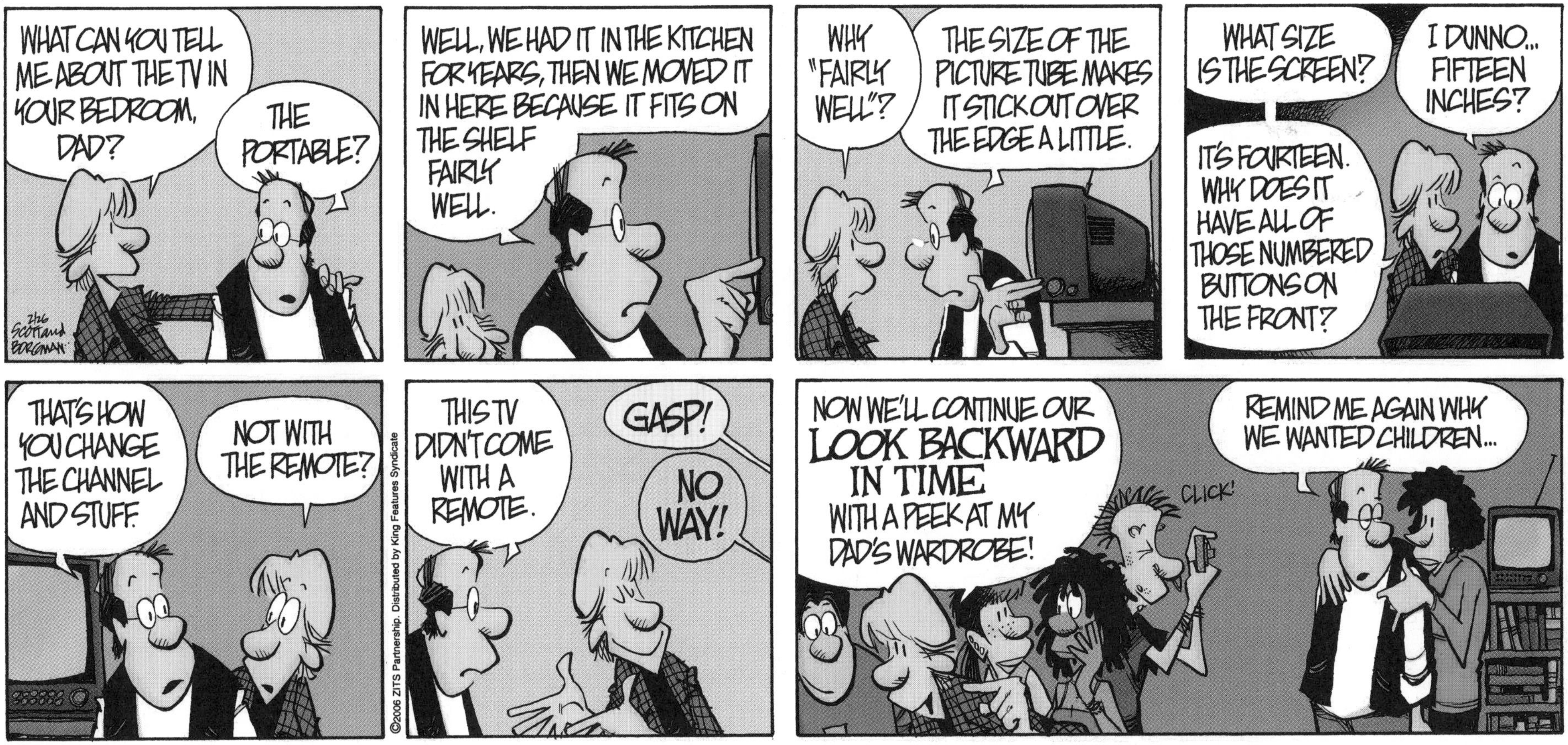
WHAT CAN YOU TELL ME ABOUT THE TV IN YOUR BEDROOM, DAD?
THE PORTABLE?
WELL, WE HAD IT IN THE KITCHEN FOR YEARS, THEN WE MOVED IT IN HERE BECAUSE IT FITS ON THE SHELF FAIRLY WELL.
WHY "FAIRLY WELL"?
THE SIZE OF THE PICTURE TUBE MAKES IT STICK OUT OVER THE EDGE A LITTLE.
WHAT SIZE IS THE SCREEN?
I DUNNO... FIFTEEN INCHES?
IT'S FOURTEEN. WHY DOES IT HAVE ALL OF THOSE NUMBERED BUTTONS ON THE FRONT?
THAT'S HOW YOU CHANGE THE CHANNEL AND STUFF.
NOT WITH THE REMOTE?
THIS TV DIDN'T COME WITH A REMOTE.
GASP!
NO WAY!
NOW WE'LL CONTINUE OUR LOOK BACKWARD IN TIME WITH A PEEK AT MY DAD'S WARDROBE!
CLICK!
REMIND ME AGAIN WHY WE WANTED CHILDREN...
©2006 ZITS Partnership. Distributed by King Features Syndicate

Jerry: If I could have given curiosity tours of my parents' bedroom furniture, I might have done it, too.

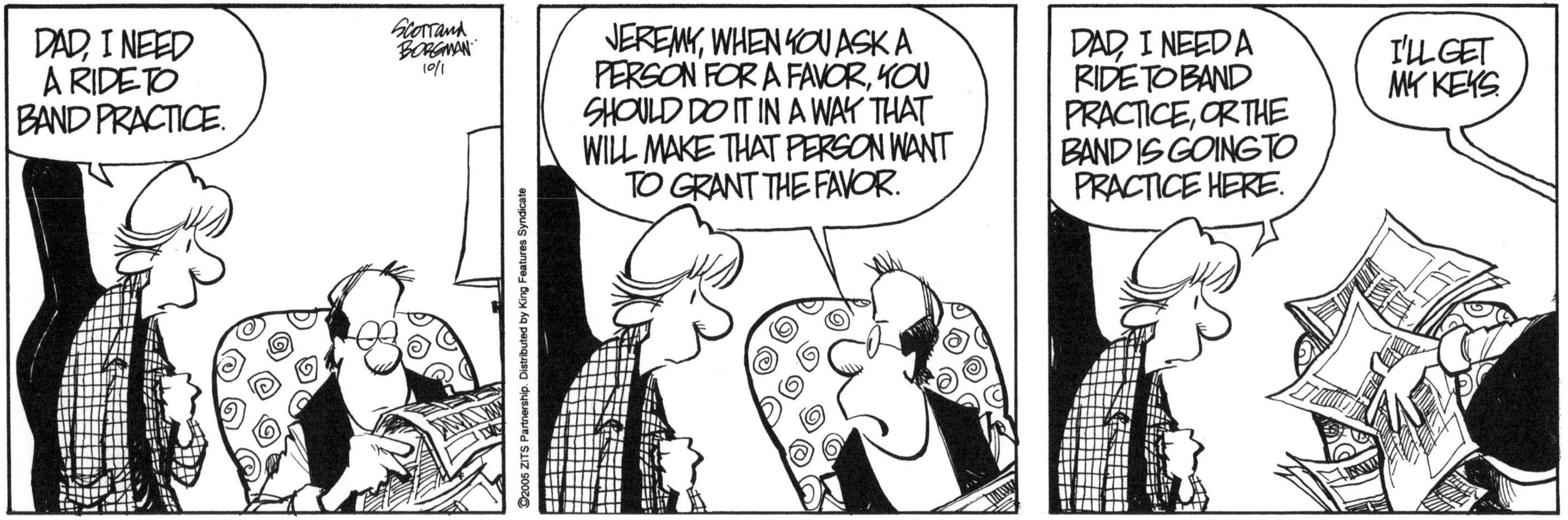
DAD, I NEED A RIDE TO BAND PRACTICE.
JEREMY, WHEN YOU ASK A PERSON FOR A FAVOR, YOU SHOULD DO IT IN A WAY THAT WILL MAKE THAT PERSON WANT TO GRANT THE FAVOR.
DAD, I NEED A RIDE TO BAND PRACTICE, OR THE BAND IS GOING TO PRACTICE HERE.
I'LL GET MY KEYS.
©2005 ZITS Partnership. Distributed by King Features Syndicate

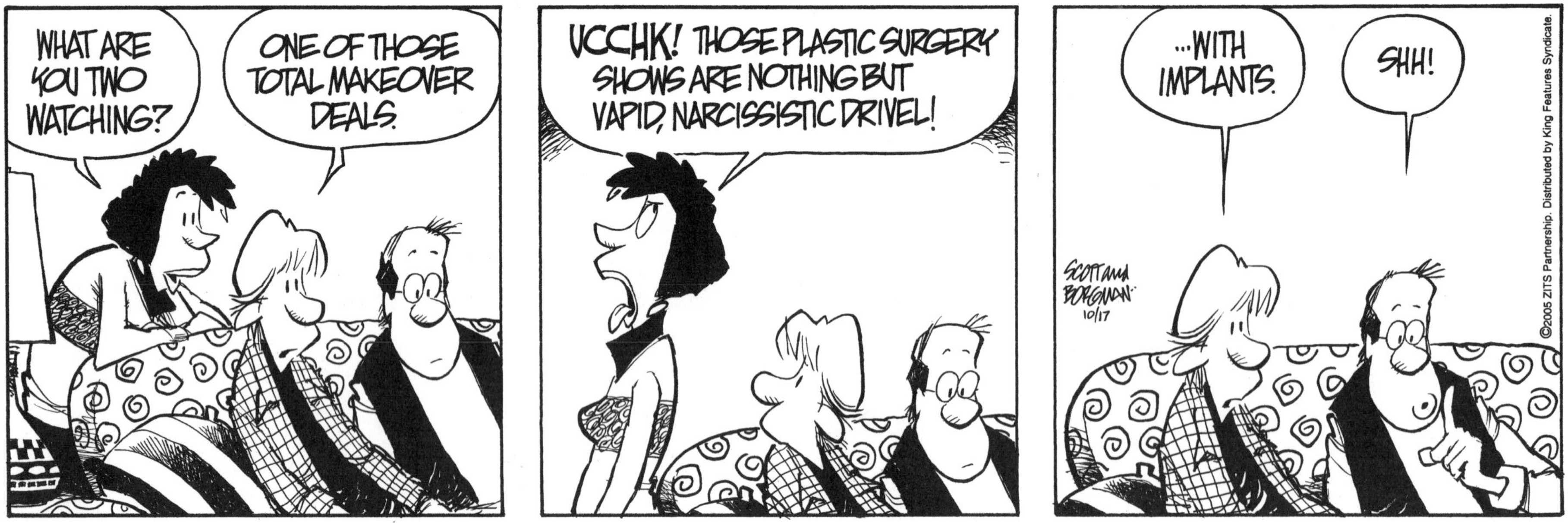
WHAT ARE YOU TWO WATCHING?
ONE OF THOSE TOTAL MAKEOVER DEALS.
UCCHK! THOSE PLASTIC SURGERY SHOWS ARE NOTHING BUT VAPID, NARCISSISTIC DRIVEL!
...WITH IMPLANTS.
SHH!
©2005 ZITS Partnership. Distributed by King Features Syndicate.

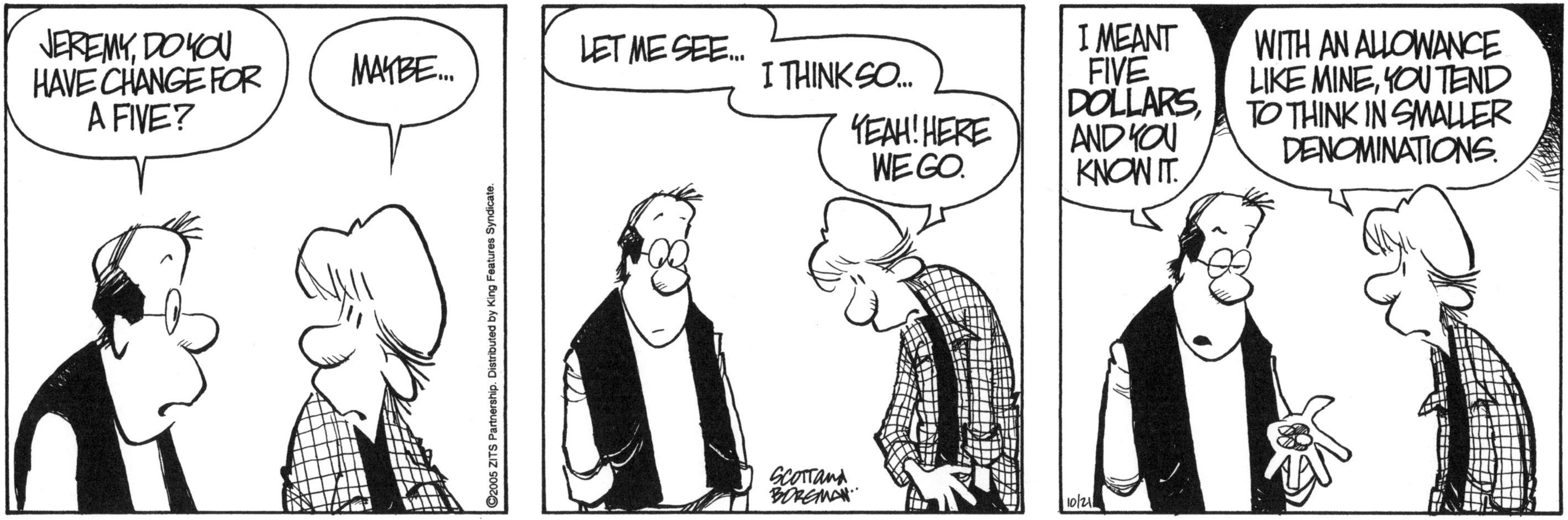
JEREMY, DO YOU HAVE CHANGE FOR A FIVE?
MAYBE...
©2005 ZITS Partnership. Distributed by King Features Syndicate.
LET ME SEE... I THINK SO...
YEAH! HERE WE GO.
I MEANT FIVE DOLLARS, AND YOU KNOW IT.
WITH AN ALLOWANCE LIKE MINE, YOU TEND TO THINK IN SMALLER DENOMINATIONS.

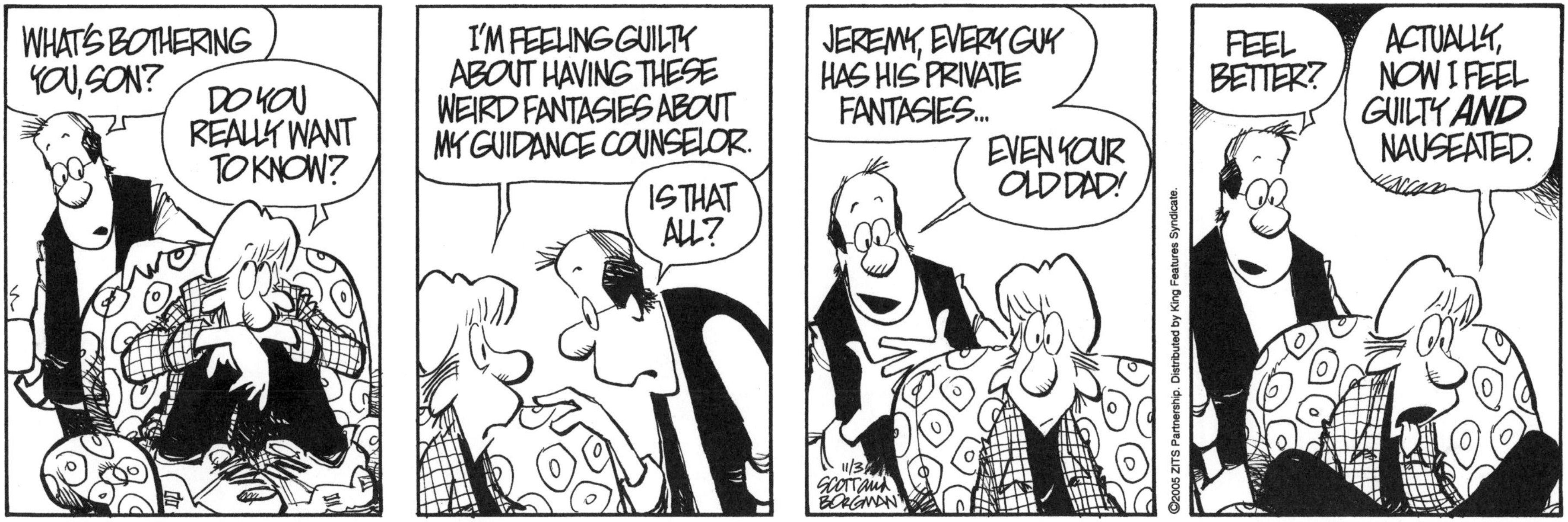
WHAT'S BOTHERING YOU, SON?
DO YOU REALLY WANT TO KNOW?
I'M FEELING GUILTY ABOUT HAVING THESE WEIRD FANTASIES ABOUT MY GUIDANCE COUNSELOR.
IS THAT ALL?
JEREMY, EVERY GUY HAS HIS PRIVATE FANTASIES...
EVEN YOUR OLD DAD!
©2005 ZITS Partnership. Distributed by King Features Syndicate.
FEEL BETTER?
ACTUALLY, NOW I FEEL GUILTY **AND** NAUSEATED.

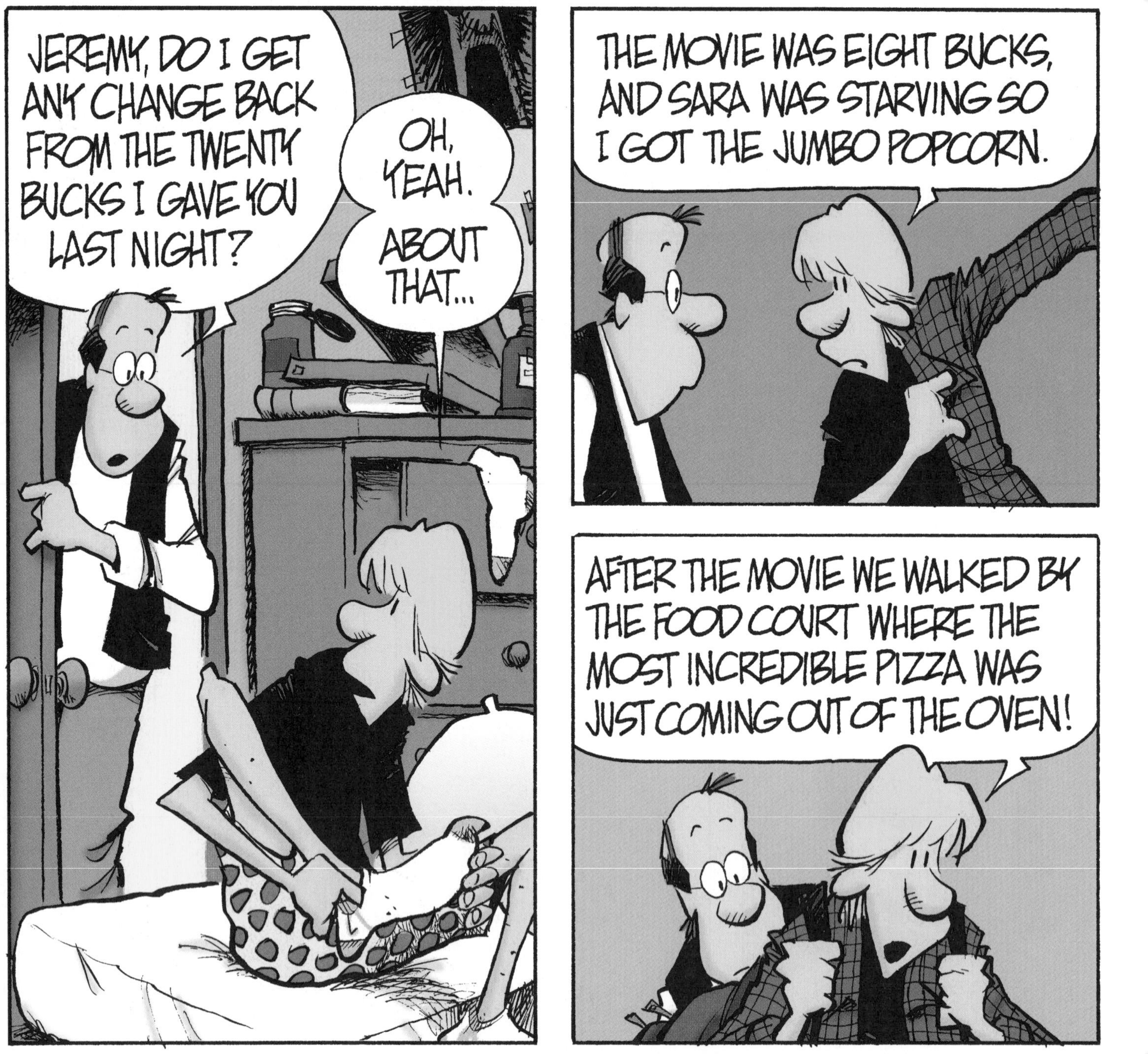
JEREMY, DO I GET ANY CHANGE BACK FROM THE TWENTY BUCKS I GAVE YOU LAST NIGHT?
OH, YEAH.
ABOUT THAT...
THE MOVIE WAS EIGHT BUCKS, AND SARA WAS STARVING SO I GOT THE JUMBO POPCORN.
AFTER THE MOVIE WE WALKED BY THE FOOD COURT WHERE THE MOST INCREDIBLE PIZZA WAS JUST COMING OUT OF THE OVEN!

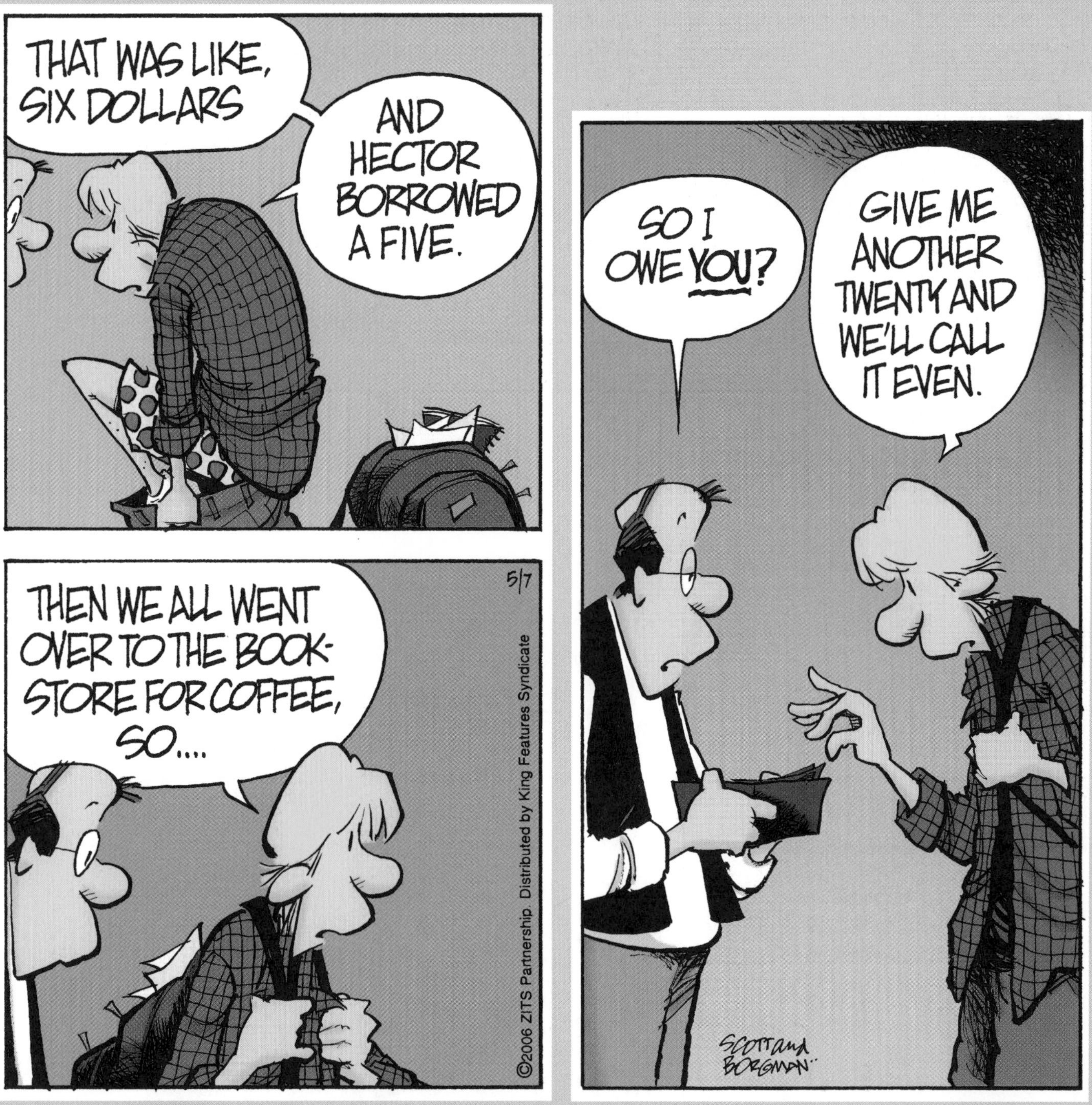
THAT WAS LIKE, SIX DOLLARS
AND HECTOR BORROWED A FIVE.
THEN WE ALL WENT OVER TO THE BOOK-STORE FOR COFFEE, SO....
5/7
©2006 ZITS Partnership. Distributed by King Features Syndicate
SO I OWE YOU?
GIVE ME ANOTHER TWENTY AND WE'LL CALL IT EVEN.
SCOTT and BORGMAN

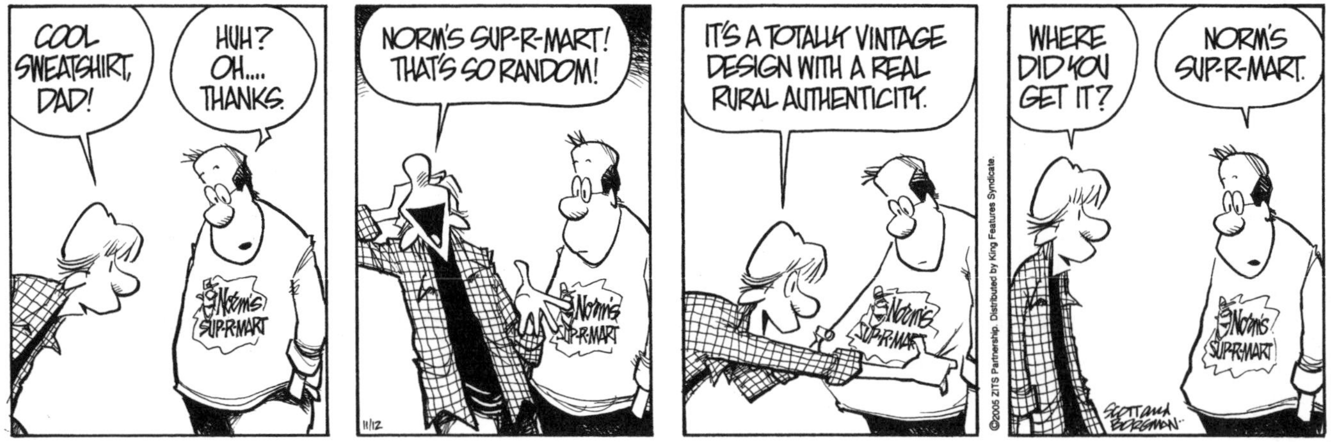
COOL SWEATSHIRT, DAD!
HUH? OH.... THANKS.
NORM'S SUP-R-MART! THAT'S SO RANDOM!
IT'S A TOTALLY VINTAGE DESIGN WITH A REAL RURAL AUTHENTICITY.
WHERE DID YOU GET IT?
NORM'S SUP-R-MART.
©2005 ZITS Partnership. Distributed by King Features Syndicate.
SCOTT AND BORGMAN

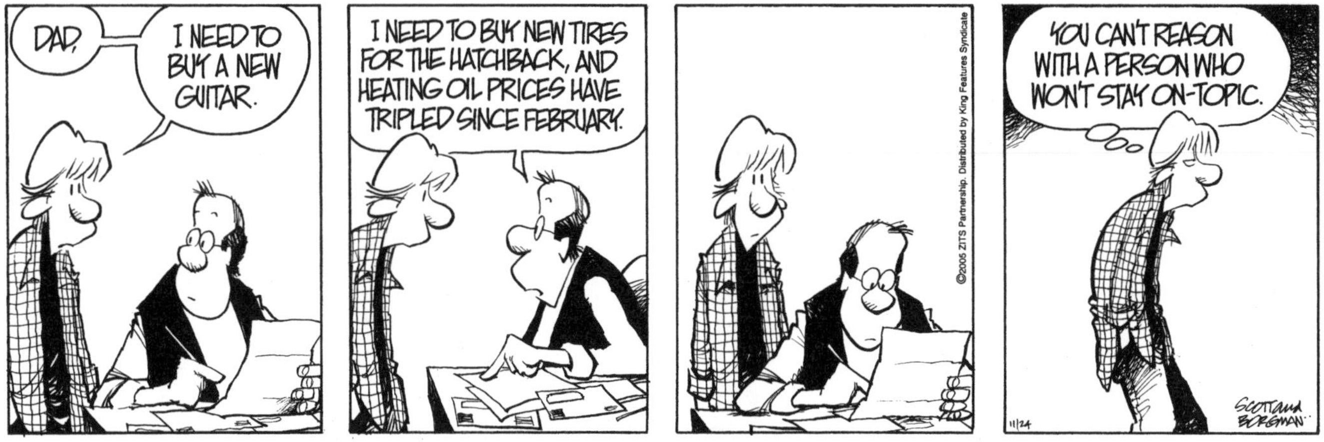
DAD,
I NEED TO BUY A NEW GUITAR.
I NEED TO BUY NEW TIRES FOR THE HATCHBACK, AND HEATING OIL PRICES HAVE TRIPLED SINCE FEBRUARY.
©2005 ZITS Partnership. Distributed by King Features Syndicate
YOU CAN'T REASON WITH A PERSON WHO WON'T STAY ON-TOPIC.
SCOTT AND BORGMAN

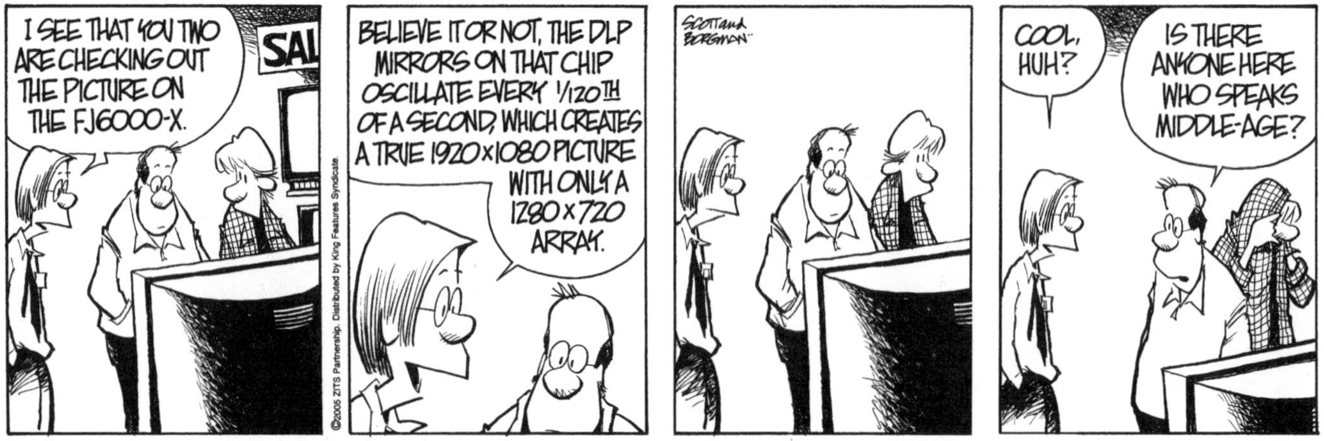
I SEE THAT YOU TWO ARE CHECKING OUT THE PICTURE ON THE FJ6000-X.
SAL
©2005 ZITS Partnership. Distributed by King Features Syndicate.
BELIEVE IT OR NOT, THE DLP MIRRORS ON THAT CHIP OSCILLATE EVERY 1/120TH OF A SECOND, WHICH CREATES A TRUE 1920 x 1080 PICTURE WITH ONLY A 1280 x 720 ARRAY.
SCOTT AND BORGMAN
COOL, HUH?
IS THERE ANYONE HERE WHO SPEAKS MIDDLE-AGE?

As the father of an almost-fifteen-year-old daughter, I want to express my immense gratitude for your Zits comic strip. I live in Maine and my daughter lives with her mother in Massachusetts. Even though the two of us get together at least monthly, as a result of the distance between us, it is sometimes difficult for us to find regular points of connection. Zits provides us an important opportunity to do just that. I have given my daughter a couple of books of Zits cartoons over the past year, and now I religiously clip the daily and Sunday strips and mail them to her every couple of weeks. They make each of us laugh independently and we subsequently laugh together over the phone about the strips that we found most amusing (often hers seem to be related to some comment made by Jeremy's all-too-square father—she can't be drawing any comparisons to me, can she?).

Once again, thank you so very much for your creative approach to dealing with the wonders of the teenage years. It isn't an overstatement to say that you are making a significant contribution to our society by enabling so many parents and teenagers to look at development and relationship issues with an injection of humor. Keep up your marvelous creations!

Sincerely,

E.B.

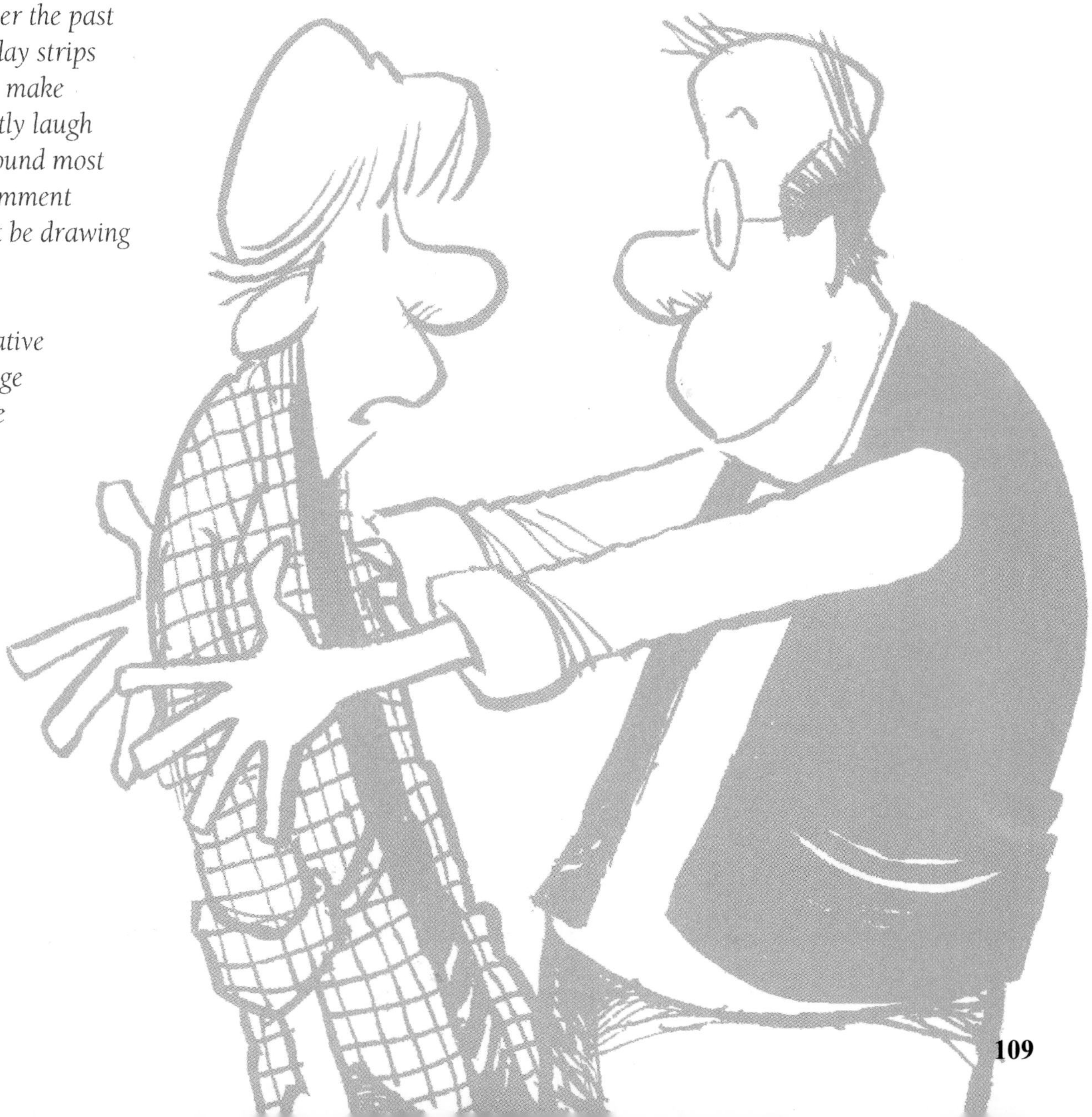

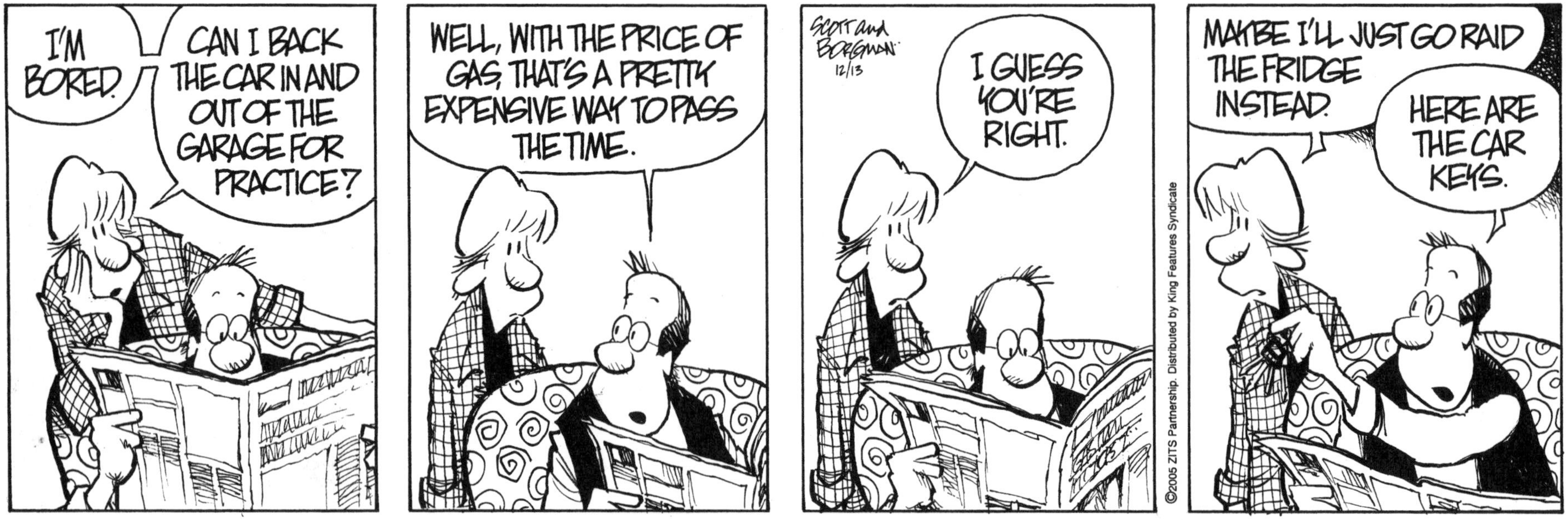
SCOTT and BORGMAN 12/13
I'M BORED.
CAN I BACK THE CAR IN AND OUT OF THE GARAGE FOR PRACTICE?
WELL, WITH THE PRICE OF GAS, THAT'S A PRETTY EXPENSIVE WAY TO PASS THE TIME.
I GUESS YOU'RE RIGHT.
MAYBE I'LL JUST GO RAID THE FRIDGE INSTEAD.
HERE ARE THE CAR KEYS.

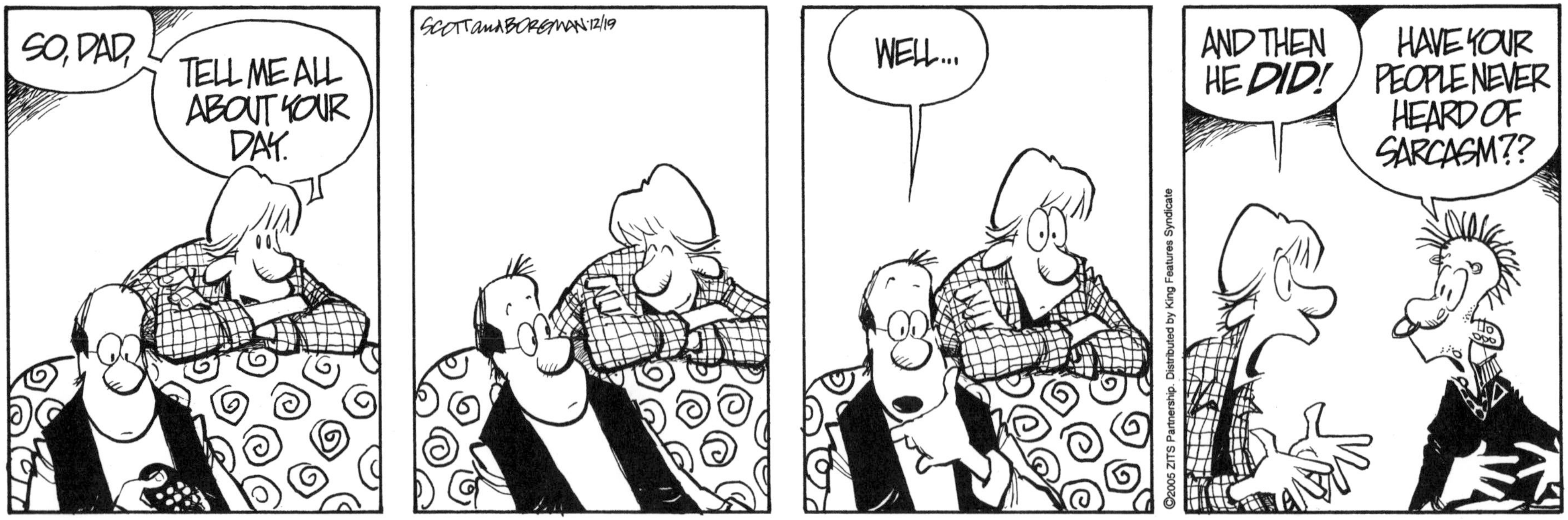
SO, DAD,
TELL ME ALL ABOUT YOUR DAY.
SCOTT and BORGMAN 12/19
WELL...
AND THEN HE *DID*!
HAVE YOUR PEOPLE NEVER HEARD OF SARCASM??

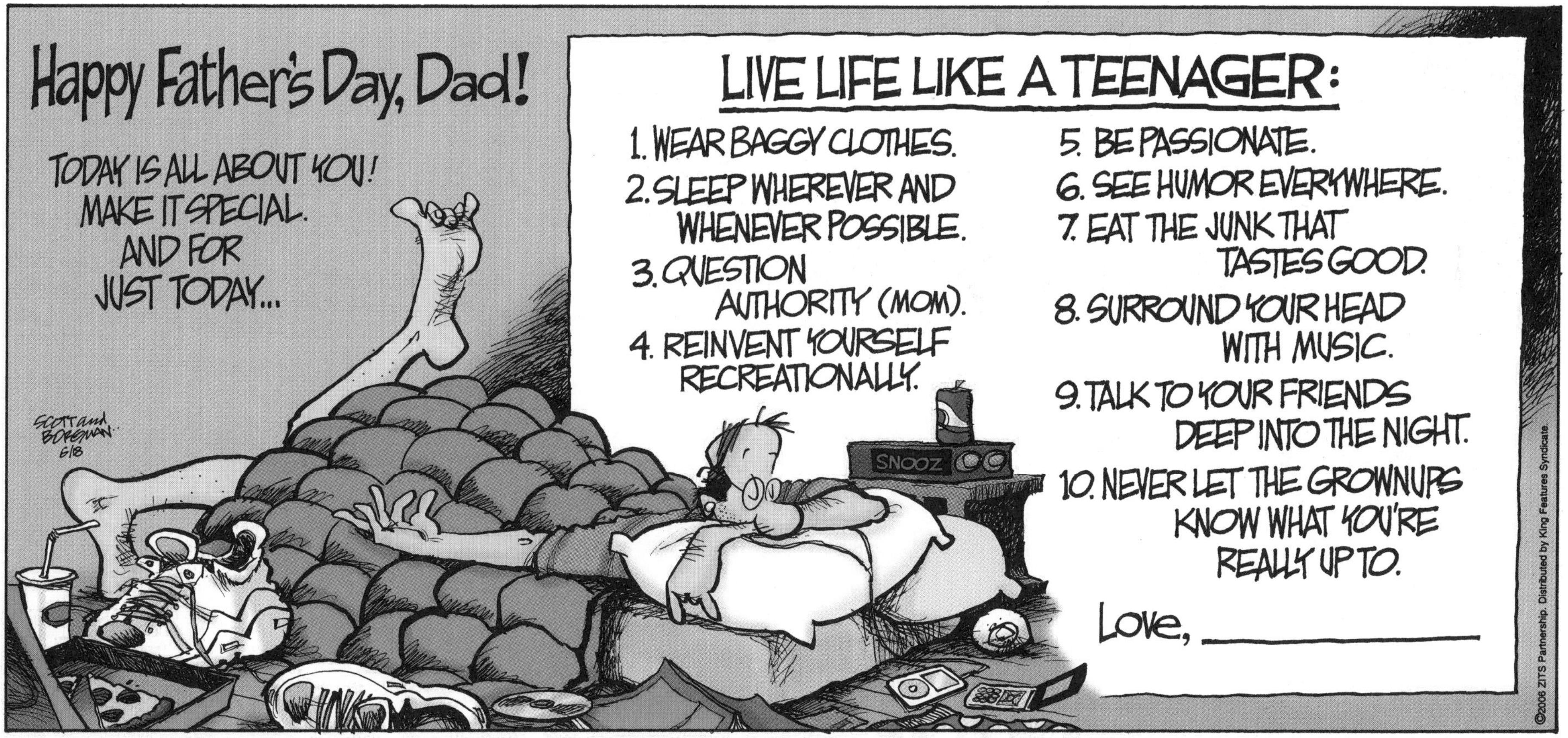
Happy Father's Day, Dad!
TODAY IS ALL ABOUT YOU! MAKE IT SPECIAL. AND FOR JUST TODAY...
LIVE LIFE LIKE A TEENAGER:
1. WEAR BAGGY CLOTHES.
2. SLEEP WHEREVER AND WHENEVER POSSIBLE.
3. QUESTION AUTHORITY (MOM).
4. REINVENT YOURSELF RECREATIONALLY.
5. BE PASSIONATE.
6. SEE HUMOR EVERYWHERE.
7. EAT THE JUNK THAT TASTES GOOD.
8. SURROUND YOUR HEAD WITH MUSIC.
9. TALK TO YOUR FRIENDS DEEP INTO THE NIGHT.
10. NEVER LET THE GROWNUPS KNOW WHAT YOU'RE REALLY UP TO.
Love, ________
SNOOZ
SCOTT and BORGMAN 6/18
©2006 ZITS Partnership. Distributed by King Features Syndicate.

Jim: Part of the problem we dads face with our sons is that, while we're civilizing them and pulling them into line, we secretly wish we were them.

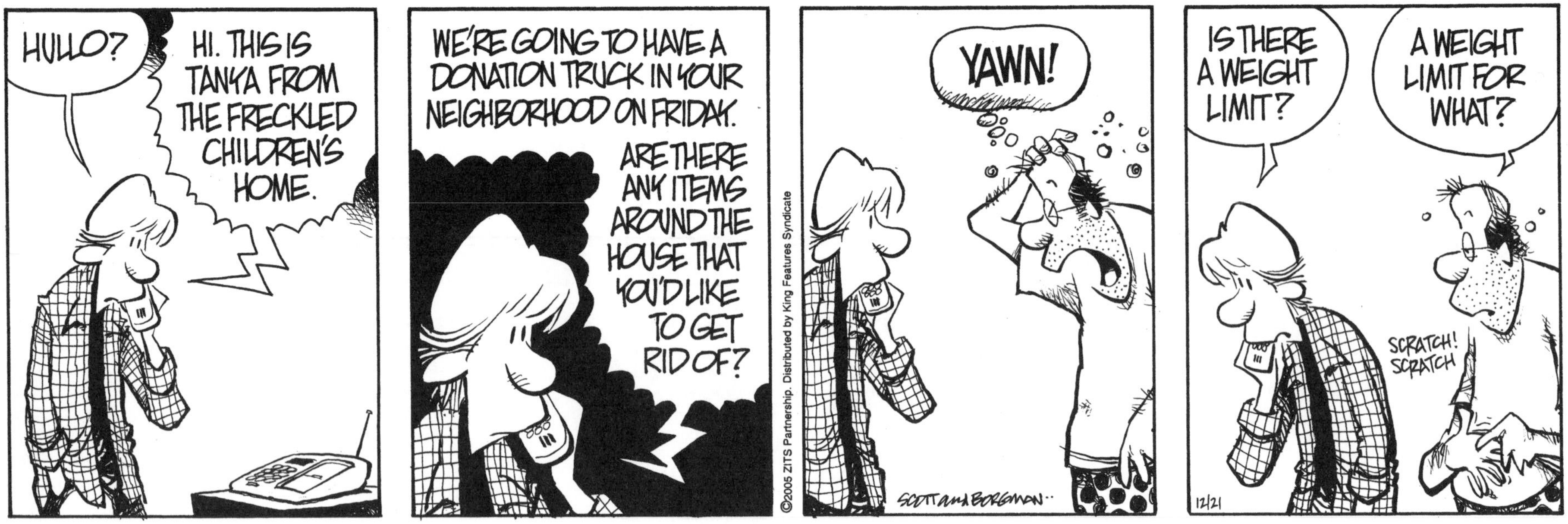
HULLO?
HI. THIS IS TANYA FROM THE FRECKLED CHILDREN'S HOME.
WE'RE GOING TO HAVE A DONATION TRUCK IN YOUR NEIGHBORHOOD ON FRIDAY.
ARE THERE ANY ITEMS AROUND THE HOUSE THAT YOU'D LIKE TO GET RID OF?
©2005 ZITS Partnership. Distributed by King Features Syndicate
YAWN!
SCOTT and BORGMAN
IS THERE A WEIGHT LIMIT?
A WEIGHT LIMIT FOR WHAT?
SCRATCH! SCRATCH
12/21

Jerry: Speaking as a former Freckled Child, I urge you to donate the next time our organization calls.

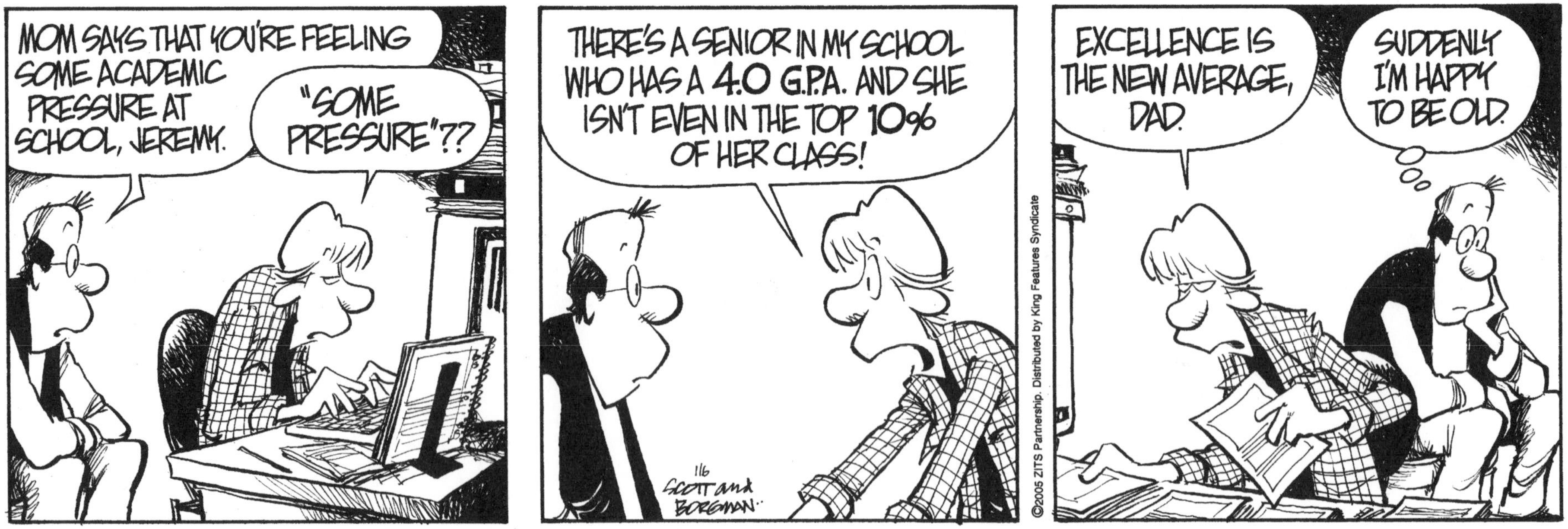
MOM SAYS THAT YOU'RE FEELING SOME ACADEMIC PRESSURE AT SCHOOL, JEREMY.
"SOME PRESSURE"??
THERE'S A SENIOR IN MY SCHOOL WHO HAS A 4.0 G.P.A. AND SHE ISN'T EVEN IN THE TOP 10% OF HER CLASS!
1/6
SCOTT and BORGMAN
©2005 ZITS Partnership. Distributed by King Features Syndicate
EXCELLENCE IS THE NEW AVERAGE, DAD.
SUDDENLY I'M HAPPY TO BE OLD.

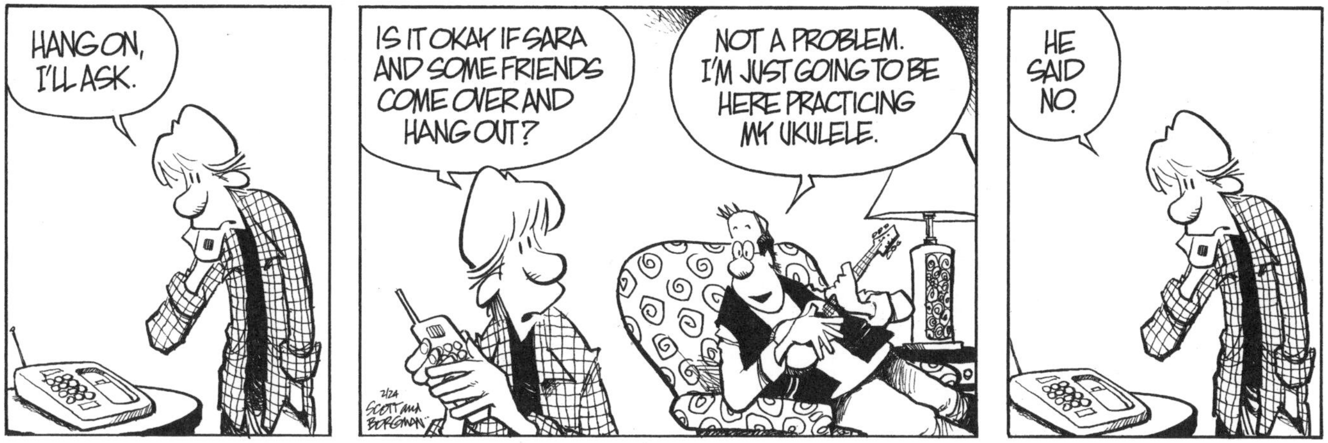
HANG ON, I'LL ASK.
IS IT OKAY IF SARA AND SOME FRIENDS COME OVER AND HANG OUT?
NOT A PROBLEM. I'M JUST GOING TO BE HERE PRACTICING MY UKULELE.
HE SAID NO.

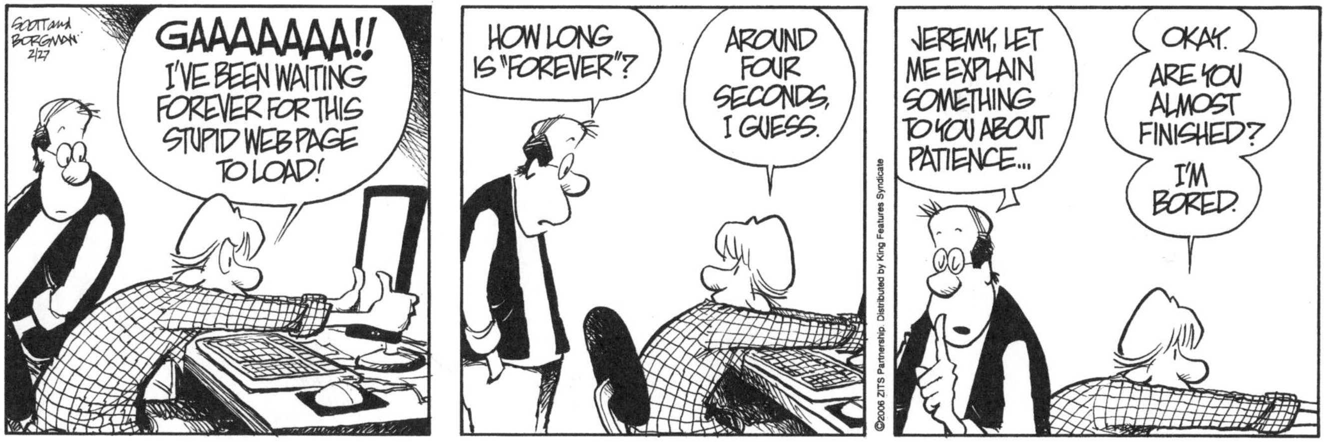
GAAAAAAA!! I'VE BEEN WAITING FOREVER FOR THIS STUPID WEB PAGE TO LOAD!
HOW LONG IS "FOREVER"?
AROUND FOUR SECONDS, I GUESS.
©2006 ZITS Partnership. Distributed by King Features Syndicate
JEREMY, LET ME EXPLAIN SOMETHING TO YOU ABOUT PATIENCE...
OKAY. ARE YOU ALMOST FINISHED?
I'M BORED.

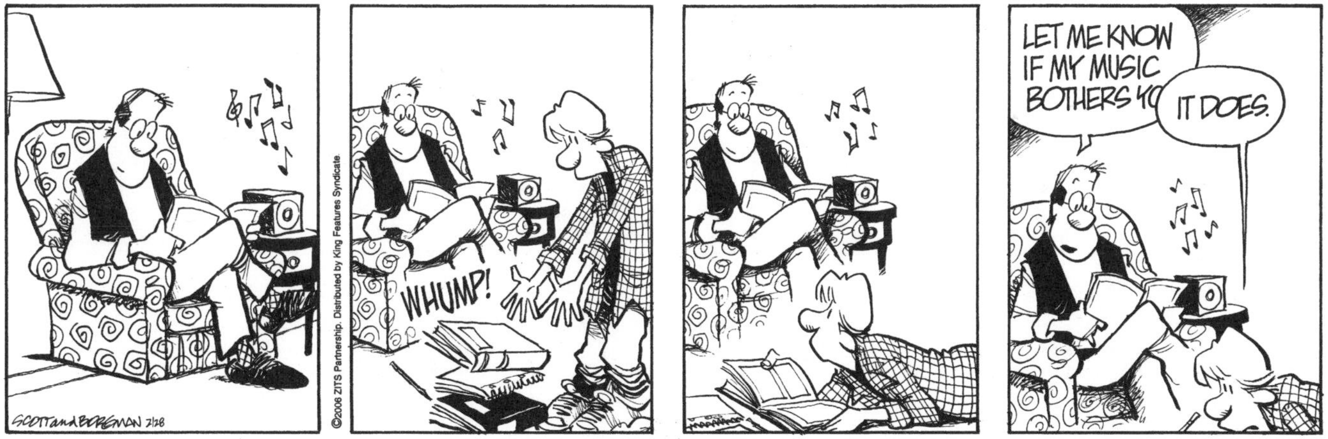
©2006 ZITS Partnership. Distributed by King Features Syndicate.
WHUMP!
LET ME KNOW IF MY MUSIC BOTHERS YO
IT DOES.

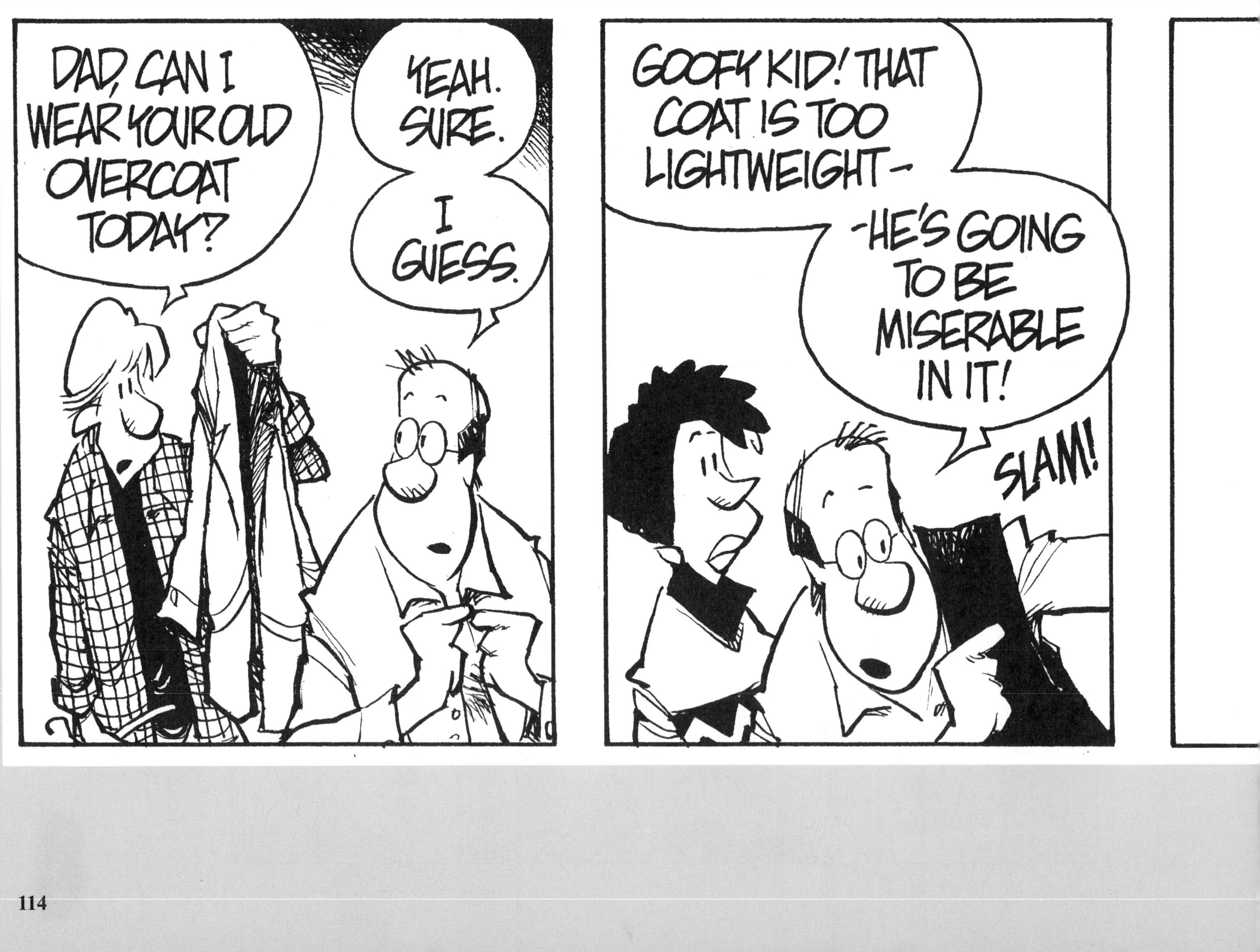
DAD, CAN I WEAR YOUR OLD OVERCOAT TODAY?
YEAH. SURE.
I GUESS.
GOOFY KID! THAT COAT IS TOO LIGHTWEIGHT-
-HE'S GOING TO BE MISERABLE IN IT!
SLAM!

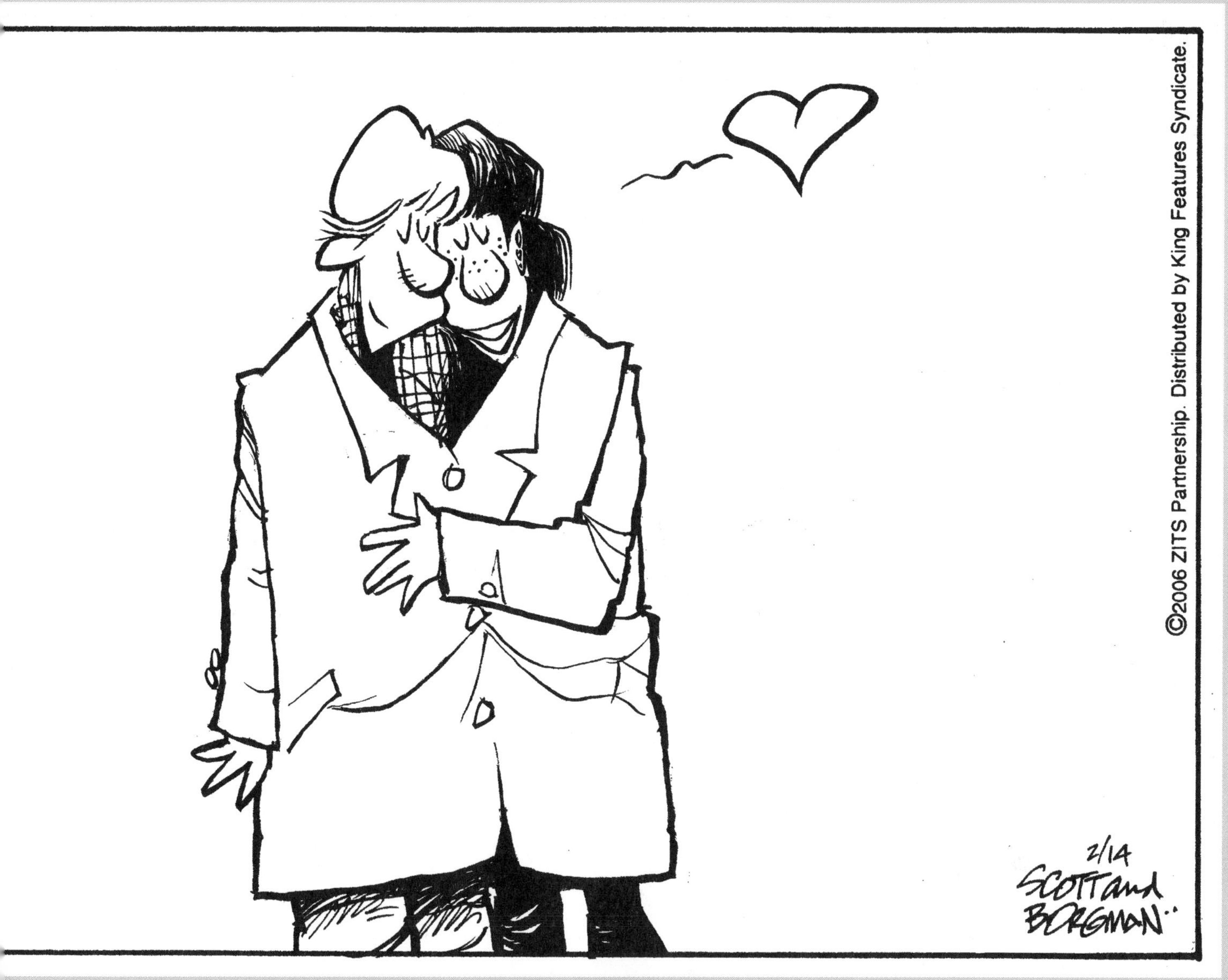
©2006 ZITS Partnership. Distributed by King Features Syndicate.
2/14
SCOTT and BORGMAN

Jim: I couldn't help thinking of David Byrne in that huge Talking Heads suit as I drew this.

Jim: I never consciously decided to give Jeremy more hair or Dad less as *Zits* has developed over the years, so sometimes it even surprises me. Look at that little sprig shooting up in the air! We've shown the young, fully Afroed Walt several times over the years.

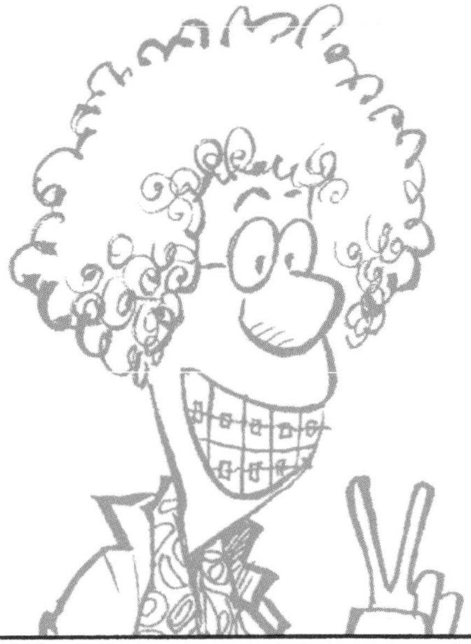

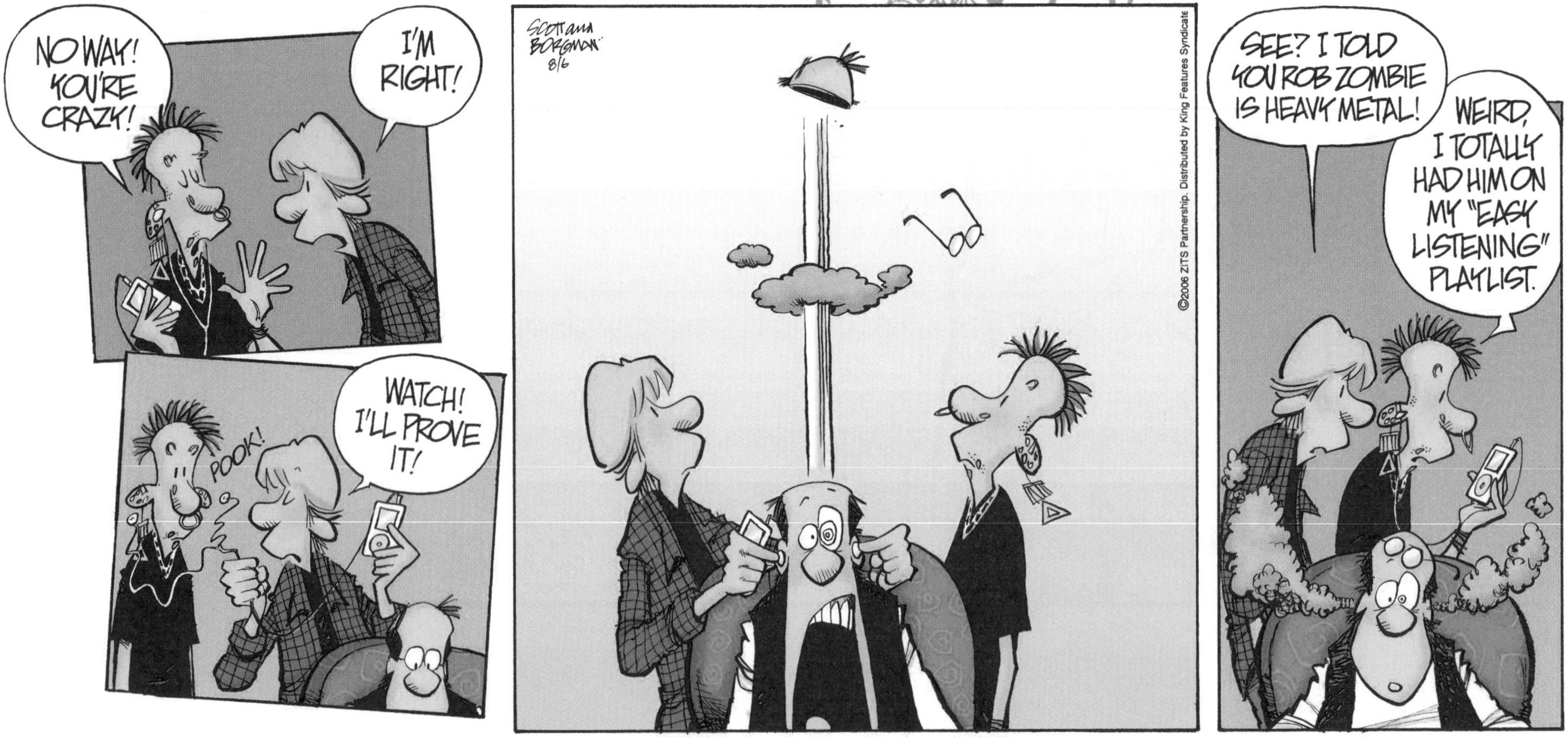

NO WAY! YOU'RE CRAZY!
I'M RIGHT!
POOK!
WATCH! I'LL PROVE IT!
©2006 ZITS Partnership. Distributed by King Features Syndicate
SEE? I TOLD YOU ROB ZOMBIE IS HEAVY METAL!
WEIRD, I TOTALLY HAD HIM ON MY "EASY LISTENING" PLAYLIST.

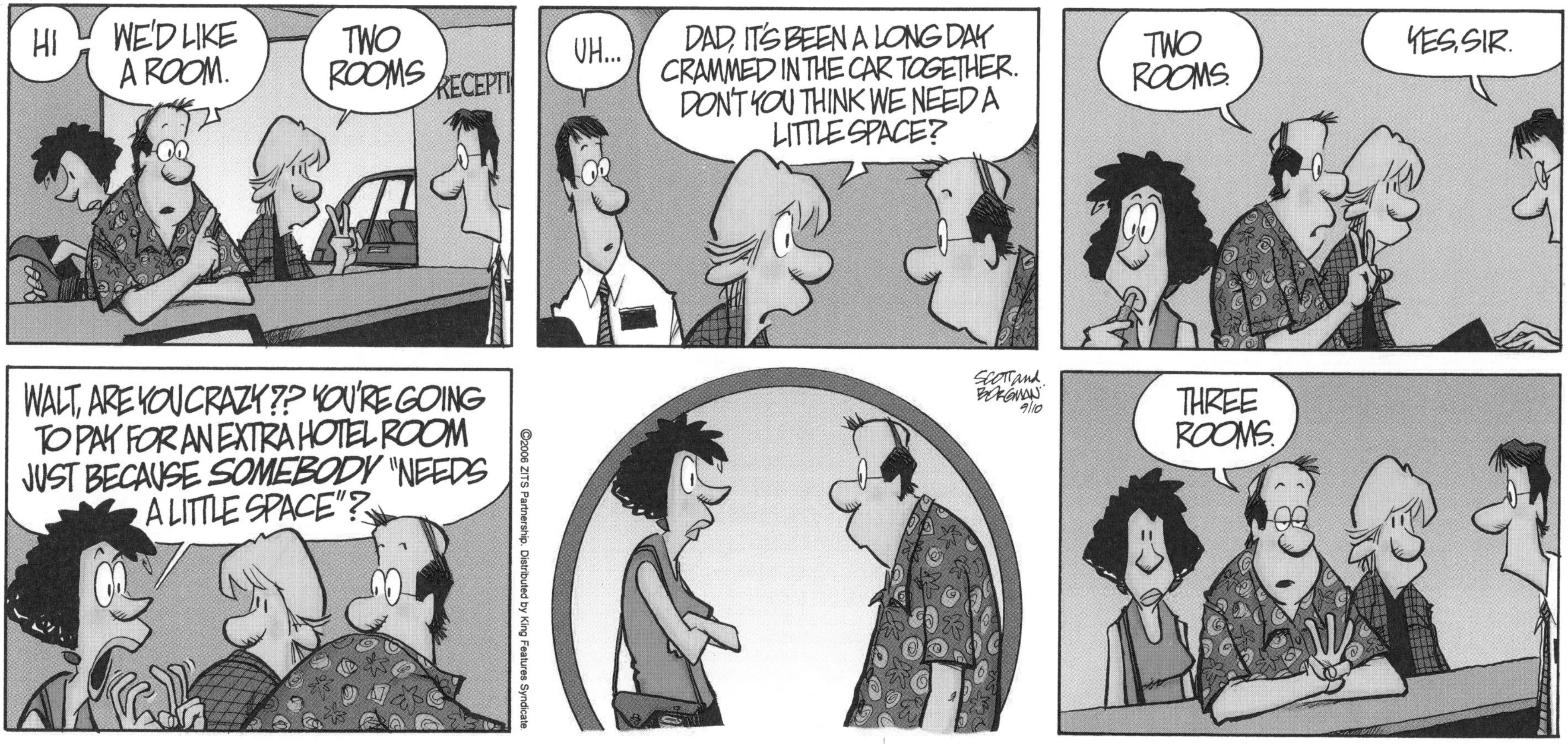
HI
WE'D LIKE A ROOM.
TWO ROOMS
RECEPTI
UH...
DAD, IT'S BEEN A LONG DAY CRAMMED IN THE CAR TOGETHER. DON'T YOU THINK WE NEED A LITTLE SPACE?
TWO ROOMS.
YES, SIR.
WALT, ARE YOU CRAZY?? YOU'RE GOING TO PAY FOR AN EXTRA HOTEL ROOM JUST BECAUSE *SOMEBODY* "NEEDS A LITTLE SPACE"?
©2006 ZITS Partnership. Distributed by King Features Syndicate
SCOTT and BORGMAN 9/10
THREE ROOMS.

Jerry: Somewhere around the third or fourth day on the road with a teenager, the term "family vacation" becomes an oxymoron.

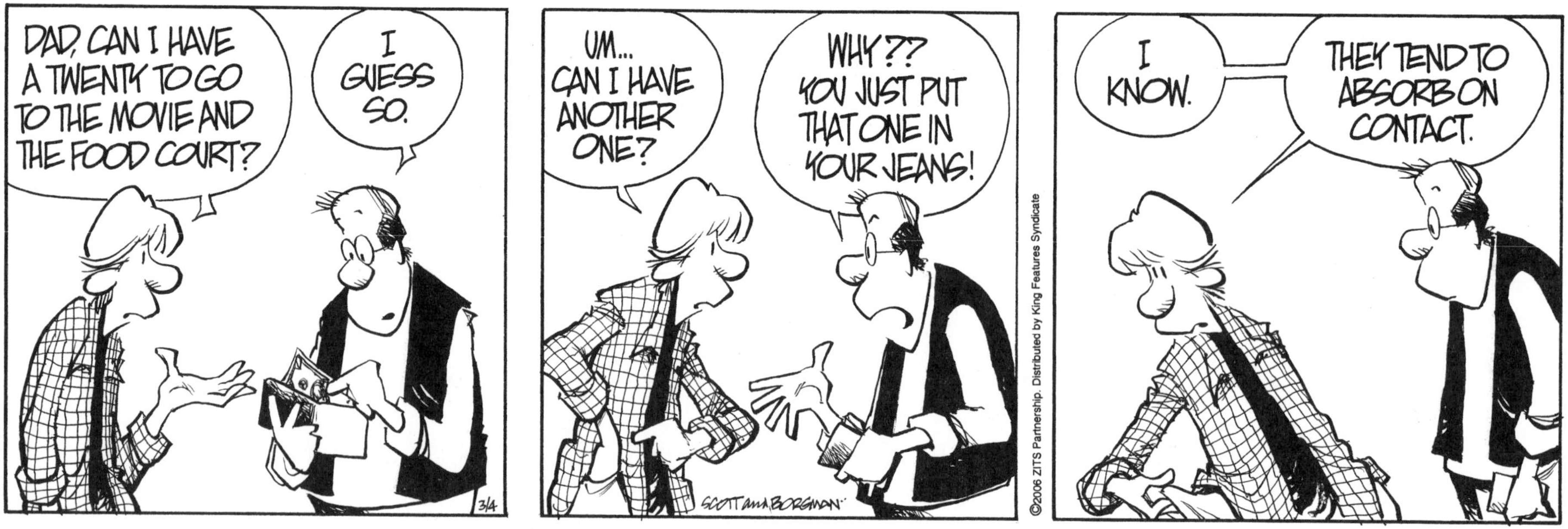
DAD, CAN I HAVE A TWENTY TO GO TO THE MOVIE AND THE FOOD COURT?
I GUESS SO.
UM... CAN I HAVE ANOTHER ONE?
WHY?? YOU JUST PUT THAT ONE IN YOUR JEANS!
I KNOW.
THEY TEND TO ABSORB ON CONTACT.
3/4
SCOTT and BORGMAN
©2006 ZITS Partnership. Distributed by King Features Syndicate

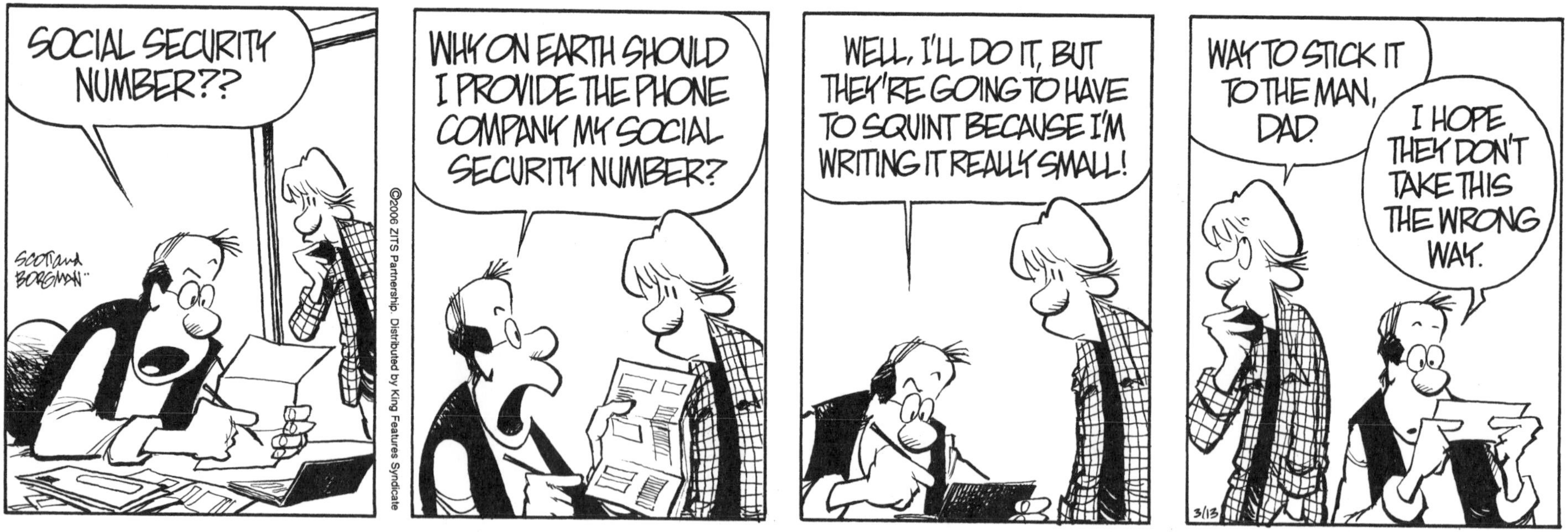
SOCIAL SECURITY NUMBER??
SCOTT and BORGMAN
©2006 ZITS Partnership. Distributed by King Features Syndicate
WHY ON EARTH SHOULD I PROVIDE THE PHONE COMPANY MY SOCIAL SECURITY NUMBER?
WELL, I'LL DO IT, BUT THEY'RE GOING TO HAVE TO SQUINT BECAUSE I'M WRITING IT REALLY SMALL!
WAY TO STICK IT TO THE MAN, DAD.
I HOPE THEY DON'T TAKE THIS THE WRONG WAY.
3/13

Jerry: Around my house, I'm known for wild outbursts of individualism like this one from Dad. My teenage daughter calls me "maverick." Then she always snickers.

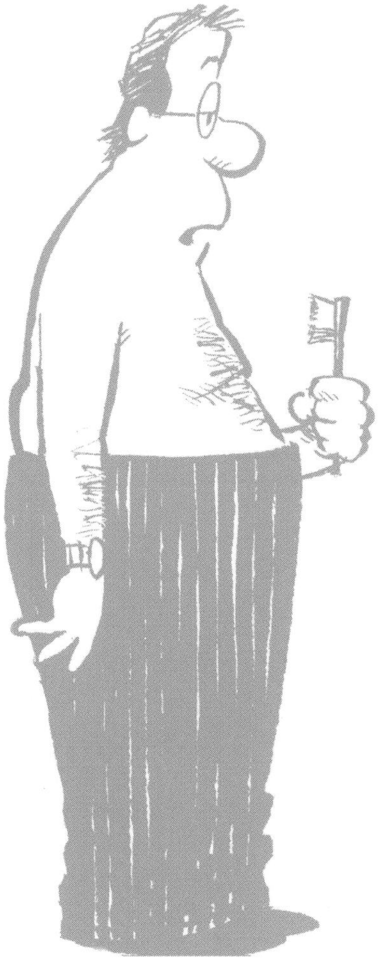

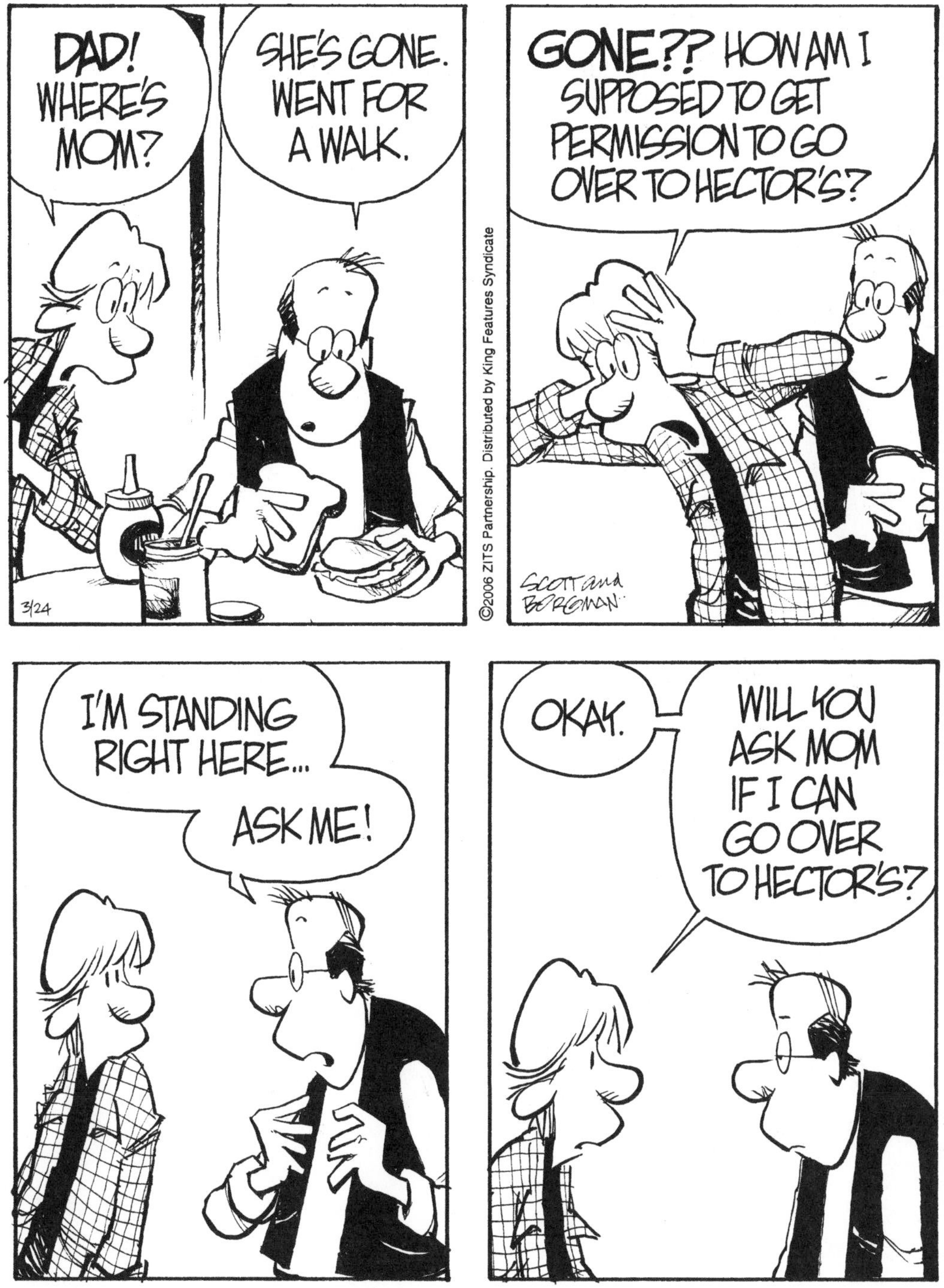
DAD! WHERE'S MOM?
SHE'S GONE. WENT FOR A WALK.
3/24
GONE?? HOW AM I SUPPOSED TO GET PERMISSION TO GO OVER TO HECTOR'S?
SCOTT and BORGMAN
I'M STANDING RIGHT HERE...
ASK ME!
OKAY.
WILL YOU ASK MOM IF I CAN GO OVER TO HECTOR'S?

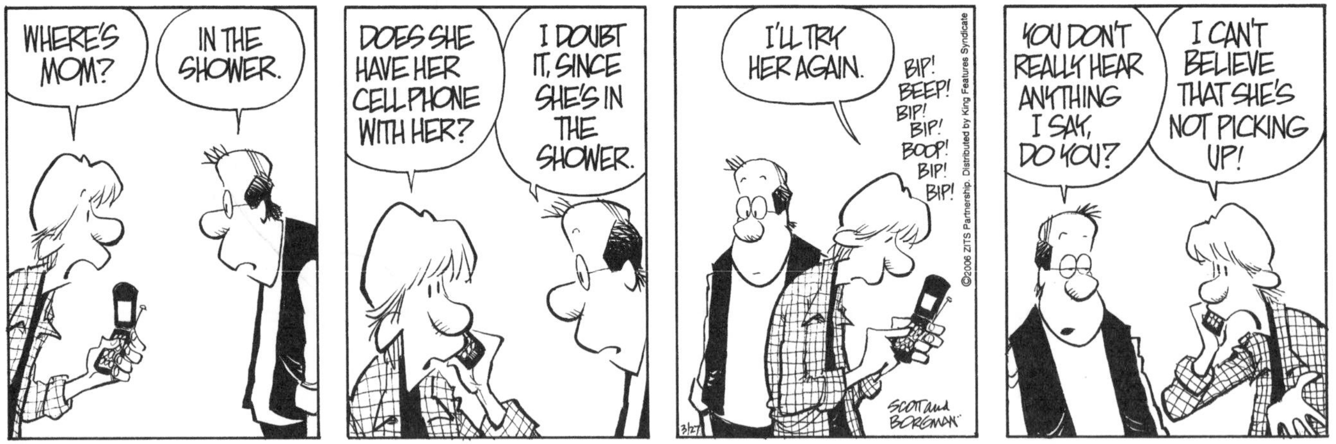
WHERE'S MOM?
IN THE SHOWER.
DOES SHE HAVE HER CELL PHONE WITH HER?
I DOUBT IT, SINCE SHE'S IN THE SHOWER.
I'LL TRY HER AGAIN.
BIP! BEEP! BIP! BIP! BOOP! BIP! BIP!
YOU DON'T REALLY HEAR ANYTHING I SAY, DO YOU?
I CAN'T BELIEVE THAT SHE'S NOT PICKING UP!
©2006 ZITS Partnership. Distributed by King Features Syndicate
SCOTT and BORGMAN
3/27

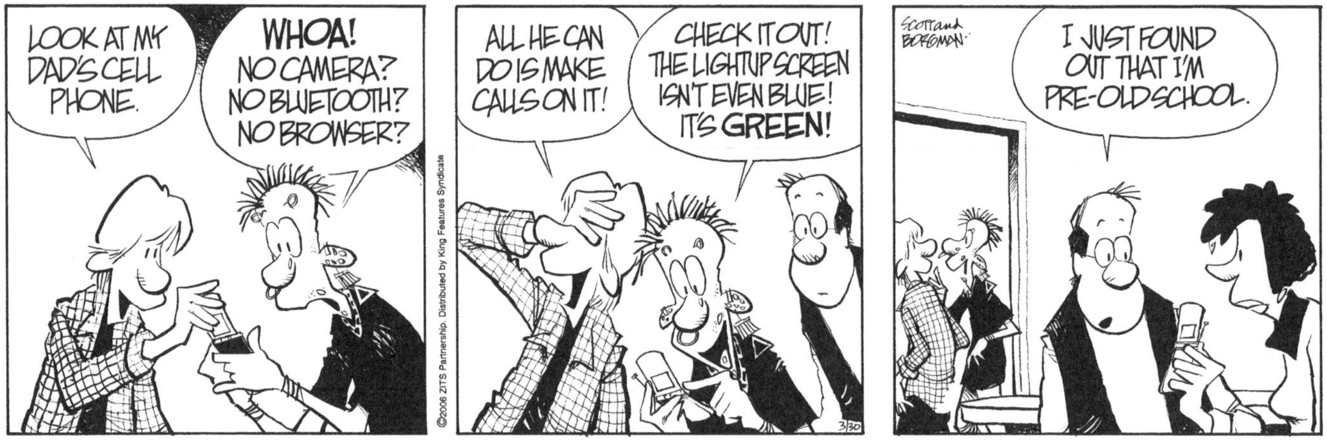
LOOK AT MY DAD'S CELL PHONE.
WHOA! NO CAMERA? NO BLUETOOTH? NO BROWSER?
©2006 ZITS Partnership. Distributed by King Features Syndicate
ALL HE CAN DO IS MAKE CALLS ON IT!
CHECK IT OUT! THE LIGHTUP SCREEN ISN'T EVEN BLUE! IT'S **GREEN!**
3/30
SCOTT and BORGMAN
I JUST FOUND OUT THAT I'M PRE-OLD SCHOOL.

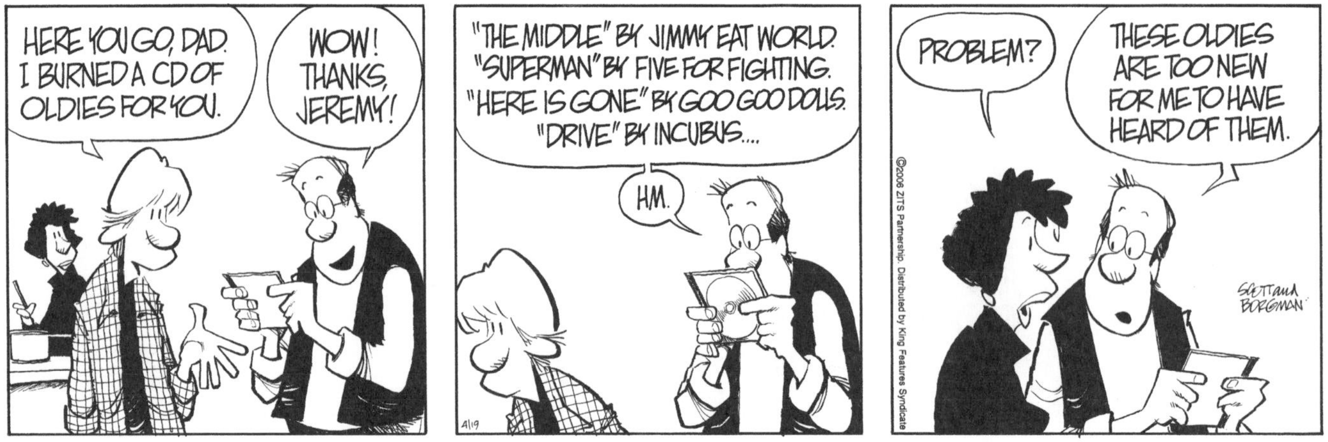
HERE YOU GO, DAD. I BURNED A CD OF OLDIES FOR YOU.
WOW! THANKS, JEREMY!
"THE MIDDLE" BY JIMMY EAT WORLD. "SUPERMAN" BY FIVE FOR FIGHTING. "HERE IS GONE" BY GOO GOO DOLLS. "DRIVE" BY INCUBUS....
HM.
4/19
©2006 ZITS Partnership. Distributed by King Features Syndicate
PROBLEM?
THESE OLDIES ARE TOO NEW FOR ME TO HAVE HEARD OF THEM.
SCOTT and BORGMAN

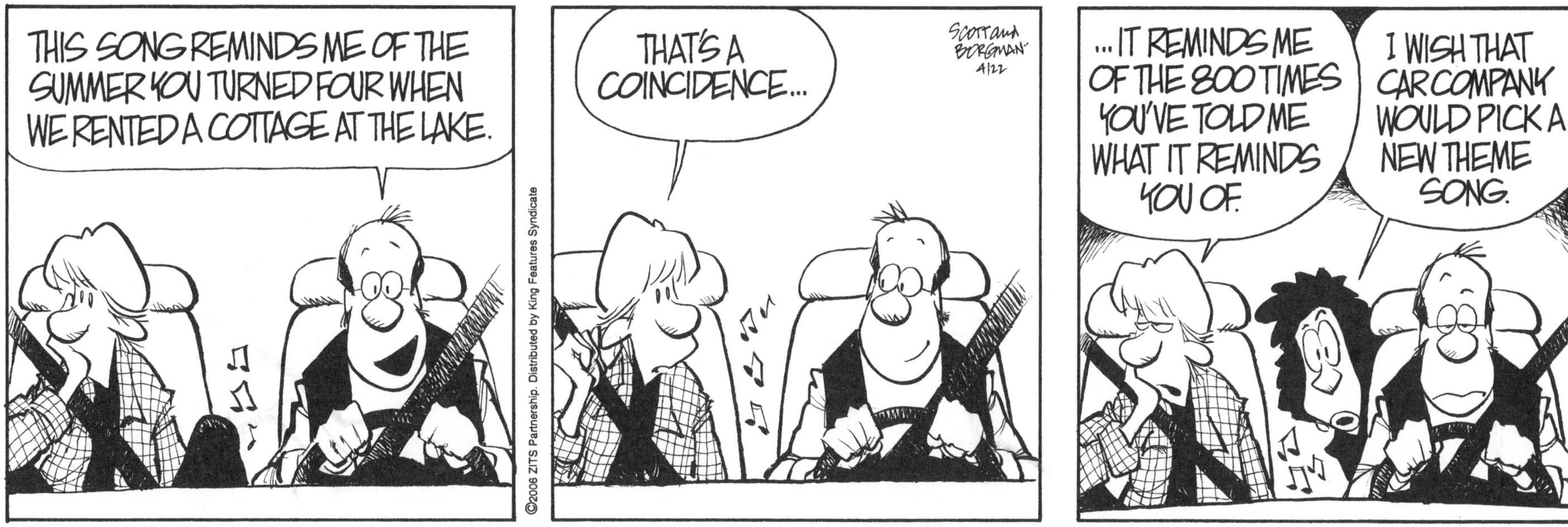
THIS SONG REMINDS ME OF THE SUMMER YOU TURNED FOUR WHEN WE RENTED A COTTAGE AT THE LAKE.
©2006 ZITS Partnership. Distributed by King Features Syndicate
THAT'S A COINCIDENCE...
SCOTT and BORGMAN 4/22
...IT REMINDS ME OF THE 800 TIMES YOU'VE TOLD ME WHAT IT REMINDS YOU OF.
I WISH THAT CAR COMPANY WOULD PICK A NEW THEME SONG.

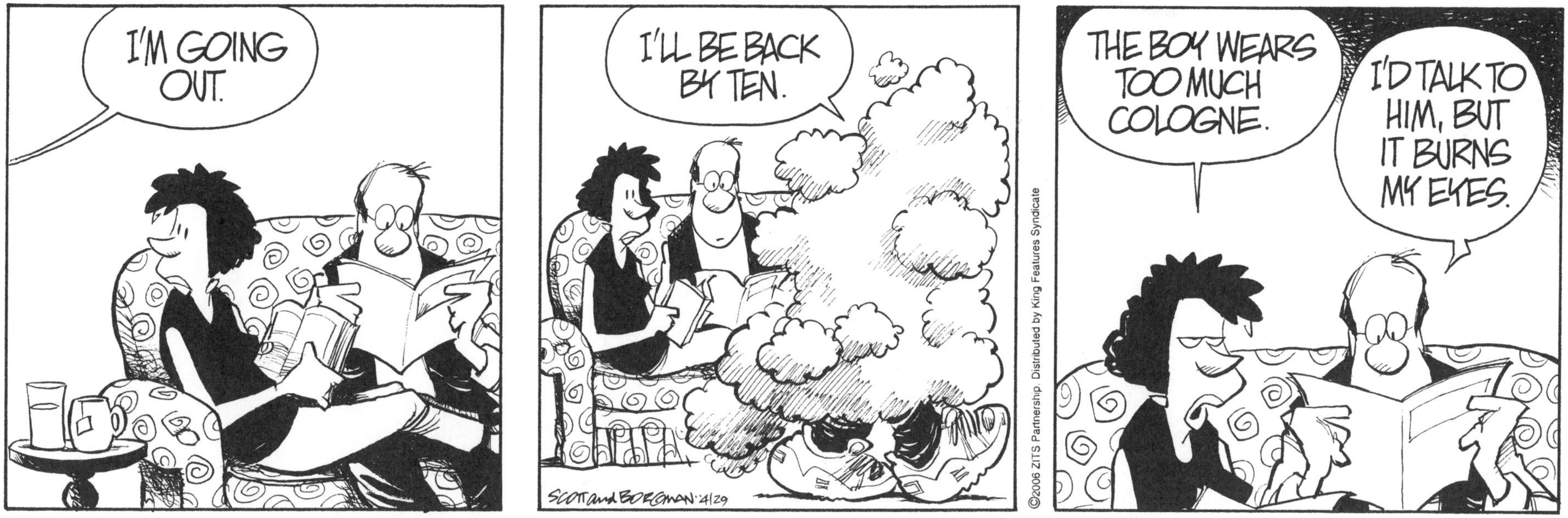
I'M GOING OUT.
I'LL BE BACK BY TEN.
SCOTT and BORGMAN 4/29
©2006 ZITS Partnership. Distributed by King Features Syndicate
THE BOY WEARS TOO MUCH COLOGNE.
I'D TALK TO HIM, BUT IT BURNS MY EYES.

Jim: Toxicologists must surely have coined the term "Axe-poisoning" by now.

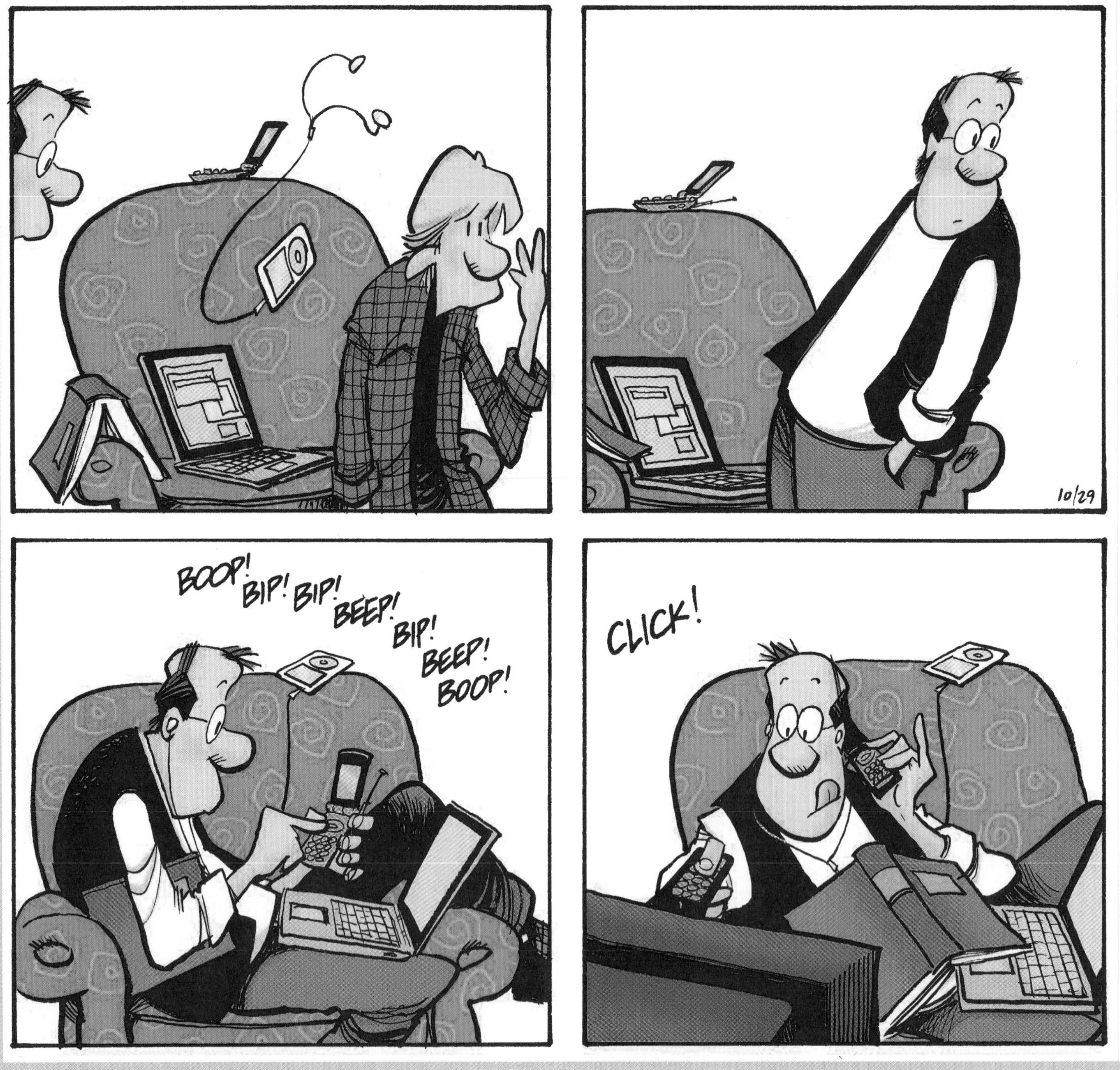
10/29
BOOP! BIP! BIP! BEEP! BIP! BEEP! BOOP!
CLICK!

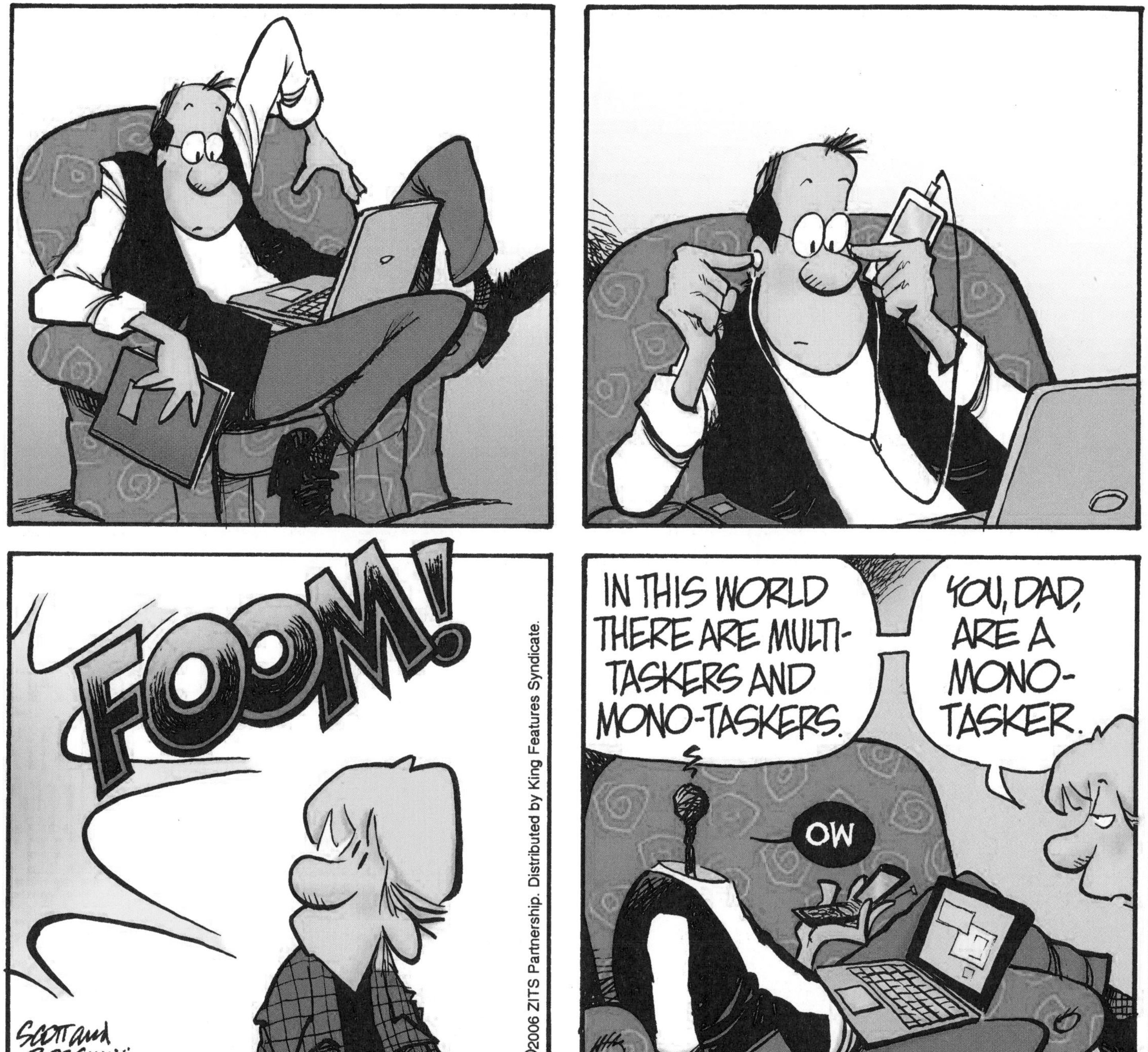
FOOM!
SCOTT and BORGMAN
©2006 ZITS Partnership. Distributed by King Features Syndicate.
IN THIS WORLD THERE ARE MULTI-TASKERS AND MONO-TASKERS.
YOU, DAD, ARE A MONO-TASKER.
OW

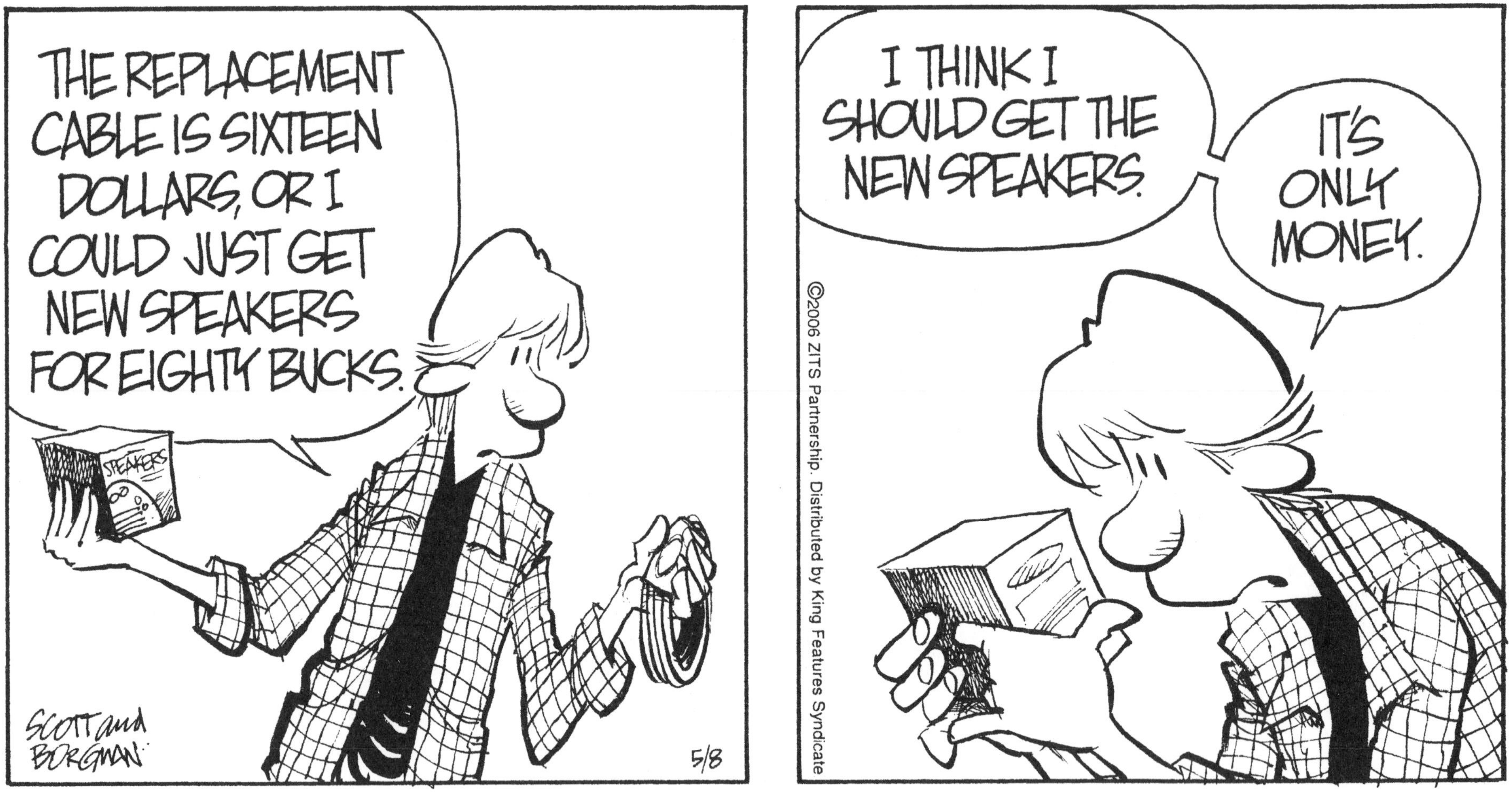
THE REPLACEMENT CABLE IS SIXTEEN DOLLARS, OR I COULD JUST GET NEW SPEAKERS FOR EIGHTY BUCKS.
SPEAKERS
SCOTT and BORGMAN
5/8
I THINK I SHOULD GET THE NEW SPEAKERS.
IT'S ONLY MONEY.
©2006 ZITS Partnership. Distributed by King Features Syndicate

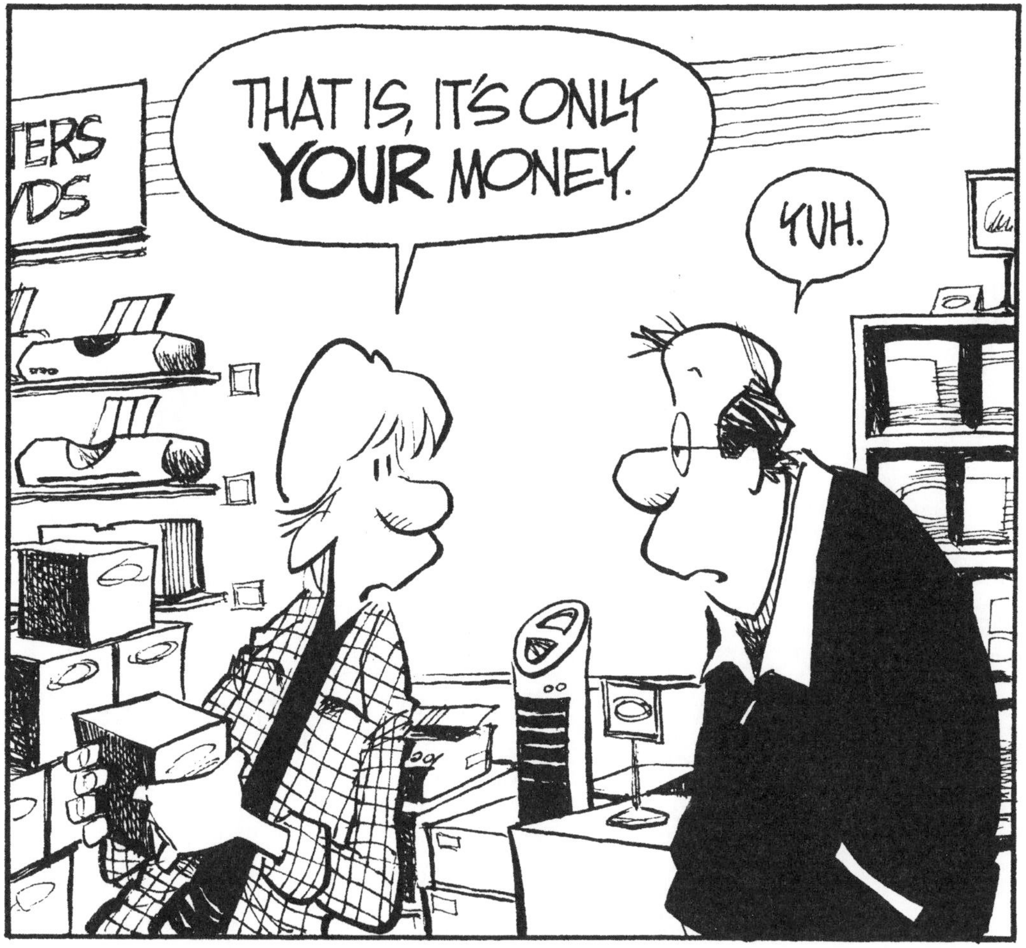
THAT IS, IT'S ONLY **YOUR** MONEY.
YUH.

Jim: Why doesn't someone make a sweatshirt for dads with a photo of a big ATM console on the back?

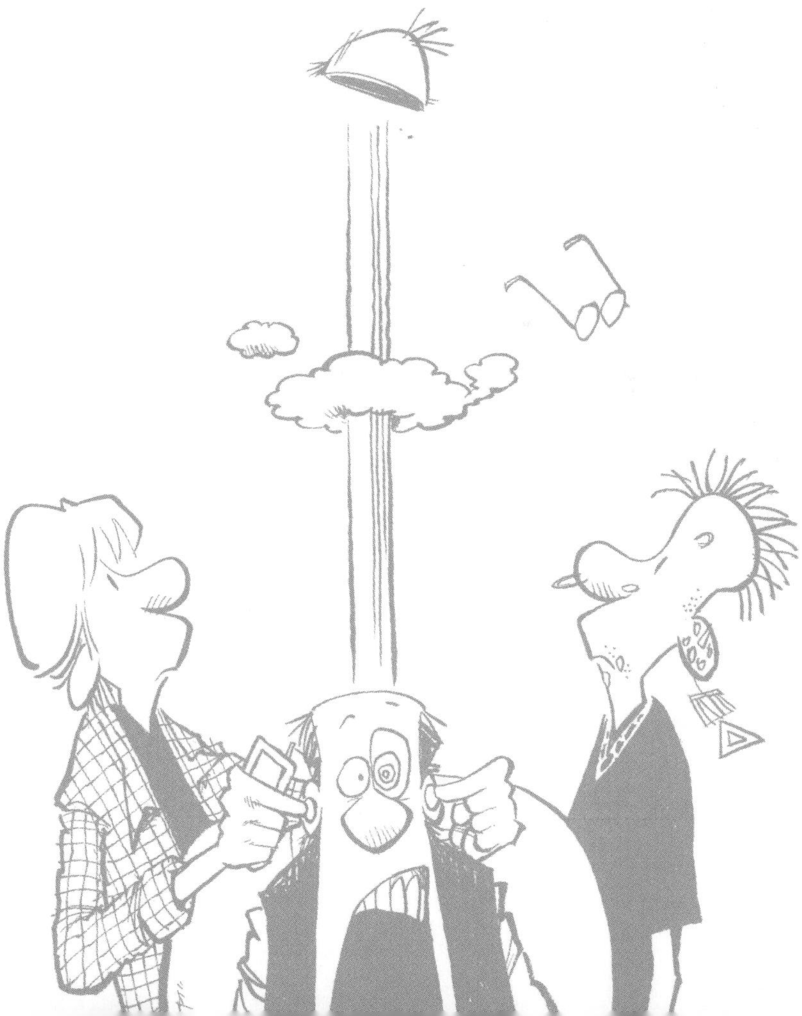

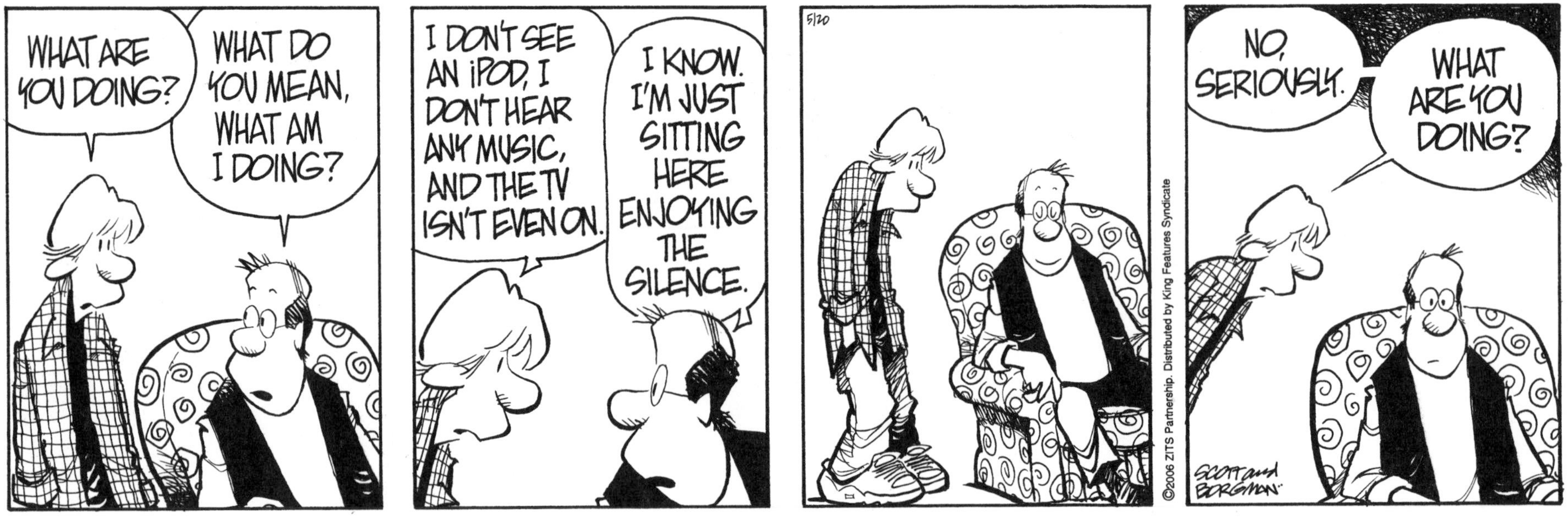
WHAT ARE YOU DOING?
WHAT DO YOU MEAN, WHAT AM I DOING?
I DON'T SEE AN iPOD, I DON'T HEAR ANY MUSIC, AND THE TV ISN'T EVEN ON.
I KNOW. I'M JUST SITTING HERE ENJOYING THE SILENCE.
5/20
©2006 ZITS Partnership. Distributed by King Features Syndicate
NO, SERIOUSLY.
WHAT ARE YOU DOING?
SCOTT and BORGMAN

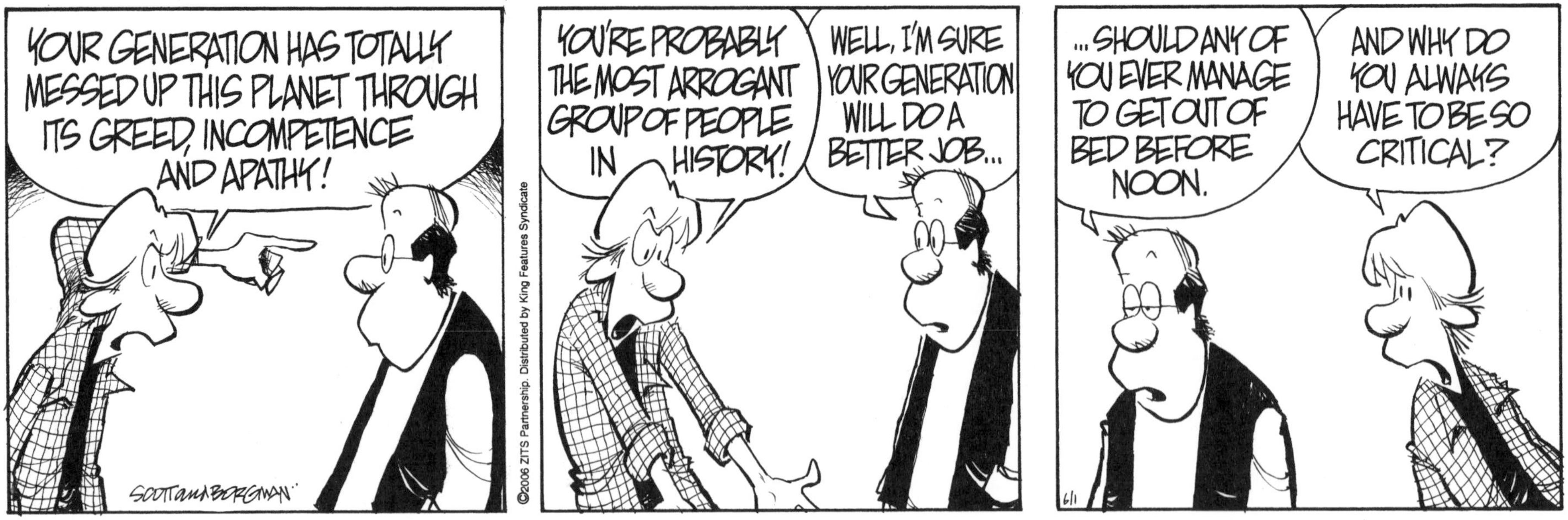
YOUR GENERATION HAS TOTALLY MESSED UP THIS PLANET THROUGH ITS GREED, INCOMPETENCE AND APATHY!
SCOTT and BORGMAN
©2006 ZITS Partnership. Distributed by King Features Syndicate
YOU'RE PROBABLY THE MOST ARROGANT GROUP OF PEOPLE IN HISTORY!
WELL, I'M SURE YOUR GENERATION WILL DO A BETTER JOB...
...SHOULD ANY OF YOU EVER MANAGE TO GET OUT OF BED BEFORE NOON.
AND WHY DO YOU ALWAYS HAVE TO BE SO CRITICAL?
6/1

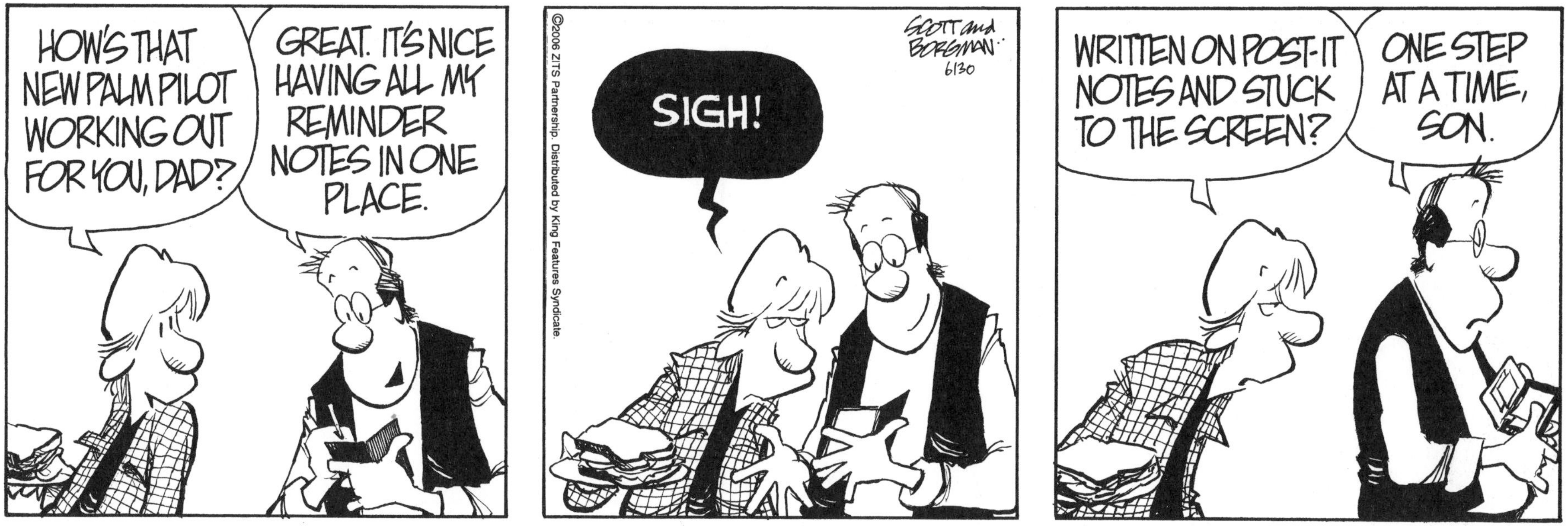
HOW'S THAT NEW PALM PILOT WORKING OUT FOR YOU, DAD?
GREAT. IT'S NICE HAVING ALL MY REMINDER NOTES IN ONE PLACE.
©2006 ZITS Partnership. Distributed by King Features Syndicate.
SCOTT and BORGMAN 6/30
SIGH!
WRITTEN ON POST-IT NOTES AND STUCK TO THE SCREEN?
ONE STEP AT A TIME, SON.

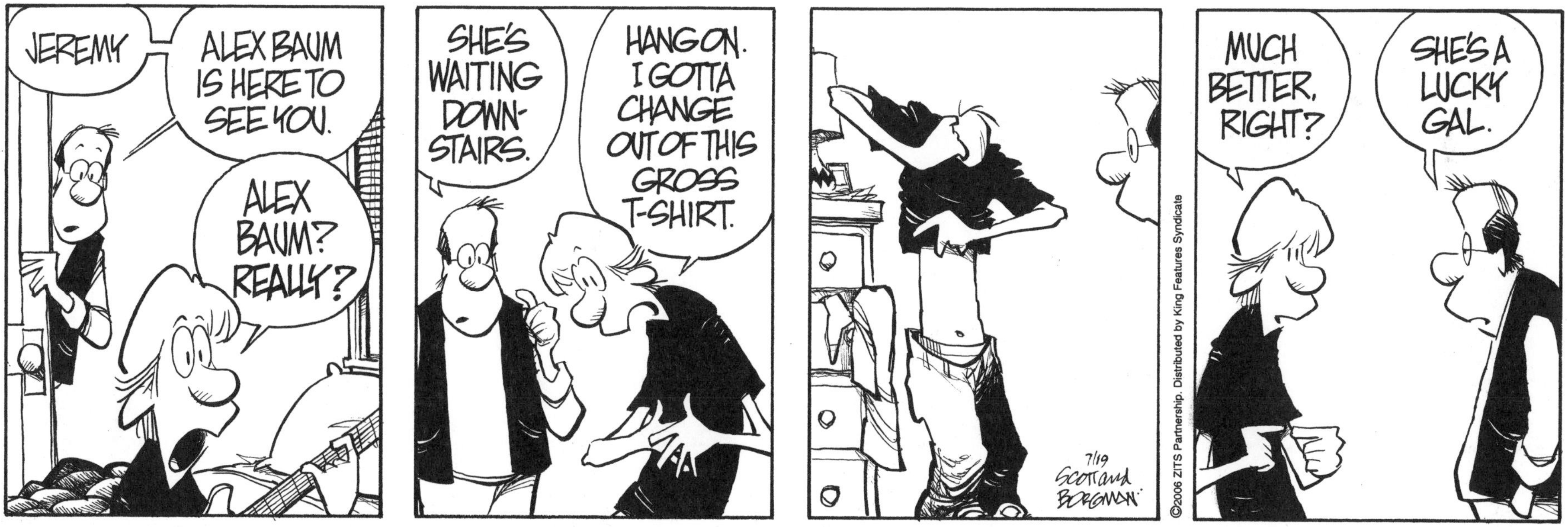
JEREMY
ALEX BAUM IS HERE TO SEE YOU.
ALEX BAUM? REALLY?
SHE'S WAITING DOWN-STAIRS.
HANG ON. I GOTTA CHANGE OUT OF THIS GROSS T-SHIRT.
7/19 SCOTT and BORGMAN
©2006 ZITS Partnership. Distributed by King Features Syndicate
MUCH BETTER, RIGHT?
SHE'S A LUCKY GAL.

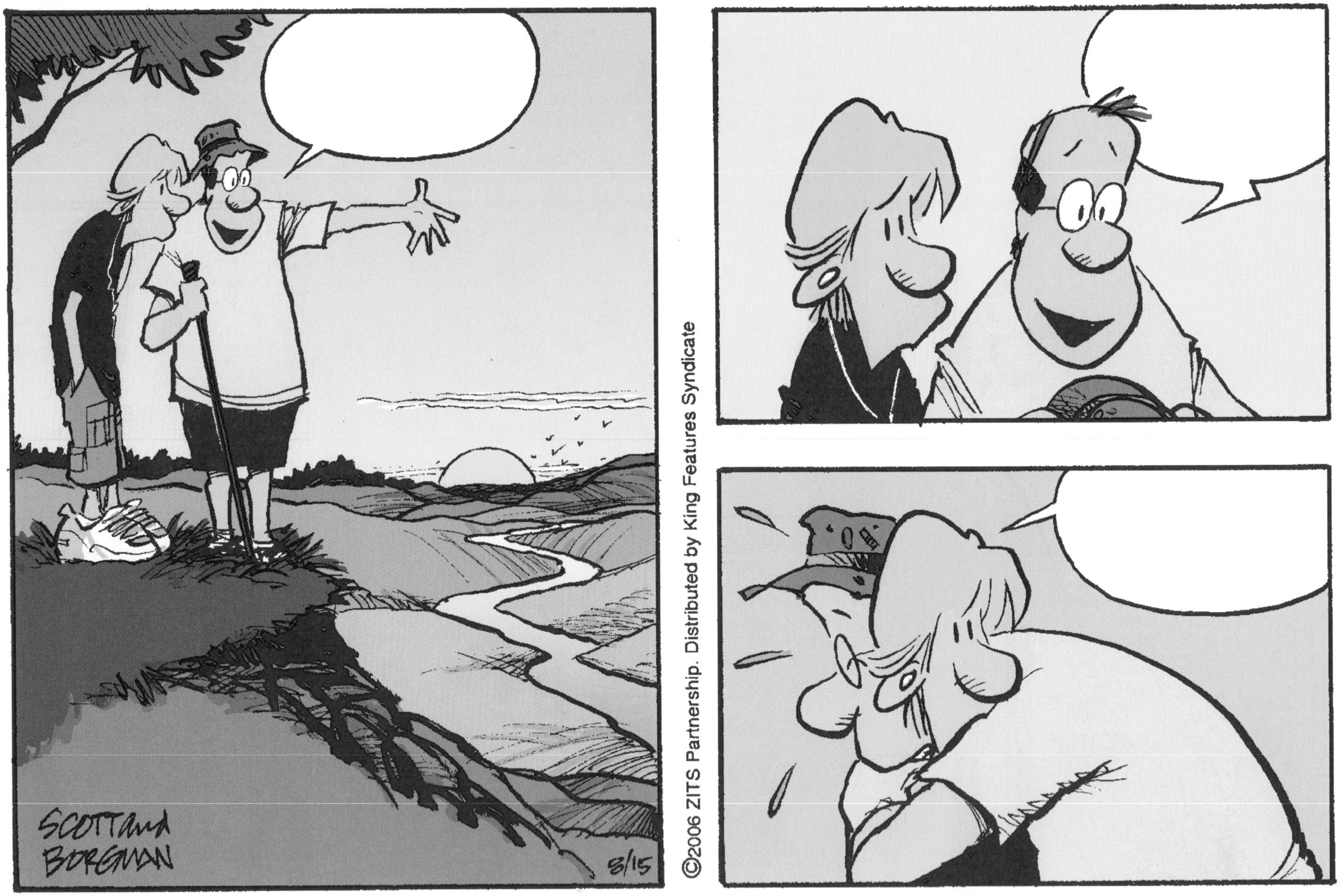
SCOTT and BORGMAN
8/15

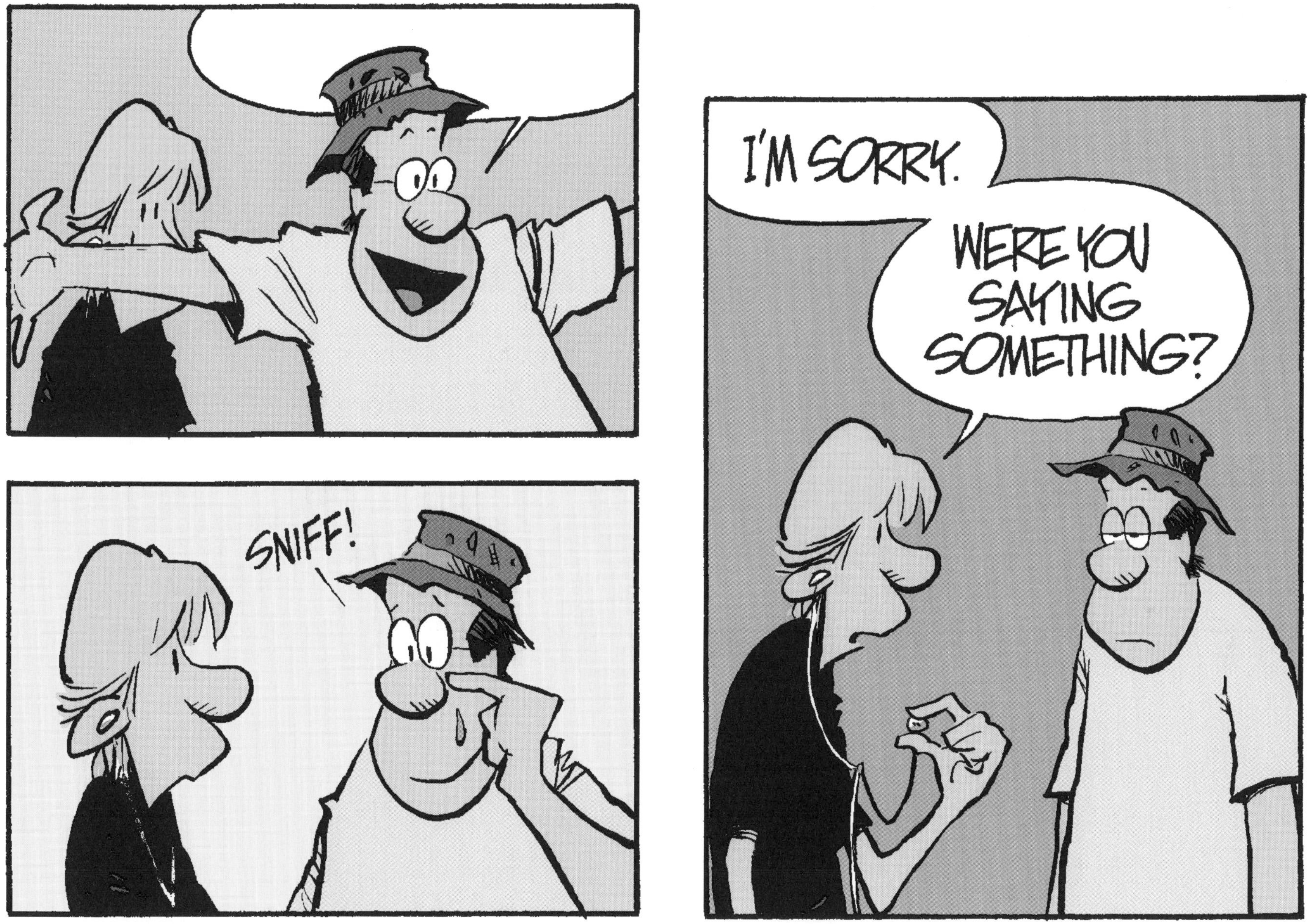
SNIFF!
I'M SORRY.
WERE YOU SAYING SOMETHING?

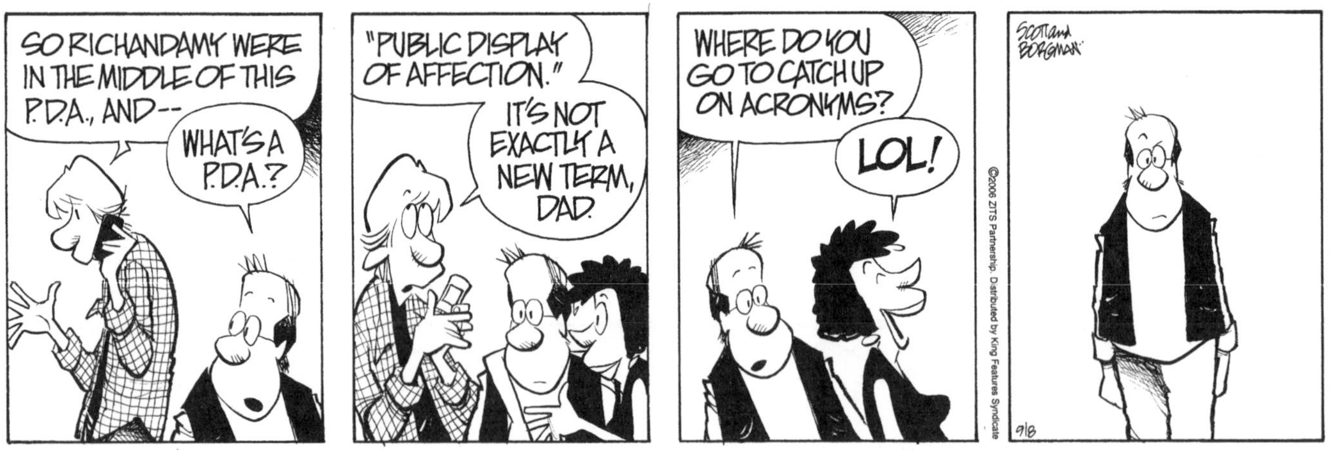
SO RICHANDAMY WERE IN THE MIDDLE OF THIS P.D.A., AND--
WHAT'S A P.D.A.?
"PUBLIC DISPLAY OF AFFECTION."
IT'S NOT EXACTLY A NEW TERM, DAD.
WHERE DO YOU GO TO CATCH UP ON ACRONYMS?
LOL!
©2006 ZITS Partnership. Distributed by King Features Syndicate
SCOTT and BORGMAN
9/8

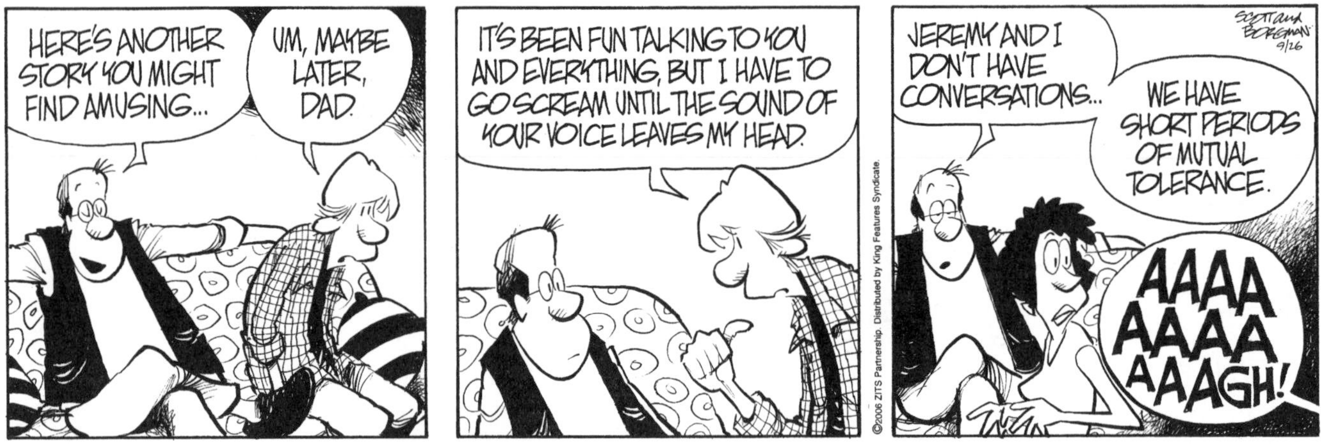
HERE'S ANOTHER STORY YOU MIGHT FIND AMUSING...
UM, MAYBE LATER, DAD.
IT'S BEEN FUN TALKING TO YOU AND EVERYTHING, BUT I HAVE TO GO SCREAM UNTIL THE SOUND OF YOUR VOICE LEAVES MY HEAD.
©2006 ZITS Partnership. Distributed by King Features Syndicate.
JEREMY AND I DON'T HAVE CONVERSATIONS...
WE HAVE SHORT PERIODS OF MUTUAL TOLERANCE.
AAAA AAAA AAAGH!
SCOTT and BORGMAN
9/26

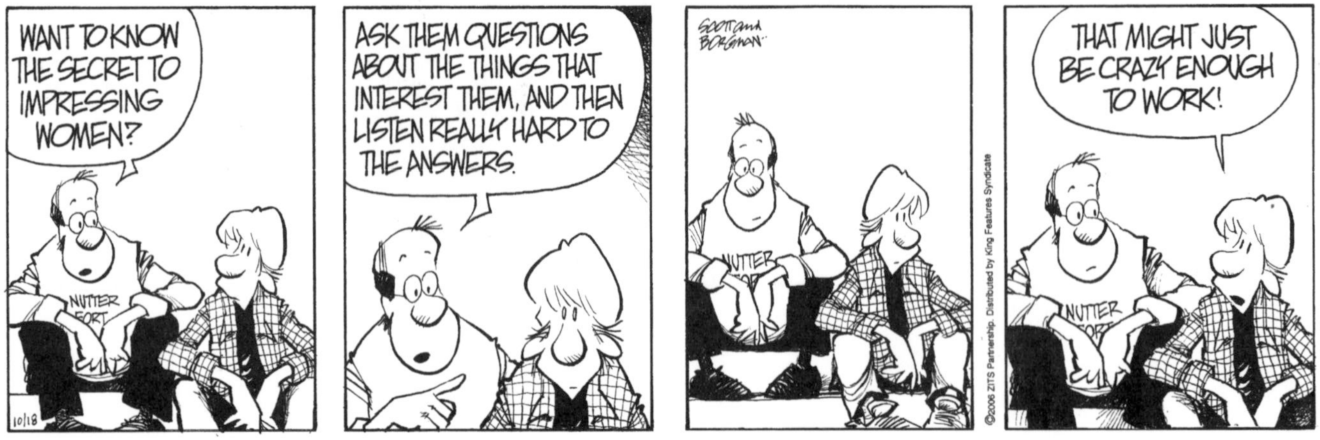
WANT TO KNOW THE SECRET TO IMPRESSING WOMEN?
NUTTER
10/18
ASK THEM QUESTIONS ABOUT THE THINGS THAT INTEREST THEM, AND THEN LISTEN REALLY HARD TO THE ANSWERS.
SCOTT and BORGMAN
NUTTER
©2006 ZITS Partnership. Distributed by King Features Syndicate
THAT MIGHT JUST BE CRAZY ENOUGH TO WORK!
NUTTER

GUESS WHAT! I FOUND THE PERFECT GUITAR!
I'VE BEEN LOOKING FOR SOMETHING LIKE THIS MY WHOLE LIFE!
©2006 ZITS Partnership. Distributed by King Features Syndicate.
YOU WON'T BELIEVE HOW COOL IT IS. I HAD TO TELL SOMEBODY!
THAT'S GREAT, JEREMY!
I DON'T KNOW A LOT ABOUT GUITARS, BUT I'D REALLY LIKE TO HEAR ABOUT IT.
SCOTT AND BORGMAN
12/10
HANG ON A SEC, HECTOR. MY DAD IS INTERRUPTING ME.

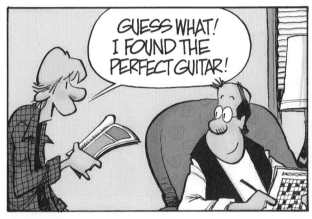

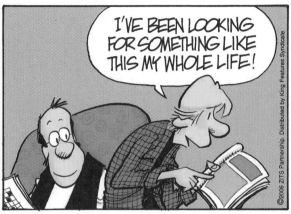

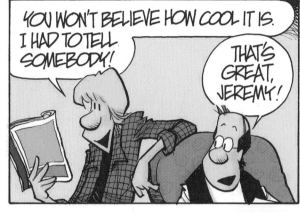

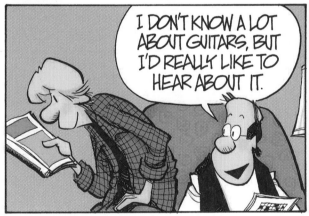

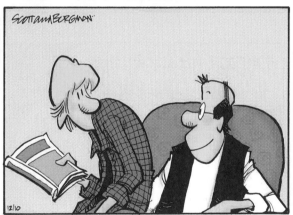

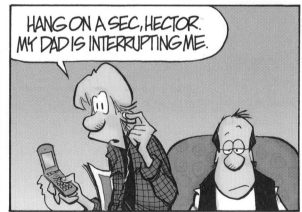

HEY! THERE ARE TWENTY MINUTES LEFT ON THIS PARKING METER!
SCOTT and BORGMAN 10/31
IF WE GET IN AND OUT OF THE MUSIC STORE FAST, THERE'S A CHANCE THAT WE'LL GET AWAY WITHOUT PAYING TO PARK!
©2006 ZITS Partnership. Distributed by King Features Syndicate.
SHOPPING WITH YOU IS LIKE RIDING WITH JESSE JAMES, DAD.
I DON'T KNOW ABOUT YOU, BUT MY PALMS ARE SWEATY!

SO, DID ANYTHING INTERESTING HAPPEN TODAY, JEREMY?
11/16
DUDE! IT'S ABOUT TIME YOU CALLED ME BACK!
WAIT'LL YOU HEAR WHAT HAPPENED TODAY!
UM... NO.
SCOTT and BORGMAN
©2006 ZITS Partnership. Distributed by King Features Syndicate

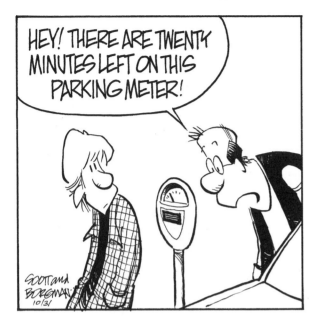

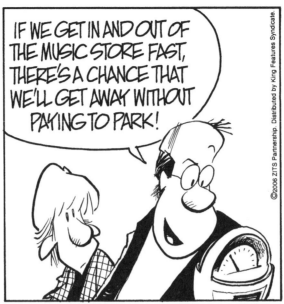

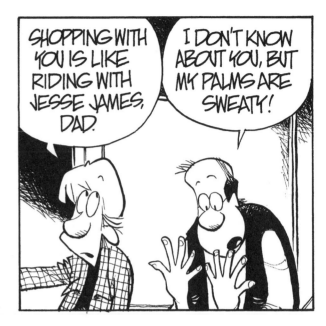

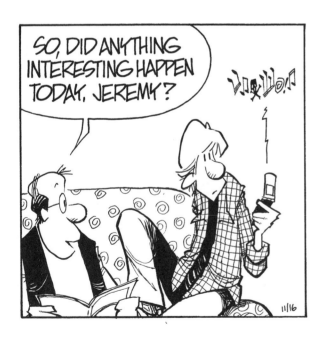

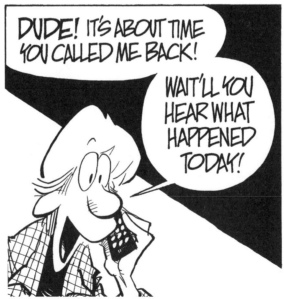

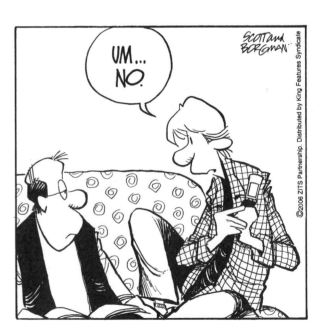

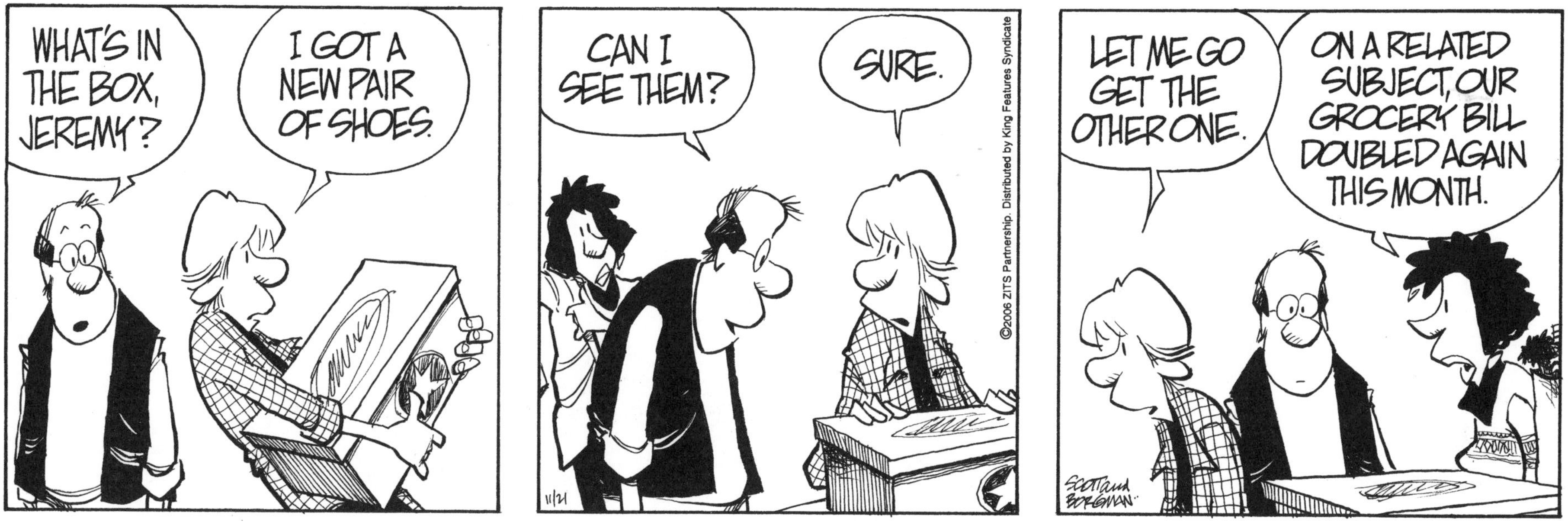
WHAT'S IN THE BOX, JEREMY?
I GOT A NEW PAIR OF SHOES.
CAN I SEE THEM?
SURE.
©2006 ZITS Partnership. Distributed by King Features Syndicate
LET ME GO GET THE OTHER ONE.
ON A RELATED SUBJECT, OUR GROCERY BILL DOUBLED AGAIN THIS MONTH.
SCOTT AND BORGMAN

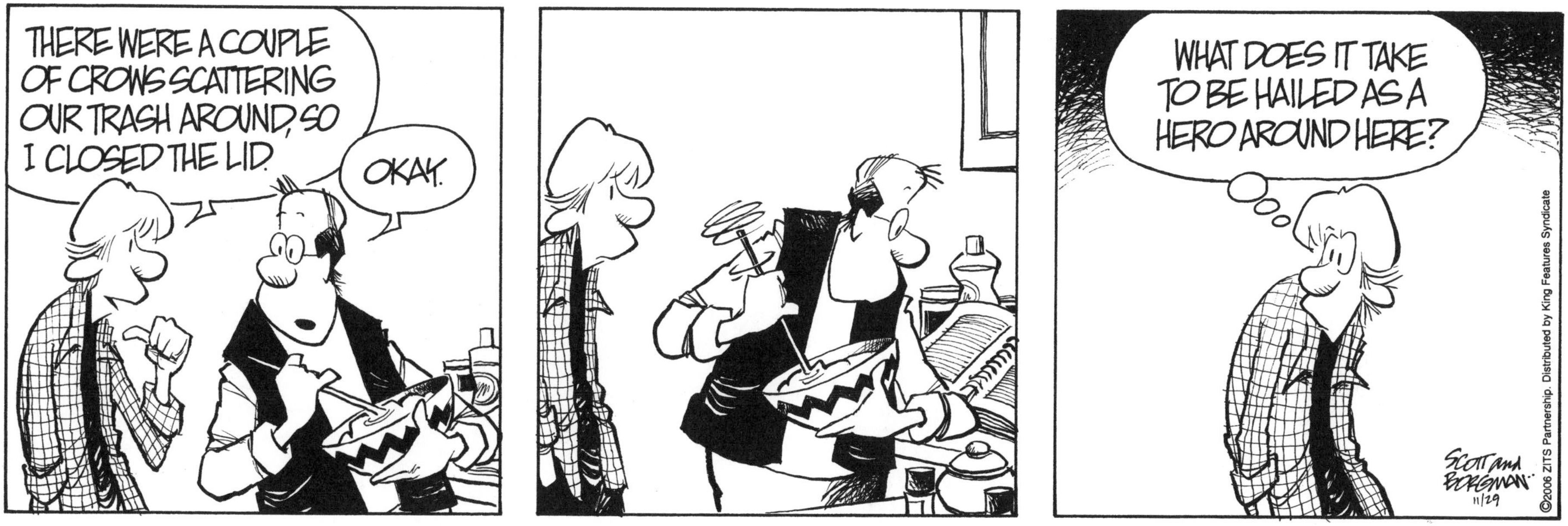
THERE WERE A COUPLE OF CROWS SCATTERING OUR TRASH AROUND, SO I CLOSED THE LID.
OKAY.
WHAT DOES IT TAKE TO BE HAILED AS A HERO AROUND HERE?
©2006 ZITS Partnership. Distributed by King Features Syndicate
SCOTT AND BORGMAN

Jerry: My wife and I took turns teaching our older daughter to drive. Next we hope to teach her how to pay for her own gas.

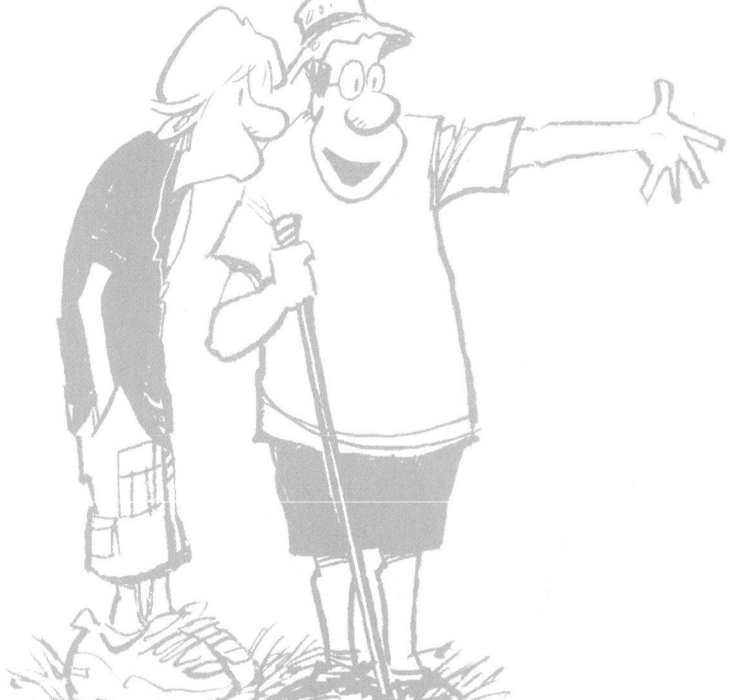

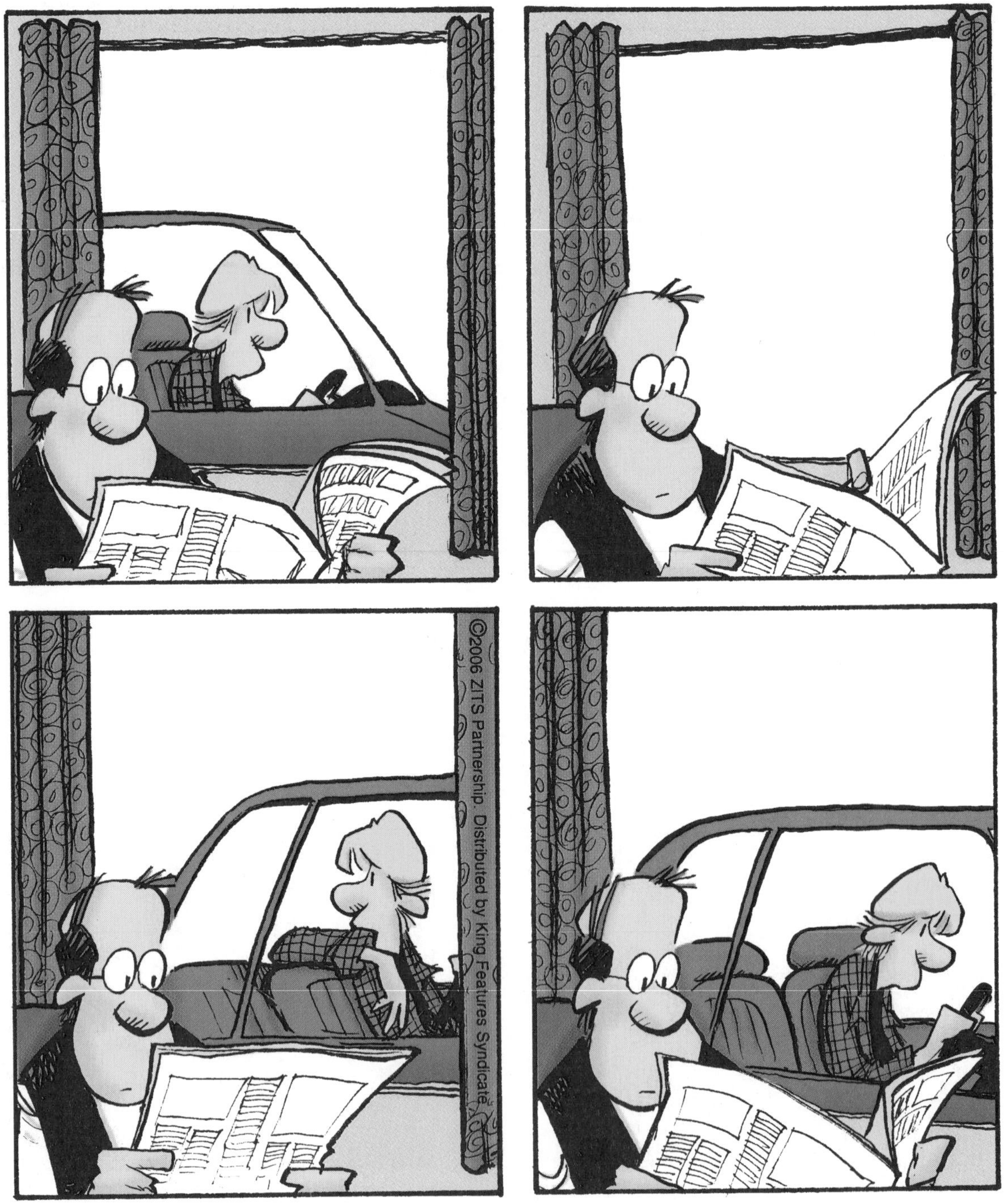
©2006 ZITS Partnership. Distributed by King Features Syndicate.

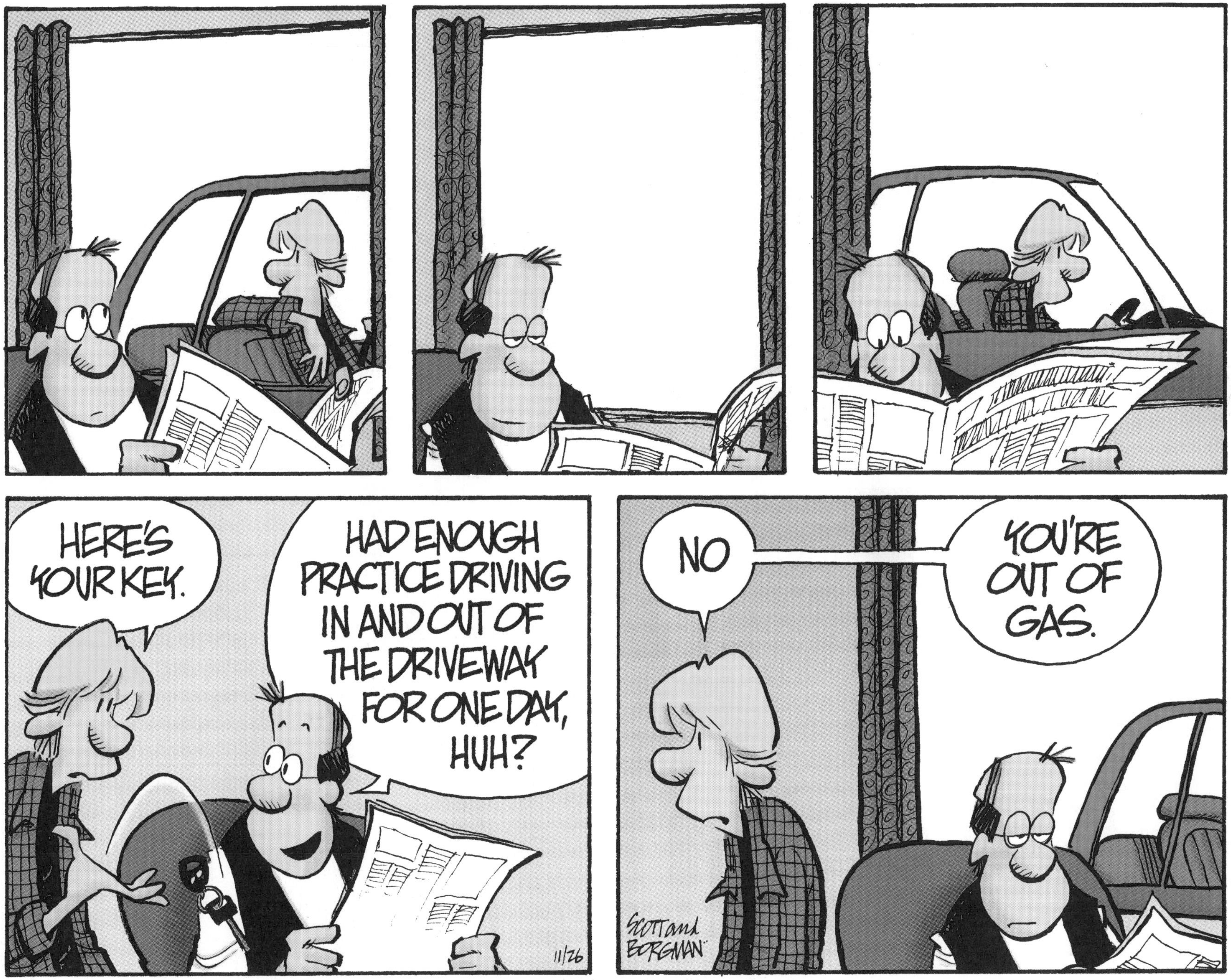
HERE'S YOUR KEY.
HAD ENOUGH PRACTICE DRIVING IN AND OUT OF THE DRIVEWAY FOR ONE DAY, HUH?
11/26
NO
YOU'RE OUT OF GAS.
SCOTT and BORGMAN

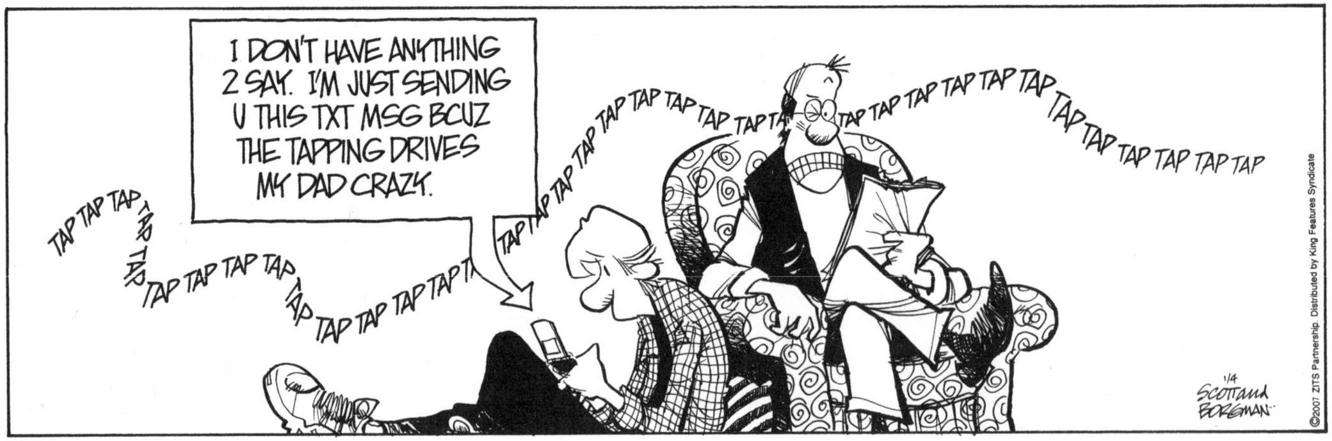
I DON'T HAVE ANYTHING 2 SAY. I'M JUST SENDING U THIS TXT MSG BCUZ THE TAPPING DRIVES MY DAD CRAZY.
1/4 SCOTT and BORGMAN
©2007 ZITS Partnership. Distributed by King Features Syndicate

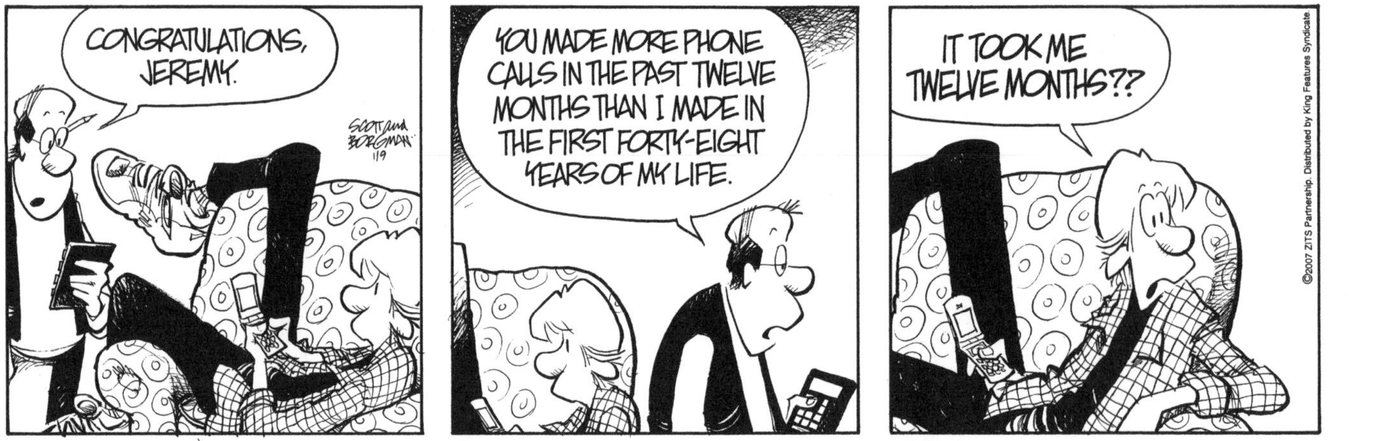
CONGRATULATIONS, JEREMY.
SCOTT and BORGMAN 1/9
YOU MADE MORE PHONE CALLS IN THE PAST TWELVE MONTHS THAN I MADE IN THE FIRST FORTY-EIGHT YEARS OF MY LIFE.
IT TOOK ME TWELVE MONTHS??
©2007 ZITS Partnership. Distributed by King Features Syndicate

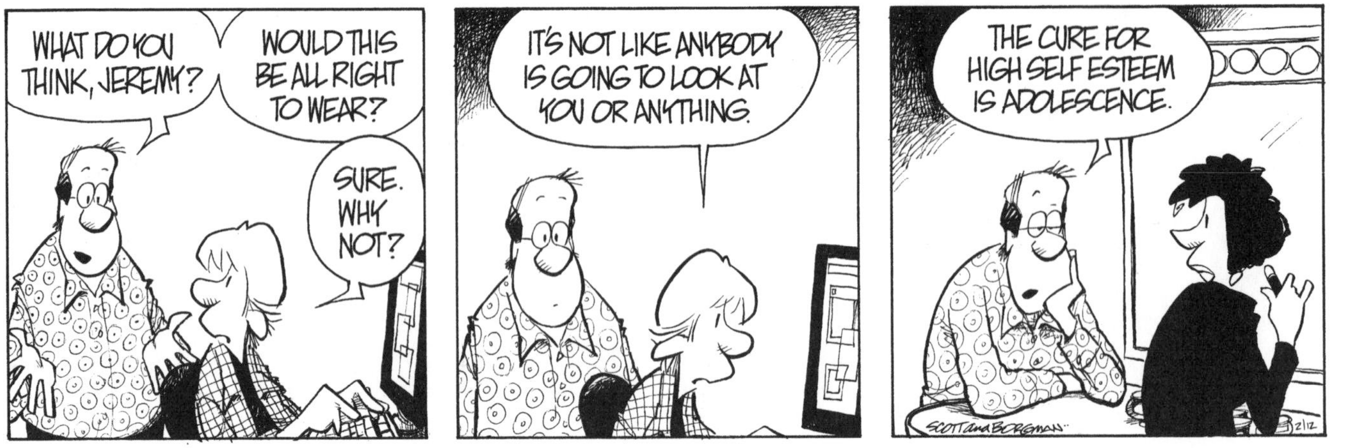
WHAT DO YOU THINK, JEREMY?
WOULD THIS BE ALL RIGHT TO WEAR?
SURE. WHY NOT?
IT'S NOT LIKE ANYBODY IS GOING TO LOOK AT YOU OR ANYTHING.
THE CURE FOR HIGH SELF ESTEEM IS ADOLESCENCE.
SCOTT and BORGMAN 2/12

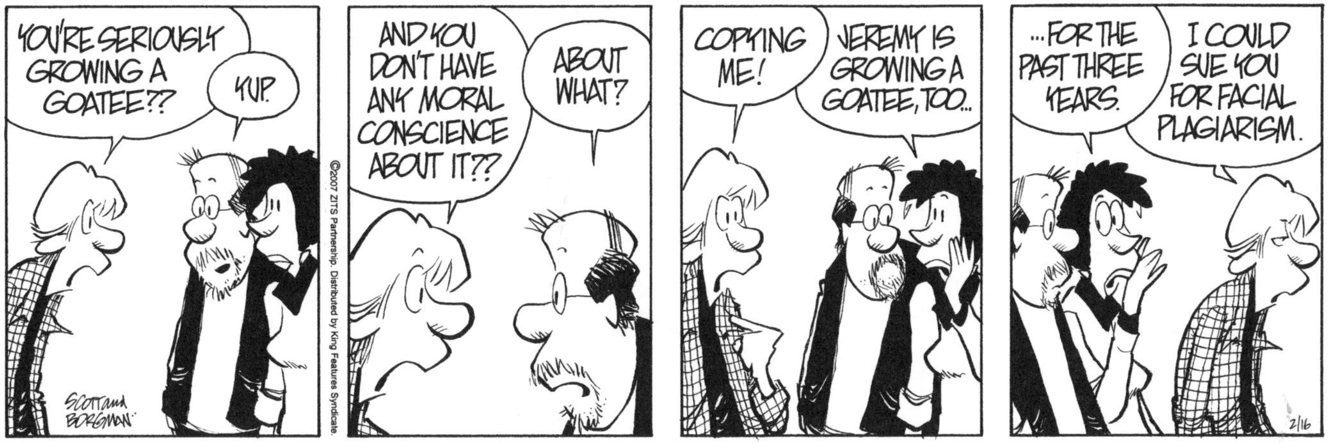
YOU'RE SERIOUSLY GROWING A GOATEE??
YUP.
AND YOU DON'T HAVE ANY MORAL CONSCIENCE ABOUT IT??
ABOUT WHAT?
COPYING ME!
JEREMY IS GROWING A GOATEE, TOO...
...FOR THE PAST THREE YEARS.
I COULD SUE YOU FOR FACIAL PLAGIARISM.
SCOTT and BORGMAN
©2007 ZITS Partnership. Distributed by King Features Syndicate.
2/16

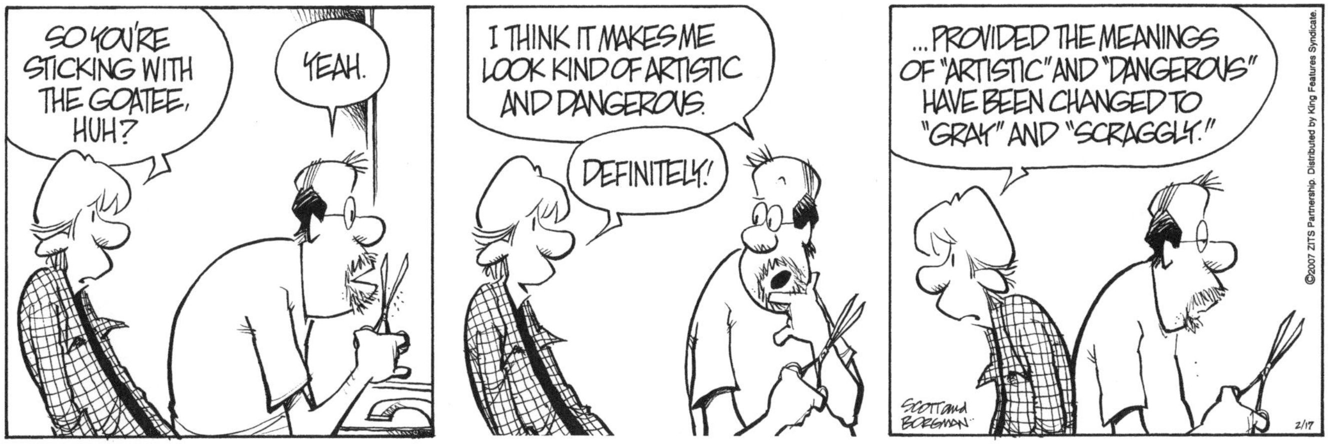
SO YOU'RE STICKING WITH THE GOATEE, HUH?
YEAH.
I THINK IT MAKES ME LOOK KIND OF ARTISTIC AND DANGEROUS.
DEFINITELY!
...PROVIDED THE MEANINGS OF "ARTISTIC" AND "DANGEROUS" HAVE BEEN CHANGED TO "GRAY" AND "SCRAGGLY."
©2007 ZITS Partnership. Distributed by King Features Syndicate.
SCOTT and BORGMAN
2/17

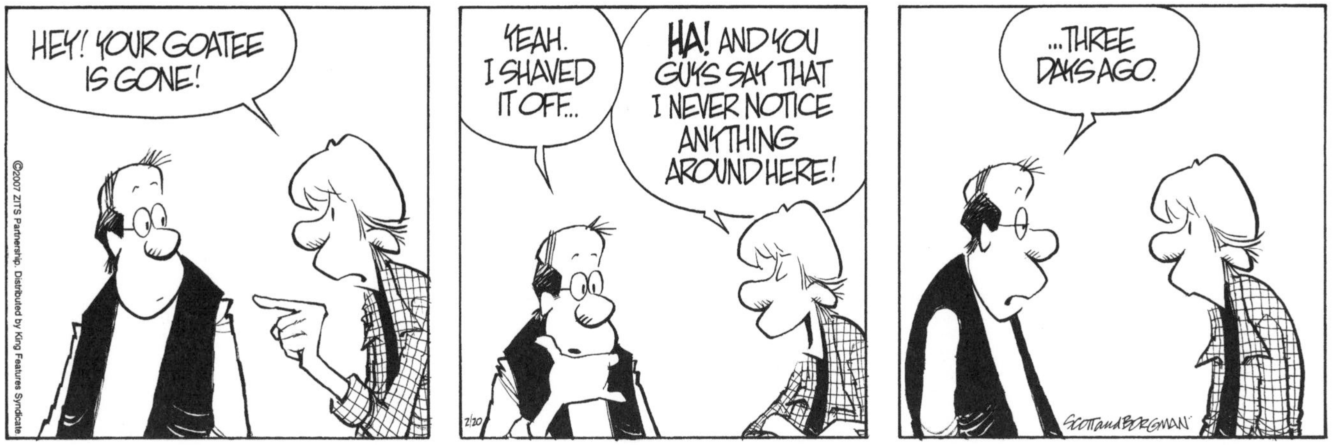
HEY! YOUR GOATEE IS GONE!
©2007 ZITS Partnership. Distributed by King Features Syndicate
YEAH. I SHAVED IT OFF...
HA! AND YOU GUYS SAY THAT I NEVER NOTICE ANYTHING AROUND HERE!
2/20
...THREE DAYS AGO.
SCOTT and BORGMAN

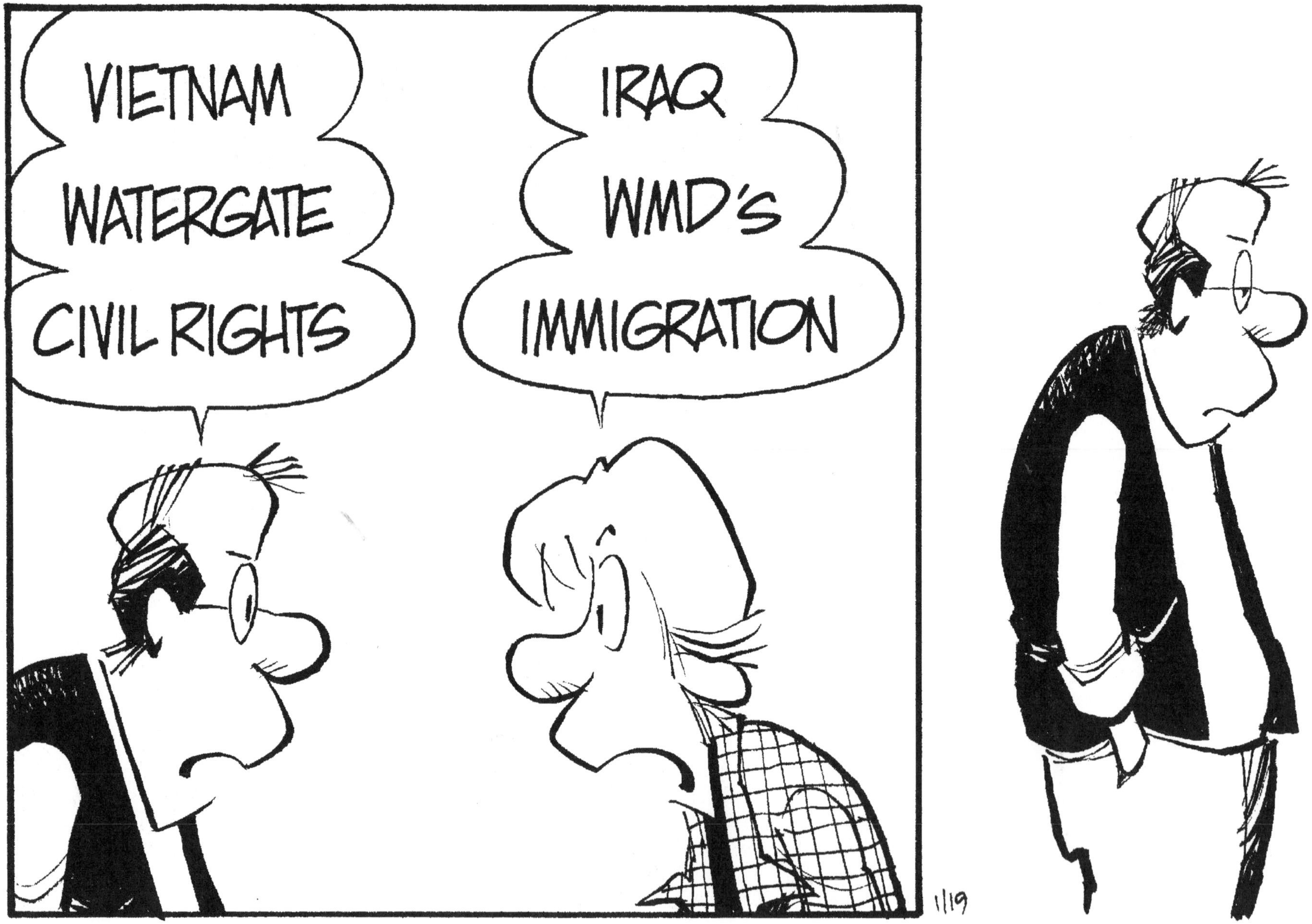
VIETNAM
WATERGATE
CIVIL RIGHTS
IRAQ
WMD's
IMMIGRATION
1/19

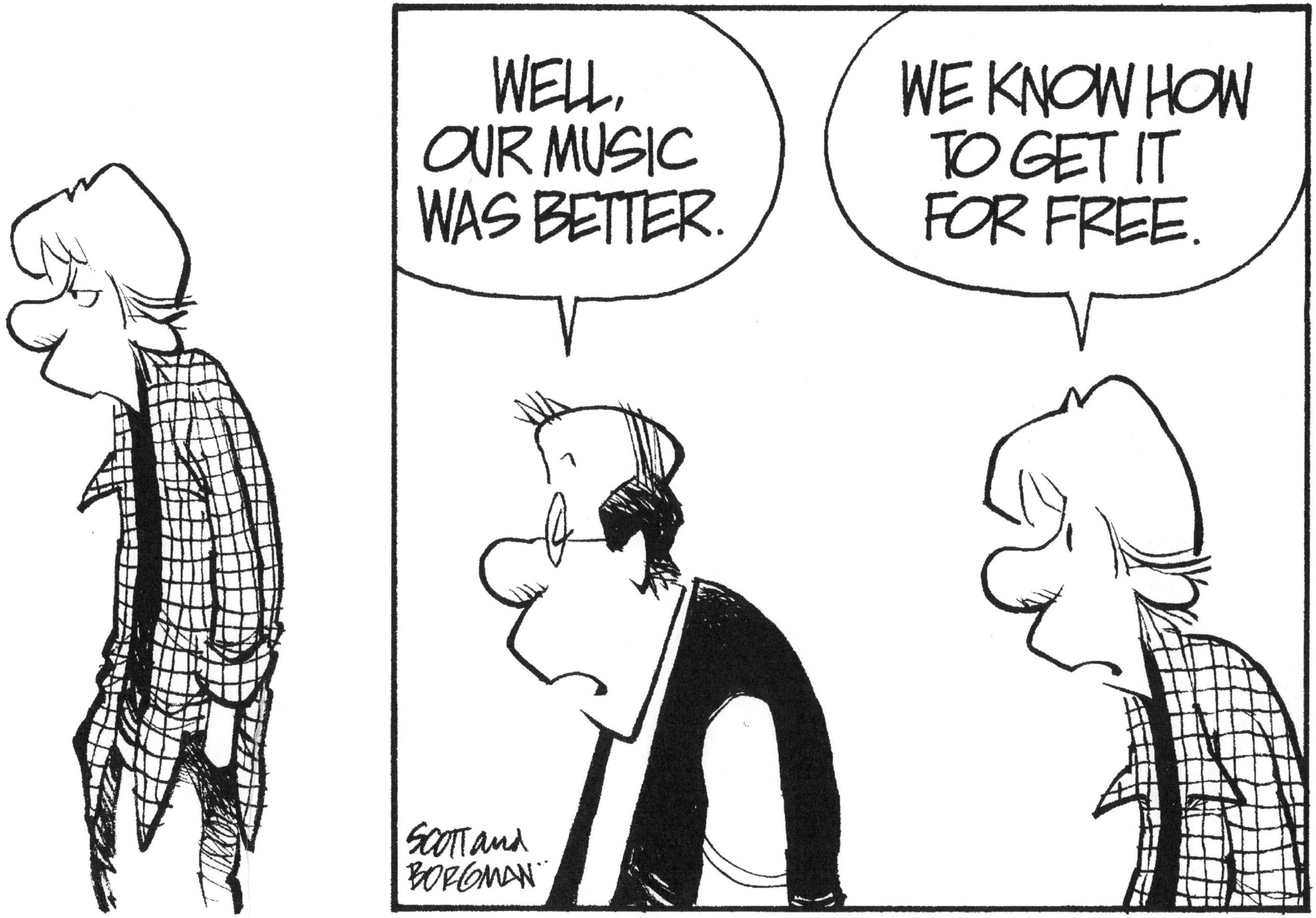
WELL, OUR MUSIC WAS BETTER.
WE KNOW HOW TO GET IT FOR FREE.
SCOTT and BORGMAN

Jim: My son and I were talking about tensions in the Middle East recently when he said, "Everybody thinks these are modern-day problems, but some of these issues date back to the '80s."

THANKS FOR THE SMOOTHIE, DAD.
SURE.
WHERE'S MY CHANGE?
WHAT?
I GAVE YOU A TEN. I WANT THE CHANGE BACK.
OH. OKAY.
SCOTT AND BORGMAN
2/11
©2007 ZITS Partnership. Distributed by King Features Syndicate
WELL...??
WHAT? YOU MEAN NOW??
YES, NOW!
FINE! I'LL GIVE YOU THE CHANGE!
I'M WAITING.
AREN'T PEOPLE YOUR AGE SUPPOSED TO BE MORE FORGET-FUL THAN THIS?

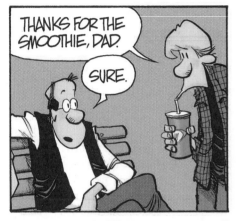

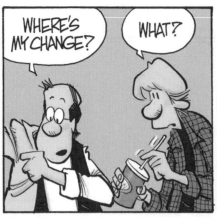

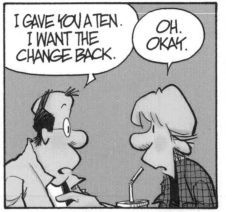

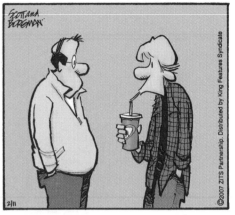

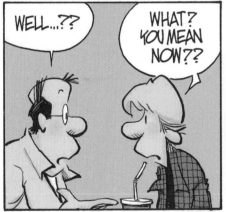

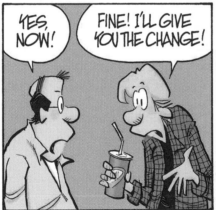

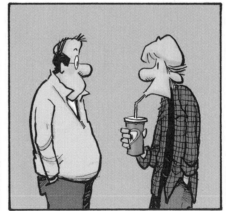

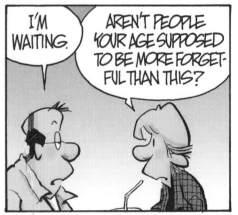

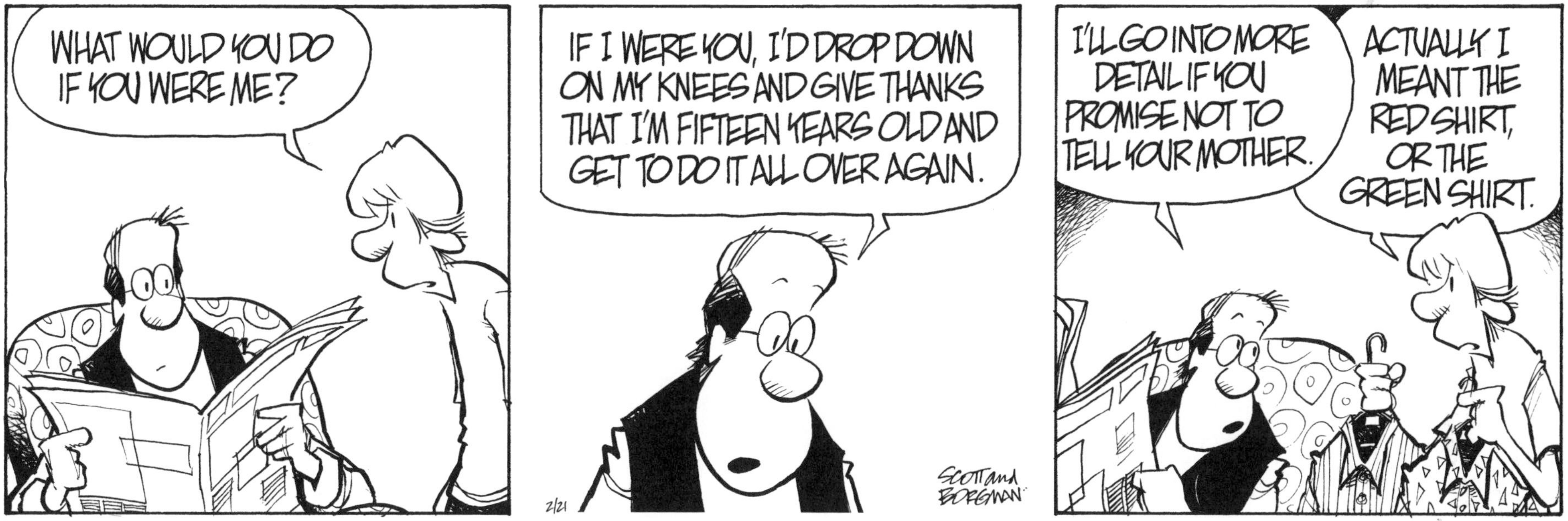
WHAT WOULD YOU DO IF YOU WERE ME?
IF I WERE YOU, I'D DROP DOWN ON MY KNEES AND GIVE THANKS THAT I'M FIFTEEN YEARS OLD AND GET TO DO IT ALL OVER AGAIN.
2/21
SCOTT and BORGMAN
I'LL GO INTO MORE DETAIL IF YOU PROMISE NOT TO TELL YOUR MOTHER.
ACTUALLY I MEANT THE RED SHIRT, OR THE GREEN SHIRT.

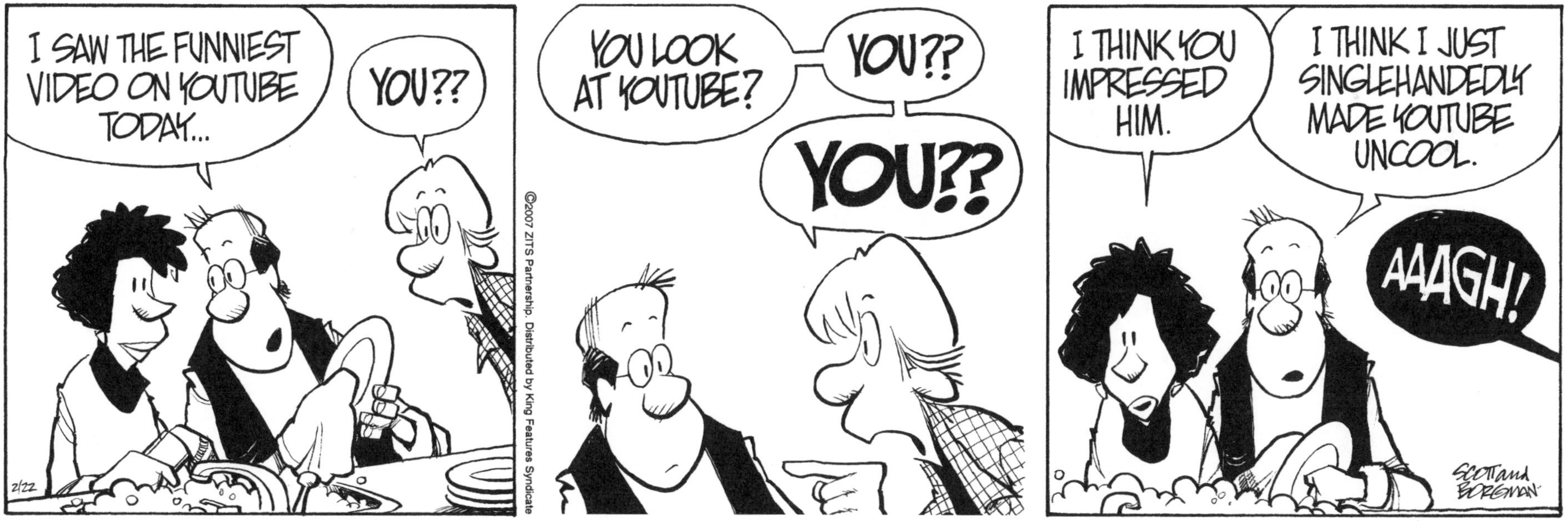
I SAW THE FUNNIEST VIDEO ON YOUTUBE TODAY...
YOU??
2/22
YOU LOOK AT YOUTUBE?
YOU??
YOU??
I THINK YOU IMPRESSED HIM.
I THINK I JUST SINGLEHANDEDLY MADE YOUTUBE UNCOOL.
AAAGH!
SCOTT and BORGMAN

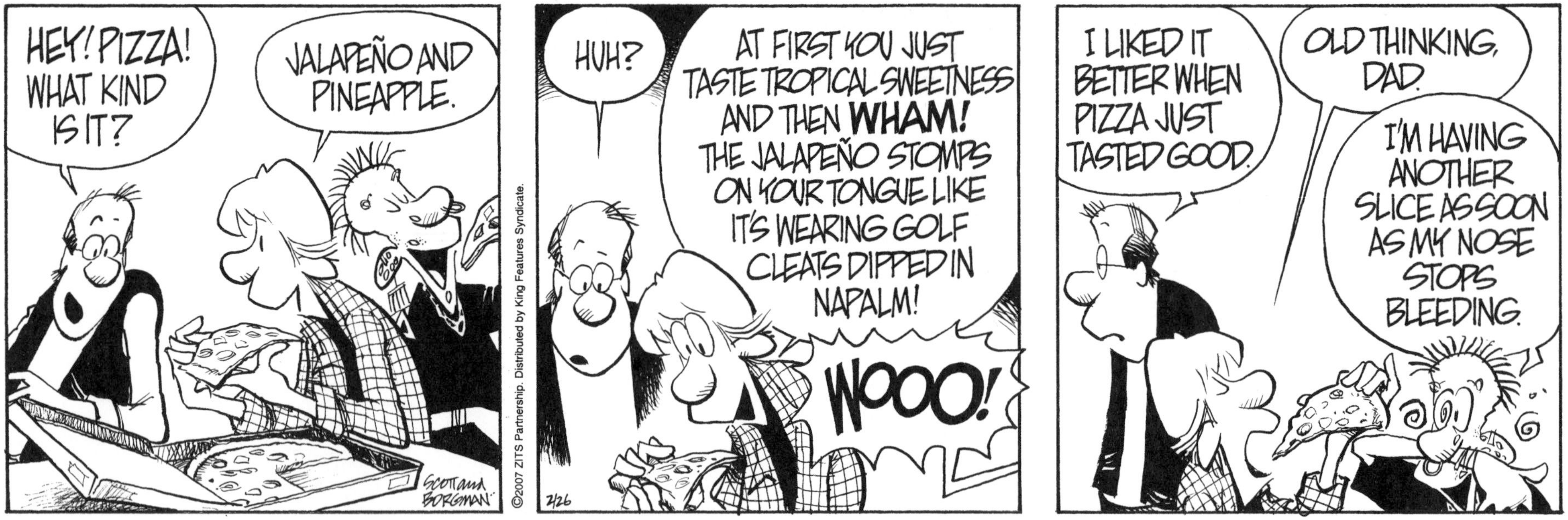
HEY! PIZZA! WHAT KIND IS IT?
JALAPEÑO AND PINEAPPLE.
SCOTT and BORGMAN
©2007 ZITS Partnership. Distributed by King Features Syndicate.
2/26
HUH?
AT FIRST YOU JUST TASTE TROPICAL SWEETNESS AND THEN **WHAM!** THE JALAPEÑO STOMPS ON YOUR TONGUE LIKE IT'S WEARING GOLF CLEATS DIPPED IN NAPALM!
WOOO!
I LIKED IT BETTER WHEN PIZZA JUST TASTED GOOD.
OLD THINKING, DAD.
I'M HAVING ANOTHER SLICE AS SOON AS MY NOSE STOPS BLEEDING.

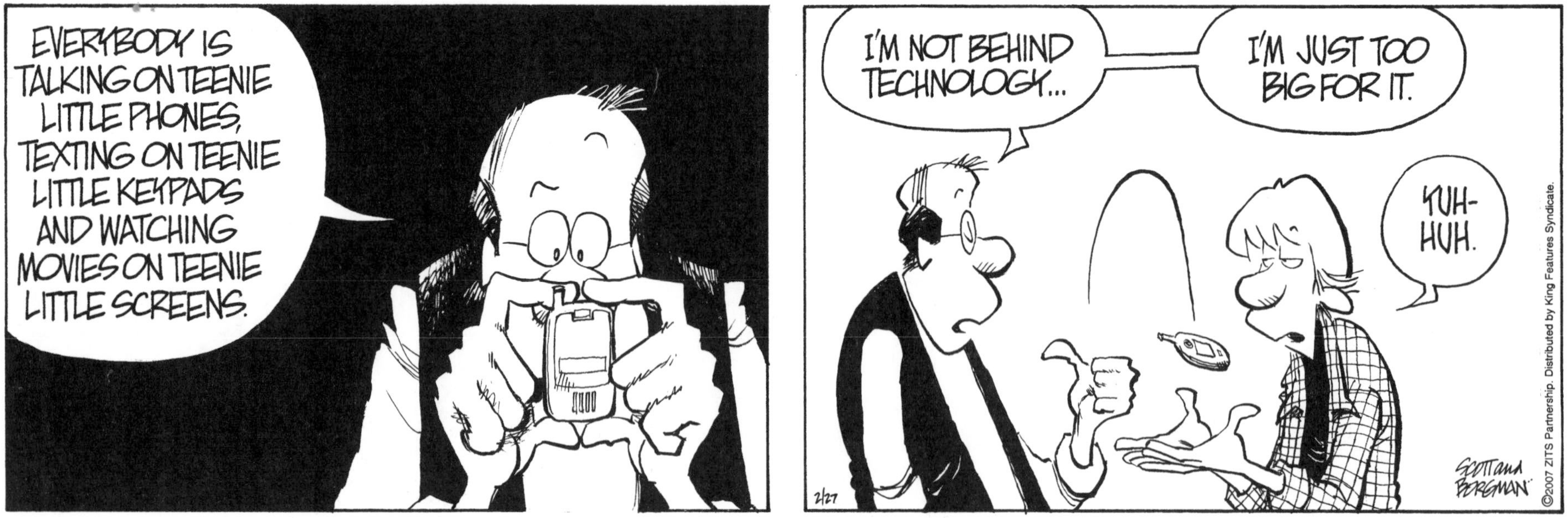
EVERYBODY IS TALKING ON TEENIE LITTLE PHONES, TEXTING ON TEENIE LITTLE KEYPADS AND WATCHING MOVIES ON TEENIE LITTLE SCREENS.
I'M NOT BEHIND TECHNOLOGY...
I'M JUST TOO BIG FOR IT.
YUH-HUH.
2/27
SCOTT and BORGMAN
©2007 ZITS Partnership. Distributed by King Features Syndicate.

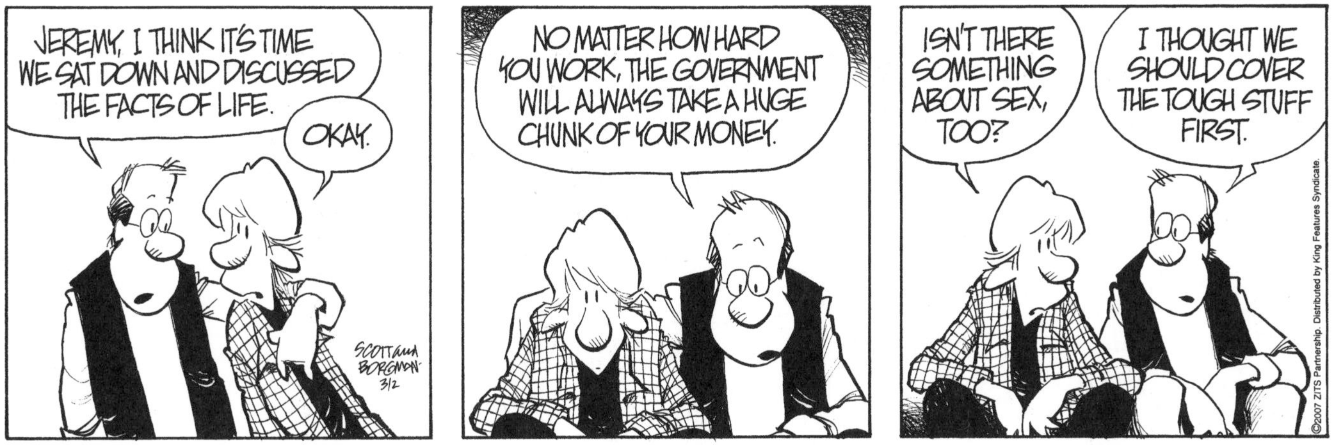
JEREMY, I THINK IT'S TIME WE SAT DOWN AND DISCUSSED THE FACTS OF LIFE.
OKAY.
SCOTT AND BORGMAN 3/2
NO MATTER HOW HARD YOU WORK, THE GOVERNMENT WILL ALWAYS TAKE A HUGE CHUNK OF YOUR MONEY.
ISN'T THERE SOMETHING ABOUT SEX, TOO?
I THOUGHT WE SHOULD COVER THE TOUGH STUFF FIRST.
©2007 ZITS Partnership. Distributed by King Features Syndicate.

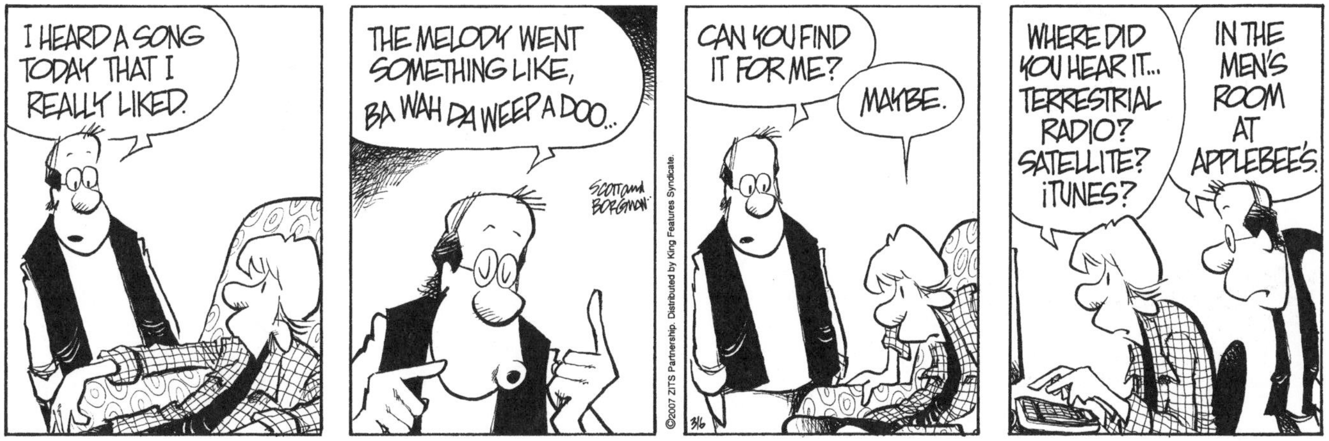
I HEARD A SONG TODAY THAT I REALLY LIKED.
THE MELODY WENT SOMETHING LIKE, BA WAH DA WEEP A DOO...
SCOTT AND BORGMAN
©2007 ZITS Partnership. Distributed by King Features Syndicate.
CAN YOU FIND IT FOR ME?
MAYBE.
3/6
WHERE DID YOU HEAR IT... TERRESTRIAL RADIO? SATELLITE? iTUNES?
IN THE MEN'S ROOM AT APPLEBEE'S.

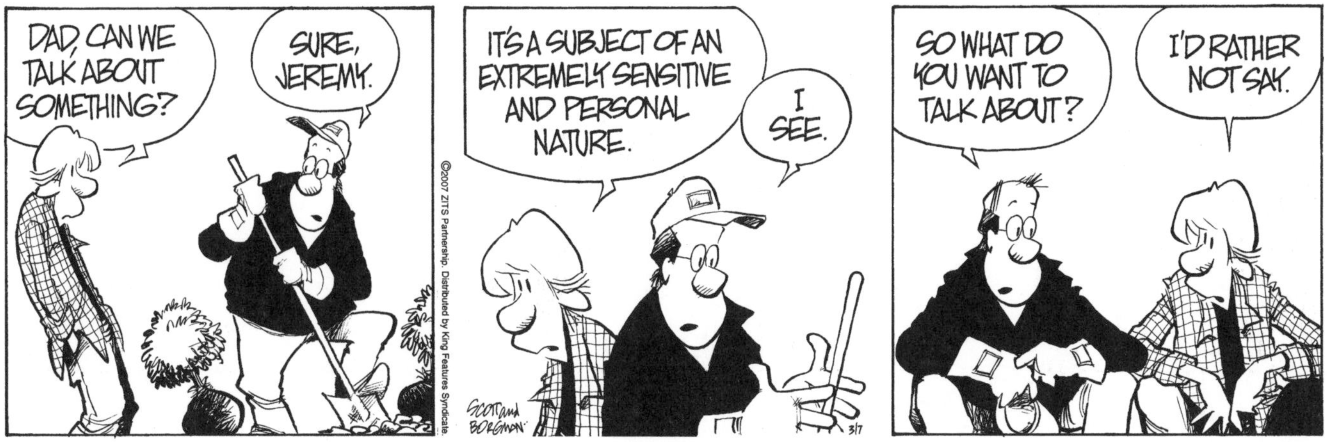
DAD, CAN WE TALK ABOUT SOMETHING?
SURE, JEREMY.
©2007 ZITS Partnership. Distributed by King Features Syndicate.
IT'S A SUBJECT OF AN EXTREMELY SENSITIVE AND PERSONAL NATURE.
I SEE.
SCOTT AND BORGMAN 3/7
SO WHAT DO YOU WANT TO TALK ABOUT?
I'D RATHER NOT SAY.

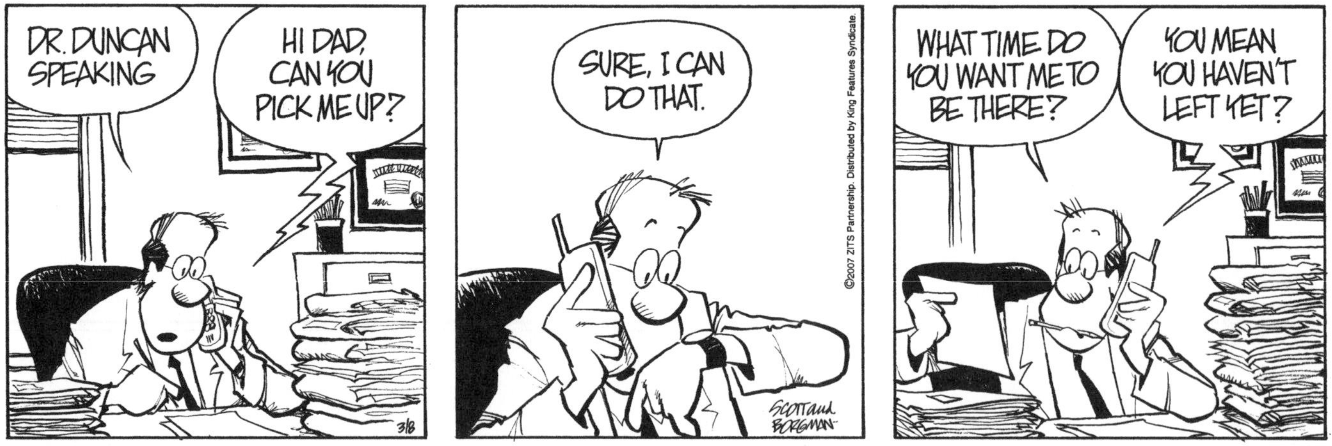
DR. DUNCAN SPEAKING
HI DAD, CAN YOU PICK ME UP?
SURE, I CAN DO THAT.
WHAT TIME DO YOU WANT ME TO BE THERE?
YOU MEAN YOU HAVEN'T LEFT YET?
3/18
SCOTT and BORGMAN
©2007 ZITS Partnership. Distributed by King Features Syndicate.

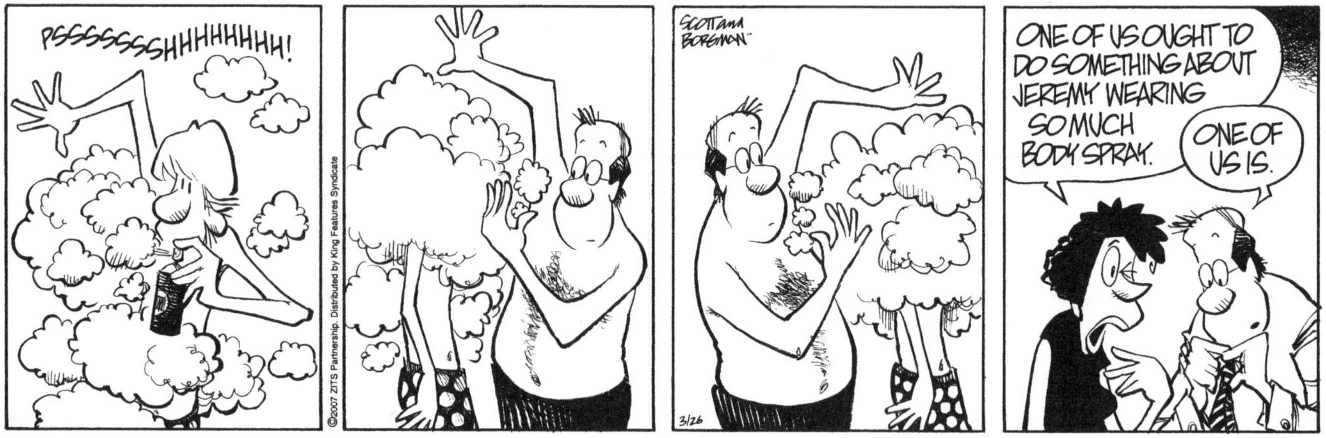
PSSSSSSSSHHHHHHHH!
©2007 ZITS Partnership. Distributed by King Features Syndicate
SCOTT and BORGMAN
3/26
ONE OF US OUGHT TO DO SOMETHING ABOUT JEREMY WEARING SO MUCH BODY SPRAY.
ONE OF US IS.

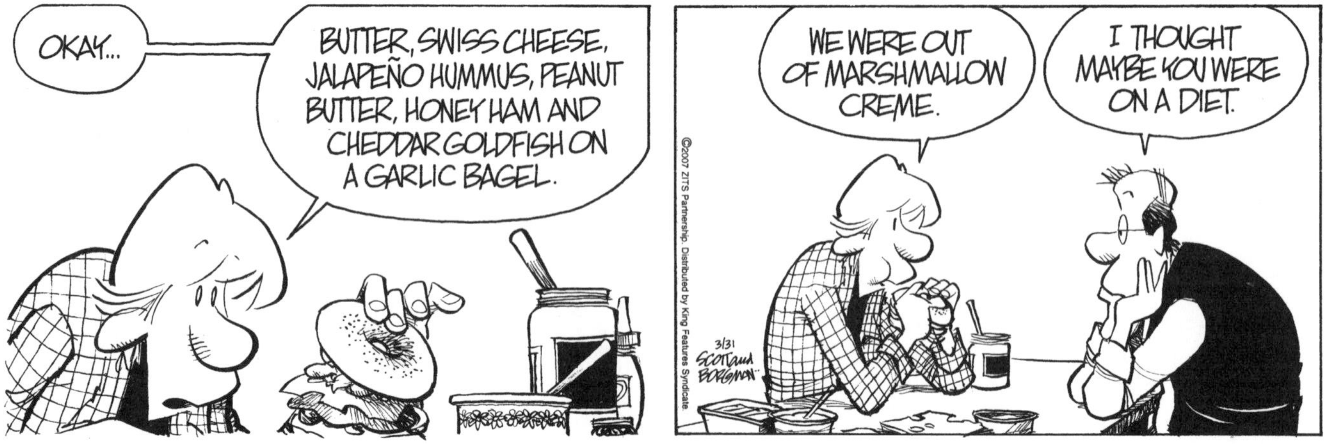
OKAY...
BUTTER, SWISS CHEESE, JALAPEÑO HUMMUS, PEANUT BUTTER, HONEY HAM AND CHEDDAR GOLDFISH ON A GARLIC BAGEL.
©2007 ZITS Partnership. Distributed by King Features Syndicate.
WE WERE OUT OF MARSHMALLOW CREME.
I THOUGHT MAYBE YOU WERE ON A DIET.
3/31
SCOTT and BORGMAN

SCRAPE!
SCRAPE!
SCRAPE!
SCRAPE!
SCRAPE!
SCRAPE!
SCRAPE!
SCRAPE!
SCRAPE!
SCRAPE!
SCRAPE!
SCRAPE!
SCRAPE!
SCRAPE!
SCRAPE!
HERE YOU GO.
I SCRAPED THE ICE OFF YOUR WINDSHIELD.
WITH MY "BEST OF FOGHAT" CD??
3/11
JEREMY, THIS THING WILL NEVER PLAY THE SAME AGAIN!
SCOTT AND BORGMAN
IN THAT CASE, I GUESS I DID US BOTH A FAVOR.
©2007 ZITS Partnership. Distributed by King Features Syndicate

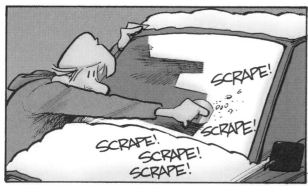

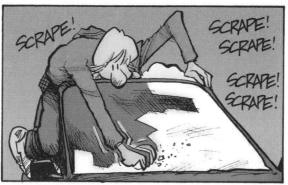

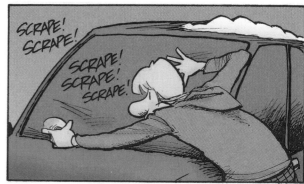

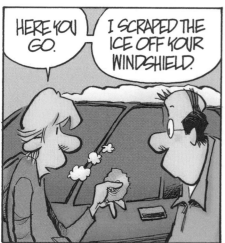

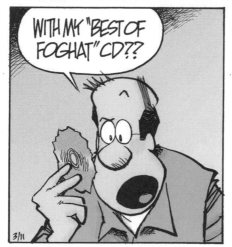

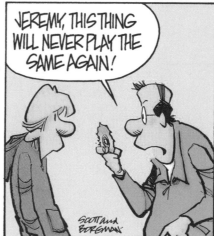

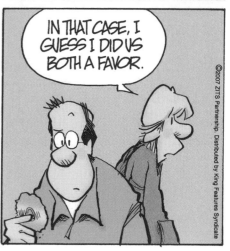

Jim: You can so see Walt drumming to "Slow Ride" on the steering wheel.

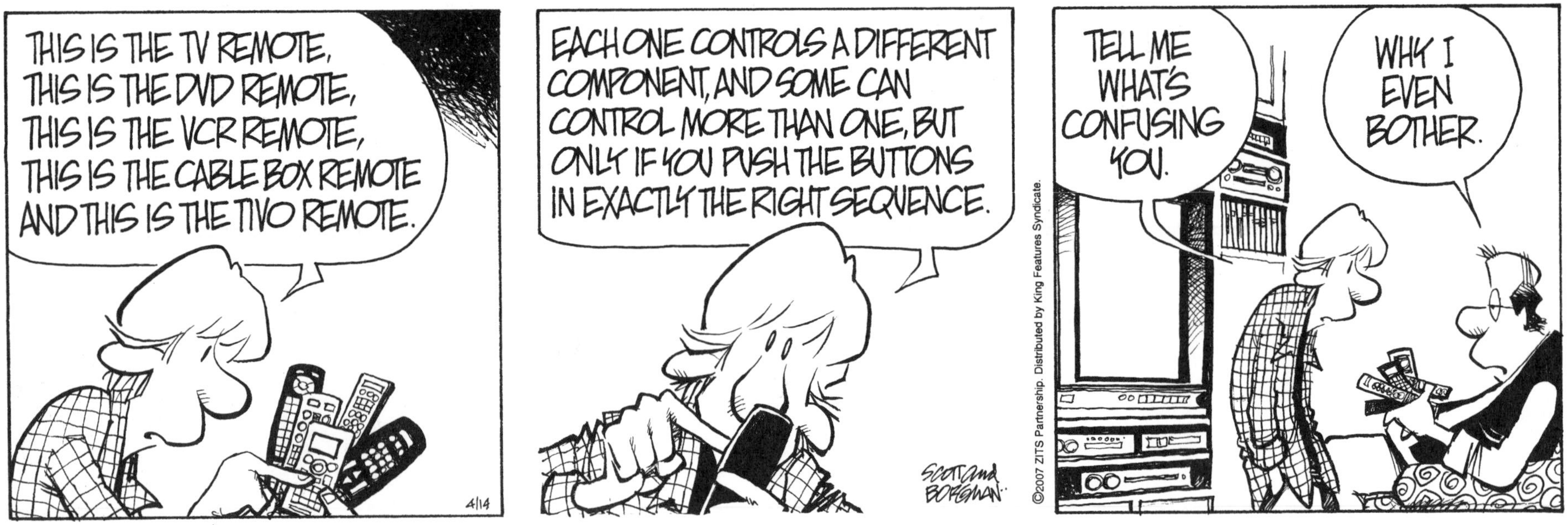
THIS IS THE TV REMOTE, THIS IS THE DVD REMOTE, THIS IS THE VCR REMOTE, THIS IS THE CABLE BOX REMOTE AND THIS IS THE TIVO REMOTE.
4/14
EACH ONE CONTROLS A DIFFERENT COMPONENT, AND SOME CAN CONTROL MORE THAN ONE, BUT ONLY IF YOU PUSH THE BUTTONS IN EXACTLY THE RIGHT SEQUENCE.
SCOTT and BORGMAN
©2007 ZITS Partnership. Distributed by King Features Syndicate.
TELL ME WHAT'S CONFUSING YOU.
WHY I EVEN BOTHER.

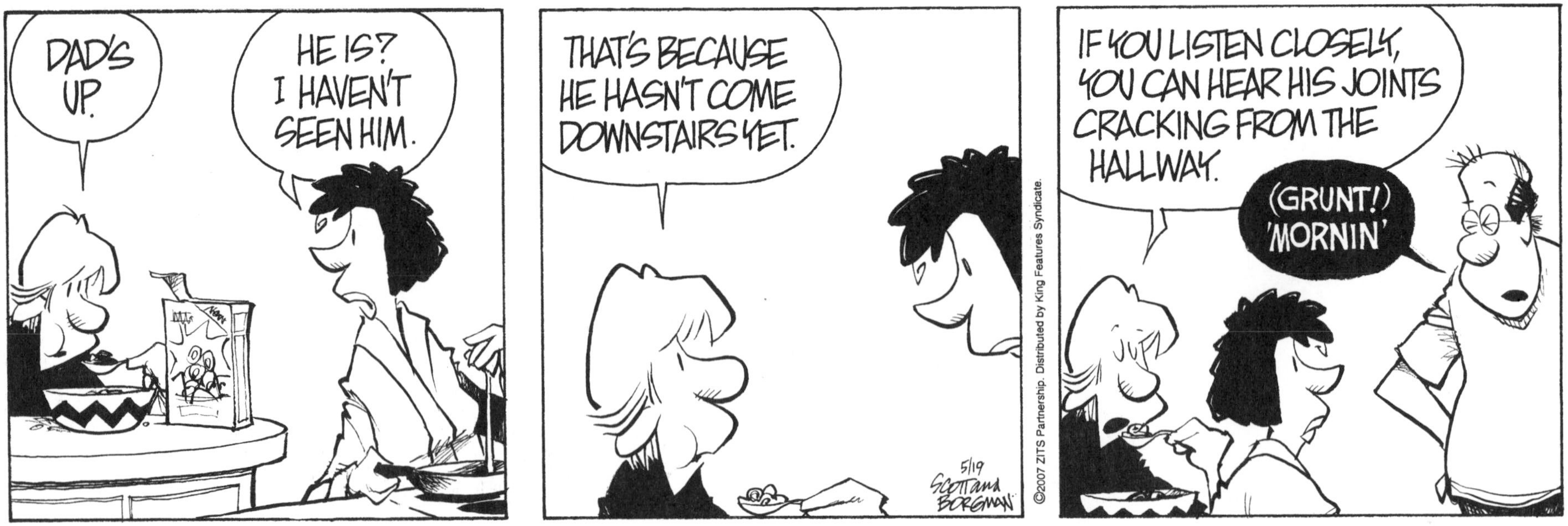
DAD'S UP.
HE IS? I HAVEN'T SEEN HIM.
THAT'S BECAUSE HE HASN'T COME DOWNSTAIRS YET.
5/19
SCOTT and BORGMAN
©2007 ZITS Partnership. Distributed by King Features Syndicate.
IF YOU LISTEN CLOSELY, YOU CAN HEAR HIS JOINTS CRACKING FROM THE HALLWAY.
(GRUNT!) 'MORNIN'

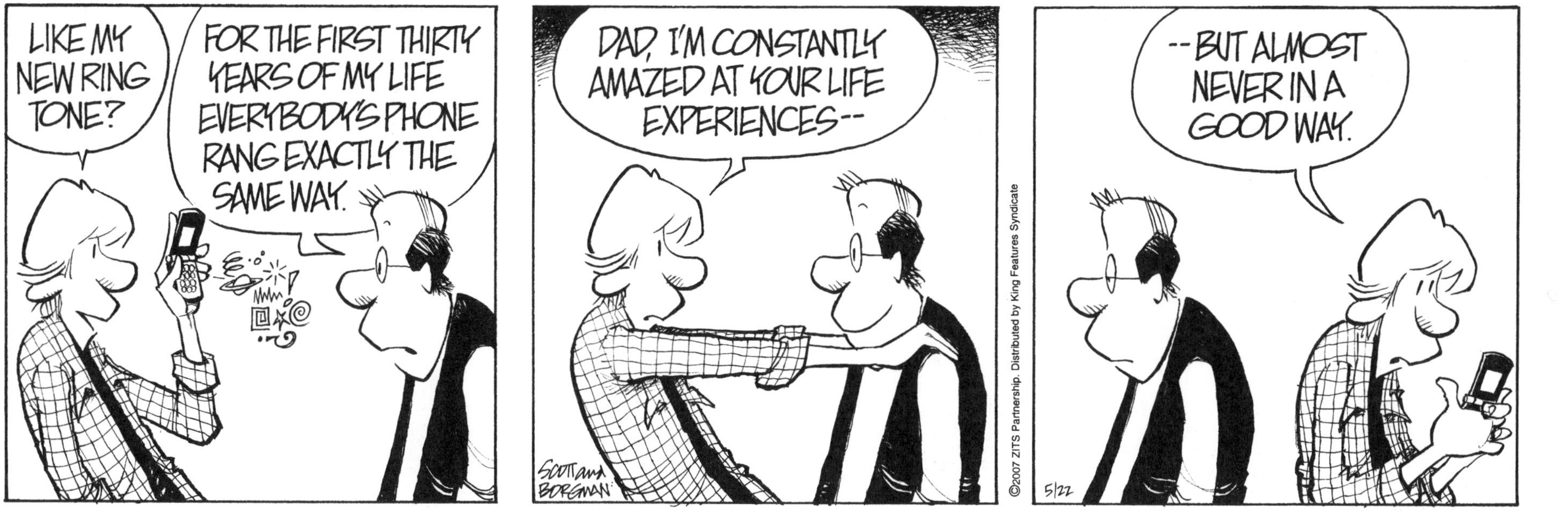
LIKE MY NEW RING TONE?
FOR THE FIRST THIRTY YEARS OF MY LIFE EVERYBODY'S PHONE RANG EXACTLY THE SAME WAY.
DAD, I'M CONSTANTLY AMAZED AT YOUR LIFE EXPERIENCES--
SCOTT and BORGMAN
©2007 ZITS Partnership. Distributed by King Features Syndicate
5/22
--BUT ALMOST NEVER IN A GOOD WAY.

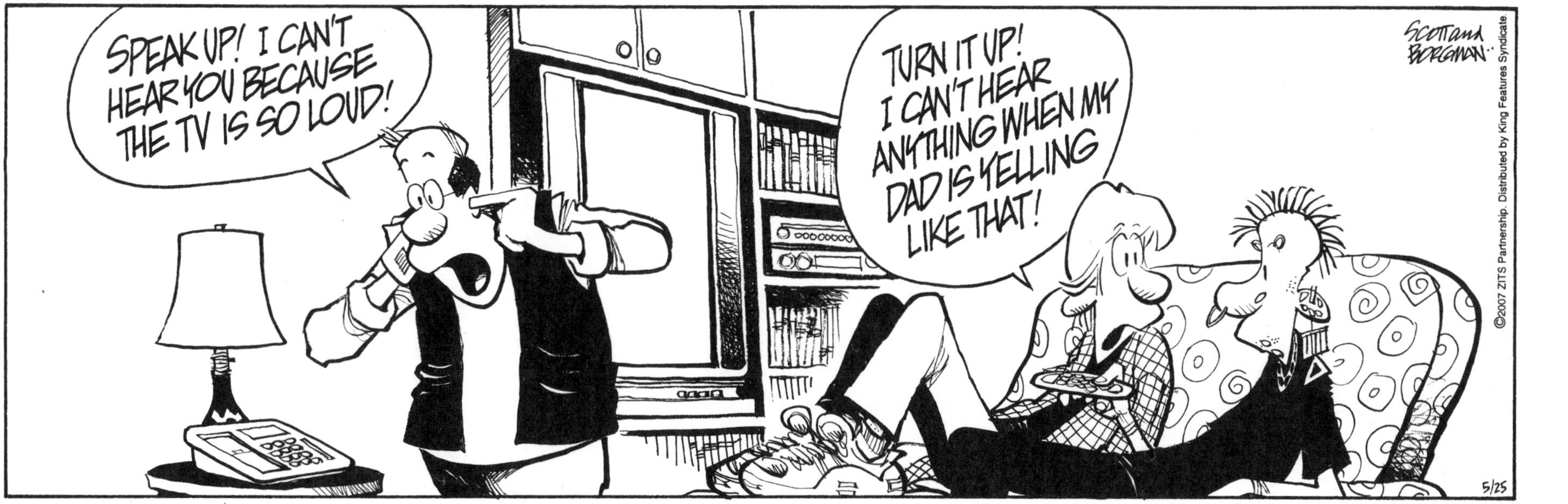
SPEAK UP! I CAN'T HEAR YOU BECAUSE THE TV IS SO LOUD!
TURN IT UP! I CAN'T HEAR ANYTHING WHEN MY DAD IS YELLING LIKE THAT!
SCOTT and BORGMAN
©2007 ZITS Partnership. Distributed by King Features Syndicate.
5/25

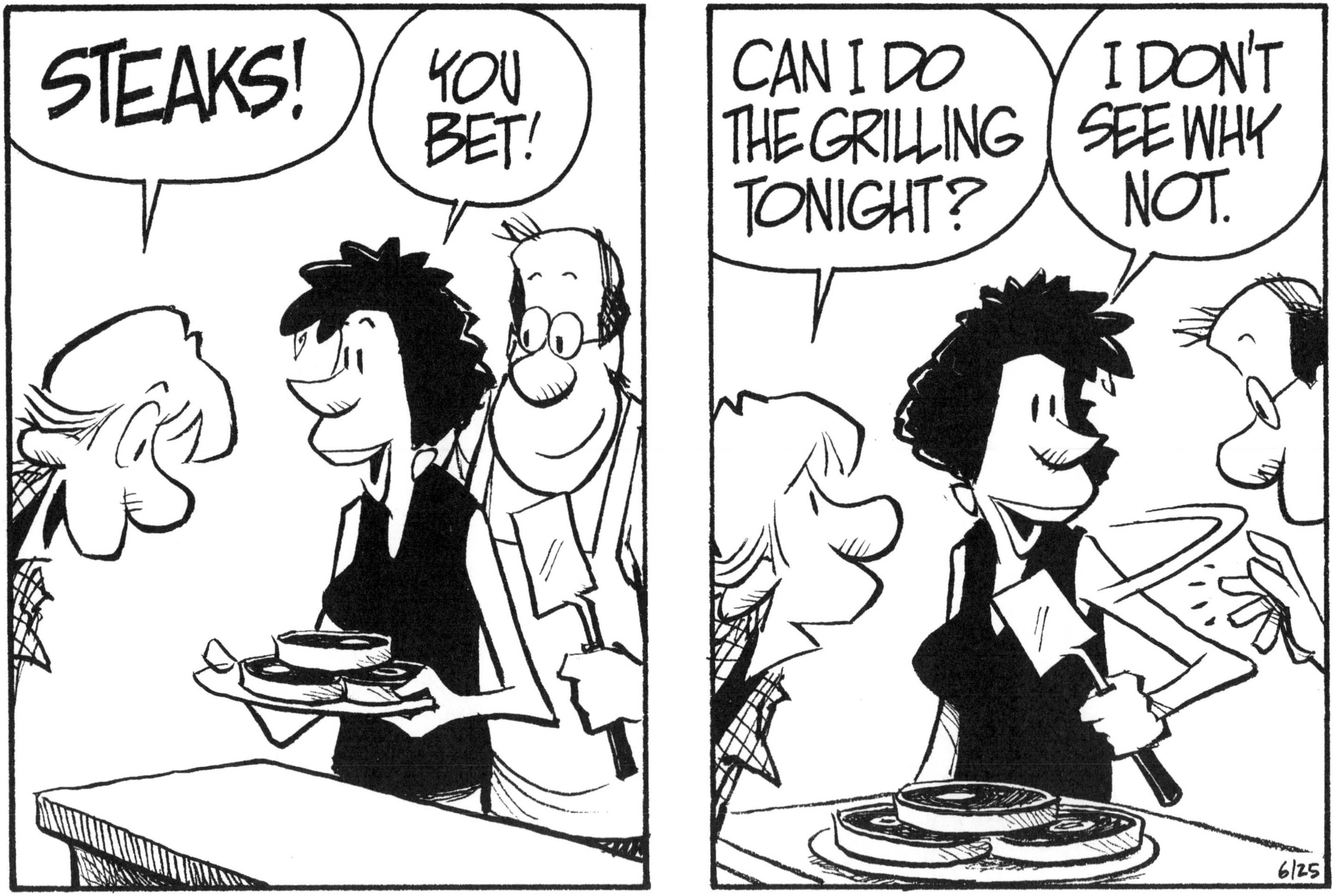
STEAKS!
YOU BET!
CAN I DO THE GRILLING TONIGHT?
I DON'T SEE WHY NOT.
6/25

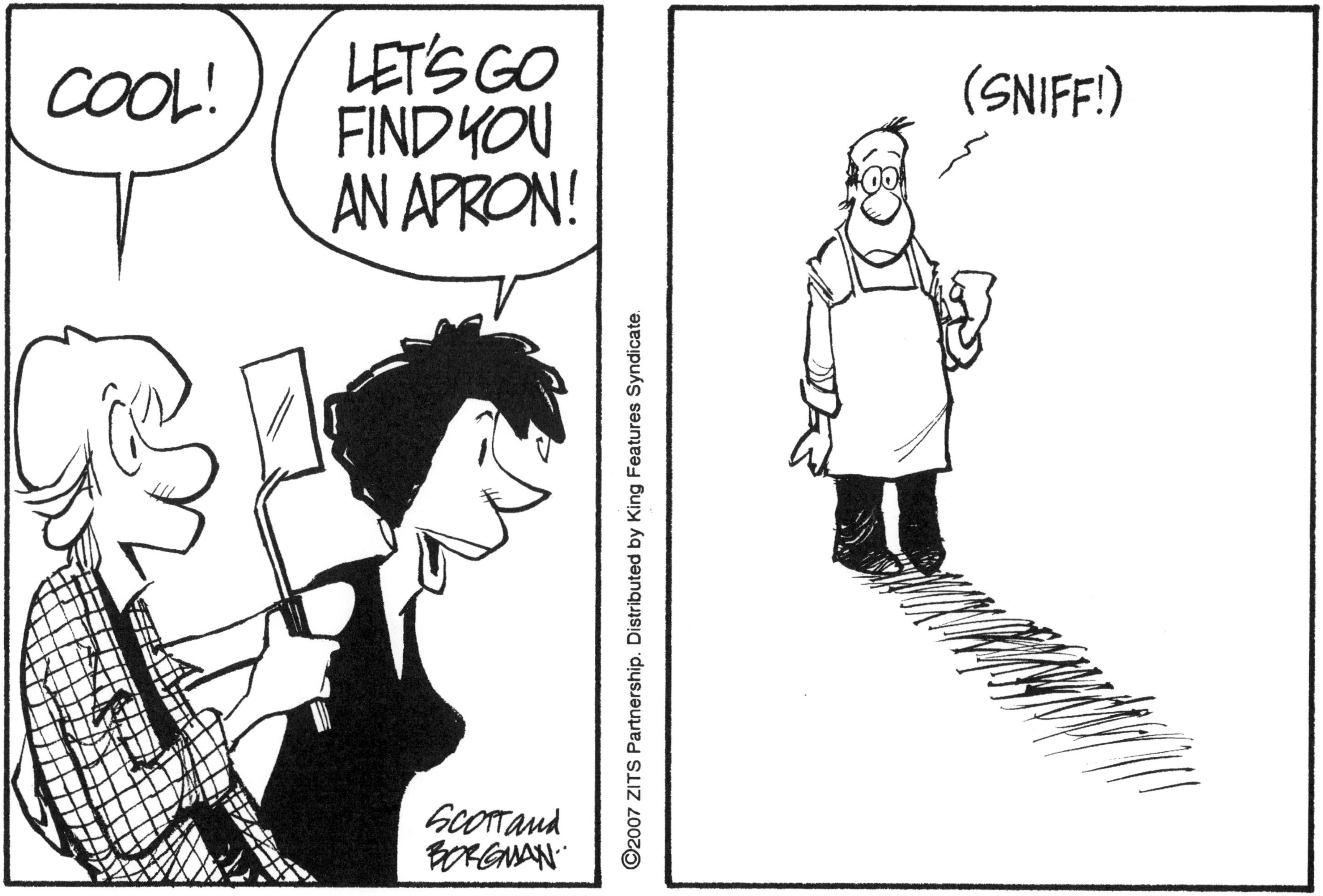
COOL!
LET'S GO FIND YOU AN APRON!
SCOTT and BORGMAN
(SNIFF!)

Jim: Thus begins a series straight from my grill to yours. Only when my stepson began mastering the art of barbecuing was it revealed that my family considered me less than a gourmet chef. But it's OK—sniff!—I'm not hurt.

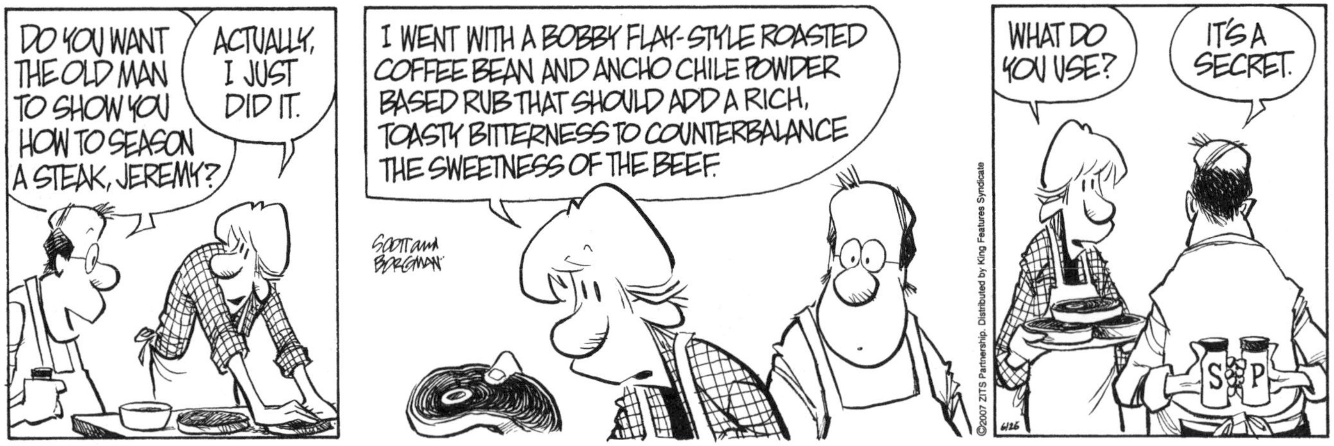
DO YOU WANT THE OLD MAN TO SHOW YOU HOW TO SEASON A STEAK, JEREMY?
ACTUALLY, I JUST DID IT.
I WENT WITH A BOBBY FLAY-STYLE ROASTED COFFEE BEAN AND ANCHO CHILE POWDER BASED RUB THAT SHOULD ADD A RICH, TOASTY BITTERNESS TO COUNTERBALANCE THE SWEETNESS OF THE BEEF.
WHAT DO YOU USE?
IT'S A SECRET.
S
P
©2007 ZITS Partnership. Distributed by King Features Syndicate

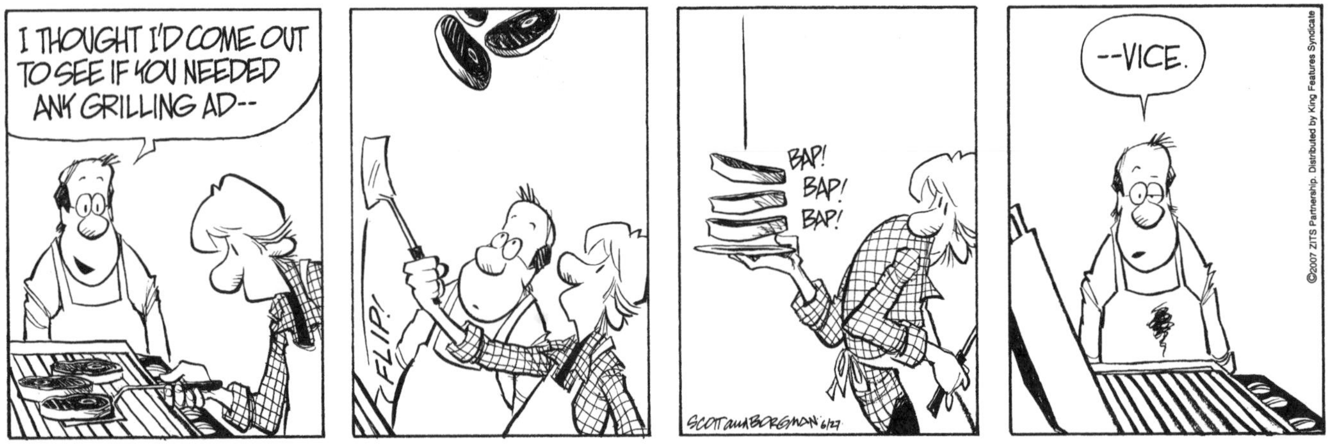
I THOUGHT I'D COME OUT TO SEE IF YOU NEEDED ANY GRILLING AD--
FLIP!
BAP! BAP! BAP!
--VICE.
©2007 ZITS Partnership. Distributed by King Features Syndicate

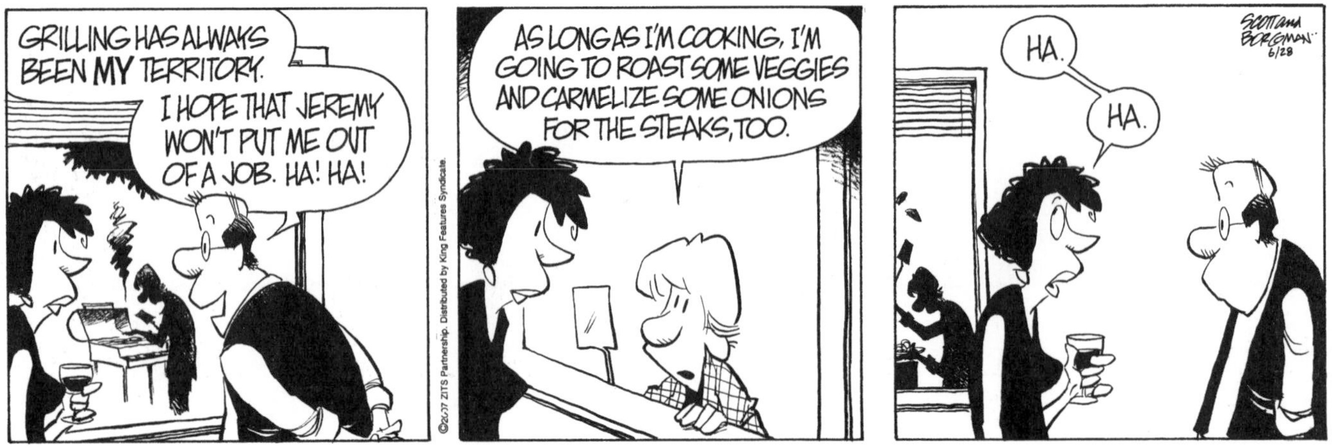
GRILLING HAS ALWAYS BEEN MY TERRITORY.
I HOPE THAT JEREMY WON'T PUT ME OUT OF A JOB. HA! HA!
AS LONG AS I'M COOKING, I'M GOING TO ROAST SOME VEGGIES AND CARMELIZE SOME ONIONS FOR THE STEAKS, TOO.
HA.
HA.

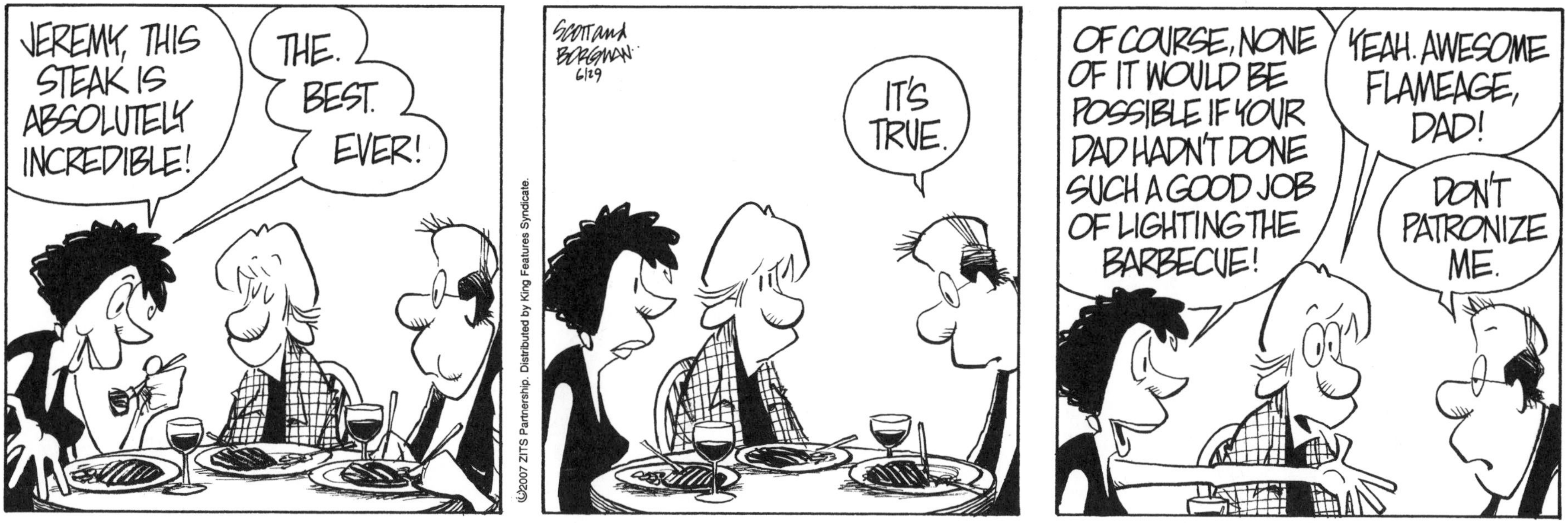
JEREMY, THIS STEAK IS ABSOLUTELY INCREDIBLE!
THE. BEST. EVER!
©2007 ZITS Partnership. Distributed by King Features Syndicate.
SCOTT and BORGMAN 6/29
IT'S TRUE.
OF COURSE, NONE OF IT WOULD BE POSSIBLE IF YOUR DAD HADN'T DONE SUCH A GOOD JOB OF LIGHTING THE BARBECUE!
YEAH. AWESOME FLAMEAGE, DAD!
DON'T PATRONIZE ME.

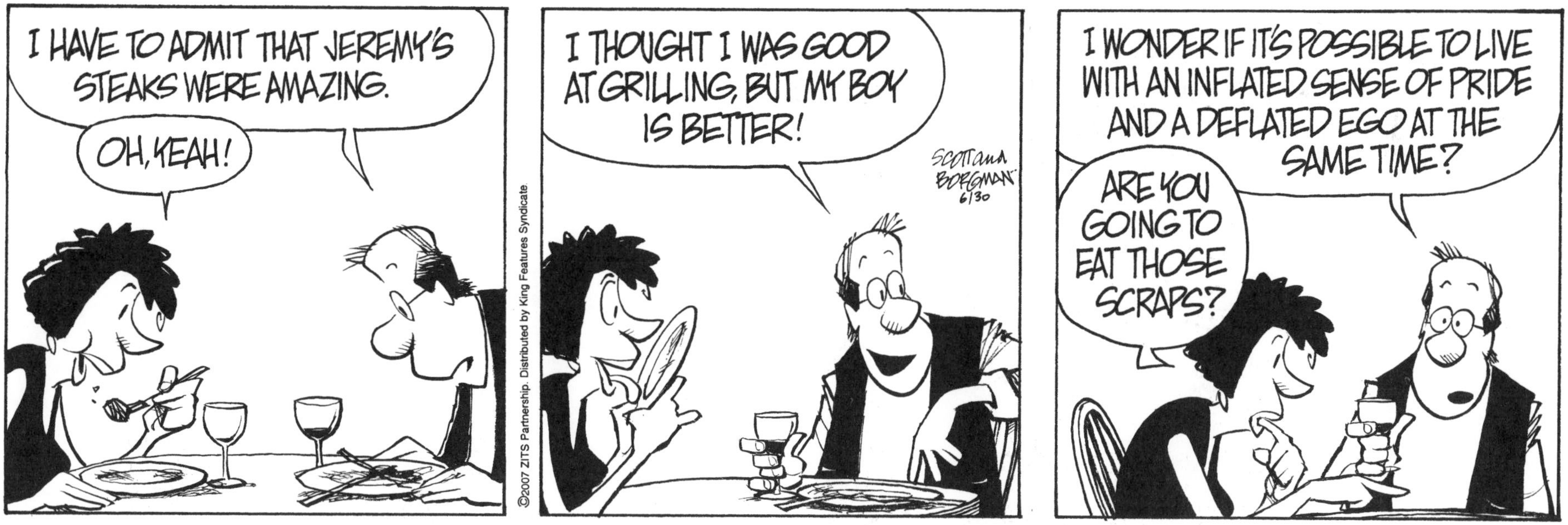
I HAVE TO ADMIT THAT JEREMY'S STEAKS WERE AMAZING.
OH, YEAH!
©2007 ZITS Partnership. Distributed by King Features Syndicate
I THOUGHT I WAS GOOD AT GRILLING, BUT MY BOY IS BETTER!
SCOTT and BORGMAN 6/30
I WONDER IF IT'S POSSIBLE TO LIVE WITH AN INFLATED SENSE OF PRIDE AND A DEFLATED EGO AT THE SAME TIME?
ARE YOU GOING TO EAT THOSE SCRAPS?

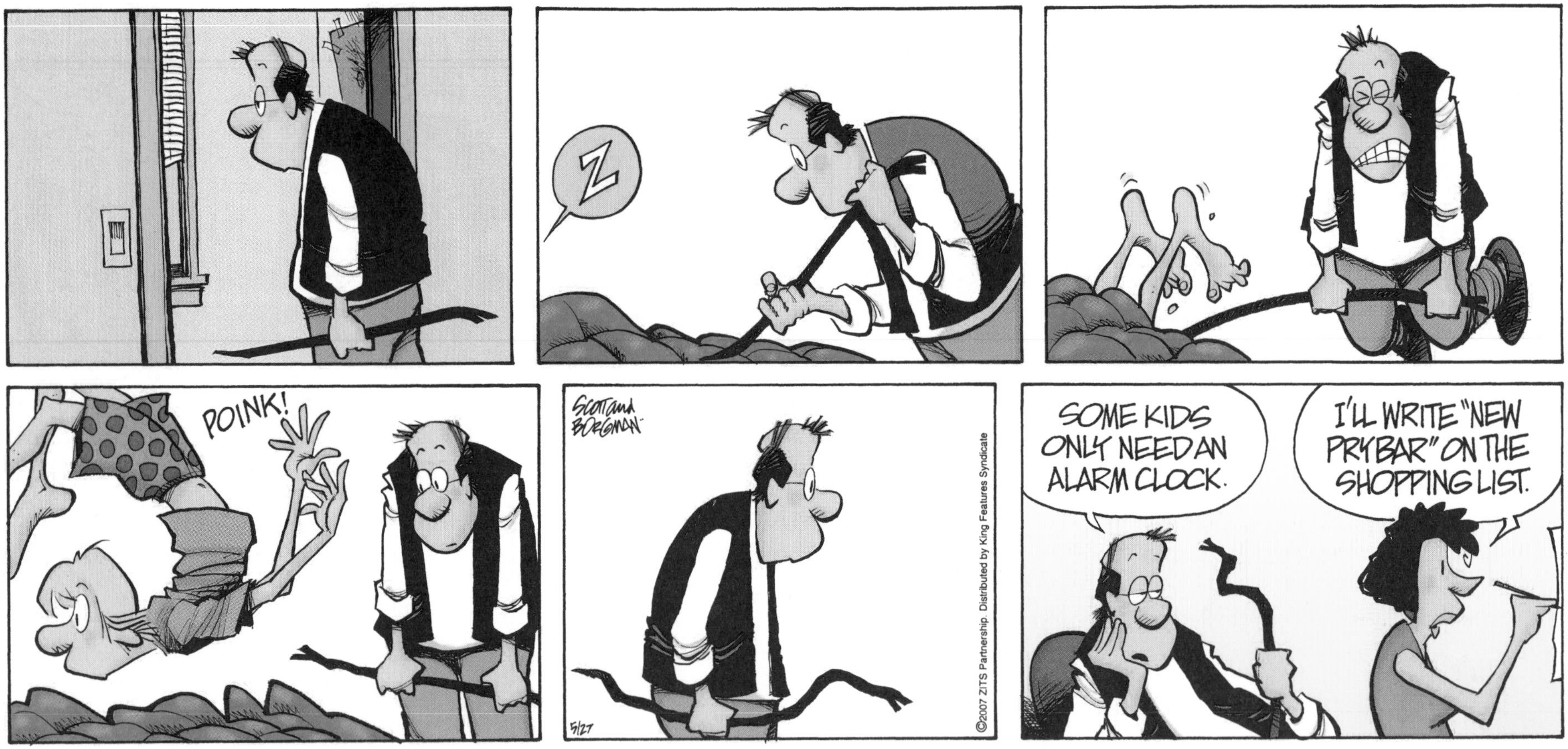
Z
POINK!
SCOTT AND BORGMAN
©2007 ZITS Partnership. Distributed by King Features Syndicate
5/27
SOME KIDS ONLY NEED AN ALARM CLOCK.
I'LL WRITE "NEW PRYBAR" ON THE SHOPPING LIST.

Jerry: Professional cartooning tip: If you're going to do a comic strip with a teenager in it, stock up on those little balloons with "Zs" in them.

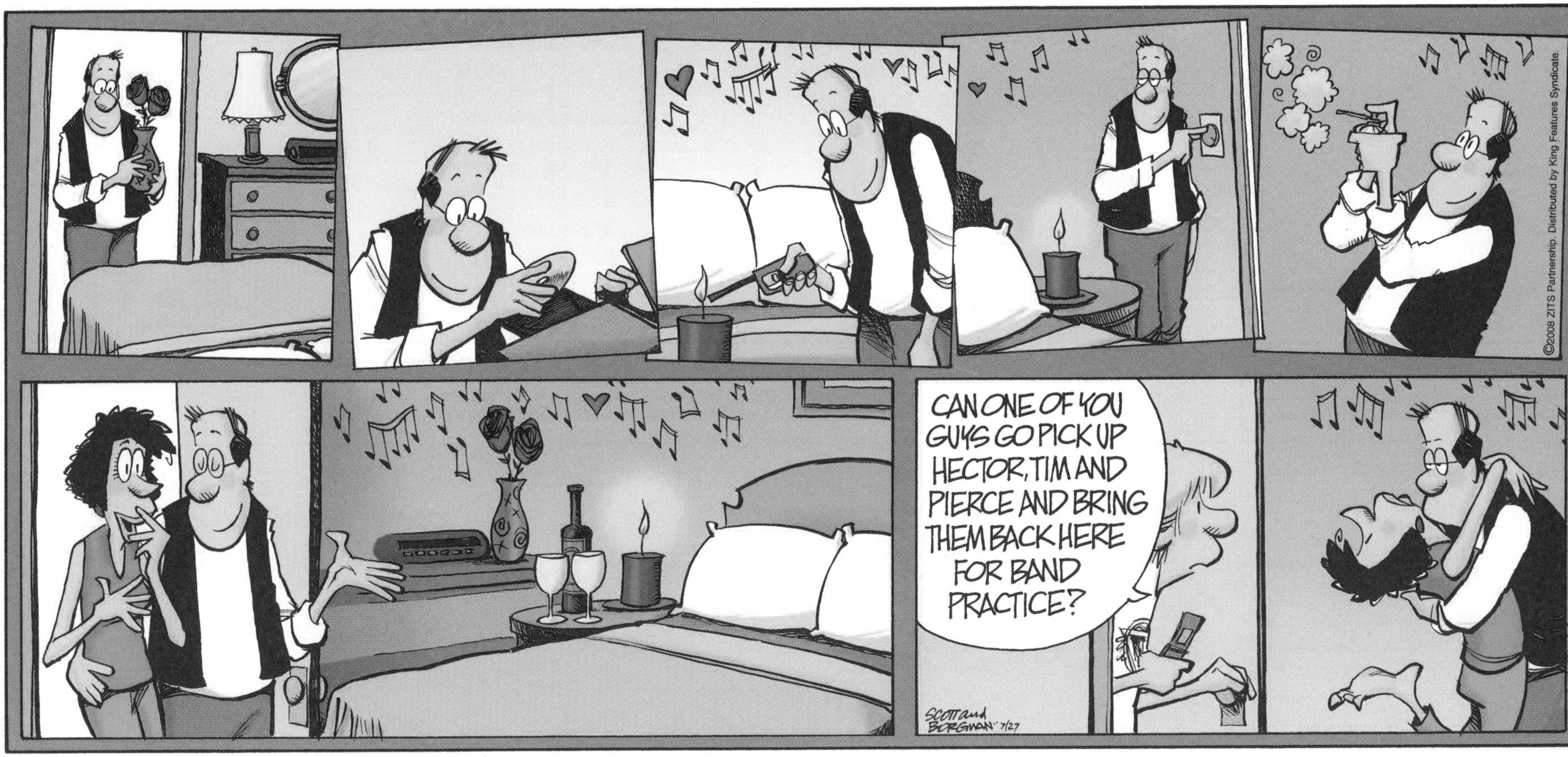
©2008 ZITS Partnership. Distributed by King Features Syndicate.
CAN ONE OF YOU GUYS GO PICK UP HECTOR, TIM AND PIERCE AND BRING THEM BACK HERE FOR BAND PRACTICE?
SCOTT and BORGMAN 7/27

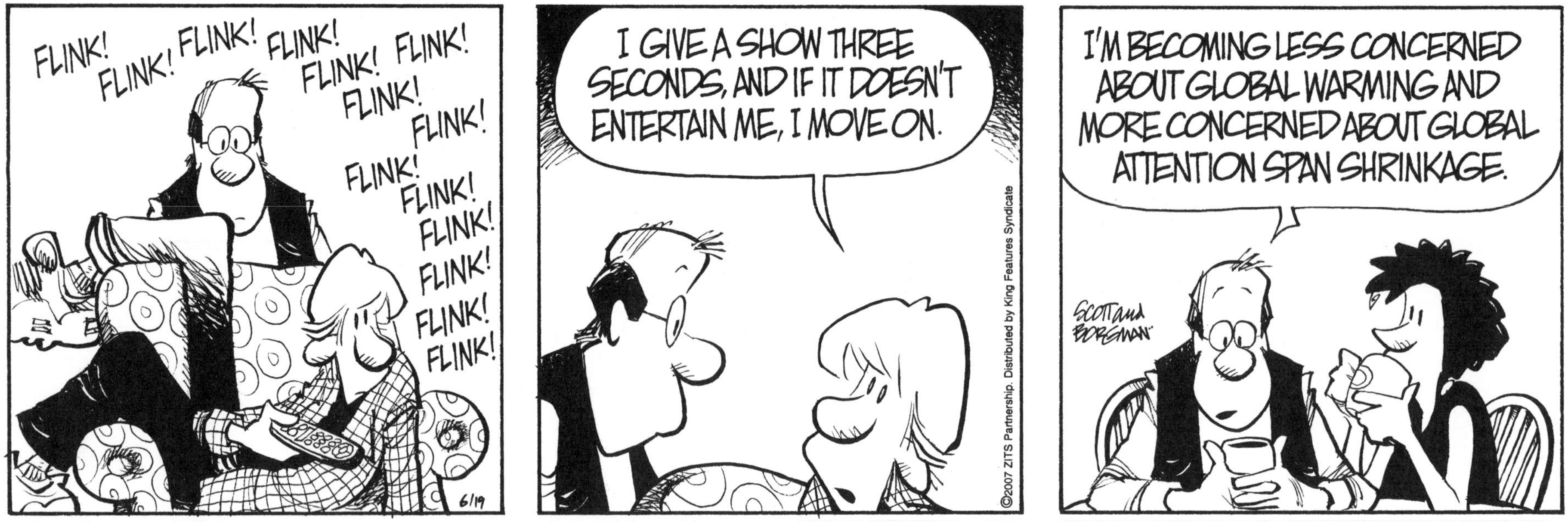
FLINK! FLINK! FLINK! FLINK! FLINK! FLINK! FLINK! FLINK! FLINK! FLINK! FLINK! FLINK! FLINK! FLINK!
I GIVE A SHOW THREE SECONDS, AND IF IT DOESN'T ENTERTAIN ME, I MOVE ON.
I'M BECOMING LESS CONCERNED ABOUT GLOBAL WARMING AND MORE CONCERNED ABOUT GLOBAL ATTENTION SPAN SHRINKAGE.
©2007 ZITS Partnership. Distributed by King Features Syndicate
SCOTT and BORGMAN

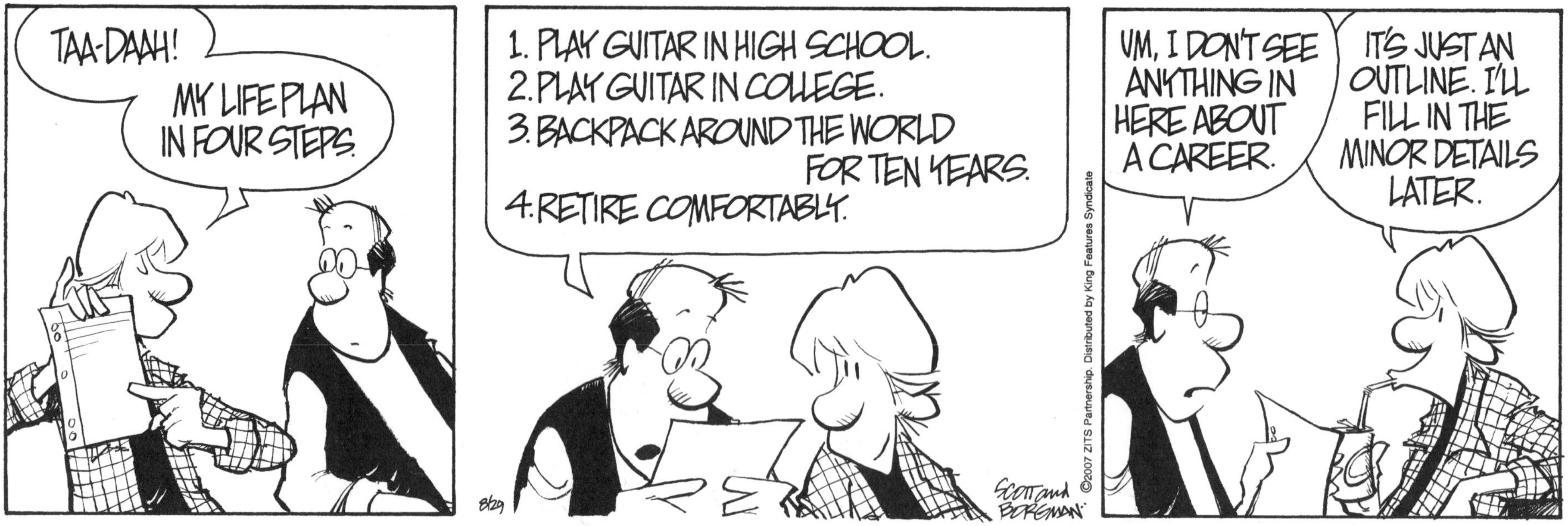
TAA-DAAH!
MY LIFE PLAN IN FOUR STEPS.
1. PLAY GUITAR IN HIGH SCHOOL.
2. PLAY GUITAR IN COLLEGE.
3. BACKPACK AROUND THE WORLD FOR TEN YEARS.
4. RETIRE COMFORTABLY.
UM, I DON'T SEE ANYTHING IN HERE ABOUT A CAREER.
IT'S JUST AN OUTLINE. I'LL FILL IN THE MINOR DETAILS LATER.
©2007 ZITS Partnership. Distributed by King Features Syndicate
SCOTT and BORGMAN

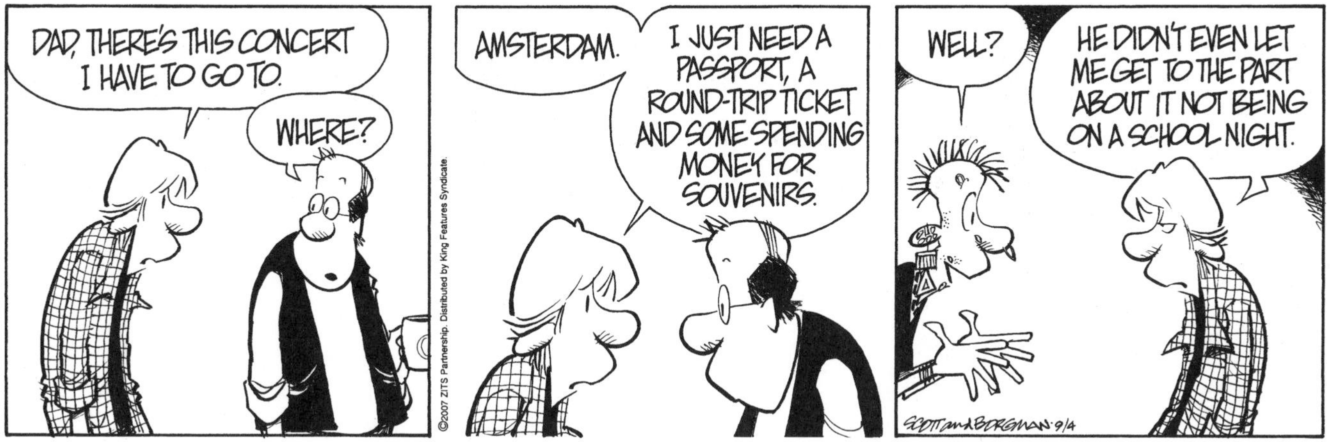
DAD, THERE'S THIS CONCERT I HAVE TO GO TO.
WHERE?
AMSTERDAM.
I JUST NEED A PASSPORT, A ROUND-TRIP TICKET AND SOME SPENDING MONEY FOR SOUVENIRS.
WELL?
HE DIDN'T EVEN LET ME GET TO THE PART ABOUT IT NOT BEING ON A SCHOOL NIGHT.
©2007 ZITS Partnership. Distributed by King Features Syndicate.
SCOTT and BORGMAN 9/4

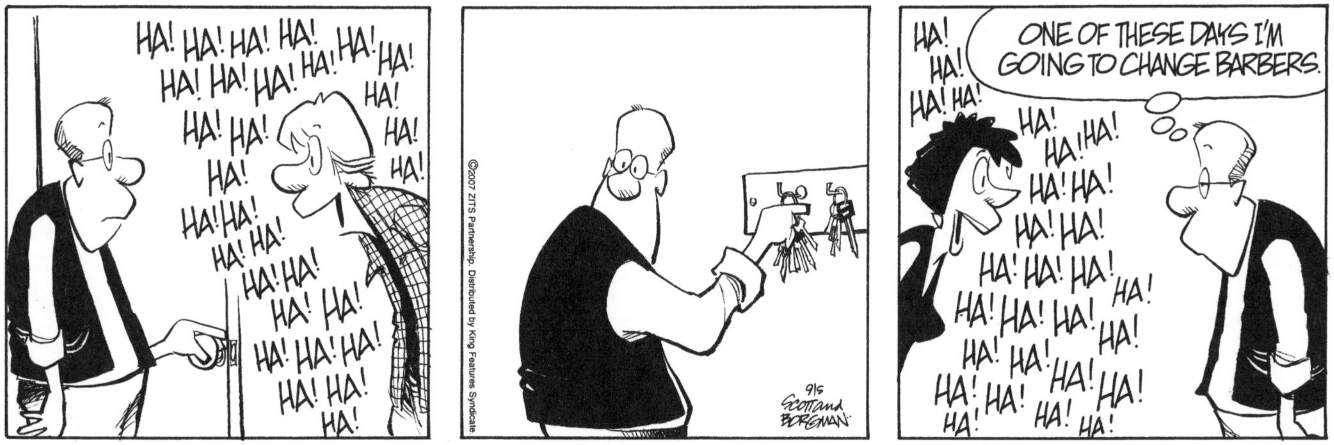
HA! HA! HA! HA! HA! HA! HA! HA! HA! HA! HA! HA! HA! HA! HA! HA! HA! HA! HA! HA! HA! HA! HA! HA! HA! HA! HA! HA! HA!
©2007 ZITS Partnership. Distributed by King Features Syndicate.
9/5 SCOTT and BORGMAN
HA! HA! HA! HA!
ONE OF THESE DAYS I'M GOING TO CHANGE BARBERS.
HA! HA! HA! HA! HA! HA! HA! HA! HA! HA! HA! HA! HA! HA! HA! HA! HA! HA! HA! HA! HA! HA! HA! HA!

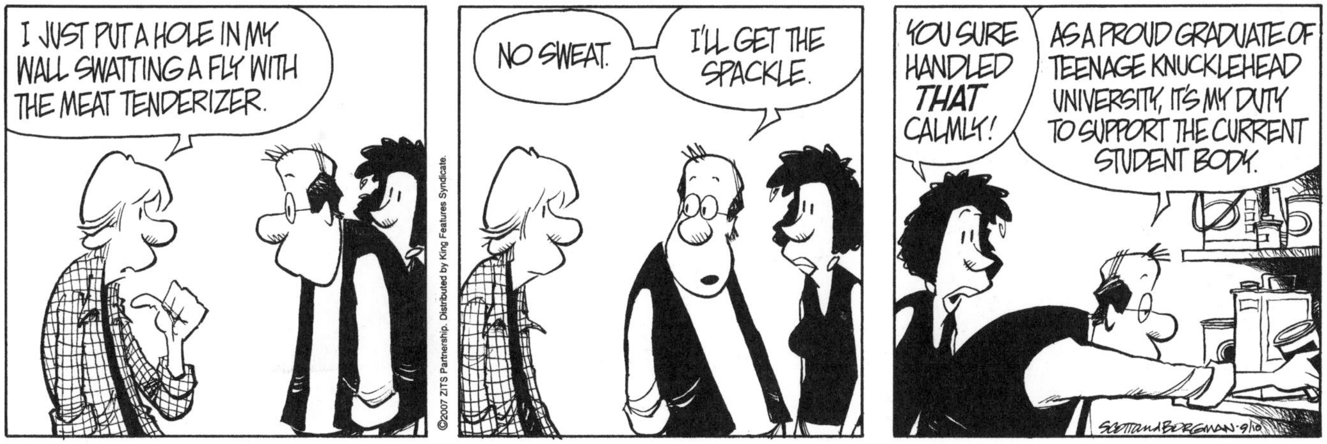
I JUST PUT A HOLE IN MY WALL SWATTING A FLY WITH THE MEAT TENDERIZER.
©2007 ZITS Partnership. Distributed by King Features Syndicate.
NO SWEAT.
I'LL GET THE SPACKLE.
YOU SURE HANDLED THAT CALMLY!
AS A PROUD GRADUATE OF TEENAGE KNUCKLEHEAD UNIVERSITY, IT'S MY DUTY TO SUPPORT THE CURRENT STUDENT BODY.
SCOTT and BORGMAN 9/10

HA! HA! NICE MOVE, MR. D.!
I CAN'T BELIEVE YOU MADE THIS PIE FROM SCRATCH!
I HAD A GREAT TIME TONIGHT.
I WISH MY DAD WAS AS MUCH FUN AS YOURS, JEREMY.
9/29
THANKS FOR EMBARRASSING ME.
SCOTT and BORGMAN

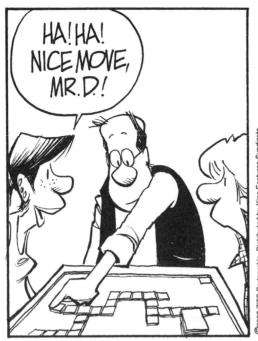

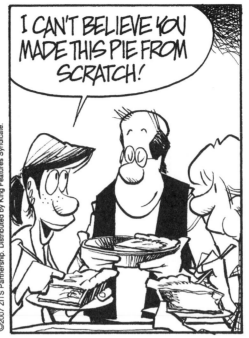

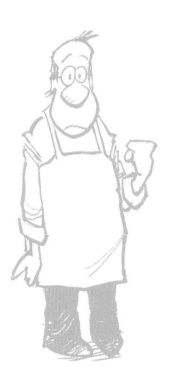

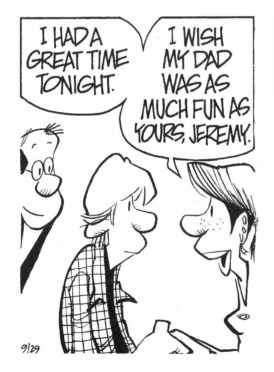

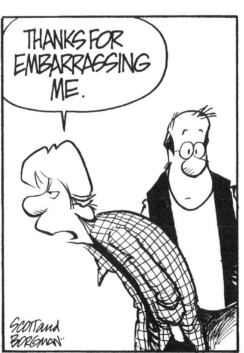

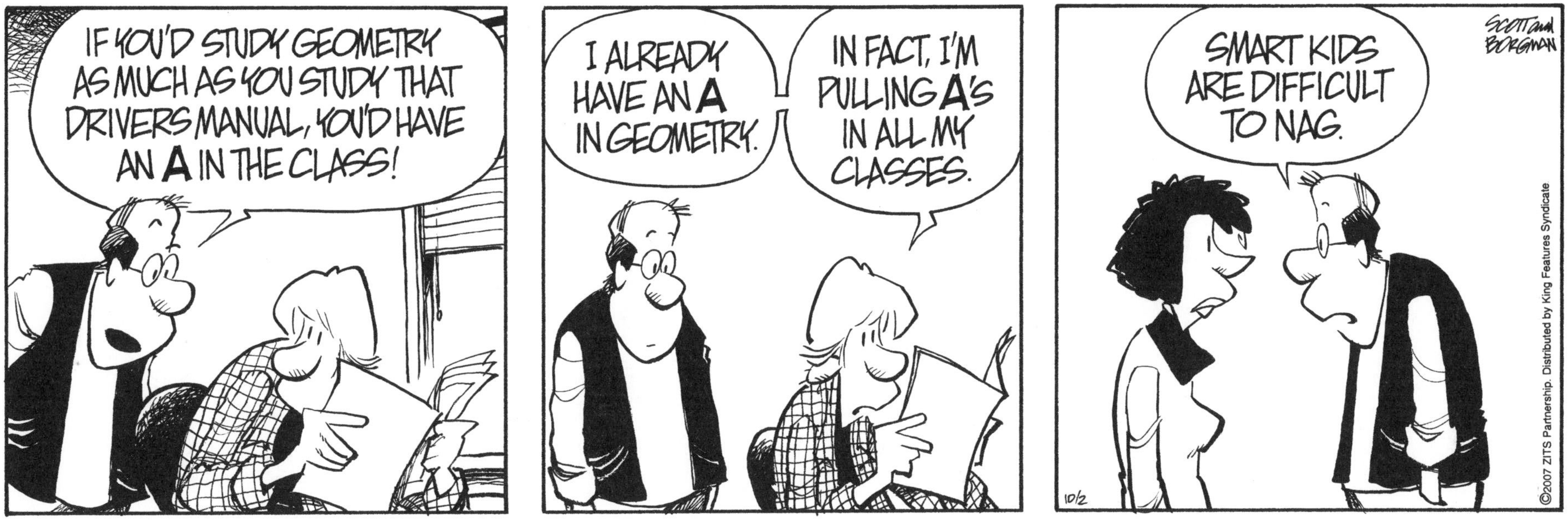
IF YOU'D STUDY GEOMETRY AS MUCH AS YOU STUDY THAT DRIVERS MANUAL, YOU'D HAVE AN A IN THE CLASS!
I ALREADY HAVE AN A IN GEOMETRY.
IN FACT, I'M PULLING A's IN ALL MY CLASSES.
SMART KIDS ARE DIFFICULT TO NAG.
SCOTT AND BORGMAN
10/2
©2007 ZITS Partnership. Distributed by King Features Syndicate

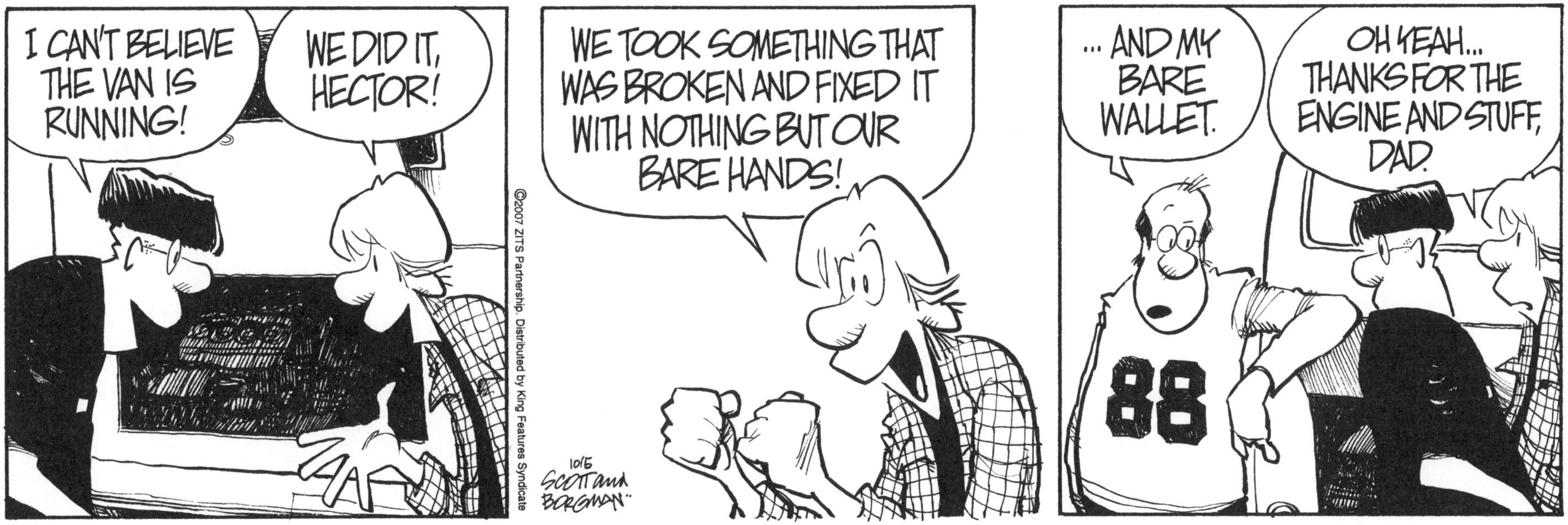
I CAN'T BELIEVE THE VAN IS RUNNING!
WE DID IT, HECTOR!
©2007 ZITS Partnership. Distributed by King Features Syndicate
WE TOOK SOMETHING THAT WAS BROKEN AND FIXED IT WITH NOTHING BUT OUR BARE HANDS!
10/5
SCOTT AND BORGMAN
... AND MY BARE WALLET.
OH YEAH... THANKS FOR THE ENGINE AND STUFF, DAD.
88

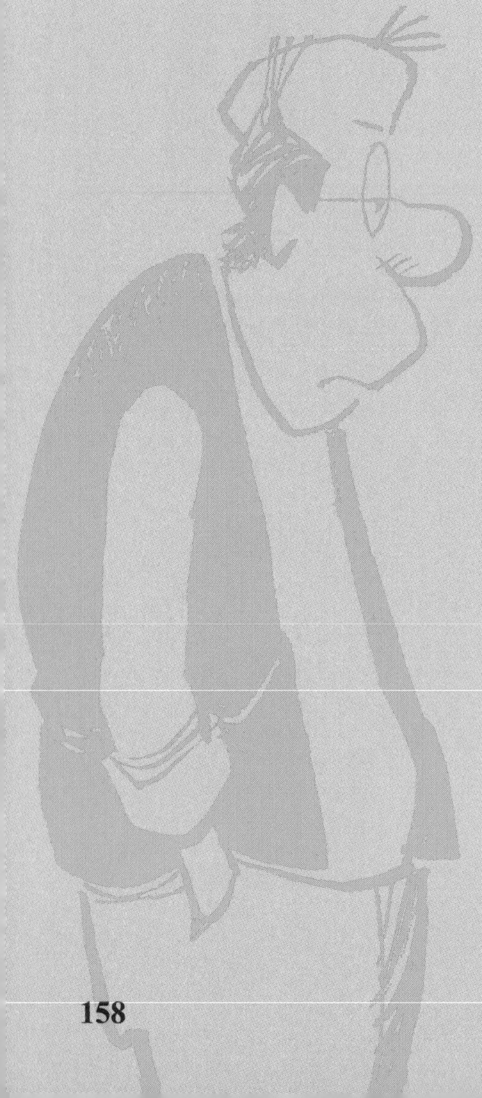

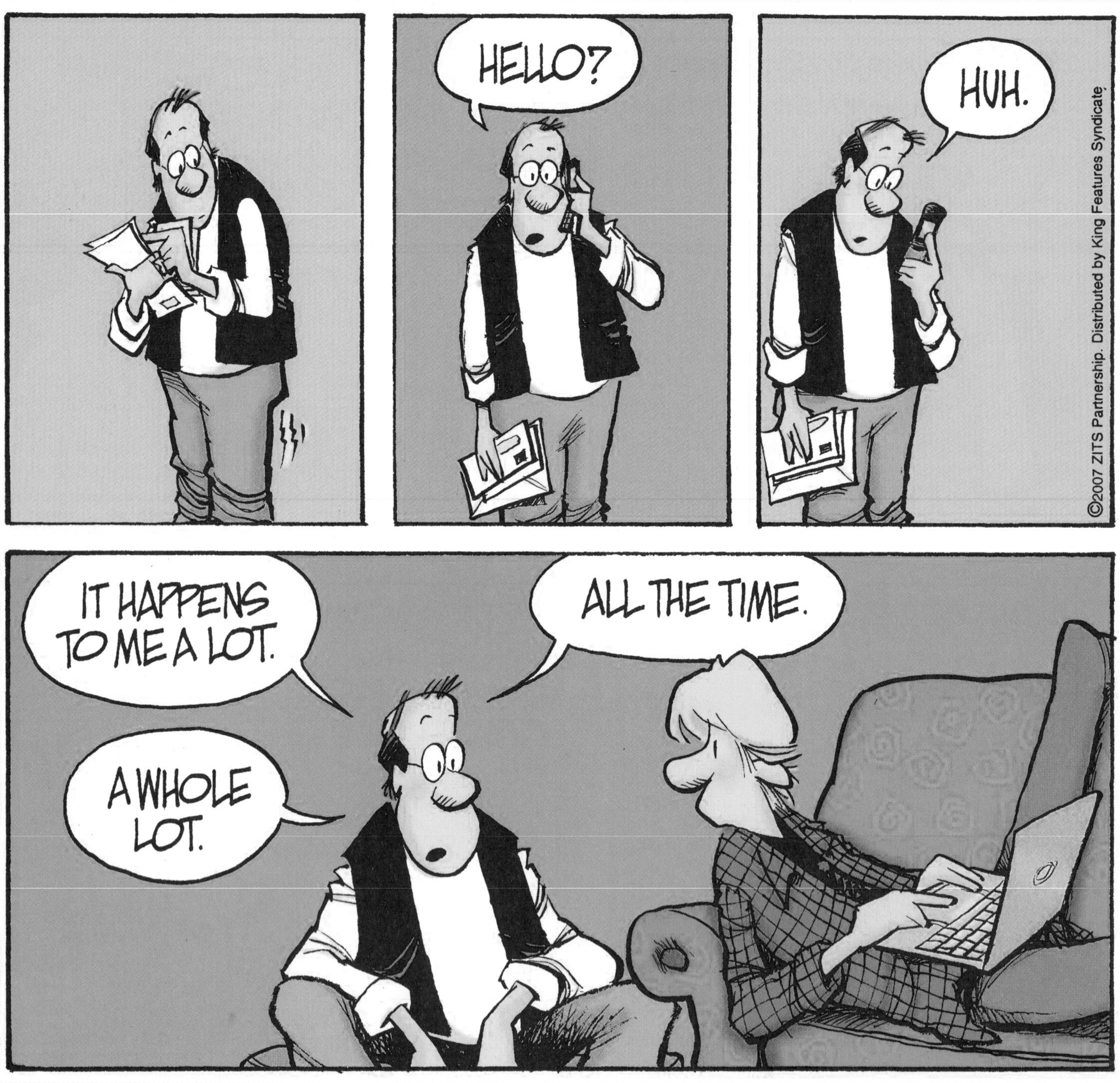
HELLO?
HUH.
©2007 ZITS Partnership. Distributed by King Features Syndicate.
IT HAPPENS TO ME A LOT.
A WHOLE LOT.
ALL THE TIME.

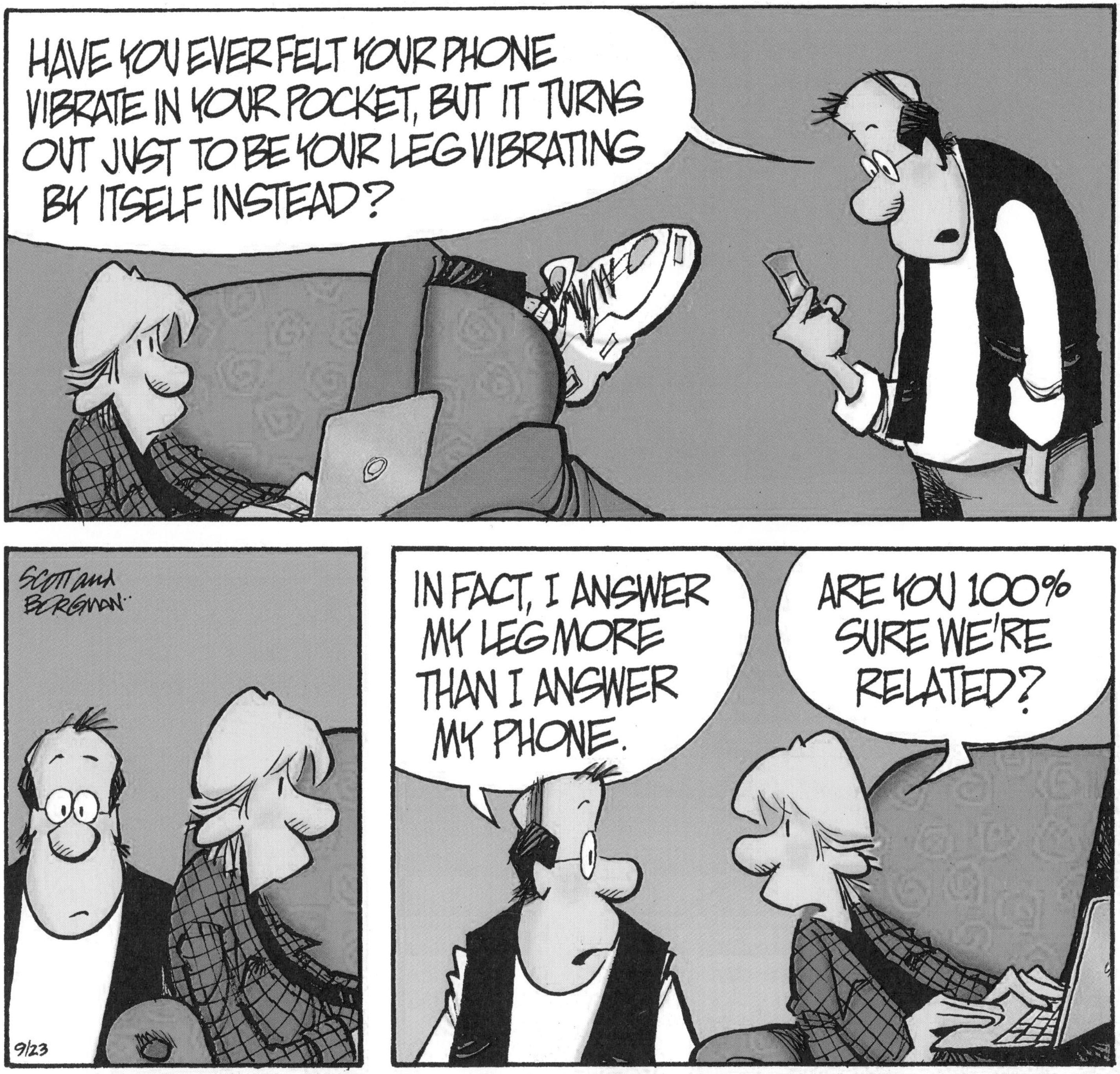
HAVE YOU EVER FELT YOUR PHONE VIBRATE IN YOUR POCKET, BUT IT TURNS OUT JUST TO BE YOUR LEG VIBRATING BY ITSELF INSTEAD?
SCOTT AND BORGMAN
IN FACT, I ANSWER MY LEG MORE THAN I ANSWER MY PHONE.
ARE YOU 100% SURE WE'RE RELATED?
9/23

Jim: There's an app for that.

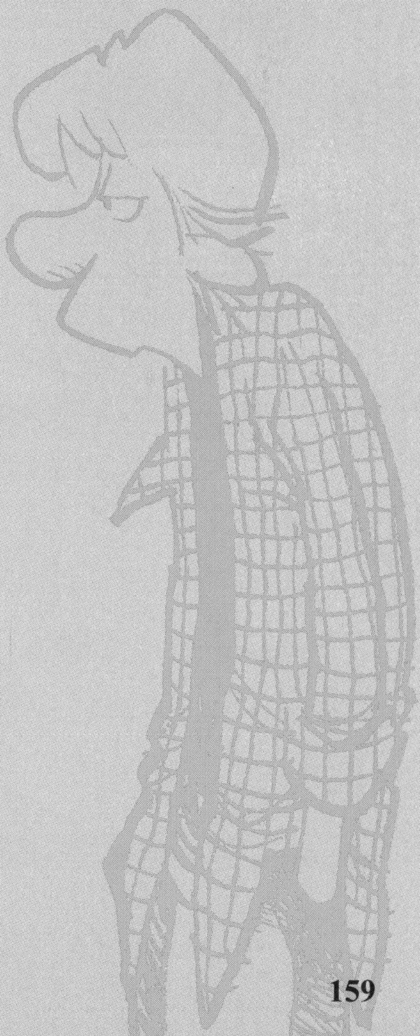

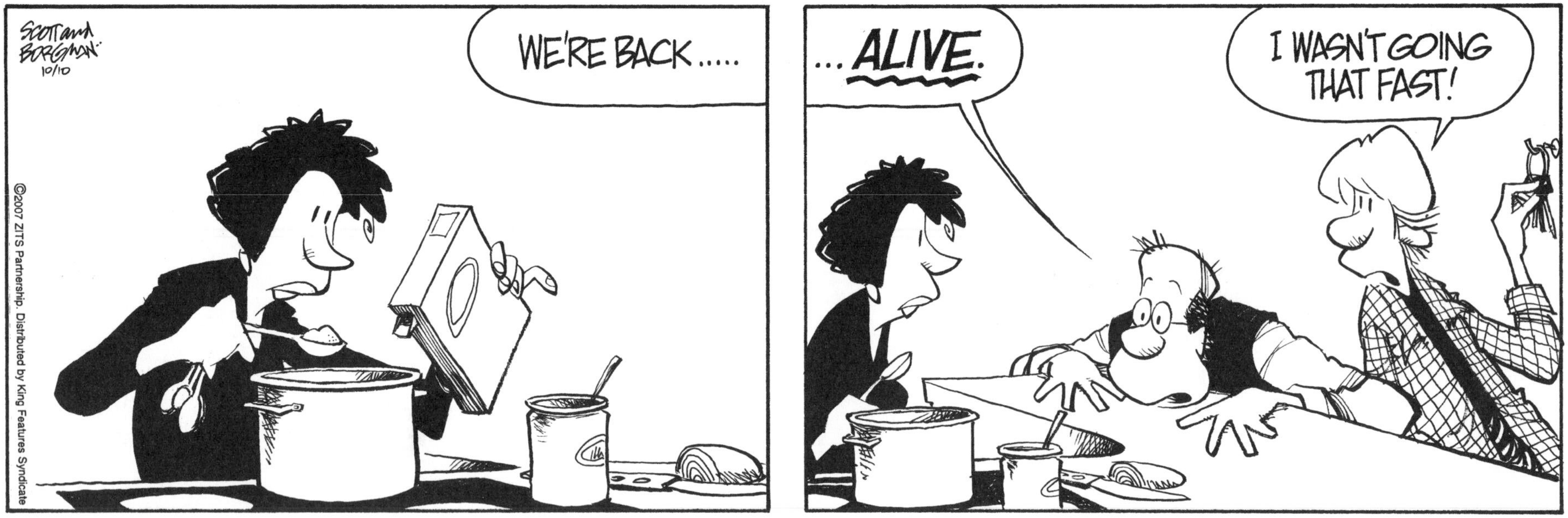
SCOTT and BORGMAN 10/10
©2007 ZITS Partnership. Distributed by King Features Syndicate
WE'RE BACK.....
...ALIVE.
I WASN'T GOING THAT FAST!

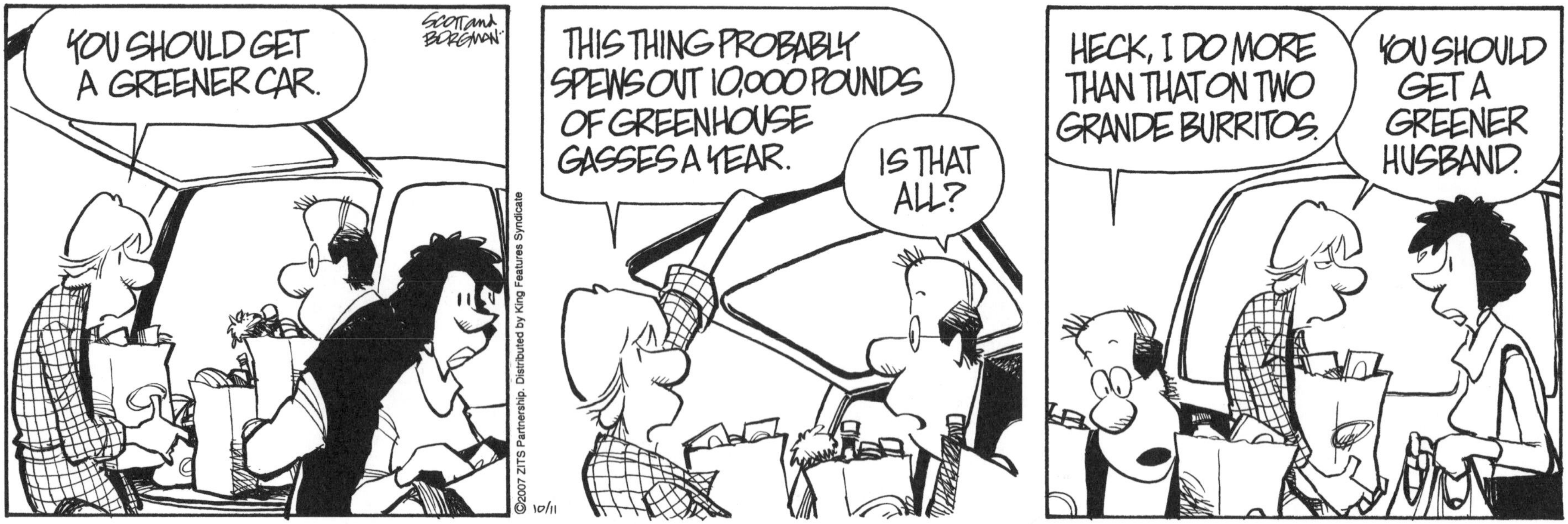
SCOTT and BORGMAN
©2007 ZITS Partnership. Distributed by King Features Syndicate 10/11
YOU SHOULD GET A GREENER CAR.
THIS THING PROBABLY SPEWS OUT 10,000 POUNDS OF GREENHOUSE GASSES A YEAR.
IS THAT ALL?
HECK, I DO MORE THAN THAT ON TWO GRANDE BURRITOS.
YOU SHOULD GET A GREENER HUSBAND.

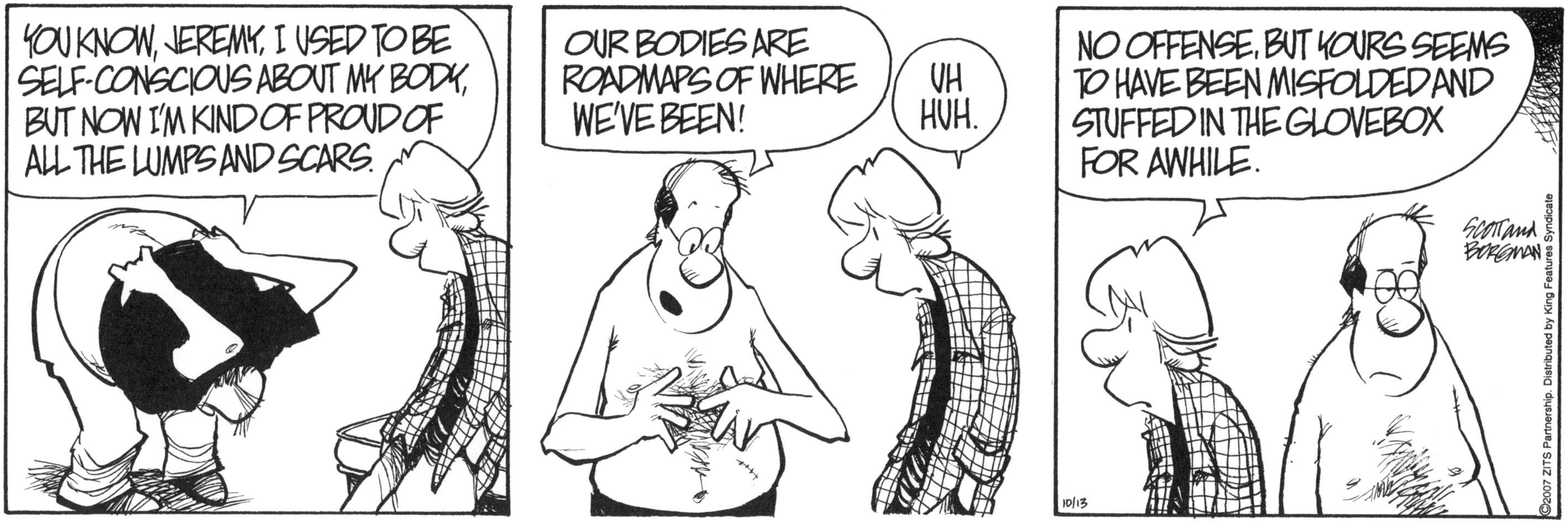
YOU KNOW, JEREMY, I USED TO BE SELF-CONSCIOUS ABOUT MY BODY, BUT NOW I'M KIND OF PROUD OF ALL THE LUMPS AND SCARS.
OUR BODIES ARE ROADMAPS OF WHERE WE'VE BEEN!
UH HUH.
NO OFFENSE, BUT YOURS SEEMS TO HAVE BEEN MISFOLDED AND STUFFED IN THE GLOVEBOX FOR AWHILE.
SCOTT and BORGMAN
10/13
©2007 ZITS Partnership. Distributed by King Features Syndicate

Jim: Jerry and I work in different parts of the country, so he e-mails me roughed-out strips. I tend to retrieve them late at night, and the bottom strip on this page made me laugh so loud I woke my daughter.

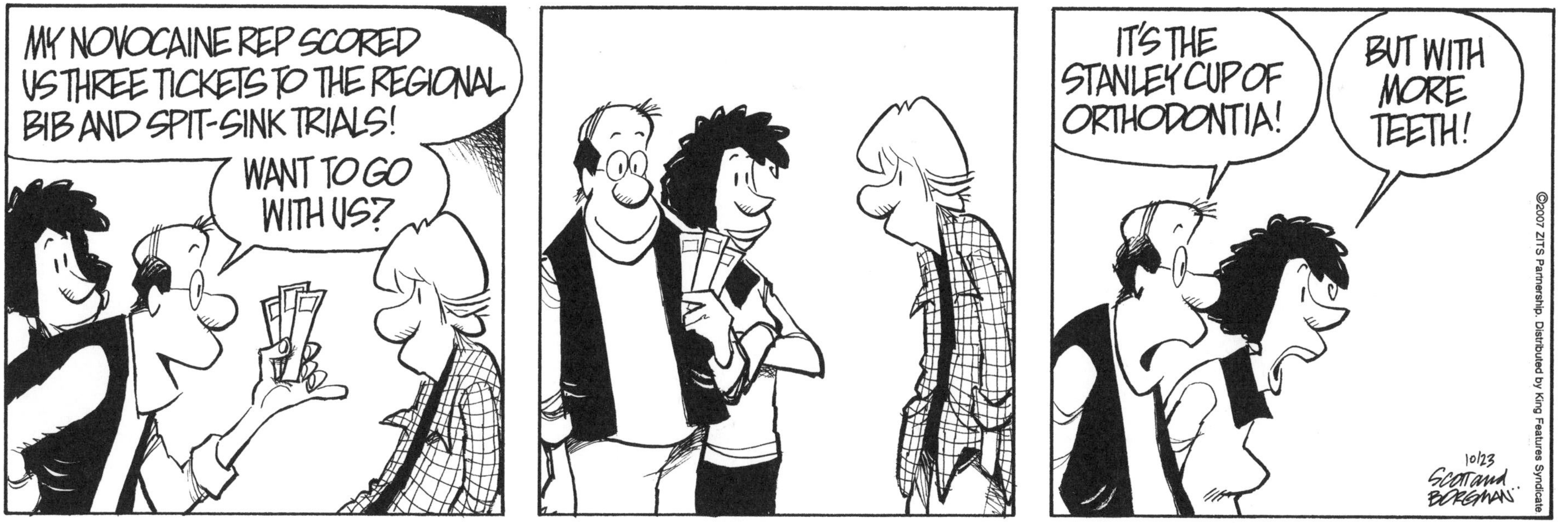
MY NOVOCAINE REP SCORED US THREE TICKETS TO THE REGIONAL BIB AND SPIT-SINK TRIALS!
WANT TO GO WITH US?
IT'S THE STANLEY CUP OF ORTHODONTIA!
BUT WITH MORE TEETH!
10/23
SCOTT and BORGMAN
©2007 ZITS Partnership. Distributed by King Features Syndicate

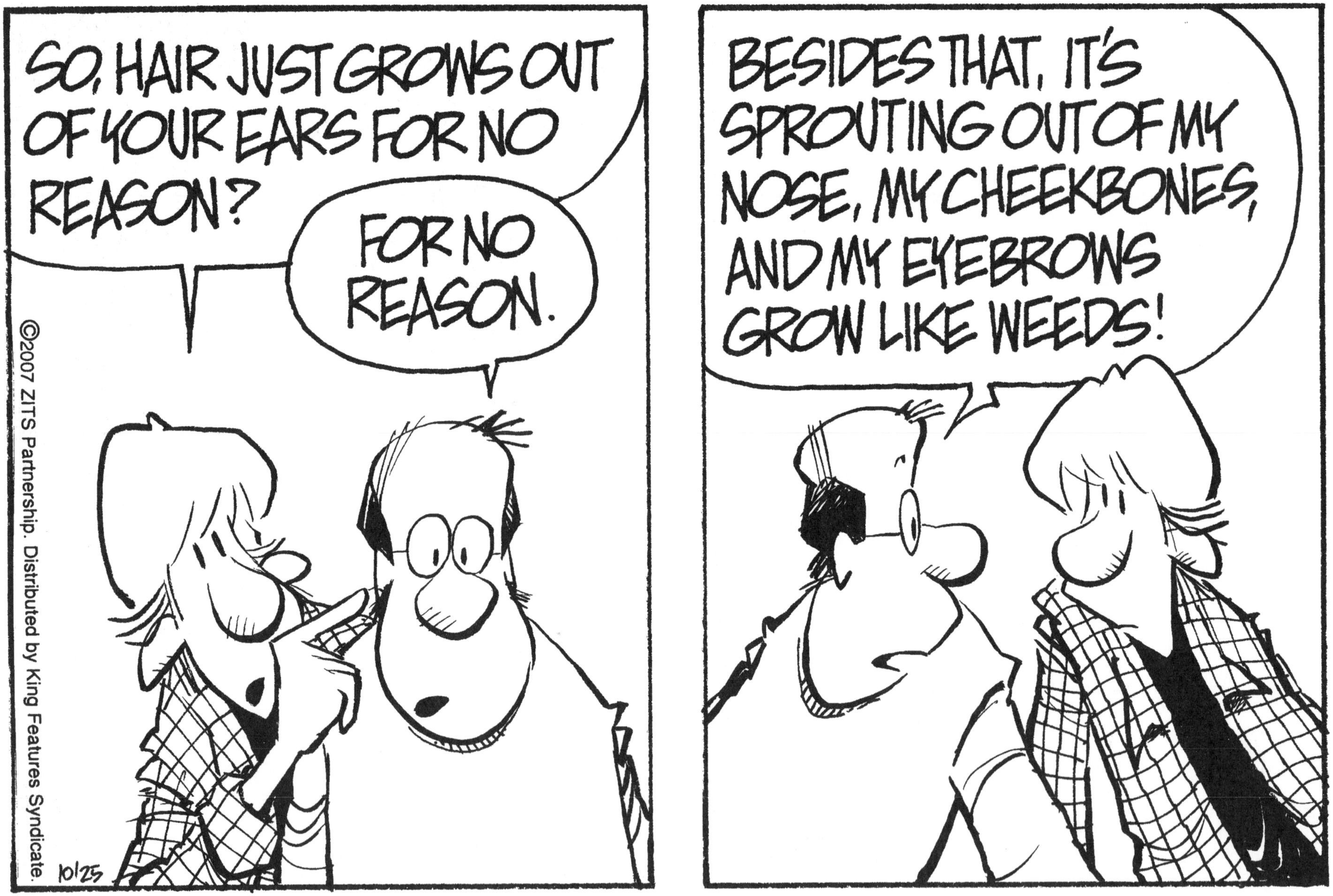
SO, HAIR JUST GROWS OUT OF YOUR EARS FOR NO REASON?
FOR NO REASON.
BESIDES THAT, IT'S SPROUTING OUT OF MY NOSE, MY CHEEKBONES, AND MY EYEBROWS GROW LIKE WEEDS!
10/25

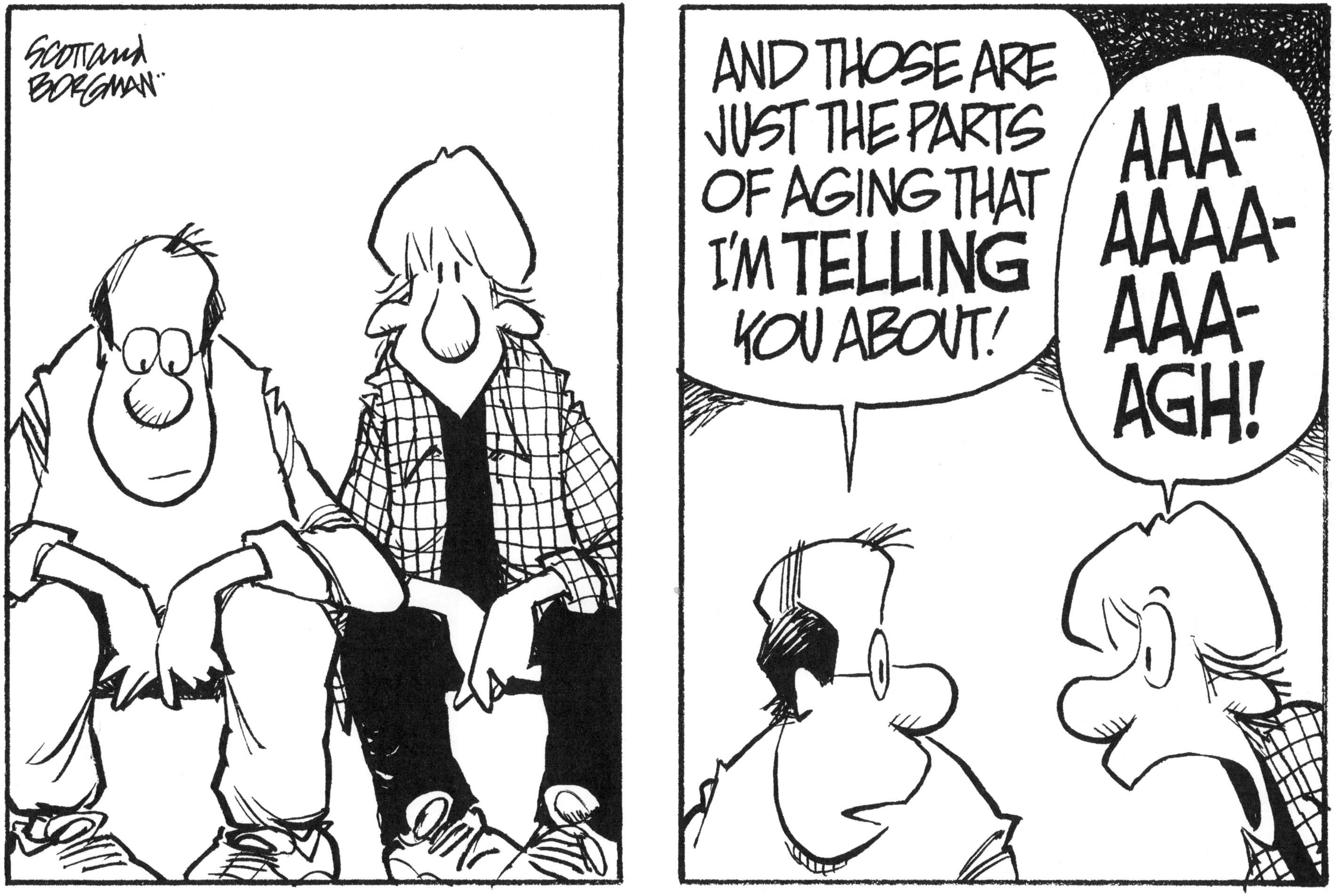
SCOTT and BORGMAN
AND THOSE ARE JUST THE PARTS OF AGING THAT I'M TELLING YOU ABOUT!
AAA-AAAA-AAA-AGH!

Jerry: What is so disagreeable about the crown of the male head to hair follicles? I mean, really!

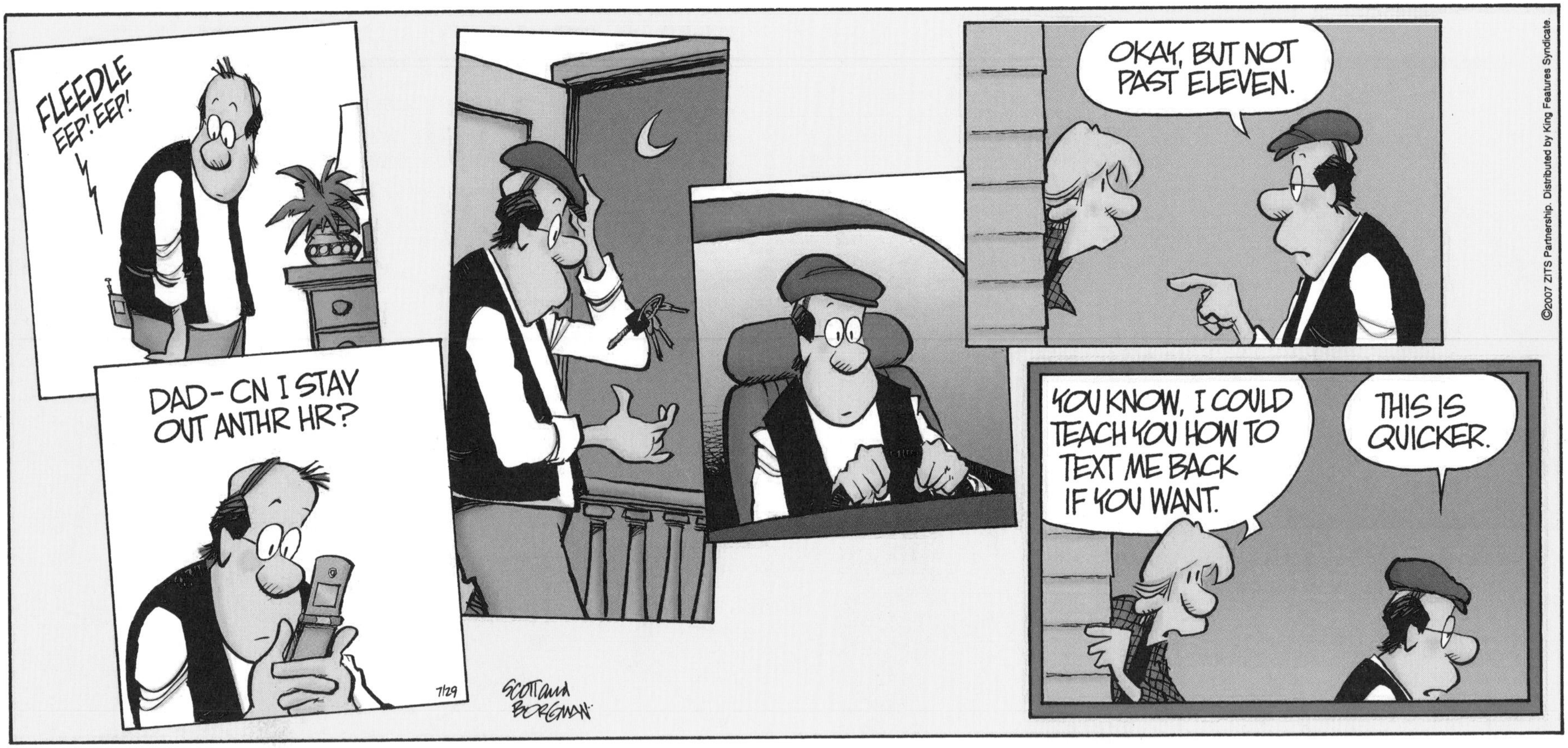
FLEEDLE EEP! EEP!
DAD- CN I STAY OUT ANTHR HR?
OKAY, BUT NOT PAST ELEVEN.
YOU KNOW, I COULD TEACH YOU HOW TO TEXT ME BACK IF YOU WANT.
THIS IS QUICKER.
7/29
SCOTT and BORGMAN

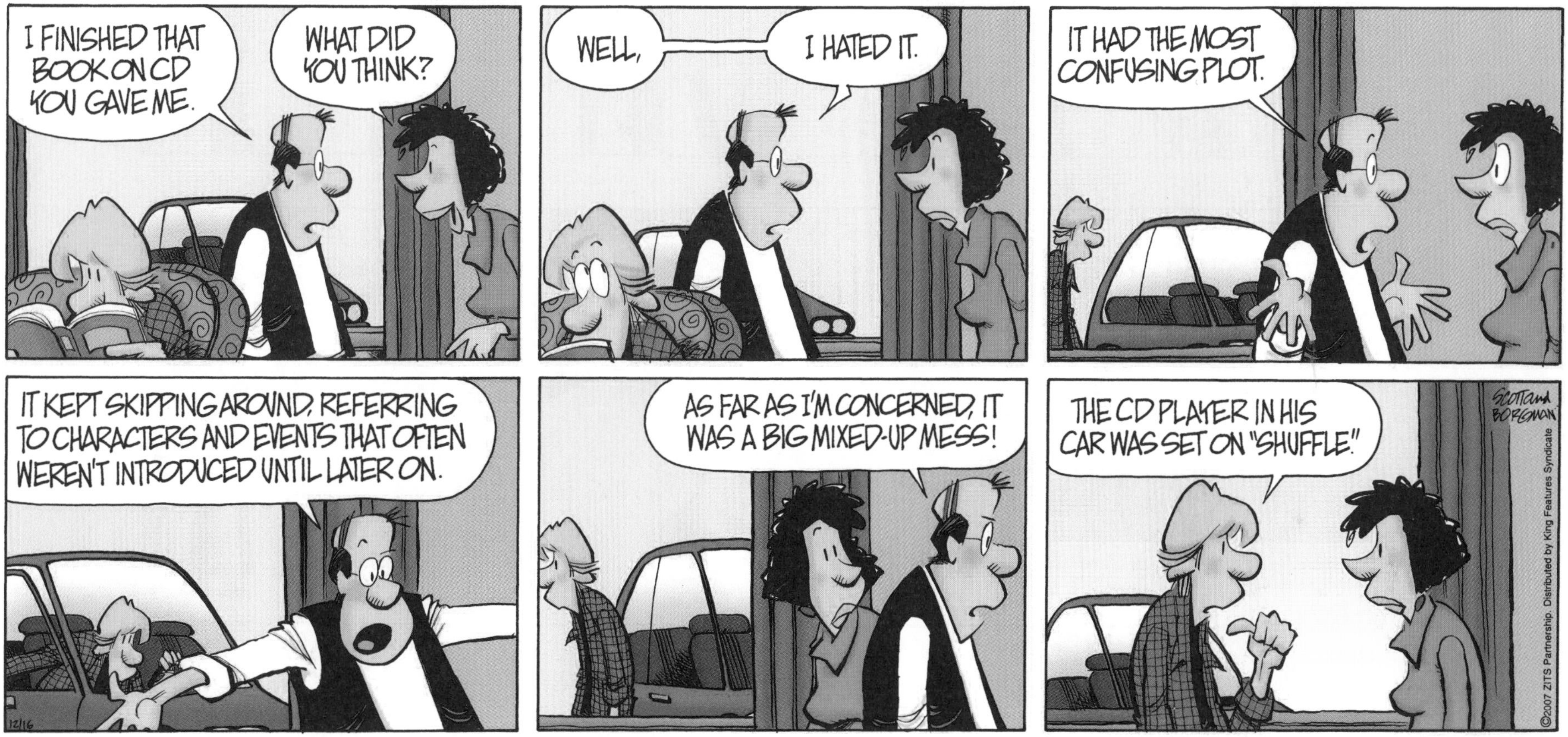
I FINISHED THAT BOOK ON CD YOU GAVE ME.
WHAT DID YOU THINK?
WELL,
I HATED IT.
IT HAD THE MOST CONFUSING PLOT.
IT KEPT SKIPPING AROUND, REFERRING TO CHARACTERS AND EVENTS THAT OFTEN WEREN'T INTRODUCED UNTIL LATER ON.
AS FAR AS I'M CONCERNED, IT WAS A BIG MIXED-UP MESS!
THE CD PLAYER IN HIS CAR WAS SET ON "SHUFFLE."
SCOTT and BORGMAN
©2007 ZITS Partnership. Distributed by King Features Syndicate

Jim: (Sigh!) Another episode ripped straight from my life. I'm the only guy on the planet who thought Morrie died before his first Tuesday conversation with Mitch Albom.

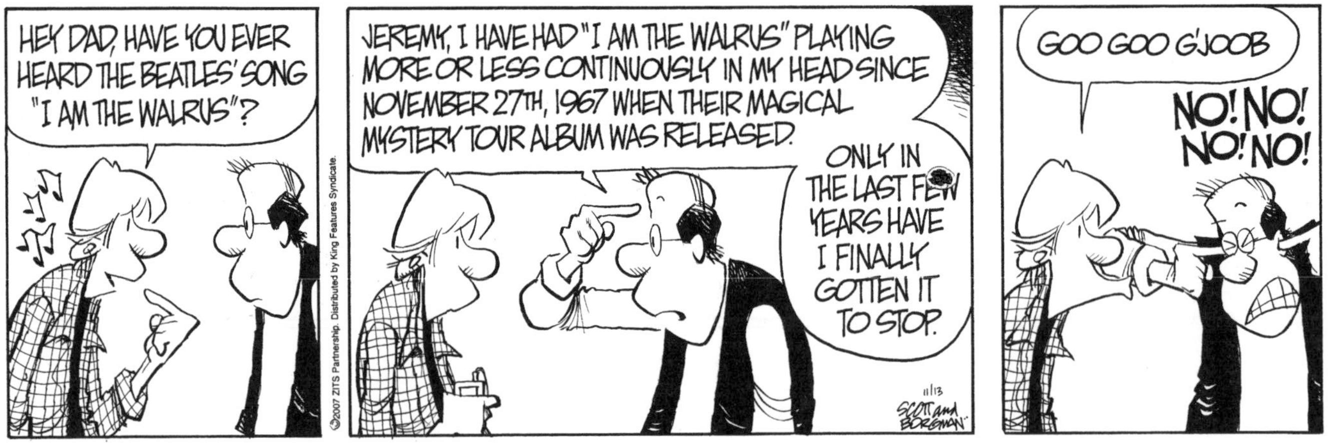
HEY DAD, HAVE YOU EVER HEARD THE BEATLES' SONG "I AM THE WALRUS"?
©2007 ZITS Partnership. Distributed by King Features Syndicate.
JEREMY, I HAVE HAD "I AM THE WALRUS" PLAYING MORE OR LESS CONTINUOUSLY IN MY HEAD SINCE NOVEMBER 27TH, 1967 WHEN THEIR MAGICAL MYSTERY TOUR ALBUM WAS RELEASED.
ONLY IN THE LAST FEW YEARS HAVE I FINALLY GOTTEN IT TO STOP.
11/13
SCOTT and BORGMAN
GOO GOO G'JOOB
NO! NO! NO! NO!

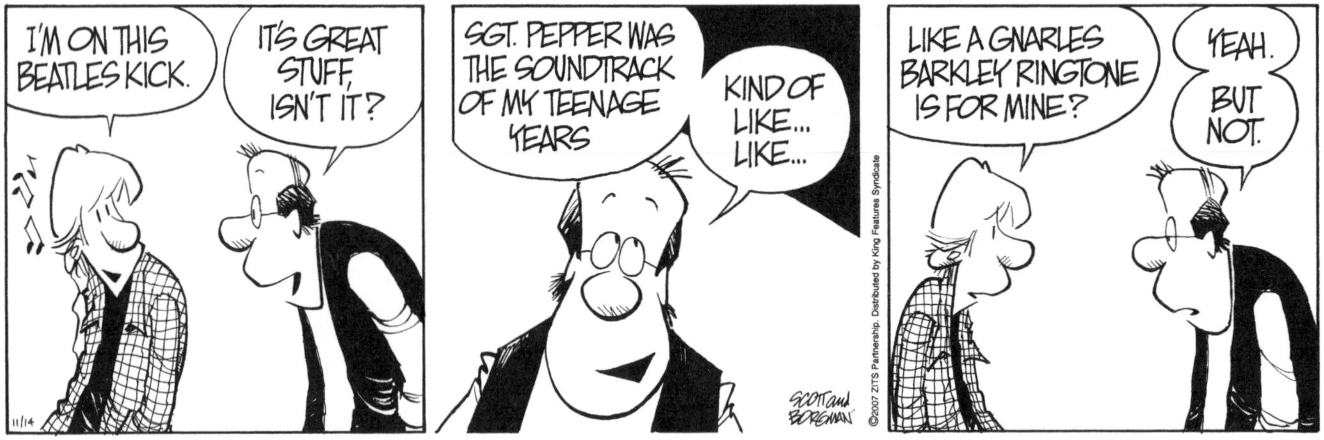
I'M ON THIS BEATLES KICK.
IT'S GREAT STUFF, ISN'T IT?
11/14
SGT. PEPPER WAS THE SOUNDTRACK OF MY TEENAGE YEARS
KIND OF LIKE... LIKE...
SCOTT and BORGMAN
©2007 ZITS Partnership. Distributed by King Features Syndicate
LIKE A GNARLES BARKLEY RINGTONE IS FOR MINE?
YEAH.
BUT NOT.

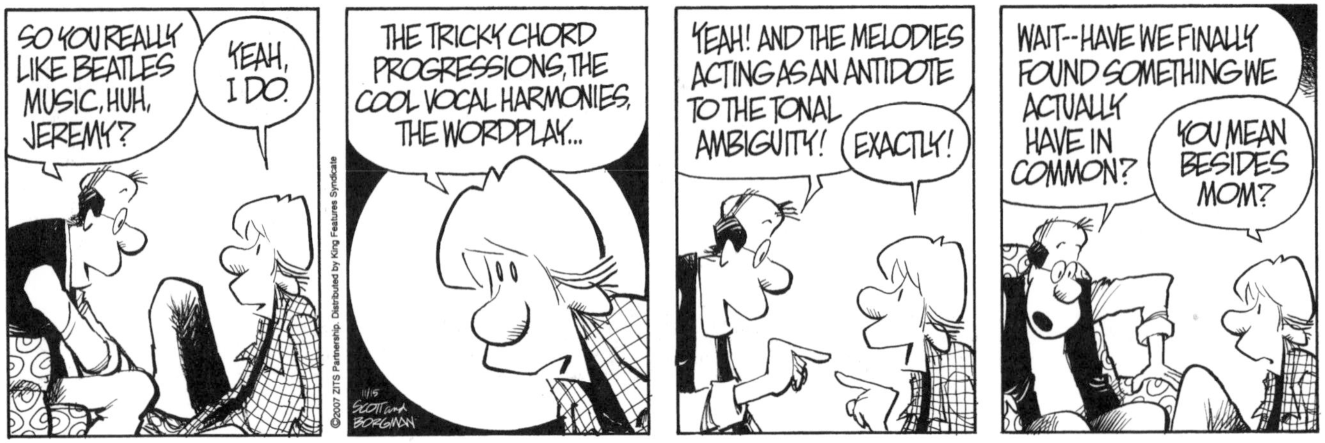
SO YOU REALLY LIKE BEATLES MUSIC, HUH, JEREMY?
YEAH, I DO.
©2007 ZITS Partnership. Distributed by King Features Syndicate
THE TRICKY CHORD PROGRESSIONS, THE COOL VOCAL HARMONIES, THE WORDPLAY...
11/15
SCOTT and BORGMAN
YEAH! AND THE MELODIES ACTING AS AN ANTIDOTE TO THE TONAL AMBIGUITY!
EXACTLY!
WAIT--HAVE WE FINALLY FOUND SOMETHING WE ACTUALLY HAVE IN COMMON?
YOU MEAN BESIDES MOM?

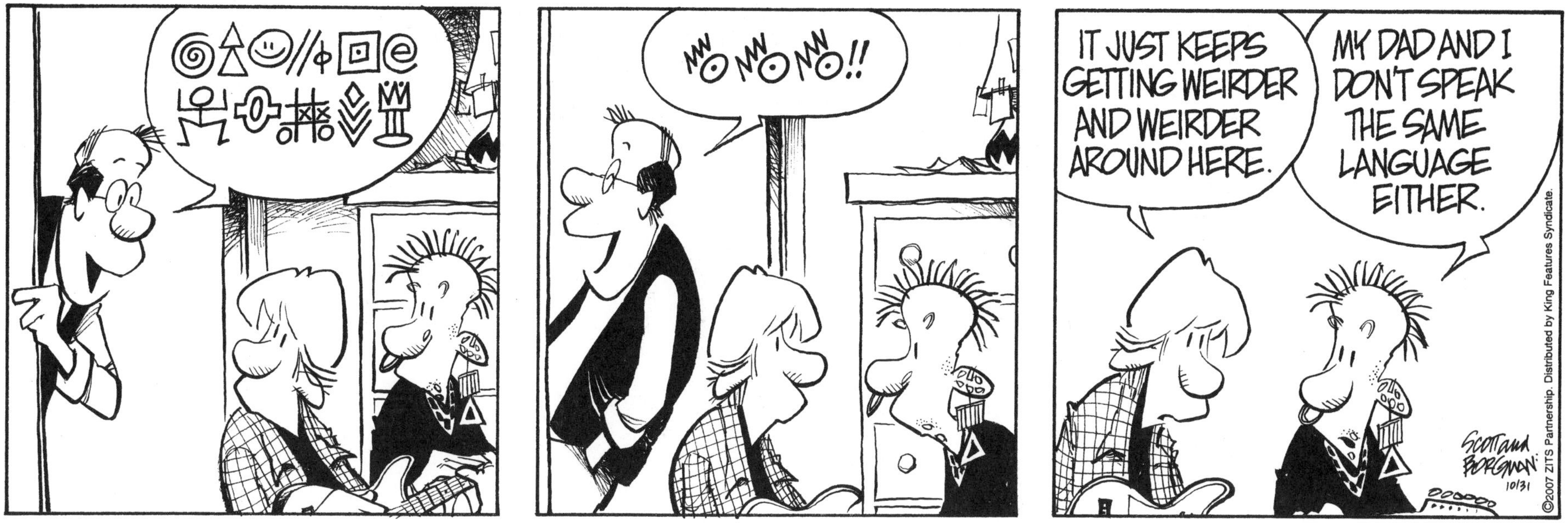

NNOMNOMNO!!
IT JUST KEEPS GETTING WEIRDER AND WEIRDER AROUND HERE.
MY DAD AND I DON'T SPEAK THE SAME LANGUAGE EITHER.
SCOTT and BORGMAN 10/31
©2007 ZITS Partnership. Distributed by King Features Syndicate.

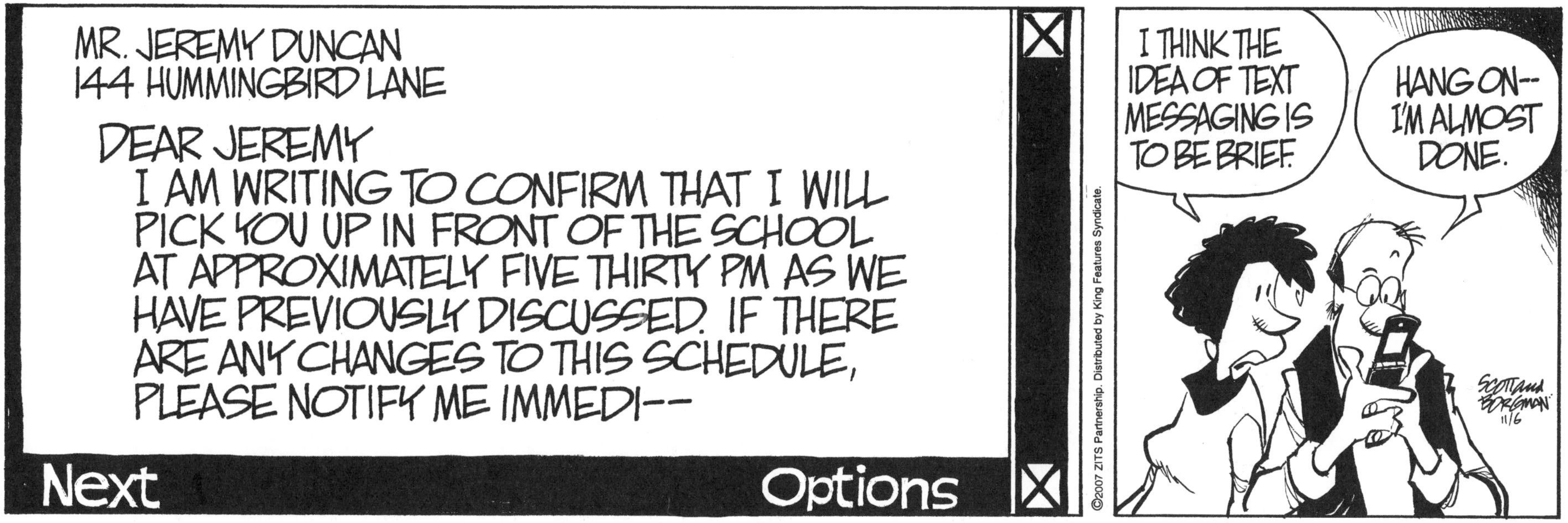

MR. JEREMY DUNCAN
144 HUMMINGBIRD LANE
DEAR JEREMY
I AM WRITING TO CONFIRM THAT I WILL PICK YOU UP IN FRONT OF THE SCHOOL AT APPROXIMATELY FIVE THIRTY PM AS WE HAVE PREVIOUSLY DISCUSSED. IF THERE ARE ANY CHANGES TO THIS SCHEDULE, PLEASE NOTIFY ME IMMEDI--
Next
Options
©2007 ZITS Partnership. Distributed by King Features Syndicate.
I THINK THE IDEA OF TEXT MESSAGING IS TO BE BRIEF.
HANG ON-- I'M ALMOST DONE.
SCOTT and BORGMAN 11/6

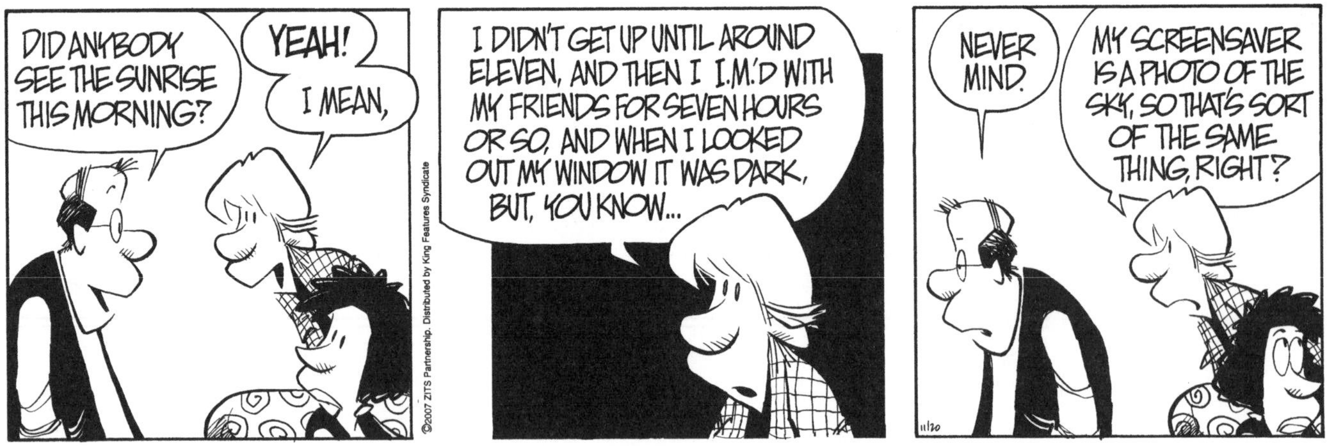
DID ANYBODY SEE THE SUNRISE THIS MORNING?
YEAH!
I MEAN,
I DIDN'T GET UP UNTIL AROUND ELEVEN, AND THEN I I.M.'D WITH MY FRIENDS FOR SEVEN HOURS OR SO, AND WHEN I LOOKED OUT MY WINDOW IT WAS DARK, BUT, YOU KNOW...
NEVER MIND.
MY SCREENSAVER IS A PHOTO OF THE SKY, SO THAT'S SORT OF THE SAME THING, RIGHT?
©2007 ZITS Partnership. Distributed by King Features Syndicate

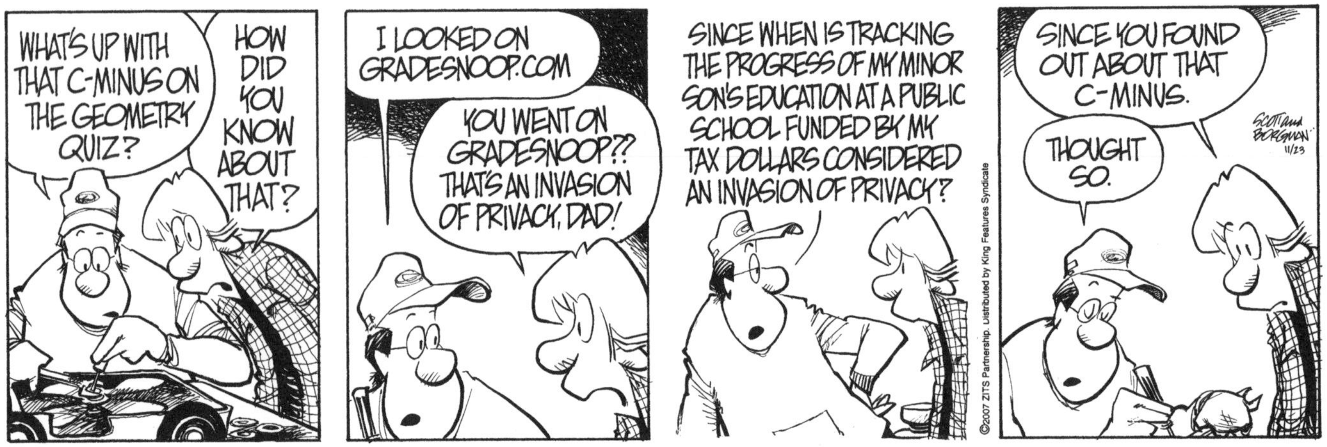
WHAT'S UP WITH THAT C-MINUS ON THE GEOMETRY QUIZ?
HOW DID YOU KNOW ABOUT THAT?
I LOOKED ON GRADESNOOP.COM
YOU WENT ON GRADESNOOP?? THAT'S AN INVASION OF PRIVACY, DAD!
SINCE WHEN IS TRACKING THE PROGRESS OF MY MINOR SON'S EDUCATION AT A PUBLIC SCHOOL FUNDED BY MY TAX DOLLARS CONSIDERED AN INVASION OF PRIVACY?
SINCE YOU FOUND OUT ABOUT THAT C-MINUS.
THOUGHT SO.
©2007 ZITS Partnership. Distributed by King Features Syndicate

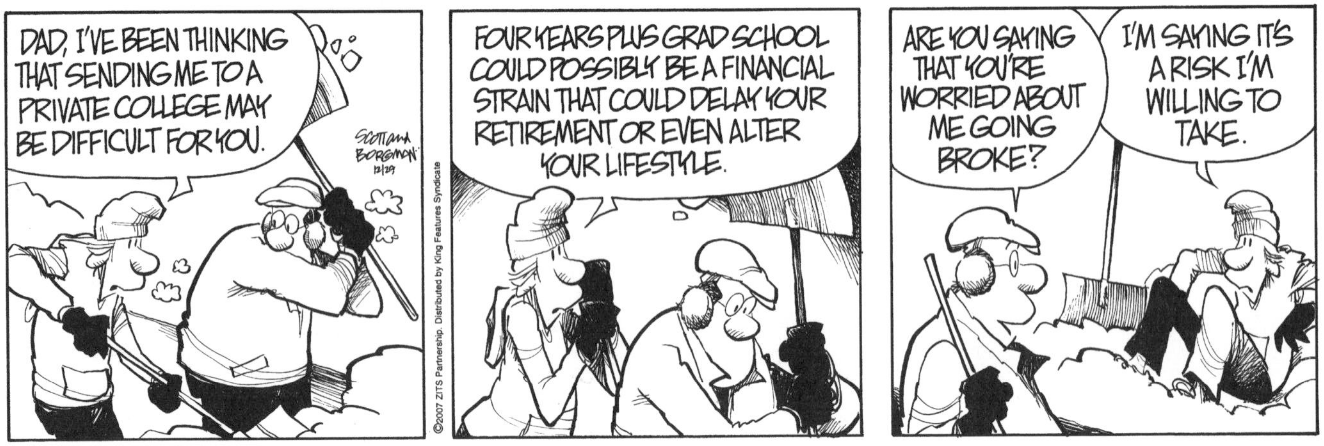
DAD, I'VE BEEN THINKING THAT SENDING ME TO A PRIVATE COLLEGE MAY BE DIFFICULT FOR YOU.
FOUR YEARS PLUS GRAD SCHOOL COULD POSSIBLY BE A FINANCIAL STRAIN THAT COULD DELAY YOUR RETIREMENT OR EVEN ALTER YOUR LIFESTYLE.
ARE YOU SAYING THAT YOU'RE WORRIED ABOUT ME GOING BROKE?
I'M SAYING IT'S A RISK I'M WILLING TO TAKE.
©2007 ZITS Partnership. Distributed by King Features Syndicate

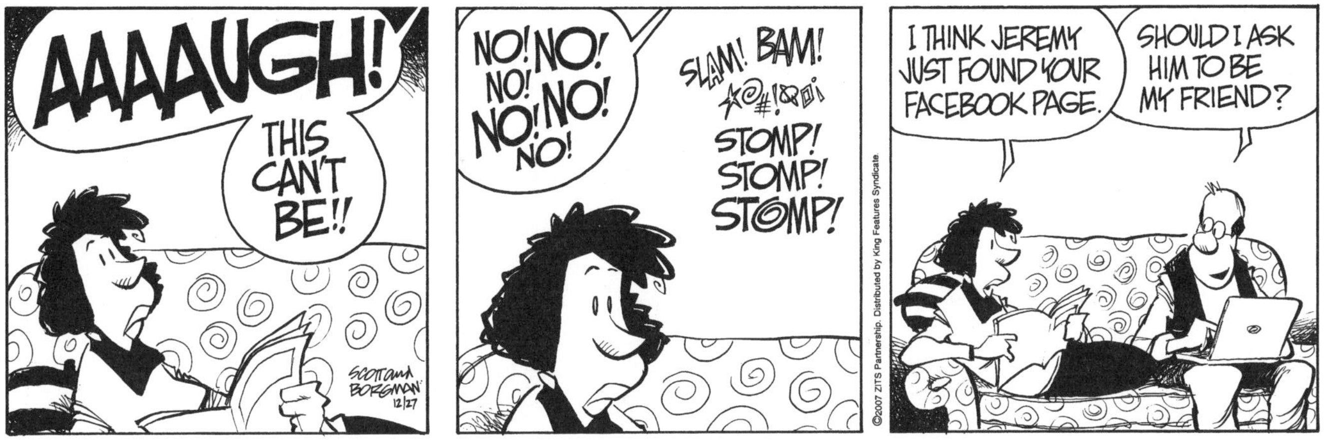
AAAAUGH!
THIS CAN'T BE!!
SCOTT and BORGMAN 12/27
NO! NO! NO! NO! NO! NO!
SLAM! BAM!
STOMP! STOMP! STOMP!
I THINK JEREMY JUST FOUND YOUR FACEBOOK PAGE.
SHOULD I ASK HIM TO BE MY FRIEND?

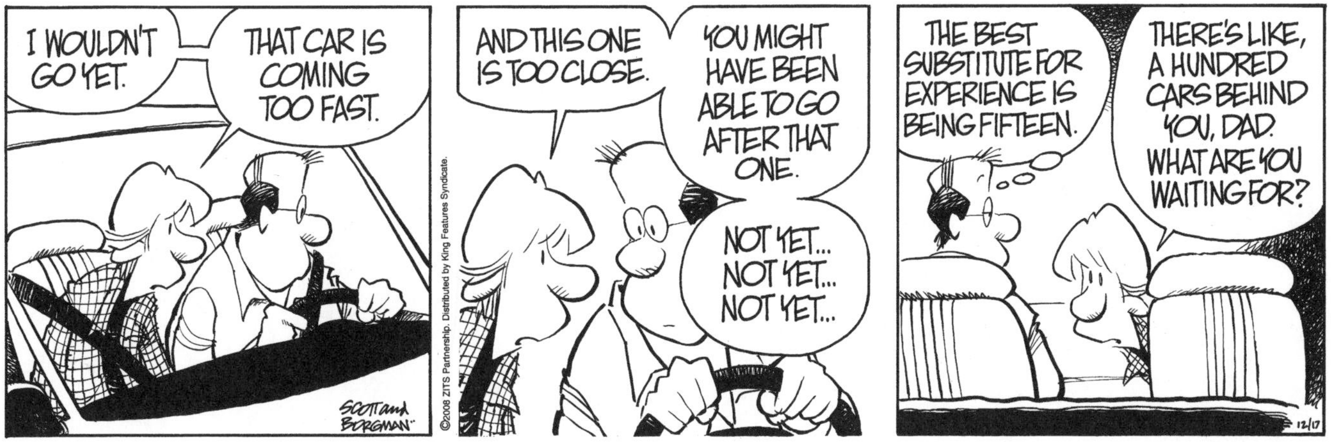
I WOULDN'T GO YET.
THAT CAR IS COMING TOO FAST.
SCOTT and BORGMAN
AND THIS ONE IS TOO CLOSE.
YOU MIGHT HAVE BEEN ABLE TO GO AFTER THAT ONE.
NOT YET... NOT YET... NOT YET...
THE BEST SUBSTITUTE FOR EXPERIENCE IS BEING FIFTEEN.
THERE'S LIKE, A HUNDRED CARS BEHIND YOU, DAD. WHAT ARE YOU WAITING FOR?
12/17

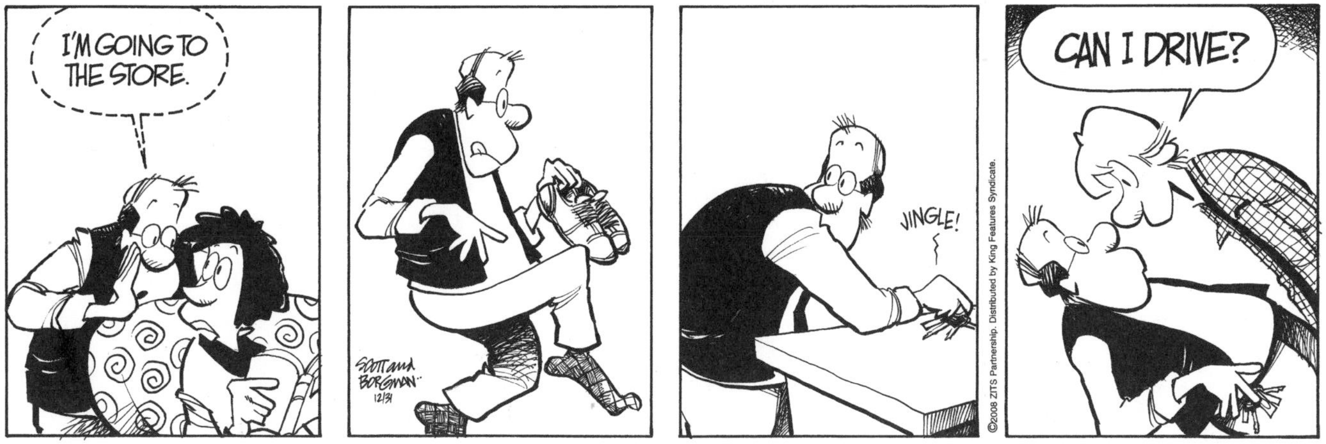
I'M GOING TO THE STORE.
SCOTT and BORGMAN 12/31
JINGLE!
CAN I DRIVE?

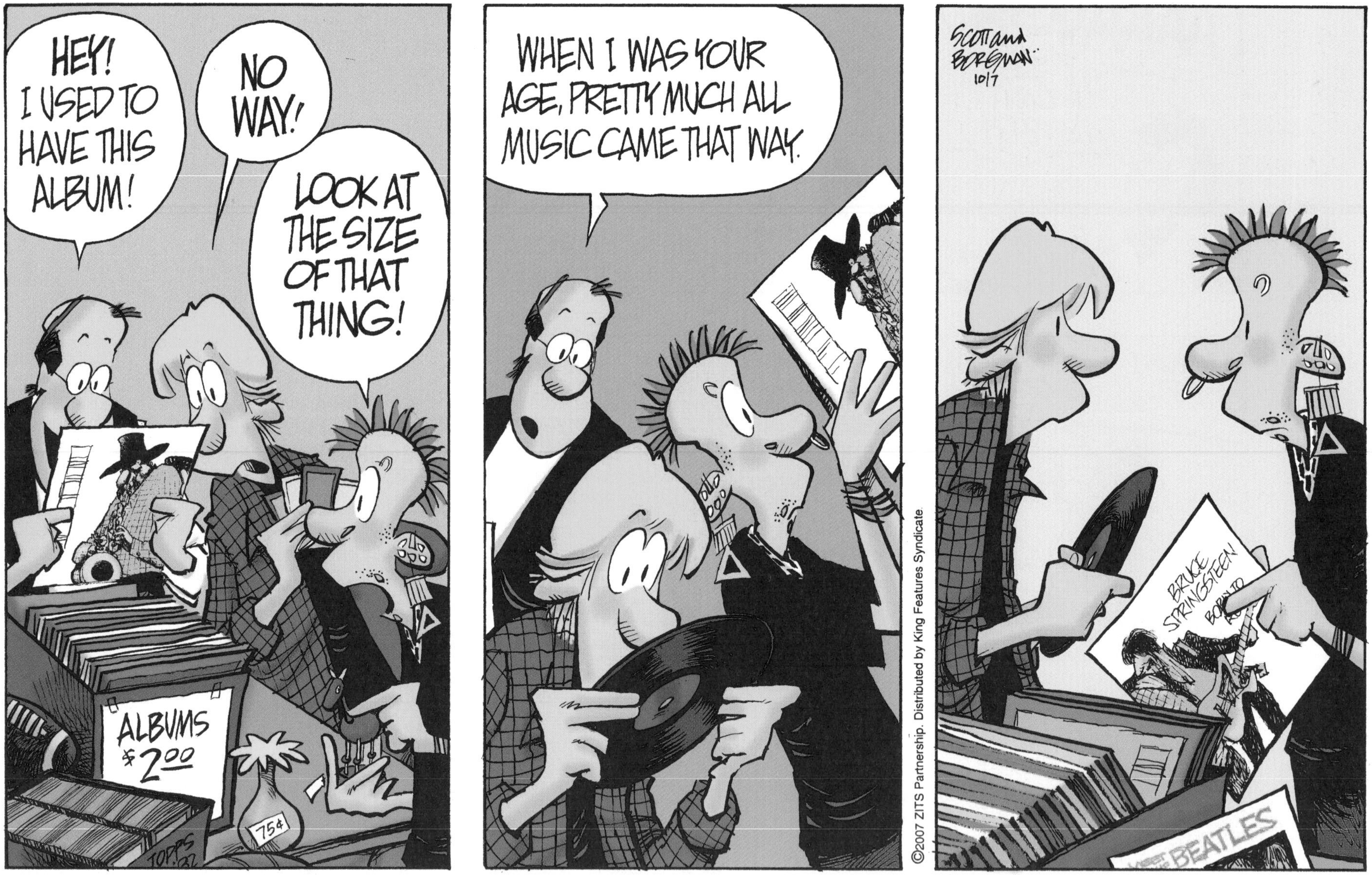
HEY! I USED TO HAVE THIS ALBUM!
NO WAY!
LOOK AT THE SIZE OF THAT THING!
ALBUMS $2.00
75¢
WHEN I WAS YOUR AGE, PRETTY MUCH ALL MUSIC CAME THAT WAY.
SCOTT and BORGMAN 10/7
BRUCE SPRINGSTEEN
BEATLES

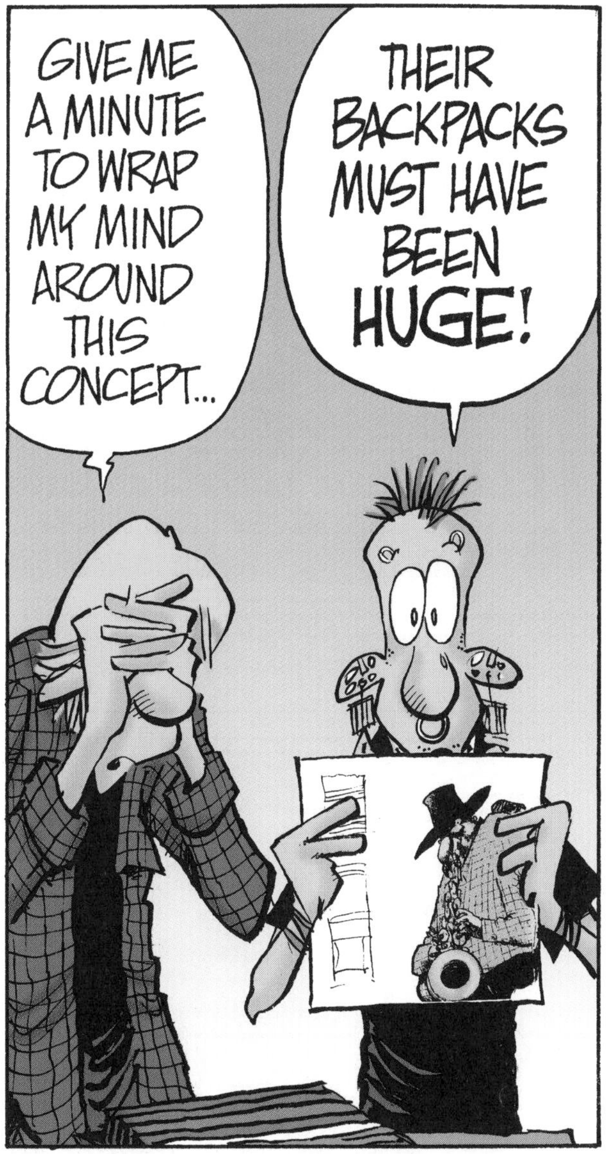
GIVE ME A MINUTE TO WRAP MY MIND AROUND THIS CONCEPT...
THEIR BACKPACKS MUST HAVE BEEN HUGE!

Jim: Pierce seems like a guy who might get into the finer points of vinyl, though he's clueless here. Don't you miss those liner notes and the great cover art? Man, I once owned a Bee Gees double album covered in velour. (Don't hate.)

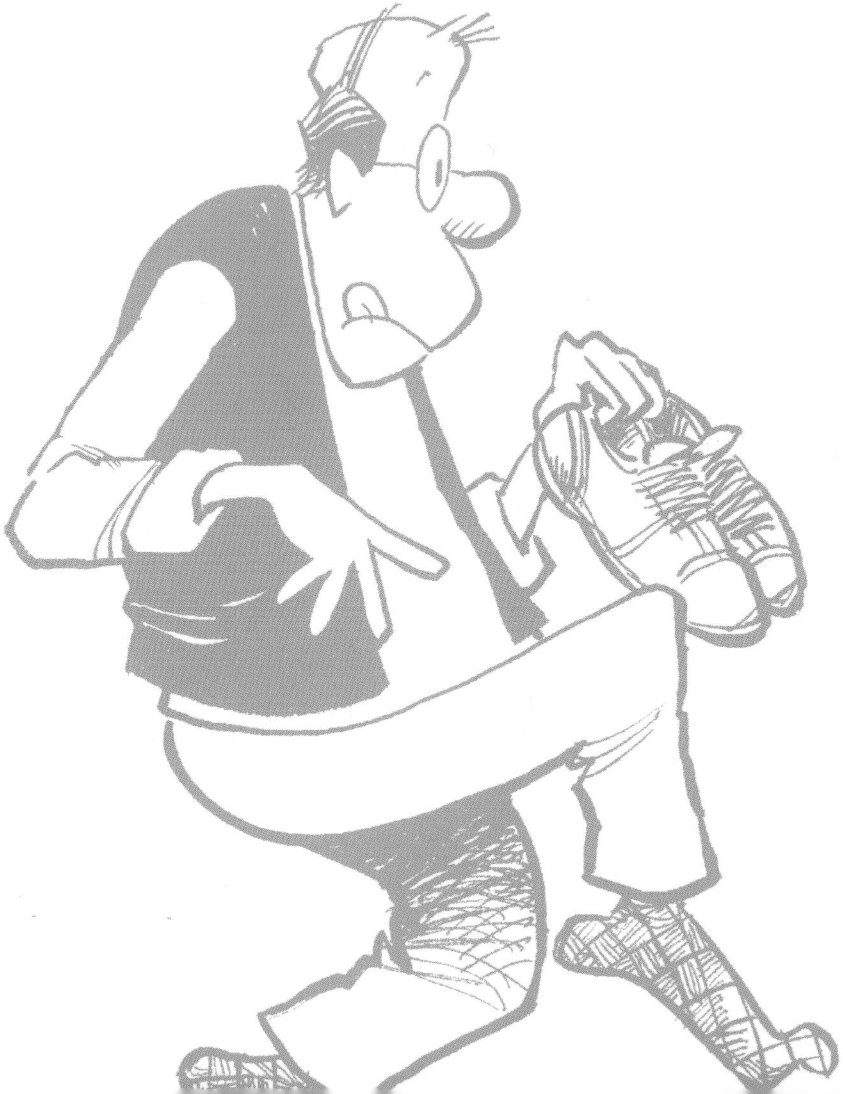

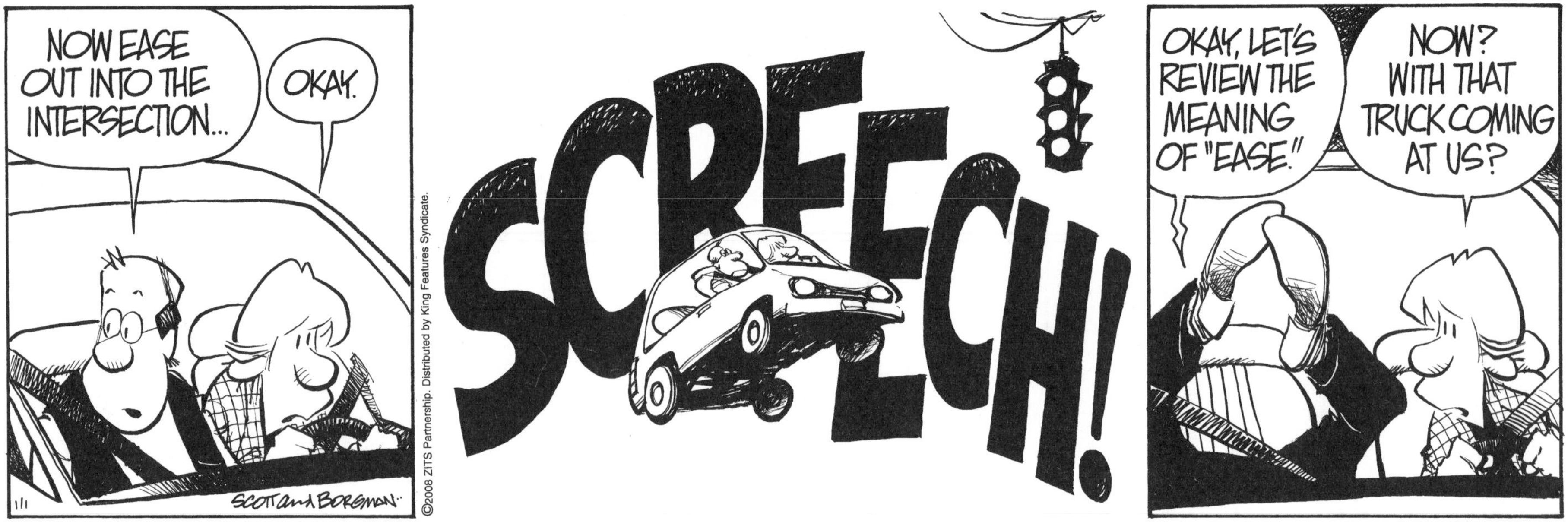
NOW EASE OUT INTO THE INTERSECTION...
OKAY.
SCREECH!
OKAY, LET'S REVIEW THE MEANING OF "EASE."
NOW? WITH THAT TRUCK COMING AT US?
1/11
SCOTT and BORGMAN
©2008 ZITS Partnership. Distributed by King Features Syndicate.

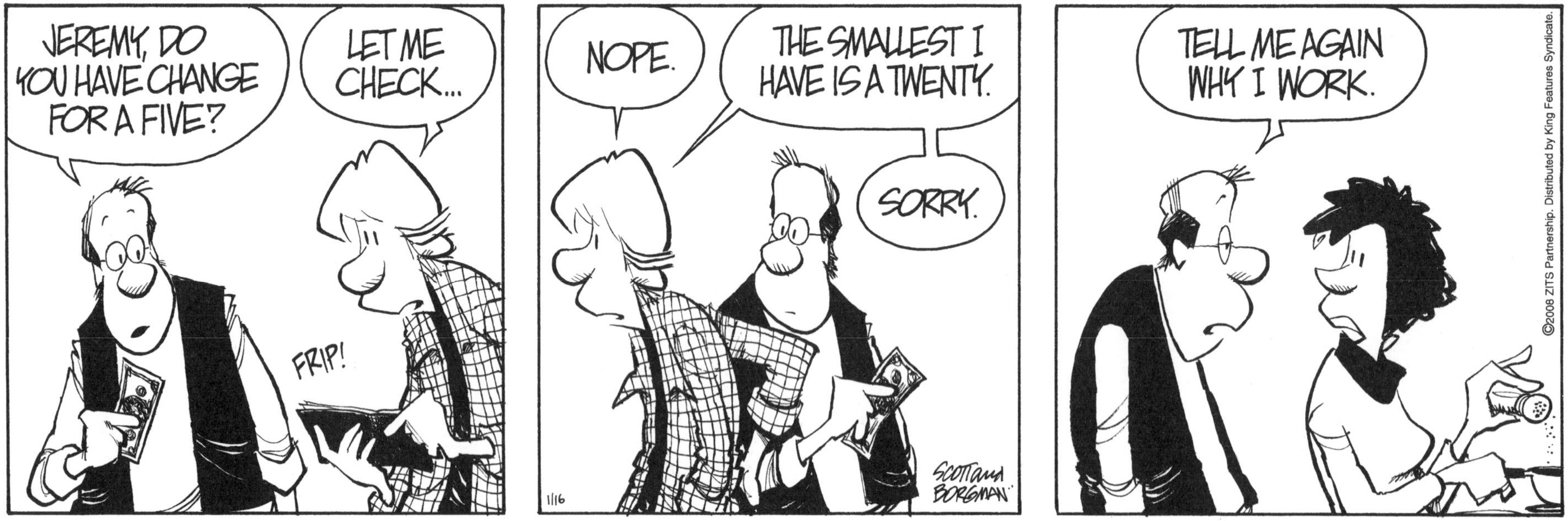
JEREMY, DO YOU HAVE CHANGE FOR A FIVE?
LET ME CHECK...
FRIP!
NOPE.
THE SMALLEST I HAVE IS A TWENTY.
SORRY.
1/16
SCOTT and BORGMAN
TELL ME AGAIN WHY I WORK.
©2008 ZITS Partnership. Distributed by King Features Syndicate.

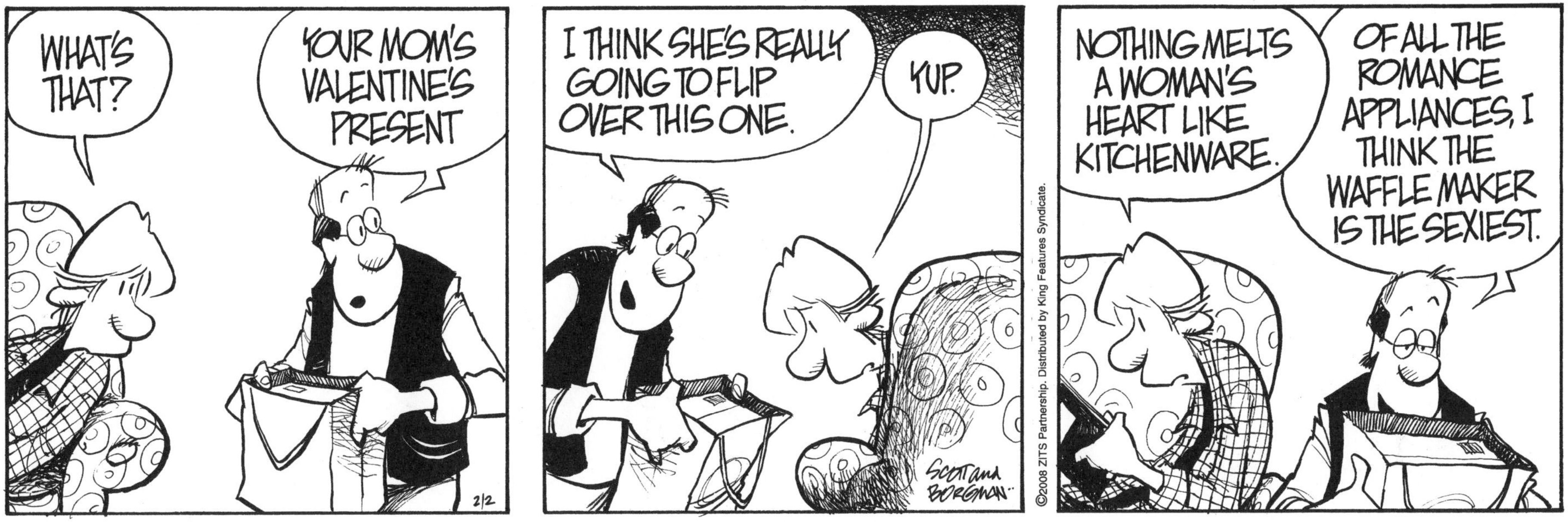
WHAT'S THAT?
YOUR MOM'S VALENTINE'S PRESENT
2/2
I THINK SHE'S REALLY GOING TO FLIP OVER THIS ONE.
YUP.
SCOTT AND BORGMAN
©2008 ZITS Partnership. Distributed by King Features Syndicate.
NOTHING MELTS A WOMAN'S HEART LIKE KITCHENWARE.
OF ALL THE ROMANCE APPLIANCES, I THINK THE WAFFLE MAKER IS THE SEXIEST.

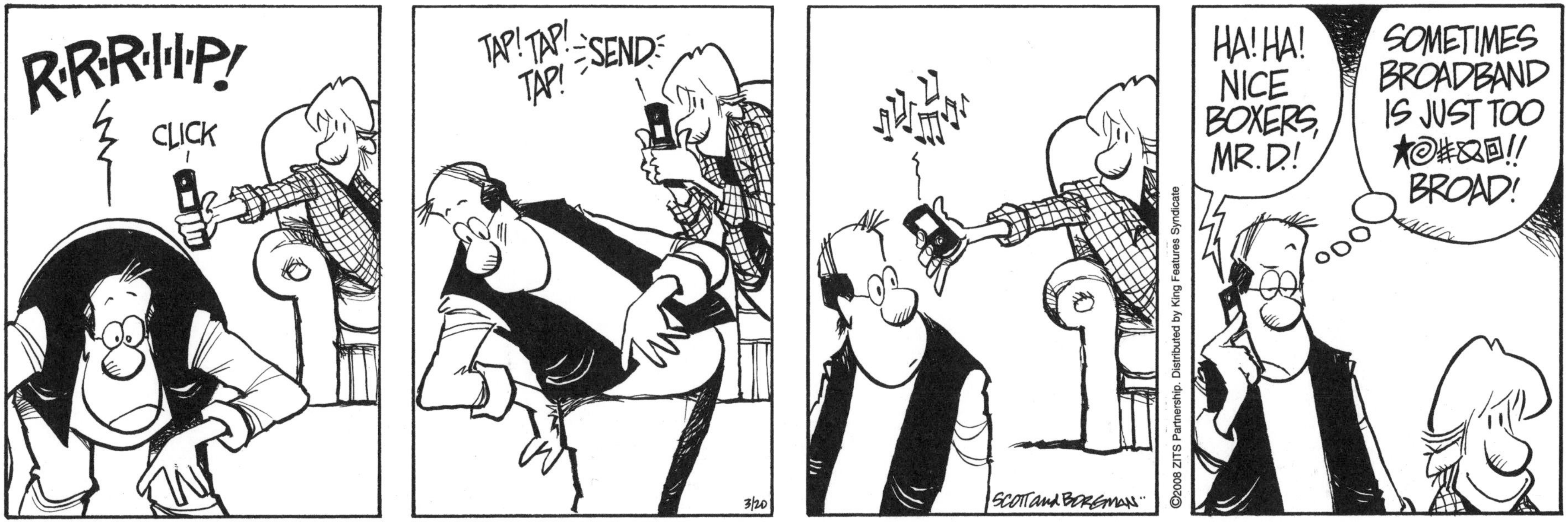
R·R·R·I·I·P!
CLICK
TAP! TAP! TAP!
SEND
3/20
SCOTT AND BORGMAN
©2008 ZITS Partnership. Distributed by King Features Syndicate
HA! HA! NICE BOXERS, MR. D.!
SOMETIMES BROADBAND IS JUST TOO ★@#&▣!! BROAD!

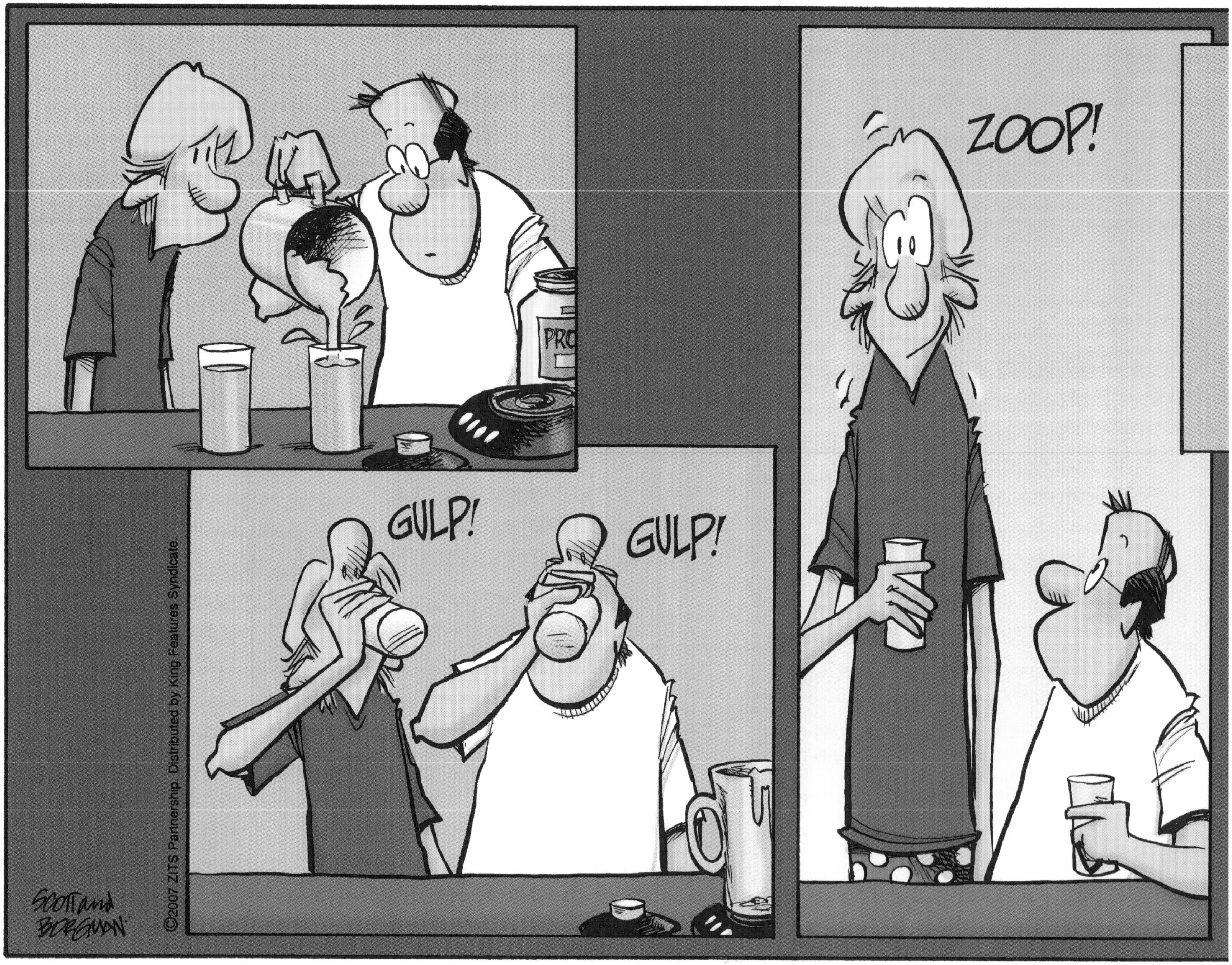
PRO
GULP!
GULP!
ZOOP!
SCOTT and BORGMAN
©2007 ZITS Partnership. Distributed by King Features Syndicate.

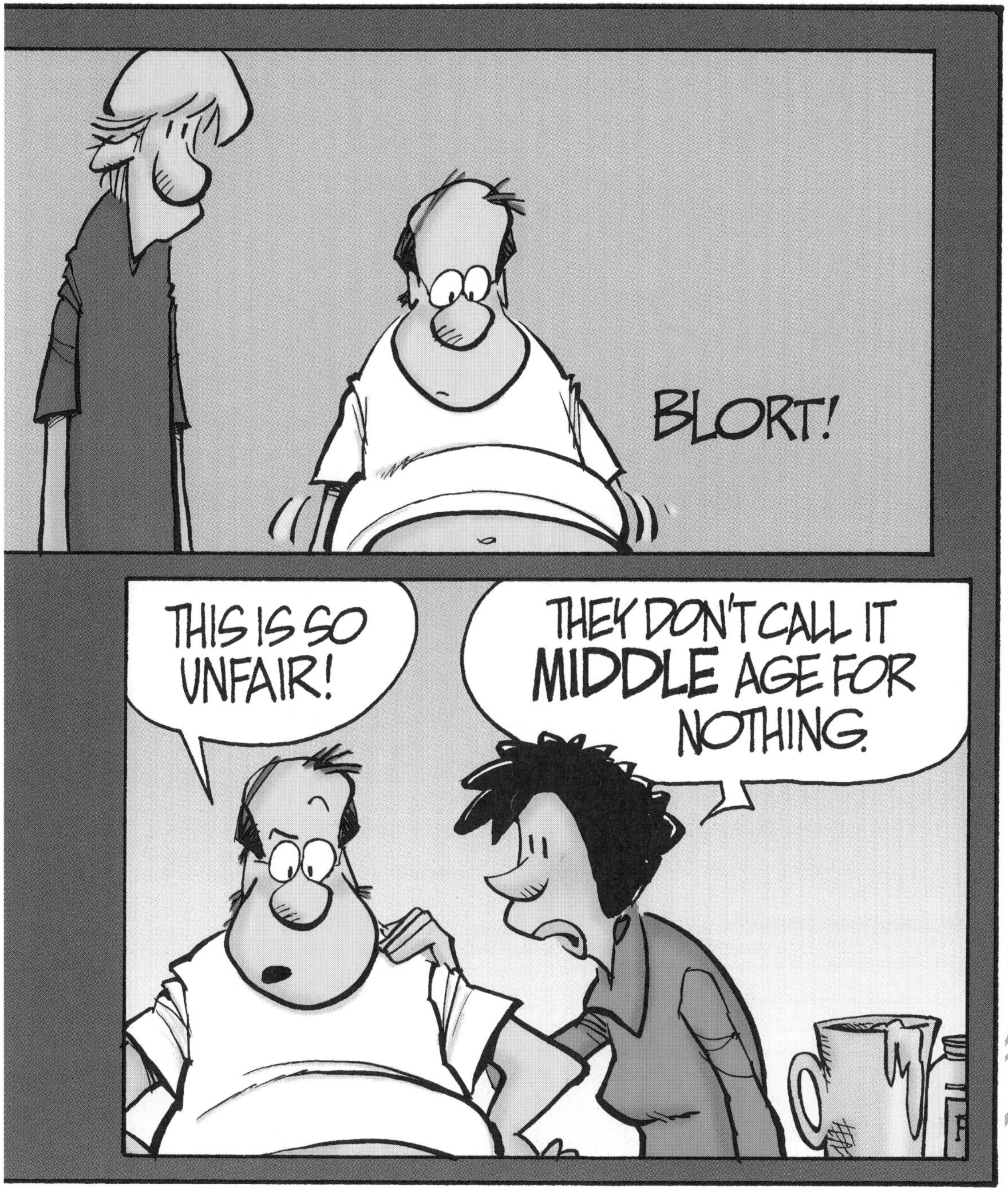
BLORT!
THIS IS SO UNFAIR!
THEY DON'T CALL IT MIDDLE AGE FOR NOTHING.

Jerry: My kid lives on Cocoa Puffs, macaroni and cheese, and ice cream and looks sensational. I eat a chocolate-covered almond and have to loosen the drawstring on my sweatpants.

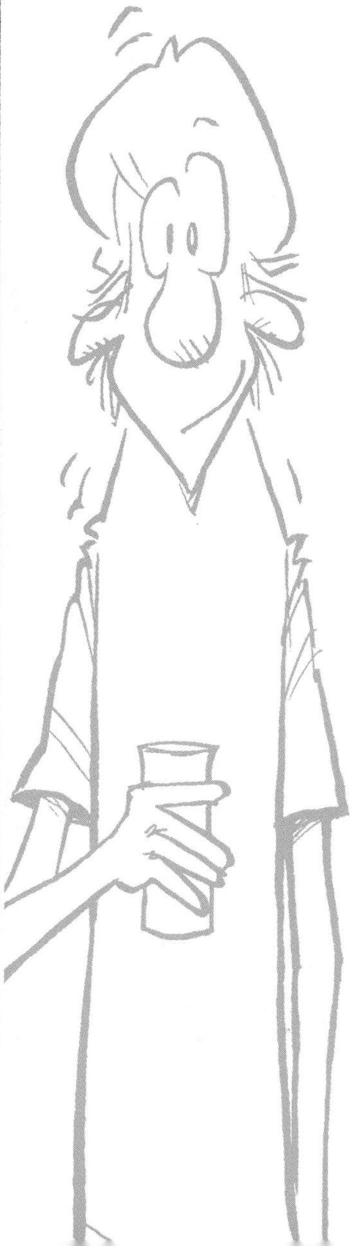

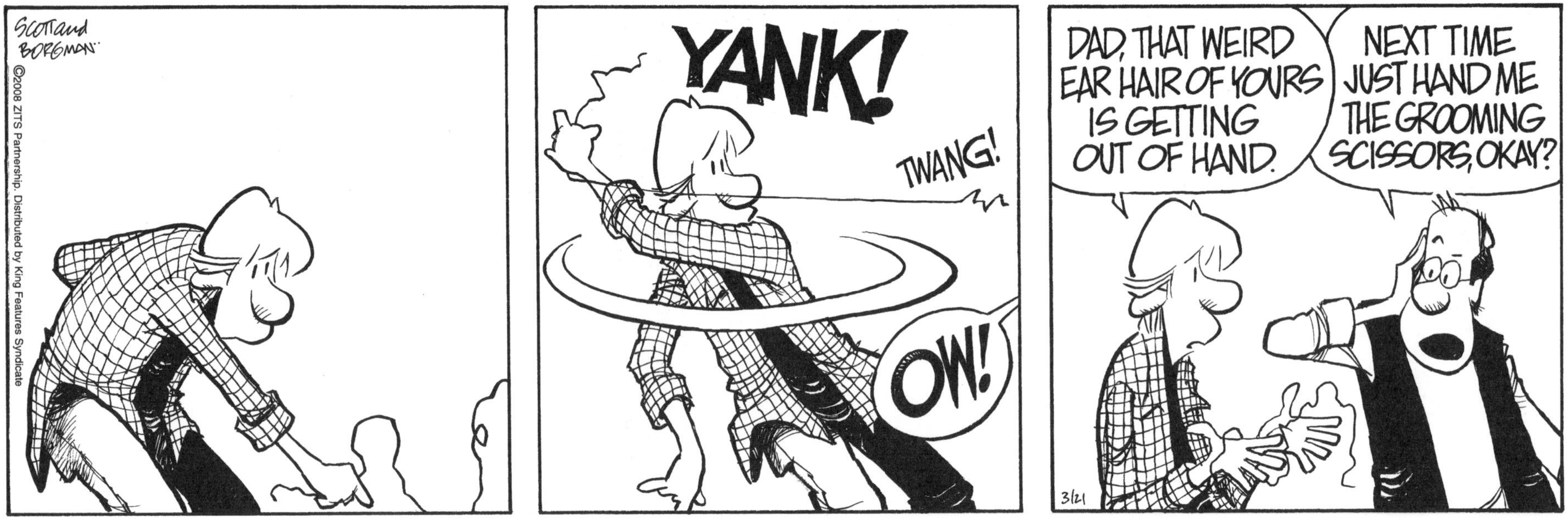
SCOTT and BORGMAN
©2008 ZITS Partnership. Distributed by King Features Syndicate
YANK!
TWANG!
OW!
DAD, THAT WEIRD EAR HAIR OF YOURS IS GETTING OUT OF HAND.
NEXT TIME JUST HAND ME THE GROOMING SCISSORS, OKAY?
3/21

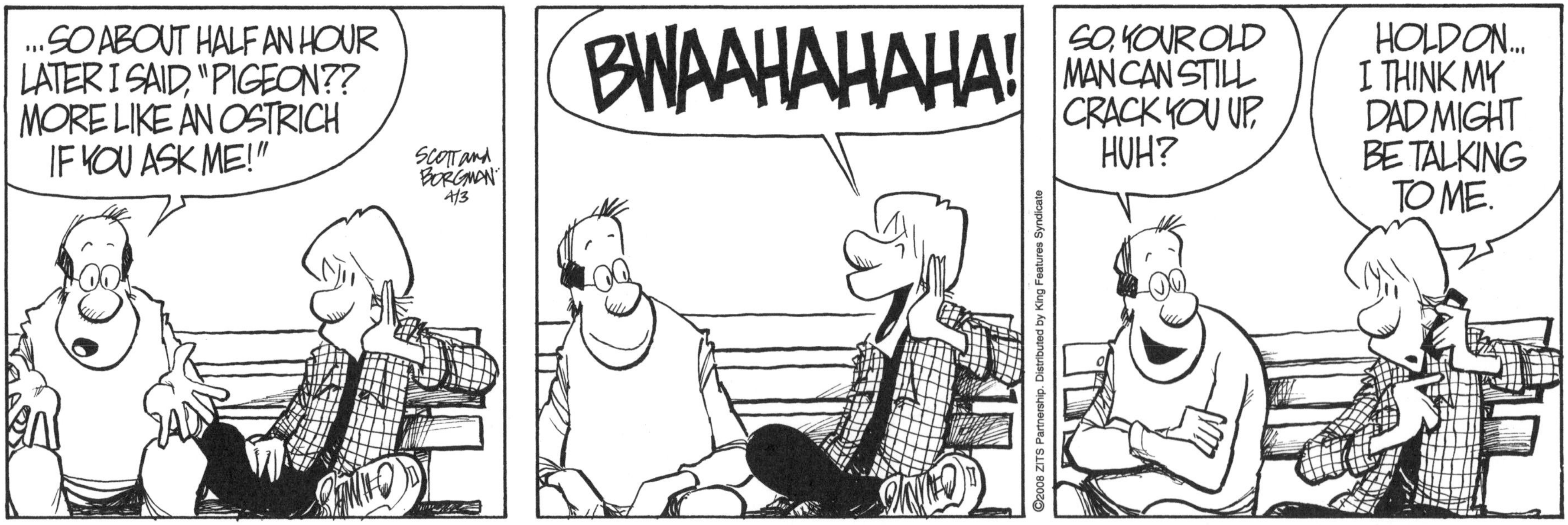
...SO ABOUT HALF AN HOUR LATER I SAID, "PIGEON?? MORE LIKE AN OSTRICH IF YOU ASK ME!"
SCOTT and BORGMAN 4/3
BWAAHAHAHAHA!
©2008 ZITS Partnership. Distributed by King Features Syndicate
SO, YOUR OLD MAN CAN STILL CRACK YOU UP, HUH?
HOLD ON... I THINK MY DAD MIGHT BE TALKING TO ME.

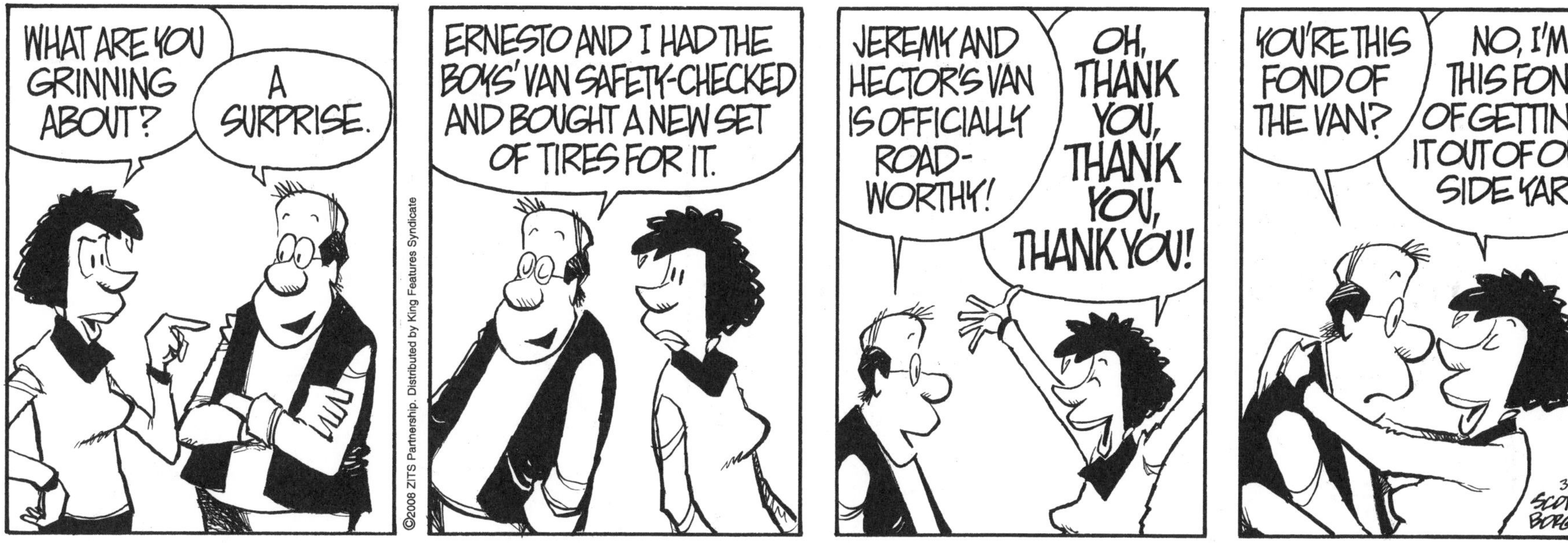
WHAT ARE YOU GRINNING ABOUT?
A SURPRISE.
©2008 ZITS Partnership. Distributed by King Features Syndicate
ERNESTO AND I HAD THE BOYS' VAN SAFETY-CHECKED AND BOUGHT A NEW SET OF TIRES FOR IT.
JEREMY AND HECTOR'S VAN IS OFFICIALLY ROAD-WORTHY!
OH, THANK YOU, THANK YOU, THANK YOU!
YOU'RE THIS FOND OF THE VAN?
NO, I'M THIS FOND OF GETTING IT OUT OF OUR SIDE YARD.
3/28
SCOTT and BORGMAN

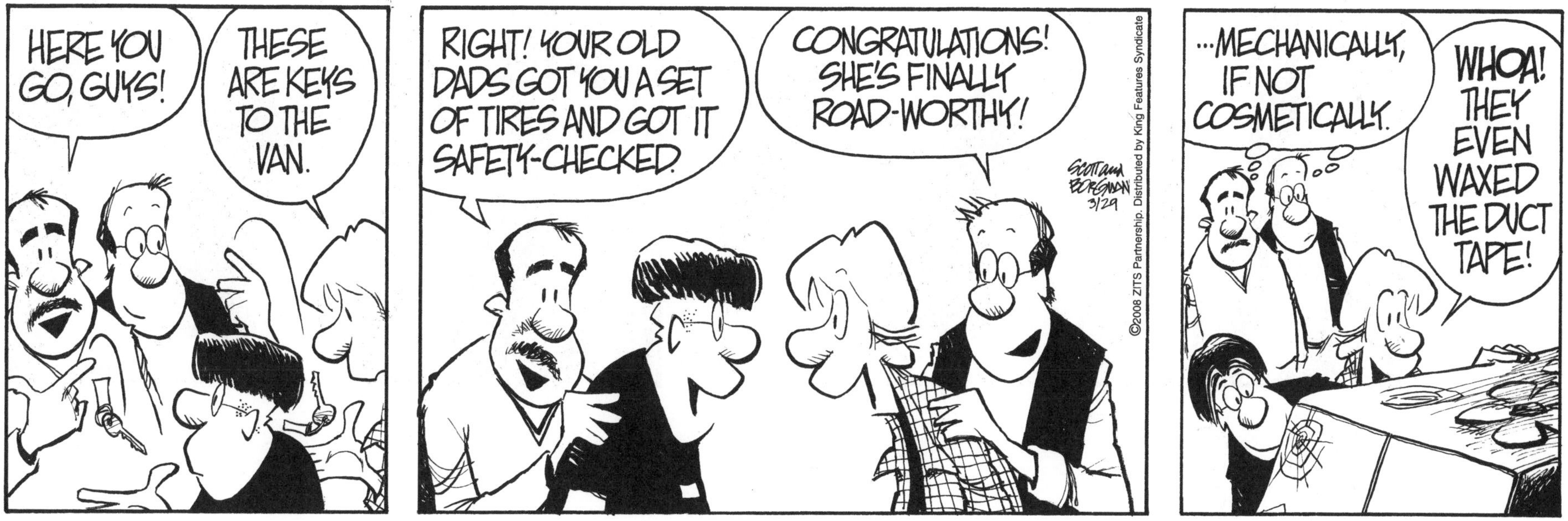
HERE YOU GO, GUYS!
THESE ARE KEYS TO THE VAN.
RIGHT! YOUR OLD DADS GOT YOU A SET OF TIRES AND GOT IT SAFETY-CHECKED.
CONGRATULATIONS! SHE'S FINALLY ROAD-WORTHY!
SCOTT and BORGMAN 3/29
©2008 ZITS Partnership. Distributed by King Features Syndicate
...MECHANICALLY, IF NOT COSMETICALLY.
WHOA! THEY EVEN WAXED THE DUCT TAPE!

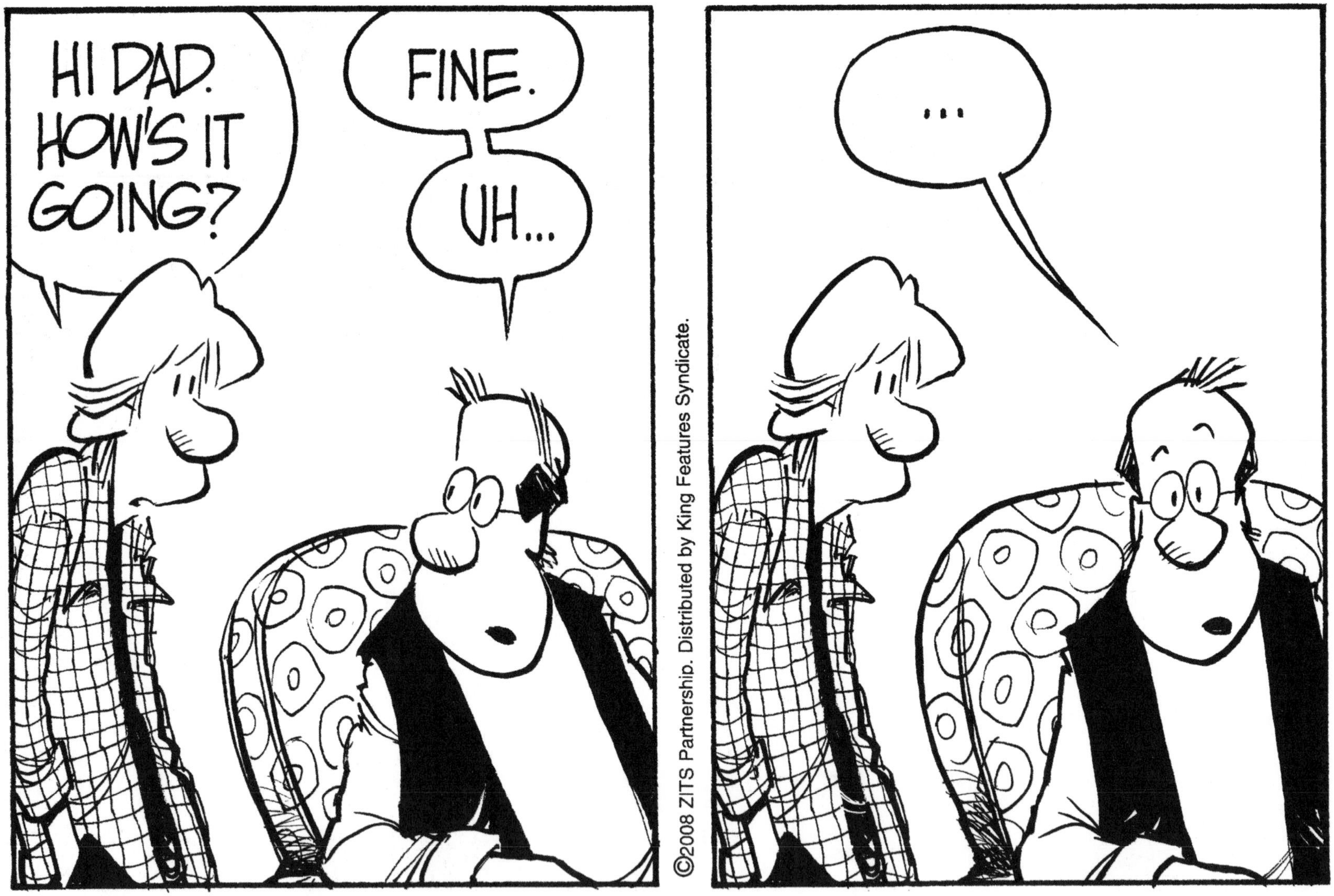
HI DAD. HOW'S IT GOING?
FINE.
UH...
...
©2008 ZITS Partnership. Distributed by King Features Syndicate.

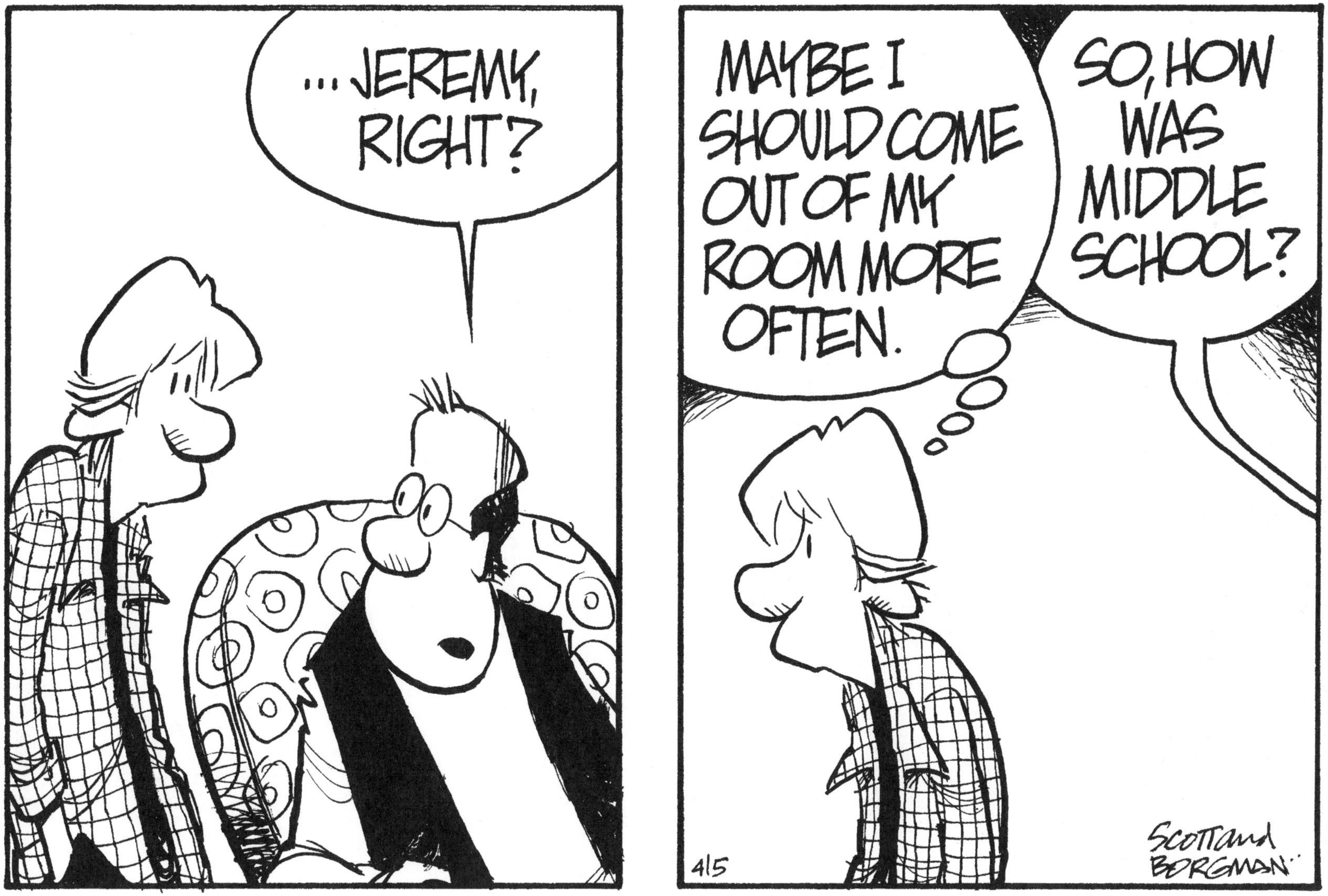
...JEREMY, RIGHT?
MAYBE I SHOULD COME OUT OF MY ROOM MORE OFTEN.
SO, HOW WAS MIDDLE SCHOOL?
4/5
SCOTT and BORGMAN

Jerry: It's a totally wonky thing, but I love the fact that Dad's speech balloon contains only an ellipsis in the second panel. We could have just had him say nothing, but this made the pause visual. Punctuation rocks!

©2008 ZITS Partnership. Distributed by King Features Syndicate
CAN SOMEBODY HELP ME WITH MY BACK?
FOR THE RECORD, I THINK IT'S GROSS WHEN DAD TRIMS HIS BODY HAIR.
I'M JUST GLAD IT'S TRASH DAY!
SCOTT and BORGMAN 1/6

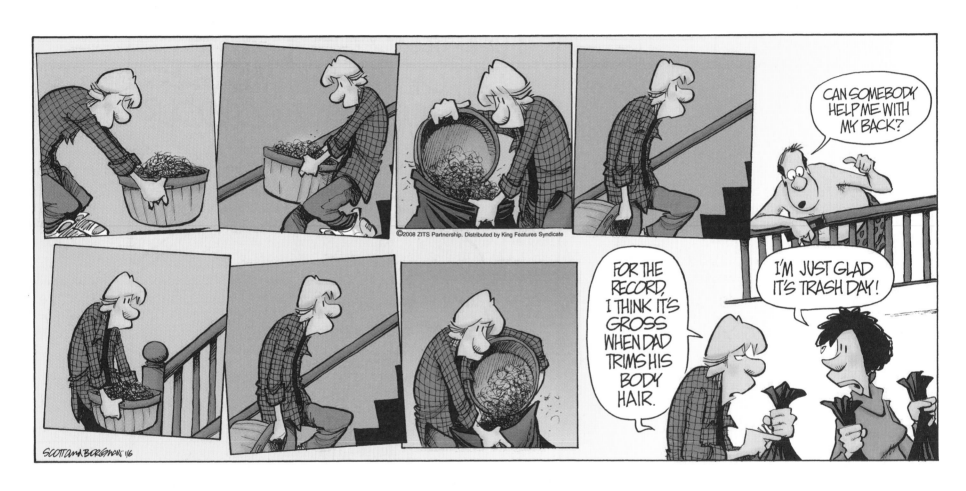

Jerry: I'll say it. Eww.

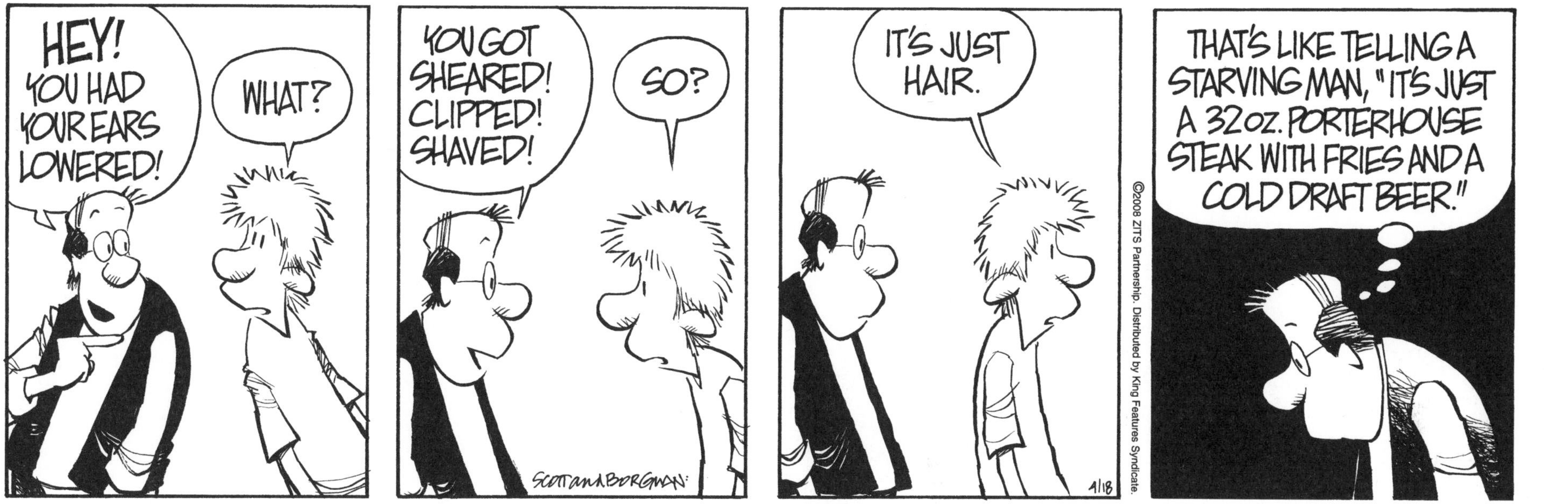
HEY! YOU HAD YOUR EARS LOWERED!
WHAT?
YOU GOT SHEARED! CLIPPED! SHAVED!
SO?
SCOTT AND BORGMAN
IT'S JUST HAIR.
4/18
©2008 ZITS Partnership. Distributed by King Features Syndicate.
THAT'S LIKE TELLING A STARVING MAN, "IT'S JUST A 32 OZ. PORTERHOUSE STEAK WITH FRIES AND A COLD DRAFT BEER."

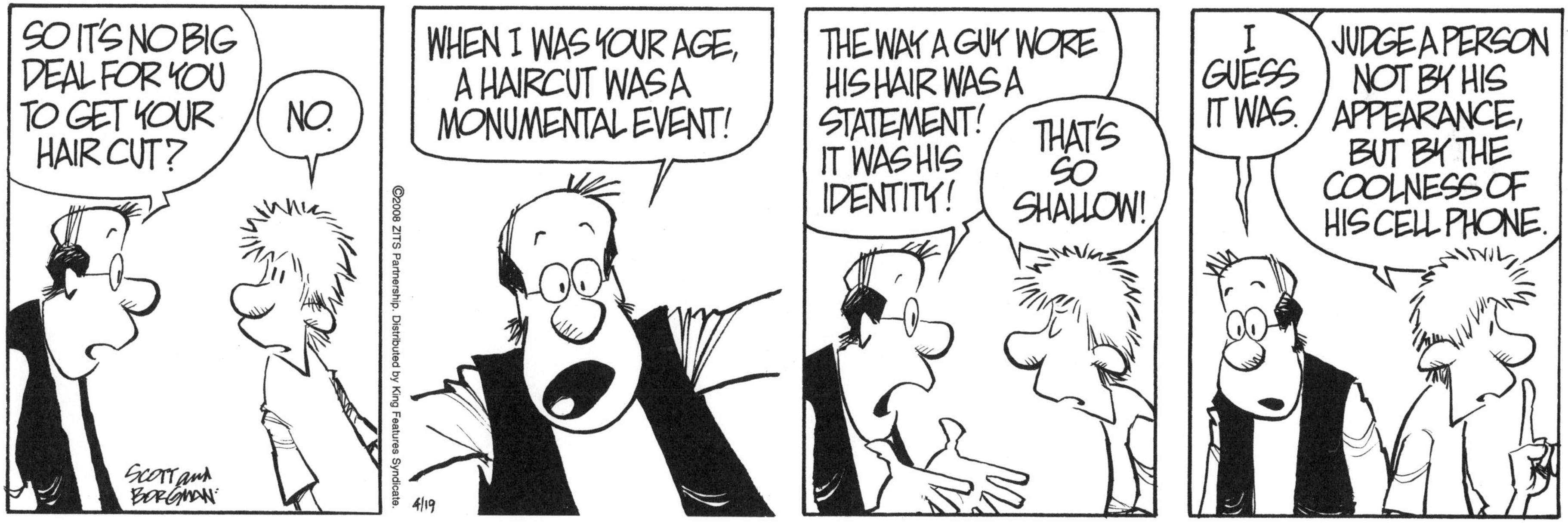
SO IT'S NO BIG DEAL FOR YOU TO GET YOUR HAIR CUT?
NO.
SCOTT AND BORGMAN
©2008 ZITS Partnership. Distributed by King Features Syndicate.
WHEN I WAS YOUR AGE, A HAIRCUT WAS A MONUMENTAL EVENT!
4/19
THE WAY A GUY WORE HIS HAIR WAS A STATEMENT! IT WAS HIS IDENTITY!
THAT'S SO SHALLOW!
I GUESS IT WAS.
JUDGE A PERSON NOT BY HIS APPEARANCE, BUT BY THE COOLNESS OF HIS CELL PHONE.

Jim: Sometimes *Zits* ideas begin with words and sometimes they begin with an image. The best ones use every tool in our box.

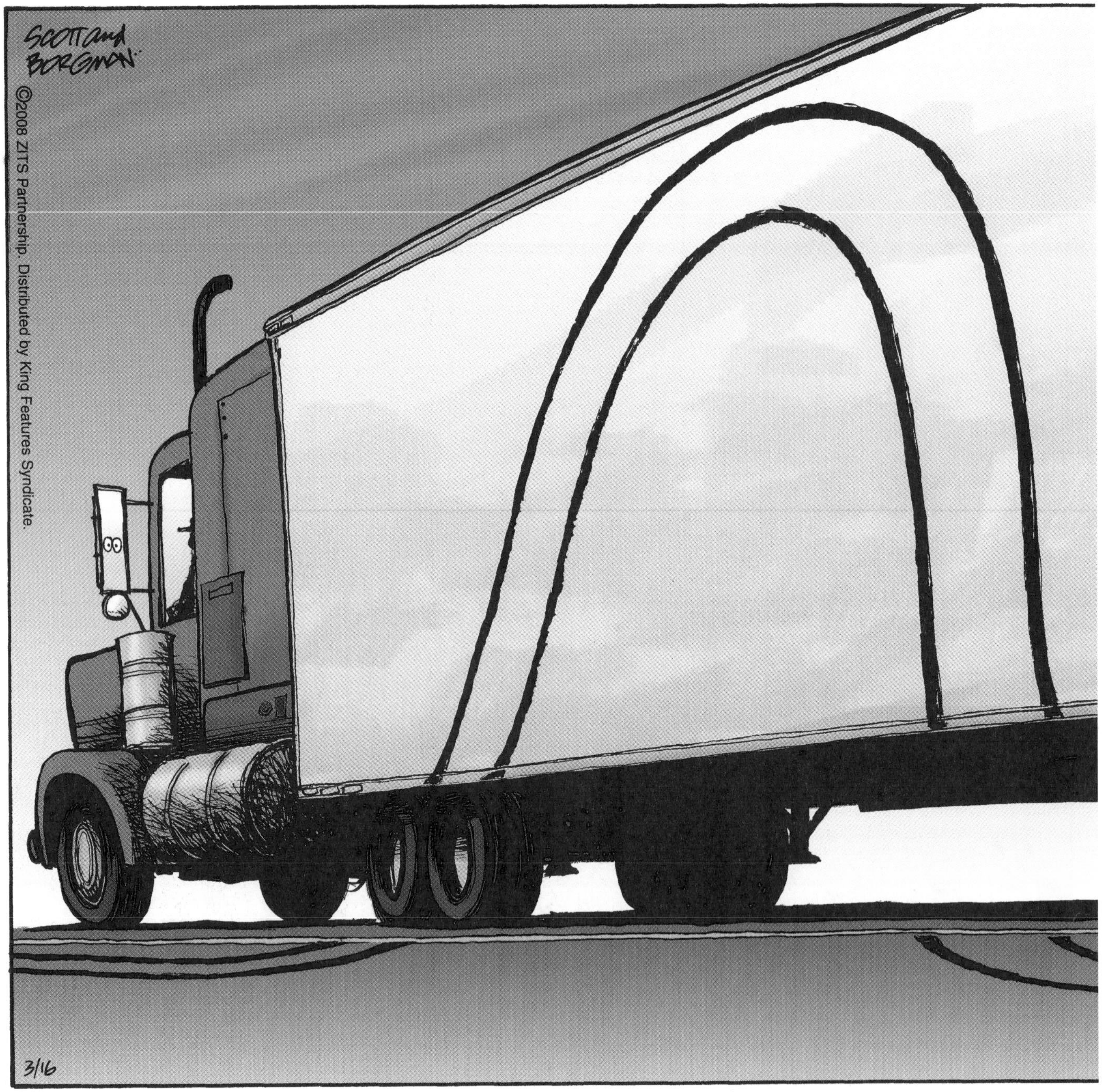
SCOTT and BORGMAN
©2008 ZITS Partnership. Distributed by King Features Syndicate.
3/16

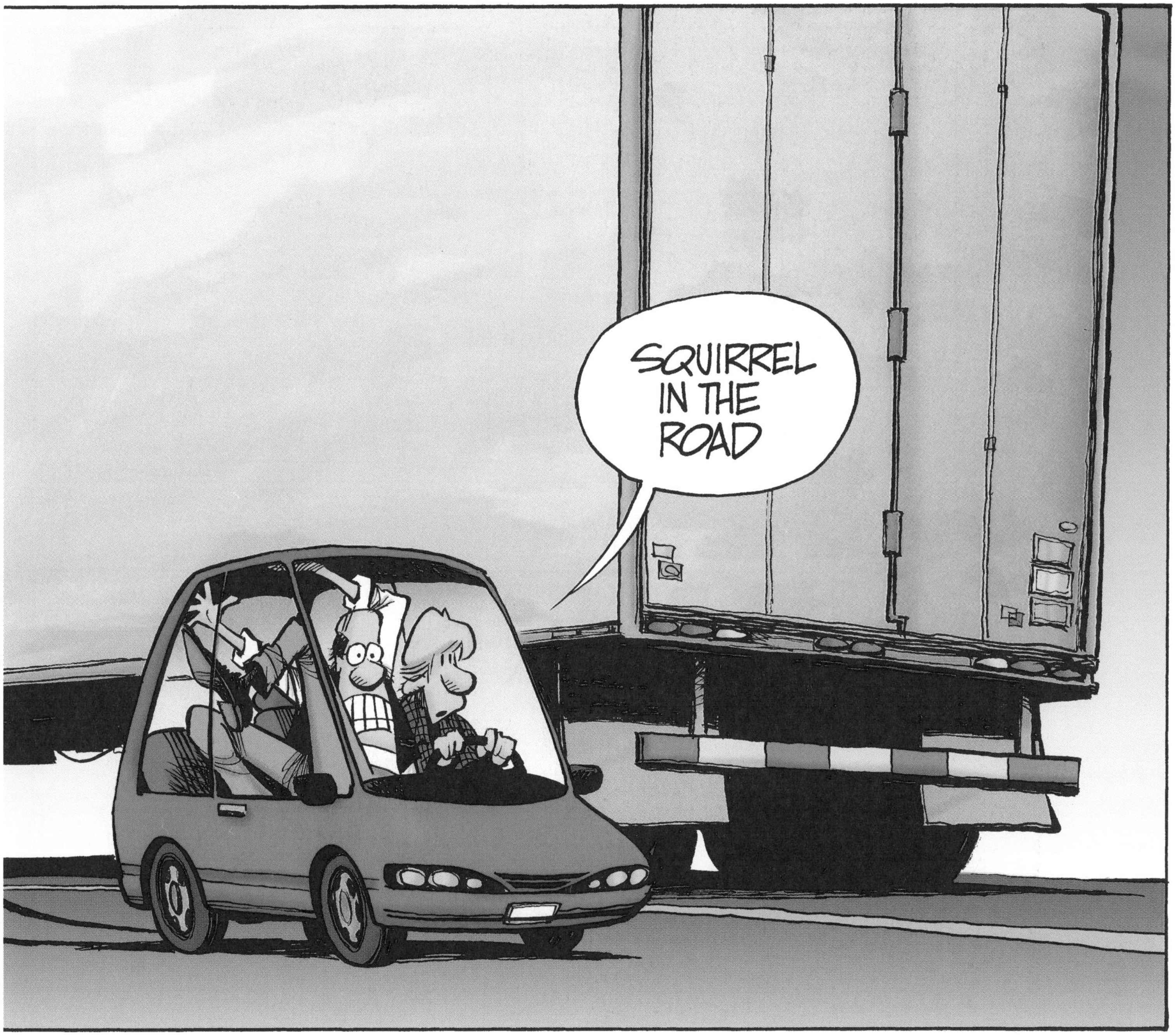
SQUIRREL IN THE ROAD

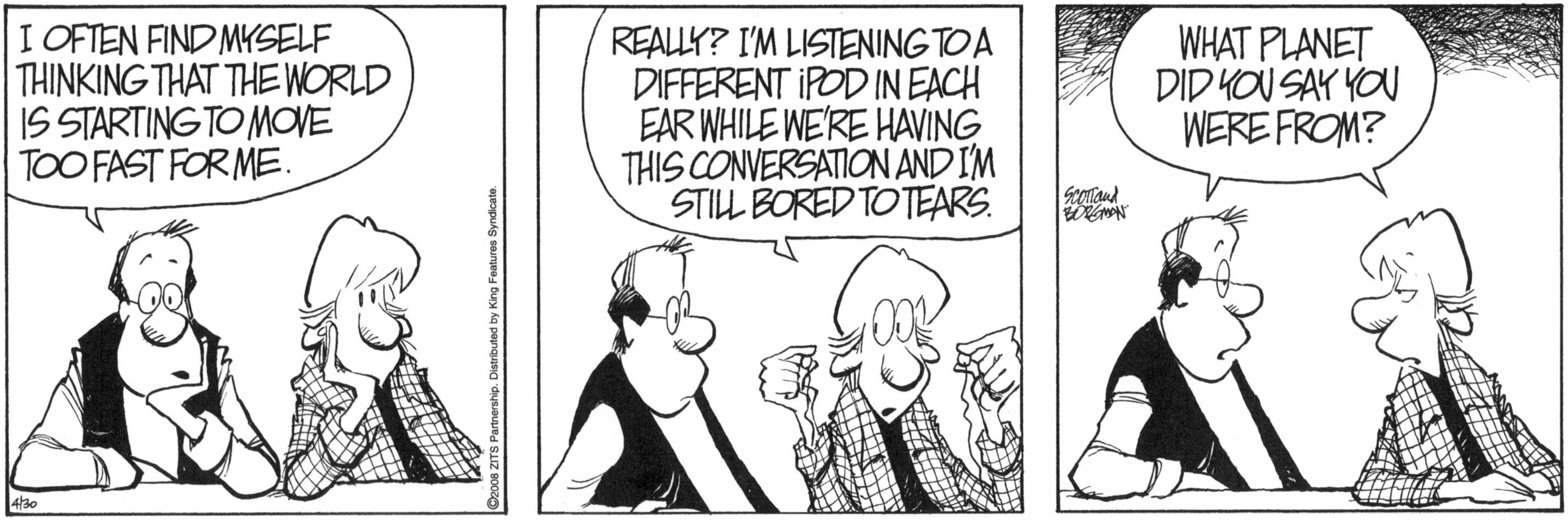
I OFTEN FIND MYSELF THINKING THAT THE WORLD IS STARTING TO MOVE TOO FAST FOR ME.
4/30
©2008 ZITS Partnership. Distributed by King Features Syndicate.
REALLY? I'M LISTENING TO A DIFFERENT iPOD IN EACH EAR WHILE WE'RE HAVING THIS CONVERSATION AND I'M STILL BORED TO TEARS.
SCOTT and BORGMAN
WHAT PLANET DID YOU SAY YOU WERE FROM?

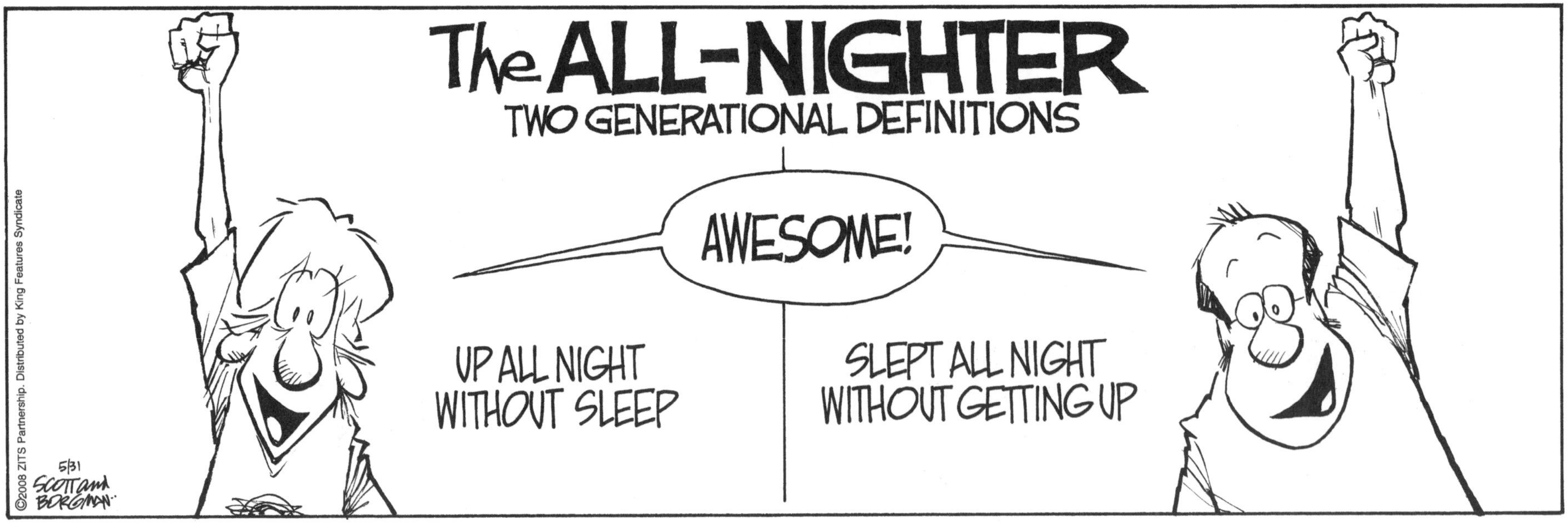
The ALL-NIGHTER
TWO GENERATIONAL DEFINITIONS
AWESOME!
UP ALL NIGHT WITHOUT SLEEP
SLEPT ALL NIGHT WITHOUT GETTING UP
5/31
SCOTT and BORGMAN
©2008 ZITS Partnership. Distributed by King Features Syndicate

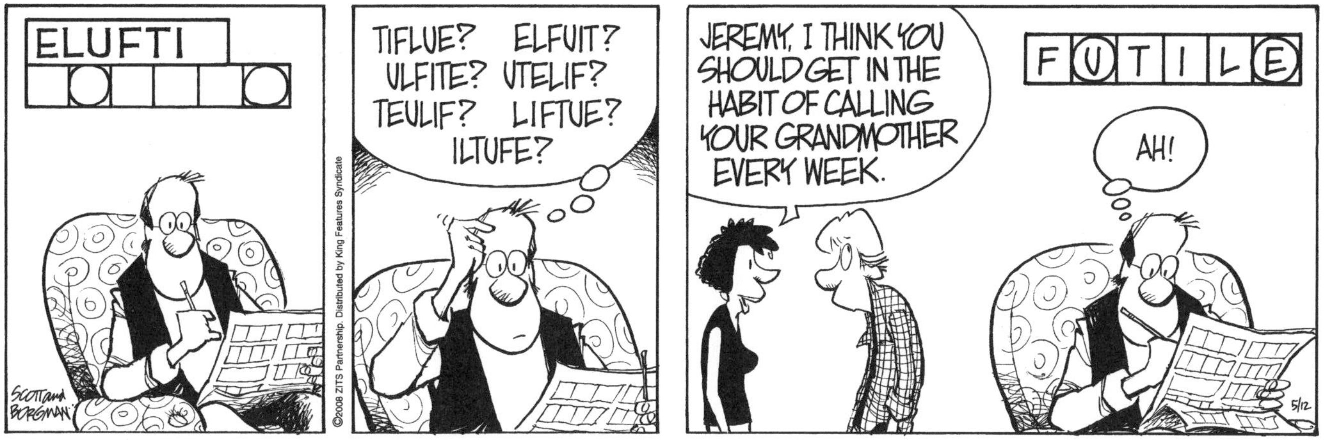
ELUFTI
TIFLUE? ELFUIT? ULFITE? UTELIF? TEULIF? LIFTUE? ILTUFE?
©2008 ZITS Partnership. Distributed by King Features Syndicate
JEREMY, I THINK YOU SHOULD GET IN THE HABIT OF CALLING YOUR GRANDMOTHER EVERY WEEK.
FUTILE
AH!

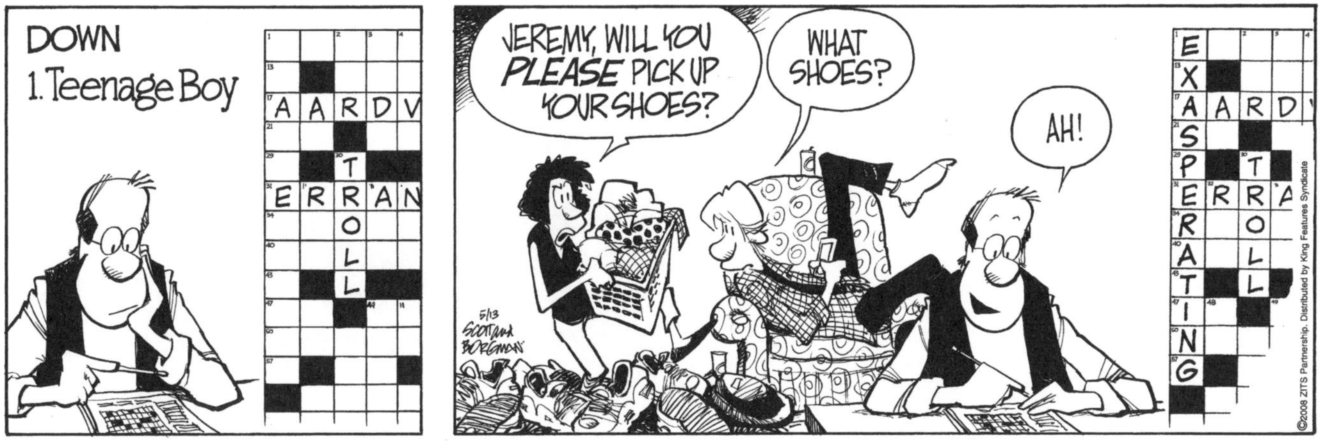
DOWN
1. Teenage Boy
AARDV
TROLL
ERRAN
JEREMY, WILL YOU *PLEASE* PICK UP YOUR SHOES?
WHAT SHOES?
AH!
EXASPERATING
©2008 ZITS Partnership. Distributed by King Features Syndicate

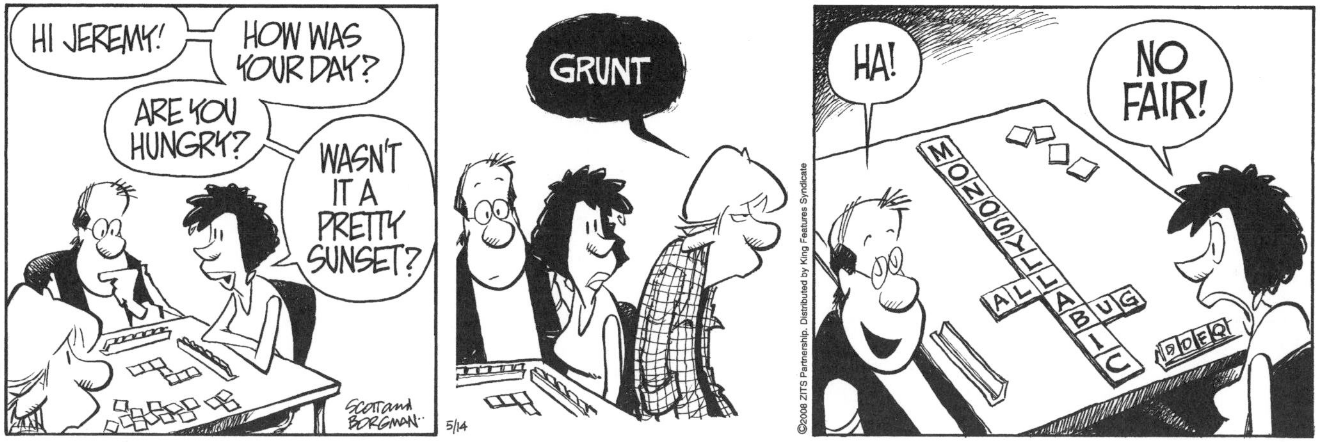
HI JEREMY!
HOW WAS YOUR DAY?
ARE YOU HUNGRY?
WASN'T IT A PRETTY SUNSET?
GRUNT
©2008 ZITS Partnership. Distributed by King Features Syndicate
HA!
NO FAIR!
MONOSYLLABIC
ALL
BUG

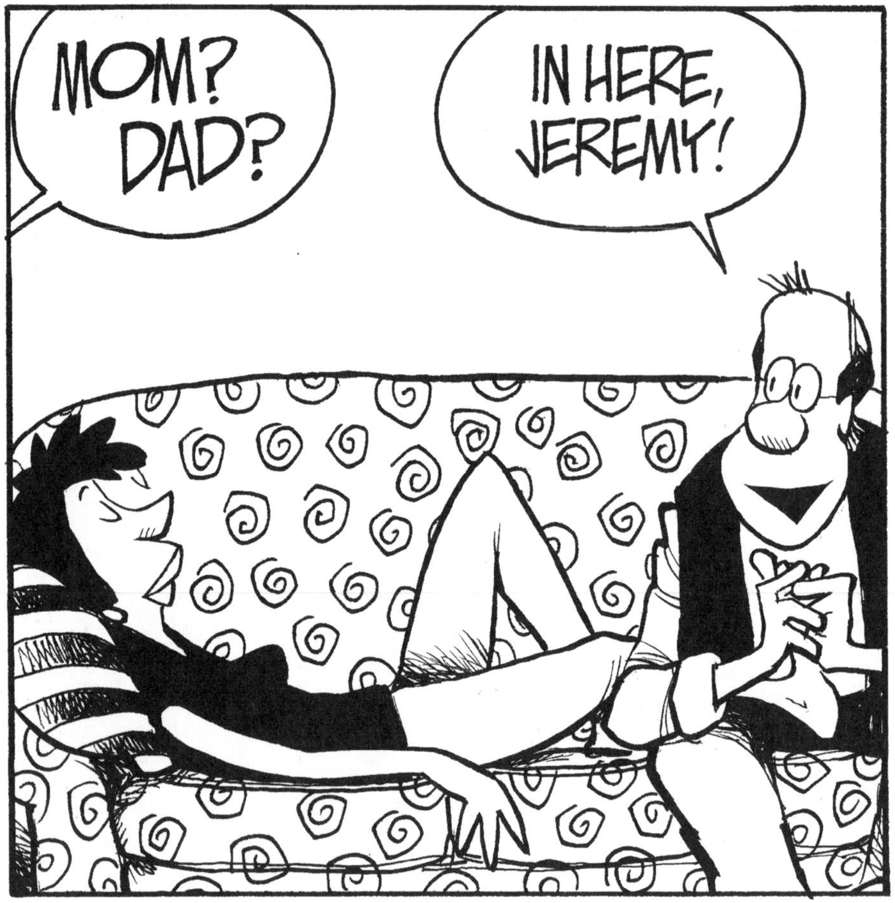
MOM? DAD?
IN HERE, JEREMY!

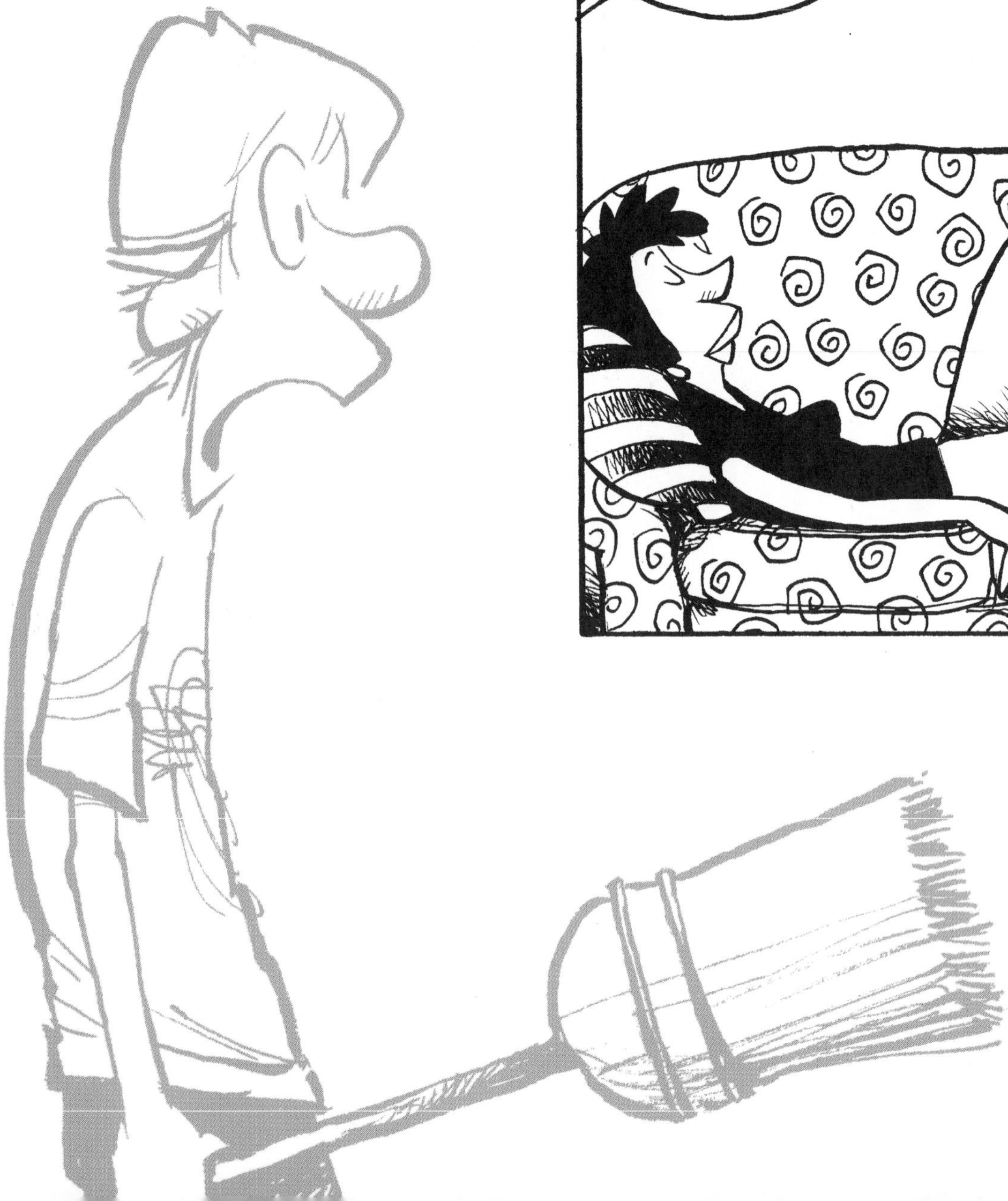

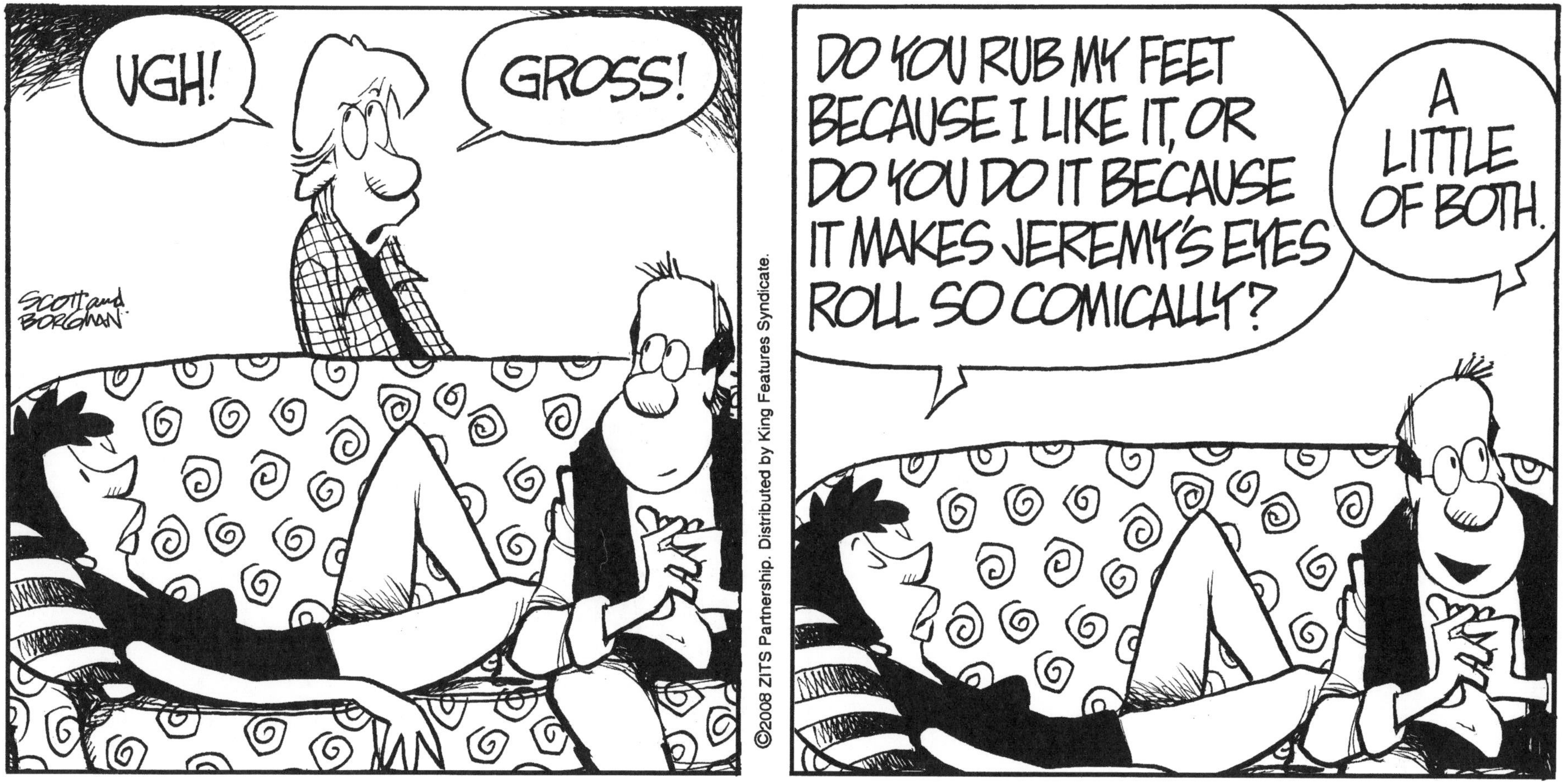
UGH!
GROSS!
SCOTT and BORGMAN
©2008 ZITS Partnership. Distributed by King Features Syndicate.
DO YOU RUB MY FEET BECAUSE I LIKE IT, OR DO YOU DO IT BECAUSE IT MAKES JEREMY'S EYES ROLL SO COMICALLY?
A LITTLE OF BOTH.

Jim: A rare glimpse at the impish side of Dad. We try to shift the butt of the jokes around so every character gets an equal chance to be ridiculed.

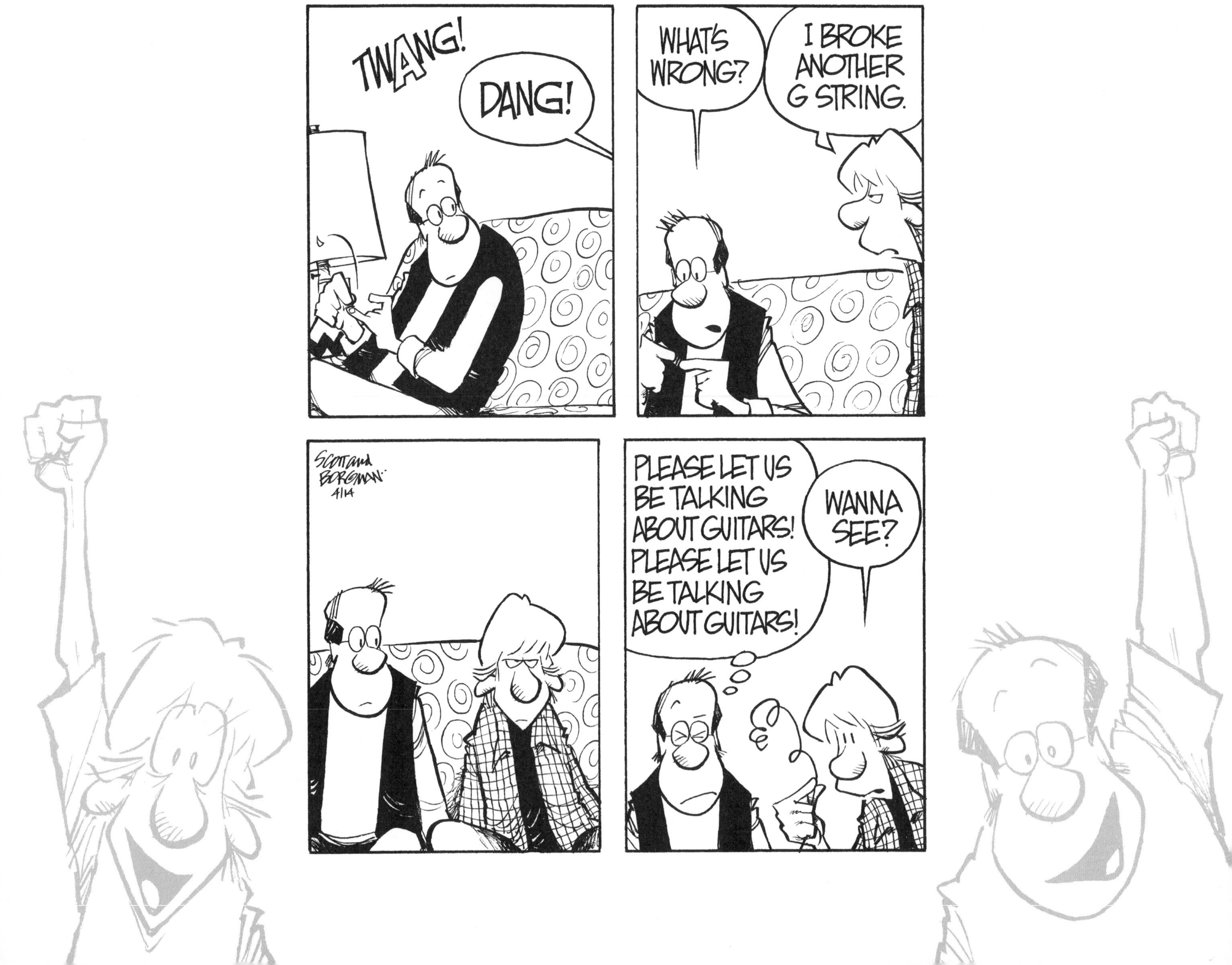
TWANG!
DANG!
WHAT'S WRONG?
I BROKE ANOTHER G STRING.
SCOTT AND BORGMAN 4/14
PLEASE LET US BE TALKING ABOUT GUITARS! PLEASE LET US BE TALKING ABOUT GUITARS!
WANNA SEE?

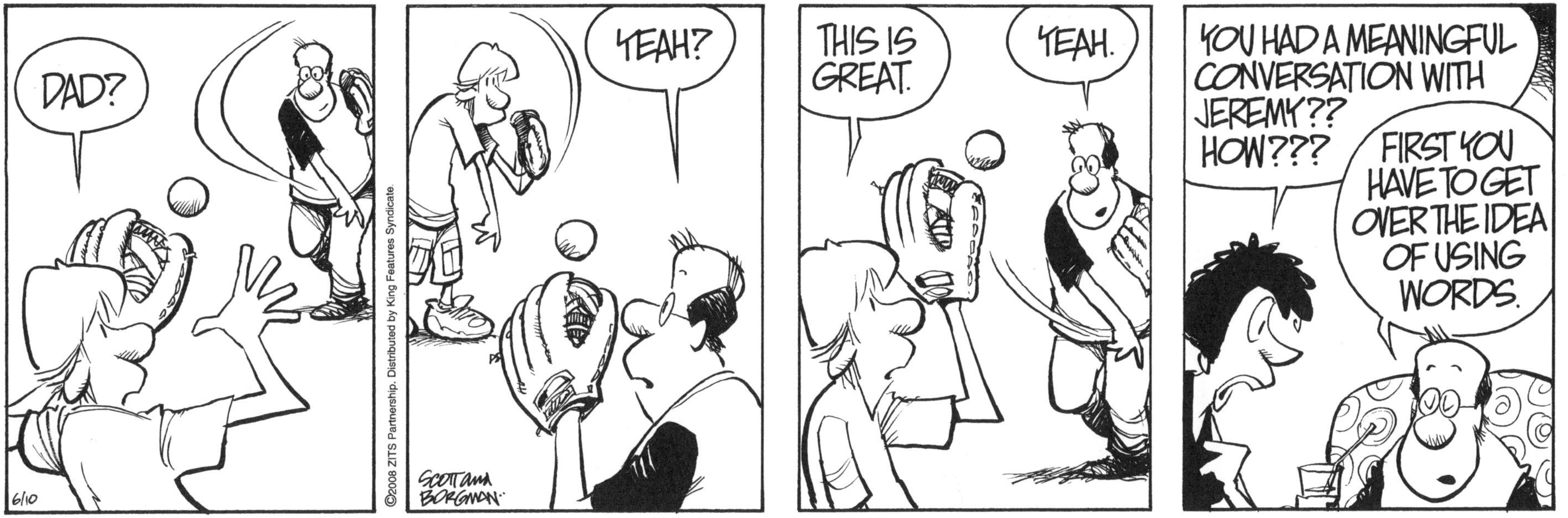
DAD?
YEAH?
THIS IS GREAT.
YEAH.
YOU HAD A MEANINGFUL CONVERSATION WITH JEREMY?? HOW???
FIRST YOU HAVE TO GET OVER THE IDEA OF USING WORDS.
6/10
©2008 ZITS Partnership. Distributed by King Features Syndicate.
SCOTT and BORGMAN

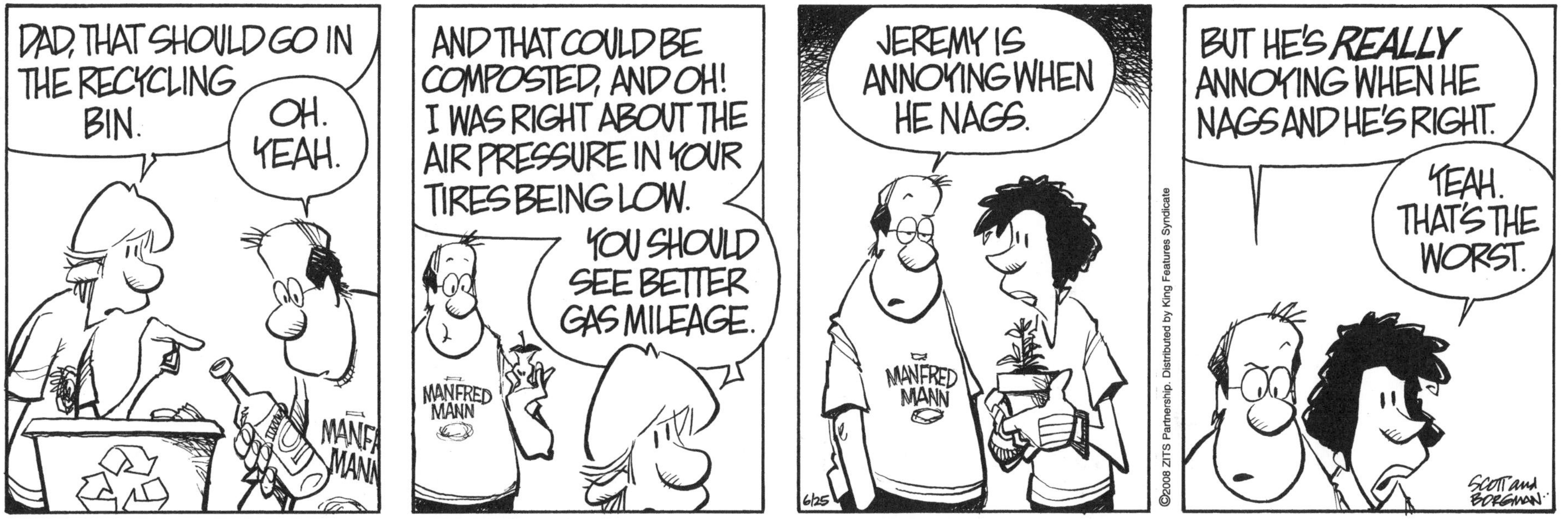
DAD, THAT SHOULD GO IN THE RECYCLING BIN.
OH. YEAH.
AND THAT COULD BE COMPOSTED, AND OH! I WAS RIGHT ABOUT THE AIR PRESSURE IN YOUR TIRES BEING LOW.
YOU SHOULD SEE BETTER GAS MILEAGE.
MANFRED MANN
JEREMY IS ANNOYING WHEN HE NAGS.
6/25
©2008 ZITS Partnership. Distributed by King Features Syndicate
BUT HE'S **REALLY** ANNOYING WHEN HE NAGS AND HE'S RIGHT.
YEAH. THAT'S THE WORST.
SCOTT and BORGMAN

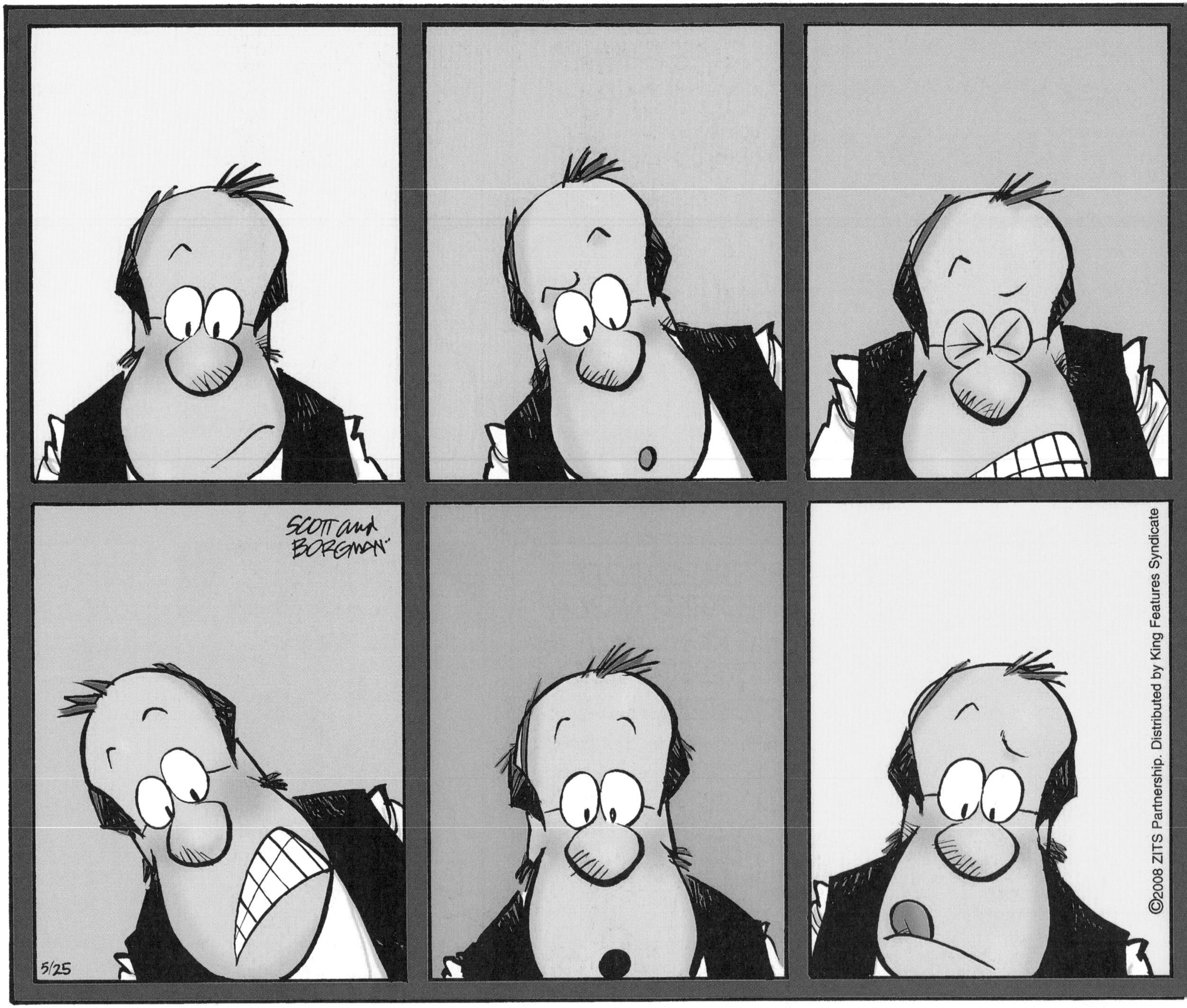
SCOTT and BORGMAN
5/25
©2008 ZITS Partnership. Distributed by King Features Syndicate

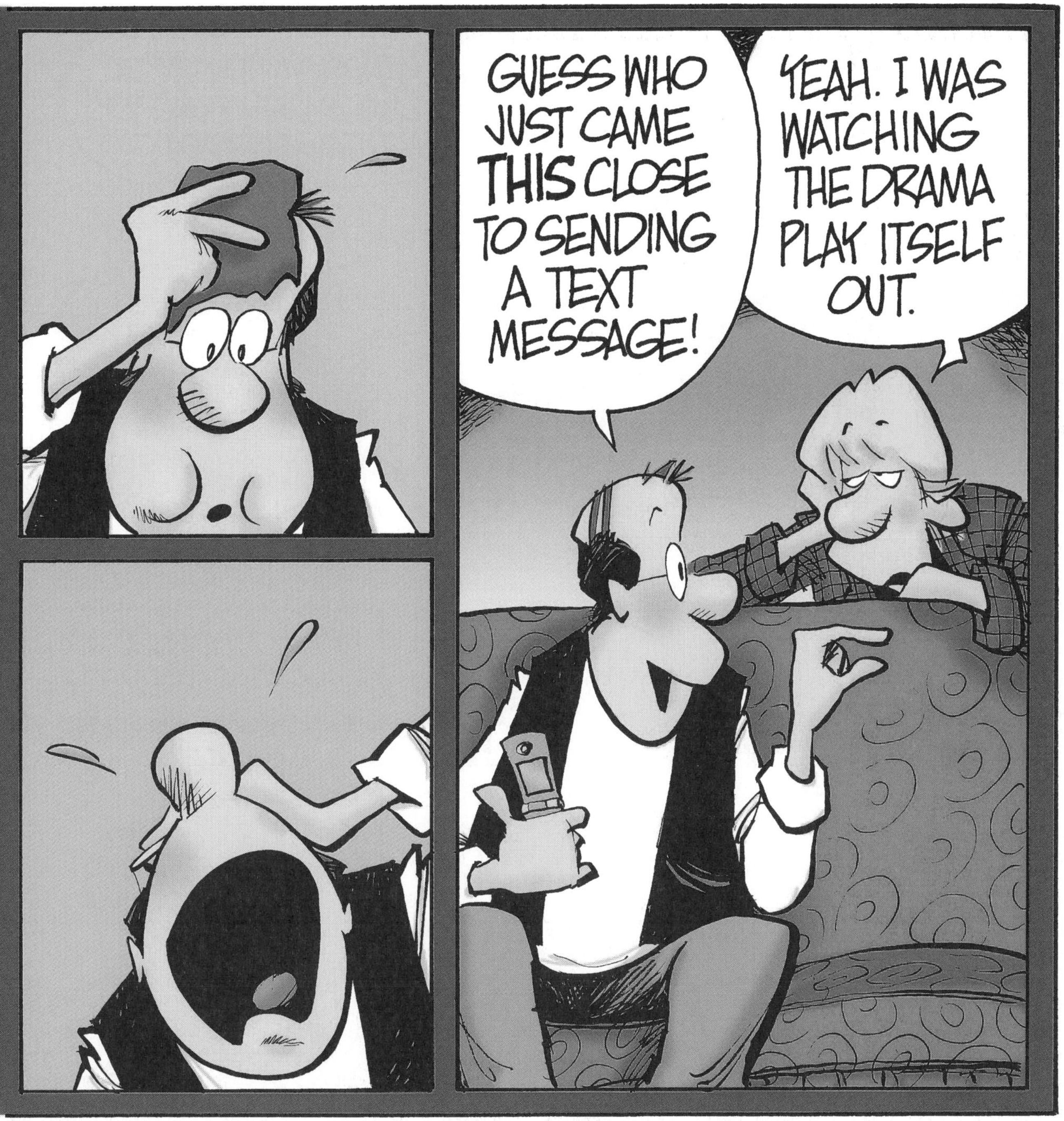
GUESS WHO JUST CAME THIS CLOSE TO SENDING A TEXT MESSAGE!
YEAH. I WAS WATCHING THE DRAMA PLAY ITSELF OUT.

Jerry: Someday somebody is going to make a phone for people with full-grown thumbs like mine.

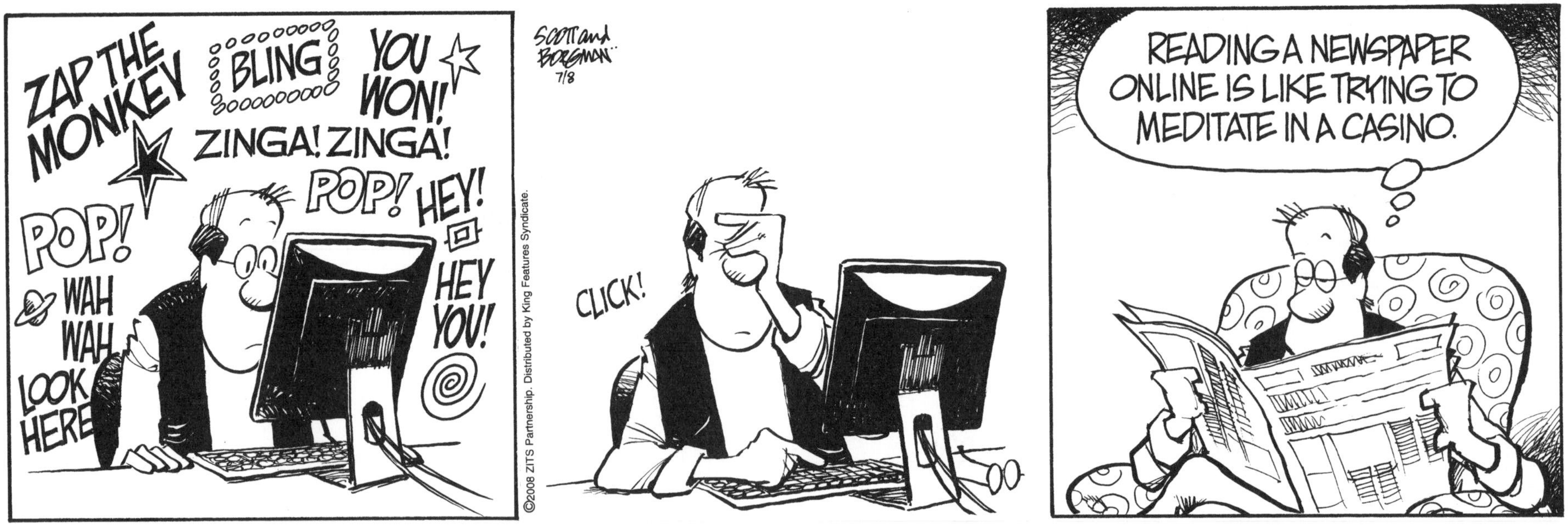
ZAP THE MONKEY
BLING
YOU WON!
ZINGA! ZINGA!
POP!
POP!
HEY!
HEY YOU!
WAH WAH
LOOK HERE
SCOTT and BORGMAN 7/8
©2008 ZITS Partnership. Distributed by King Features Syndicate.
CLICK!
READING A NEWSPAPER ONLINE IS LIKE TRYING TO MEDITATE IN A CASINO.

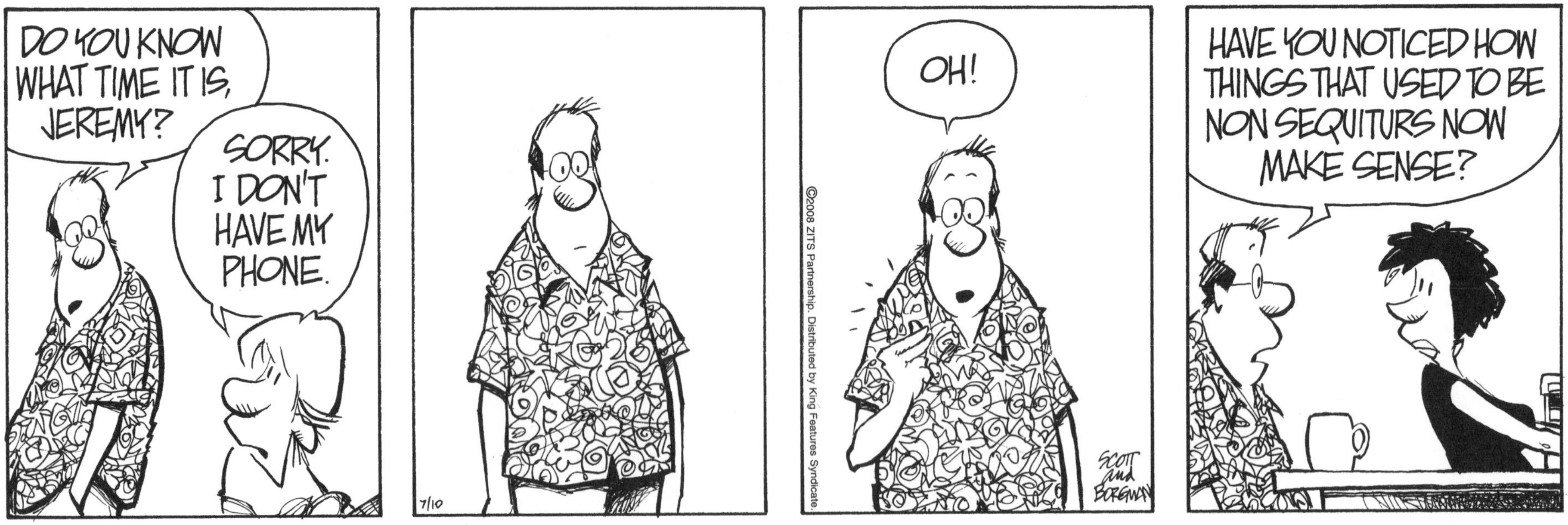
DO YOU KNOW WHAT TIME IT IS, JEREMY?
SORRY. I DON'T HAVE MY PHONE.
7/10
©2008 ZITS Partnership. Distributed by King Features Syndicate.
OH!
SCOTT and BORGMAN
HAVE YOU NOTICED HOW THINGS THAT USED TO BE NON SEQUITURS NOW MAKE SENSE?

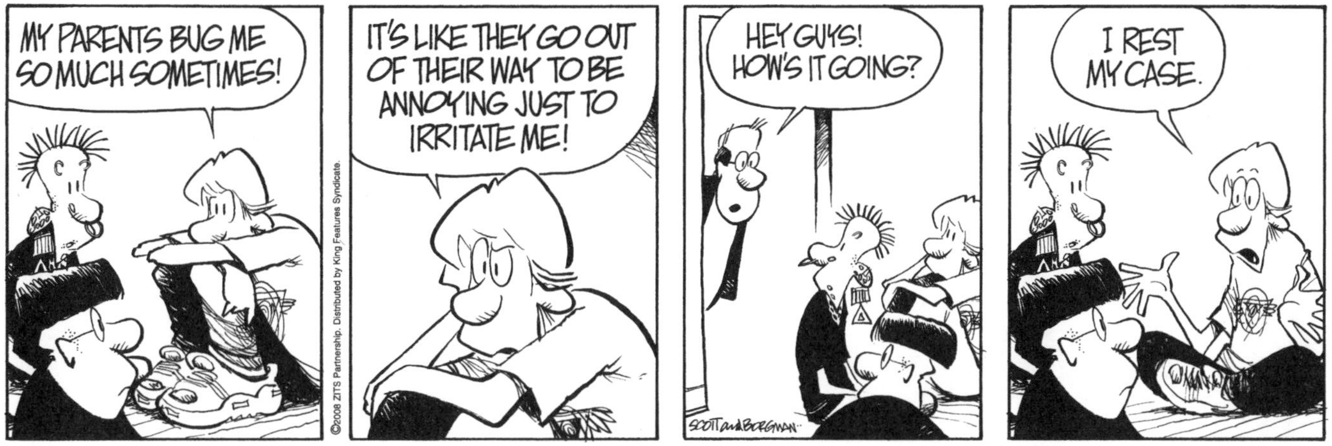
MY PARENTS BUG ME SO MUCH SOMETIMES!
IT'S LIKE THEY GO OUT OF THEIR WAY TO BE ANNOYING JUST TO IRRITATE ME!
HEY GUYS! HOW'S IT GOING?
I REST MY CASE.
©2008 ZITS Partnership. Distributed by King Features Syndicate.
SCOTT and BORGMAN

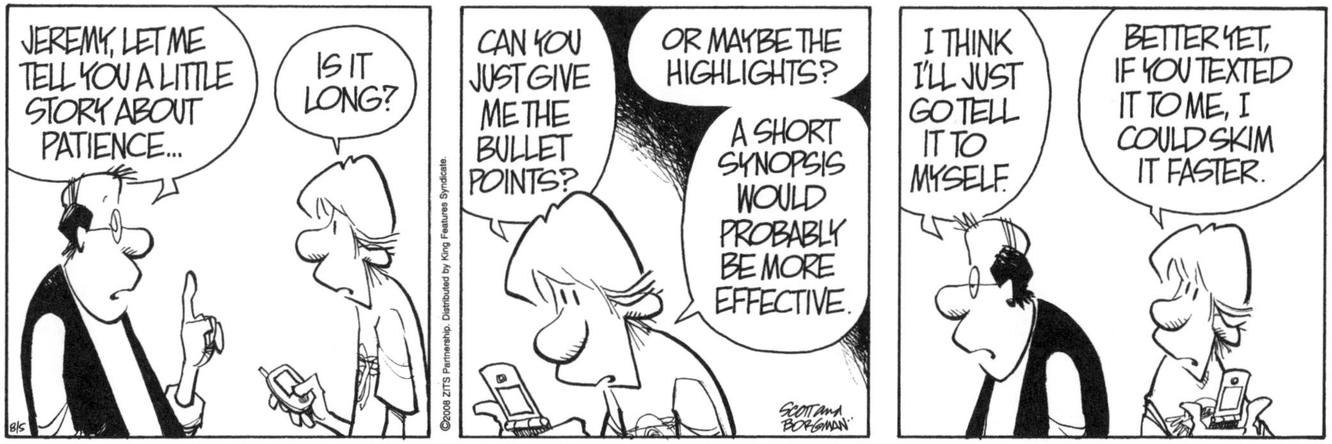
JEREMY, LET ME TELL YOU A LITTLE STORY ABOUT PATIENCE...
IS IT LONG?
CAN YOU JUST GIVE ME THE BULLET POINTS?
OR MAYBE THE HIGHLIGHTS?
A SHORT SYNOPSIS WOULD PROBABLY BE MORE EFFECTIVE.
I THINK I'LL JUST GO TELL IT TO MYSELF.
BETTER YET, IF YOU TEXTED IT TO ME, I COULD SKIM IT FASTER.
8/5
©2008 ZITS Partnership. Distributed by King Features Syndicate.
SCOTT and BORGMAN

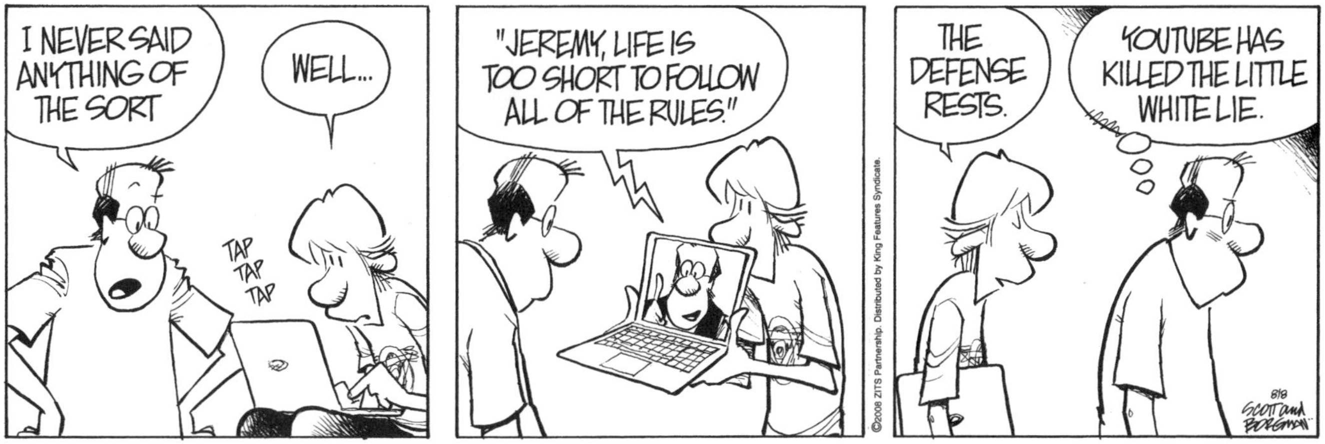
I NEVER SAID ANYTHING OF THE SORT
WELL...
TAP TAP TAP
"JEREMY, LIFE IS TOO SHORT TO FOLLOW ALL OF THE RULES."
THE DEFENSE RESTS.
YOUTUBE HAS KILLED THE LITTLE WHITE LIE.
©2008 ZITS Partnership. Distributed by King Features Syndicate.
8/8
SCOTT and BORGMAN

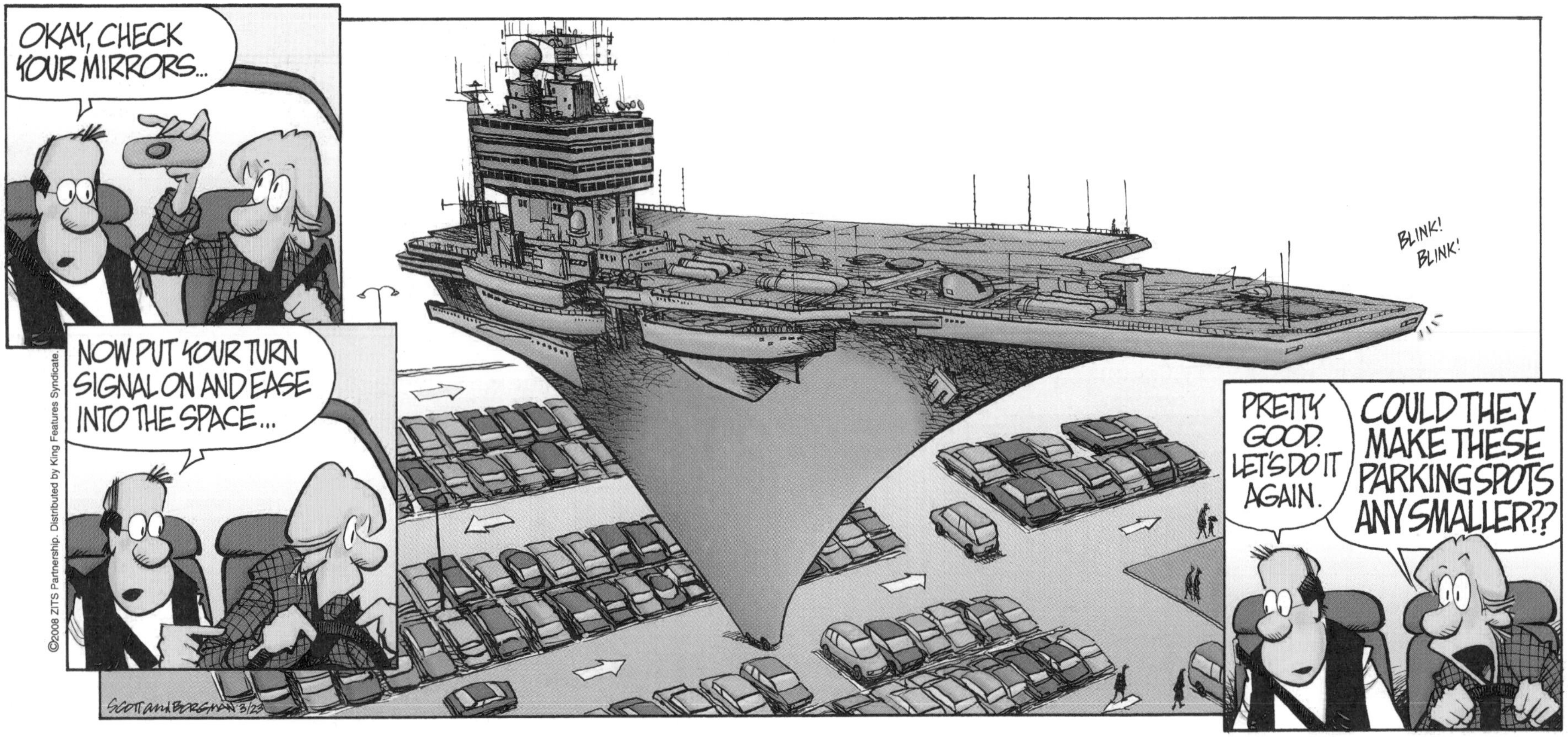
OKAY, CHECK YOUR MIRRORS...
NOW PUT YOUR TURN SIGNAL ON AND EASE INTO THE SPACE...
BLINK! BLINK!
PRETTY GOOD. LET'S DO IT AGAIN.
COULD THEY MAKE THESE PARKING SPOTS ANY SMALLER??
©2008 ZITS Partnership. Distributed by King Features Syndicate.
SCOTT AND BORGMAN 3/23

Jim: I learned to drive in my parents' hulking Ford LTD back in the '70s. It filled every inch of the lane as it swayed down the street. The phrase "parallel parking" still causes flop sweat and flashbacks.

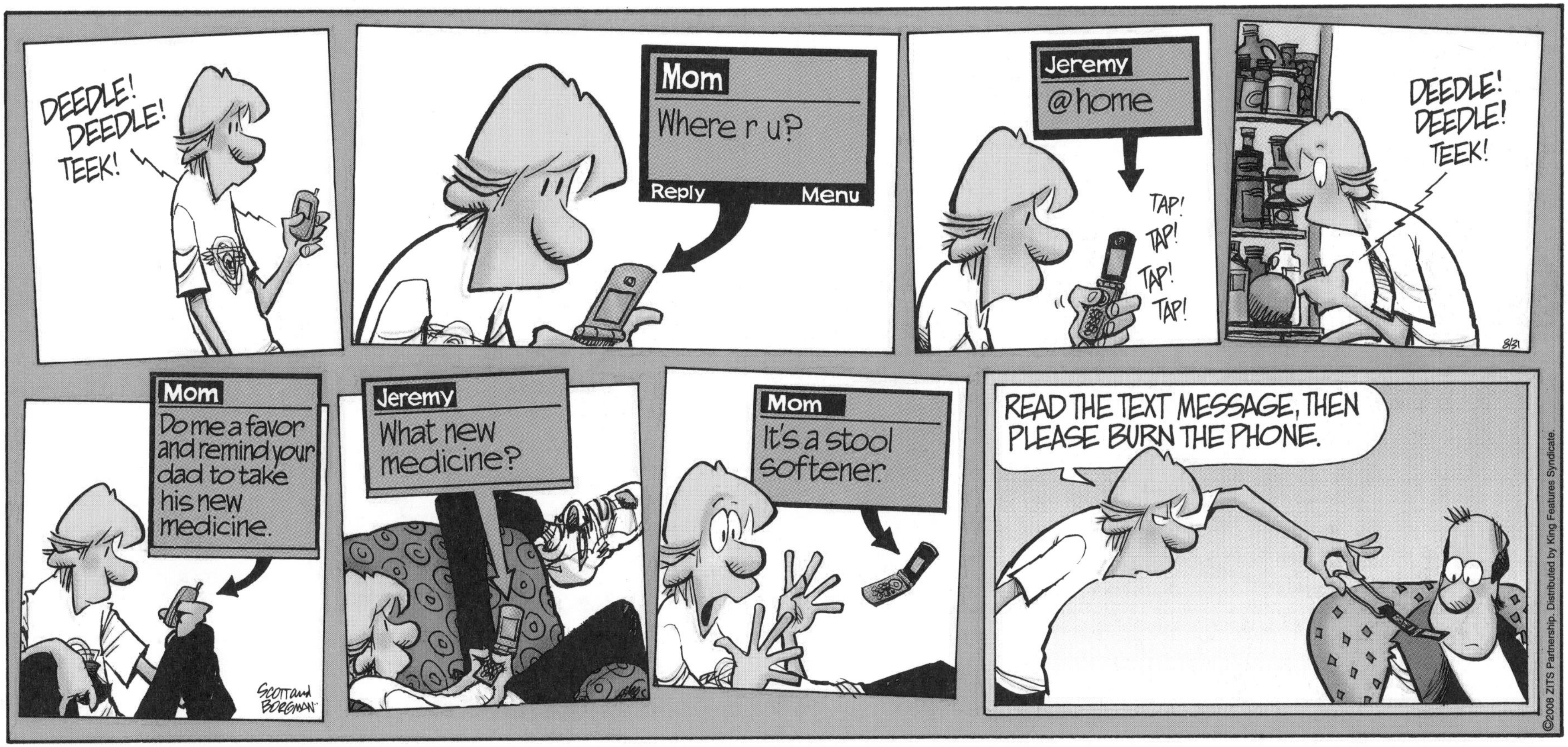
DEEDLE! DEEDLE! TEEK!
Mom
Where r u?
Reply
Menu
Jeremy
@home
TAP! TAP! TAP! TAP!
DEEDLE! DEEDLE! TEEK!
Mom
Do me a favor and remind your dad to take his new medicine.
Jeremy
What new medicine?
Mom
It's a stool softener.
READ THE TEXT MESSAGE, THEN PLEASE BURN THE PHONE.
©2008 ZITS Partnership. Distributed by King Features Syndicate.

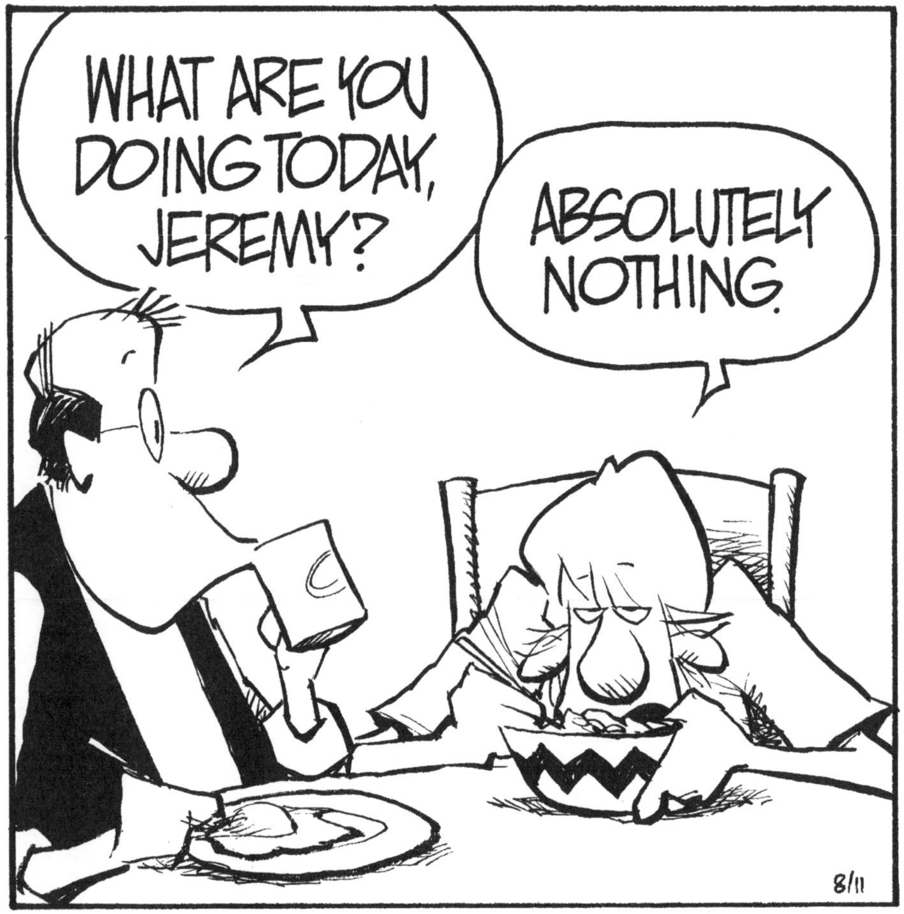
WHAT ARE YOU DOING TODAY, JEREMY?
ABSOLUTELY NOTHING.
8/11

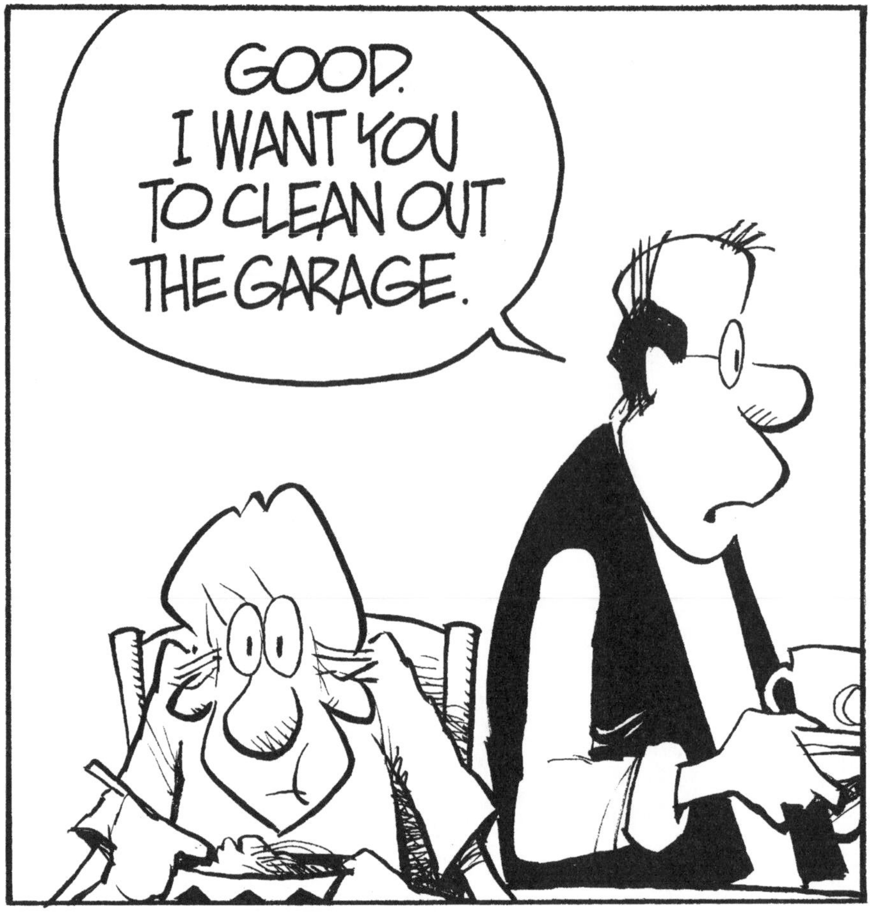
GOOD. I WANT YOU TO CLEAN OUT THE GARAGE.

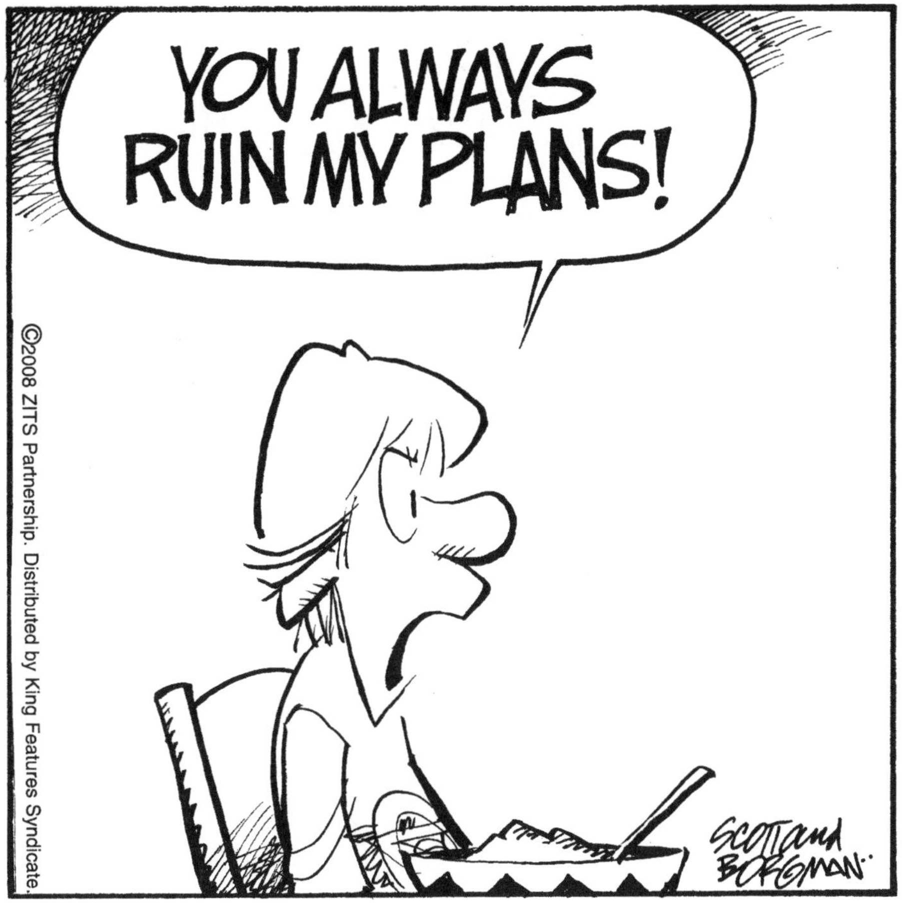
YOU ALWAYS RUIN MY PLANS!
©2008 ZITS Partnership. Distributed by King Features Syndicate.

Jerry: I write *Zits* by putting myself inside the characters and reacting to random situations. I was way deep in my inner-teenager for this one.

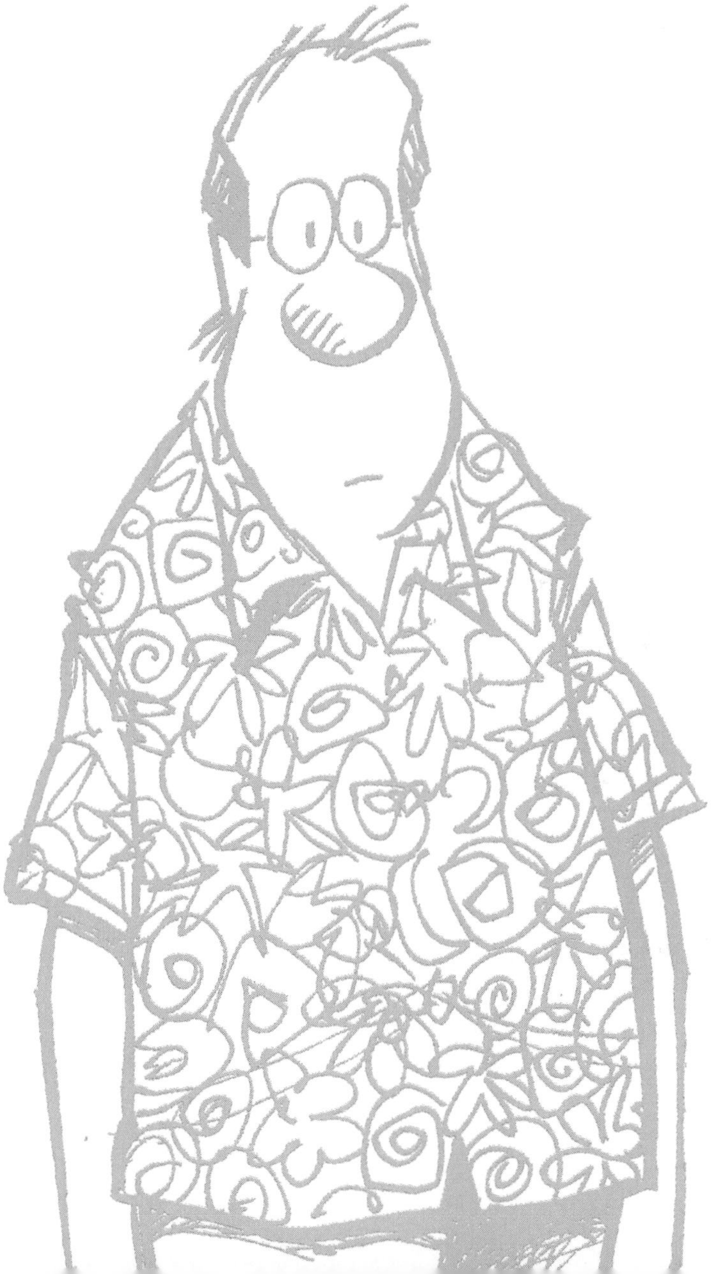

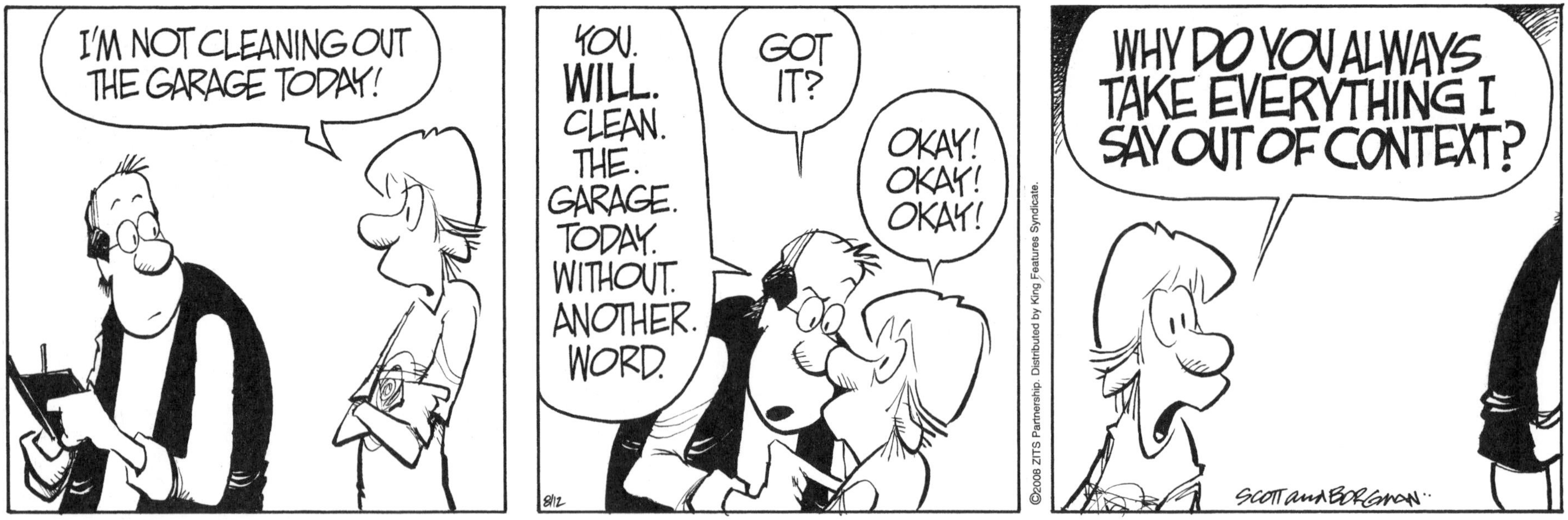
I'M NOT CLEANING OUT THE GARAGE TODAY!
YOU. WILL. CLEAN. THE. GARAGE. TODAY. WITHOUT. ANOTHER. WORD.
GOT IT?
OKAY! OKAY! OKAY!
8/12
©2008 ZITS Partnership. Distributed by King Features Syndicate.
WHY DO YOU ALWAYS TAKE EVERYTHING I SAY OUT OF CONTEXT?
SCOTT and BORGMAN

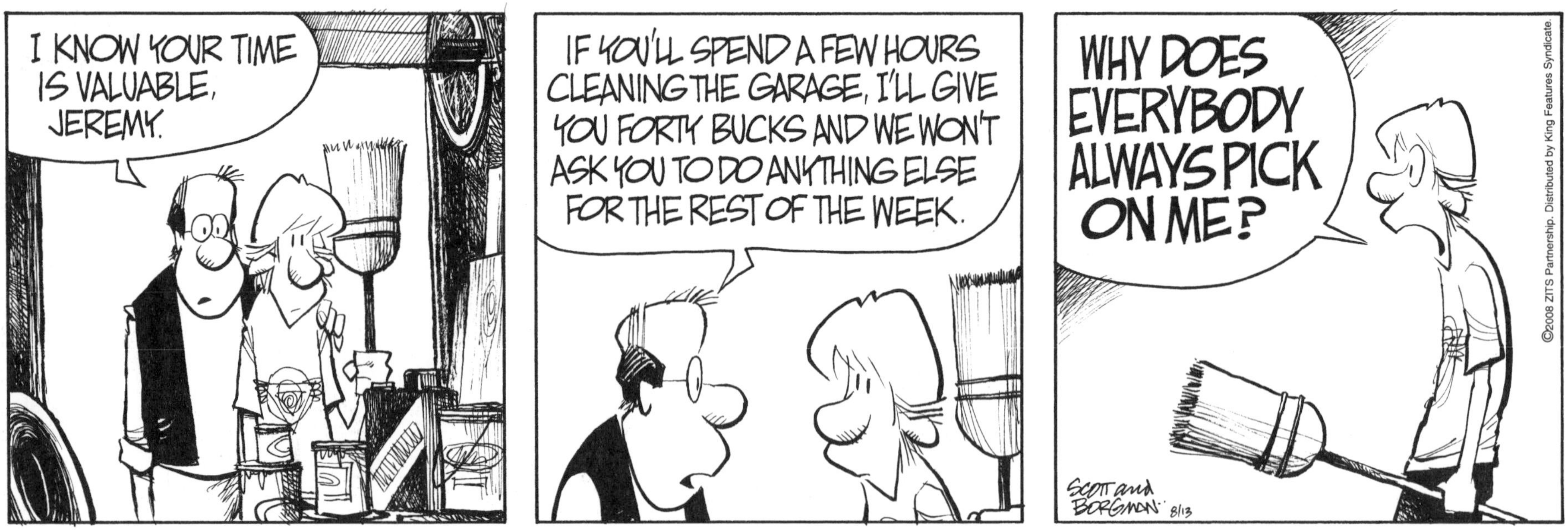
I KNOW YOUR TIME IS VALUABLE, JEREMY.
IF YOU'LL SPEND A FEW HOURS CLEANING THE GARAGE, I'LL GIVE YOU FORTY BUCKS AND WE WON'T ASK YOU TO DO ANYTHING ELSE FOR THE REST OF THE WEEK.
WHY DOES EVERYBODY ALWAYS PICK ON ME?
©2008 ZITS Partnership. Distributed by King Features Syndicate.
SCOTT and BORGMAN
8/13

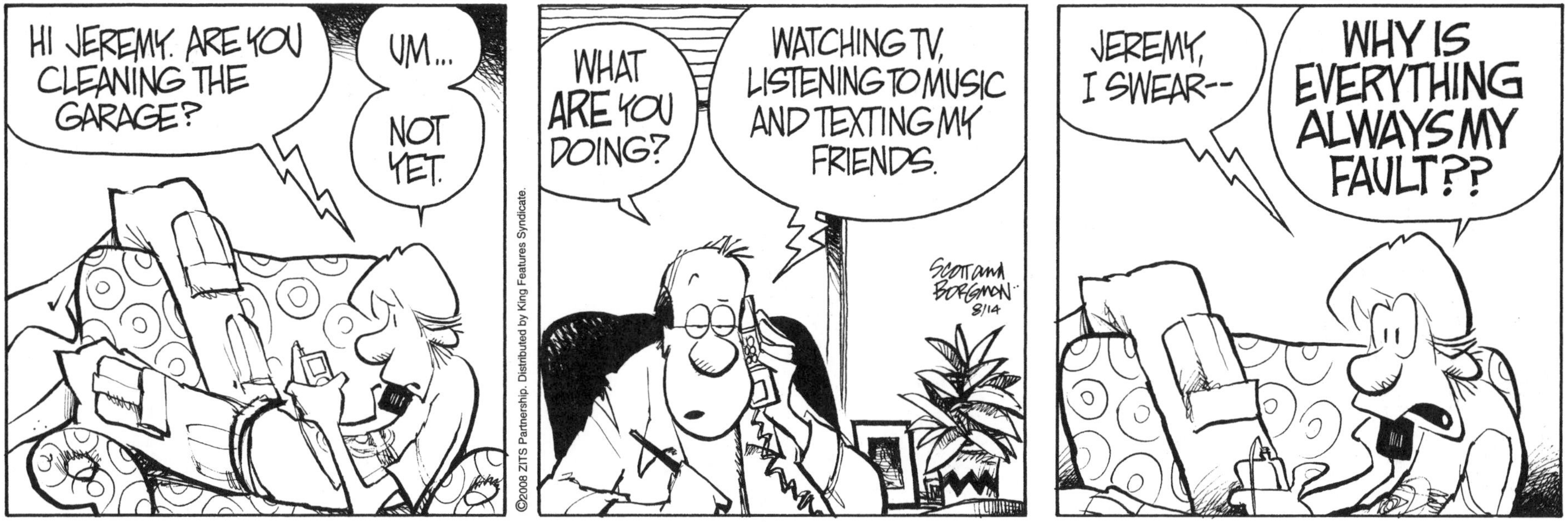
HI JEREMY. ARE YOU CLEANING THE GARAGE?
UM...
NOT YET.
©2008 ZITS Partnership. Distributed by King Features Syndicate.
WHAT ARE YOU DOING?
WATCHING TV, LISTENING TO MUSIC AND TEXTING MY FRIENDS.
SCOTT AND BORGMAN 8/14
JEREMY, I SWEAR--
WHY IS EVERYTHING ALWAYS MY FAULT??

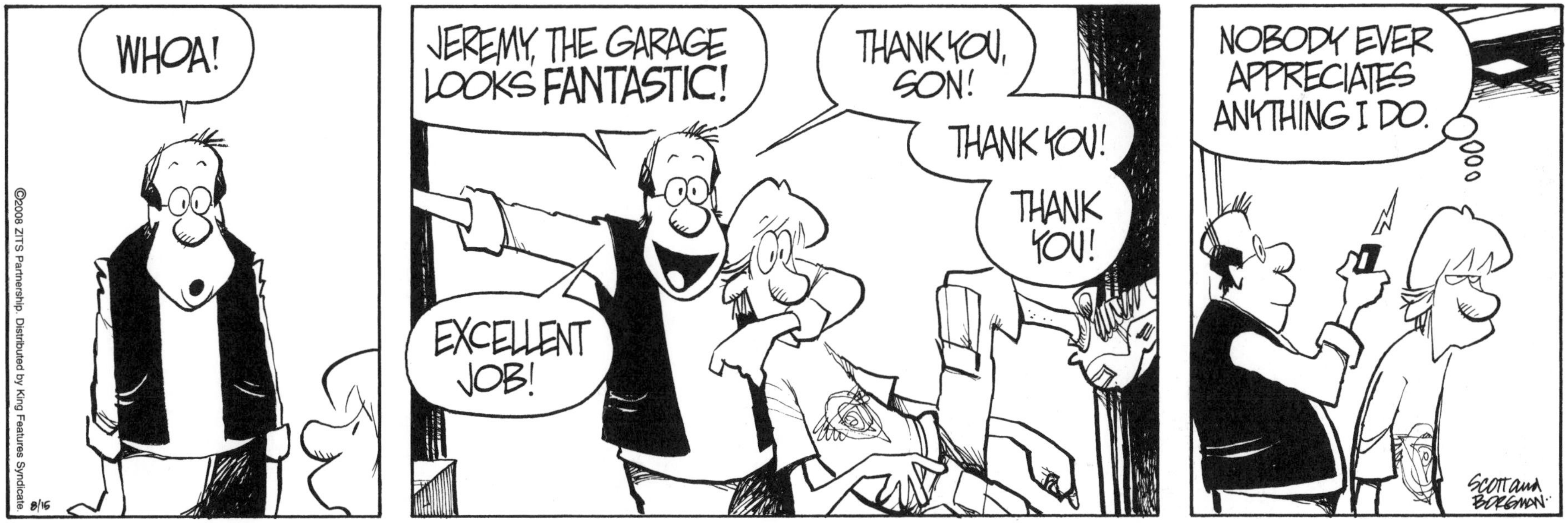
WHOA!
©2008 ZITS Partnership. Distributed by King Features Syndicate.
8/15
JEREMY, THE GARAGE LOOKS FANTASTIC!
EXCELLENT JOB!
THANK YOU, SON!
THANK YOU!
THANK YOU!
NOBODY EVER APPRECIATES ANYTHING I DO.
SCOTT AND BORGMAN

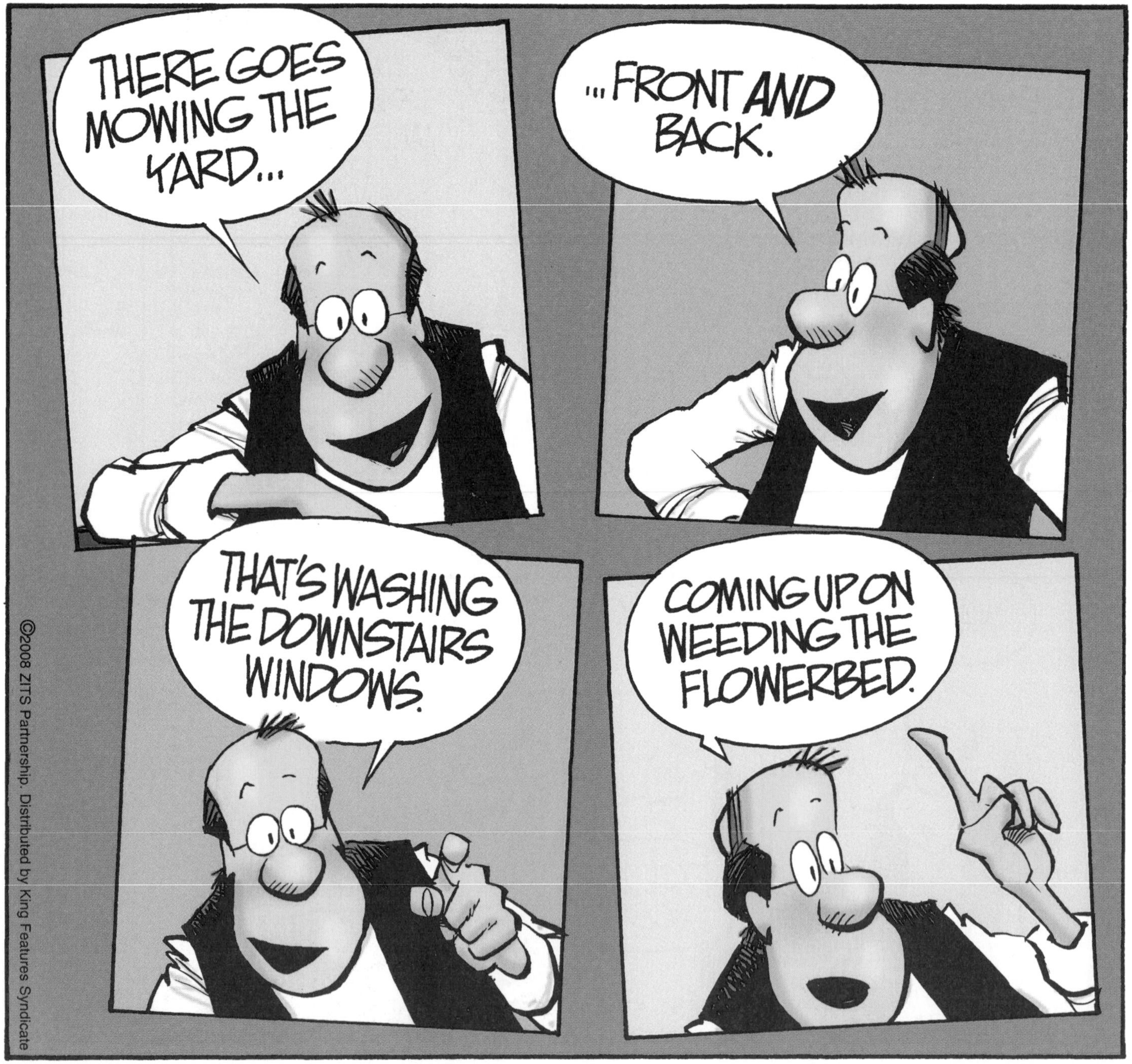
THERE GOES MOWING THE YARD...
...FRONT AND BACK.
THAT'S WASHING THE DOWNSTAIRS WINDOWS.
COMING UP ON WEEDING THE FLOWERBED.
©2008 ZITS Partnership. Distributed by King Features Syndicate

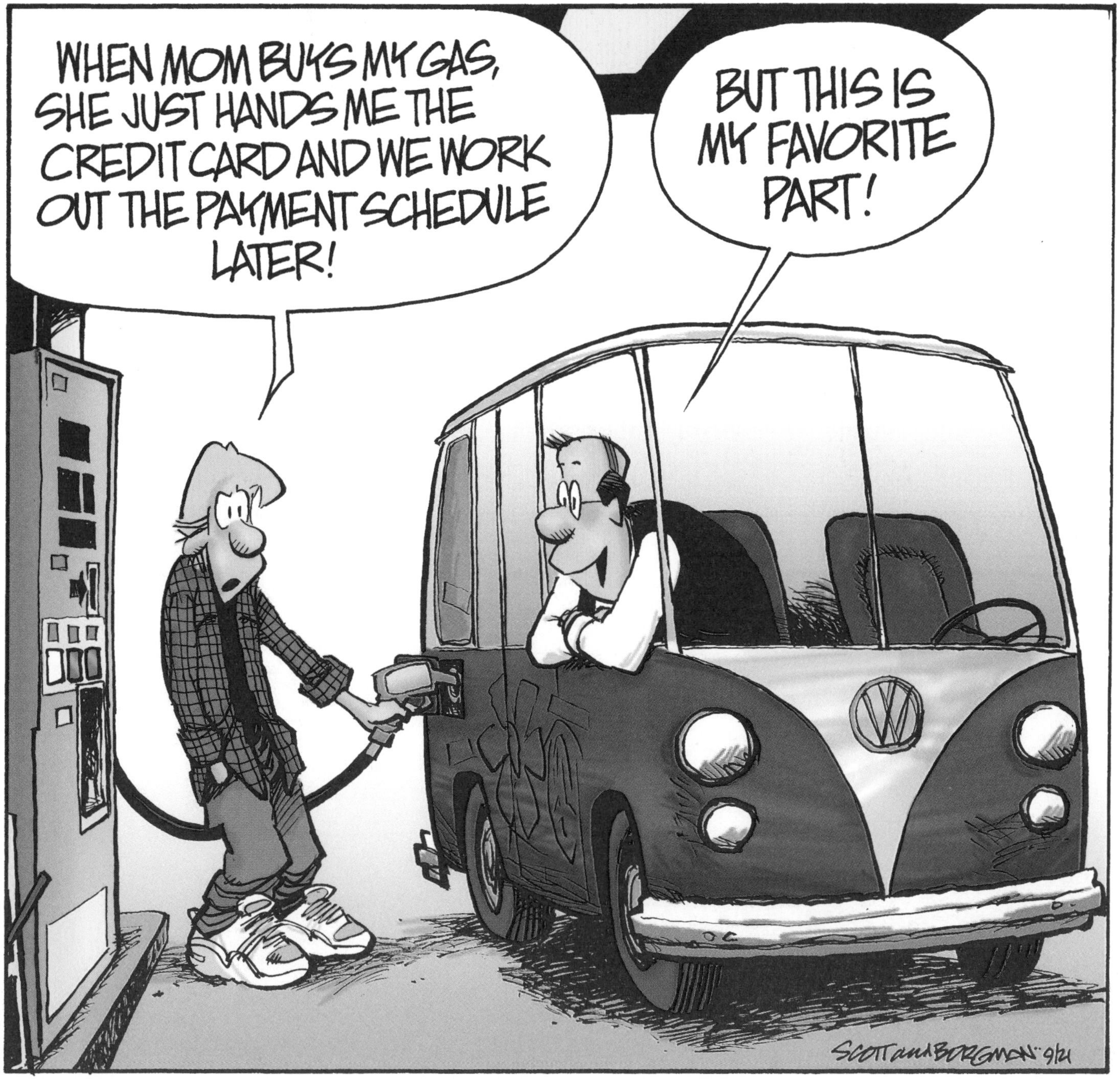
WHEN MOM BUYS MY GAS, SHE JUST HANDS ME THE CREDIT CARD AND WE WORK OUT THE PAYMENT SCHEDULE LATER!
BUT THIS IS MY FAVORITE PART!
SCOTT and BORGMAN 9/21

Jim: Dads take perverse pleasure in seeing their sons work hard. It's a guy thing.

"When I was a boy of fourteen, my father was so ignorant I could hardly stand to have the old man around. But when I got to be twenty-one, I was astonished at how much the old man had learned in seven years."

—Mark Twain

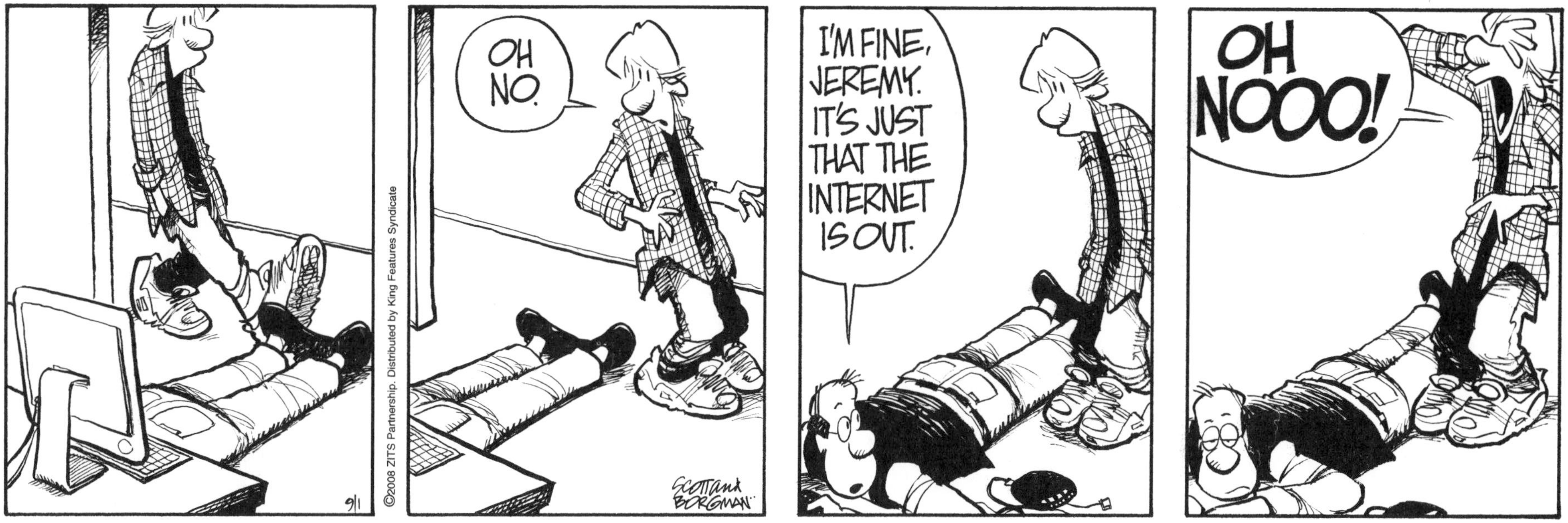
OH NO.
I'M FINE, JEREMY. IT'S JUST THAT THE INTERNET IS OUT.
OH NOOO!
©2008 ZITS Partnership. Distributed by King Features Syndicate

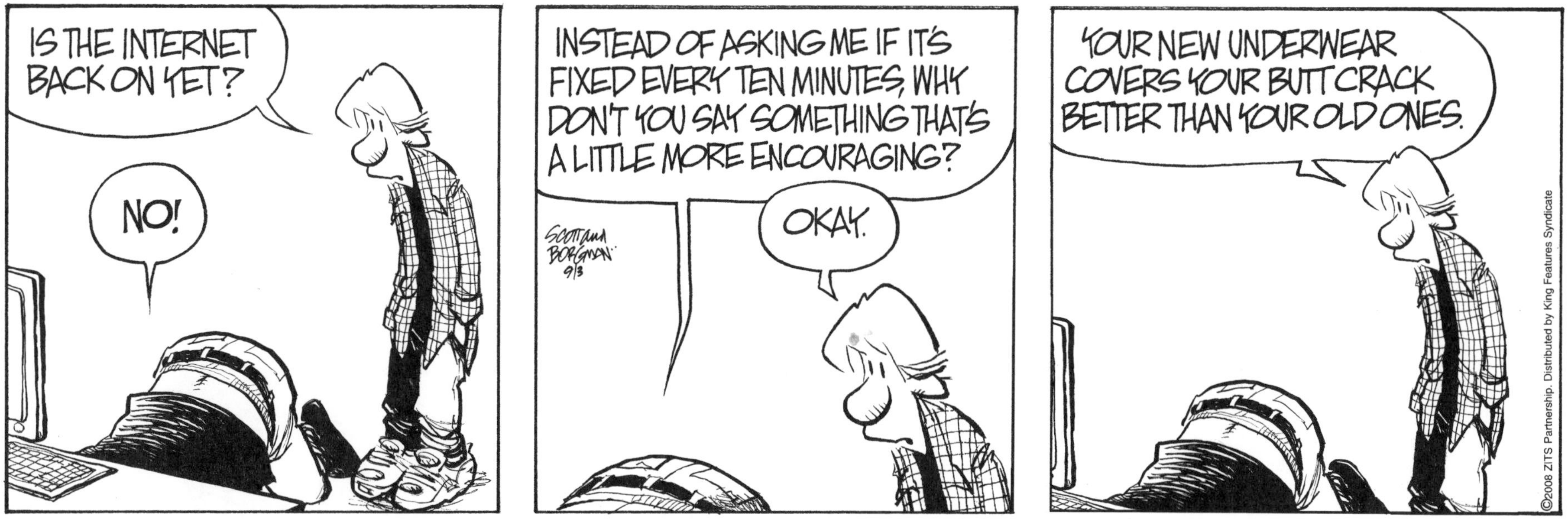
IS THE INTERNET BACK ON YET?
NO!
INSTEAD OF ASKING ME IF IT'S FIXED EVERY TEN MINUTES, WHY DON'T YOU SAY SOMETHING THAT'S A LITTLE MORE ENCOURAGING?
OKAY.
YOUR NEW UNDERWEAR COVERS YOUR BUTT CRACK BETTER THAN YOUR OLD ONES.
©2008 ZITS Partnership. Distributed by King Features Syndicate

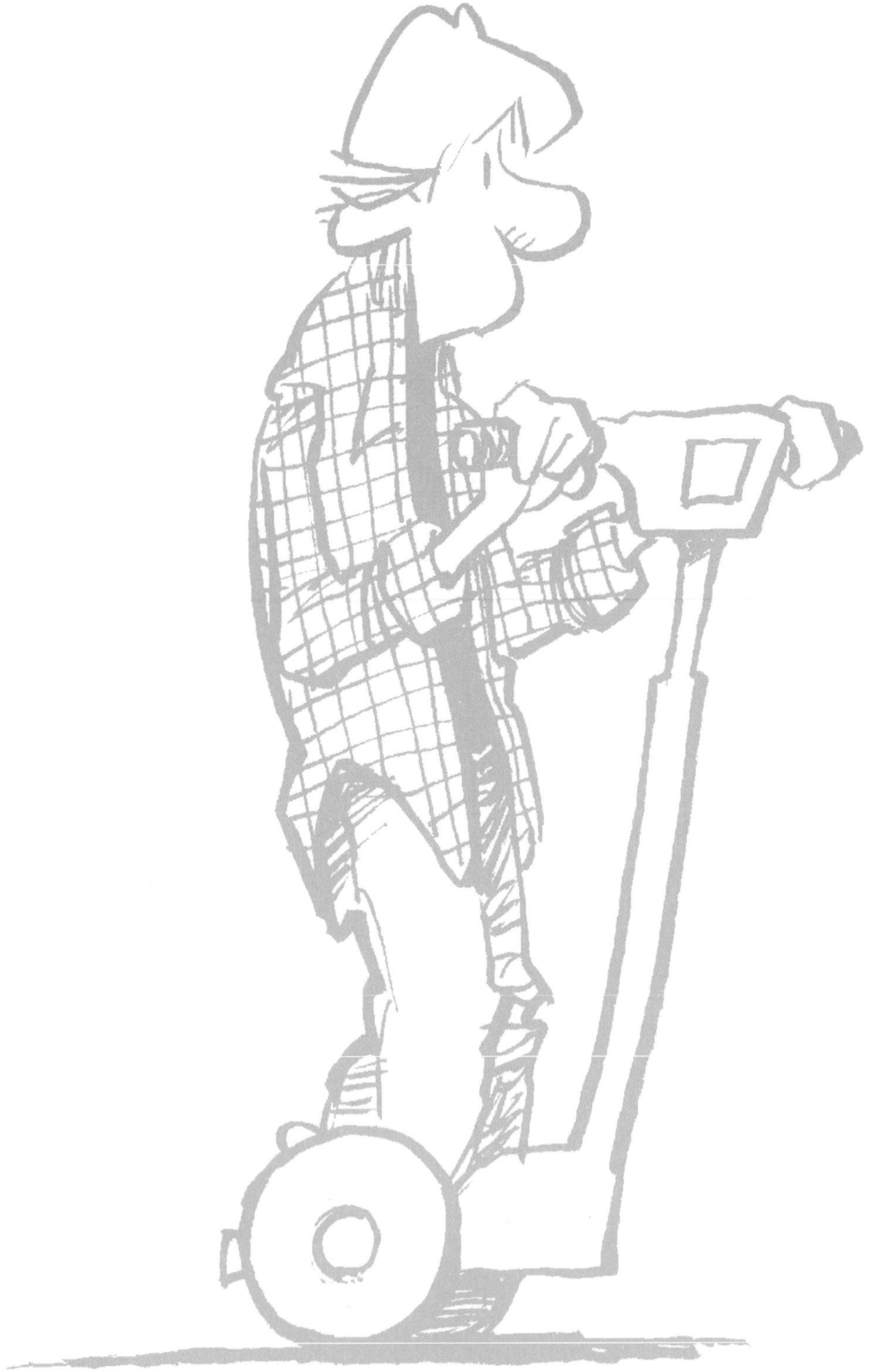

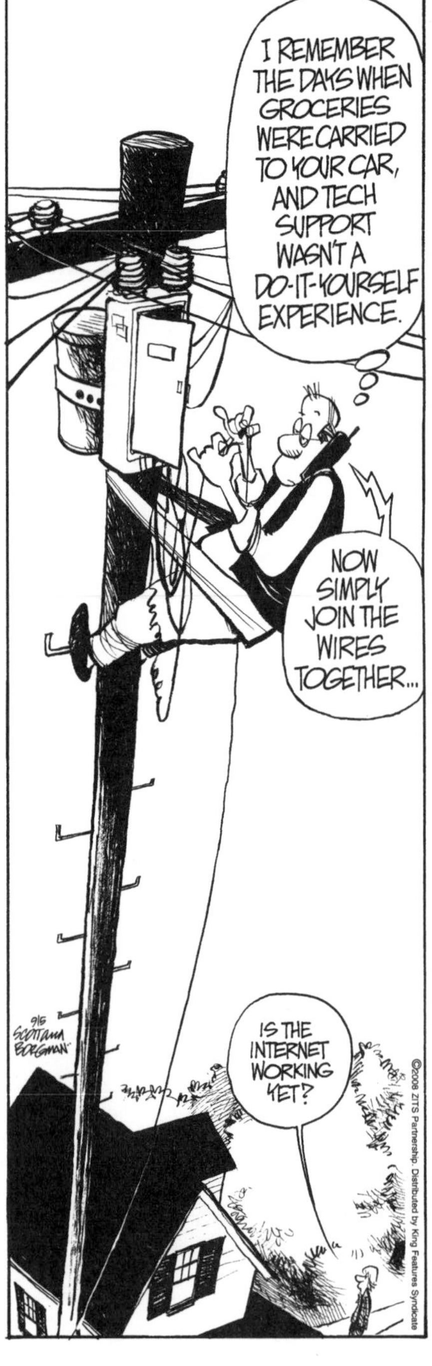
I REMEMBER THE DAYS WHEN GROCERIES WERE CARRIED TO YOUR CAR, AND TECH SUPPORT WASN'T A DO-IT-YOURSELF EXPERIENCE.
NOW SIMPLY JOIN THE WIRES TOGETHER...
IS THE INTERNET WORKING YET?
©2008 ZITS Partnership. Distributed by King Features Syndicate

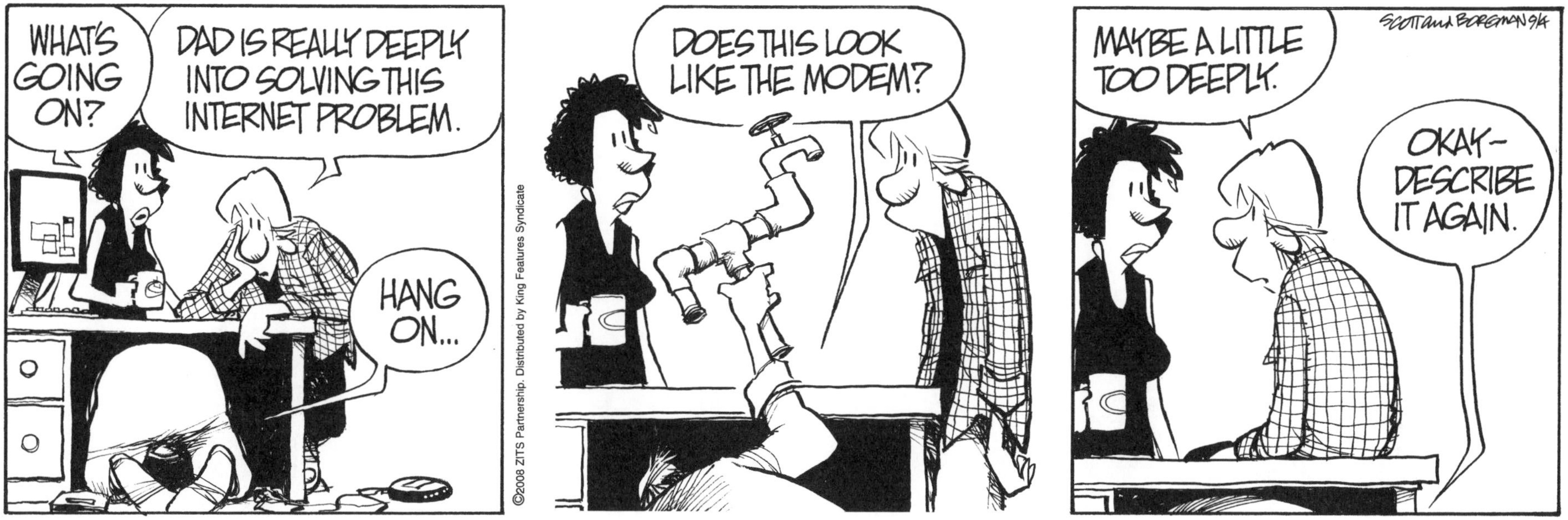
WHAT'S GOING ON?
DAD IS REALLY DEEPLY INTO SOLVING THIS INTERNET PROBLEM.
HANG ON...
©2008 ZITS Partnership. Distributed by King Features Syndicate
DOES THIS LOOK LIKE THE MODEM?
SCOTT and BORGMAN 9/4
MAYBE A LITTLE TOO DEEPLY.
OKAY- DESCRIBE IT AGAIN.

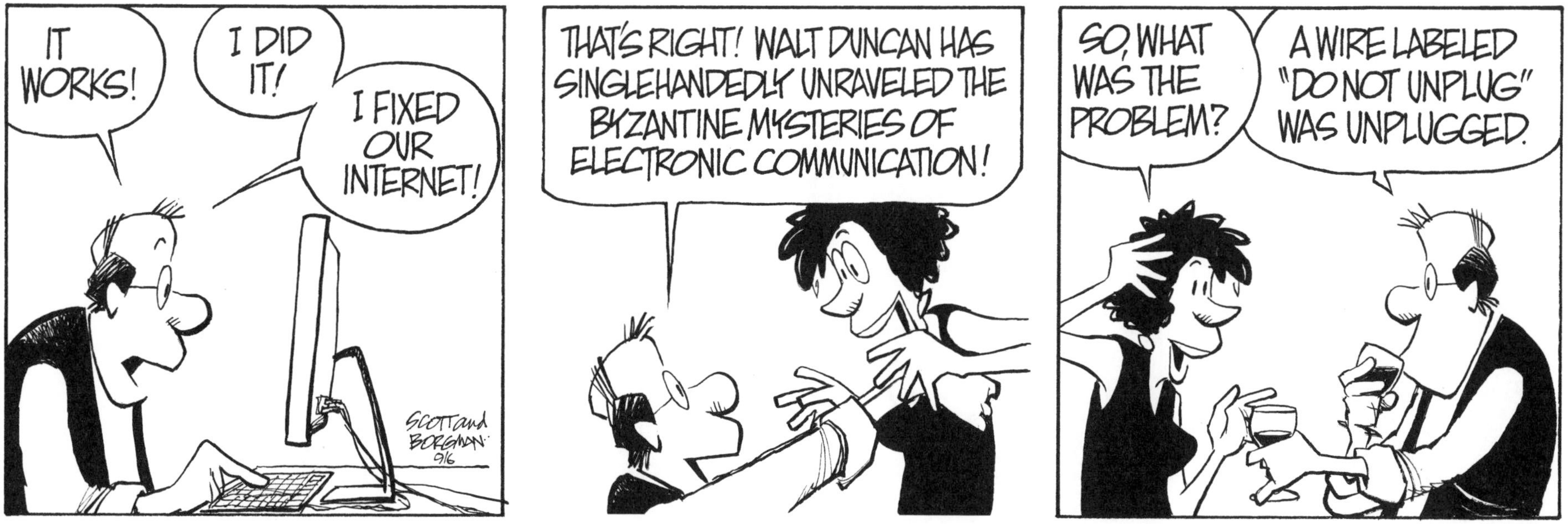
IT WORKS!
I DID IT!
I FIXED OUR INTERNET!
SCOTT and BORGMAN 9/6
THAT'S RIGHT! WALT DUNCAN HAS SINGLEHANDEDLY UNRAVELED THE BYZANTINE MYSTERIES OF ELECTRONIC COMMUNICATION!
SO, WHAT WAS THE PROBLEM?
A WIRE LABELED "DO NOT UNPLUG" WAS UNPLUGGED.

Jim: Hey, after years of frustration, Charlie Brown finally got to kick the football, too. Every dad has his day.

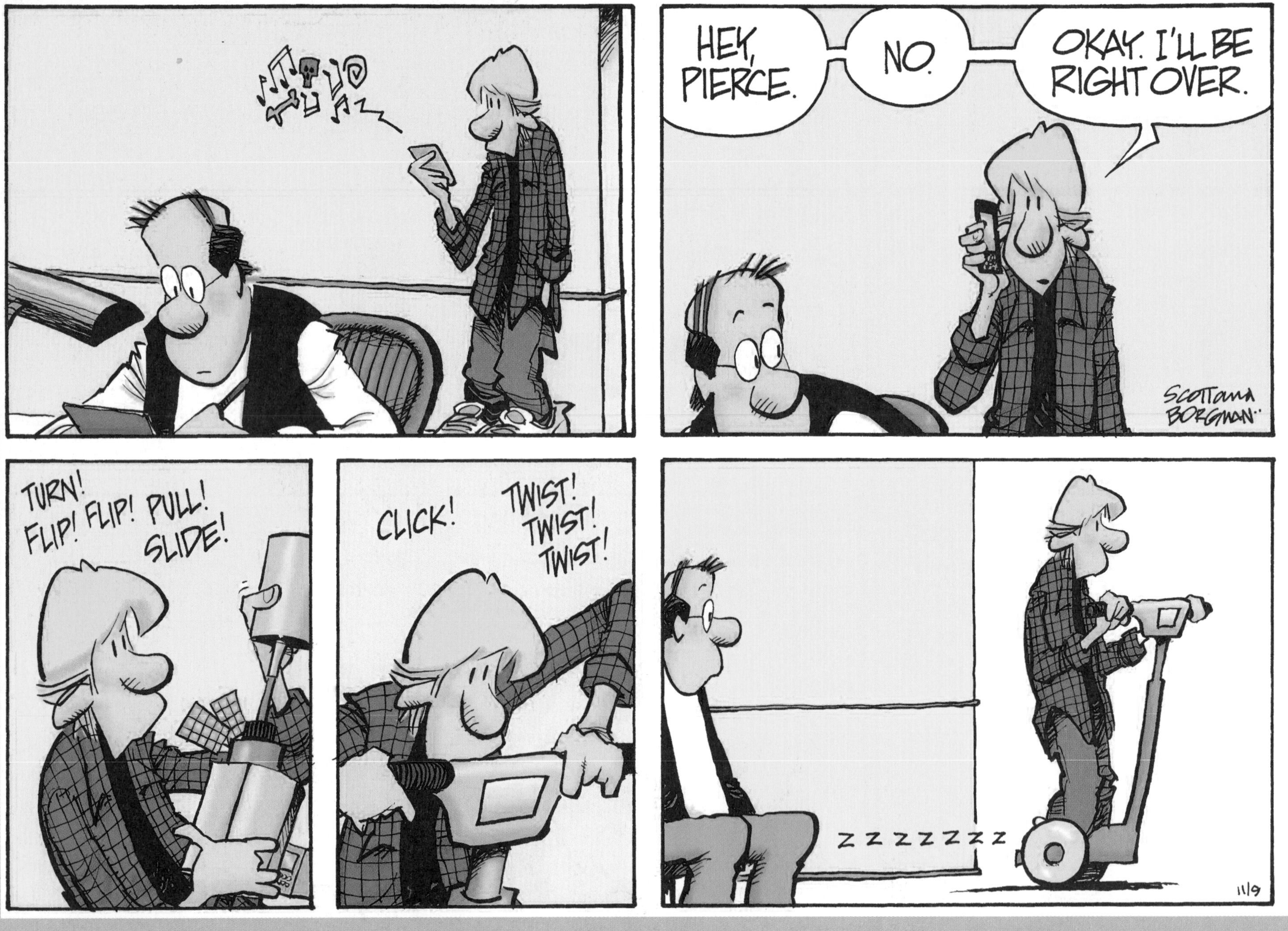
HEY, PIERCE.
NO.
OKAY. I'LL BE RIGHT OVER.
SCOTT AND BORGMAN
TURN! FLIP! FLIP! PULL! SLIDE!
CLICK!
TWIST! TWIST! TWIST!
Z Z Z Z Z Z Z Z
11/9

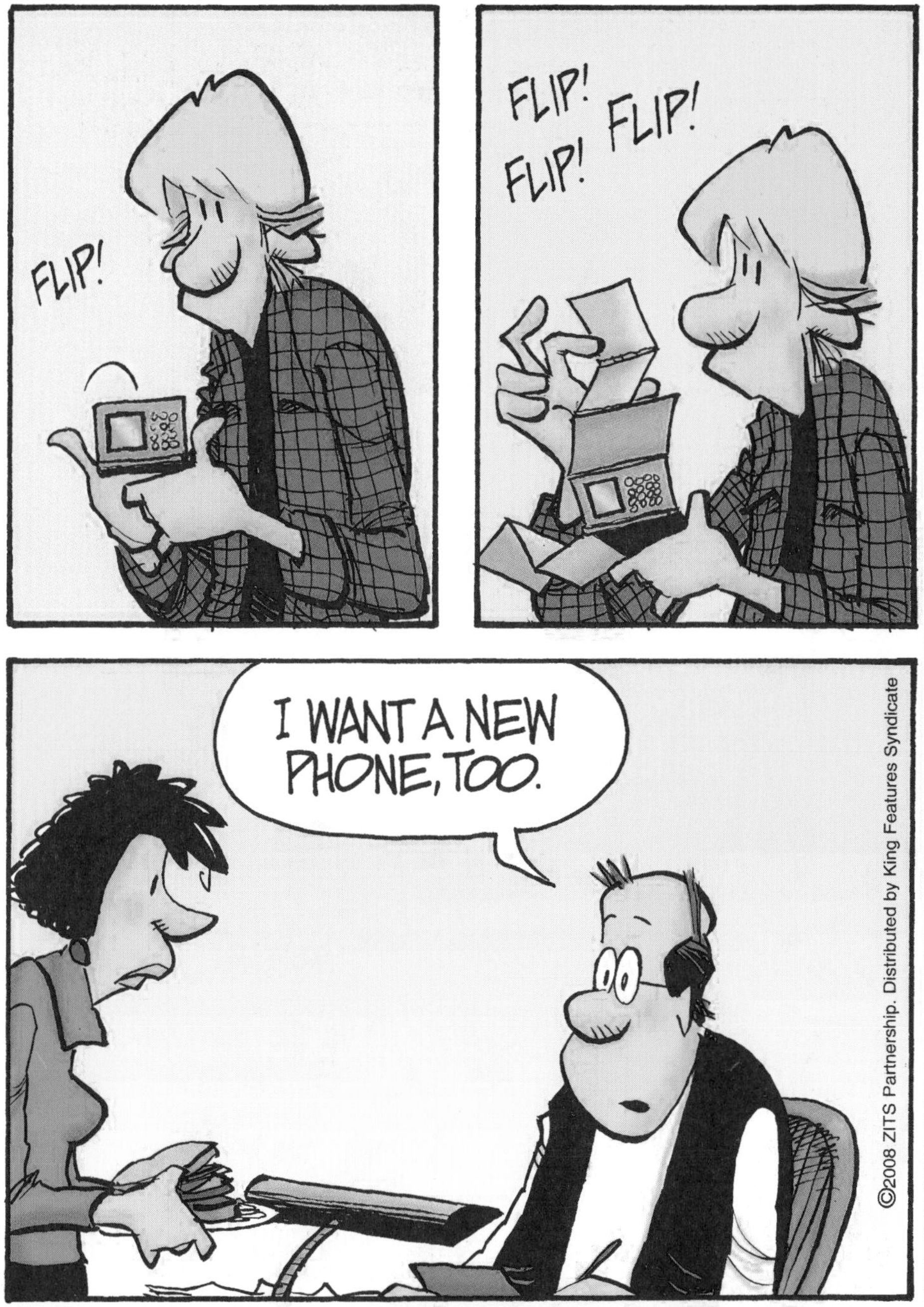
FLIP!
FLIP! FLIP! FLIP!
I WANT A NEW PHONE, TOO.
©2008 ZITS Partnership. Distributed by King Features Syndicate

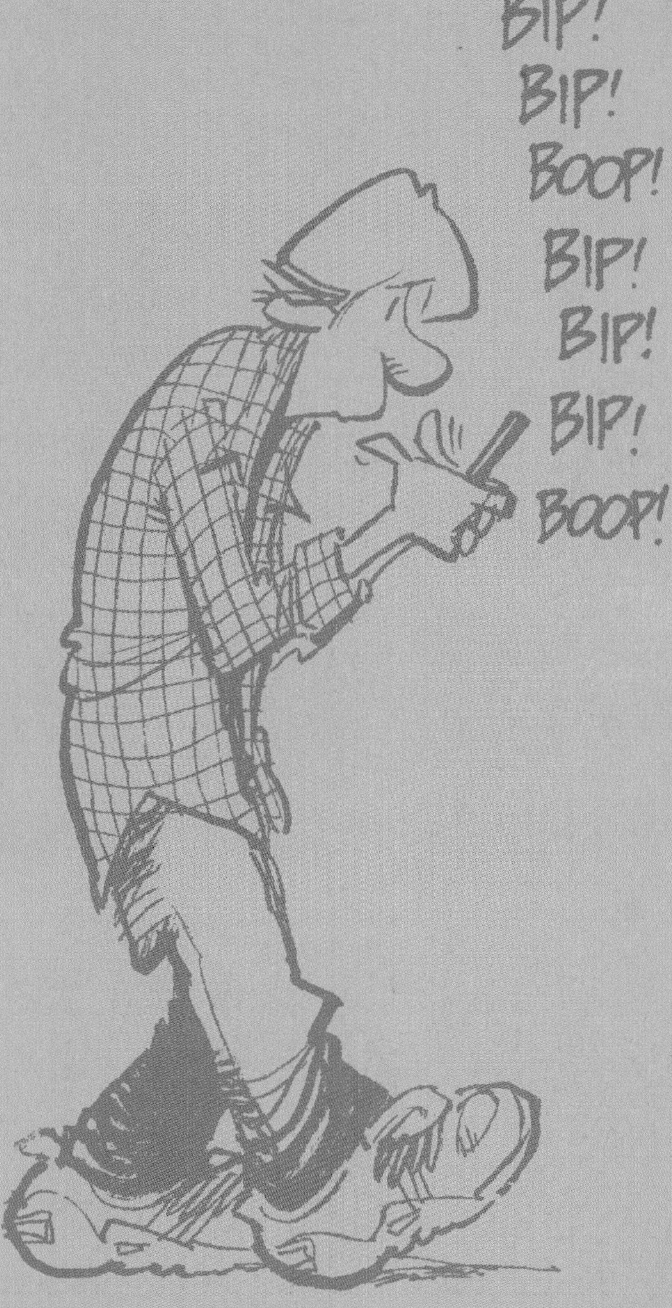
BIP!
BIP!
BOOP!
BIP!
BIP!
BIP!
BOOP!

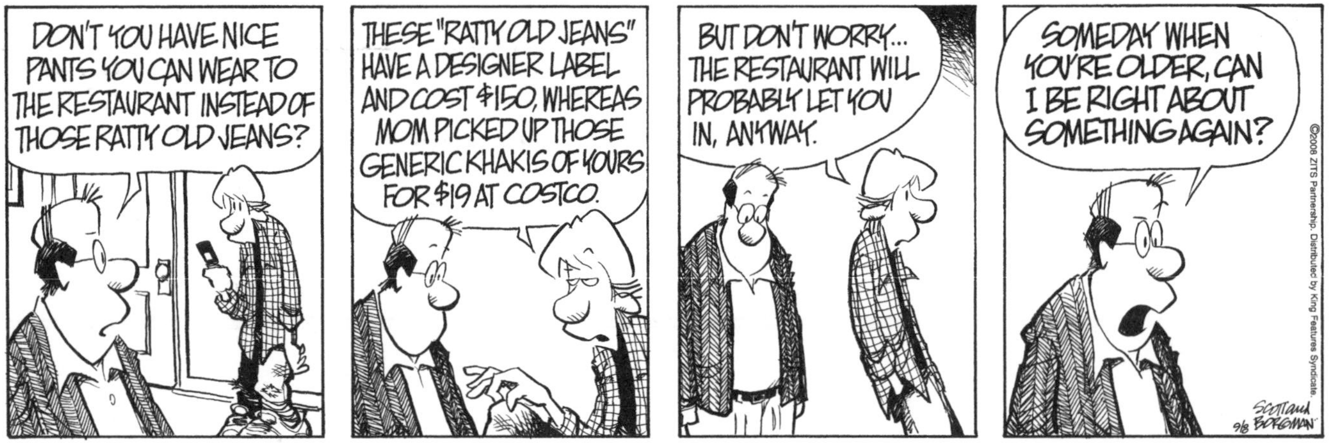
DON'T YOU HAVE NICE PANTS YOU CAN WEAR TO THE RESTAURANT INSTEAD OF THOSE RATTY OLD JEANS?
THESE "RATTY OLD JEANS" HAVE A DESIGNER LABEL AND COST $150, WHEREAS MOM PICKED UP THOSE GENERIC KHAKIS OF YOURS FOR $19 AT COSTCO.
BUT DON'T WORRY... THE RESTAURANT WILL PROBABLY LET YOU IN, ANYWAY.
SOMEDAY WHEN YOU'RE OLDER, CAN I BE RIGHT ABOUT SOMETHING AGAIN?
©2008 ZITS Partnership. Distributed by King Features Syndicate.
SCOTT and BORGMAN
9/8

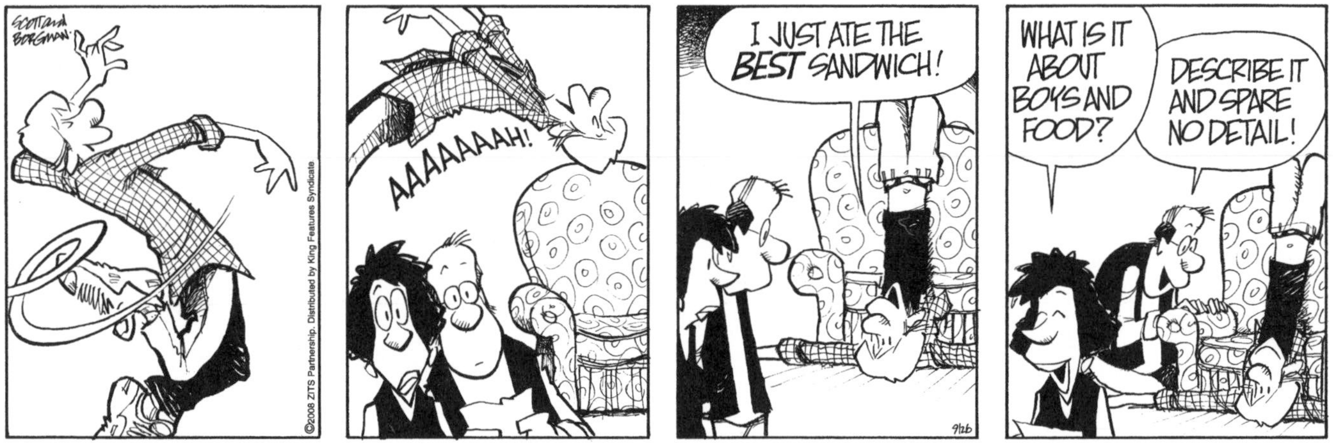
SCOTT and BORGMAN
©2008 ZITS Partnership. Distributed by King Features Syndicate
AAAAAAAH!
I JUST ATE THE *BEST* SANDWICH!
9/26
WHAT IS IT ABOUT BOYS AND FOOD?
DESCRIBE IT AND SPARE NO DETAIL!

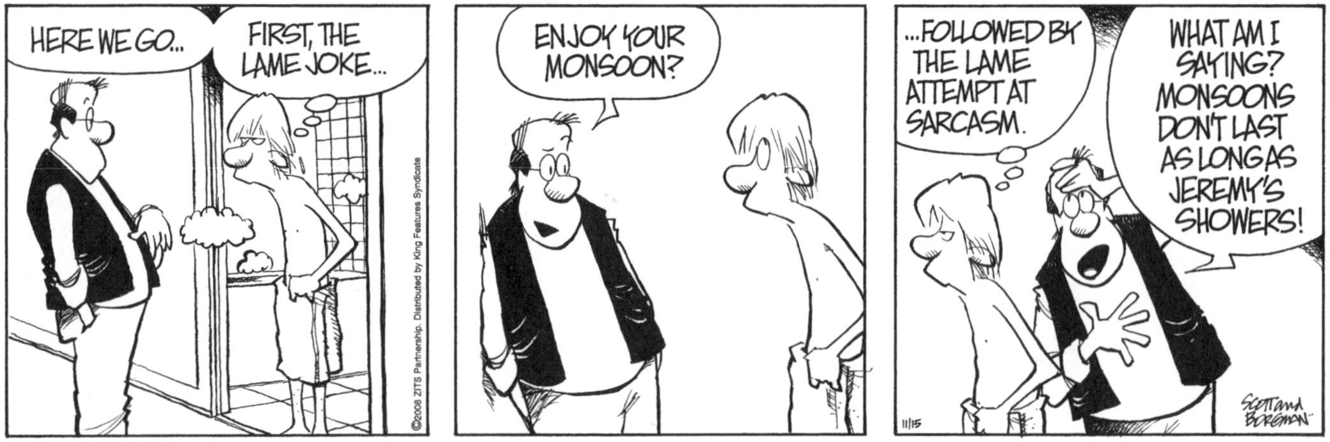
HERE WE GO...
FIRST, THE LAME JOKE...
©2008 ZITS Partnership. Distributed by King Features Syndicate
ENJOY YOUR MONSOON?
11/15
...FOLLOWED BY THE LAME ATTEMPT AT SARCASM.
WHAT AM I SAYING? MONSOONS DON'T LAST AS LONG AS JEREMY'S SHOWERS!
SCOTT and BORGMAN

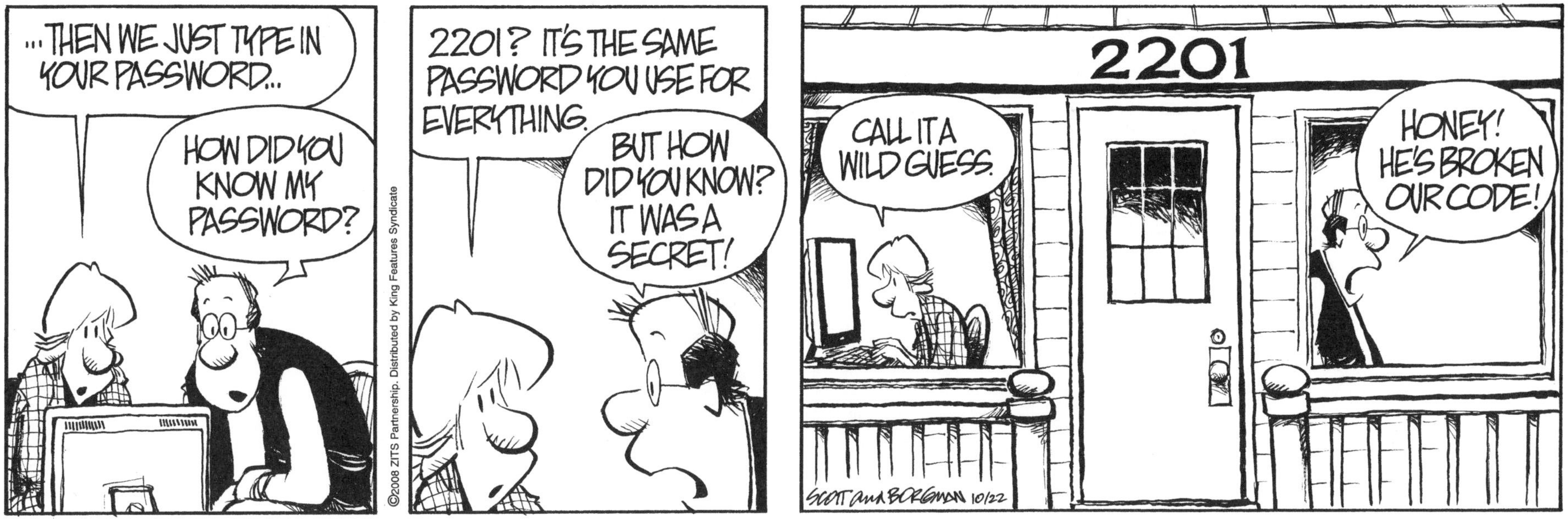
...THEN WE JUST TYPE IN YOUR PASSWORD...
HOW DID YOU KNOW MY PASSWORD?
2201? IT'S THE SAME PASSWORD YOU USE FOR EVERYTHING.
BUT HOW DID YOU KNOW? IT WAS A SECRET!
2201
CALL IT A WILD GUESS.
HONEY! HE'S BROKEN OUR CODE!
SCOTT and BORGMAN 10/22

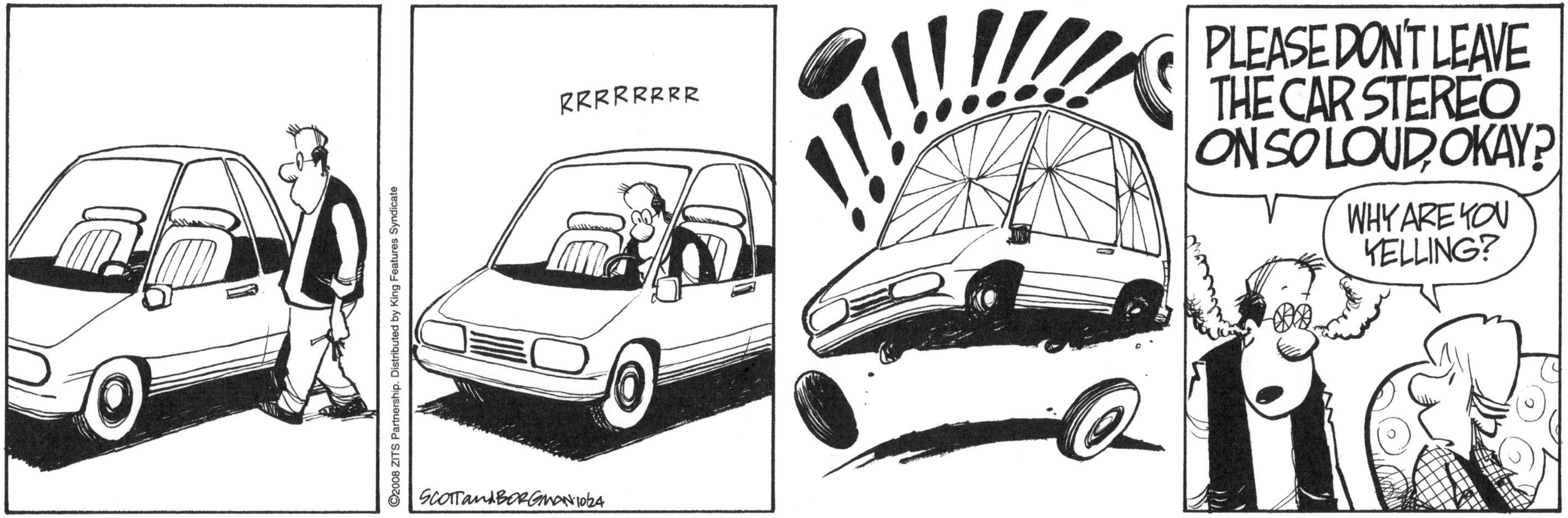
RRRRRRRR
SCOTT and BORGMAN 10/24
PLEASE DON'T LEAVE THE CAR STEREO ON SO LOUD, OKAY?
WHY ARE YOU YELLING?

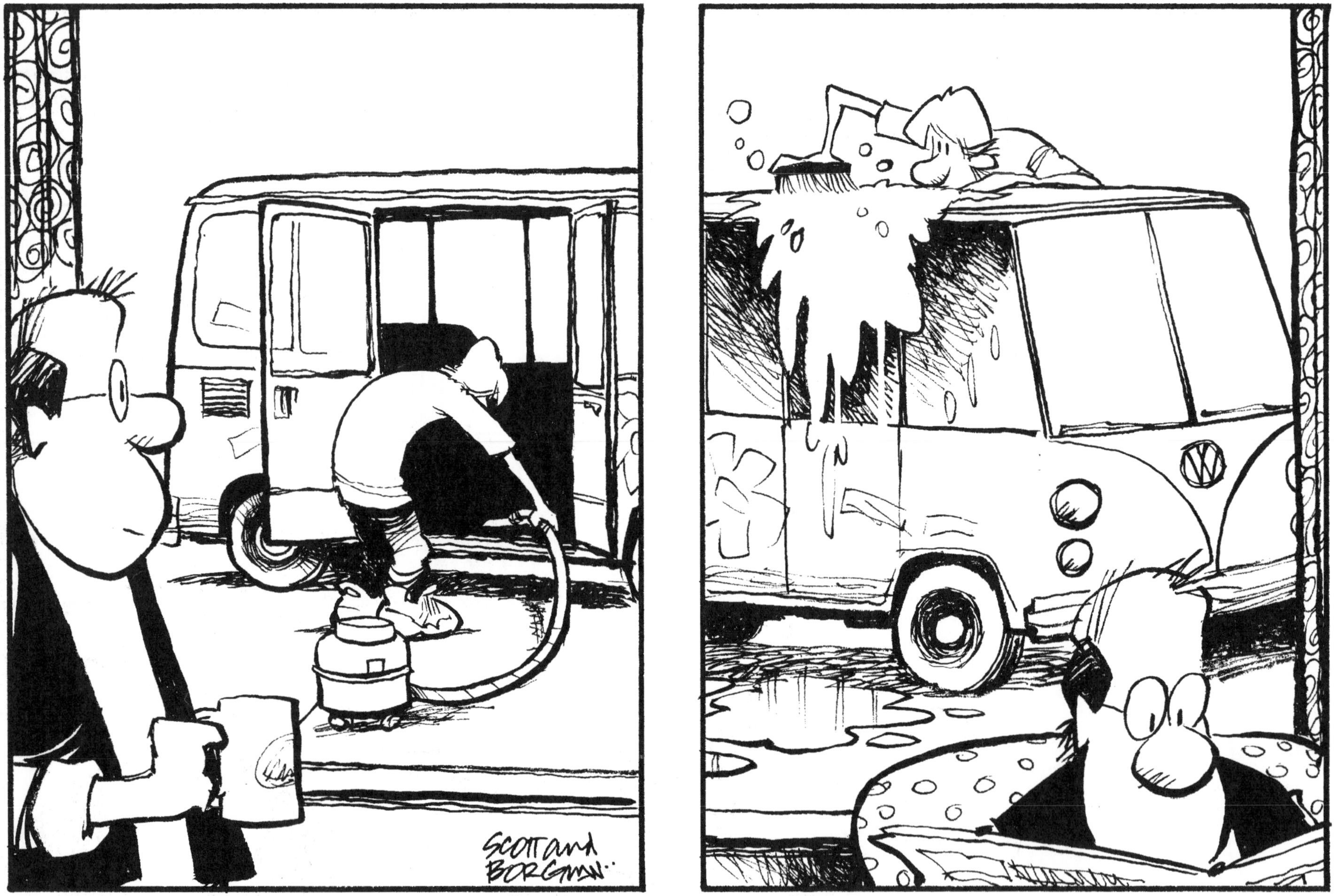
SCOTT and BORGMAN

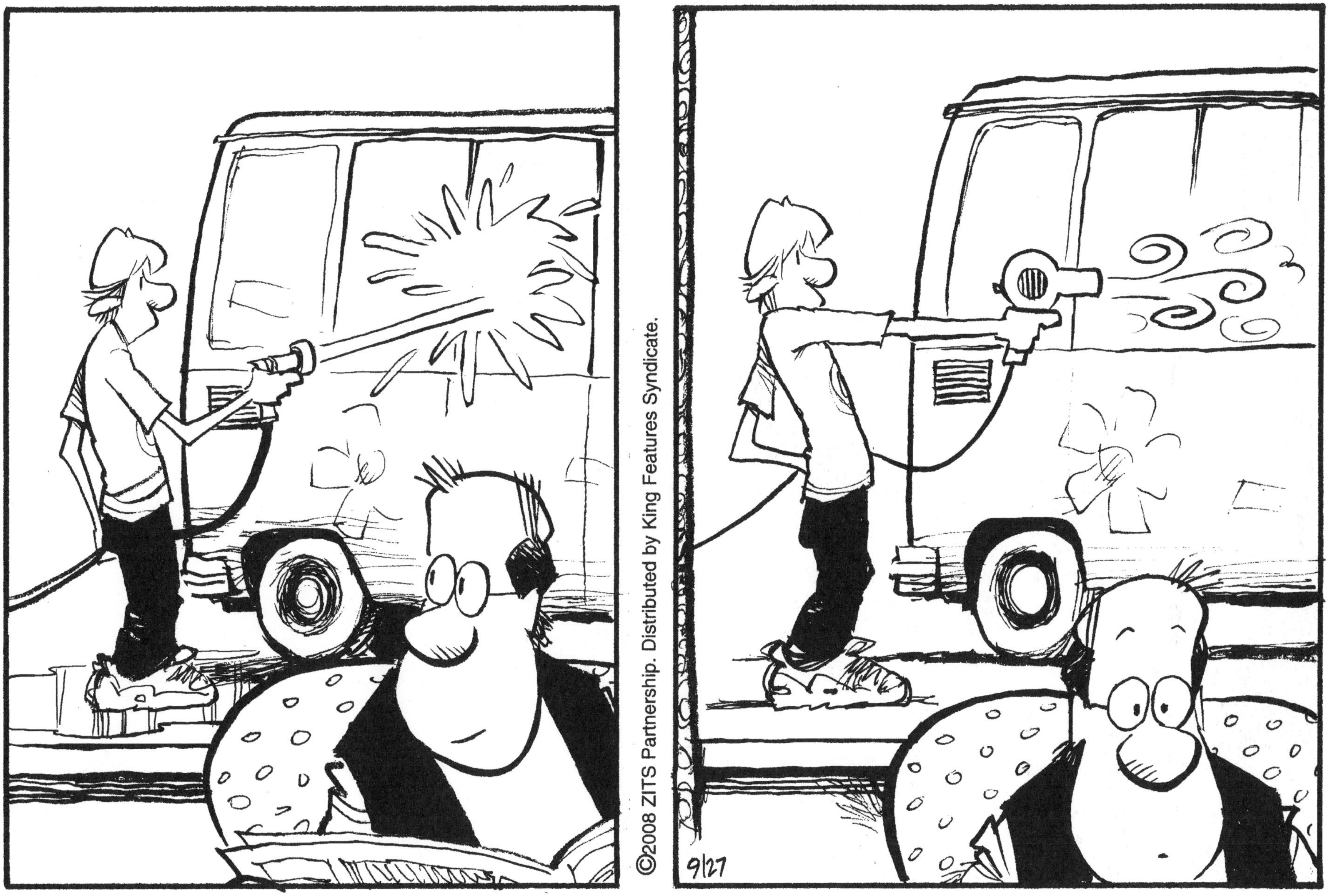
9/27

Jim: You think we're exaggerating, but this behavior has been documented numerous times among the male members of certain remote automotive-centric tribes on YouTube.

DAD!
CHECK OUT THIS VIDEO ON YOUTUBE!
(SNICKER!)
BWAAHAHA HAHA!
HA! HA!HA! HA! HA! HA! HA!
SNORT!
HA HA HAHA!
HAHA! HAHA HA!
HOO!
HEE!
THAT HAS TO BE THE MOST HILARIOUS THING I'VE EVER SEEN!
THE HUMOR GENE HAS APPARENTLY SKIPPED A GENERATION.
SCOTT AND BORGMAN 1/11
©2009 ZITS Partnership. Distributed by King Features Syndicate.

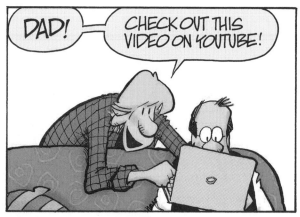

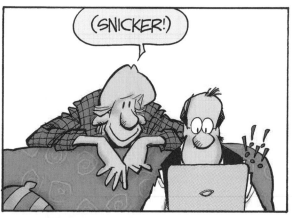

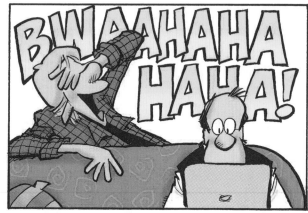

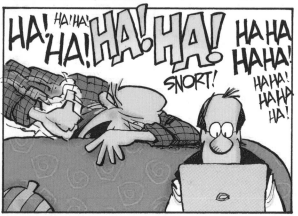

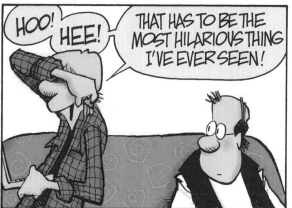

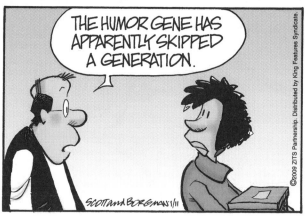

YANK!
VROOM!
HURRAY!
THAT'S WHAT I'M TALKIN' ABOUT!
(SHUDDER!)
WHAT'S WRONG, JEREMY?
NOTHING.
IT'S JUST THAT WHENEVER DAD USES A SLANG PHRASE THAT'S THE LEAST BIT CURRENT, THE WORLD SEEMS TOTALLY OUT OF BALANCE AND WEIRD.
WELL, EXCUSE ME FOR BEING JIGGY WITH THE LINGO!
BEING WHAT??
OKAY, NOW WE'RE BACK TO NORMAL!
SCOTT and BORGMAN
©2009 ZITS Partnership. Distributed by King Features Syndicate.

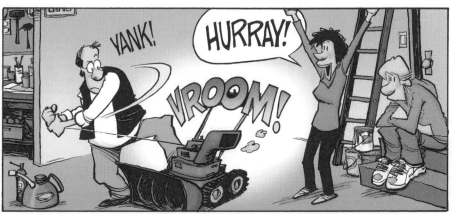

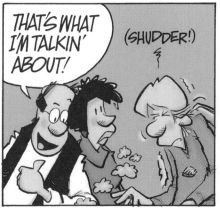

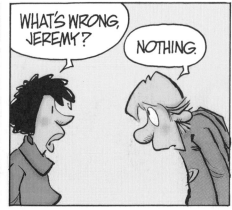

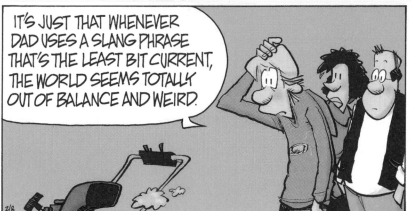

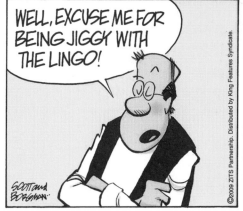

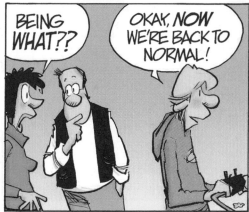

Jerry: Want to get a laugh from your kids? Repeat aloud almost anything you hear somebody say on the MTV Video Music Awards. Guaranteed hilarity.

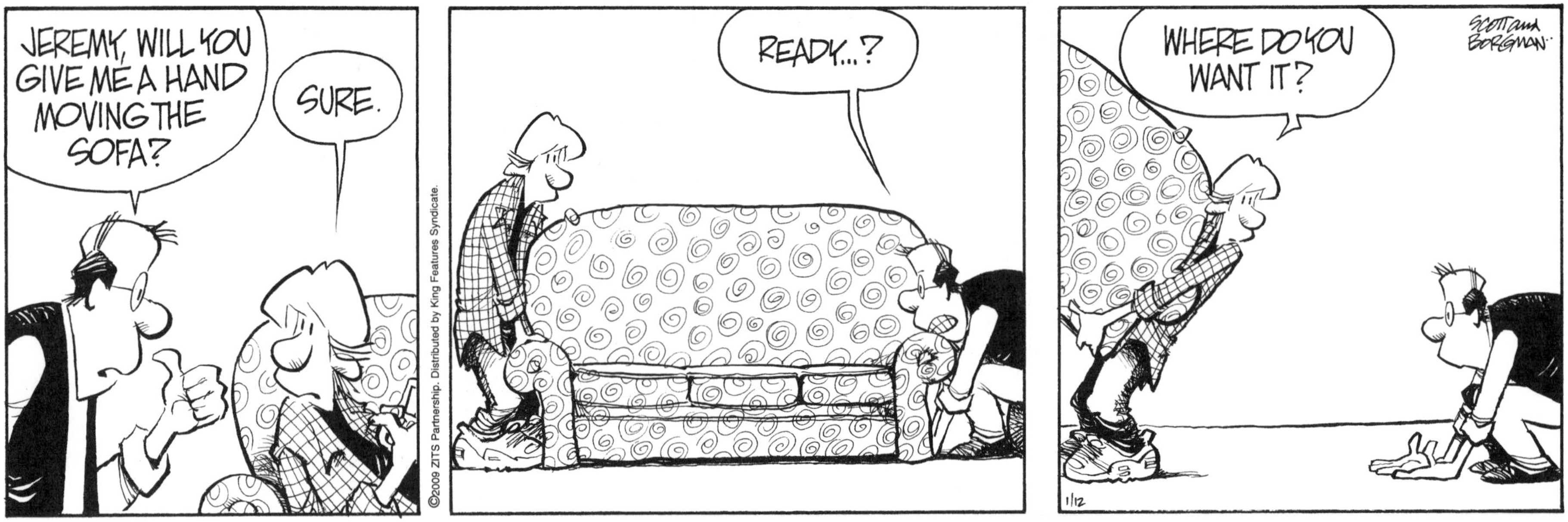
JEREMY, WILL YOU GIVE ME A HAND MOVING THE SOFA?
SURE.
©2009 ZITS Partnership. Distributed by King Features Syndicate.
READY...?
WHERE DO YOU WANT IT?
SCOTT and BORGMAN
1/12

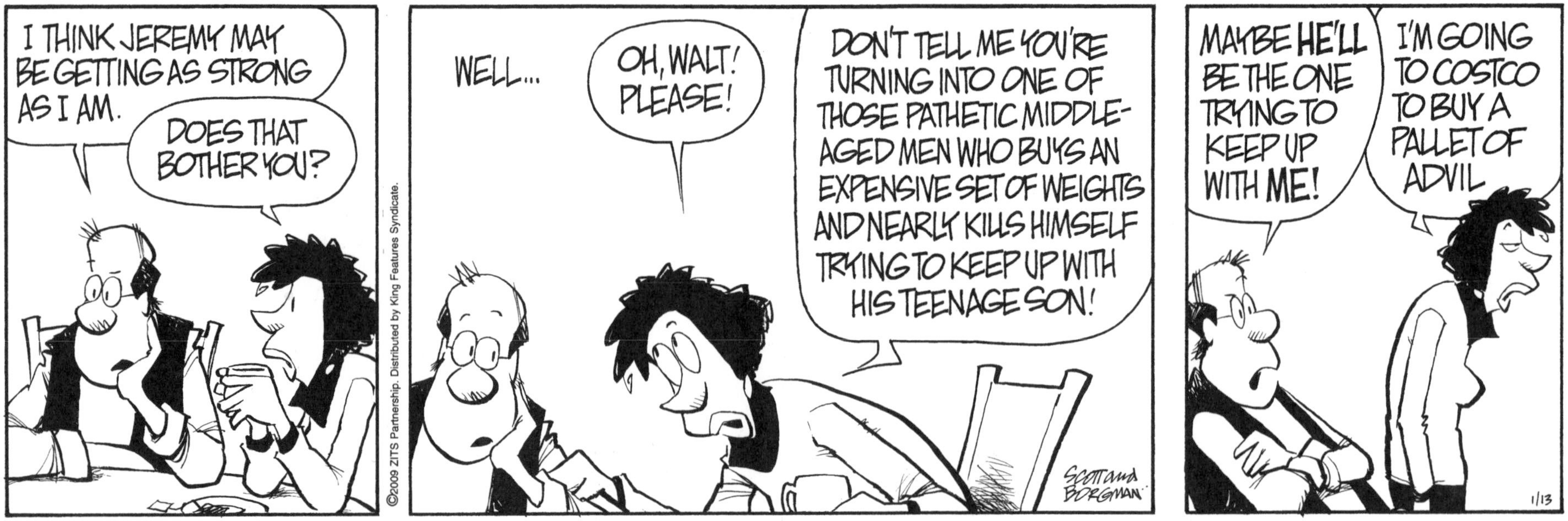
I THINK JEREMY MAY BE GETTING AS STRONG AS I AM.
DOES THAT BOTHER YOU?
©2009 ZITS Partnership. Distributed by King Features Syndicate.
WELL...
OH, WALT! PLEASE!
DON'T TELL ME YOU'RE TURNING INTO ONE OF THOSE PATHETIC MIDDLE-AGED MEN WHO BUYS AN EXPENSIVE SET OF WEIGHTS AND NEARLY KILLS HIMSELF TRYING TO KEEP UP WITH HIS TEENAGE SON!
SCOTT and BORGMAN
MAYBE HE'LL BE THE ONE TRYING TO KEEP UP WITH ME!
I'M GOING TO COSTCO TO BUY A PALLET OF ADVIL
1/13

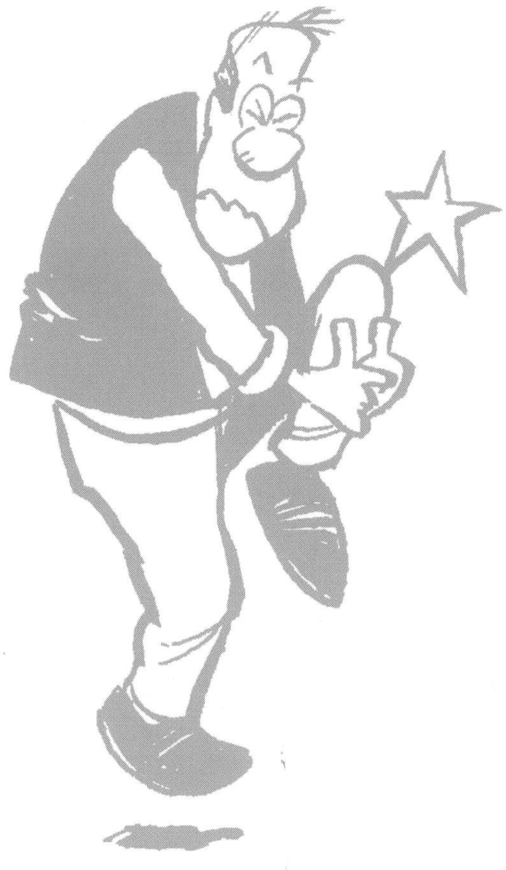

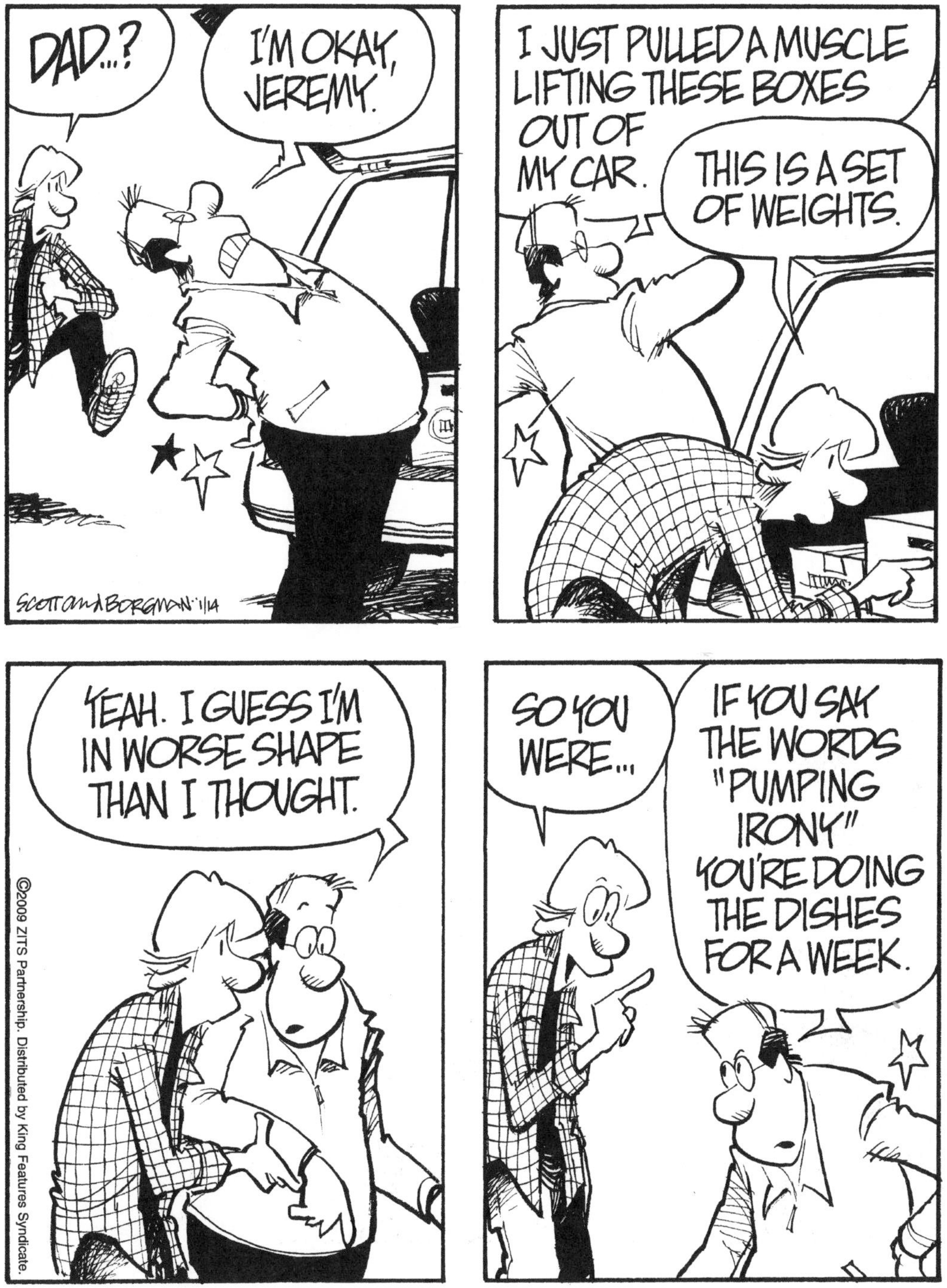
DAD...?
I'M OKAY, JEREMY.
SCOTT and BORGMAN 1/14
I JUST PULLED A MUSCLE LIFTING THESE BOXES OUT OF MY CAR.
THIS IS A SET OF WEIGHTS.
YEAH. I GUESS I'M IN WORSE SHAPE THAN I THOUGHT.
©2009 ZITS Partnership. Distributed by King Features Syndicate.
SO YOU WERE...
IF YOU SAY THE WORDS "PUMPING IRONY" YOU'RE DOING THE DISHES FOR A WEEK.

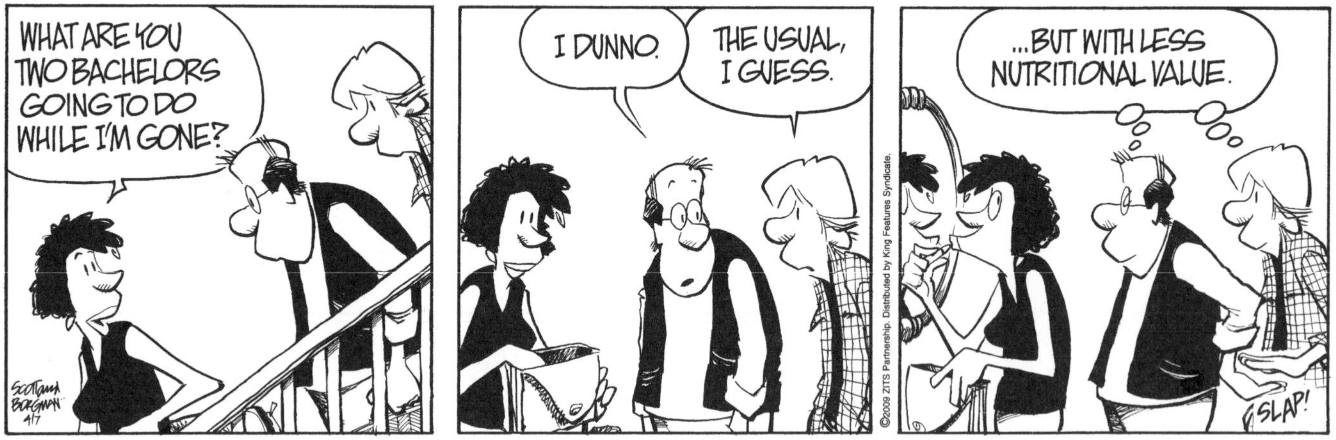
WHAT ARE YOU TWO BACHELORS GOING TO DO WHILE I'M GONE?
SCOTT and BORGMAN 4/7
I DUNNO.
THE USUAL, I GUESS.
©2009 ZITS Partnership. Distributed by King Features Syndicate.
...BUT WITH LESS NUTRITIONAL VALUE.
SLAP!

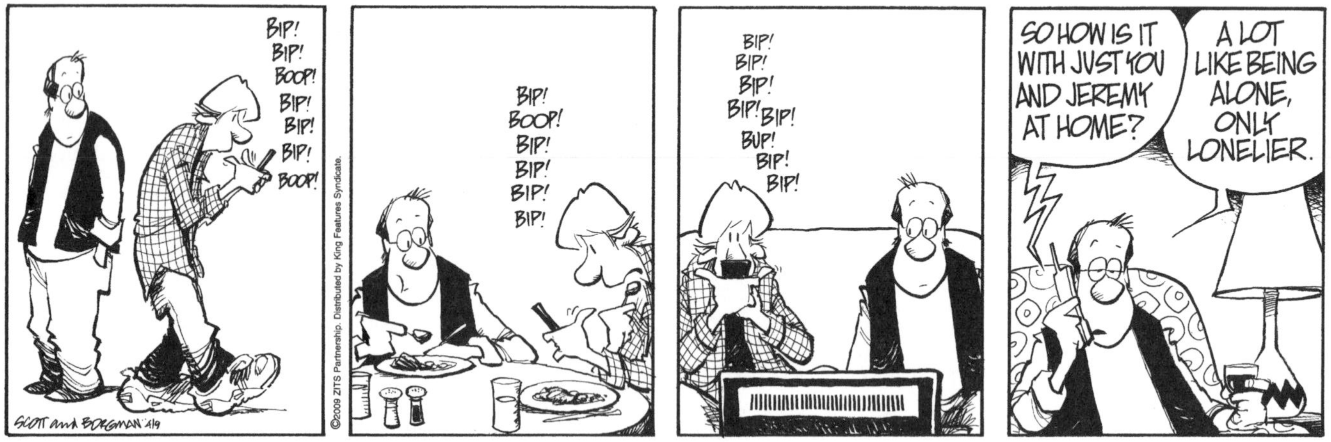
BIP! BIP! BOOP! BIP! BIP! BIP! BOOP!
SCOTT and BORGMAN 4/9
©2009 ZITS Partnership. Distributed by King Features Syndicate.
BIP! BOOP! BIP! BIP! BIP! BIP!
BIP! BIP! BIP! BIP! BIP! BUP! BIP! BIP!
SO HOW IS IT WITH JUST YOU AND JEREMY AT HOME?
A LOT LIKE BEING ALONE, ONLY LONELIER.

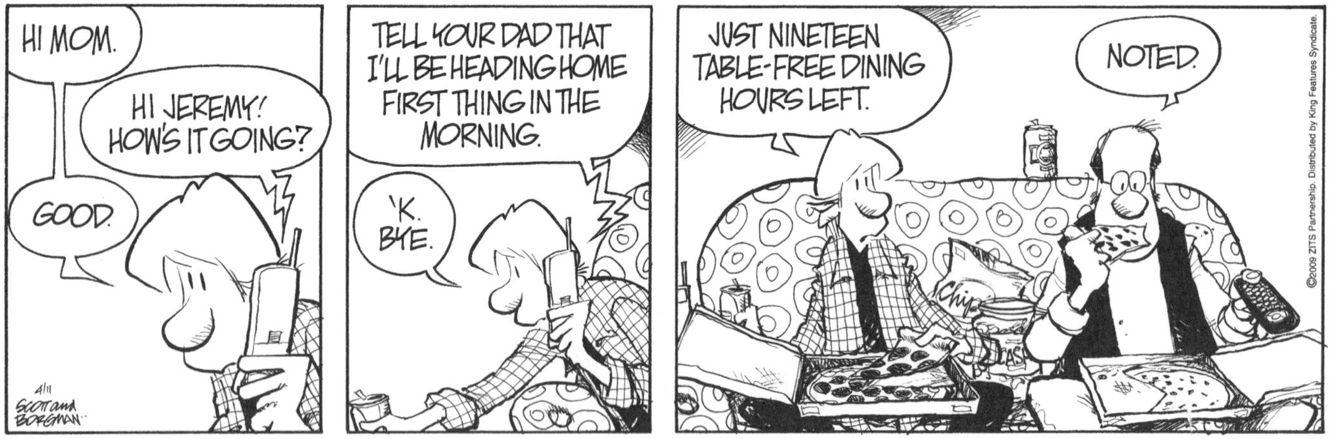
HI MOM.
HI JEREMY! HOW'S IT GOING?
GOOD.
4/11 SCOTT and BORGMAN
TELL YOUR DAD THAT I'LL BE HEADING HOME FIRST THING IN THE MORNING.
'K. BYE.
JUST NINETEEN TABLE-FREE DINING HOURS LEFT.
NOTED.
Chips
©2009 ZITS Partnership. Distributed by King Features Syndicate.

JEREMY, I'M GOING TO THE GROCERY STORE.
DO YOU NEED ANYTHING BESIDES LUGNUTS, MUSK OX AND SARDINE BRAS?
SCOTT AND BORGMAN
THAT SAYS "LUNCHMEAT, MUSTARD AND SANDWICH BAGS."
I TAKE IT YOU'RE NOT SHOOTING FOR A CAREER IN CALLIGRAPHY.
1/31

DAD, IS IT OKAY IF I PUT ON SOME MUSIC?
SURE.
©2009 ZITS Partnership. Distributed by King Features Syndicate.
SCOTT AND BORGMAN
2/12
I'M SORRY...
DID YOU SAY TURN IT DOWN OR TURN IT UP?
DOWN, PLEASE.

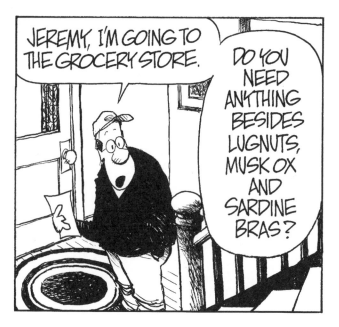

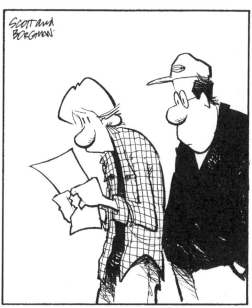

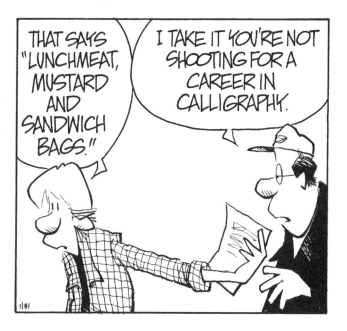

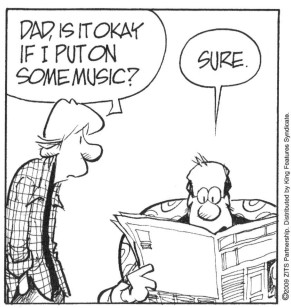

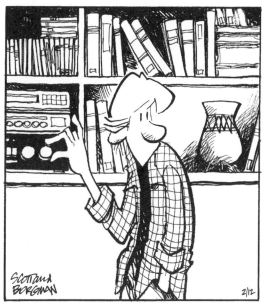

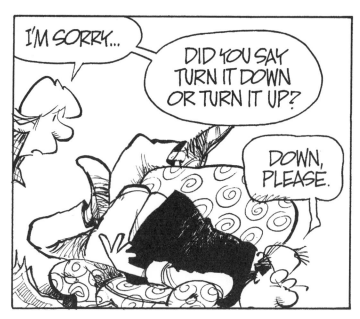

Jim: If you give a teenager clean laundry, he will be clothed for a day. If you teach a teenager to do his own laundry, it will accumulate on his bedroom floor for a lifetime.

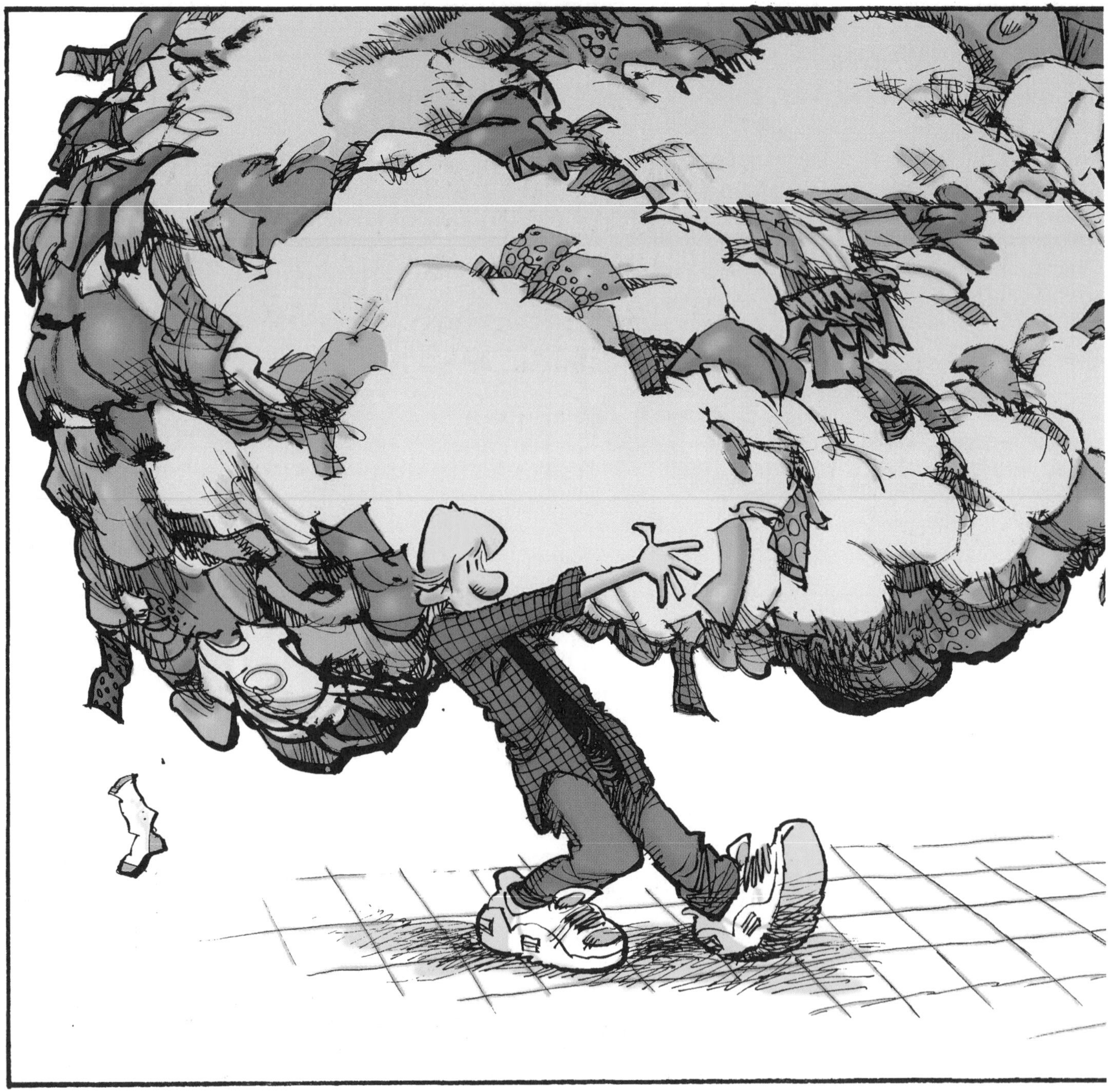

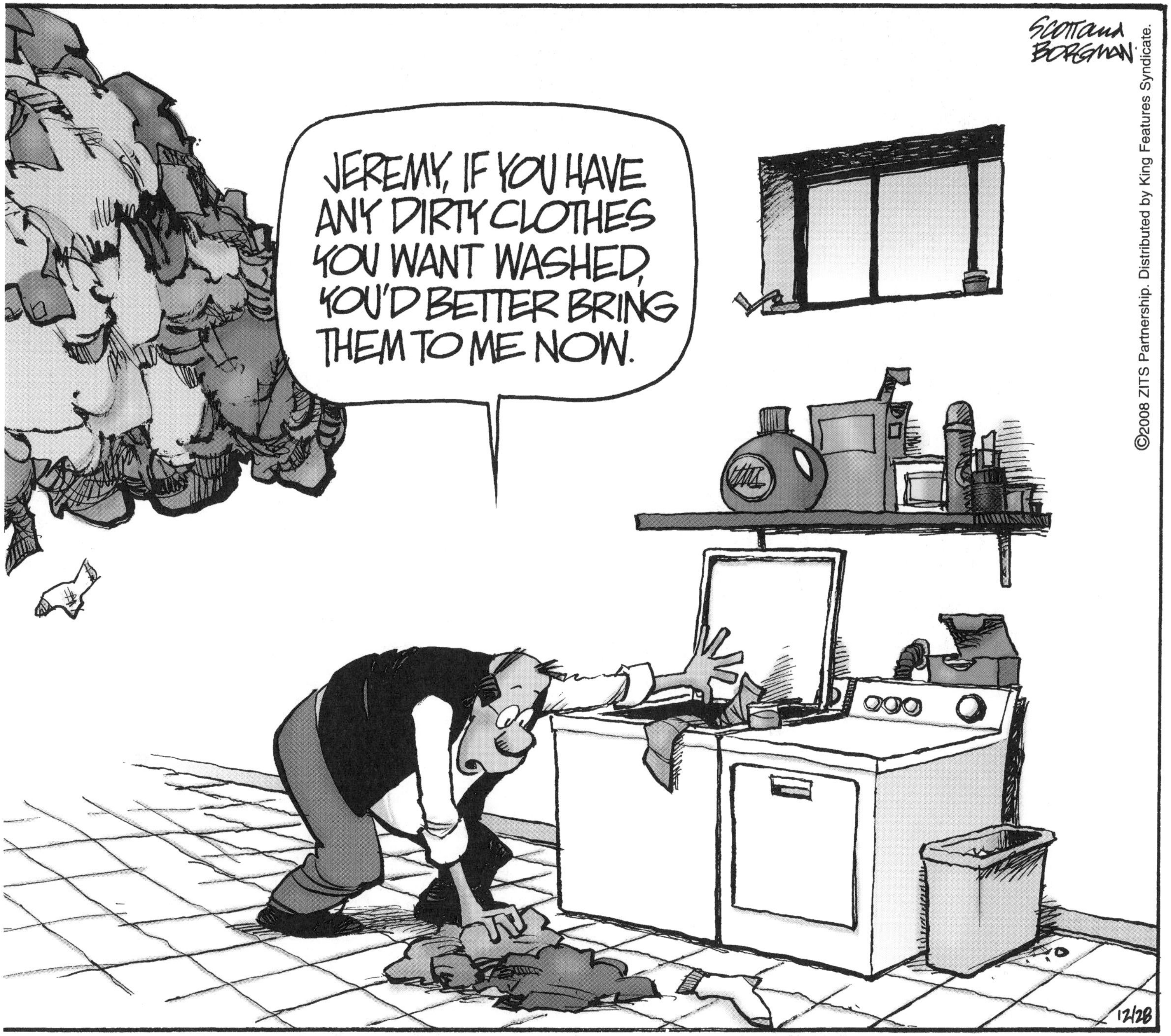
JEREMY, IF YOU HAVE ANY DIRTY CLOTHES YOU WANT WASHED, YOU'D BETTER BRING THEM TO ME NOW.
SCOTT and BORGMAN
©2008 ZITS Partnership. Distributed by King Features Syndicate.
12/28

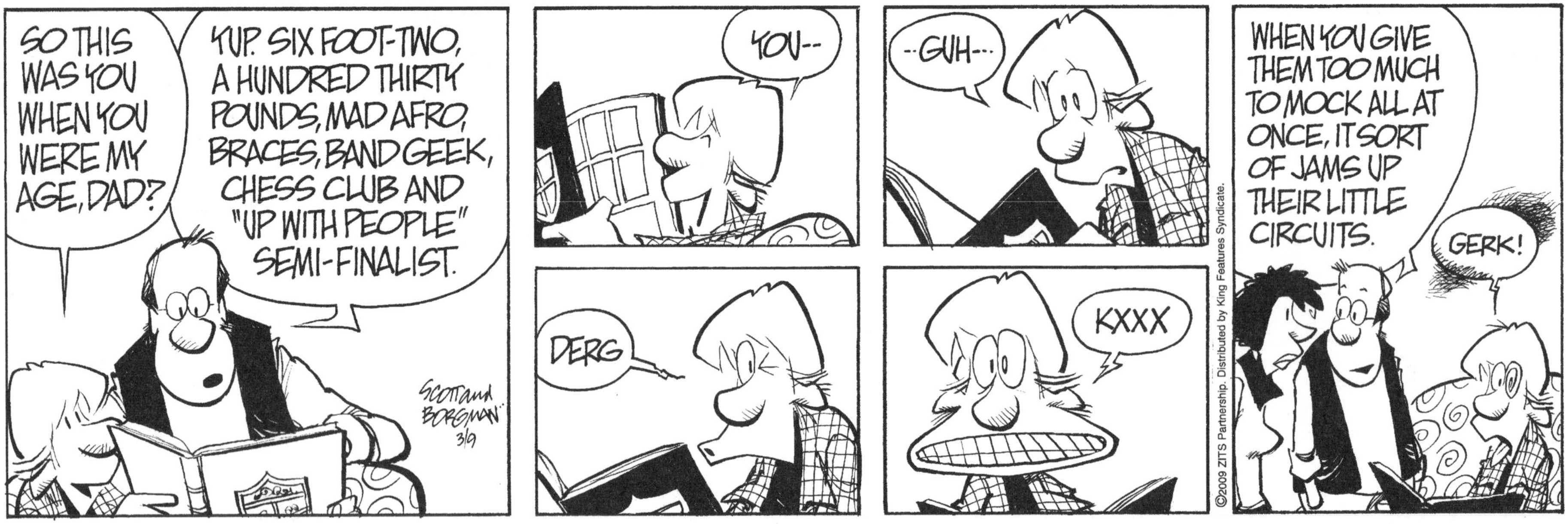
SO THIS WAS YOU WHEN YOU WERE MY AGE, DAD?
YUP. SIX FOOT-TWO, A HUNDRED THIRTY POUNDS, MAD AFRO, BRACES, BAND GEEK, CHESS CLUB AND "UP WITH PEOPLE" SEMI-FINALIST.
SCOTT and BORGMAN 3/9
YOU--
--GUH---
DERG
KXXX
WHEN YOU GIVE THEM TOO MUCH TO MOCK ALL AT ONCE, IT SORT OF JAMS UP THEIR LITTLE CIRCUITS.
GERK!
©2009 ZITS Partnership. Distributed by King Features Syndicate.

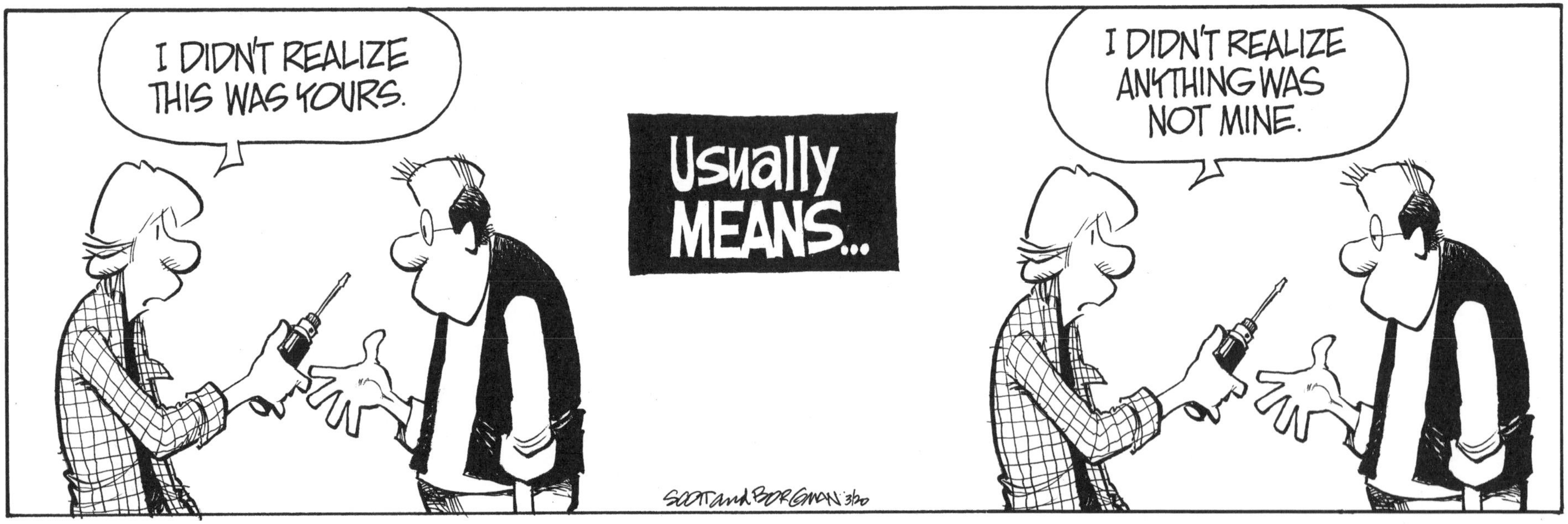
I DIDN'T REALIZE THIS WAS YOURS.
Usually MEANS...
I DIDN'T REALIZE ANYTHING WAS NOT MINE.
SCOTT and BORGMAN 3/20

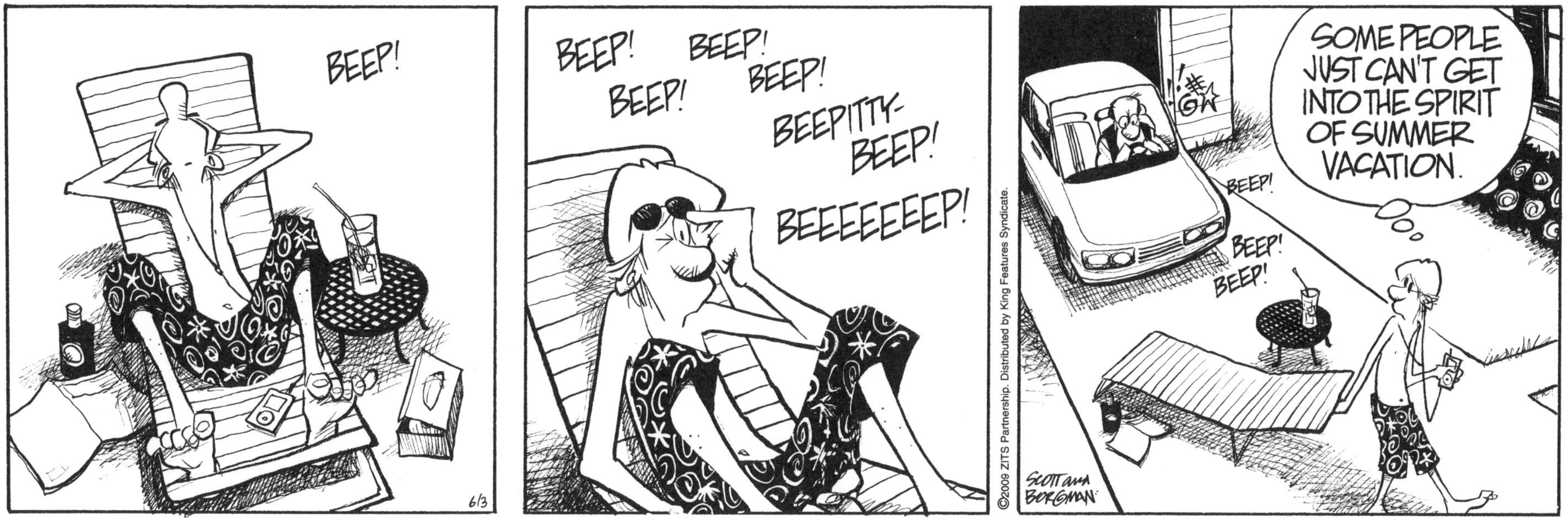
BEEP!
BEEP! BEEP! BEEP! BEEP! BEEPITTY-BEEP! BEEEEEEEEP!
!#!@*
BEEP! BEEP! BEEP!
SOME PEOPLE JUST CAN'T GET INTO THE SPIRIT OF SUMMER VACATION.
©2009 ZITS Partnership. Distributed by King Features Syndicate.
SCOTT and BORGMAN
6/3

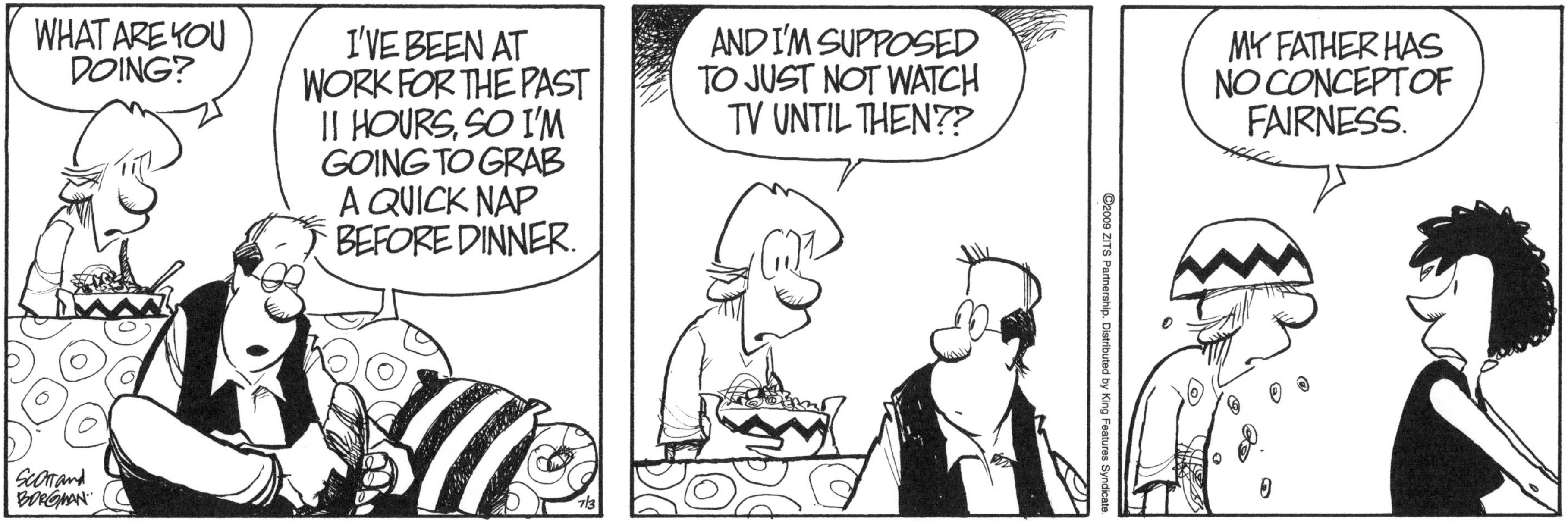
WHAT ARE YOU DOING?
I'VE BEEN AT WORK FOR THE PAST 11 HOURS, SO I'M GOING TO GRAB A QUICK NAP BEFORE DINNER.
AND I'M SUPPOSED TO JUST NOT WATCH TV UNTIL THEN??
MY FATHER HAS NO CONCEPT OF FAIRNESS.
©2009 ZITS Partnership. Distributed by King Features Syndicate.
SCOTT and BORGMAN
7/3

"A father carries pictures where his money used to be."
—author unknown

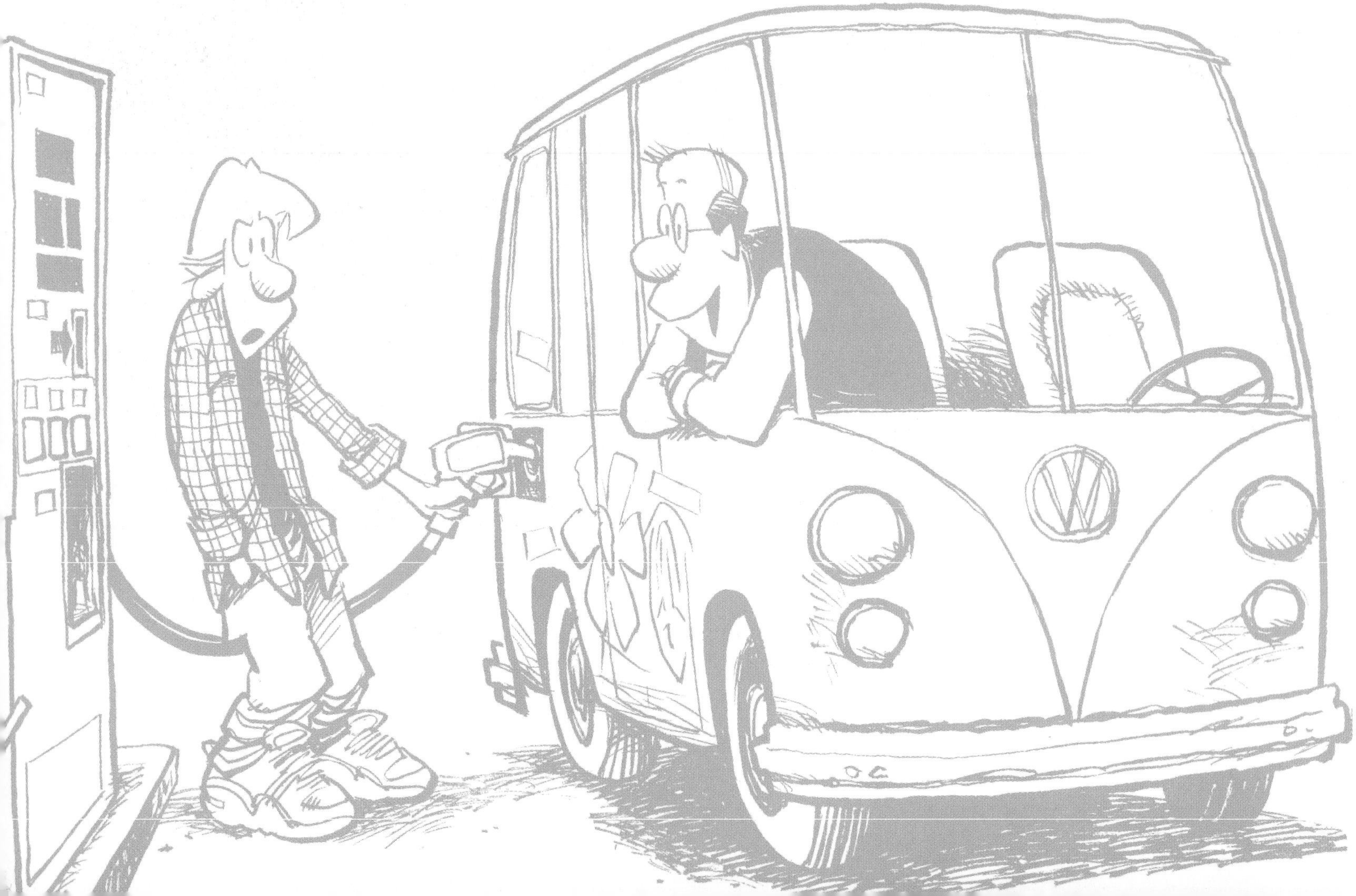

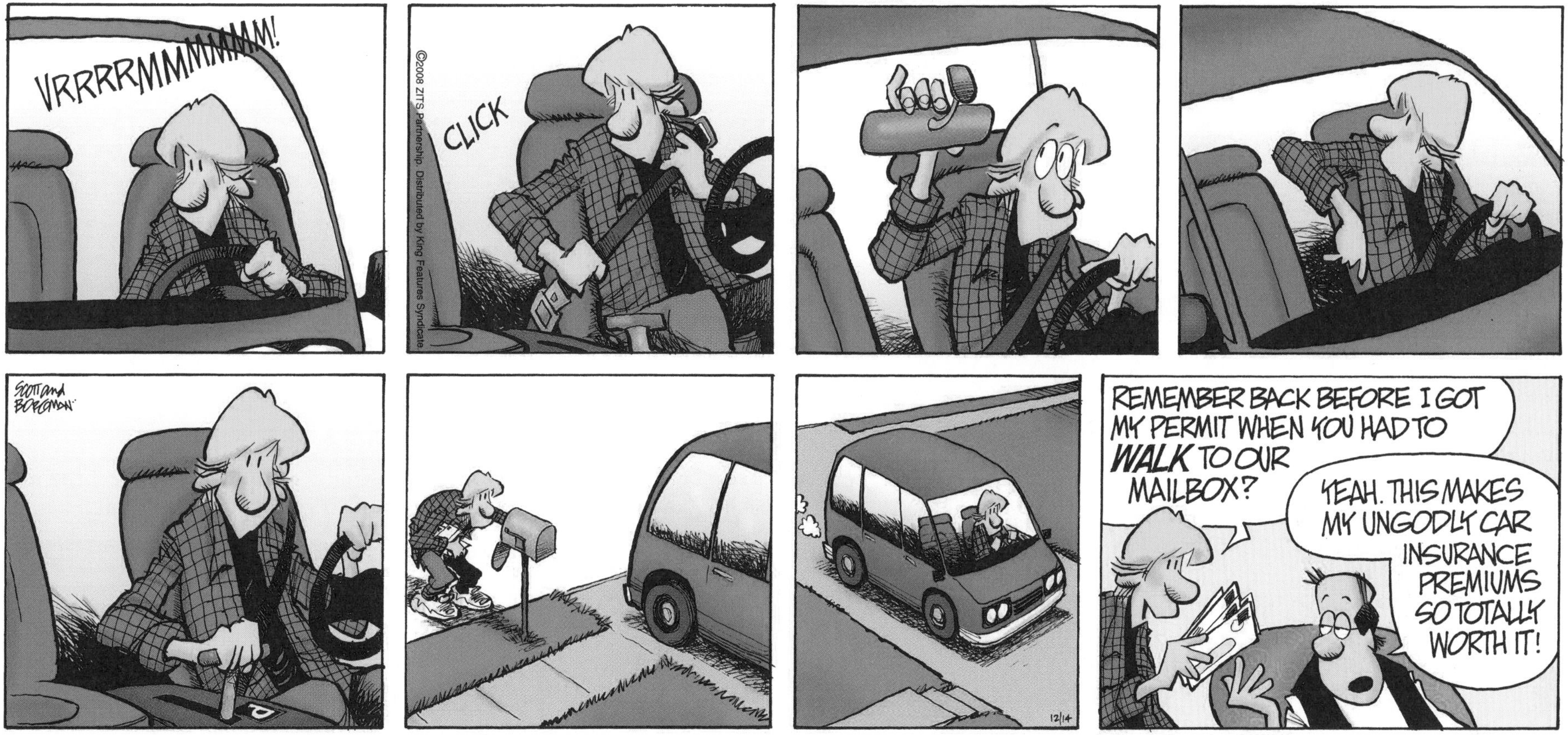
VRRRRMMMMMMM!
©2008 ZITS Partnership. Distributed by King Features Syndicate
CLICK
SCOTT AND BORGMAN
12/14
REMEMBER BACK BEFORE I GOT MY PERMIT WHEN YOU HAD TO **WALK** TO OUR MAILBOX?
YEAH. THIS MAKES MY UNGODLY CAR INSURANCE PREMIUMS SO TOTALLY WORTH IT!

Jerry: We have a pretty long driveway, and when our daughter had her permit we would let her drive to the mailbox for practice. Now we have a teenager who is a very good driver and a Volvo with 107,000 miles on it.

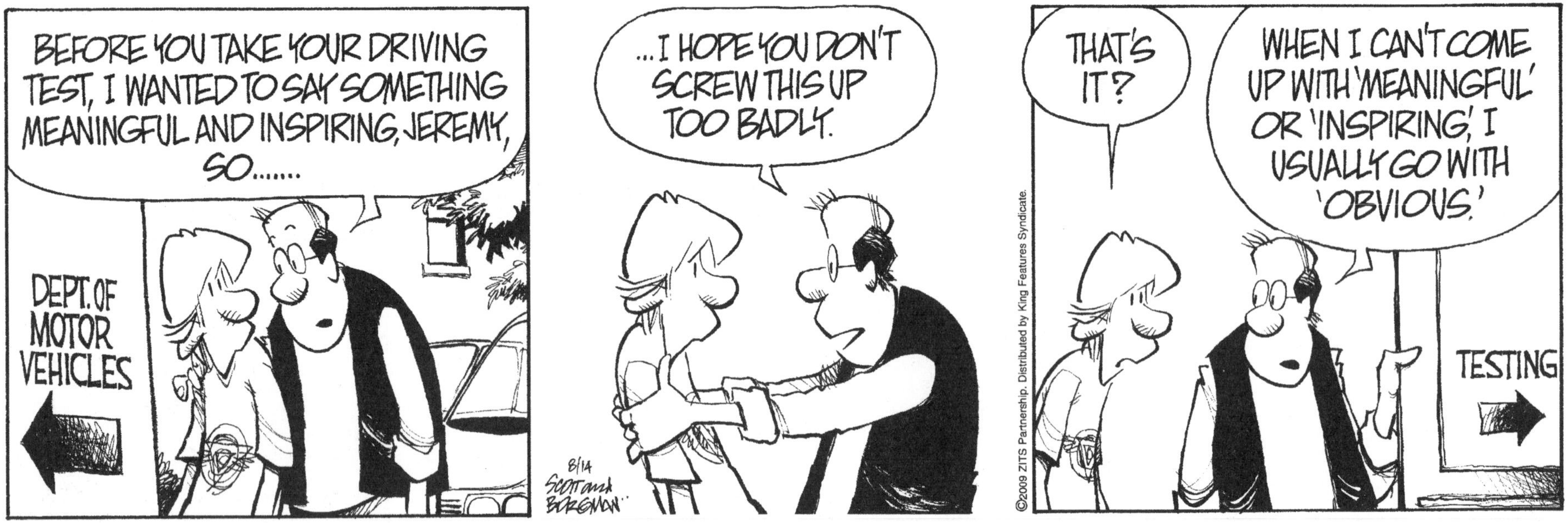
BEFORE YOU TAKE YOUR DRIVING TEST, I WANTED TO SAY SOMETHING MEANINGFUL AND INSPIRING, JEREMY, SO.......
DEPT. OF MOTOR VEHICLES
...I HOPE YOU DON'T SCREW THIS UP TOO BADLY.
8/14 SCOTT and BORGMAN
©2009 ZITS Partnership. Distributed by King Features Syndicate.
THAT'S IT?
WHEN I CAN'T COME UP WITH 'MEANINGFUL' OR 'INSPIRING,' I USUALLY GO WITH 'OBVIOUS.'
TESTING

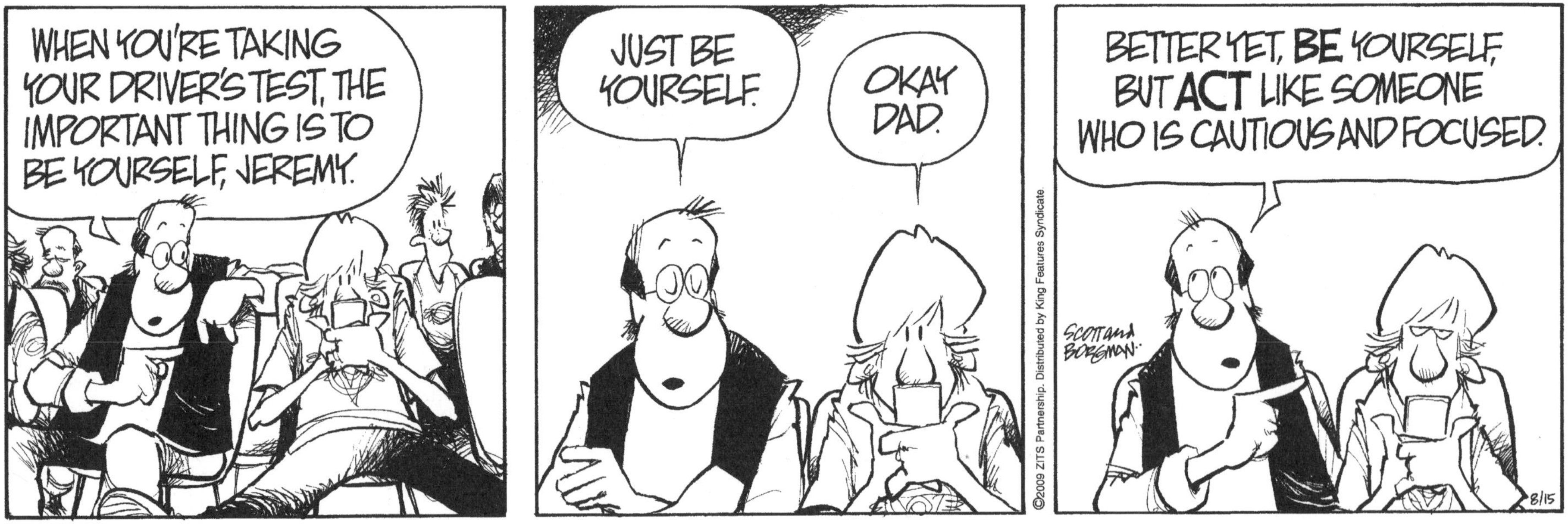
WHEN YOU'RE TAKING YOUR DRIVER'S TEST, THE IMPORTANT THING IS TO BE YOURSELF, JEREMY.
JUST BE YOURSELF.
OKAY DAD.
©2009 ZITS Partnership. Distributed by King Features Syndicate
BETTER YET, BE YOURSELF, BUT ACT LIKE SOMEONE WHO IS CAUTIOUS AND FOCUSED.
SCOTT and BORGMAN
8/15

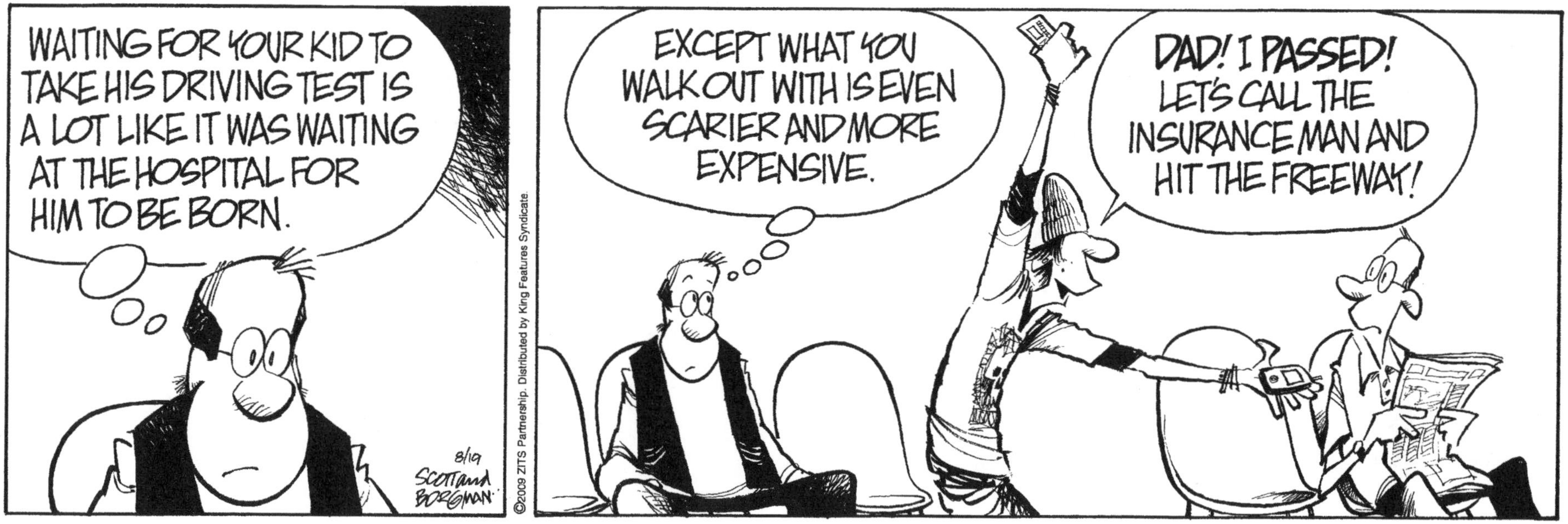
WAITING FOR YOUR KID TO TAKE HIS DRIVING TEST IS A LOT LIKE IT WAS WAITING AT THE HOSPITAL FOR HIM TO BE BORN.
8/19
SCOTT and BORGMAN
©2009 ZITS Partnership. Distributed by King Features Syndicate.
EXCEPT WHAT YOU WALK OUT WITH IS EVEN SCARIER AND MORE EXPENSIVE.
DAD! I PASSED! LET'S CALL THE INSURANCE MAN AND HIT THE FREEWAY!

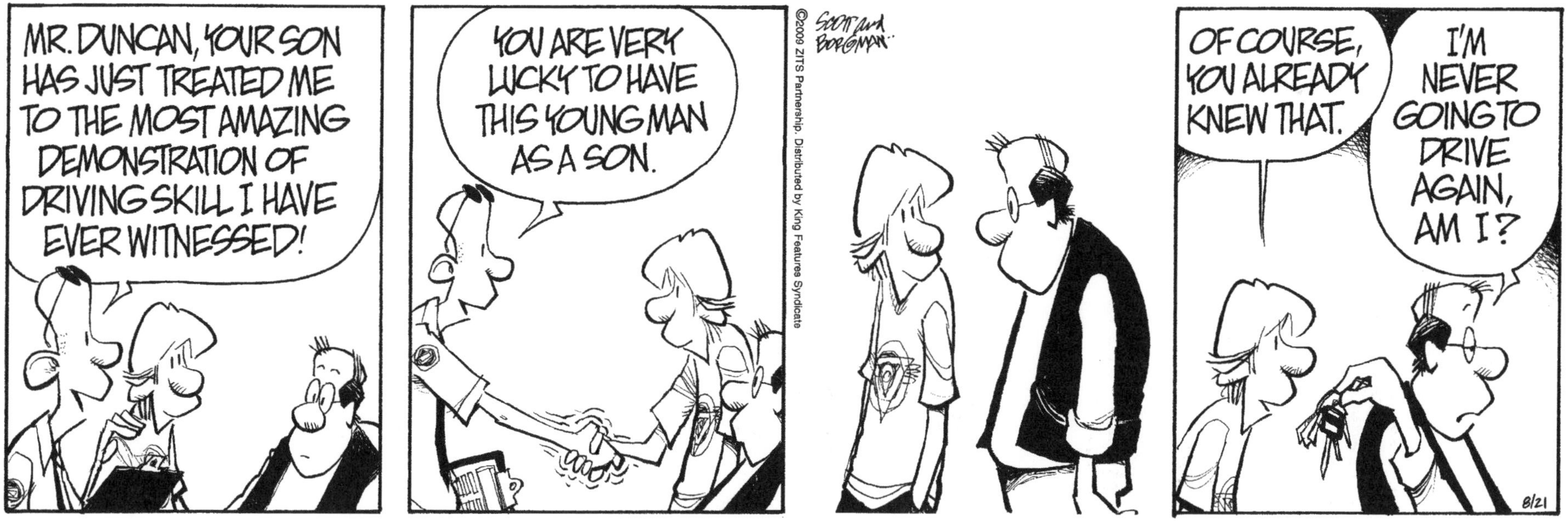
MR. DUNCAN, YOUR SON HAS JUST TREATED ME TO THE MOST AMAZING DEMONSTRATION OF DRIVING SKILL I HAVE EVER WITNESSED!
YOU ARE VERY LUCKY TO HAVE THIS YOUNG MAN AS A SON.
©2009 ZITS Partnership. Distributed by King Features Syndicate
SCOTT and BORGMAN
OF COURSE, YOU ALREADY KNEW THAT.
I'M NEVER GOING TO DRIVE AGAIN, AM I?
8/21

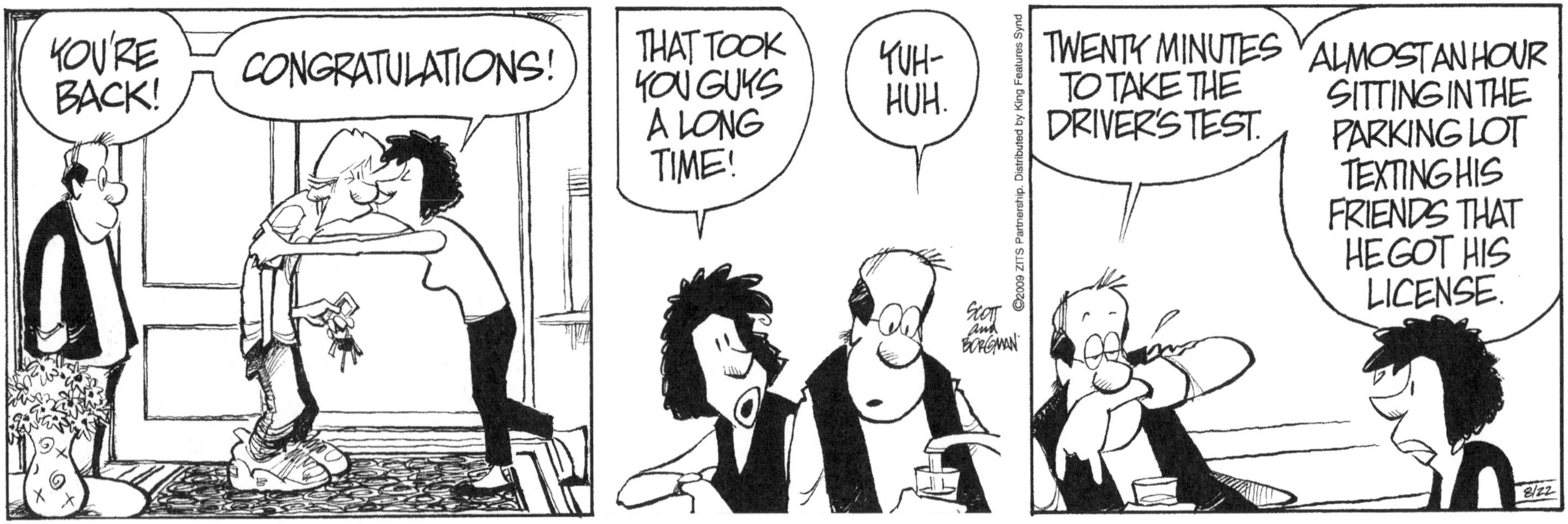
YOU'RE BACK!
CONGRATULATIONS!
THAT TOOK YOU GUYS A LONG TIME!
YUH-HUH.
©2009 ZITS Partnership. Distributed by King Features Synd
SCOTT and BORGMAN
TWENTY MINUTES TO TAKE THE DRIVER'S TEST.
ALMOST AN HOUR SITTING IN THE PARKING LOT TEXTING HIS FRIENDS THAT HE GOT HIS LICENSE.
8/22

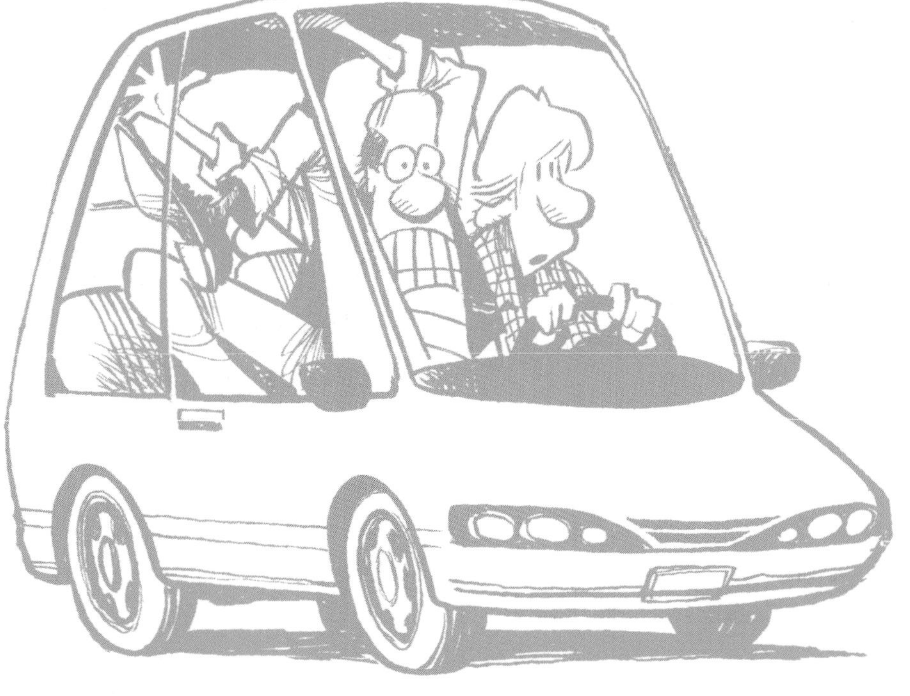

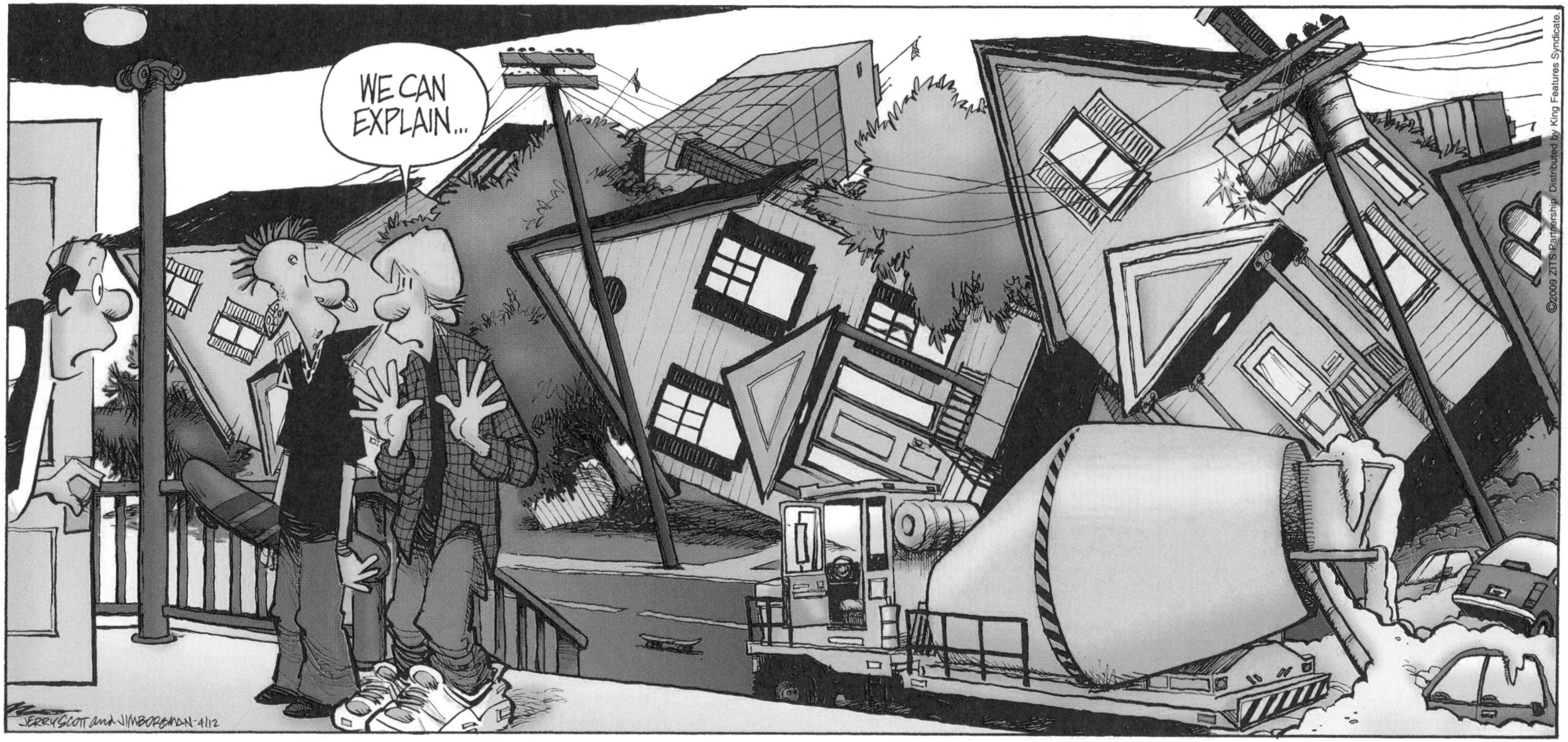
WE CAN EXPLAIN...
©2009 ZITS Partnership. Distributed by King Features Syndicate.

Jim: Sometimes I ask Jerry to "just give me something fun to draw."
Invariably, I immediately regret it.

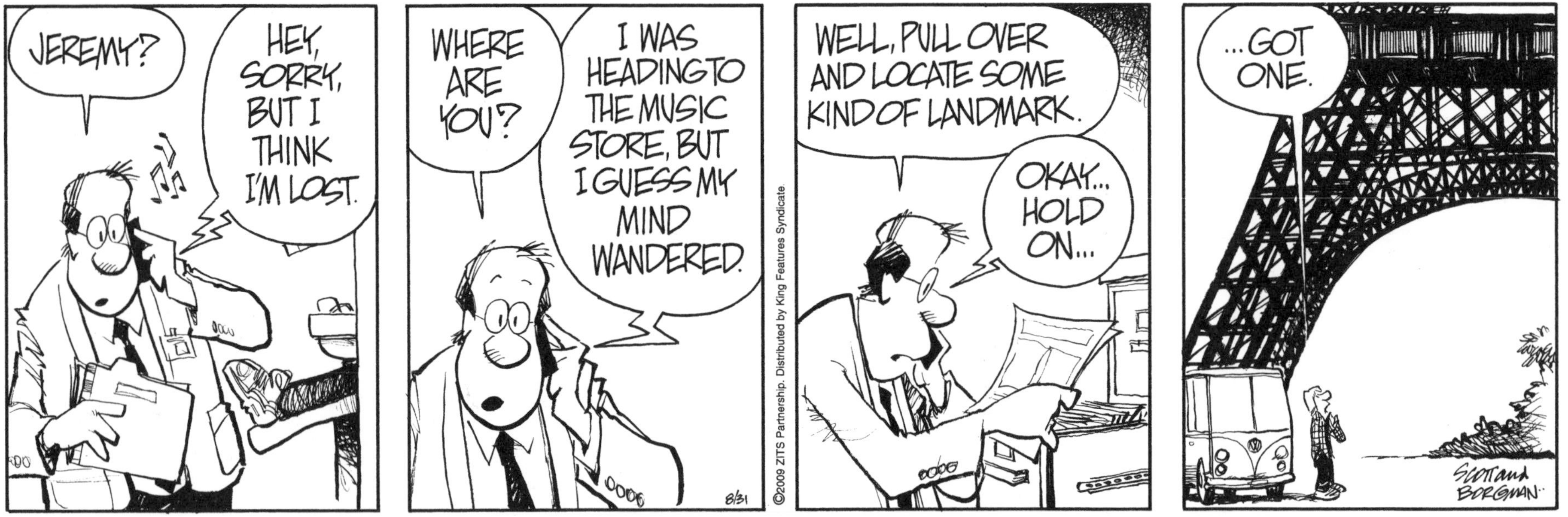
JEREMY?
HEY, SORRY, BUT I THINK I'M LOST.
WHERE ARE YOU?
I WAS HEADING TO THE MUSIC STORE, BUT I GUESS MY MIND WANDERED.
8/31
©2009 ZITS Partnership. Distributed by King Features Syndicate.
WELL, PULL OVER AND LOCATE SOME KIND OF LANDMARK.
OKAY... HOLD ON...
...GOT ONE.
SCOTT and BORGMAN

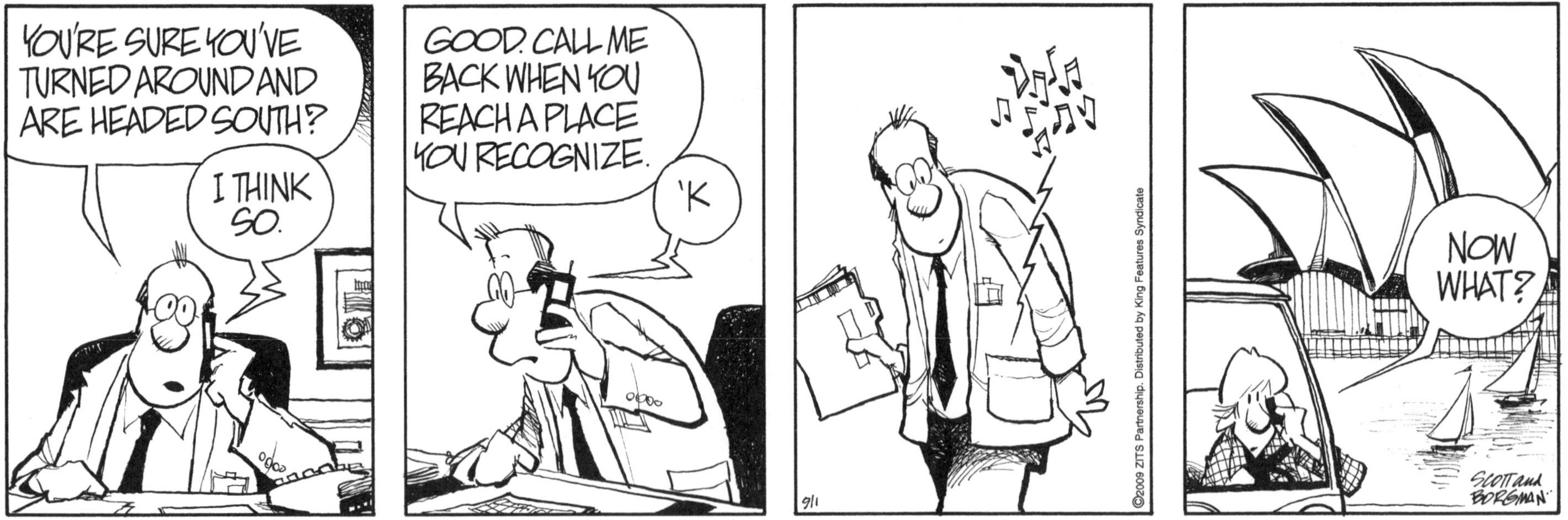
YOU'RE SURE YOU'VE TURNED AROUND AND ARE HEADED SOUTH?
I THINK SO.
GOOD. CALL ME BACK WHEN YOU REACH A PLACE YOU RECOGNIZE.
'K
9/1
©2009 ZITS Partnership. Distributed by King Features Syndicate
NOW WHAT?
SCOTT and BORGMAN

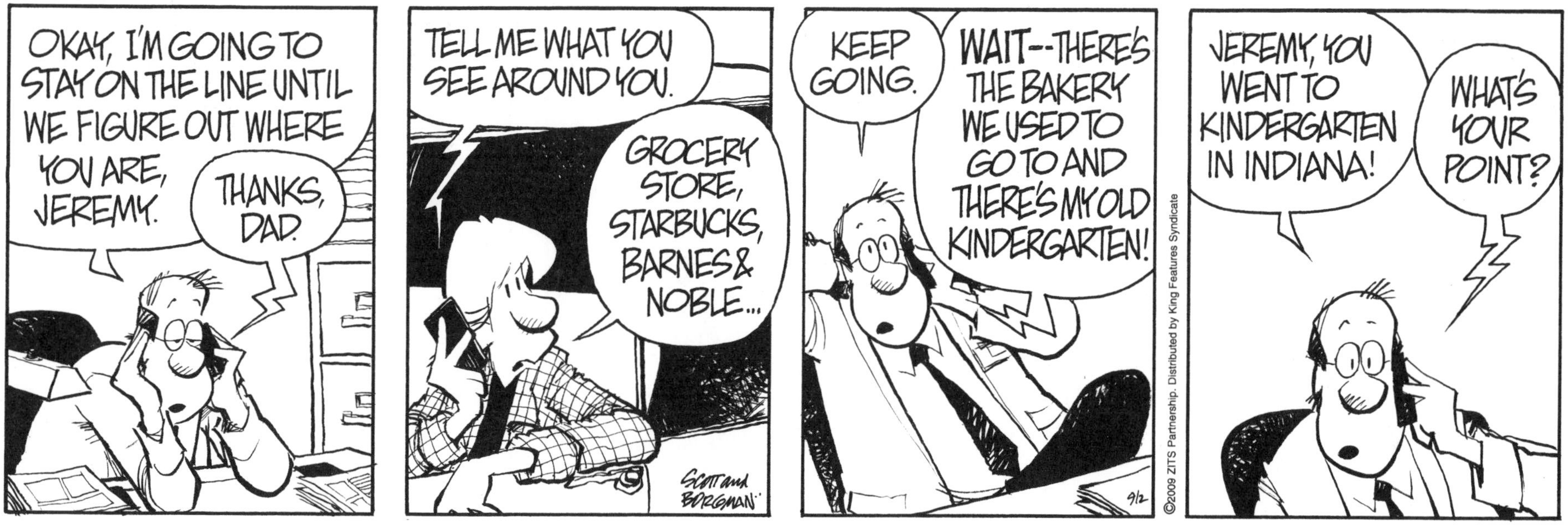
OKAY, I'M GOING TO STAY ON THE LINE UNTIL WE FIGURE OUT WHERE YOU ARE, JEREMY.
THANKS, DAD.
TELL ME WHAT YOU SEE AROUND YOU.
GROCERY STORE, STARBUCKS, BARNES & NOBLE...
SCOTT and BORGMAN
KEEP GOING.
WAIT--THERE'S THE BAKERY WE USED TO GO TO AND THERE'S MY OLD KINDERGARTEN!
9/2
©2009 ZITS Partnership. Distributed by King Features Syndicate
JEREMY, YOU WENT TO KINDERGARTEN IN INDIANA!
WHAT'S YOUR POINT?

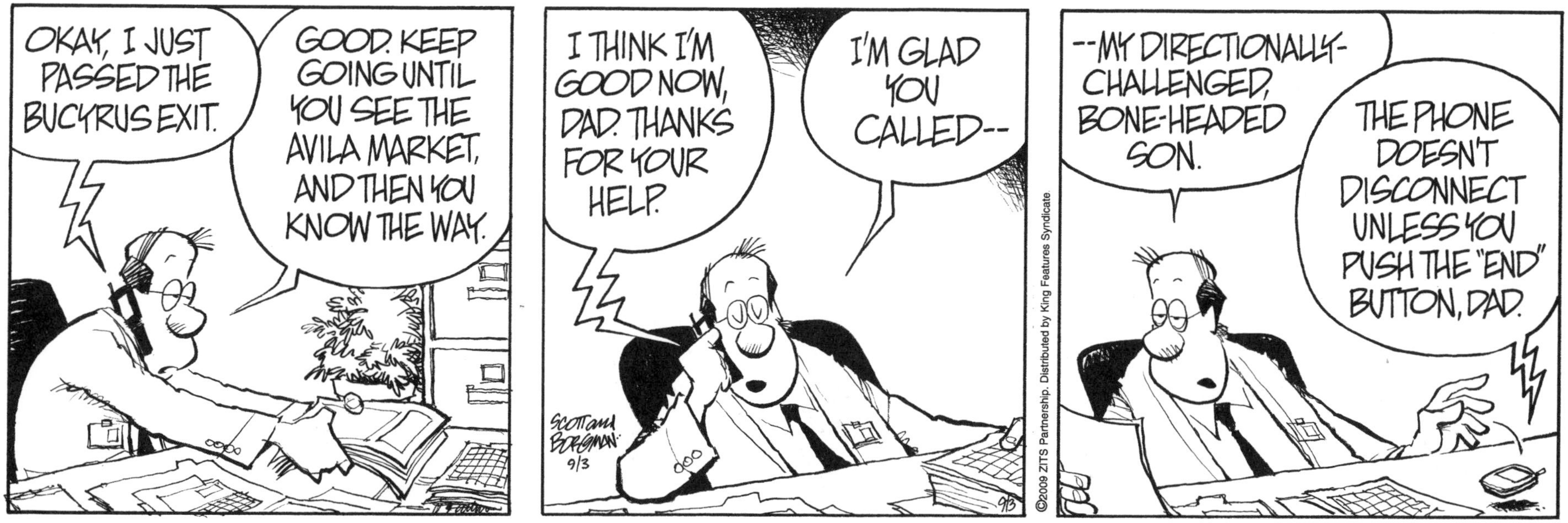
OKAY, I JUST PASSED THE BUCYRUS EXIT.
GOOD. KEEP GOING UNTIL YOU SEE THE AVILA MARKET, AND THEN YOU KNOW THE WAY.
I THINK I'M GOOD NOW, DAD. THANKS FOR YOUR HELP.
I'M GLAD YOU CALLED--
SCOTT and BORGMAN
9/3
©2009 ZITS Partnership. Distributed by King Features Syndicate
--MY DIRECTIONALLY-CHALLENGED, BONE-HEADED SON.
THE PHONE DOESN'T DISCONNECT UNLESS YOU PUSH THE "END" BUTTON, DAD.

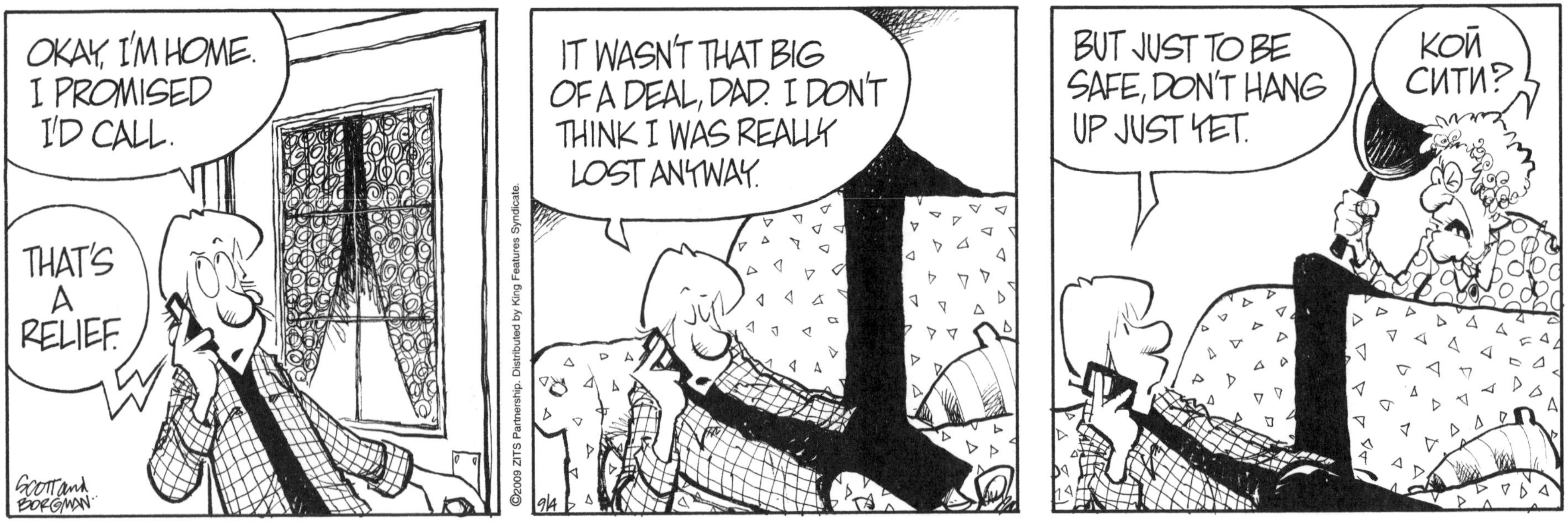
OKAY, I'M HOME. I PROMISED I'D CALL.
THAT'S A RELIEF.
SCOTT and BORGMAN
©2009 ZITS Partnership. Distributed by King Features Syndicate.
IT WASN'T THAT BIG OF A DEAL, DAD. I DON'T THINK I WAS REALLY LOST ANYWAY.
9/4
BUT JUST TO BE SAFE, DON'T HANG UP JUST YET.
КОЙ СИТИ?

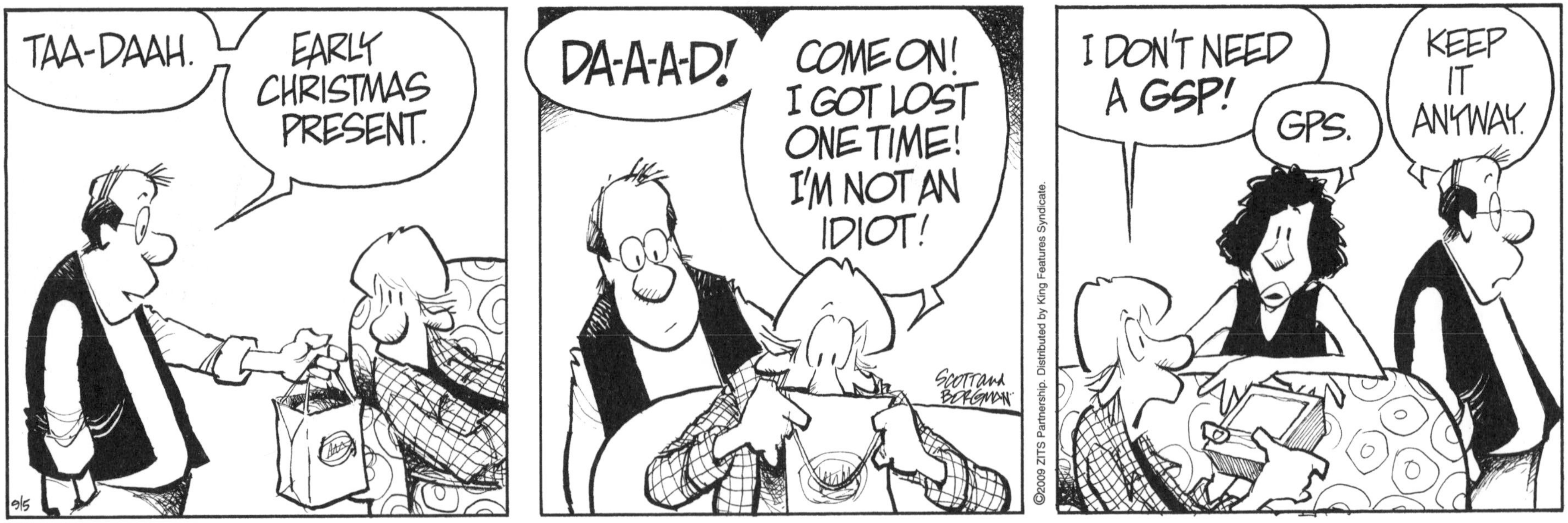
TAA-DAAH.
EARLY CHRISTMAS PRESENT.
9/5
DA-A-A-D!
COME ON! I GOT LOST ONE TIME! I'M NOT AN IDIOT!
SCOTT and BORGMAN
©2009 ZITS Partnership. Distributed by King Features Syndicate.
I DON'T NEED A GSP!
GPS.
KEEP IT ANYWAY.

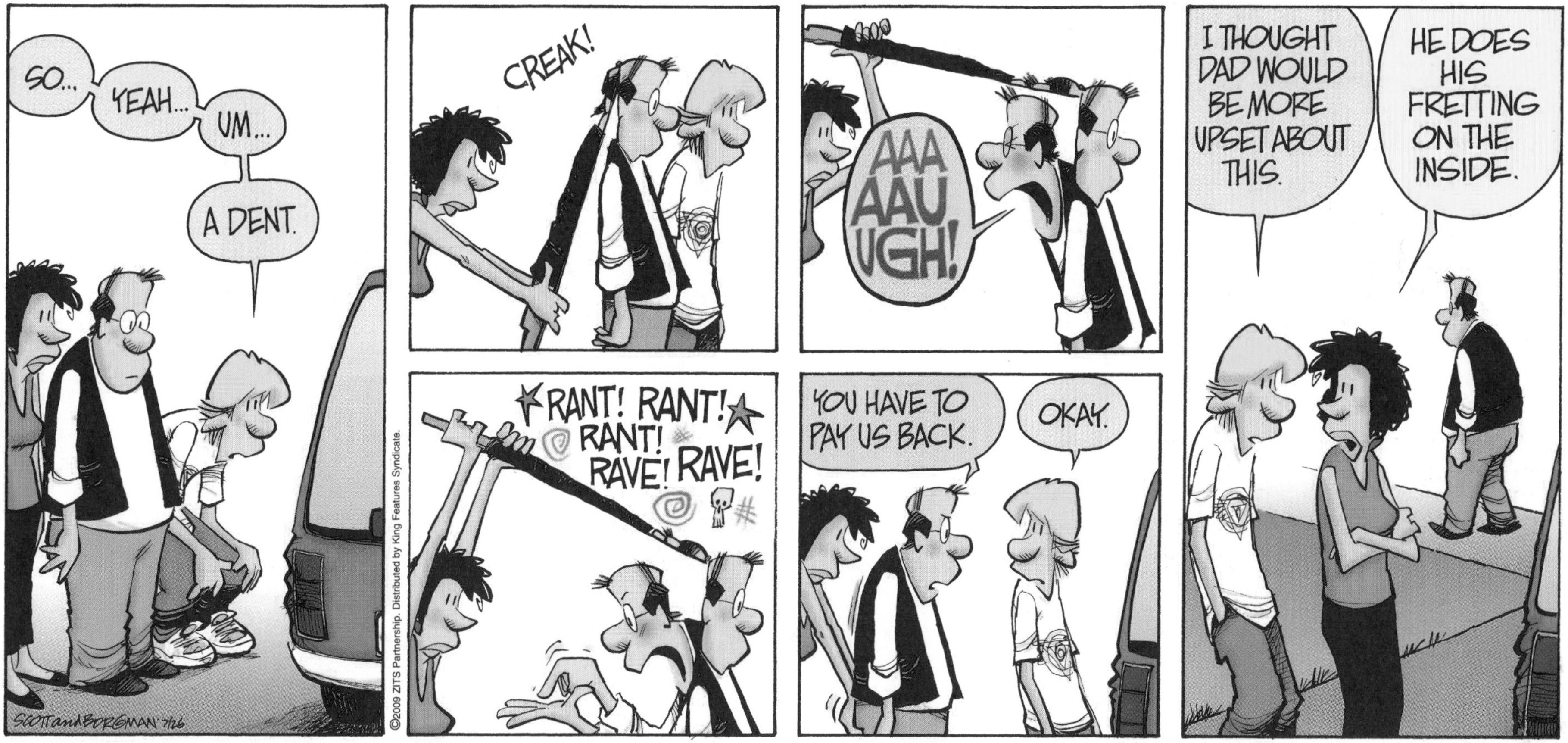
SO...
YEAH...
UM...
A DENT.
SCOTT and BORGMAN 7/26
©2009 ZITS Partnership. Distributed by King Features Syndicate.
CREAK!
AAAAAUUGH!
RANT! RANT! RANT! RAVE! RAVE!
YOU HAVE TO PAY US BACK.
OKAY.
I THOUGHT DAD WOULD BE MORE UPSET ABOUT THIS.
HE DOES HIS FRETTING ON THE INSIDE.

Jerry: This is kind of how I operate as a dad. Calm in a crisis, but it's best not to look under the hood.

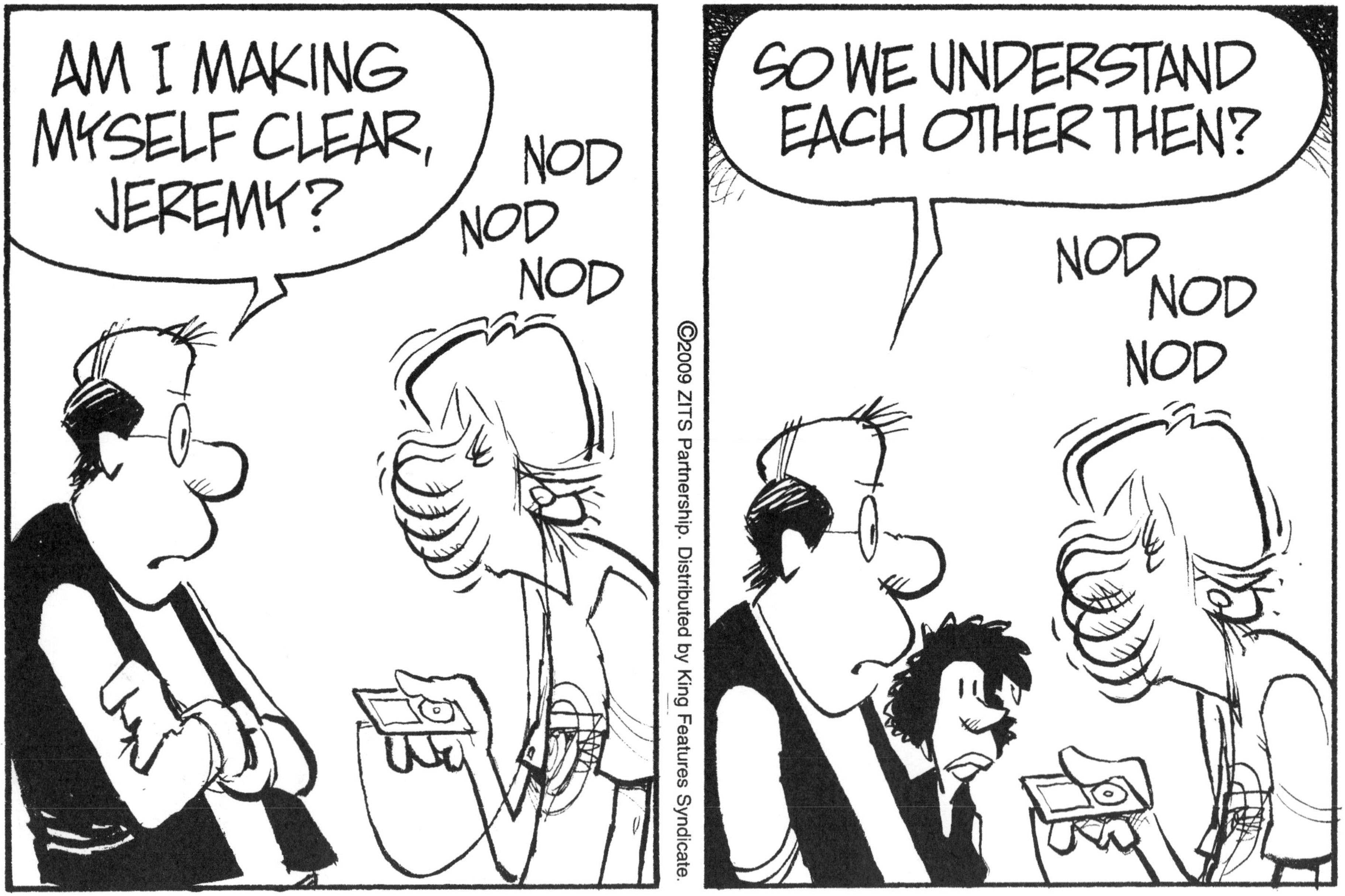
AM I MAKING MYSELF CLEAR, JEREMY?
NOD NOD NOD
SO WE UNDERSTAND EACH OTHER THEN?
NOD NOD NOD

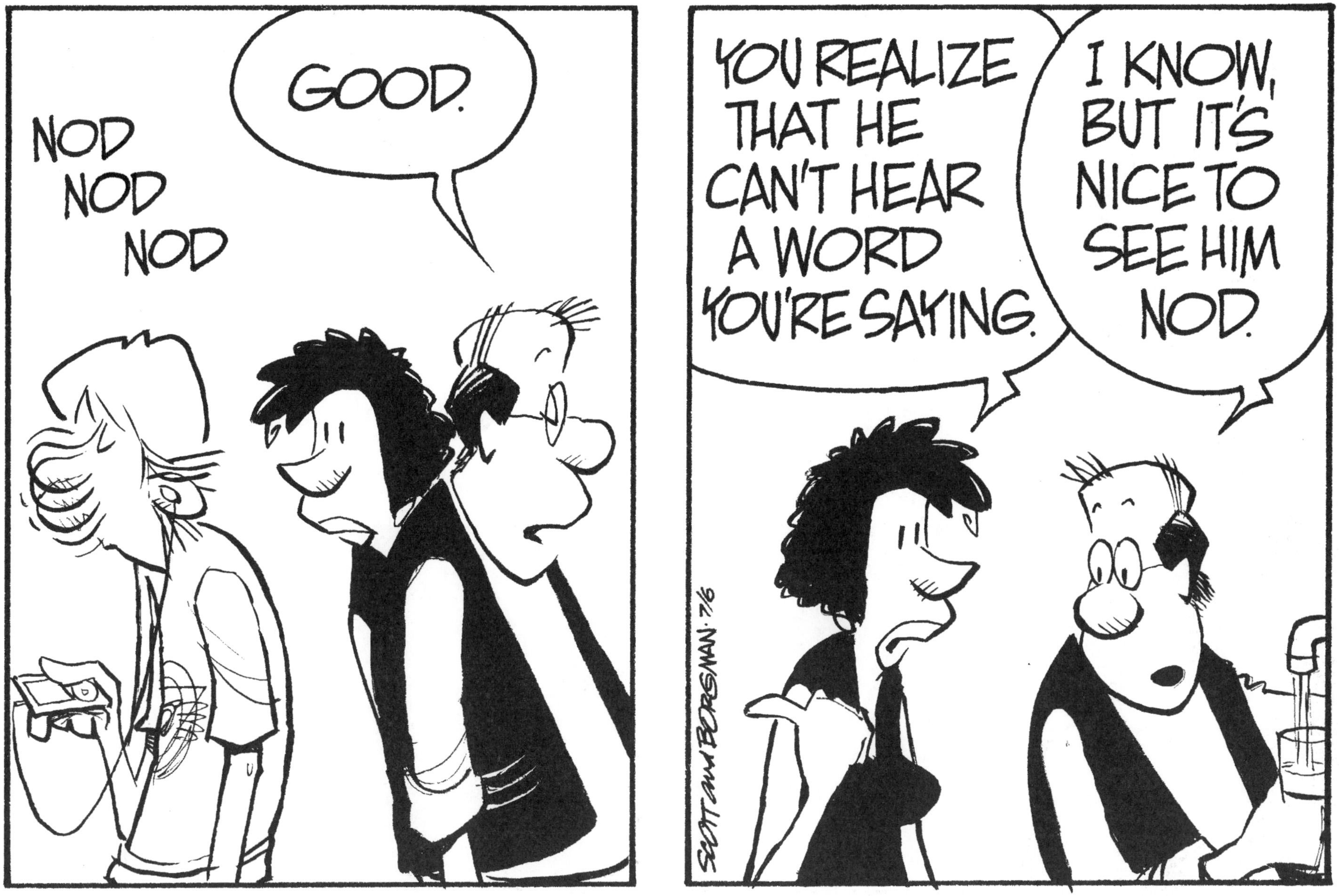
NOD
NOD
NOD
GOOD.
YOU REALIZE THAT HE CAN'T HEAR A WORD YOU'RE SAYING.
I KNOW, BUT IT'S NICE TO SEE HIM NOD.
SCOTT AND BORGMAN 7/6

Jim: Appreciate the small moments of agreement, Dad, even if they are an illusion.

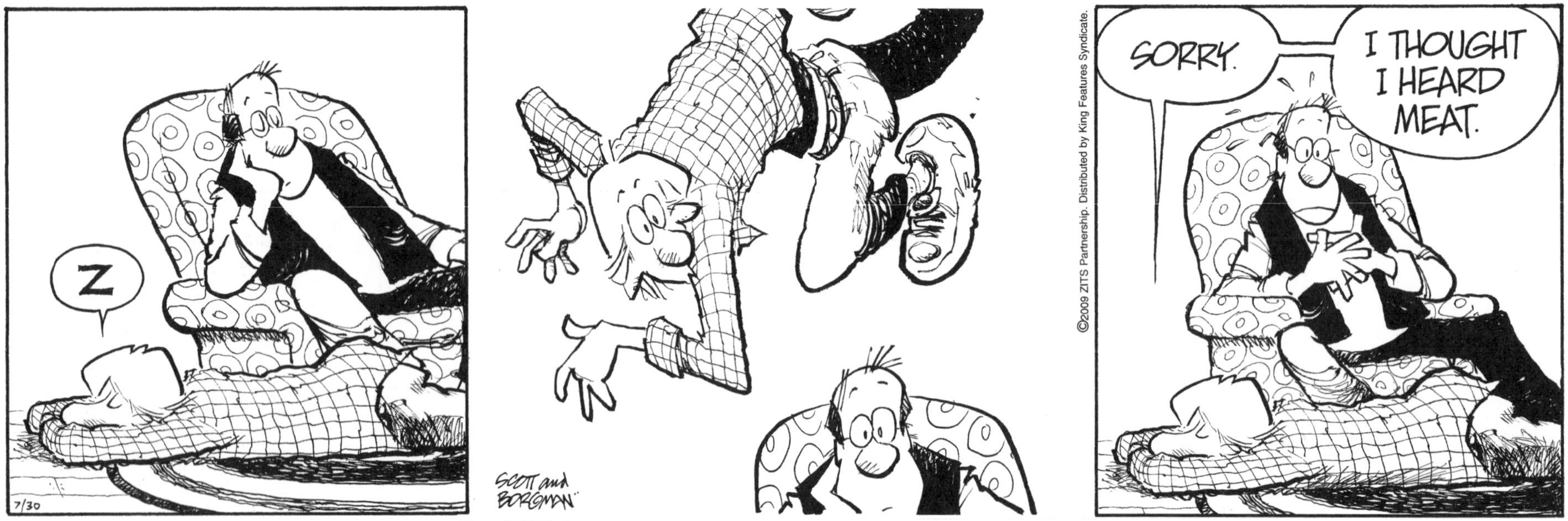
Z
SCOTT and BORGMAN
SORRY.
I THOUGHT I HEARD MEAT.
©2009 ZITS Partnership. Distributed by King Features Syndicate.

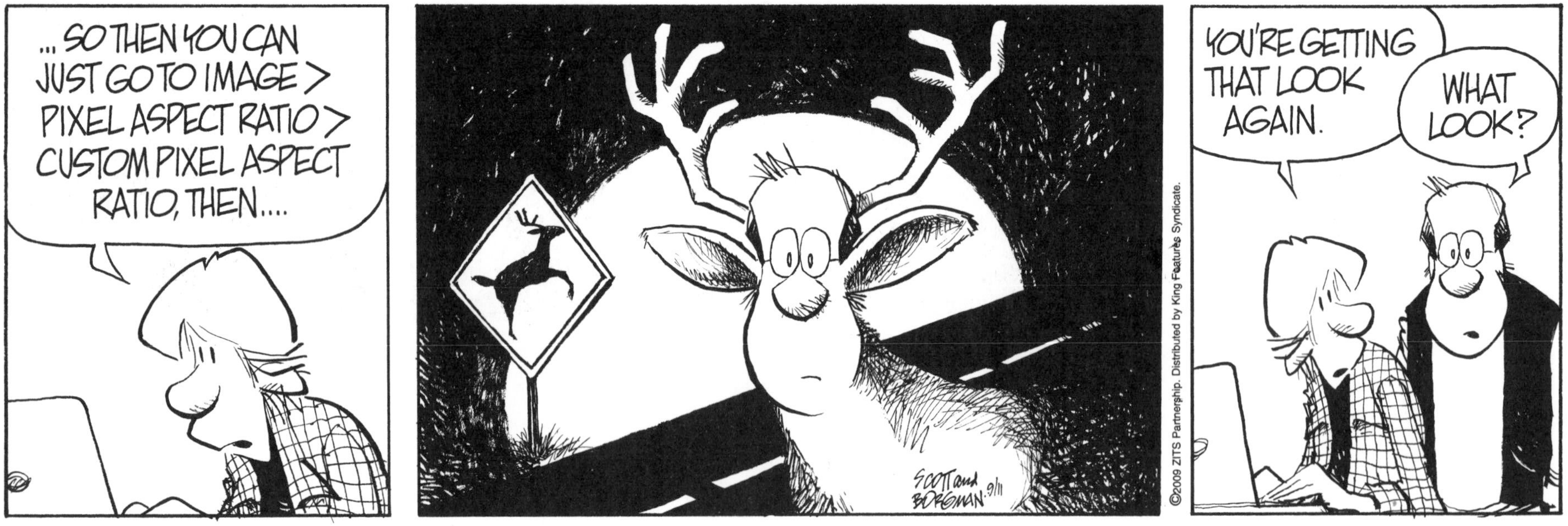
... SO THEN YOU CAN JUST GO TO IMAGE > PIXEL ASPECT RATIO > CUSTOM PIXEL ASPECT RATIO, THEN....
SCOTT and BORGMAN
YOU'RE GETTING THAT LOOK AGAIN.
WHAT LOOK?
©2009 ZITS Partnership. Distributed by King Features Syndicate.

DAD, ARE YOU USING THIS COMPUTER?
WELL, I.....
'CUZ MOM IS ON HER LAPTOP AND I LEFT MINE AT HECTOR'S HOUSE.
I'M RIGHT IN THE MIDDLE OF BALANCING THE CHEC--
SCOTT and BORGMAN
I JUST NEED IT FOR A SECOND TO CHECK THE MOVIE SCHEDULES-OH!-AND I SAW THIS HILARIOUS VIDEO THAT PIERCE TOLD ME ABOUT, SO I SHOULD POST A THANKS ON HIS FACEBOOK TO, YOU KNOW... BE POLITE, AND--
--ARE YOU DRINKING THIS COKE?

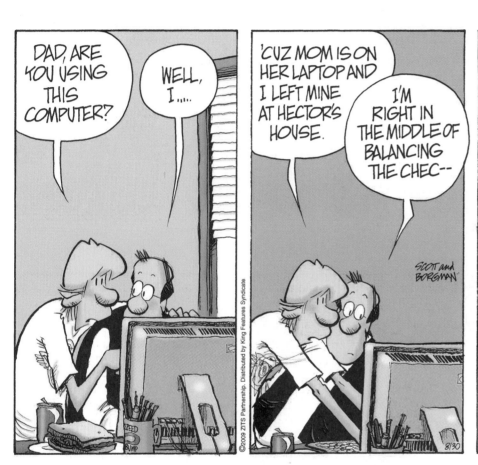

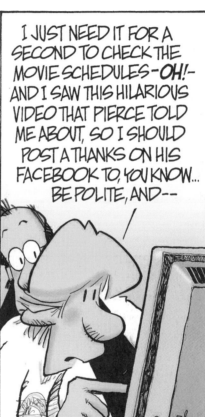

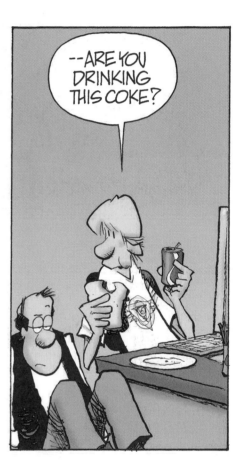

Jim: To your teenager, YourSpace is also MySpace.

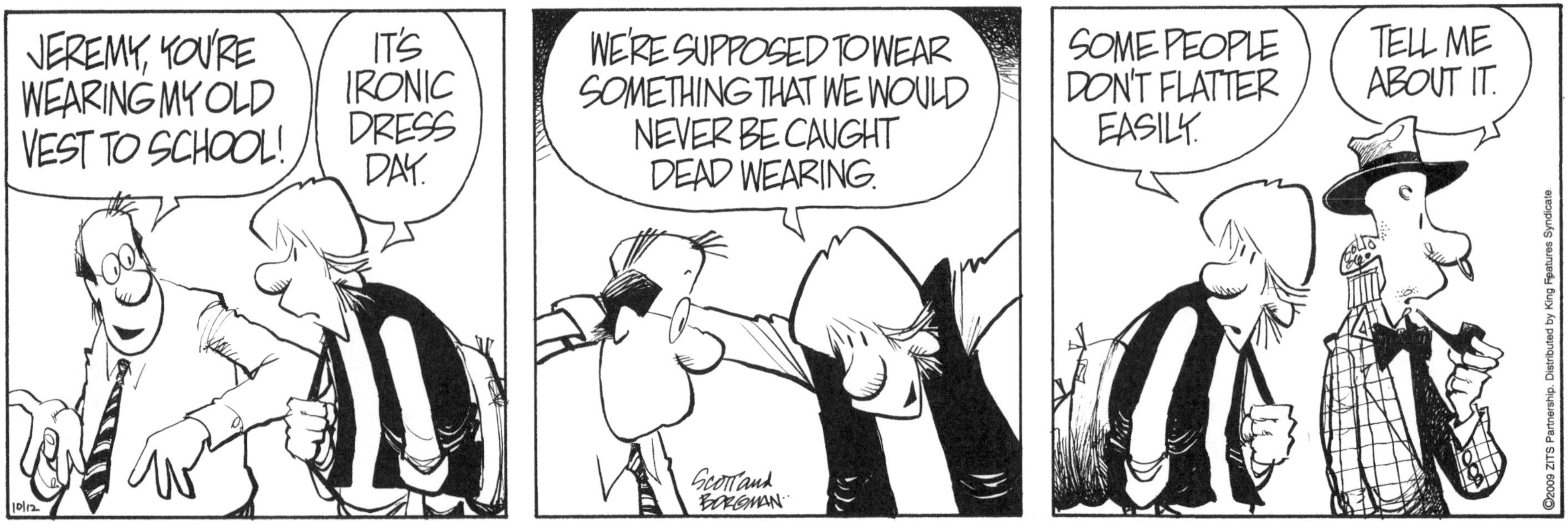
JEREMY, YOU'RE WEARING MY OLD VEST TO SCHOOL!
IT'S IRONIC DRESS DAY.
WE'RE SUPPOSED TO WEAR SOMETHING THAT WE WOULD NEVER BE CAUGHT DEAD WEARING.
SOME PEOPLE DON'T FLATTER EASILY.
TELL ME ABOUT IT.
10/12
SCOTT and BORGMAN

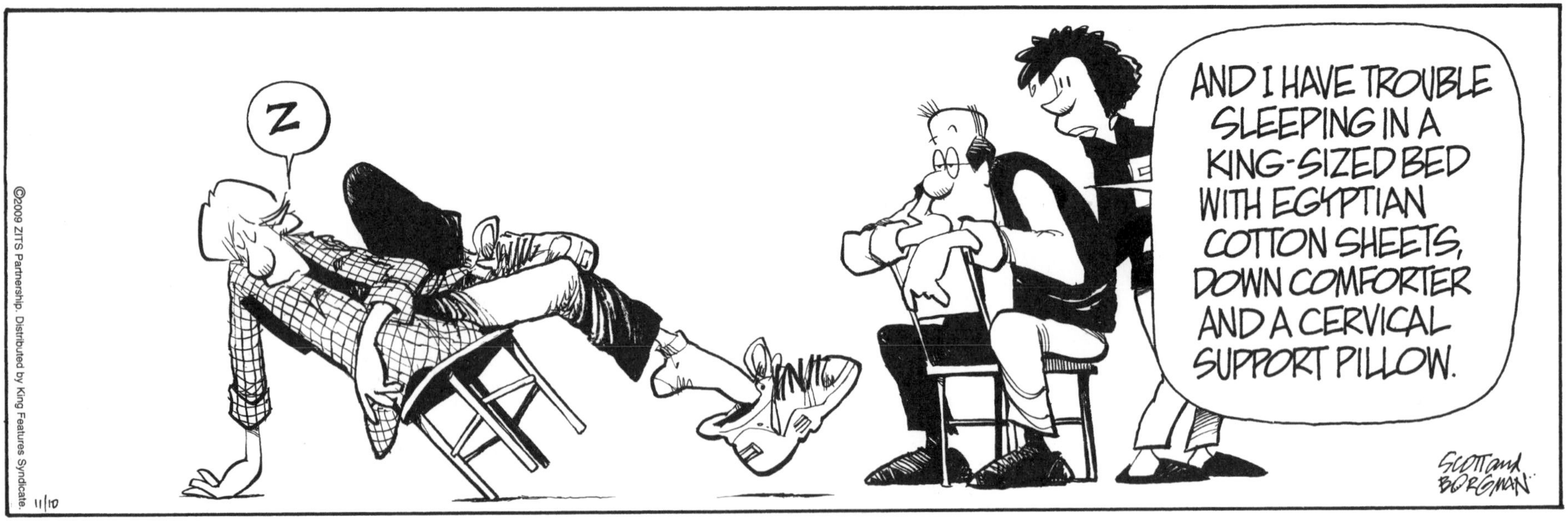
Z
AND I HAVE TROUBLE SLEEPING IN A KING-SIZED BED WITH EGYPTIAN COTTON SHEETS, DOWN COMFORTER AND A CERVICAL SUPPORT PILLOW.
11/10
SCOTT and BORGMAN

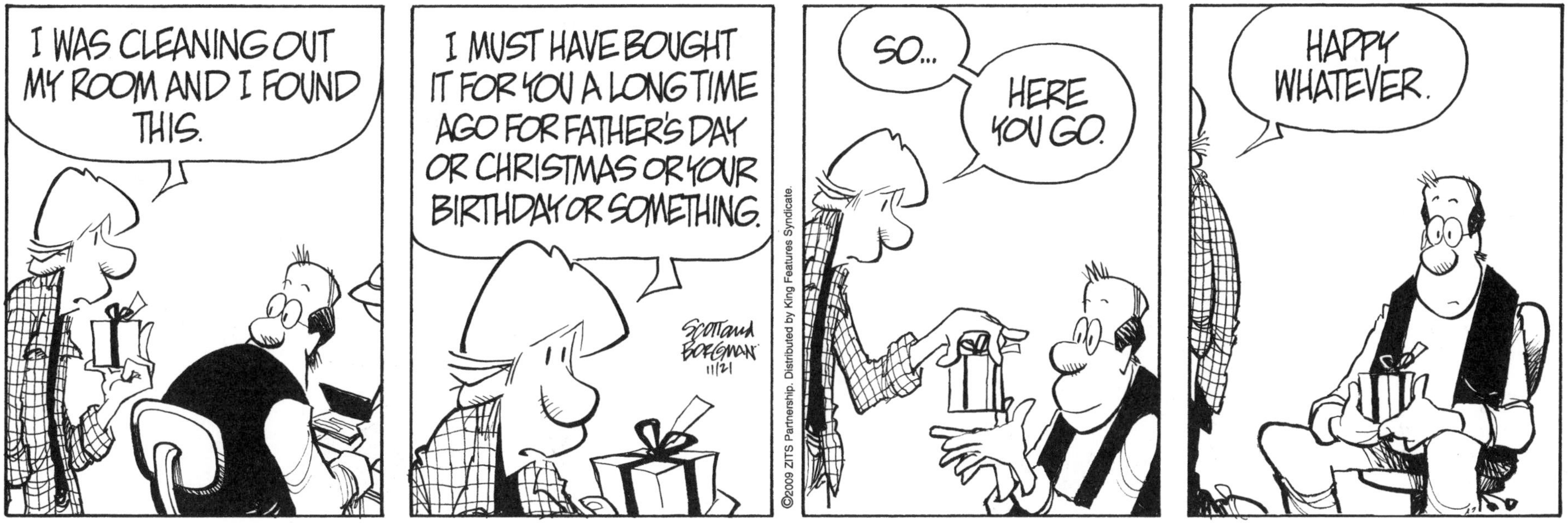
I WAS CLEANING OUT MY ROOM AND I FOUND THIS.
I MUST HAVE BOUGHT IT FOR YOU A LONG TIME AGO FOR FATHER'S DAY OR CHRISTMAS OR YOUR BIRTHDAY OR SOMETHING.
SCOTT and BORGMAN 11/21
©2009 ZITS Partnership. Distributed by King Features Syndicate.
SO...
HERE YOU GO.
HAPPY WHATEVER.

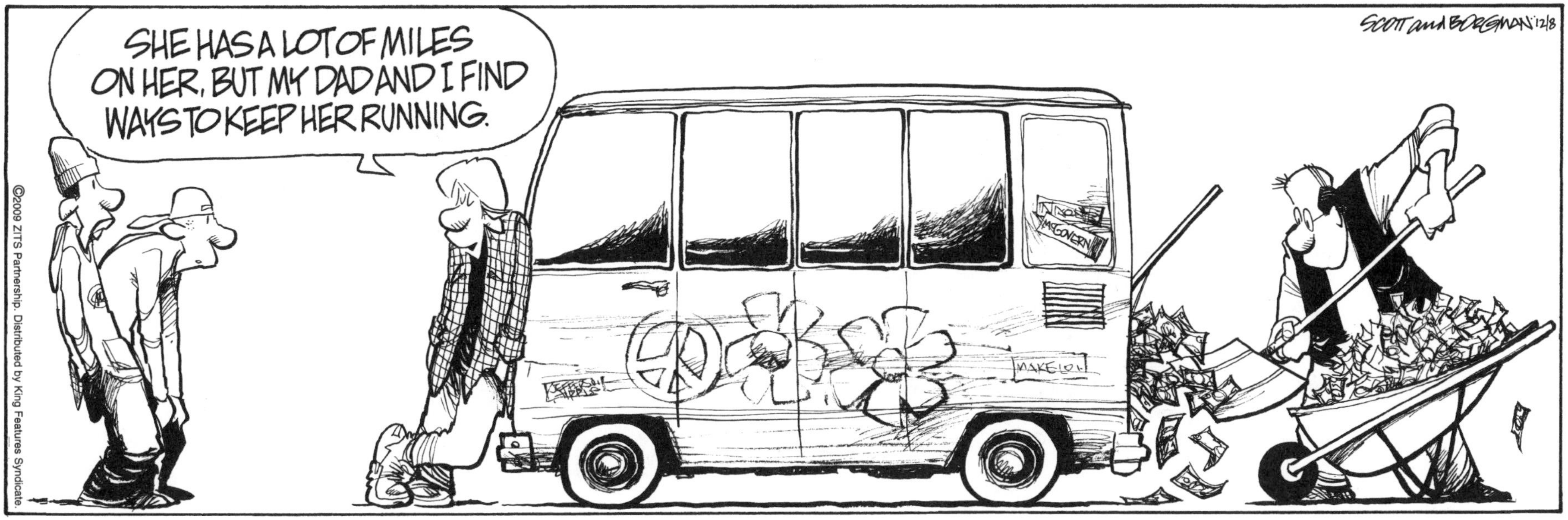
SCOTT and BORGMAN 12/8
SHE HAS A LOT OF MILES ON HER, BUT MY DAD AND I FIND WAYS TO KEEP HER RUNNING.
©2009 ZITS Partnership. Distributed by King Features Syndicate.

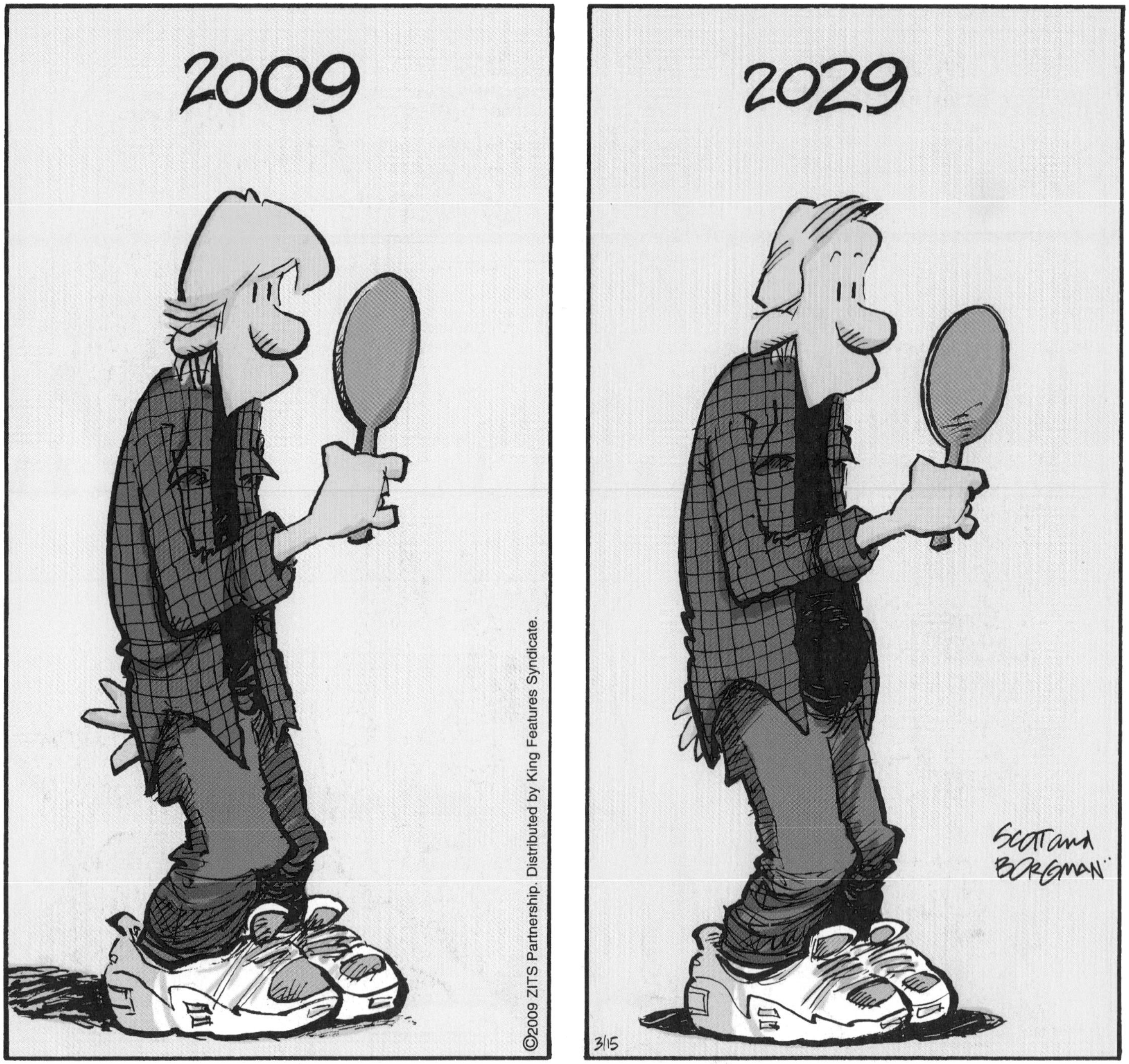
2009
2029
SCOTT and BORGMAN
3/15

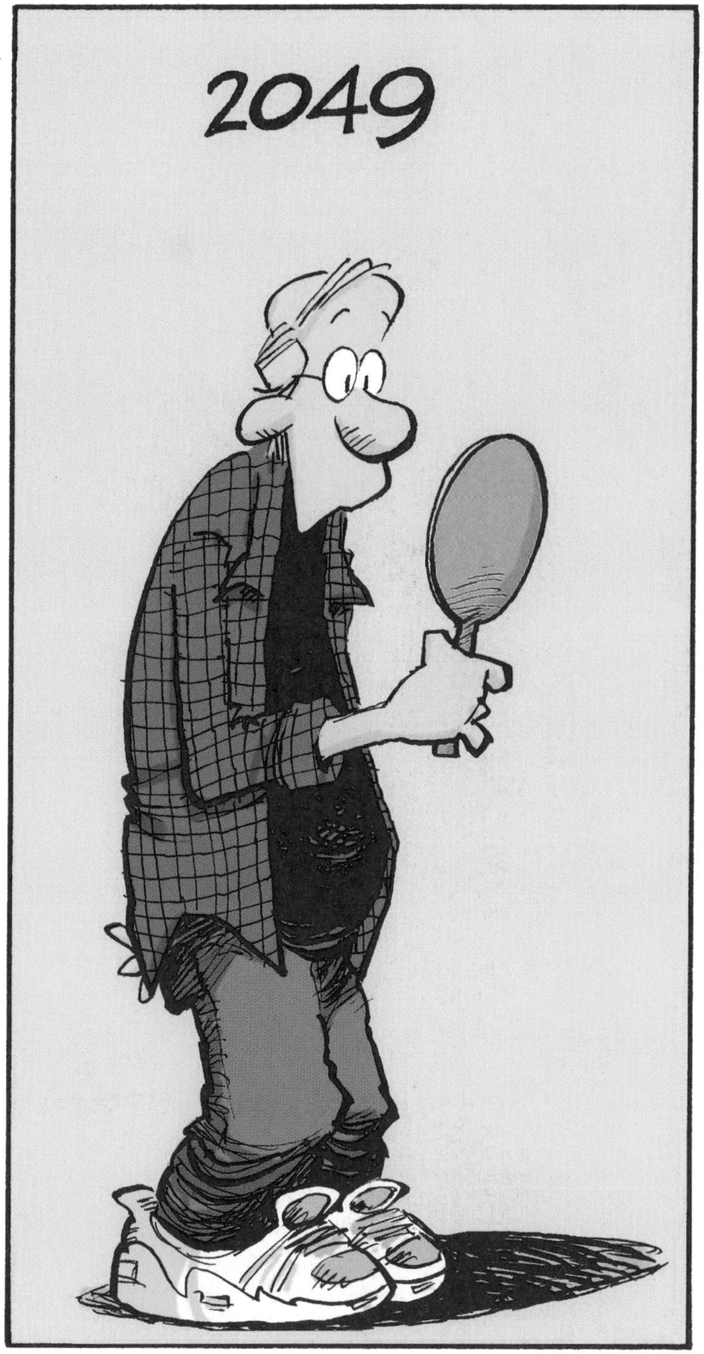
2049

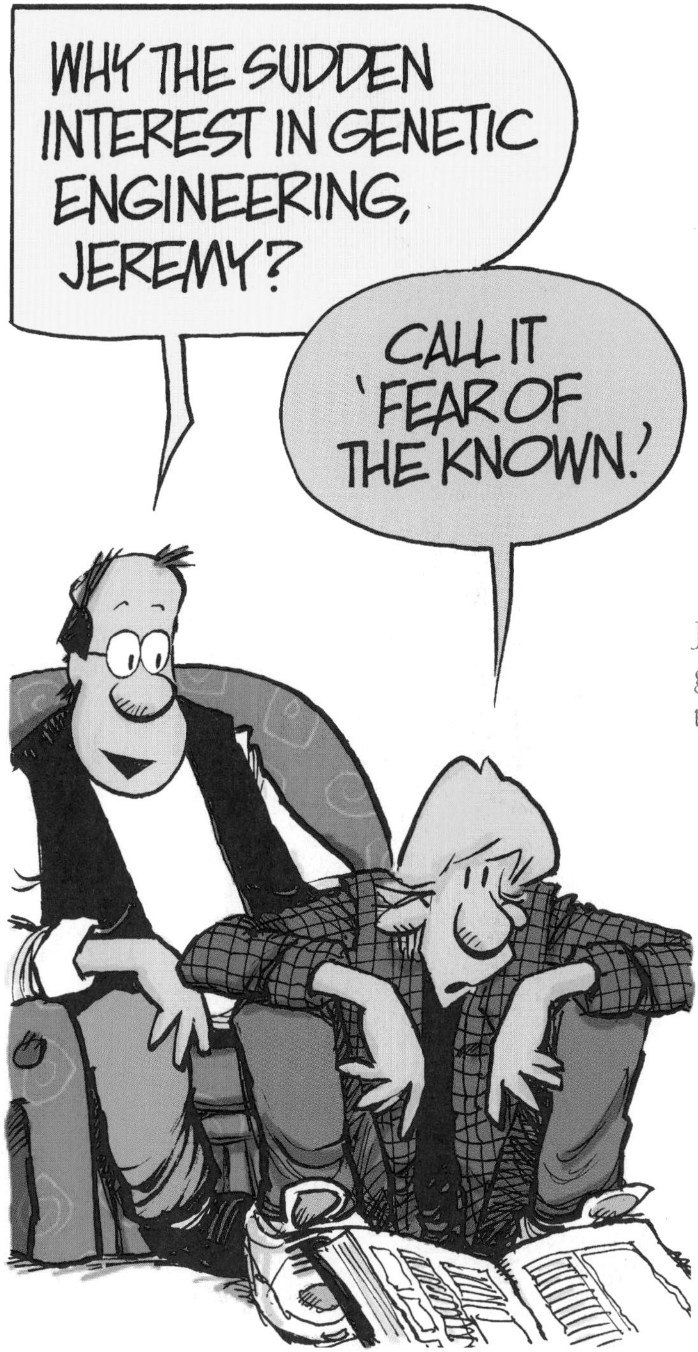
WHY THE SUDDEN INTEREST IN GENETIC ENGINEERING, JEREMY?
CALL IT 'FEAR OF THE KNOWN.'

Jerry: And in the end, the genes you take are equal to the genes you make.